DA

PLOTS AND CHARACTERS
IN THE WORKS OF MARK TWAIN

PLOTS AND CHARACTERS
IN THE WORKS OF
MARK TWAIN

Robert L. Gale

with a foreword by
Frederick Anderson

VOLUME ONE

Archon Books
1973

Published in two volumes

Library of Congress Cataloging in Publication Data

Gale, Robert L.
    Plots and characters in the works of Mark Twain.

    1. Clemens, Samuel Langhorne, 1835-1910—Plots.
2. Clemens, Samuel Langhorne, 1835-1910—Characters.
I. Title.
PS1341.G3   818'.4'09   73-5745
ISBN 0-208-01242-7

Printed in the United States of America

As a token of my profound and lasting love
I dedicate this book to
My Wife
Maureen Dowd Gale
and
Our Children
John Lee Gale
James Dowd Gale
Christine Ann Gale

CONTENTS

FOREWORD

In a commendably selfless and extraordinarily ambitious project, Robert L. Gale has brought together all of the principal and minor plots and characters in the fictional and many of the biographical pieces written by Mark Twain. Without critical commitment, but in an even and steady fashion, Mr. Gale presents spacious summaries of the entire range of Mark Twain's imaginative writing.

Even with as wide and durable an audience as Mark Twain captured with his first major book and maintains to the present day, it is unlikely his most dedicated readers can encompass and remember the interlocking characters and overlapping plots of so prolific an author. It is even more unlikely that anyone else could have compiled as comprehensive and objective a survey as Mr. Gale has given us. He painstakingly records variant forms of personal names, the appearance of nicknames no matter how infrequently used, and the alternate forms of titles of even minor pieces. Although this detail seems sometimes to go beyond the bounds of probable usefulness, it is impossible to anticipate what may have lodged in the imperfect memories of a wide range of readers. Such meticulous inclusiveness is a far safer approach to a catalogue than the easier alternatives. A relaxed use of idiom and the adoption of a point of view closely paralleling that of the original author embellishes factual description with a sense of the style and narrative method of the original.

A somewhat unexpected benefit of this drawing together of characters and plots is the pleasure and education of browsing. As with a dictionary, the specific piece of information originally sought diminishes in immediate importance as the eye is diverted by surrounding material. Perhaps this is not the most efficient or logical method of accumulating information, but it is surely the most fascinating and in a surprising number of cases it is immediately productive.

In addition to the alphabetical listings of characters and plots, this volume contains a full chronology of Clemens' life and work continuing the record of posthumous publications to the present. This account is amplified by a bibliography of the shorter pieces listed according to the year of their composition with the notation of the date in which they were incorporated into later collections. The reader can quickly determine the pieces written during a given period and by turning to the plot and character summaries he can establish a perspective for the use of themes, names and character development at any point in Mark Twain's career.

For the major English writers of the Victorian era there have long been lovingly-compiled concordances, but until very recently few American writers of the period had such guides. This neglect has imposed upon readers frequent, and often long, searches for a character, an incident or an anecdote whose location lies just beyond the edge of memory. It is gratifying at last to be able to turn to a single volume instead of a set of collected works supplemented by a dozen or more imperfectly related collections. That the patient industry of one man has provided a source for this information in recent years for Poe, Hawthorne, Melville, Henry James—and now Mark Twain—places students of American literature deeply in Mr. Gale's debt.

Anyone who deals frequently with Mark Twain's writings and biography always has at hand Merle Johnson's *Bibliography of the Works of Mark Twain* and Albert Bigelow Paine's *Mark Twain: A Biography*. Many biographies, critical studies and other reference works correct errors in those two pioneering volumes and are frequently used but none of them has attained the central status of "Johnson" and "Paine." Those incomparable resources appear finally to have a companion in "Gale."

Frederick Anderson
Editor of the Mark Twain Papers

University of California, Berkeley
January, 1973

PREFACE

This book is a companion volume to my *Plots and Characters in the Fiction of Henry James* (1965), *Plots and Character in the Fiction and Sketches of Nathaniel Hawthorne* (1968), *Plots and Characters in the Fiction and Narrative Poetry of Herman Melville* (1969), and *Plots and Characters in the Fiction and Poetry of Edgar Allan Poe* (1970), all of which have been published by Archon Books. *Plots and Characters in the Works of Mark Twain* proved to be a more difficult undertaking than the other four books in the series combined.

Problems were numerous. To begin with, it was hard to decide what to include and what to exclude. After consulting with many experts and friends, I decided to summarize all of Twain's novels, travel pieces, short stories, essays, critical articles, collected speeches, plays, and collected poems, and in addition some of those few letters which have been anthologized; and to exclude notebook material, autobiographical dictation (including *Mark Twain in Eruption*), and collected letters. I had to draw the line somewhere. As it is, I have summarized more than eight hundred items by Twain totaling about 18,000 pages. And I identify in my alphabetized sequence all fictional characters and all real-life people as well, provided they move, speak, or otherwise have a part in action which Twain vivifies (except where indicated in footnotes after certain titles). Well over seven thousand characters are collected from Twain's works and identified here—considerably more than twice as many as I considered earlier from Hawthorne, Poe, Melville, and James combined. I also include animals here if Twain names them and gives them speaking or thinking parts.

Upon publication of Mark Twain's definitive bibliography, which Professor William B. Todd is now compiling, I presume a diligent collator will find that I have missed a few items. In fact, I have a very short list of such titles myself, of items I cannot lay my hands on (for example, "A Birthplace Worth Saving," The Lincoln Farm Association, n.d., n.p. [1906]). All but the most demanding reader, however, ought to find enough here—perhaps more than enough.

A word about the mechanical features of this book may be helpful. The chronology of main events in Twain's life will enable the reader to parallel the author's literary productions with his activities. It also dramatizes the recent and current intense interest in Twain's writing. The chronological list of his works will serve the same purposes, among others more routine and obvious. In this sequence, dates in parentheses are of first book publication. Those titles not followed by parenthetical dates have not yet been published in book form. Alternate titles, which with Twain constitute a formidable problem, are interspersed, in alphabetical order, in the section of plot summaries with *See* references to enable the reader to locate material which he might have expected to find under different titles. The titles I use, no doubt inconsistently at times, are those which Twain or reputable editors have seemed to prefer. I also include titles of popular episodes or parts of larger works extrapolated and separately reprinted (for example, "Abelard and Heloise" [from *The Innocents Abroad*]). Any reader who cannot find the title he seeks would be well advised to consult Merle Johnson's *Bibliography of the Works of Mark Twain* (New York and London: Harper & Brothers, 1935), at the back of which is an index including variant titles and much else. Titles in italics are of works more than about 50,000 words in length. Titles in double quotation marks are of prose works, including plays, under about 50,000 words in length. Titles in single quotation marks are of speeches. And titles in roman type without quotation marks are of poems. Each title in the summary section is followed by a parenthetical notation or a footnote. Abbreviations in parentheses refer to titles of the twenty-two most important works of Twain (for example, WMT 1 means the first volume of *The Writings of Mark Twain*, Definitive Edition, 1922-1925—see Abbreviations for full information). Locations of titles not followed by parenthetical notations are indicated in footnotes (see, for example, the footnote following my summary of "Address to His Imperial Majesty Alexander II, Emperor of Russia"). Material which appears in brackets constitutes information supplied from sources other than the work under consideration: editors have sometimes provided titles for Twain's untitled published works (for example, see ["Several Items by Mark Twain"]), and I occasionally complete the names of real-life persons whom Twain too briefly mentions (see Aguinaldo, [Emilio]). Please note that when I use ellipsis dots in my summaries, such dots indicate Twain's incompleteness, never mine (see ["Affeland"]).   Alphabetizing the names of the characters proved arduous in the extreme. Varying from the usual form, I list first a person—male or female—whose first name or nickname as well as his last name is known, then a person with no indicated first name but with the same last name and a title, then a man with that same last name, then a married woman of that name, and then a single woman of that name. I deviate from this pattern only to place a wife immediately following her husband, unless she has a first name which should be alphabetized earlier. Where doing so seems informative, I distinguish between Mrs. and Miss. (I never employ the Ms. designation.) If inconsistencies seem outrageous, please use a little ingenuity in seeking what you need and also be tolerant: I had eighty inches of 3"x5" cards to shuffle.

I have tried to incorporate all nicknames, handling them as in this example: Finn, Huckleberry; Huck, Hucky. Alternate names and honorific titles are separately alphabetized, with *See* references. (Note, for example, the twenty-six names assigned to Joan of Arc, from the Bashful to the Witch.) When a character appears in more than one of Twain's works, I list him once and then in chronological order of works summarize his activities. (See, for example, Tom Sawyer, who appears in a dozen works; or see Adam, Eve, or Satan.) De —, de —, d' —, La —, L' —, Mac—, Mc—, St.—, Van—, Von—, and von—characters were a troublesome lot, and I again ask your indulgence. Finally, if a person is unnamed but his designation is capitalized, I include him (for example, Captain, Landlady, and You).

It remains for others to say what uses my work may be put to. But I may be permitted to note briefly here that my extensive reading of Twain has made me revise my notion of the man. He is not only far more wide-ranging stylistically and substantively than I realized but also a great deal more profound and *au courant*. It is really not necessary to peruse his notebooks, letters, and autobiography, ignored here, to confirm this conclusion.

It is a pleasure to record my sense of gratitude to many people who have been generous and helpful to me during the seven years I have intermittently worked on this book. Mr. Frederick Anderson, Editor, Mark Twain Papers, University of California at Berkeley, gave me access to the unpublished materials there, and was most hospitable, helpful, knowledgeable, and patient; in addition, he read parts of my manuscript and offered valuable suggestions. Mr. Charles E. Aston, Jr., Curator, Special Collections, Hillman Library, University of Pittsburgh, Pittsburgh, Pennsylvania, made available a splendid edition of Twain. Mrs. Peggy Batten, bibliographer, English Department, University of Pittsburgh, was always efficient and cooperative. Professor Edgar M. Branch, Miami University, Oxford, Ohio, prevented my making one big mistake and a couple of little ones. Dr. John C. Broderick, Manuscript Division, the Library of Congress, Washington, D.C., answered my questions promptly and helpfully. Mr. Cyril Clemens, Editor, the *Mark Twain Journal*, Kirkwood, Missouri, has been a pen pal of mine for years and has been unfailingly gracious and encouraging. Professor John C. Gerber, University of Iowa, Iowa City, Iowa, gave me sound advice. Professor William M. Gibson, New York University, New York City, New York, improved one summary and offered encouragement. Mr. Alan D. Gribben and Mr. Bruce T. Hamilton, editorial assistants, Mark Twain Papers, Berkeley, were cooperative and generous when I appealed to them for help. Professor Hamlin Hill, University of Chicago, Chicago, Illinois, answered a few questions wisely and wittily. Mr. George M. Jones, librarian, Darlington Room, University of Pittsburgh, has always been generous when I have called upon him for aid. Professor E. Hudson Long, Baylor University, Waco, Texas, answered a plea with flattering speed. Professor Walter J. Meserve, Indiana University, Bloomington, Indiana, provided expert advice. So did Professor Henry Nash Smith, University of California, Berkeley, who illuminates every topic he touches. Dr. Jerome L. Rosenberg, Dean, Faculty of Arts and Sciences, University of Pittsburgh, expeditiously allocated funds for travel, research, and photocopying, without which this book would have been smaller in scope and would have been delayed in appearing. Professor William B. Todd, University of Texas, Austin, through his efficient associate Martha Hartzog Stocker, sent me a copy of his invaluable "Index of Minor Works [of Mark Twain]," without which my book would have taken much longer and would inevitably have been less complete. And Professor John S. Tuckey, Calumet Campus of Purdue University, Hammond, Indiana, answered questions before the publication of his edition of *Mark Twain's Fables of Man*, galleys of which Mr. Anderson had generously given me.

The Mark Twain Company has kindly allowed me to summarize Twain's works, including slightly more than a hundred unpublished pieces, and to identify the characters therein. Harper & Row, Publishers, generously gave me permission to summarize material in their copyrighted Twain books, *Letters from the Earth* and *A Pen Warmed-up in Hell*. The Beinecke Rare Book and Manuscript Library, Yale University Press, Yale University, New Haven, Connecticut, granted me whimsically phrased permission to summarize two pornographic poems by Twain. The Rare Book Department, Alderman Library, University of Virginia Library, University of Virginia, Charlottesville, Virginia, sent me a photocopy of Twain's ludicrous lecture on onanism. I am also most grateful to the staffs of Hillman Library, University of Pittsburgh; Hill Library, Carnegie-Mellon University, Pittsburgh; Duquesne University Library, Duquesne University, Pittsburgh; Pattee Library, Pennsylvania State University, University Park, Pennsylvania; and the Library of Congress, Washington, D.C.

Many people named above—and others too—have saved me from mistakes. All the same, it has seemed best to allow a few to remain, as testimony of my imperfection. Twain would be pleased. Which reminds me: I should be remiss if I did not commend that ill-tempered and badly remunerated person who typed my entire manuscript twice (and parts of it thrice)—namely, myself.

Robert L. Gale

University of Pittsburgh
Pittsburgh, Pennsylvania 15260

Man's mind is a clever machine, and can work up materials into ingenious fancies and ideas, but it can't create the material; none but the gods can do that.

Mark Twain's Letters (New York and London: Harper & Brothers Publishers, 1917), II, 815

. . . hang these names . . . , they warp my jaw . . .

Mark Twain, "A Horse's Tale"

CHRONOLOGY

1835   Born on November 30 in Florida, Missouri, the fifth child of John Marshall Clemens (1797-1847) and Jane Lampton Clemens (1803-90)

1839   Moved with Clemens family to Hannibal, Missouri

1848   Apprenticed to various Hannibal newspapers

1853-57   Worked as a printer in St. Louis, New York, Philadelphia, Muscatine, Keokuk, and Cincinnati

1857-61   Worked as a cub pilot and then a pilot on Mississippi River steamboats

1861   Served briefly in the Missouri militia; went with his brother Orion by stagecoach to Nevada, where he prospected for silver (to 1862, and again 1864-65)

1862-64   Worked as a reporter on the Virginia City *Territorial Enterprise*

1864-66   Wrote for San Francisco newspapers, including the *Morning Call*, and magazines

1865   "Jim Smiley and His Jumping Frog"

1866   Visited Hawaii as a correspondent for the Sacramento *Union*, lectured in San Francisco

1866-67   Was the New York correspondent for the San Francisco *Alta California*

1867   Traveled aboard the *Quaker City* to Europe and the Holy Land; *The Celebrated Jumping Frog of Calaveras County, and Other Sketches*

1867-69   Was an intermittent correspondent (contributing to the *Galaxy*, 1868-71) and lecturer

1869   Bought an interest in the Buffalo *Express* and contributed to it (to 1871); *The Innocents Abroad*

1870   Married Olivia Langdon (1845-1904) in Elmira, New York; their son Langdon was born (died 1872)

1871   Sold his *Express* interest; moved to Hartford, Connecticut; resumed lecturing

1872   Daughter Susan was born (died 1896); Twain lectured in England (again in 1873); *Roughing It*

1873   *The Gilded Age* (with Charles Dudley Warner)

1874   Daughter Clara was born (died 1962)

1875   *Sketches, Old and New*

1876   Privately printed "1601"; *The Adventures of Tom Sawyer*

1877	Delivered his disastrous Whittier birthday speech in Boston
1878-79	Traveled extensively in Europe and visited London
1880	Daughter Jean was born (died 1909); *A Tramp Abroad*
1881	Began ruinously investing in the Paige typesetting machine (until 1894); *The Prince and the Pauper*
1882	Revisited the Mississippi River region; *The Stolen White Elephant*
1883	*Life on the Mississippi*
1884	*Adventures of Huckleberry Finn*
1884-85	Lectured with George Washington Cable
1885	Founded the publishing firm of Charles L. Webster & Co. (failed 1894)
1889	*A Connecticut Yankee in King Arthur's Court*
1891-95	Lived in Europe
1892	*The American Claimant*
1893	*The £1,000,000 Bank-Note*
1894	Refused to accept bankruptcy (was solvent again by 1896); *Pudd'nhead Wilson* and *Tom Sawyer Abroad*
1895	Lectured around the world (until 1896)
1896	*Personal Recollections of Joan of Arc* and *Tom Sawyer, Detective*
1897	Orion Clemens, Mark Twain's brother (born 1825), died; *Following the Equator* and *How to Tell a Story*
1897-1900	Lived in Europe and London
1899	Publication of the first uniform edition of works was begun (to 1907)
1900	Lived in New York
1901	"To the Person Sitting in Darkness"
1902	*A Double Barrelled Detective Story*
1903-04	Lived in Italy
1904	Death of Olivia; *A Dog's Tale*
1905	*King Leopold's Soliloquy*
1906	*The $30,000 Bequest* and *Eve's Diary*
1907	Final visit to England; *Christian Science* and *A Horse's Tale*
1908	Began his residence in Redding, Connecticut
1909	*Is Shakespeare Dead?* and *Extracts from Captain Stormfield's Visit*
1910	Died on April 21 at Redding; *Speeches* (expanded 1923)
1916	*The Mysterious Stranger*
1917	*What Is Man?* and *Letters*

1919	*The Curious Republic of Gondour*
1922-25	*The Writings of Mark Twain*, 37 vols.
1923	*Europe and Elsewhere*
1924	*Autobiography* (expanded 1959)
1926	*Sketches of the Sixties* (with Bret Harte, rev. 1927)
1928	*The Adventures of Thomas Jefferson Snodgrass*
1935	*Notebook*
1938	*Letters from the Sandwich Islands, The Washoe Giant in San Francisco,* and *Mark Twain's Western Years*
1939	*Letters from Honolulu*
1940	*Mark Twain in Eruption* and *Mark Twain's Travels with Mr. Brown*
1941	*Mark Twain's Letters to Will Bowen* and *Republican Letters*
1942	*Letters in the Muscatine Journal*
1943	*Washington in 1868*
1949	*The Letters of Mark Twain to Mrs. Fairbanks* and *The Love Letters of Mark Twain*
1952	*Report from Paradise*
1957	*The Complete Short Stories of Mark Twain* and *Mark Twain of the Enterprise*
1958	*Traveling with the Innocents Abroad*
1960	*Mark Twain-Howells Letters*
1961	*Ah Sin* (with Bret Harte), *Contributions to the Galaxy,* and *Life as I Find It*
1962	*Letters from the Earth*
1963	*The Forgotten Writings of Mark Twain* and *Mark Twain's San Francisco*
1967	*Mark Twain's Letters to His Publishers, 1867-1894* and *Which Was the Dream?*
1968	*Satires & Burlesques*
1969	*Hannibal, Huck and Tom; Mark Twain's Correspondence with Henry Huttleston Rogers, 1893-1909;* and *Mysterious Stranger Manuscripts*
1970	*Clemens of the Call*
1972	*Fables of Man, The Great Landslide Case: Three Versions,* and *A Pen Warmed-up in Hell*
1973	*Mark Twain's What Is Man?* and *Other Philosophical Essays*

CHRONOLOGICAL LIST OF MARK TWAIN'S WORKS*

1852
"The Dandy Frightening the Squatter" (1930)

1853
The Burial of Sir Abner Gilstrap (1934)
"Correspondence" (1942)
[Good-by, Good-by] (1920)
The Heart's Lament (1966)
Love Concealed (1934)
Married in Podunk (1934)
"Original Correspondence" (1942)
["Several Items by Mark Twain"], 1853, 1869, 1879 (1935)

1854
"For the Journal" (1942)

1855
"Correspondence of the 'Journal'" (February) (1942)
"Correspondence of the 'Journal'" (March) (1942)

1856
The Adventures of Thomas Jefferson Snodgrass, 1856, 1857 (1928)

1859
"River Intelligence" (1962)

1862
[How Sleep the Brave . . . ?] (1966)

---

*For bibliographical information, grateful acknowledgment is hereby made to Merle Johnson, A Bibliography of the Works of Mark Twain (New York and London: Harper & Brothers, rev. ed., 1935); to Jacob Blanck, Bibliography of American Literature (New Haven: Yale University Press, 1957), II, 173-254; and to Professor William B. Todd and his bibliographical associate Martha Hartzog Stocker, the University of Texas at Austin, for an invaluable copy of "Index of Minor Works [of Mark Twain]," soon to be published. Please note that for each year items are listed alphabetically rather than chronologically. Usually I give here only short titles. Dates in parentheses are of first book publication. Often these titles are revised ones.

"The Chapman Family" (1938)
"A Complaint about Correspondents" (1867)
"Concerning Chambermaids" (1867)
"An Epistle from Mark Twain" (1938)
"Fashions" (1938)
"Fitz Smythe's Horse" (1886)
"Honored as a Curiosity" (1867)
"An Inquiry about Insurances" (1867)
"The Kearny Street Ghost Story" (1938)
Letters from Honolulu (1939)
Letters from the Sandwich Islands (1938)
"Mark Twain on the New Wild Cat Religion" (1938)
'"Mark Twain's" Farewell' (1938)
"Mark Twain's Interior Notes" (1938)
"Miseries of Washoe Men" (1938)
"The Moral Phenomenon" (1926)
"More Spiritual Investigations" (1938)
"Mysterious Newspaper Man" (1938)
"New Year's Day" (1938)
"On Boot-Blacks" (1938)
"On California Critics" (1938)
"On Linden" (1926)
"Origin of Illustrious Men" (1867)
Polonius' Advice to His Son (1947)
"Reflections on the Sabbath" (1938)
"Remarkable Instances of Presence of Mind" (1867)
"Sabbath Reflections" (1973)
"A San Francisco Millionaire" (1938)
'The Sandwich Islands' (1923)
"The Signal Corps" (1938)
"So-Long" (1938)
"Spiritual Insanity" (1938)
"A Strange Dream" (1867)
"What Have the Police Been Doing?" (1938)

1867
'The American Vandal' (1923)
"The Facts in the Case of the Senate Doorkeeper" (1961)
"Female Suffrage" (1961)
Good Bye (1966)

"Map of Paris" (1871)
"A Medieval Romance" (1871)
"A Memory" (1871)
"Misplaced Confidence" (1872)
"My Bloody Massacre" (1871)
[My Name It Was "Old Chris"] (1963)
"My Watch" (1871)
"A Mysterious Visit" (1872)
Napoleon after Hagenau (1966)
"A New Crime" (1872)
"The Noble Red Man" (1871)
"The Office Bore" (1871)
Old Time and I (1963)
["Oneida"] (1871)
"Our Precious Lunatic" (1919)
["A Patriarch"] (1871)
Personal (1963)
"A Personal Explanation" (1961)
"The Petrified Man" (1871)
"Political Economy" (1871)
["Portrait"] (1961)
"Post Mortem Poetry" (1871)
"The 'Present' Nuisance" (1871)
["Professor Silliman"] (1871)
"The Reception at the President's" (1871)
"Riley" (1871)
"A Royal Compliment" (1871)
"Running for Governor" (1871)
"Science vs. Luck" (1871)
The Story of a Gallant Deed (1871)
"The Story of the Good Little Boy" (1870)
Three Aces (1963)
"To Correspondents" (1871)
"To Raise Poultry" (1872)
"The 'Tournament' in A.D. 1870" (1871)
"A Tribute to Anson Burlingame" (1923)
"Unburlesquable Things" (1871)
"The Undertaker's Chat" (1871)
"The Widow's Protest" (1871)
"Wit Inspiration of the 'Two-Year-Olds'" (1870)

"Putting Up Stoves" (1872)
"Rev. Henry Ward Beecher's Farm" (1872)
Roughing It (1872)
"The Siamese Twins" (1872)
'The Union Right or Wrong?' (1910)

1873
"British Benevolence" (1961)
The Gilded Age (1873)
'License of the Press' (1923)
"Mark Twain on Foster" (1961)

1874
'Cats and Candy' (1910)
"A Curious Pleasure Excursion" (1875)
"Life as I Find It" (1961)
"A Memorable Midnight Experience" (1874)
"Property in Opulent London" (1874)
"Rogers" (1874)
"A True Story" (1875)

1875
'Accident Insurance' (1875)
"The 'Blind Letter' Department" (1875)
"A Couple of Poems by Twain and Moore" (1875)
"The Curious Republic of Gondour" (1919)
"An Encounter with an Interviewer" (1878)
"Experience of the McWilliamses with Membranous Croup" (1875)
"'Party Cries' in Ireland" (1875)
"Some Learned Fables" (1875)
'Speech at the Scottish Banquet in London' (1875)
Those Annual Bills (1875)

1876
The Adventures of Tom Sawyer (1876)
"The Canvasser's Tale" (1878)
"The Facts Concerning the Recent Carnival of Crime in Connecticut" (1877)
"Letter Read at a Dinner of the Knights of St. Patrick" (1878)

1877
"Duncan of the *Quaker City*" (1961)
"Duncan Once More" (1961)
"Francis Lightfoot Lee" (1961)
"Mark Twain's War Experiences" (1877)
'The Sandwich Islands,' c. 1877 (1901)
"Some Rambling Notes of an Idle Excursion" (1878)
"The Story of a Speech," 1877, 1907 (1910)

1878
"About Magnanimous-Incident Literature" (1882)
"The Loves of Alonzo Fitz Clarence and Rosannah Ethelton" (1878)
"O'Shah" (1923)
"Punch, Brothers, Punch" (1878)

1879
'The Babies' (1896)
"The Great Revolution in Pitcairn" (1882)
'Some Thoughts on the Science of Onanism' (1952)
"Salutatory" (1923)
'Unconscious Plagiarism' (1910)

1880
"A Boston Girl" (1961)
"Edward Mills and George Benton" (1906)
"Mrs. McWilliams and the Lightning" (1882)
'On Adam,' c. 1880 (1923)
'On After-Dinner Speaking' (1923)
"On the Philosophy of Shaving" (1961)
"The Postal Order Business" (1880)
"Remarkable Gold Mines" (1885)
"1601" (1880)
"A Tale for Struggling Young Poets" (1892)
"A Telephonic Conversation" (1906)
A Tramp Abroad (1880)

1881
"A Curious Experience" (1882)
'Mistaken Identity' (1910)
'Plymouth Rock and the Pilgrims' (1910)

1893
"About All Kinds of Ships" (1893)
"The Californian's Tale" (1897)
"A Cure for the Blues" (1893)
"The Esquimau Maiden's Romance" (1900)
"Extracts from Adam's Diary" (1893)
"Is He Living or Is He Dead?" (1900)
'Lotos Club Dinner in Honor of Mark Twain' (1910)
"The £1,000,000 Bank-Note" (1893)
"Traveling with a Reformer" (1897)

1894
"In Defense of Harriet Shelley" (1897)
"Private History of the 'Jumping Frog' Story" (1897)
Pudd'nhead Wilson (1894)
"Those Extraordinary Twins" (1894)
Tom Sawyer Abroad (1894)

1895
L'Arbre Fée de Bourlemont (1895)
Contract with Mrs. T. K. Beecher (1912)
"Fenimore Cooper's Literary Offenses" (1897)
"How to Tell a Story" (1897)
"Mental Telegraphy Again" (1897)
'The Morals Lecture,' 1895-96 (1968)
'Obituary Poetry' (1910)
'Pudd'nhead Wilson Dramatized' (1910)
"Talk about Twins" (1895)
'An Undelivered Speech' (1910)
"What Paul Bourget Thinks of Us" (1897)

1896
"A Little Note to M. Paul Bourget" (1896)
Personal Recollections of Joan of Arc (1896)
Tom Sawyer, Detective (1896)

1897
Following the Equator (1897)
'The Horrors of the German Language' (1910)
In Memoriam: Olivia Susan Clemens (1900)
Invocation (1897)

To the Above Old People (1923)
'Welcome Home' (1901)
'Woman's Press Club' (1910)

1901
'Business' (1910)
"The Death Disk" (1902)
'Dinner to Hamilton W. Mabie' (1910)
'The Dinner to Mr. Choate' (1910)
'Edmund Burke on Croker and Tammany' (1901)
'Municipal Corruption' (1910)
'Osteopathy' (1910)
'Princeton' (1910)
"To My Missionary Critics" (1923)
"To the Person Sitting in Darkness" (1901)
"Two Little Tales" (1902)
'University Settlement Society' (1910)
'Votes for Women' (1910)
'Water Supply' (1910)
'Watterson and Twain as Rebels' (1910)

1902
"Amended Obituaries" (1906)
"The Belated Russian Passport" (1903)
"A Defence of General Funston" (1902)
"Did Not Hurt the Mule" (1902)
"Does the Race of Man Love a Lord?" (1906)
"A Double Barrelled Detective Story" (1902)
"The Five Boons of Life" (1906)
'Missouri University Speech' (1910)
"New Ideas on Farming" (1902)
'The St. Louis Harbor-Boat "Mark Twain"' (1910)
'Sixty-Seventh Birthday' (1910)
"Thomas Brackett Reed" (1923)
"Was It Heaven? Or Hell?" (1906)

1903
"A Dog's Tale" (1903)
"Instructions in Art" (1923)
"The Yacht Races" (1920)

1907
'The Alphabet and Simplified Spelling' (1910)
'The Ascot Gold Cup' (1932)
'Books, Authors, and Hats' (1910)
"Captain Stormfield's Visit to Heaven," 1907-08 (1952)
'Charity and Actors' (1910)
Christian Science (1907)
'Educating Theatre-Goers' (1910)
'The Educational Theatre,' 1907, 1908 (1923)
'Fulton Day, Jamestown' (1910)
'General Miles and the Dog' (1910)
'Independence Day' (1910)
'The Savage Club Dinner' (1910)
'A Visit to the Savage Club' (1907)

1908
'Books and Burglars' (1910)
'Booksellers' (1910)
'Compliments and Degrees' (1910)
'Courage' (1910)
'Dedication Speech' (1910)
'Dinner to Whitelaw Reid' (1910)
'Dress Reform and Copyright' (1910)
'Education and Citizenship' (1910)
'Queen Victoria' (1910)

1909
'Advice to Girls' (1910)
'Carnegie the Benefactor' (1910)
'Dinner to Mr. Jerome' (1910)
'Dr. Mark Twain, Farmeopath' (1910)
"A Fable" (1922)
Is Shakespeare Dead? (1909)
"Marjorie Fleming, the Wonder Child" (1923)
"The New Planet" (1923)
["The Omitted Chapter of *The Prince and the Pauper*"] c. 1909 (1961)
"Queen Victoria's Jubilee" (1909)
'Rogers and Railroads' (1910)

1910
'Cigars and Tobacco' (1910)
'The Dress of Civilized Woman' (1910)

'Girls,' n.d. (1910)
"Preface" to *Mark Twain's Speeches* (1910)
["The Suppressed Chapter of *Life on the Mississippi*"[, c. 1910 (1942)
"The Turning Point of My Life" (1917)
'The Weather,' n.d. (1910)

1911
"The Death of Jean" (1917)

1912
"Address to His Imperial Majesty Alexander II, Emperor of Russia"
    (1912)
Cushion First (1912)
Kiditchin (1966)
"A Monument to Adam" (1912)
"My Platonic Sweetheart" (1922)
"Petition Concerning Copyright" (1912)

1914
"How to Make History Dates Stick" (1917)
"A Scrap of Curious History" (1917)

1917
"As Concerns Interpreting the Deity" (1917)
"The Bee" (1917)
["Concerning a Bear"] (1917)
"Concerning Tobacco" (1917)
["Letter to Sylvester Baxter"] (1917)
["Letter to William T. Snead"] (1917)
"The Memorable Assassination" (1917)
"A Simplified Alphabet" (1917)
"Taming the Bicycle" (1917)

1920
[Mammoth Cod], c. 1920 (1937)

1923
"Adam's Soliloquy" (1923)
"As Regards Patriotism" (1923)
"Bible Teaching and Religious Practice" (1923)

"The Cholera Epidemic in Hamburg" (1923)
"Corn-Pone Opinions" (1923)
"The Dervish and the Offensive Stranger" (1923)
"Dr. Loeb's Incredible Discovery" (1923)
"Down the Rhône" (1923)
"Dueling" (1923)
"Eve Speaks" (1923)
"The Finished Book" (1923)
"Letters to Satan" (1923)
"The Lost Napoleon" (1923)
"Samuel Erasmus Moffett" (1923)
"Skeleton Plan of a Proposed Casting Vote Party" (1923)
"Sold to Satan" (1923)
"Some National Stupidities" (1923)
"The Temperance Crusade and Women's Rights" (1923)
"That Day in Eden" (1923)
"The United States of Lyncherdom" (1923)
"The War Prayer" (1923)
"A Word of Encouragement for Our Blushing Exiles" (1923)

1927
"Quaker City" (1927)

1931
[Goodnight, Sweetheart, Goodnight] (1931)

1935
The Derelict, c. 1935 (c. 1935)
Mark Twain's Margins on Thackeray's "Swift" (1935)
[A Parody on Swift] (1935)

1942
Poem to Margaret (1966)

1944
["The Gorky Incident"] (1962)

1946
"Fenimore Cooper's Further Literary Offenses" (1962)
"Letter from the Recording Angel" (1952)

1947
The Mysterious Chinaman (1966)

1948
["Ghost Life on the Mississippi"]
Mark Twain in Three Moods (1948)

1958
Battle Hymn of the Republic (Brought down to Date) (1958)

1959
"The Autobiography of Belshazzar" (1959)
["A Cat Tale"] (1962)

1960
The Earth Invoketh the Sun (1960)

1961
Ah Sin (1961)

1962
["The French and the Comanches"] (1962)
["From an English Notebook"] (1962)
["From an Unfinished Burlesque of Books on Etiquette"] (1962)
"In the Animals' Court" (1962)
["The Intelligence of God"] (1962)
["Letters from the Earth"] (1962)
["The Lowest Animal"] (1962)
["Official Report to the I.I.A.S."] (1962)
["Papers of the Adam Family"] (1962)
["Simplified Spelling"] (1962)
["Something about Repentance"] (1962)
"Was the World Made for Man?" (1962)
["Zola's 'La Terre'"] (1962)

1963
Simon Wheeler, Detective (1963)
S'klk! G'lang! (1966)

1966
Apostrophe to Death (1966)

1972
"Abner L. Jackson (About to Be) Deceased" (1972)
["Ancients in Modern Dress"] (1972)
["Asa Hoover"] (1972)
["Colloquy Between a Slum Child and a Moral Mentor"] (1972)
"Concerning 'Martyrs' Day'" (1972)
["The Emperor-God Satire"] (1972)
"The Fable of the Yellow Terror" (1972)
["Flies and Russians"] (1972)
"Goose Fable" (1972)
["History 1,000 Years from Now"] (1972)
"The Holy Children" (1972)
["In My Bitterness"] (1972)
"The International Lightning Trust" (1972)
"A Letter from the Comet" (1972)
["Letter to Jules Hart"] (1972)
["Letter to the Editor of *Free Russia*"] (1972)
"Little Bessie" (1972)
"Little Nelly Tells a Story Out of Her Own Head" (1972)
["The Lost Ear-ring"] (1972)
["Mock Marriage"] (1972)
"Newhouse's Jew Story" (1972)
"Old Age" (1972)
"The Private Secretary's Diary" (1972)
["Randall's Jew Story"] (1972)
"The Recurrent Major and Minor Compliment" (1972)
"The Refuge of the Derelicts" (1972)
"The Second Advent" (1972)
"The Secret History of Eddypus, the World Empire" (1972)
"The Stupendous Procession" (1972)
"The Synod of Praise" (1972)
["The Ten Commandments"] (1972)
"Thoughts of God" (1972)
["The Victims"] (1972)
"You've Been a Dam Fool, Mary. You Always Was" (1972)

1973
"The Character of Man" (1973)
["Macfarlane"] (1973)
["Man's Place in the Animal World"] (1973)
"Things a Scotsman Wants to Know" (1973)

["Three Statements of the Eighties"] (1973)

Unpublished
"About Cities in the Sun"
"Adopted Boy"
"Aguinaldo"
"The American Claimant"
"American Representation in Austria"
["Anecdote about Captain Jones"]
"The Aquarium"
["Baron Tauchnitz and Copyright"]
Behold—the Penis Mightier Than the Sword
"Bells in Buffalo"
"The Black Prince's Cat"
["Boarding House Novel"]
["Burlesque News Item"]
["Burlesque Review of *Allen Bay*"]
["Burlesque Sea Story"]
["Changing Definitions of 'Lady' and 'Gentleman'"]
"Charade"
"The Christening Yarn"
"Concerning a Reformed Pledge"
"Concerning the 'Interview'"
"Concerning the Scoundrel Edward H. House"
"The Countess Massiglia (Reality)"
"The Countess Massiglia (Romance)"
["Criticism of the Bible"]
"The Curse of McAllister"
"The Death Wafer"
"The Death-Wafer"
"A Defence of Royalty & Nobility"
["Dialogue on the Philippines"]
"Discovery of Anesthetics"
"Dr. Van Dyke as a Man and as a Fisherman"
["Doré Gallery"]
"The Drinking & Tobacco Habits Cured"
["English Phone and Postal Service"]
"An Extraordinary Case"
["For Free Silver"]
"The Force of 'Suggestion'"
"Fragments of Prussian History"

ABBREVIATIONS

CG   *Contributions to the Galaxy 1868-1871,* ed. Bruce R. McElderry, Jr. (Gainesville, Florida: Scholars' Facsimiles & Reprints, 1961)

CJF   *The Celebrated Jumping Frog of Calaveras, and Other Sketches,* ed. John Paul (New York: C. H. Webb, 1867)

CRG   *The Curious Republic of Gondour and Other Whimsical Sketches* (New York: Boni and Liveright, 1919)

FM   *Mark Twain's Fables of Man,* ed. John S. Tuckey (Berkeley, Los Angeles, London: University of California Press, 1972)

FW   *The Forgotten Writings of Mark Twain,* ed. Henry Duskis (New York: Philosophical Library, 1961)

HHT   *Mark Twain's Hannibal, Huck & Tom,* ed. Walter Blair (Berkeley and Los Angeles: University of California Press, 1969)

LAIFI   *Life as I Find It,* ed. Charles Neider (Garden City, New York: Hanover House, 1961)

LFE   *Letters from the Earth,* ed. Bernard DeVoto (New York: Harper & Row, 1962)

LSI   *Letters from the Sandwich Islands,* ed. G. Ezra Dane (San Francisco: Grabhorn Press, 1937)

MSM   *Mark Twain's Mysterious Stranger Manuscripts,* ed. William M. Gibson (Berkeley and Los Angeles: University of California Press, 1969)

MTP   The Mark Twain Papers, General Library, University of California at Berkeley

MTWY Ivan Benson, *Mark Twain's Western Years: Together with Hitherto Unprinted Clemens Western Items* (Stanford: Stanford University Press, 1938)

P   Arthur L. Scott, *On the Poetry of Mark Twain, with Selections from His Verse* (Urbana: University of Illinois Press, 1966)

RL   *Republican Letters,* ed. Cyril Clemens (Webster Groves, Missouri: International Mark Twain Society, 1941)

S   *Mark Twain's Speeches,* with Introduction by William Dean Howells (New York: Harper & Brothers, 1910)

SB   *Mark Twain's Satires & Burlesques,* ed. Franklin R. Rogers (Berkeley and Los Angeles: University of California Press, 1967)

l

SS   Bret Harte and Mark Twain, *Sketches of the Sixties* (San Fran-
         cisco: John Howell, 1926, rev. 1927)
W 1868   *Washington in 1868,* ed. Cyril Clemens (Webster Groves,
         Missouri: International Mark Twain Society, 1943)
WG   *The Washoe Giant in San Francisco,* ed. Franklin Walker (San
         Francisco: George Fields, 1938)
WIM   *What is Man? and Other Philosophical Essays,* ed. Paul
         Baender (Berkeley, Los Angeles, London: University of
         California Press, 1973)
WMT   *The Writings of Mark Twain,* Definitive Edition (New York:
         Gabriel Wells, 1922-1925), 37 vols. (The number in
         arabic numerals after the abbreviation WMT indi-
         cates the volume number.)
WWD   *Mark Twain's Which Was the Dream?,* ed. John S. Tuckey
         (Berkeley and Los Angeles: University of California
         Press, 1967)

PLOTS

"Abelard and Heloise." From *The Innocents Abroad*.

"Das Abenteuer des Hochwürdiger Sam Jones." See "A Singular Episode."

"Abner L. Jackson (About to Be) Deceased," 1972 (FM).

Nathaniel E. Harrison, executor of Abner L. Jackson's will, writes to Rodney Dennis, an insurance official, about Jackson, whose home town now mourns his loss. Jackson was born in Connecticut in 1810, was orphaned in his early teens, attended Yale but was unable to finish, read for the law, entered the ministry but had a change of conscience and resigned, moved to Elmira in 1840, raised a company for the Mexican War but never fought, was elected in 1854 to the legislature but was disqualified because of an election irregularity, raised a company at the outbreak of the Civil War but was struck by a passing elephant on his way to take up his commission, and was employed as a Presbyterian sexton during his last ten years. Last week something seemed amiss with him. He was in debt and had only $130 to his name. So he took out a travel-insurance policy in the amount of $100,000, bid farewell to his wife and seven children, begged their forgiveness for what he was about to do, and went to New York to take a trip on an excursion boat. Now he is gone. Harrison asks whether he may now draw upon Dennis to fulfill the terms of Jackson's will. The man left $90,000 to his family and specified various sums to other relatives, various strange religious outfits, odd charities, pet societies, and the like.

> Rodney Dennis, Nathaniel E. Harrison, Robert G. Ingersoll, Abner L. Jackson, Mrs. Abner L. Jackson, Jackson, Mrs. Jackson, Jackson, Jackson, Jabez Parks, Abel Thompson, Miss Wright, Miss Wright.

"About a Remarkable Stranger," 1871 (CG).

The narrator no sooner finishes telling about a chimney than Markiss caps the account by explaining that his chimney has smoke in it so thick that it must be dug out with an axe. Later he says that he knows of a tree much bigger than one the narrator has been describing. Still later he says that he has a faster horse than the narrator's. Finally he tells a better story about mean employers: he knew a miner who was blown up by some blasting powder, and his bosses docked him for the sixteen minutes he was in flight. Finally when Markiss hanged himself, the jury doubted his suicide note, because he had never told the truth before. (In *Roughing It*.)

> Captain Bilgewater, John James Godfrey, the High Sheriff, Jones, Markiss, Muckawow, Captain Perkins, Captain Saltmarsh.

"About All Kinds of Ships," 1893 (WMT 22).

First the author contrasts the modern steamer and the obsolete one. He walks about the great vessel the *Havel* and notes changes. It is as comfortable as a Continental hotel, quiet, well lighted, sumptuously appointed, handled by signals from gongs, with varied menu, dry decks, walls of steel, and water-tight compartments for variable ballast. Next the author implicitly compares Noah's ark to a modern vessel, remarking that the inspector at Bremen would never allow Noah to clear his harbor. Noah could not satisfactorily answer questions concerning destination—Chicago, perhaps, for the Exposition?—crew, cargo, maintenance of animals aboard, and the like. Then the author contrasts the luxury of the *Havel* with the squalor of Columbus's ships. They rolled and pitched, darkness was as thick as gum, their rats and cockroaches marched in brigades, and the illustrious Admiral had only bacon, beans, and gin for his fare. Finally the author regrets that romance at sea is gone forever. What passengers indulge in sea-songs now? Who is pleasantly becalmed, as the author once was between San Francisco and the Sandwich Islands, for fourteen straight days? When the wind finally sprang up, a column of barnacles held the vessel fast.

Columbus, Noah, the King of Spain.

"About Barbers," 1871 (WMT 7).

Barbers and their surroundings never change. A man approaches a shop door, enters a split-second ahead of the narrator, and therefore takes the only vacant chair. The second and third barbers are finishing customers neck and neck, and the less proficient barber is through first; so the narrator leaves the shop to avoid him. When he returns, four people are waiting. He whiles away the time looking at bottles and shaving cups, and examining cheap prints and stale papers. The worst barber finally yells "Next!", and soon rubs and scrubs and lathers him terribly, interrupts his labors to watch a dog fight—and lose his bet—and finally rakes and cuts the narrator's tender chin. The barber takes so long that the narrator misses his train. Still, he happily delays a day, in order to attend the funeral of that barber, who fortunately dies of apoplexy two hours after soaking, slapping, and generously sprinkling and powdering him.

No. 1, No. 2.

"About Cities in the Sun" (MTP).

Twain reviews George Woodward Wander's *Cities of the Sun*, praising it for making St. John's description of the New Jerusalem imaginable, but then criticizing it for regarding John as a real-estate agent, giving the celestial city wrong dimensions and a pyramidal shape rather than a box shape, and getting the walls incorrect. How nice it would be to go to that heavenly city, and to hear Shakespeare, Milton, and Bunyan read from their works.

Senator [Chauncey M.] Depew, George Woodward Wander.

'About London,' 1872 (WMT 28).

Twain expresses his pleasure at being invited to the Savage Club, says that he will not pun on its name, but instead tells of his joy at being here in London. Hyde Park is fun to see, though one must have a private carriage to ride through it. He likes the zoological gardens, but the British Museum uniquely thrills him. He can read in its library for hours and hardly make a dent. People in London measure distance by coin. For example, it is a shilling by cab to Charing Cross. Twain closes by thanking the Savage Club for being hospitable to his friend Artemus Ward.

"About Magnanimous-Incident Literature," 1878 (WMT 19).

Twain has long read stories about good deeds. Now he determines to investigate and report their consequences. A physician set a poodle's broken leg only to have the dog bring a crowd of other dogs needing similar attention, then bite the physician as he was about to shoot the animals. The doctor died of hydrophobia. A celebrated author, Snodgrass, helped an unknown writer named Snagsby place an article, then several more, only to have his heart broken by Snagsby's publication of a satirical private life of Snodgrass. Thompson McSpadden was grateful when a grocery-wagon driver named William Ferguson rescued his wife and little son during a runaway—grateful, that is, until Ferguson asked for a job, help for his sick mother, then his sisters, then little brother, etc. After a while, McSpadden rebeled and threw the lazy Ferguson clan out of his house. Twain closes in an unsermonlike way with the text at the end: President Lincoln once commended an actor for his Falstaff, only to have the man ask to be named consul to London.

Jimmy Ferguson, Julia Ferguson, Mary Ferguson, William Ferguson, Mrs. Ferguson, Thompson McSpadden, Mrs. Thompson McSpadden, McSpadden, Snagsby, Snodgrass.

"About Play-Acting," 1898 (WMT 23).

The author has a project to suggest but will first describe a tremendously popular play he recently saw in Vienna. It was *The Master of Palmyra* by [Adolf von] Wilbrandt. The scene is Palmyra in Roman times, and the action covers many years. The play features not only an actress reincarnated several times—first she

is a Christian girl among pagans, then a luxury-loving Roman, next
a mother who combines traits of both previous identities, and
finally a beautiful boy also mixing previous natures—but also an
unaging hero who finally asks for the ultimate gift from Death
personified on stage. The play is a sardonic laugh at life, which is
childish, ridiculous, trivial, cheap, capricious, miserable, humiliating,
wearisome, and monotonous. Over and over in the play, hope is
ruined and blight settles upon everyone. Now for the project. The
author suggests that to a New York whose theaters now offer too
many comedies and farces we ought to bring *The Master of Palmyra*,
to satisfy the graver moods of an intelligent public.

[Adolf von] Wilbrandt.

"About Signs." See FW, 1869.

"About Smells," 1870 (CRG).
    In a recent essay, the Rev. Dr. T. De Witte Talmage says that he
has a good Christian friend with such a sensitive nose that when
laborers enter church he can smell them instantly. Talmage says
that we must not kill the church with bad odors. Twain responds
by saying that heaven will be populated with Negroes, Esquimos,
Arabs, Indians, and even a few Spaniards. Talmage and his finicky
friend will want to leave. Christ's very disciples might have smelled
fishy to Talmage. Surely Christianity has a stronger stomach.

The Master, Rev. Dr. T. De Witte Talmage.

'Accident Insurance,' 1875 (WMT 28).
    Twain rises to express his delight at being able to help welcome
[to Hartford] a distinguished visitor [Cornelius Walford]. This
city has a group of people working together: the Colt Arms Company destroys people, insurance companies pay, Batterson erects
monuments for the dead, and fire-insurance companies care for
their hot hereafter. Now that the speaker is a director in an accident-insurance company, he looks with affection on cripples and
freshly mutilated men, provided they have policies. The Hartford
Accident Insurance Company has noted that when a man takes
out a policy he is crippled within a year. One man, who was dis-

appointed with other companies, is bright and happy now, with the Hartford Company, for he has a steady income and new bandages every day. The speaker closes by admitting that he talks nonsense and can say the same for the other speakers.

Batterson, [Cornelius Watford].

'Accident Insurance—Etc.' See 'Accident Insurance.'

"Adam's Diary." See "Extracts from Adam's Diary."

"Adam's Soliloquy," 1923 (WMT 29).

Adam is visiting New York City in spirit. He goes into the Museum of Natural History, pauses before a dinosaur skeleton, and is amazed by its size. Neither he nor Eve ever heard of such a creature until yesterday. They spoke then to Noah about it, and he confessed with some embarrassment that he and his sons failed to stock the ark with any dinosaurs, since they would have taken up too much room and would also have been hard to feed and water. Anyway, it was obvious that they would be needed as fossils for museums eventually. A number of other interesting species were excluded from the ark as well. Next Adam goes out and sits on a bench in the park. He is delighted to think that all of the swarms of people out there are his relatives. A young woman with a baby in a baby carriage comes by, sits down, and begins to read a newspaper. When she scoffs at something she is reading, Adam courteously asks what is the matter. She shows him the article, but he confesses that he cannot read. She asks where he is from. He challenges her to guess. She judges from his accent that he is not an American, and says that he is partly citified and yet partly countrified too. To more questions he replies that his home is huge but has no electric lights, railroads, hospitals, colleges, or police. He gives her a hint: his home has gates of pearl. She thinks he is joking. He tells her that his name is simply Adam. She laughs and says that his name reminds her of the old original, whom she would be afraid to meet. Adam counters by saying that she should not be, since Adam is her kin. When a young fellow sidles up and makes some fresh remarks about the weather to the girl, she stiffly walks away.

Adam, Eve, Ham, Japheth, Noah, Shem.

"Address to His Imperial Majesty Alexander II, Emperor of Russia,"
1912.*

Twain from the *Quaker City* in Yalta sends greetings from a handful of private American travelers, to express their gratitude for
steadfast Russian friendship. The Emperor was right to free twenty million men, and America has profited by the example. Twain
closes by praying for continued Russo-American friendship.

Emperor Alexander II of Russia.

*In Albert Bigelow Paine, *Mark Twain: A Biography* (New York and London:
Harper & Brothers, 1912).

"Adopted Boy" (MTP).

The narrator's family is composed of daughters. So they adopt a
ten-year-old boy for variety. He arrives and becomes adjusted the
same day. He shows curiosity for everything, cannot learn to close
doors, forgets where he has dropped things he is through with,
tastes everything he can (including ink), loves to climb dangerously,
does everything noisily, and knows a hundred ways to hurt himself.

"An Adventure in Remote Seas," 1967 (WWD).

The narrator, George Parker (who told the story to Mark Twain
in New Zealand in 1895), was born in Ohio in 1860, the son of the
village blacksmith, who was killed during the war. The mother died
when the boy was fifteen. He was apprenticed to another blacksmith but three years later made his way to San Francisco and then
ran off to sea. He is now a sailor out of Australia on a ship commanded by Philip Hardy, a good but dull Englishman. The thirteen
men go due south until they are well below Auckland Island, then
east into snow for many days. They lose their bearings and finally
are blown into a rocky bay, where they anchor and begin to kill
seals. Ashore they find an old weather-beaten house, made of
rough boards, and near it a cave. One stormy night, half the men
sit around drinking in the little hovel while the others stay aboard
the ship out in the harbor. A talkative seaman named Sandy Mc-
Pherson gets into a debate with Captain Hardy and argues that
the word "intrinsic" is useless, since nothing has value apart from
circumstantial use. Hardy interrupts to suggest that they check

the ship for lights and also explore the cave. The ship seems to be all right. In the cave they find 120 tons of gold coin, worth at least $60,000,000. When the storm clears, they observe that their vessel is missing. They are so intrigued by their valuable find that they do not worry at first. But then Sandy questions the captain's theory that Abel Jones, the mate, rightly sought safety at sea during the storm and will be back soon. Hardy figures and figures the value of their gold.

> John Boyd, "Brush," Jan Dam, Captain Philip Hardy, Tom Hayes, Charley Holmes, Abel Jones, Jorgensen, Kalani, Sandy McPherson, "Melbourne," George Parker, Parker, Mrs. Parker, "Yaller-Jacket."

"Adventures in Hayti." See ["Several Items by Mark Twain"].

Adventures of Huckleberry Finn, 1884 (WMT 13).

In a prefatory note, Mark Twain explains that he has used a number of dialects in this story, then adds that no one should try to find a motive, a moral, or a plot in it.

Huckleberry Finn begins his account where Mr. Mark Twain ended *The Adventures of Tom Sawyer.* Tom and Huck live in St. Petersburg by the Mississippi River and are rich now, with six thousand dollars apiece from the cave. The money has been invested by Judge Thatcher. The Widow Douglas takes Huck in as her son, to "sivilize" him. Her skinny sister, Miss Watson, lives with her and assists in the process. One midnight, for diversion, Tom and Huck fool Miss Watson's slave Jim into believing that witches flew him around the world. Tom organizes a gang of robbers, to rob and murder men and to ransom women. One day the gang attacks some Spanish merchants and rich Arabs, all of whom are enchanted, as in *Don Quixote,* and look like a group on a Sunday-school picnic. Months pass, and winter comes. Then various omens lead Huck to believe that bad luck is in the offing; so he asks Judge Thatcher to safeguard his money by "buying" it. Misfortune duly enters: Pap Finn the town drunk returns, verifies that his son Huck can now read, and soon thereafter in great discontent spirits the boy up river to a log hut on the Illinois shore. Except for regular whippings, Huck welcomes the return of his lazy old life. More months pass. Pap drinks and rants too much; therefore, Huck, in fear of his life, awaits his chance, saws his way out of the locked hut, stages his own murder so that no one will follow him, and heads for Jackson's Island one long June night.

Huck enjoys his new domain, quite well satisfied with his exploit. He even spies on a boatload of friends searching for his drowned corpse. But after three days, trouble appears: Huck runs across signs of a recent campfire. Overcoming his fear, he investigates and soon finds Miss Watson's Jim, who has heard that he may be sold down the river and has therefore run off to the island. Huck promises not to tell on him. The two enjoy each other's companionship for ten or twelve days. They live in a cavern, explore a floating house which comes by and has a corpse in it but also much useful plunder, and have some anxious moments when Jim is bitten by a rattlesnake, the mate to a dead one which Huck foolishly put in Jim's blanket for a joke. Wondering one day what is happening in town, Huck disguises himself as a girl, paddles his canoe to shore, and raps at the door of a shanty unoccupied until recently. Kind Judith Loftus tells him that Huck Finn was murdered, that Pap was suspected until Jim ran off, and that her husband is about to investigate signs of life on the island. In spite of his elaborate lies, Mrs. Loftus guesses that Huck is a boy, not a girl; but his confession, which is a string of new lies, is satisfactory. In a few minutes, he is rushing back to Jim to roust him out with a terrifying report—"They're after us!"

Huck and Jim gather their numerous belongings and shove off in their canoe and a raft which Jim found earlier and which they have fitted up very comfortably. Timber on the Illinois shore is heavy; so they drift south, past St. Louis during the fifth night. Five nights after that, they encounter a steamboat named the *Walter Scott* and evidently abandoned during a violent storm. Boarding it, though Jim wants to leave well enough alone, they eavesdrop on a band of murderers whose skiff they take when their own raft becomes untied. Huck tries to send help back but soon sees that the boat, wallowing low in the stormy water, has become a house of death. Huck and Jim enjoy some fine cigars from the lost men's loot, talk about European royalty and Biblical harems and foreign languages, and plan to head for Cairo, the Ohio River, and freedom by following it. One night a terrible fog separates Jim, on the raft, and Huck, in their canoe. After hours of loneliness, Huck naps and then spies the raft far ahead. He sneaks aboard and fools Jim into thinking that he only dreamed that they were parted. Learning the truth at last, Jim is so unsmiling and scornful that Huck, abashed, apologizes and vows to himself to treat his companion better.

That night the two float on toward Cairo. When Jim announces that he wants to free his wife and two children, or hire an Abolitionist to do so, Huck is distressed at the man's lack of respect for white folks' property. While Jim hides on the raft, Huck takes the canoe and approaches two white strangers on the river to find out where Cairo is. When the two men are suspicious that the nearby raft might harbor a fugitive slave, Huck hints that the man aboard has smallpox. Each of the men gives Huck $20, and then they back quickly off. Jim is tremendously impressed and grateful. But before daybreak they pass Cairo. Huck surmises that this bad luck came from handling snakeskins. They must buy a big canoe and work their way carefully back to the Ohio. But during the evening the weather gets so thick that a steamboat crashes into their raft, forcing them to dive for their lives.

When Huck bobs to the surface of the water, he cannot find Jim; so he swims to shore and soon comes upon an old-fashioned log house. Challenged by the guns of several residents there, he timidly enters the house to be inspected. Soon the entire Grangerford family—Colonel Saul Grangerfield, his wife Rachel, and their children Bob, Tom, Charlotte, Sophia, and Buck—give him a hospitable welcome, explaining that they thought he might be a member of the Shepherdson clan, with which they have been feuding for thirty years. Huck gets along wonderfully with young Buck, but after a couple of weeks the interlude ends: when Sophia elopes with Harney Shepherdson, the murderous feud erupts and leaves all of the Grangerford males dead. Huck chances to witness Buck's death. Covering the corpse's face, he cries a little, runs to a place in the swamp where a friendly Grangerford slave has already told him Jim and their mended raft are waiting, and seeks with his faithful companion the safety of the river.

Two or three more days and nights swim by. Everything is beautiful. Then one morning while Huck is canoing along the shore he rescues two men who are being pursued by a gang with dogs and horses, and gets them to the raft. One is a bald-headed, gray-whiskered old fellow about seventy; the other, an equally ornery-looking man of thirty or so. The old man lectures at temperance and revival meetings, and has also done doctoring, fortune-telling, and preaching, he explains. The younger man admits to being a journeyman printer, patent-medicine salesman, actor, mesmerist, phrenologist, and teacher. After resting up, the younger man abruptly confesses that he is really the lineal heir of the Duke of Bridgewater. Not to be outdone, the old fellow reveals that he is "Looy the Seventeen," the missing Dauphin of France. Huck and Jim obligingly wait on the two, whom the boy quickly labels in his own mind as frauds. He explains to the king and the duke that Jim is his slave and that they are on their way to orphaned Huck's Uncle Ben in New Orleans. The rapscallions rehearse a couple of scenes from Shakespeare—the balcony scene from *Romeo and Juliet* and a sword fight from *Richard III*—and then go into Pokeville, where the king attends a camp meeting, confesses there that he is a reformed pirate, and collects $87.75 by passing the hat, while the duke sneaks into a printing shop, makes some dishonest sales, and returns to the raft with $9.50. He shows Huck and Jim a reward poster he composed about Jim, so that the group can pretend to have captured the fugitive and thus continue south in safety.

At the next lazy Arkansas town (later named Bricksville) Huck sees proud Colonel Sherburn shoot the harmless town drunk, Boggs, to death for alcoholically insulting him. When a mob swarms up to lynch the murderer, he outfaces them all, with a sneer and a shotgun. Huck drifts away with the crowd and soon dives under a circus tent and enjoys a gaudy performance, highlighted by the emergence of a drunk from the audience who volunteers to ride a circus horse, and does so, to the obvious discomfiture of the ringmaster, who did not know that the drunk was one of his own men! That same evening the king and the duke put on their Shakespearean scenes, but to an audience so small and sleepy that the two decide to present the *Royal Nonesuch* for three nights—ladies and children not admitted. The first performance is wild but so brief that it disappoints the large audience, which, however, decides to say nothing and thus let the second performance claim its victims too. On the third night, everyone returns armed with rotten eggs and dead cats, but the king and the duke skip out early and escape by the raft. While the two rapscallions sleep in triumph—the *Royal Nonesuch* netted them $465—Huck improves Jim's mind with a long lecture on the villainy of royalty in general. Late the same night, Jim, reminded by chance of his daughter, 'Lizabeth, confesses to

Huck that he slapped her once when she refused to obey a command from him which she had not heard because she had been rendered deaf by scarlet fever—and he did not know.

A few days later, in store clothes now, the king, the duke, and Huck leave Jim temporarily and take a steamboat into the next town. On the way to it, the king encounters a young lad (later named Tim Collins) from the town and learns in lavish detail that a well-to-do citizen named Peter Wilks has just died, before the arrival of his brothers, Harvey, a minister, and William, a deaf-and-dumb younger man, both living in England. The king gets enough information about survivors, including Peter's nieces Mary Jane, Susan, and Joanna Wilks, and their numerous neighbors, to feel that he and the duke can successfully impersonate the minister and his mute brother. So the king orders Huck to bring up their baggage and hide Jim and the raft. They enter town, and the villagers quickly fall upon them in sympathy and take them to the fine home of their dead "brother," where they enjoy kissing their "nieces" and talking soulfully of the deceased. They are so completely trusted by everyone but iron-jawed Dr. Robinson— lawyer Levi Bell is out of town—that soon they are in the basement counting Peter's six thousand dollars in gold. The sum is a trifle short of the amount mentioned in a letter left by the dead man; so the two frauds add from their own loot to make up the deficit.

Night comes, and the impostors go to their bedrooms to rest. Huck has been treated so considerately by the girls, especially beautiful Mary Jane, that he decides to take the bag of gold and return it somehow to the Wilks family. After considerable trouble, he finds it in the king's room and hopes to be able to hide it somewhere outside; but when he discovers the front door locked and mourners approaching the coffin, he thrusts it under the lid beside the corpse's cold hands. Embarrassingly soon after the funeral, which is interrupted by a dog with a rat in the basement, the king and the duke begin to auction off Wilks property, including the slaves, prior to the departure of all the Wilkses for England. When the two scoundrels discover the gold gone and query Huck, he harmlessly puts the blame on members of a now broken slave family. Mary Jane later cries so piteously at the separating of the slaves that Huck compassionately bursts out with the information that the sale was illegal and that the Negroes will therefore be together again soon. He tells Mary Jane everything and then urges her to go visit some friends for a day or so outside town so that her beautifully expressive face will not give everything away prematurely, before he can arrange to expose the king and the duke, and yet save some one else (that is, Jim). He writes notes for Mary Jane to read later, about the *Royal Nonesuch* at Bricksville and also about the location of the bag of gold. With a promise to pray for him, Mary Jane then leaves. Huck pauses to remark that he has never seen the gritty girl since but has thought of her millions of times. He quickly tells her sisters that she has gone to nurse a sick friend— with contagious "pluribus-unum mumps"—on the other side of the river but that if they tell their "uncles" their trip to England might be delayed. Huck feels that not even Tom Sawyer could have managed things any better. But then suddenly comes the announcement from the river that two more men calling themselves Harvey and William Wilks have arrived by steamboat.

Levi Bell, the canny town lawyer, has returned from Louisville and now queries the four men and Huck. Most of the citizens suspect that the new pair are frauds, until the king when asked to produce the bag of gold says lamely that a slave stole it from his bed. Talk of lynching frightens Huck, who wishes that Mary Jane were here to help him. Suddenly the new Harvey Wilks challenges the king to describe the tatoo on dead Peter's chest. The king says that it was a small blue arrow. The other Harvey says that his brother had his initials on his chest. But the men who prepared the corpse for burial cannot confirm either story. So the irate crowd rushes through an impending storm to the cemetery, where they dig up the corpse and find the gold. In the ensuing excitement, Huck breaks loose, runs to the river, grabs a canoe, and paddles to the towhead where Jim, their raft, and safety lie. Behind him, however, come the king and the duke in a borrowed skiff. Soon the four are on the raft together. Fortunately for Huck, the duke throttles the king until he "confesses," to save his life, that he hid the gold in the coffin. Within minutes the two scoundrels are drunk and friendly again, and Huck can quietly tell Jim the entire story.

The four float down the river for several days. The king and the duke work towns along the way, lecturing on temperance, teaching dancing, and trying "yellocution," fortune telling, and so on. Then, one morning, they tie up near shabby Pikesville, the king goes to town—the two rascals think that they might put on the

Royal Nonesuch here—Huck and the duke soon follow, and then the king sneaks back and sells Jim for $40. Huck reconnoitres in extreme anguish, learns that Jim is at Silas Phelps's farm two miles away, thinks that if Jim must be a slave it would be better for him to be one back at home with his family, writes out a letter to Jim's owner Miss Watson, but then begins to reminisce. He can recall only good things about Jim and therefore tears up the letter and decides to go to hell—that is, to steal Jim out of bondage. On the road, he sees the duke, who without intending to do so confirms Jim's location. Soon Huck is heading for the Phelps farm. Suddenly a kind-looking woman almost fifty years old bursts from a farm house and greets him, calling him Tom and identifying herself as Aunt Sally. Dogs and children mill about. The woman's confused old husband Silas comes up. Soon Huck is relieved to learn that he is supposed to be Tom Sawyer. Trusting to Providence to help him with the answers, he tells the Phelpses all they might care to know about Aunt Polly, Sid, and Mary back home.

After a while, Huck takes a wagon to the wharf, ostensibly to get his baggage, and runs into the real Tom Sawyer, who, after momentarily doubting that Huck is really alive, decides to pretend that he is Sid. When Huck reveals his intention to steal Jim, Tom surprises his friend by agreeing to help. The two boys part, so that Tom can make a dramatic entrance, which he does. That night they slip down the lightning rod outside their bedroom and rush to town to try to warn the king and the duke that the townspeople plan to tar and feather them when they start their *Royal Nonesuch,* details of which plan the boys have learned from Uncle Silas. But they are too late, and the last they see of the rapscallions is a cruel sight.

For the next three weeks or so, Tom engineers a mixed-up and splendid rescue of Jim, whom they find languishing in chains in a hut near a lean-to behind the Phelps house. They fashion a ladder of sheet shreds, make Jim keep a journal by writing in blood on a shirt borrowed from Silas, have Jim scratch messages on tin plates and throw them out his little window, use digging tools to get to his bunk, bake a witch pie in which to smuggle things to him, steal spoons and other objects for him, convert various things into makeshift pens and saws, fill his hut with rats and spiders and snakes, and finally even post anonymous letters warning the white adults that a rescue is impending. In the climactic midnight scramble, Tom and Huck free Jim, run together to the towhead where Huck's raft is hidden, and get away from a neighborhood posse of armed farmers and barking dogs. But in the melee Tom catches a bullet in his calf. Huck returns to town for a doctor, whom Jim gives up his freedom to assist in treating dangerously feverish Tom.

The wounded boy is soon out of danger and begins to boast of his successful exploit. When he learns that Jim has been recaptured, Tom orders him released, revealing for the first time that Miss Watson freed him on her deathbed. Suddenly Aunt Polly appears. It seems that she became alarmed not only when her sister Sally wrote about Sid in addition to Tom but also when her queries went unanswered. Tom confesses that he intercepted Aunt Polly's letters to Sally. When Tom suggests that he, Huck, and Jim go west for a while and have some adventures among the Indians, Huck is willing but says that he lacks funds for an outfit since Pap has surely collared all of his money by this time. Tom replies that Pap has not been heard from, and Jim mournfully explains that the corpse in the house floating down the river back north was Pap's. Tom soon recovers. Aunt Sally wants to adopt Huck and "sivilize" him; but he plans to resist, since he has been there.

Andy, Marry Antonette, Apthorp, Mrs. Apthorp, Balum's Ass, Tommy Barnes, Mrs. Barnes, Mrs. Bartley, Levi Bell, Mrs. Levi Bell, Uncle Ben, Betsy, Bill, Bill, Bob, Boggs, Miss Boggs, Stephen Dowling Bots, Misto Bradish, the Duke of Bridgewater, the Duke of Bridgewater, the Duke of Bridgewater, the Duke of Bridgewater, Buck, Lafe Buckner, Bud, Hank Bunker, Burton, Tim Collins, Mrs. Collins, Sister Damrell, Widow Douglas, the Duke, Sister Dunlap, Huckleberry Finn, Pap Finn, Mrs. Finn, Abram G. Foster, G. G., Bob Grangerford, Buck Grangerford, Charlotte Grangerford, Emmeline Grangerford, Mrs. Rachel Grangerford, Colonel Saul Grangerford, Sophia Grangerford, Tom Grangerford, Grangerford, Sowberry Hagan, Hank, Buck Harkness, Joe Harper, Hatfield, Brer Hightower, Hines, Hines, Rev. Mr. Hobson, Mrs. Hobson, Miss Hooker, Jim Hornback, Sister Hotchkiss, Deacon Lot Hovey, Mrs. Lot Hovey, Ike, Jack, Jack, Bill Jackson, Mary Ann Jackson, Mort Jackson, Tom Jackson, Jackson, Jim,

Joe, Joe, John, Johnny, the King, 'Lizabeth, Lize, Mrs. Judith, Loftus, Loftus, Looy the Sixteen, Lothrop, Louis XIV, Brer Marples, Mary, Abner Moore, Nat, Archibald Nichols, Pa, Jake Packard, Parker, Brer Penrod, Jimmy Phelps, Matilda Angelina Araminta Phelps, Mrs. Sally Phelps, Silas Phelps, Thomas Benjamin Franklin Jefferson Elexander Phelps, Aunt Polly, Hanner Proctor, Proctor, Sister Ridgeway, Dr. Robinson, Mrs. Robinson, Ben Rogers, Ben Rucker, Mrs. Ben Rucker, St. Jacques, Sid Sawyer, Tom Sawyer, Abner Shackleford, Mrs. Abner Shackleford, Baldy Shepherdson, Harvey Shepherdson, Shepherdson, Colonel Sherburn, Bessie Thatcher, Judge Thatcher, Ben Thompson, William Thompson, Ab Turner, Jim Turner, Sister Utterback, Miss Watson, Miss-What-you-may-call-her, Bill Whipple, Whistler, George Wilks, Mrs. George Wilks, Rev. Mr. Harvey Wilks, Joanna Wilks, Mary Jane Wilks, Peter Wilks, Susan Wilks, William Wilks, Deacon Winn.

[*The Adventures of Thomas Jefferson Snodgrass*], 1856, 1857.*

Thomas Jefferson Snodgrass writes back home to Keokuk from St. Louis that he has been living in a Dutch boardinghouse. One of his hairy friends there suggests that they see Nealy in *Julius Cesar*. They climb up and around to their seats in the many-storeyed theater, which sports an orchestra, ragged lads eating peanuts, and fancy men and women. When the fiddlers tune up, Snodgrass chimes in with a comb-and-paper rendition of "Auld Lang Syne." A policeman starts to put him out, until he explains that St. Louis can hardly survive without patronage from Keokuk. The play finally begins. The scenery is intricate. Cesar, Antony, Mr. Cashus, and grand Brutus engage the attention of the audience, including a woman who is seated in front of Snodgrass and has a turkey-tail hat and a spy glass. Killing Cesar is most unfair. Snodgrass changes his seat, props his feet on the railing, and is booed for doing so. He starts to offer a speech of explanation, but the policeman deposits him in the street.

Next, Snodgrass reports his strange trip from Keokuk to Chicago, on his way to Indianapolis and Cincinnati. He buys a wad of tickets, suffers when his baggage is spilled on the levee, and gets a packet to Quincy. The ship sticks on a sand bar in spite of the

Captain's profanity. The iron horse to Chicago chews red coal, snorts, and shakes the ground. At first Snodgrass is terrified, but soon he feels like such a veteran traveler that he answers passengers' questions—wrongly. The conductor asks him where he plans to stop, but Snodgrass explains that he is going to Chicago, not stopping at all. He starts to make a speech, but the train jerks suddenly and flops him back into his seat. Once the train arrives in Chicago, baggage smashers tear everything apart, and Snodgrass retrieves only part of his vallis. Concluding that Chicago resembles hell, he sets out next day for Cincinnati. The train goes so fast that the tracks behind it melt in places.

Finally, Snodgrass reports that Cincinnati is bitter cold. Everything is frozen, even the miserable little Ohio River. Coal dust is so expensive that the Jews begin to adulterate it with ground pepper. One night Snodgrass is sauntering up a street when a young lady asks him to hold her big basket while she runs over to the grocery store. After he obliges her for more than an hour, he grows suspicious, peeks under the basket cover, and finds a baby, which he transports to his room, where the thing squalls to such an extent that he tries to poke it under the river ice. He is caught and jailed as the child's unnatural father.

> Belding, Jeemes Gordon Bennett, the Captain, Clennam, the Constable, the County Clerk, the Curoner, Dutch, Gentlemen, Dr. H., Lady, the Marshal, the Mayor, Nealy, the Postmaster, the Recorder, Thomas Jefferson Snodgrass, Squire.

*Edited by Charles Honce (Chicago: Pascal Covici, 1928).

The Adventures of Tom Sawyer, 1876 (WMT 8).

In the little village of St. Petersburg by the Mississippi River, Tom Sawyer's Aunt Polly is about to switch the irrepressible boy for stealing jam; but he amusingly escapes, plays hookey from school and goes swimming, watches the little slave boy Jim saw wood in the yard, and then goes in for supper. Tom successfully evades his aunt's questions until his sissified younger half-brother Sid observes that Polly sewed Tom's collar shut with white thread but that it is now fastened with black thread. Shouting a threat to Sid, Tom darts into the street, where he soon encounters a big, citified new boy (later named Alfred Temple). They trade taunts, and then Tom thoroughly beats him up and chases him home. When Tom finally returns to his house, late, he finds his aunt waiting for him, resolved to turn tomorrow—a school-free Saturday—into captivity at hard labor.

The lovely morning dawns, but Tom must whitewash a board fence thirty yards long and nine feet high. Ben Rogers comes by, prepared to flaunt his freedom to go swimming until Tom, pretending that his chore is fun, tricks him—and other lads who come along—into trading such treasures as apples, marbles, and door. knobs for the privilege of daubing the fence. Aunt Polly is amazed to find the chore completed and gives Tom an apple and a little sermon on the rewards of work. Tom hurls some clods at Sid, plays at war with Joe Harper and other cronies, and then is smitten by the charms of a new girl in town. She is blue-eyed, yellow-haired, and summery. Showing off gymnastically, he follows her to his friend Jeff Thatcher's house, where she is staying. At supper, he is whacked for stealing sugar and is later sent sprawling after Sid breaks the sugar bowl doing the same thing and Aunt Polly blames Tom. When the truth comes out, she turns contrite but cannot quite admit her error. Tom relishes the situation and even imagines her greater sorrow should he be brought home drowned. Late in the evening he finds himself under the window of the adorable new girl, but suddenly he is aroused from his reverie when the maid dumps a bucket of water on him.

Sunday morning arrives. Mary, Tom's cousin who has been away but has just returned, teaches the boy some lines from the Bible, scrubs him for church, and rewards him with the present of a new knife. He trades some of his recently acquired loot for tickets given at Sunday-school to reciters of biblical verses. Mr. Walters, the Sunday-school superintendent, marshalls his squirming charges with special rigor this day, because lawyer Thatcher has brought his brother Judge Thatcher, who is from Constantinople, twelve miles away, and that illustrious man's wife and daughter— the blue-eyed angel. Amy Lawrence, a former girl friend, gradually understands that Tom is smitten by the newcomer, Becky Thatcher. Doubly anxious to show off now, he presents the required number of tickets and asks for a Bible as prize. Judge Thatcher loftily quizzes him on his accumulated religious lore and is reluctantly informed that the first two disciples were David and Goliah. Church now begins. The Widow Douglas, forty years of age and smart in appearance, enters. So does the Model Boy of the village, Willie Mufferson by name, who escorts his mother as though she were made of cut glass. The minister, the Rev. Mr. Sprague, delivers a sermon about predestination which is so boring that Tom starts to play with a fly and then turns a pinchbug loose on a dog. The resulting torture of the animal provides welcome relief for all.

Monday comes. Tom feigns illness, has a loose tooth pulled by his aunt for his pains, and trudges off to school. On the way, he meets juvenile pariah Huckleberry Finn, son of the town drunkard. The two boys discuss the best way to remove warts. Huck favors taking a dead cat—he has one with him—to a cemetery at midnight after a wicked person has been buried. They agree to try Huck's method this night. Arriving at school late, Tom sees Becky there and acts up so that he will be assigned by the cruel teacher, Mr. Dobbins, to sit with the girls as a punishment. Soon he is happily flirting with his new love, who blushes with pleasure. Back at his own seat again, Tom grows bored in the summery heat, until he thinks of a tick he has in a little box. He and his friend Joe Harper play with it until Dobbins interrupts them. At noon Tom and Becky rendezvous in the deserted schoolhouse, where she lets him chew her gum and they decide to become engaged, then seal the bargain with a kiss. But when Tom foolishly talks about his previous engagement, with neglected Amy Lawrence, Becky flounces off—even though he gives her his best jewel—a brass knob from an andiron. So Tom marches away, to return to school no more on that day. He is so miserable that he wishes he could die temporarily. He considers becoming a soldier, an Indian chief, and then a pirate. As the Black Avenger of the Spanish Main, he might stride into church at St. Petersburg years after people had given him up for lost. When Joe, also a truant from school, arrives on the summit of Cardiff Hill behind the Widow Douglas's house, the two boys play at Robin Hood.

That night Huck Finn, swinging his cat, gives the catcall signal, and Tom sneaks out of the house to walk with him to the graveyard to try wart cures at the burial spot of Hoss Williams. Once there, they barely manage to hide before Dr. Robinson, drunken Muff Potter, and villainous Injun Joe enter and unearth the corpse, which they tie to a barrow. Potter then cuts the rope with his knife. Then he and Injun Joe suddenly demand more money.

The doctor protests, is threatened, and knocks the half-breed down. Potter then grapples with Robinson, who fells him with a grave board. But at this instant Injun Joe stabs the doctor to death with Potter's knife. Tom and Huck disappear as the moon goes under a cloud. When Potter reels back to consciousness, the half-breed convinces him that he did the killing but promises not to tell. Potter is grateful. Then the two part. Meanwhile Tom and Huck have run as hard as they can to the old tannery, where they solemnly vow never to tell on Injun Joe, who might murder them if he were tried and escaped hanging. Home again and in bed, Tom fancies that he is undetected. But gently snoring Sid is really awake and tells on him in the morning. Aunt Polly weeps and lectures, making Tom feel worse than if he were flogged. When he gets to school, he is whipped for playing hookey the day before. Becky then returns his andiron knob. Life is too depressing.

News of the murder spreads fast. Potter's knife is found. Then Potter himself wanders in, is accused, becomes rattled, and finally confesses in the presence of Injun Joe, whose corroborating lies astound Tom and Huck. When God does not strike the half-breed dead, the boys are convinced that he has sold himself to the devil. For a week or so, Tom is so gloomy that he mutters in his sleep, to Sid's delight. More time passes. To ease his conscience, Tom smuggles gifts to Potter, who is languishing in the little brick jail at the edge of town. So formidable is Injun Joe that no one takes the lead in trying to have him punished for grave-robbing.

Becky, now sick, is absent from school. Tom grows even more listless, and his aunt doses him with all sorts of medicine until he feeds some of his Pain-killer to the family cat and almost destroys it. Becky returns to school, and Tom instantly clowns in the play yard until the haughty little girl sniffs derisively. Crestfallen, Tom decides to run away for good. Joe Harper will go with him, since his mother has just whipped him for something he did not do. Huck agrees to join the pair. At midnight they meet two miles above the village with filched supplies, borrow a log raft, and float like pirates out of romantic literature down to Jackson's Island, a long, narrow, wooded island three miles below the town. They build a fire, eat, talk, and then fall asleep—Huck first, because he has no conscience to make him restless.

Glorious morning dawns. The boys swim, build up their fire, catch some fish and fry them with bacon. Incipient homesickness is dispelled by the booming of a distant cannon—fired over the water from a ferryboat searching for drowned bodies. The boys are elated again, because they suddenly realize that the town regards them as dead. But when the shadows of night begin to fall, Joe tentatively suggests that they might return to civilization— later. Tom turns derisive. Huck sides with him and soon falls asleep, as does Joe. Tom lies awake, writes messages on two pieces of sycamore bark, puts one in the pocket of his jacket and the other—along with some gifts—in Joe's hat, wades and swims to the Illinois shore, and under the twickling stars hooks a ride behind a ferryboat going to the other shore. Soon he is at his house spying on a scene of mourning: Aunt Polly, Sid, Mary, and Joe Harper's mother are noisily lamenting the demise of Tom and Joe. Tom almost cries, is tempted to skip out and overwhelm his aunt with joy, but decides not to when he learns that four days hence—on Sunday—if the boys' corpses are not recovered there will be a funeral service. Instead of leaving the bark message for Aunt Polly, who has now retired and is moaning in her sleep, he sneaks into her room and kisses her gently and then returns to Jackson's Island, bursting dramatically into camp precisely at breakfast time.

After a long sleep, Tom again leads his friends in romping on the beach and playing a variety of games. When Joe and Huck again grow anxious to return to town, Tom runs after them and unfolds his secret, after which they willingly stay. Huck teaches the other two how to smoke, but at first they frequently have to retire to the woods in search of a lost knife. About midnight Joe wakes up and calls the others. They hardly have time to rush to their old tent for protection before a titanic storm breaks over the island, crashing and smashing all about them. The next day they spend in playing Indians, eating, and smoking. Meanwhile, back in St. Petersburg there is no joy. Saturday gives way to Sunday. During the funeral speech given by the minister, who extols the dead boys' virtues, the three burst into the church and soon find themselves smothered in kisses—even the outcast Huck. Tom is incredibly proud.

First thing next morning Tom describes as a dream the scene of mourning he furtively observed the previous Wednesday night. His aunt is thrilled, but Sid is suspicious. Tom then swaggers off to school, where he is treated like a sunburned hero. When Becky skylarks near him, he ignores her and talks only to Amy; so Becky loudly discusses plans for a picnic to be given when vacation starts. She is reduced to tears by Tom's apparent indifference but soon begins flirting with the new boy, Alfred Temple. Tom observes them, revels in visions of again beating up the hated interloper, then rushes home, at which point Becky tells Alfred that she really hates him. So he sneaks into the vacant schoolroom and pours ink all over Tom's spelling book to get his rival into trouble. Becky sees the act but decides not to tell anybody, so that Tom will get punished instead. Home again, Tom is roundly scolded by his aunt, who through Joe's mother has learned that Tom eavesdropped on the mourners and that therefore the wonderful dream was all a lie. When he explains everything, including the bark message— still in his jacket, he adds—she forgives him, kisses him, and happily sends him off to school. Reluctant to do so, she gets out his old jacket, finds the bark, and dissolves in tears. By this time Tom is back at school, where he forthrightly apologizes to Becky, who, however, tosses her head scornfully. She walks past the teacher's desk, finds the key in his drawer, opens it, and starts to look at his favorite book—an anatomy text with a nude for a frontispiece. Tom happens to step near, and Becky in fright tears the picture. She shouts through her tears that she will now be whipped but that she also knows something dreadful about him too. He is puzzled. Soon he is occupied with his own misery, because Dobbins has found the lad's ruined spelling book and whips the innocent owner while Becky says nothing in his defense. But then real trouble follows, when the master discovers his torn anatomy book and furiously goes down the line of frightened pupils quizzing them one after another. Tom knows that Becky's face will give her away. Feeling nothing but pity for her now, he shouts out that he did the deed. Dobbins flays him mercilessly. After school, Becky tells all and melts in utter adoration.

As vacation approaches, Dobbins redoubles his sadistic efforts in order to get the most out of his charges at examination evening. On the big night, with beaming parents in the audience, he is slightly tipsy. Pupils recite insipid material, Tom breaks down over his "Give me liberty or give me death" speech, and then the teacher begins to draw a map on the blackboard. Suddenly through the scuttle in the garret above him a jaw-tied cat is lowered by a string. Down she comes, clawing the air. Finally she snatches off Dobbins's wig, revealing a gilded pate. The son of the sign painter, in whose house the teacher rooms and boards, did the job while the hated man was snoozing immediately after supper. Vacation is now here.

At first time passes listlessly. Tom joins the Cadets of Temperance but soon quits. He keeps a diary, helps to organize a minstrel show, sees Senator [Thomas H.] Benton at the Fourth of July ceremony, plays at circus, and observes some itinerant showmen. Becky has gone to her Constantinople home for vacation. Tom gets the measles. Finally Muff Potter's trial begins. As it drags on, day after day, Potter becomes more haggard in appearance, until his lawyer calls Tom to the stand. The conscience-stricken boy has decided to testify. When he dramatically names Injun Joe, that iron-faced scoundrel, who has been callously attending the trial, leaps through a window and is gone. Tom becomes a hero once again, though a worried one, because there is no sign of the real murderer now. Huck, who took no part in the courtroom revelation, hopes only for continued anonymity.

Then one day Tom is consumed with the desire to hunt for hidden treasure. With Huck as his only available crony, he tries digging on Jackson's Island and then under trees with dead limbs. When Tom says that if they find money he will get married, Huck advises against such a course. At night they dig under a tree on Cardiff Hill behind the Widow Douglas's property, but without luck. They feel uneasy, as though something is behind them. All the same, they decide to try their luck next at the haunted house up the Still-house branch. Shortly after they enter the deserted place and explore its second floor, two men burst in. The terrified boys peer down through knotholes and recognize one of the men as Injun Joe, even though he is disguised as a deaf and dumb Spaniard with white hair and green glasses. The two men talk about a job of revenge remaining to be accomplished before they head for Texas. Then they nap. Then they decide to bury their swag of $650 in silver. They start digging a suitable hole but soon strike an iron-bound box, which the Indian unearths with the boys' own pick, which happens to be nearby. They have found thousands of dollars, in gold, probably loot left there by [John A.] Murrel[l]'s gang. Suddenly Injun Joe remembers that the pick had fresh dirt on it. The men decide to take the money to the half-breed's den— Number Two under the cross. Still suspicious, the Indian starts up the stairs to see if anyone is there but falls through the rotten steps, grumbles, and soon leaves with his partner in crime—and the chest of money. The boys wait a while and then creep out, terrified at the hideous words about revenge. Is the Indian after both boys, or only Tom?

The following morning Tom half thinks that perhaps he only dreamed about Injun Joe and the treasure, until he finds Huck and the two boys talk about it. Tom wants that money. He and Huck wonder what the Number Two den could refer to, think that it might be Room No. 2 in the less ostentatious of the two local taverns, and therefore plan to collect spare keys to try to open that room and also plan to keep a lookout for the half-breed—to follow him. The next several nights, however, are too clear for the boys to scout around the tavern with any impunity. Thursday night is better. So while Huck stands guard, Tom takes a lantern, goes into the back room, then suddenly flies out of it, warning his friend to run for his life. They make for the shelter of the deserted slaughterhouse at the lower end of town, just as rain begins to flood the place. Only then does Tom explain that when he entered the room he found Injun Joe drunk, asleep, and still in his Spanish disguise. The boys decide to wait for a chance, when the half-breed is away at night, to slip in and search his room for the money. Huck will sleep in the Rogers family hayloft during the day, will watch at night, and when he sees the Indian leave will rush to get Tom.

Good news for Tom comes next day. Becky is back in town, with her parents. He promptly forgets both treasure and Huck, especially when the girl obtains permission to have the long-delayed picnic. It is now scheduled for the following day. The group of youngsters, watched over by only a few girls of eighteen and some young gentlemen of twenty-three, go by chartered ferryboat three miles below town to the mouth of a woody grove. Sid is sick and therefore cannot participate, and kind Mary obligingly remains behind to care for him. The children work up appetites by exploring the forest nearby and then McDougal's cave in the hillside. When they emerge, it is nearly dark. Soon the bell of the boat is clanging. The vessel pushes offshore. Meanwhile that night Huck has been at his post watching for Injun Joe, who long after eleven o'clock suddenly emerges with his confederate. They have a box with them. Huck, thinking that it might contain the gold, follows them to Cardiff Hill, past the house of old Jones the

Welshman, beyond the quarry, and onto the Widow Douglas's land. Huck overhears the Indian mutter to his companion that he intends to slit the woman's nostrils and notch her ears, because her husband when a justice of the peace arrested him for vagrancy and had him whipped. Huck sneaks off to Jones's house and alerts the man and his two sons to their neighbor's danger. Minutes later the men are armed and off to the rescue. Huck hears shots and a cry. He runs down the hill and away.

Early the following day, which is Sunday, Huck returns to Jones's house, learns that the two criminals got away, tells Jones some details, and reveals that one of the men about to mutilate the widow was the deaf and dumb Spaniard. When the Jones sons leave to go for the sheriff, Huck reluctantly adds that the Spaniard is really Injun Joe. Huck is still afraid of the Indian's revenge. Jones promises secrecy. Then to the boy's relief, the contents of the box which the fugitives were carrying and dropped in panic turn out to be burglar tools and not coins. The widow comes over to thank Jones, who is genuinely modest and hints that another person deserves the real credit. Suddenly, after church, it is learned that Tom and Becky are still in the cave. Becky's mother thought that the girl was staying overnight with the Harpers. Would-be rescuers pour out of town. But no luck.

Next morning the inept rescuers try again. Meanwhile, Huck has grown feverish from exposure and excitement, and remains at Jones's house, with the widow watching over him. Still no news from the cave, beyond mention that the names of Tom and Becky have been found traced in candle smoke on a cave wall and that her ribbon was nearby. Three days drag on, hopelessly.

Now let us return to Tom and Becky. Once in the cave, they walk past murky aisles and a trickling spring. Bats attack their candles. They find a lake. Suddenly they realize that they are lost and begin to shout uselessly, rousing only the echoes. Tom blames himself bitterly for their predicament. Becky goes into a frenzy of tears. They conserve their candles and wander on and on, aimlessly. Becky falls asleep, then wakes up with a groan. Their last candle flickers and dies. Utter darkness reigns. They sleep in each other's arms, are stirred by a faint noise, and creep toward it. Tom goes on ahead, shouts joyfully, but then spies Injun Joe with a light. The half-breed rushes out of sight. Tom returns and tells Becky that he yelled only for luck. They sleep again. When they rouse themselves once more, they are uncertain what day it is. They fear that any search for them must be abandoned by this time. Becky grows very weak. Tom searches side passages for a way out.

In the village all is gloomy as Tuesday night comes, with no word. But at midnight the bells ring in jubilation. The two children are safe. Tom lies in glory at Judge Thatcher's house and tells his story. Playing out his kite line, he clambered all about until he finally glimpsed a light, thrust his head through a crevice, and saw the glorious Mississippi rolling by. He returned for Becky, and the two emerged to safety, five miles below the valley of the cave, hailed a skiff, and soon were home. The two are sick for some time, especially Becky. Tom is up and about again by Friday and goes to see Huck, who cannot see him for days, however, because of continued sickness. Tom learns of the Cardiff Hill shooting and that the ragged companion of the missing "Spaniard" has been found, drowned near the ferry landing while trying to escape. A couple of weeks pass. Then one day while on his way to confer with Huck, who is well again, Tom stops at the Thatcher house to see Becky. The judge reports that curious children will no longer be in danger of getting lost in the cave, because two weeks ago he ordered the door of its mouth sheathed with boiler iron and locked. Tom blurts out the dire news that Injun Joe is inside.

News of the murderous Indian's death spreads through town. Tom and Judge Thatcher, among dozens of others, quickly go to the cave, behind the heavy door of which they find the half-breed's body. Tom feels both pity and relief. Next morning he and Huck discuss the fact that in the Indian's alcoholic room in the tavern no money was ever found. Tom suddenly announces that the treasure is in the cave. The boys get some equipment together, borrow a skiff, and enter the subterranean cavern through the crevice which provided Tom his means of escape. He reasons that No. 2 means a second cross on a cave wall. He points out such a mark to Huck. The two boys soon unearth the heavy box, transfer its rich contents to bags which they have brought, and by sundown are skimming along shore back to town. While they are hiding the money in the Widow Douglas's woodshed loft, Jones enters to tell them to go along to the woman's drawing room, which is ablaze with lights. The whole village seems to be there. Jones announces that Huck was responsible for saving the Widow Douglas's life. The woman thanks the boy, and promises to adopt him and later to start him in business. Tom asserts that Huck is in no need of money and produces the bags of gold—$12,000 in all—half of it his and half Huck's. The astonished villagers do not interrupt the thrilling story which Tom then reels off.

The entire town of St. Petersburg idolizes the two boys. Their money is safely invested. Their futures are the subject of much talk. Becky tells her father how Tom took a whipping for her, and the big man compares the boy to George Washington. Within three weeks Huck has grown wretched under the well-meaning widow's civilizing influence and sneaks off to the old slaughter-house where Tom ferrets him out. Tom induces him to return by telling him that he can be a member of their projected robbers' gang only if he becomes respectable.

Novels concerning adults end with marriage. But since this is a story about boys, it must stop here.

Mary Austin, Johnny Baker, Senator [Thomas H.] Benton, Billy, Dobbins, the Widow Douglas, Douglas, Huckleberry Finn, Pap Finn, Mrs. Finn, Billy Fisher, Judge Frazer, Harbison, Joseph Harper, Mrs. Sereny Harper, Susy Harper, Harper, Hays, Jimmy Hodges, Jim Hollis, Mother Hopkins, Injun Joe, Uncle Jake, Jim, Jim, Jones the Welshman, Jones, Amy Lawrence, Mary, Grace Miller, Johnny Miller, Willie Mufferson, Mrs. Mufferson, [John A.] Murrel[l], Nance, Miss Peters, Aunt Polly, Muff Potter, Riverson, Dr. Robinson, Robinson, Benjamin Rogers, Sally Rogers, Rogers, Thomas Sawyer, the Sheriff, Sidney, Professor Somebody, Rev. Mr. Sprague, Bob Tanner, Benny Taylor, Alfred Temple, Jeff Thatcher, Rebecca Thatcher, Judge Thatcher, Mrs. Thatcher, Thatcher, Bill Turner, Walters, Major Ward, Mrs. Ward, Hoss Williams.

"Advice for Good Little Girls," 1865 (WMT 24).

Don't make mouths at teachers except under really stressful circumstances, don't swap your rag doll for a costly one unless you have conscience and superior strength on your side, and don't take your little brother's gum away from him but instead rope him in with a promise to give him any money you see floating down the river on a grindstone. It is better to scald your brother than to throw mud at him; this way, your hot water will remove impurities from him, and maybe a bit of skin too. Don't tell your mother you won't obey a certain order; instead intimate that you will, then do as you please. Humor your kind parents, at least until they crowd you. And don't sass old people except in retaliation.

'Advice to Girls,' 1909 (S).
Briefly addressing a graduating class, Twain advises the girls not to smoke, drink, or marry to excess. He also tells them that honesty is the best policy.

    Martin.

"Advice to Little Girls" (WMT 24). See "Advice for Good Little Girls."

"Advice to Parents." See FW, 1870.

"Advice to the Unreliable on Church-Going," c. 1863.*
Twain advises the Unreliable to avoid mixing perfumes while dressing for church, to get up long enough before arriving there to avoid looking puffed from sleep, and to stop his trick of appearing to be praying while the collection box is being passed.

    *In *Wit and Humor of America*, ed. Kate M. Rabb, Vol. 5 (Indianapolis: Bobbs-Merrill, 1907).

'Advice to Youth,' c. 1882 (WMT 28).
Twain was asked to say something instructive to young people. So here goes. Obey your parents, because if you do not they will make you. They think they know best; so humor their superstitions. Be respectful to your superiors, if you have any. Do not argue with an offensive person; simply hit him with a brick. Get up with the lark; if you try hard, you can catch a lark and train it to get up at 9:30. Be careful about lying; otherwise you will get caught. Practice lying until you are an expert. Do not handle unloaded firearms, because they are the only kind that do the many

killings of grandmothers we hear about. Read only edifying books, for example, sermons and *The Innocents Abroad*. Follow this advice, and you will grow up to resemble everyone else.

"Affecting." See FW, 1870.

"Affeland (Snivelization)," 1967 (SB).
He [Albert] is grave, big-eyed, precocious, studious, and solitary. The villagers expect much of him until they notice that he shifts from one preoccupation to another. He becomes a Methodist, then a Presbyterian, then a Baptist, always flitting. At the age of nine he begins to study for the ministry. At twelve he starts to pattern his life on that of Benjamin Franklin. At fifteen he studies law, but soon he decides to . . .

[Albert].

'After Dinner Speech by Mark Twain.' See 'Mistaken Identity.'

"'After' Jenkins," 1865 (WMT 7).
The following notes concerning the Pioneers' Ball at the Occidental some time back may interest the reader, and Jenkins may get an idea or two from them. Mrs. W. M. was admirably dressed in *pate de foie grus*. Mrs. C. N. was arrayed in white kid gloves and had modest manners. Mrs. L. R.'s sustained smile heightened the *bon jour* effect of her new and pretty false teeth. Miss R.P.'s eyes displayed quite a contrast: one was sparkling, the other placid glass. Miss C.L.B. blew her enameled nose with modulated tones. And so on.

Miss C.L.B., Miss M.M.B., Jenkins, Mrs. W.M., Mrs. C.N., Miss R. P., Mrs. L. R., Miss S., Mrs. G. W.

'After-Dinner Speech' (WMT 70). See 'Americans and the English.'

The Aged Pilot Man, 1872 (P).
One summer day a violent storm descends upon a boat on the Erie Canal. Everyone aboard is terrified; but Dollinger, the old

pilot, insists that he will fetch the boat through. The storm grows worse. Finally a farmer brings a plank, and everyone walks ashore to safety.

Dollinger.

"Agricultural Twaddle at the Institute Farmer's Club." See FW, 1870.

"Aguinaldo" (MPT).

Twain reviews Edwin Wildman's biography of Aguinaldo, summarizes its facts, praises the native Philippine leader—even comparing him to Joan of Arc—and castigates American treatment of him, his people, and their land.

President [Emilio] Aguinaldo, Edwin Wildman.

Ah Sin, 1961.*

Ferguson, Boston, Masters, and some other miners are having no luck finding gold, when York, a fashionable Britisher, enters. Broderick jeers at him and then goes to Plunkett's empty cabin to help himself to a drink. Offstage a carriage breaks down, and Miss Shirley Tempest enters, escorted by Plunkett. Broderick steps aside and, listening, learns that the girl is the daughter of rich Judge Tempest of San Francisco. Plunkett is loud in offers of protection. The pretty girl tells about being rescued from a runaway one dark night by a mysterious stranger. Suddenly she notices York's photograph. Plunkett foolishly lies, saying that the handsome fellow is his son, who is engaged to a New York girl. Revealing that York was her rescuer, though he did not see her face, Shirley takes his picture and gives Plunkett one of herself in exchange. Plunkett regrets his lies at once. They go back to the carriage, and Broderick slips forward and notices Shirley's picture. Ah Sin enters, samples Plunkett's whiskey, digs up a gold rock in Broderick's claim, and steals a cup. Broderick shakes the cup loose and chases the hapless Chinese offstage. York enters, reveals in an aside that he will not give Plunkett the $15 he requested for his worthless mine, and then sees the picture of Miss Tempest, who, lies Plunkett—now entering—is his daughter. York then

forces money on the man, receives the picture, and offers to have
a game of cards. York, who does not play, suggests that Broderick,
just coming in, be his substitute, and leaves. Broderick flatters
Plunkett by exaggerating rumors of his war record, and soon the
two are busy at poker. Ah Sin, spying on them, sees Broderick
starting to cheat, fires a revolver to get them away, and stacks
their hands: four kings for Broderick but four aces for Plunkett,
whom Ah Sin likes. The two players bet everything, including
their mines. Plunkett wins and soon finds gold where Ah Sin did,
whereupon Broderick accuses him of cheating at their card game.
The two fight; and soon Broderick, thinking he has killed the older
man, hides his own bloodied jacket, which Ah Sin finds. Broderick
offers the Chinese a share in his mine for the jacket, which he then
has Ah Sin wrap for him. He throws the package in the river, but
the wily Chinese has retained the jacket after all.

Three months later, in Deadwood, York is seen impatiently
awaiting the stage coach. In an effort to learn about Plunkett's
disappearance, he hires Ah Sin, who, he thinks, may know something. Broderick enters with three other miners and voices his
reluctance to question Ah Sin, since he hates the Heathen. The
miners interrogate him so roughly that York threatens them with
the law and thus saves Ah Sin. York leaves. Judge Tempest enters,
gives Ah Sin a note for York, and leaves. Mrs. Tempest and Shirley enter. The daughter is annoyed that her parents want her to
marry York, since she is in love with the man whose photograph
she now has. York enters, sees in Shirley the original of his lovely
photograph, but showing her the picture addresses her as the
daughter of missing Plunkett. When he leaves to get them a carriage to take them to Plunkett's place, mother and daughter discuss
the mystery. Shirley agrees to accept the hospitality of York but
only as young Plunkett. Mrs. Tempest promises to support this
procedure. York returns and escorts them offstage. Ah Sin opines
that Plunkett has two wives, Chinese fashion. Next enter Mrs.
Plunkett, lamenting her husband's disappearance, and their
daughter Caroline Plunkett, who is busy hoping that here she
can land a gold-laden man. Perhaps York, who has sent for them,
is rich and wants to marry one of the Plunkett women. Mrs. Plunkett sobs that she last saw her husband thirteen years ago when
she threw a skillet at him and he left. The daughter cannot cry,
though, because she hardly ever saw him. The women ask Ah Sin

to find York. As the Chinese exits, Broderick enters and almost faints when they introduce themselves as the late Plunkett's wife and daughter. But the two women fuss over him, each jealous of the other and hoping to attract him; soon, therefore, he offers them the hospitality of his place. When the three leave, Plunkett appears and then disappears, and Ah Sin has a drink. A group of miners—including Boston, Ferguson, and Masters—enters bent on hanging Ah Sin. They suspect him, and York as well, of killing Plunkett. But when they dive for Ah Sin, he scampers away.

Broderick bribes Ah Sin to bloody a jacket of York's. When the miners enter, Broderick arouses their suspicions that York is guilty. They all leave, whereupon Mrs. Tempest, upset that she is representing someone else for her daughter's sake, sees Ah Sin and gives him a lesson in table-setting. He repeats everything, including her mistakes. She leaves, and York and Shirley enter apparently in some embarrassment. While he mouths endearments to "Miss Plunkett," she corrects Ah Sin's manner of setting the table. York stammers that he loves her; she puts him at a distance, then repels him by saying that the woman was really her aunt. She wishes that he had followed up his heroic rescue act by meeting her—her aunt, that is—then tells him to leave and return for lunch and stop calling her Caroline but Shirley instead. The girl is annoyed with herself for lying. She concludes that she must be under the influence of that old liar, Plunkett. Then Mrs. Plunkett and her daughter Caroline enter, each accusing the other of wanting Broderick. Shirley advances to clear up the situation; she asks if the two are Plunketts, introduces herself, confesses that she has been misleading the man they want to meet, but promises soon to restore York. At the name York, the Plunkett woman start and reveal that they are after Broderick. With a laugh, Shirley invites them to lunch and talks Miss Plunkett into impersonating Miss Tempest in front of York, and Mrs. Plunkett into impersonating Mrs. Tempest. They agree. They leave and soon return with Mrs. Tempest calling Mrs. Plunkett Mrs. Tempest, to eavesdropping Ah Sin's bewilderment. When York comes in, Mrs. Tempest introduces the Plunkett women as Tempests. He is confused but bows to hide the fact. After Mrs. Plunkett confuses him with mispronouncements, Mrs. Tempest expresses sadness that Broderick, whom they invited, cannot be here for lunch. Ah Sin spills fruit on entering, and the manners of the Plunkett women disenchant

York completely. He encourages Ah Sin to sing; but then in troop the diffident miners, led by apologetic Ferguson, who reluctantly arrests York for the murder of Plunkett. York calls on Ah Sin to testify on his behalf but is dragged off while Ah Sin says that he cannot testify in court because he is Chinese.

On a woody hill, Judge Tempest is talking with his daughter Shirley. He says he knows she loves York, who is about to be lynched, but she must not go to him in that rough camp. She says that she will do so, since she is no longer a child but a woman. The scene shifts to a country store and bar, where the trial has just been held. Jurymen miners are playing cards but are interrupted by a dogfight. Masters, who is in charge, replaces one juryman because he does not know how to play poker. The trial summary starts. Ferguson ticks off the shoddy evidence against York, in spite of Judge Tempest's protests, which Masters squelches. Masters leaps up to prevent a premature lynching, and Broderick whispers something to Ferguson, who shouts that two women were seen masquerading with York as Plunkett's widow and daughter. Does York want the bogus widow to deed Plunkett's mine to him? At this point, just as Judge Tempest wishes he had not ordered Shirley to stay away, she enters and guilelessly answers Masters' questions, revealing that she assumed Miss Plunkett's identity because York thought her nice photograph was Miss Plunkett's and because she loves York. The Judge then formally queries his daughter, who reveals that she acted as she did all on her own and then decided to testify here in spite of his order not to do so and also in spite of Broderick's threat to prevent her appearance in court. Further, she says that Broderick told her to discard York for him if she wanted to see York escape the noose. The judge urges that York be acquitted at once. But at this point Ferguson makes the sarcastic suggestion that all the miners ought to buy York some gloves so that when he condescends to shake hands with them he will not catch any germs. The other miners then recall that York bilked a sad widow and daughter out of their rightful mine. The jury promptly votes to hang the fellow, in spite of the judge's assertion that they have failed to prove guilt. But when the judge says that the verdict is an insult to Shirley, who loves York, the jury begins to waver. So Broderick must play his trump card: he orders Ah Sin to produce the bloody jacket which York was wearing on the night of the murder. Ah Sin promptly flourishes a jacket; and Broderick is in fine fettle until Masters points out that the jacket is Broderick's, not York's. Ah Sin then produces a revolver which helps the others to collar Broderick. Ah Sin taunts his former torturer by asking what he would give to save his neck now. Everything, says Broderick, whereupon Ah Sin scoots out; just before the miners are about to lynch Broderick, Ah Sin returns with Plunkett. The miners are so surprised that they ask if he is really Plunkett. His wife and daughter enter. Much rejoicing. Even a hurrah for the Chinaman.

Ah Sin, Boston, Silas Broderick, Fergy Ferguson, Juryman, Grace Astor Livingstone, Masters, Jake Miller, Miner, Abner Plunkett, Mrs. Abner Plunkett, Caroline Anastasia Plunkett, Spectator, Becky Simpson, Shirley Tempest, Judge Tempest, Mrs. Tempest, Hank Williamson, Henry York.

*Ed. Frederick Anderson (San Francisco: Book Club of California, 1961).

'Ah Sin, the Heathen Chinee,' 1884 (LAIFI).

Twain observes that the play *Ah Sin, the Heathen Chinee,* which he and Bret Harte wrote, is most remarkable, and was the result of research, inventiveness, and plagiarism. Its most original feature is the stagecoach breakdown, which they may have overdone. The play is didactic rather than amusing, and instructs all with respect to the Chinese and also the game of poker. Originally, the play was too long; so the manager cut and cut and cut. It would have been better if he had cut everything.

"Aix, the Paradise of the Rheumatics," 1891 (WMT 29).

The author is at enchanting Aix-les-Bains, which the occasional presence of kings advertises well. The valley is geologically old. After unrecorded pagans, came the Romans (symbolized by a graceful, battered arch), then Catholicism (symbolized by a church), and now modern times (symbolized by a telegraph office). Aix is handsome and well situated, with its crooked little streets, pleasant park, hotels, baths, and gambling establishments. In spite of incredible noise, one sleeps wonderfully here. The author visits a gambling hall and could be persuaded to stay a while if he could borrow the croupier's sculling oar. To treat a rheumatic right arm, the author tries the baths and soon feels fresher. The drives outside Aix are beautiful, especially the one through Eden-like gardens to Annecy, which has a heartbreakingly beautiful lake. Beyond it is an abbey complete with cloister, arcade, weeds, ruined wall, and silence so serene that it could cure anyone's blistered spirit.

"Aladdin, or the Wonderful Scamp." See FW, 1869.

"All About the Fashions," 1863 (WG).

Twain answers a brief, confidential letter from Bettie, who inquires into San Francisco ladies' fashions, by reporting that he recently attended a Lick House parlor party given to celebrate his board-bill payment. Mrs. B. wore a speckled foulard with embroidered dogs; Mrs. J. W., a polonais of ruche *a la vielle*; Mrs. J. B. W., nankeen pique balloon sleeves and an imported sage brush bouquet; Miss C., a Garibaldi shirt with her hair in greenbacks; and Miss A. H., a Lucia de Lammermoor with stringed-sardine coiffure. Twain himself borrowed apparel from nine friends and looked salubrious.

> Mrs. B., Bettie, Miss C., Camp, Judge Gilchrist, Miss H. A., Lawlor, Jerry Long, Dr. Toll-road McDonald, Paxton, Ridgway, the Unreliable, Miss J. W., Mrs. J. B. W., Dr. Wayman.

'The Alphabet and Simplified Spelling,' 1907 (WMT 28).

Twain has just heard compliments about Carnegie delivered to his face, a face sparkling with fictitious innocence. In truth, Carnegie is bringing destruction to mankind, through his sponsoring of simplified spelling. We should not simply reform the spelling of such words as "pneumatic" and "pterodactyl"; we should invent a new alphabet which could accurately spell all the different sounds. For example, what word does b-o-w spell? Like chastity, simplified spelling is all right but can be carried too far.

> [Andrew] Carnegie.

"Amended Obituaries," 1902 (WMT 24).

Mark Twain writes the Editor to inform him that since Twain is approaching the age of seventy it is only wisdom on his part to set his worldly house in order now, before confusion begins in connection with arranging his other house. He wants at once therefore to correct his obituaries. Facts in standing obituaries of him are probably satisfactory, but what about verdicts deriving from those facts? So he wants copies sent to him for correction. He will pay double rates for all corrections and quadruple rates for obituaries so wisely worded as to need no correction. He intends to bind all of these obituaries together for family consolation and entertainment, and as an heirloom which may later have value. He will even offer a prize—a pen-and-ink sketch of himself by himself—for the obituary best calculated to inspire regret.

The Editor.

"American Authors and British Pirates," 1888 (LAIFI).

Twain begins with a letter to his friend Brander Matthews, who has just complained in print about English literary pirates. He said that in times past they cheated such American authors as Hawthorne and Longfellow, and more recently John Habberton. Twain observes that the English have changed their copyright law, which now permits a foreign author to establish a three-day residence in Canada, or to publish in England before doing so at home, and thus obtain an iron-clad English copyright. (No similar American law protects non-American authors.) Twain therefore rebukes Matthews for flogging a dead issue and compares his doing so to a present-day Mohammedan slave trader in Africa criticizing America for tolerating slavery before the Civil War. Next Twain shows that American authors are capable of plagiarism, by printing parallel passages from E. H. House's "Martyrdom of an Empire" (*Atlantic Monthly*, 1881) and plagiarist James King Newton's "Obligations of the United States to Initiate a Revision of Treaties between the Western Powers and Japan" (*Bibliotheca Sacra*, 1887). Twain closes by urging American authors not only to abide by the generous British law if they expect to be internationally protected but also to admit that our own villainous Congress wrongly refuses to reciprocate, and by gently telling Matthews to mend his logic if he does not wish to wind up in the asylum.

John Habberton, [Nathaniel] Hawthorne, E[dward]. H. House, [Henry Wadsworth] Longfellow, Brander Matthews, Rev. James King Newton.

The American Claimant, 1892. (WMT 15).

The author explains that there is no weather in his story. The interested reader may turn to the Appendix for samples of weather written by experts. He then explains that the name Eschol Sellers, which appeared in the first edition of *The Gilded Age,* was changed to Beriah Sellers, and then to Mulberry Sellers for the play version.

At Cholmondeley Castle, England, Earl Rossmore is bidding good-bye to his son Viscount Berkeley, who favors letting the American claimant to the family estates and titles have it all while Berkeley tries to make his fortune in America by talent and work. As he leaves, a letter comes from Mulberry Sellers announcing that the claimant, Simon Lathers, has died and that Sellers, his heir, is claiming everything.

Back to Colonel Mulberry Sellers before he wrote Rossmore. Sellers is in the "library" of his delapidated, ugly, but homey house on the outskirts of Washington, D.C. His faithful wife Polly is with him. All but one of their children are dead. He is working indifferently on a little toy. His only job is that of flint-picker in the War Department at three dollars a week. Suddenly his Negro servant Dan'l shows Washington Hawkins in. He and Sellers have not seen each other for fifteen years. Washington now unofficially represents his home town, Cherokee Strip, where his wife Louise and his children are now awaiting news of his success. Sellers agrees to help get him recognition and influence. While Sellers goes outside for something, Polly tells Washington that her husband is the same as ever generous to others, periodically impoverished, the humorous friend of the illustrious. He returns and confides in his house guest that he is about to materialize ghosts, who will take over for policemen, armies, leaders, etc. He will make billions. Then a bill collector named Suggs appears, and Sellers stalls him by giving him a chromo which the colonel calls a Fra Angelico. He and Washington then send a message to a Baltimore newspaper to trap One-Armed Pete, for whom there is a reward out west for bank robbery. Washington soon leaves to draw up a contract with a Yankee furniture repairman to manufacture Sellers's toy, then returns to find the colonel sad at news that Lathers has died but joyful at being the new Earl of Rossmore. Polly objects to his romantic dreams but lets him wire the news to their daughter Sally—now to be named Gwendolen—at Rowena-Ivanhoe College, where everything is inspired by Sir Walter Scott. Sellers orders the corpses of the Lathers twins to be sent to England—collect.

After three days, Sally writes her parents all about the arrival of the telegram and her consequent snubbing of formerly pretentious rich schoolmates at Rowena-Ivanhoe. Sally comes home, and Sellers soon introduces the strikingly beautiful girl as Lady Gwendolen to "Major " Hawkins, who is instantly smitten. The girl takes in sewing to support the family while awaiting her title. One-Armed Pete answers the ad by suggesting a rendezvous in Black Horse Alley. Sellers concludes that the outlaw's hotel is the New Gadsby near the alley, and when he reconnoitres he sees a one-armed cowboy in the elevator. Another man there, whom he does not recognize, is Berkeley, over from England, where the Lathers twins have arrived and been buried. That night Berkeley records his initial impressions of America in his diary, retires, is awakened in the night by the cry of fire, gropes into an adjoining room and dresses in One-Armed Pete's clothes, and escapes. In the morning he reads in the papers of his own death! He is glad, because now he can make it on his own. Sellers and his group also read of Berkeley, who is reported to have died heroically, saving others. Sally wishes that she had known him. Sellers goes to the morgue and fills three baskets with corpse ashes, hoping that part is young Berkeley and planning to send them to the victim's father in England. But Polly says that as long as the bereaved father does not receive any shipment of ashes he will hope that his son escaped the hotel fire. Sellers agrees and thanks his wife profusely for saving him from a crime.

Berkeley changes his name to Howard Tracy, deposits five hundred dollars of the money found in One-Armed Pete's coat in a bank so that he will not touch it, and cables his father that he escaped the fire unhurt and has taken a fictitious name. Then he attends a lecture, at the Mechanics' Club, on the virtues of American journalistic frankness and irreverence. "Tracy" is delighted. But when he tries for days without success to find a job, he becomes discouraged. He contracts for room and board at $4.50 a week with chatty Mrs. Rachel Marsh, who tells him something about the laborers who also stay in her establishment; then she introduces him to Hattie—nicknamed "Puss"—her lively eighteen-year-old daughter. She and Tracy discuss what constitutes a lady, in England and in America. Barrow, a journeyman chairmaker, casually enters and joins in the conversation. Tracy is a little uneasy but soon develops deep respect for the sandy-haired, freckled fellow and his frank opinions on the artificiality of British titles. Soon there is a scramble for dinner, which is a coarse, smelly event at a big basement table, presided over by kindly Aunt Rachel's swarthy, sarcastic husband, who takes pleasure in being abusive to an unemployed tinner named Nat Brady. After supper, Barrow and Tracy take a walk and discuss the fact that prosperity and position constitute rank in America. Tracy becomes a little apprehensive and homesick.

Days pass, and Tracy finds himself about as unpopular as Brady, whom the boardinghouse bully, an amateur boxer named Allen, treats so abusively that Tracy challenges him and repeatedly knocks him down. Tracy now becomes popular with the others, including Hattie, who tells him to call her Puss. But he still can find no work. So he cables his American name to his father in England and at once feels better. Soon he may be going home. That evening he and Barrows attend a debate at the Mechanics' Club, during which a blacksmith named Tompkins gives a speech against British titles which seems like a reproach to Tracy until, on the way home, Barrows pronounces it hypocritical. He says that if offered a British title Tompkins would take it in a second. Barrows would fight against hereditary titles in general but would take one himself. Tracy is relieved and vows to pick up his title when he can. He awakens light-hearted next morning, but his mood quickly changes when he discovers that he has been robbed by Allen and therefore cannot pay his room-and-board bill when it is demanded by sarcastic Marsh. Tracy blurts out that he is an English earl's son, sends Brady to the cable office for his father's reply, but is cast into despair when he reads the answer—"Thanks." The other men doubt and taunt him until he defies them all. Then Barrow tells him not to give up the ship and hints that he has a plan.

Brady, sent out by Barrow, returns with a box of atrociously ugly portraits with cannon and sea in each background. Barrow explains that Andy Handel paints the figures and Captain Saltmarsh the rest. These two worthies enter, and talking with them about their lucrative trade brightens Tracy immensely. He soon promises Barrow that he will not mention earldoms again. He waits vainly for a second cable from England, then decides that he can paint non-cannon backgrounds in Saltmarsh-Handels and improve their trade. He rushes to the ratty studio of the men, converts a cannon to a hearse, and thrills the "artists" upon their return. Tracy is ecstatic to be working.

Meanwhile, back to Washington Hawkins, who is depressed at lack of success in the materializing line—One-Armed Pete is still absent—and to Colonel Sellers, who cheers Washington up by showing him his cursing phonograph for timid sea captains and tells him of his plan to light homes with decomposed sewer gas. Then when Washington guesses that Sellers must be seeking a colossal sum of money for a special project, the old man confesses that he plans to buy Siberia and start a republic of intellectuals there. At about this time, Tracy has been taking an afternoon stroll and happens to see the Rossmore hatchments all over the front of Sellers's little house. So here is where the American claimant lives. Sellers fancies that the stroller is One-Armed Pete. The clothes match. Tracy innocently enters, chats with Sellers and "General" Hawkins, reveals that he is an artist, and agrees to restore one of Sellers's chromos— identified as a Del Sarto. Sellers and Washington retire to the "laboratory," where the old man explains that "It" is One-Armed Pete's English ancestor and then decides to incorporate It, sell stock—there are millions in it—and gradually materialize It down to the present time for a variety of rewards. All this time, Tracy is painting away, when suddenly Sally enters: it is love at first sight.

Next day, Tracy returns in a nice new suit, but the fresh flower in his buttonhole bothers Sally. Who is giving flowers to her young man? Thinking that he will not stay to dinner this evening, since when invited the day before he declined (in order to buy a suit to replace his awkward cowboy outfit), Sally invites herself to the home of the neighboring Thompsons. Then, however, Sellers invites Tracy to dine, and he accepts. Sally must leave. Sellers shows Tracy a wretched chromo which he says is a portrait of young Rossmore, burned in the hotel fire, then analyzes the late nobleman as irresolute. Though concluding that his host is mentally unbalanced, especially for having Rossmore hatchments all about, Tracy privately acknowledges the justice of the old man's criticism. But then Sellers reveals that he has some baskets containing young Rossmore's ashes. Tracy grows rather unresponsive until Sally returns, Sellers retires, and Washington follows suit. In a flash Tracy and Sally express their love with a kiss. Washington, peeking through the doorway, is aghast. She is kissing It! Washington is sad. Just to think that Sally loves an imperfectly materialized criminal belonging in Sheol! But he is soon thrilled, when Sellers returns and announces that he intends to leave Tracy in his present stage, not bring him down to the present, and let the reward for One-Armed Pete go.

Back to Sally, who for the first time regards herself as real and put on the earth for a purpose. She asks Tracy if he wants her for her title—that of Lady Gwendolen—and then confesses that her father is no earl and that her name is Sally. He says that he is glad she is a commoner. Just as she begins to admit that she could never love an earl, he hastily interrupts to comment on her beauty. When she praises the heroism of the late young Rossmore, Tracy begins to envy him and asks whether she disapproves of real earls. She says not and adds that she hates only sham titles like those of the common Sellerses. He is relieved. Late that night in bed, she uneasily concludes that Tracy's query means that the young man secretly hankers after her title.

Next Tracy writes the whole truth, including his desire to marry the daughter of the pretender to the Rossmore estates, to his father, who promptly takes ship for America without answering. For the next ten days Tracy happily reports to the Sellers house to paint the colonel. He is often alone with lovely Sally. But she periodically grows suspicious that he wants her for her title. They argue, and he blurts out that he is Viscount Berkeley and that he came to America to rise on his own merit. She tells him to leave until he can provide proof from home; then she confesses to herself that she adores the liar.

No proof comes from England, naturally. Tracy is in agony for ten days. Sally cries most of the time. Her father prepares for a temperance lecture by getting drunk, must take to his bed, and is most apologetic when Sally weeps beside him (for absent Tracy). The little toy which the colonel invented sweeps the nation suddenly, and on proceeds from its sales he and his wife start for England, prepared to settle their claim in the House of Lords. Meanwhile, to discourage Sally, Washington tells her that Tracy is really a peculiar character named Spinal Meningitis Snodgrass from Cherokee Strip. But, though disliking his odd name, Sally only defends him the more and determines to marry him if his moral character is good. Washington reluctantly promises to fetch him in the morning and wires Sellers to return and thus prevent Sally from marrying the materializee. Tracy duly arrives, does not turn a hair when the girl hints about Snodgrasses, but denies that he was ever an earl's son. But then—Rossmore from England enters! Tracy, turned Lord Berkeley in a trice, greets his father, who soon approves volubly of Sally and clears up all difficulties. Washington learns that One-Armed Pete must have died in the hotel fire and philosophically consigns the lost rewards to oblivion.

Rossmore Towers in Washington, D.C., becomes very busy. Rossmore and the colonel take to each other at once. The wedding of Berkeley and Sally is a quiet one. Saltmarsh, Handel, and Barrow attend; Hattie Marsh is invited but cannot come, because she is nursing her sick fiancé, Brady. Sellers cannot join his new allies on their trip to England because he is busy making arrangements to purchase Siberia with money to be realized from altering certain climates in the world by controlling sunspots.

An appendix provides seven literary descriptions of weather, for use in this book.

Allen, Barrow, Graham Bell, Viscount Kirkcudbright Llanover Marjoribanks Berkeley, Billy, Nat Brady, Dan'l, Fairfax, [Ulysses S.] Grant, Augusta-Templeton-Ashmore Hamilton, Andy Handel, Louise Hawkins, Washington Hawkins, Hawkins, Dave Hopkins, Jinny, John, [Joseph B.] Johnston, Simon Lathers, Lathers, Lathers, Maggie Lee, [Robert E.] Lee, [James] Longstreet, Hattie Marsh, Rachel Marsh, Marsh, McAllister, Billy Nash, Naylor, One-Armed Pete, Sir Oracle, Parker, the Earl of Rossmore, Rossmore, Rossmore, Captain Saltmarsh, Colonel Mulberry Sellers, Polly Sellers, Sally Sellers, [Philip H.] Sheridan, [William T.] Sherman, Miss Skimperton, Spinal Meningitis Snodgrass, Zylobalsamum Snodgrass, Dr. Snodgrass, Suggs, Sumner, Lord Tanzy of Tollmache, Belle Thompson, Thompson, Tom, Tompkins, William 'the Conqueror, X. Y. Z.

"The American Claimant" (play) (MTP).*

In Washington, Mary Sellers tells her mother that her father the Colonel is impractical and then tells their Negro servant, Aunt Sally, that she wishes the handsome stranger had let her drown instead of saving her and then going off to rescue still another person. Lafayette Hawkins arrives from Hannibal, inspects many of the Colonel's inventions, embraces Cousin Mary, and tells her that the heir of the Earl of Dover will arrive soon, according to the Colonel. When Lafayette explains that he has sold his house to support the Colonel's claim to the earldom, Mary is outraged. The Colonel enters, showing his latest invention—a fire extinguisher— explaining his invention to capture profanity phonographically, and announcing his plan to materialize the dead and make police-

/

men and soldiers out of them. The Colonel wants Lafayette to go to England to buy out Reginald De Bohen, thus improving the Sellers claim to the earldom. Meanwhile Mrs. Sellers enters in a shabby dress and announces that De Bohen has been killed in the Tolliver House fire. The Colonel weeps at the death of this thirteenth cousin and promises to ship the remains to England C.O.D. But suddenly R. De Bohen sends in his card to the Colonel.

Colonel Sellers thinks for sure he has materialized De Bohen, who humors the odd fellow, says that he is happy to meet the American claimant to the earldom, and mentions the Colonel's letters to England on the subject. De Bohen would have been here sooner but went to Missouri first and then became involved in a steamboat sinking. He even saved an unknown girl, is really in love with her now, but cannot locate her anywhere. The Colonel offers to materialize her. While he excuses himself to go talk to a business acquaintance, De Bohen plays with the invention of the phonograph and hears Mary's voice. The young man is ecstatic, and the girl enters almost immediately. The two embrace and kiss. He introduces himself as Rupert De Bohen, her father's distant cousin, and explains that caddish Reginald De Bohen was the one who perished in the hotel fire. Mary tells him that her father thinks he has materialized burned R. De Bohen. The Colonel re-enters with a New York businessman, meets R. De Bohen, and scares off the New Yorker by talking about the materializee. When the Negro servant, Daniel, announces the arrival of some temperance ladies, the Colonel decides to sample the tempter and gets thoroughly drunk on Lafayette's Missouri brandy. He offers to show the ladies what drink can bring a man to, by leading their procession until he passes out.

Mrs. Sellers comforts her husband that evening. Soon he is trying on a pair of wings to enable him to play his fire extinguisher into upper windows, until his wife distracts him with the news that it was De Bohen who rescued their daughter and that the couple are now in love. But the Colonel does not want Mary engaged to a ghost! Lycurgus Suckers, a journalist, comes to interview the inventor; they discuss flying, the price of pork in Germany, hotel fires, and jewelry allegedly lost in such fires, a state church, copyright laws, immorality, and sunspots. De Bohen enters and meets Suckers. Mrs. Sellers is afraid to touch the ghost. Mary sees De Bohen and rushes into his arms. He identifies himself as the living

Rupert, not Reginald, who also is alive though now the worse for too much wine. Rupert says that he was planning to give the earldom to Colonel Sellers anyway, in exchange for Mary, but Reginald's being alive changes all that. The Colonel graciously tells Rupert to marry the girl anyway and adds that if Reginald drinks himself to death, Rupert will become the rightful earl and his radiant wife will grace his court.

> Abner, Boone, Braden, British Minister, Uncle Daniel, Reginald De Bohen, Rupert De Bohen, Senator Dilworthy, the Earl of Dover, Lafayette Hawkins, Jones, Meissonnier, Portage Joe, Richard Lion Heart, Aunt Sally, Mary Sellers, Colonel Mulberry Sellers, Mrs. Polly Sellers, Colonel Sellers, Sister of Siloam, Lycurgus Suckers, Vanderbilt, Watson.

*Twain's manuscript of this play is somewhat different from the version on which he collaborated with William Dean Howells. See "Colonel Sellers as a Scientist," in *The Complete Plays of William Dean Howells,* ed. Walter J. Meserve (New York: New York University Press, 1960). There are other variations, as Professor Meserve points out in his introduction and notes.

"American Representation in Austria" (MTP).

Twain deplores the fact that Americans are being badly represented in Vienna by Addison Harris, an undistinguished man—uncultured, monolingual, not rich enough, inhospitable, and ill-mannered. Twain also criticizes some of the other officials here.

> The Emperor [of Austria], Beechler, Addison Harris, Herdliski, General Ruger, Tower.

'The American Vandal,' 1867 (WMT 28).

The American Vandal is a roving, independent, free-and-easy traveler who is not gilded with education and social graces. He gallops over England and then down to Italy, where he takes a piece of stone from Columbus's house in Genoa, is impressed by the cathedral in Milan but laughs at the worn-and-torn condition of "The Last Supper" there, paddles around the Lake of Como, and delights in Venice—especially at night when moonbeams dance in the shadows. After Florence and Naples, he goes to Athens. Twain and three other Vandals avoided the quarantine to see the

Parthenon by moonlight. Twain wishes that he could take time to describe their visit to Alexander II of Russia. In closing, Twain recommends that American Vandals continue to travel, because it makes them more tolerant and compassionate.

[King] Alexander II of Russia, the American Vandal.

'The American Vandal Abroad,' 1868-1869.*

Twain says that he feels like a relic when he is introduced publicly in this fashion. He hates relics and therefore used to respond like an imbecile to them in Europe. An American vandal is simply a free and easy-going traveler without much education, at home everywhere abroad and anxious to satisfy his curiosity about everything, including harems, Turkish pipes and baths, figs, camels, and especially St. Peter's and the thinking, lonely Sphinx. The vandal is inordinately happy in Paris, Genoa, the Crimea, and Milan. Twain saw a statue in Milan of a skinned man and also the faded "Last Supper." The typical vandal prefers Lake Como, Venice (with its canals, gondolas, and bridges), and Athens by moonlight. Time does not permit Twain to tell of the vandals' audience with Alexander II of Russia. America is best of all, with its beautiful women, corruption, energy, and monogamy. If this lecture has a moral, it is a suggestion that all vandals should travel to remove prejudices and gain a liberalizing tolerance.

[King] Alexander II of Russia, the Doctor, the Sultan of Turkey, the American Vandal.

*In Fred W. Lorch, *The Trouble Begins at Eight: Mark Twain's Lecture Tours* (Ames: Iowa State University Press, 1968).

'American Vandals in the Old World.' See 'The American Vandal Abroad.'

'Americans and the English,' 1872 (WMT 28).

The author greets the Chairman, and the ladies and gentlemen present at a Fourth of July gathering of Americans in London, tells them that it is better for Americans and Englishmen to do as they have recently been doing, that is, settle misunderstandings by arbitration rather than by cannon. The English are beginning to accept things American. The United States is progressive, and has produced Washington, Longfellow, and Jay Gould, a strange trial system, manslaughtering railroads, and a fine, non-aristocratic respect for individual rights. Well, the author would so greet and address his audience but for the fact that General Schenck presided, harangued everyone at dull length, and ordered no further oratory.

    General [Robert C.] Schenck.

"Among the Fenians," 1866.*

    Wishing to be agreeable, the narrator Mark tries out his Gaelic on Dennis McCarthy, editor of the new Fenian journal in San Francisco. It is called the *Irish People*. But after saying "Arrah," "Erin go brach," and "Tare an' ouns," Mark runs out of niceties.

    Mark, Dennis McCarthy.

    *In *The Celebrated Jumping Frog of Calaveras County, and Other Sketches* (New York: 1867).

"Among the Spirits," 1866 (WG).

    Along with about four hundred others, in addition to reporters, Twain attends Mrs. Foye's séance. An *Examiner* reporter asks the woman about a man he knew named Gus Graham, and the responding raps indicate that he was shot to death in Illinois in 1854. It is all true. Twain asks about John Smith and learns that everyone in hell is named Smith until a correction can be made. Seriously, Mrs. Foye is perplexing, and Twain wonders what connection there might be between spiritualism and clairvoyance.

    The Prince Apollyon, Mrs. [Ada Hoyt] Foye, Gus Graham, John Smith, Smith.

["Ancients in Modern Dress"], 1972 (FM).

    In a letter recently discovered, Gainsborough answers a lady who complained that her portrait does not look like her. Of course it does not, the artist replies. She insisted on sitting in an outlandish, unnatural costume. Not even her friends would know her. Twain ponders all of this and concludes that the reason portraits of historical idols look strange is that their dress is not up to date. So he copies several portraits, each accurately as to face but with clothing modernized. The people now seem like old friends. One which he copied and which causes him to weep is Adam's portrait, reputedly taken from life and now in the collection of the Armenian Patriarch of Jerusalem.

The Armenian Patriarch of Jerusalem.

"Andy on Grant." See FW, 1869.

["Anecdote about Captain Jones, Who Ate the Awful Candy"] (MTP).

A small boy named Harry likes old bachelor Captain Jones and therefore decides to give him something. Harry's sister is having a party one night; so, during the molasses pull, the boy pitches in but forgets to butter his hands, gets the sticky candy in his hair and some hair in it, drops it in some ashes, and finally puts it in an old sack with bits of tobacco left behind. Harry then sleeps the sleep of the just, and in the morning trudges off to present his candy to Captain Jones. The rugged old fellow sees its ingredients but, to spare the boy's feelings, eats it anyway—in an act truly heroic and delicate.

Harry, Captain Jones.

"Another Big Thing." See FW, 1870.

"Another Fossil." See FW, 1869.

"Another View of the Great Jubilee." See FW, 1869.

"Answer to an Inquiry from the Coming Man," 1871 (CG).

Twain says yes to the young man who has written to ask whether Agassiz really recommends fish as a diet for authors. As to the amount of fish an author should eat? Twain suggests that if the specimen of writing the young man sent is about his average, he should probably try a couple of middle-sized whales for now.

"An Answer to That Conundrum" (SS). See "Concerning the Answer to That Conundrum."

"Answers to Correspondents," 1865 (WMT 7).

The author must answer a number of his correspondents. To the Moral Statistician, he issues a rebuke. Who cares how much a nonagenarian has spent on tobacco if he has enjoyed it? Critics of smokers save money; but they do not contribute it to charities, and when the contribution box is passed in church they are busy kneeling with eyes downcast. To the Young Author who asks whether fish is really brain food, the author replies in the affirmative and adds that, judging by the specimen of writing the fellow sent, he needs to eat two medium-sized whales. Simon Wheeler deserves the author's thanks for sending a poem about the parson who always "done his level best." The author continues by sending pertinent advice to others, including a beggar, a would-be poet, two persons frustrated in love, a mathematician, a scholar, a flower tosser, and a happy young mother. (See also [*Mark Twain's San Francisco*].)

> Ambitious Learner, Arithmeticus, Arthur Augustus, Discarded Lover, St. Clair Higgins, Jim, Mrs. Edwitha Howard Jones, Jones, Moral Statistician, Melton Mowbray, Professional Beggar, Signorina ——, Mark Twain, Simon Wheeler, Young Author, Young Mother.

Apostrophe to Death, 1966 (P).

Death is the only god which confers gifts instead of trading, peddling, and demanding things in return. Other gods are like gas companies selling light at exorbitant rates and giving light to none. Death gives peace to all—to sinners, innocent ones, rich, poor, unloved, and loved ones. Death is a sweet, gracious friend, worthy of worship.

"Appendix Concerning Dreams." See FW, 1869.

"The Approaching Epidemic," 1870 (CRG).

Now that Charles Dickens has died, everyone who can do so will offer readings from his works and those who associated with him in even the slightest capacity will lecture about the relationship. People who heard him read will reminisce, and his cigar ash and toothpick will be exhibited.

John Brown, John Gray, John Jones, Serena Amelia Try-
phenia McSpadden, Mrs. J. Hooligan Murphy, John Smith,
John Thomas, John White.

"The Aquarium" (MTP).

As the Admiral of the Aquarium, Twain prepares an elaborate
handbook. Innocence at Home, his residence at Redding, Connecticut, was designed, he says in 1908, around the Aquarium. Now the
Aquarium is an exclusive club, composed of a dozen little girls,
called Fish and Angel-Fish, who have as their private headquarters
the billiard room, and have certain privileges with respect to that
room, also the loggia, the type of trial following alleged unbecom-
ing conduct, their portraits, the badge (a pin in the form of an
angel-fish from the West Indies), and membership.

The Admiral of the Aquarium, Helen Allen, Margaret
Blackmer, Margaret Breckinridge, Dorothy Butes, the
Chatelaine, Fish, Dan Frohman, Margaret Illington Frohman, Irene Gerken, Dorothy Harvey, the Legal Staff, Hel-
len Martin, the Mother Superior, Frances Nunnally, Officer, Louise Paine, Dorothy Quick, Servant, Jean Spurr,
Dorothy Sturgis.

L'Arbre Fée de Bourlemont: Song of the Children, 1895 (P).

The marvelous tree of Bourlemont keeps green because of the
children's tears and strong because of their love. (In *Personal Recollections of Joan of Arc.*)

"The Arkansas Traveler Comes to Light." See FW, 1869.

["Arrival at Honolulu"]. See LSI.

"The Art of Composition," 1890 (LAIFI).

Twain says that he probably has some methods of composition
but cannot really define them. When he reads a sentence that he
likes, he stores it away as a model. He rejects others if he dislikes
them. But the process is mostly unconscious. He dislikes long sentences if they resemble partly underwater serpents rather than

torchlight parades. He also prefers the exact rather than the almost
exact word.

'Artemus Ward,' 1871.*

Twain begins by introducing himself as a man devoted to philosophy, accuracy, and the love of truth. Artemus Ward was America's
greatest humorist, although he became famous so fast that he
lacked time to polish his wit. Artemus Ward was born Charles F.
Browne of Puritan stock in Waterford, Maine, in 1834. He was
skinny and red-haired. He became an apprentice to a printer in
Skowhegan, then a typesetter for the Boston *Carpet Bagger,* and
next a Cleveland reporter. After he penned his first misspelled
letter, he quickly became famous, went to New York—where he
wrote *Vanity Fair* columns—and then lectured—notably on "The
Babes in the Woods"—with great success in California and abroad.
Twain says that Artemus Ward's genius lay in his delivery, which
was always perfectly timed. He was also a master at moving without transition from important facts to something ridiculous. The
English climate worsened his poor health, and he died in South-
ampton in his thirty-fourth year.

Browne, Twain, Artemus Ward.

*In Fred W. Lorch, *The Trouble Begins at Eight: Mark Twain's Lecture Tours,* 1968.

"Artemus Ward Announces His Coming to Washoe . . . ," (1863)
(MTWY).

The narrator understands that Artemus Ward is coming to Washoe to lecture and perhaps to add items to his sho. The narrator will
help him find todes, snaix, a wax model of a wash-owe man, and
maybe the skulp of the layte Missus Hoppins. Busts of Mark
Twain are too common around here to merit inclusion of one.

Mrs. Hoppins, Artemus Ward.

'Artemus Ward, Humorist.' See 'Artemus Ward.'

"As Concerns Interpreting the Deity," 1917 (WMT 26).

A line of hieroglyphics puzzled Rosetta-stone scholars for fourteen years, but Champollion finally translated it. Then three years

of work by rival scholars produced eleven new translations. More years followed, and more translations, until Rawlinson's won almost universal approval. Demotic writing is similarly challenging. American Indians have left records scratched on boulders, some of which on the Dighton Rocks are still the despair of would-be interpreters. We have trouble solving man-made mysteries; by comparison, God's seem easy. The ancient Roman augurs read the Deity's intentions in birds' entrails, also in thunder claps and dreams. Eleven hundred and thirty or forty years later we find Henry of Huntington lamenting in his chronicles over King Stephen's seizure of the throne of England from dead King Henry's daughter. Henry of Huntington explains that the Lord struck down the Archbishop of Canterbury for crowning wicked Stephen, who later died comfortably. Now, how did the ecclesiast earn such punishment? Henry of Huntington also explains God's apparently capricious adverse treatment of certain warriors in battles between Scotland and England. Perhaps the chronicler was only a guesser. He seems little better than the old Roman entrail-gazers.

Henry of Huntington.

"As Regards Patriotism," 1923 (WMT 29).

Some countries, for example, Austria, have an official religion and the individual must conform. Not so in America. Yet patriotism is merely a religion, a mechanical devotion to country and flag. In monarchies, the throne provides the patriotism. In America, politicians and newspapers do so. At the beginning of a political upheaval, most people are tempted to revolt but usually let political leaders and journalists dissuade them. Potential real patriots thus turn traitor to keep from being called traitor. People can seldom fight against their training; so the result is shop-worn patriotism in those who merely side with the majority. Since training can do anything, however, people can surely be trained to create their own patriotism instead of taking it by command as Austrians do their religion.

The Patriot, the Traitor.

["Asa Hoover"], 1972 (FM).

Old Walters comes by on September 6, and he and the narrator reminisce about old times in their village by the Mississippi River, where John Tolliver lived. Then Walters tells about Asa Hoover, the richest man in the village during Walters's youth. Everyone looked up to Hoover, even though he was evil. When anyone annoyed him, he always got even. But his cruelties people assigned to others; and even good deeds performed by others they thanked him for. He had several children. One of them fell into the fire, but Hoover would do nothing to save it. Two of his other children saved it and were burned in the process. But Hoover got credit for the heroic deed.

Asa Hoover, Hoover, Hoover, Hoover, Hoover, John Tolliver, Walters.

'The Ascot Gold Cup,' 1907 (S).

Twain begins by saying that he did not steal the Ascot Cup, in spite of the recent combination of British headlines—"Mark Twain Arrives—Ascot Cup Stolen." He is growing more and more honest, perhaps because of his surroundings. An eloquent charity worker at a fund-raising meeting once almost persuaded Twain to give hundreds of dollars, or even a blank check—with someone else's signature on it. But the orator was followed by such a dull speaker that Twain contributed only a dime and took a quarter for change. He then voices serious appreciation for the greatest honor he ever received—a degree from Oxford University. It is a compliment partly addressed to America as well. He closes by commenting that given his age he is unlikely ever to visit England again and says goodbye with lips and heart.

"Assassination in Carson," 1863 (MTWY).

Twain reports that Joe Magee, suspected of killing Jack Williams in Virginia last winter, was killed by a bullet through a saloon window this very morning.

Joe Magee, Jack Williams.

["At Sea Again"]. See LSI.

"At the Appetite Cure," 1898 (WMT 22).

The author is at an establishment called Hochberghaus, a short distance out of Vienna and into Bohemia, so remote and quiet that every day seems like Sunday. Hochberghaus is situated in a lonely spot on the top of a wooded mountain, and it is here that lost appetites are restored. The founder is Professor Haimberger. When the author explains that the mere sight of food is revolting, the professor carefully goes over the rules: if the patient does not wish to order anything at this time from an elaborate menu—including tough tripe, scrambled cat, and even raw sailor boots—he must obtain the professor's approval for anything ordered later. Rather reluctantly, the author agrees, retires for the night, tries unsuccessfully to get some coffee in the morning, notices that he is locked in his room, and finally surrenders and agrees to eat anything approved. Haimberger is delighted and instantly permits his subdued patient to have beefsteak, potatoes, Vienna bread, and coffee. It seems that thirty years earlier Haimberger took a long voyage, was shipwrecked, watched his fellow survivors at the end of fifteen days happy to gnaw on anything available, but was disheartened to see that when rescued most, though in fine condition after their enforced fast, lapsed back into the habit of nibbling at and complaining about too much food. Haimberger then concluded that the best remedy for loss of appetite is for one to become exceedingly hungry and then rejoice in one's food. His system at Hochberghaus combines a good deal of exercise and exposure to repulsive fare. Modified starvation cures many ailments, including loss of appetite.

Professor Haimberger.

"At the Shrine of St. Wagner," 1891 (WMT 26).

Twain and his party join the waves of music-lovers rolling in upon Bayreuth from as far away as San Francisco. The only persons to be accommodated properly are those who obtained reservations months in advance. The way here was fatiguing, by slow train. Stragglers look like wet cats. Twain arrives on Saturday. On Sunday he reports to the opera house by mid-afternoon. The interior is simple and impressive, seating 1,650 persons, who enter smoothly by eighteen doors. The floor slopes sharply down to the stage. When the music begins, Twain has an eerie feeling that dead Wagner is conducting music which at just that moment is passing through his brain. Twain much prefers the non-vocal parts of the music, compares the gestures of the singers to those of persons trying to catch flies, and can detect nothing melodic in the *Parsifal* arias. They seem to be combinations of long notes and peremptory barks. During intermission some go out and eat, if they have reservations. On Monday Twain attends his only operatic favorite, which is *Tannhäuser*. At the end of the intermission, buglers recall straggling members of the audience. An imperial princess appears on a balcony; but when she notices that people are stopping to stare and that therefore she is halting traffic back into the theater, she graciously re-enters. The presence of princes at the rear loft of the theater occasions Twain's thought that our interest in nobility is generated by a combination of envy and worship, because a prince is the only type on earth with accidental, unearned, but permanent good fortune. Twain recalls a British friend in London who was late in keeping a social appointment with him because she had delayed to stand in freezing weather to see the Prince of Wales. When Twain commented that he would not do so even to see Grant for the first time, she replied that he was only a president. Twain relishes the last act of *Tannhäuser*. Next he comments on Bayreuth food, which is so bad that it remains in the eater's crop forever and is hence rather like a souvenir. On Wednesday Twain attends *Tristan and Isolde,* and is fascinated by the rapt attention of the audience, which, unlike people at the New York Metropolitan, worship in reverential silence. Twain feels out of place here, like a uniquely sane person among the mad or perhaps a heretic in heaven. On Thursday he sees *Parsifal* again and likes it better. Then he learns that the critics lambasted that performance, which proves to him again that art work which he likes is poor.

> [Max] Alvary, General and President [Ulysses S.] Grant, [Amalie] Materna, Uhlic, [Richard] Wagner, Madame [Richard] Wagner, the Prince of Wales.

"The Athenian and the Frog." Part of "Private History of the 'Jumping Frog' Story."

"Aurelia's Unfortunate Young Man," 1864 (WMT 7).

The author receives a letter from a young lady who signs herself "Aurelia Maria" of San Jose. Her story is touching. She is seeking advice. It seems that when she was sixteen years old she fell passionately in love with Williamson Breckinridge Caruthers of New Jersey, six years her senior. They were engaged when a series of misfortunes befell Caruthers. Smallpox pitted his face until it looked like a waffle mold; he fell into a well, broke a leg, and had it amputated; he lost his other leg; and finally he was scalped by sion and then the other in a carding machine; erysipelas blinded him in one eye; he lost his other leg; and finally he was scalped by the Owens River Indians. What to do? The author advises Aurelia Maria to furnish her diminished lover with wooden limbs, a glass eye, and a wig, give him ninety days to avoid breaking his neck, then marry him. Odds are he will be dead first; and if not, he probably will die soon, and the limbs and such will revert to the widow. We must do our best under all circumstances.

Aurelia Maria, Williamson Breckinridge Caruthers.

"The Austrian Edison Keeping School Again," 1898 (WMT 23).

Jan Szczepanik, a twenty-four-year-old Austrian inventor, was a schoolmaster in a small Moravian village a few years ago. Then, when he invented a process for applying photography to pattern-designing for the textile industry, he journeyed without permission to Vienna to try unsuccessfully to market it, lost his teaching post, ran out of money, returned home, and was reinstated. Later he invented a telelectroscope, sold it to a French syndicate, and began to work in comfort in a fine laboratory. But now it seems that when he gave up teaching he lost his exemption from military duty. Instead of drafting him for three years, the authorities have ordered him to return home and teach one morning every two months. The spectacle is romantic, and the children periodically love the fruits and toys he brings, and his almost magical scientific lectures.

Jan Szczepanik.

"Author's Advertisement," 1872.*

Twain explains that George Routledge and Sons are his only valid English publishers. They pay him, and let him edit and revise his material, which piratical British printers do not let him do.

George Routledge, Routledge.

*In *Mark Twain's Sketches* (London: Routledge, 1872).

'Authors'Club,'1899 (WMT 28).

Twain thanks members of the Authors' Club for saying pleasant things about his books. Sir Walter Besant and Sir Spencer Walpole were especially kind. Twain will repeat their compliments when he reports to his family. When he was a boy, he read the *Walpole Letters* and put them away for later use. Since he has paid his club dues, he hopes to use their lawyer, to avoid personal contact with publishers and to lose his case.

Sir Walter Besant, Sir Spencer Walpole.

'An Author's Soldiering,'1887 (LAIFI).

Twain is happy to speak to the Union veterans in Baltimore and to clear up at last the mystery of his military service. He was a rebel soldier in the Civil War for two weeks. In that time he rose from private to second lieutenant. He and several cohorts were being surrounded one night by a stranger who seemed to be an enemy, and so they killed him. The battle was unique in military annals: an entire enemy force was exterminated to the last man. Twain could not go on killing all opponents every two weeks; so he withdrew his support of the Confederacy and let it collapse, which was good, because we now have a majestic democracy here.

Union Veteran of Maryland.

["Autobiography of a Damned Fool"], 1967 (SB).

The partly Presbyterian and partly papistical Scotch-Irish father of the narrator, who is named Bolivar and is a printer's apprentice, dies when the lad is eighteen. Thoughts of death intrude upon Bolivar, and he gives up smoking, making a little pyre of his unused cigars on the sidewalk. But then when he returns to work, he is so late that Mr. Sprague, his employer, an irascible man of forty, hurls things at him; so he goes to the Methodist minister, and together they pray for Sprague. Bolivar then joins the church, starts teaching Sunday School, and points out to his agreeable charges that the ark could not have contained so many animals and the earth could not have been submerged after only forty days of rain.

Bolivar's master (now called Milton Bangs) is small, wiry, red-haired, and bad-tempered. Mrs. Bangs, three years older than her husband, is a tall, thin, flat-chested Yankee woman, a former school teacher who has the only false teeth in town. The Bangses have been married only four years; and in their large frame house live Hank Flanders, the other apprentice, and Tom Rogers, a journeyman, in addition to Bolivar. The young fellow grows so worried about Bangs's spiritual condition that he gives the man a tract called "The Pit Yawns for You" to read; but the angry man tears it to fragments and dances upon them. The Methodist minister, the Rev. Mr. Soper, then takes Bolivar to task for disturbing his Sunday-School pupils' theological beliefs. Soper gives the lad an infidel tract to read, just to show him how specious some reasoning can be; but he instantly becomes unconverted and burns his tracts, to the discomfiture of Mrs. Bangs, who wants him to read a sample to her unregenerate husband. Tom and Hank laugh riotously.

Bolivar begins a study of Benjamin Franklin's autobiography and is impressed by the similarities in their attitudes: both aim to improve the welfare of others, have progressive ideas, thirst for knowledge, are reverent, avoid frivolities, and act upon principle. Franklin, however, accumulated money, whereas Bolivar has no such instinct. He now begins to study by the light of embers, practice secret oratory until Mrs. Bangs objects, and bathe in the cold creek. He is soon expelled from church, but that does not distress him because he has taken to reading the Koran and has become such a thorough Mahometan that he decides to keep a harem. He writes to five mature ladies; but Mrs. Bangs refuses to enlarge the family, and the ladies themselves descend upon him with umbrellas and slippers.

When he recovers, Bolivar sallies forth into the street, only to be abused there also by several young people. One of them is a fellow named Simpson, who flings mud in Bolivar's direction but instead splatters a bully named Jim Frisbie, who berates Simpson so much that Bolivar beats up Frisbie among others. Hank Flanders helps Bolivar in some later fights, for the fun of it. About this time a temperance movement hits the village, and Bolivar happily joins the Paladins of Purity. He is elected lodge secretary, then its constable, and then its marshal. He would have reigned as grand duke but for an unfortunate circumstance. He undertakes to reform Si Higgins, the town drunkard, and appears to be succeeding until Hank gives Bolivar a bottle of rye just before the ceremony at which he is to present Higgins and lecture on the man's reformation. Bolivar reasons that he does not know about wishkey; so before he can lecture on the enemy, he should face it. He gets staggering drunk, and so does Higgins. A new grand duke quickly replaces Bolivar. Hank is a friendly, gangling youth. Some accuse him of being a practical joker, but Bolivar knows this to be untrue. Such people joy inflicting pain, but not kind Hank. For example, he once left a wasps' nest in Bolivar's chair, forgot about it, and was volubly sorry for the pain thus caused. Hank likes animals and urges Bolivar to be gentle with stray cats and dogs. He brings a bad-breathed dog to Bolivar's room one night and begs his friend to comfort it in his bed. Bolivar tries but finally has to take to the sofa. In addition, Mrs. Bangs is angry because the dog turned the feather pillow into a snowstorm.

Bolivar absent-mindedly goes very late one night to his fianceé's home, and the girl's father opens the door in his night-shirt. Bolivar sits down in the parlor. The old man returns wrapped in a green blanket, sits and talks and talks about himself, until finally Bolivar grows so bored that he gets up to leave, whereupon the old man with a sneer offers him breakfast. Walking home, Bolivar notices that dawn is breaking. In the afternoon the girl sends a chaffing note, in which she reminds him of the preacher Alexander Campbell. It seems that two years earlier Campbell came to town and delivered a ringing sermon so good that it simply had to be printed. Bolivar set it up in type and abbreviated the name J. Iscariot, which outraged the volatile minister. Bolivar never could understand the fuss.

> Milton Bangs, Mrs. Milton Bangs, Bolivar, Alexander Campbell, Grand Duke, Miss Dunlap, Hank Flanders, Jim Frisbie, Miss Hatcher, Si Higgins, Sam Jenkins, Lawson, Paladin, Miss Rankin, Tom Rogers, the Most Noble Deputy Scribe, the Most Noble Grand Secretary, Most Faithful Dauntless and Renowned Seneschal of the Castle-Keep, Simpson, Molly Sims, Rev. Mr. Soper, Miss Tunstall, Miss Watson.

"The Autobiography of Belshazzar," 1959.*

Belshazzar, a cat, was born one summer noon in a meadow with a few fruit trees. Across the valley is a town so far away that it seems like part of another world. Belshazzar's papa, however, was there one night long ago and has some marvelous stories about the place.

Belshazzar's family are guests of the Wagner family at Sunset Farm. Mr. Wagner is rather clumsy and lazy, drawls and wobbles, but has nice hair. His wife is young, nice, and sensible; and so are her sister and brother-in-law Mr. and Mrs. Staveley. Workers for the Wagners include ex-slaves Aunt Rachel and Uncle Loomis. The Wagners have three little daughters—Lucy, Carrie, and Irene. Sorrow is unknown as yet at Sunset Farm. The Wagners spread out the new litter of kittens, which includes Belshazzar, three sisters, and two brothers. Belshazzar is proud of his mother Sour Mash, so named by Mr. Wagner, who names all the pets foolishly. The family dog Alexander Hamilton likes Sour Mash and her kittens. But the Baptist collie neighbor Carlo Hopkins tries to get fresh with the new litter, and Sour Mash has to ride him off. She cannot stand his religious and political notions. The kittens are placed on the floor of the big, cozy porch. With the sailcloth curtains up, they could look out beyond the valley to the twinkling town in the distance. All is peaceful. While the dogs look on, Mr. Wagner names the new kittens: first Belshazzar, then the others, and finally Belshazzar's baby sister the Grand Duchess of Baden.

> Alexander Hamilton, Belshazzar, Carlo Hopkins, Fräulein, the Grand Duchess of Baden, Henry VIII, Uncle Loomis, Aunt Rachel, Sour Mash, Staveley, Mrs. Staveley, Carrie Wagner, Irene Wagner, Lucy Wagner, Wagner, Mrs. Wagner.

*In *Concerning Cats: Two Tales by Mark Twain,* ed. Frederick Anderson (San Francisco: The Book Club of California, 1959).

"Awful, Terrible Medieval Romance." See "A Medieval Romance."

'The Babies,' 1879 (WMT 28).

Twain begins by saying that we all stand on common ground through all having been babies. When a baby arrives at family headquarters, he takes command. Soldiers who could face enemy fire surrender to their babies' cries. Our future leaders, mere babies now, must be well cared for and properly trained. In a cradle somewhere, right now, is a baby who will become the commander-in-chief of the American armies one day [like General U. S. Grant, being honored tonight]. Now that baby is worried only about putting his big toe into his mouth. Fifty-six years ago that was all General Grant was concerned with; and if the child is a prophecy of the man, he succeeded.

General U. S. Grant.

"Back from 'Yurrup.'" See FW, 1869.

"Baker's Blue-jay Yarn." From *A Tramp Abroad*.

"Baker's Cat." See "Dick Baker's Cat."

A Ballotd: Owed phor the Tymz; Not the Knusepaper, 1966 (P).

I, Twark Main, have been thinking about the Kunnettykut elexuns of 1871. An Inglish mon, supposedly backt bi Twead, is running against Jewill for govennur. When Twead di'nt kumm through, a cawkuss was helld and it was decided to have the Forth Waurde stuff the ballod-bocks again. Some Republykans soon demand a count, and a moderator reports to the Hi Bored. People begin to damn each other, but the victory of Inglish is soon announced. He plans a triumphal procession. The awphul mawn arrives when the Ledgislachur meats with members of both sides seated. Committees convene to check into frawdz at the poles. Eaton's men resine. Soon the investigation proves fraud by the Demokrats, who quickly blame desperait gamblers for stuffing the boxes by stelth. The Republikans feel obliged to march out the phive hunderd who voted for thair man. Inglish's men stand firm but know that all is lost, and their leader soon shows the whight fether. Alas, in daze of yoar those men wore Jaxon's knaim. But they solde thair principals, till tru Republykans hav gaynd the relm. Old Hickoree would not stand for any aristocratic nonsense, but later the Demokrats became oppressurs and even called it Konstitutishanall to shute a runaway slaiv but unkonstitushunall to deter a Ku Klux nave. Well, the partiegh's dedd now, and Demokrats mourn while Republikans cheer their new Govenor. Modest Juel, meanwhile, eggstends to his defunkt ennymyes the ollive braunch.

> Alderman, Demokrat, Eaton, Gard, Hall, Hi Bored, Hi Kanvasier, the Hoss Gardz, Inglish, Jaxon, Jeffurson, Jewill, Jueller, Kanva-sir, Kommitteigh man, Lowgan,

Mack chord, Twark Main, the Millertareigh, Nashunals, Phedral, the Phoot Gardz, the Putnam Falank, Republykan, the Sassphields, Sur, Treet, Twead, Wallow, Wate.

["Baron Tauchnitz and Copyright"] (MTP).

O, the son of Baron Tauchnitz, has been here arranging terms for publishing the works of some American authors. He and his father are the only honest publishers Twain has ever known. All the others steal from authors, because the copyright laws permit them to do so.

O, Baron Tauchnitz.

"The Bathing Tutor." See TW, 1870

Battle Hymn of the Republic (Brought down to Date), 1958 (P).

My eyes have seen the launching of the sword which seeks out strangers' wealth. They have built the sword an altar in the East. His night marches on. His gospel is written in steel. Greed marches on. We now guard sin. Since Christ died to make people holy, let us force men to die to increase our riches.

"Bearding the Fenian in His Lair." See "Among the Fenians."

"The Bee," 1917 (WMT 26).

Important bees are female. In a hive, only one bee is married. She is the queen and has fifty thousand children, a hundred of which are sons and the rest all maiden daughters. Each spring the queen goes on a honeymoon with one of her sons, soon divorces him, returns home, and begins to lay two million eggs. When the queen gets slack, substitutes fight to replace her, and rather unfairly too. She lives in gilded darkness and has no friends. Opinionated scientists agree that bees are not human; yet bees are master fools. After the queen, the next in importance in the hive are the virgin workers, numbering into the thousands. Males do no work. Hive assignments are distributed according to specialization, as in a big American factory. Workers take a bony pride in the uniqueness of their work, in hives as in life.

Behold—the Penis Mightier Than the Sword (unpublished poem).*
See this phallus, once so mighty but now dreaming of the past,
unmoved.

*Original in the Collection of American Literature, Beinecke Rare Room and
Manuscript Library, Yale University, New Haven, Connecticut.

"The Belated Russian Passport," 1902 (WMT 23).
In Berlin some young Americans are drinking beer. Several try
to persuade Alfred Parrish, of Yale, not to cut his vacation short.
But he confesses to homesickness, although he adds that he would
like to see St. Petersburg. His friends soon leave. Then a total
stranger, who introduces himself as Major Jackson, also of America but intimately familiar with St. Petersburg, advances and soon
talks him into venturing on. While Parrish waits, the major rushes
off with the lad's railroad ticket to Paris, baggage checks, and
money, to make all necessary arrangements. Just as Parrish decides
to sneak out of the beer saloon, since he now lacks money to pay
his bill, Jackson returns and rushes him into a cab and off to the
major's friend the Russian consul for a visa. But the man is away
in the country; so they leave instructions to mail the document
to the Hôtel de l'Europe, St. Petersburg, and off they clatter to the
train. Jackson is an adorable companion, full of sunshiny charm.
But suddenly Parrish realizes that he lacks any passport. The major
talks their way past a frontier inspector, and soon they are at the
hotel in St. Petersburg. But the clerk refuses to assign Parrish a
room without a passport. So Jackson takes his quaking, fainting
friend to Prince Bossloffsky, the head of the Secret Police. He gives
Parrish twenty-four hours to produce the passport, or it is off to
Siberia with him. The boy writes a touching letter of farewell to
his mother back home and then spends a harrowing night. In the
morning, the major charms him until they overhear some Englishmen complaining that a train accident will delay the Berlin mail
unduly. Parrish swoons again. So Jackson takes him to the American legation, where his friend the minister will surely issue a
duplicate passport in ample time. But he is away hunting. His
secretary refuses all aid, until suddenly he decides to question Parrish. Where does he come from? Where did he live? Describe the
house! Pinned down, Parrish confesses that his clergyman father
once called a certain picture in the family dining room a hellfired

nightmare. All is well. It appears that the secretary once lived in
the Parrish house in New Haven and painted that very picture. He
saves Parrish by signing a duplicate passport.

Prince Bossloffsky, the Chief Inspector, Archy Hale, Major Jackson, Alfred Parrish, Will Parrish, Rev. Mr. Parrish,
Mrs. Parrish, Henry Taylor.

"Bells in Buffalo" (MTP).
The person who gave those bells to the city of Buffalo was beneficent. They comfort everyone. Even when people who grew up in
Buffalo wander afar, the memory of those harmonious bells never
fades.

"Benjamin Franklin." See FW, 1869.

"Bible Teaching and Religious Practice," 1923 (WMT 29).
Religion has always had the lion's share in the changes of civilization. The Christian's Bible is like a drug store. Its contents remain
the same, but medical practice changes. At first the practice was
crudely allopathic: the patient was drenched with repulsive doses,
and yet all along the store had homeopathic medications. Leeches
were once used; later Christ's love was administered. The text
remained the same, but the practice changed. It was the same with
slavery. At first the Roman Church sanctioned it with suitable
biblical references. Christian England supported it and even
knighted that great slave hunter John Hawkins, whose ship was
the *Jesus*. But then slavery was abolished, first in England and later
in the United States, and always with appropriate textual citations.
The same with witchcraft, hell fire, and infant damnation. In each
instance, the text remains but the practice has changed. In the
evolution of mankind, no good and useful text has ever been
obliterated. Perhaps in a few billion more years man will develop
something fine and his religious practice may even become
decent.

Sir John Hawkins, the Pope.

"A Big Thing." See FW, 1870.

"Bigler vs Tahoe," 1863 (WG).

To a man named Grub who writes in calling Lake Bigler by the ugly name of Tahoe, the author replies that Indian names may be more fitting but that the word *Tahoe* is repulsive and slobbering. He intends to start for Lake Bigler and Grub next Monday.

    Grub.

'Billiards,' 1906 (WMT 28).

Twain recalls playing billiards with a stranger in Virginia City once. The man said that he wanted to be fair and would therefore play lefthanded. He did so, and won easily. Twain asked the man how he would do righthanded. The stranger replied that he could not play righthanded at all because he was lefthanded.

"Biographical Sketch of George Washington" (WG). See "Brief Biographical Sketch of George Washington."

"Biography A La Mode." See FW, 1870.

"The Black Prince's Cat" (MTP).

While at Windsor, Twain learns from the castle cook that a cat is there which is five hundred years old. It once belonged to the Black Prince and is named the Black Prince because it is pure black. When the human Black Prince died, his father King Edward decreed that the royal cook should care for the cat and receive £500 a year for so doing as long as the cat should live. Well, curiously enough, heirs of that cook have kept this cat alive for centuries and have even proved the fact in court from time to time. Even if the cat should be banished, the antiquity-loving British would rescue it and finance its longevity. The cook is pleased with the attention Twain shows to her story and promises him a kitten.

    The Black Prince, [Oliver] Cromwell, King Edward III, [King] Richard II.

"The 'Blind Letter' Department, London, P.O.," 1875.*

A curious feature of the London Post Office is its Blind Letter

Department, which employs one man with the ability to decipher poor handwriting. He keeps copies of especially atrocious penmanship and also has facsimiles of envelopes with curious pictures drawn beside the addresses. Twain presents some samples.

"Blue-Jays." From *A Tramp Abroad.*

*In *Mark Twain's Sketches, New and Old* (Hartford: American Publishing Co., 1875).

["Boarding House Novel"] (MTP).
The narrator agrees that his friend has a good idea. The narrator will move to the boardinghouse where his friend stays, observe the various people there, change their names and occupations, and put them into a novel.

Blakely, Mrs. Blakely, Blakely, Miss Blakely, Miss Blakely, Col. Bloomer, Mrs. Bloomer, Bloomer, Bloomer, Bullard, John Douglas, Emma, Col. Gaspipe, Mrs. Gaspipe, Gaspipe, Archibald Grandison, Mrs. Archibald Grandison, Susan Grandison, Silas Gurley, Mrs. Silas Gurley, Thomas Hawksley, Parker Jones, Lamb, George Ridgeway, Ruggles, William Sawyer, Simpson, Thompson, Mrs. Thompson, Thompson, Miss Thompson, Miss Thompson, Wolf.

"A Book Review," 1871 (CG).
R. B. W. of Philadelphia undertakes to review Thomas Henry Huxley's *Inquiry into the Origin, Development, and Transmission of the Games of Childhood, in All Ages and of Every Nation, with Notes, Critical, Analytical, and Historical,* published by Shelton & Brothers of New York. The book suggestively posits the following brilliant theories, among others: Druids behaved like superstitious children, certain childish games are reminiscent of conduct of Shakers today, and hopscotch may be traced back to Cain and Abel. Twain adds a note that the review is incomprehensible enough to warrant the conclusion that Huxley's book is good but that he intends not to read it.

Bruce, Disraeli, Douglass, Professor Thomas Henry Huxley, Shelton, Shelton, R. B. W.

'Books and Burglars,' 1908 (S).

Twain asks the Redding Library Association to consider the burglars who recently broke into his house and took a lot of useless
things. Imagine those men breaking instead into this library. Here
they are, seated on the floor reading by the light of tiny lanterns
and thus absorbing moral truths. Their lives would have been
changed. As it is, they went their immoral ways, were sent to jail,
and might even wind up in Congress. Burglars, however, deserve
some praise. They avoid disturbing people's sleep while they work.
But if any go near his house now, the elaborate new alarms will
ring and spring, and the trespassers will be heard of no more.

'Books, Authors, and Hats,' 1907 (WMT 28).

Twain thanks his audience in London for honoring him and then
voices his gladness that some undergraduates from Oxford are also
present, because their presence reminds him of his youth. He remembers that Professor Norton of Harvard, related by marriage to
Darwin, once told him that Darwin read himself to sleep with
Twain's books. Twain told his friend Joseph Twichell, who later
read that Darwin once claimed to have an appreciation for literature, which, however, had atrophied. Twichell explained that that
was the reason Darwin had liked to read Twain. Twain says that
he was sorry the headline in a recent British newspaper lacked punctuation. It read "Mark Twain arrives Ascot Cup stolen." He did
steal a hat once, or rather he took Archdeacon Wilberforce's hat but
only after that worthy had walked off with Twain's. Wilberforce
was then complimented for saying witty things while under the
influence of Twain's hat. Twain now becomes serious. He chaffs
a lot, he says, but no one can reach the age of seventy-two without
having his share of heartbreak. England is connected with one such
tragedy. He was here when he received word that his oldest daughter, only twenty-four, had just died. He is happy to be responsible
for helping to unite England and America. Since arriving in England
this time, he has received hundreds of letters from people expressing their praise of him but, more important, their affection. In England he may be an alien, but he is also at home.

> Birrell, Chatterton, [Clara Clemens], [Olivia Langdon
> Clemens], [Susan Clemens], [Charles] Darwin, Sir Thom-
> as Hooker, [William Dean] Howells, Professor [Charles

Eliot] Norton, Otway, Rev. Joseph [H.] Twichell, Archdeacon Wilberforce.

'Booksellers,' 1908 (WMT 28).

To this national gathering of booksellers Twain feels that he
owes an accounting. For more than forty years he has earned his
bread by print. For thirty-six years his books sold by subscription.
But for the last four years his publishers have released his work
through booksellers, and they have done well by him. In four years
they have sold 489,000 copies of his books. The titles which have
done best are, in order, *The Innocents Abroad, Roughing It,* and *Tom Sawyer.* Twain is especially delighted that in four years the booksellers
have sold 16,000 copies of his serious *Joan of Arc,* which he never
expected to be popular. When Kipling was sick in America, England and America united in sympathy. Twain closes by hoping
that the two countries may never be severed by Twain.

"A Boston Girl," 1880 (LAIFI).

A Boston girl wrote Twain to chide him for splitting his infinitives with adverbs and for the tautology of "rise up." Twain replies
by confessing that he will never learn where to place adverbs. They
are his devil. He defends "rise up" as meaning rising to one's full
height and promises to use the expression again. He boasts about
his spelling prowess. He also gently ridicules the Boston girl's
punctuation, which is imperfect and therefore is evidently her
devil. He concludes that everyone has some weaknesses and should
confess them freely.

A Boston Girl.

"A Boy's Adventure." See ["The Omitted Chapter of *The Prince and
the Pauper* "].

"A Boy's Ambition." From *Life on the Mississippi.*

"A Brace of Brief Lectures on Science," 1871 (LAIFI).

Twain observes that paleontologists have concluded from examining ancient bones, ashes, and chips of flint that Primeval Man,

who lived in the quaternary period—whenever that was—had weapons, wore clothes, were artistic, roasted their meat, liked bone marrow, did not domesticate dogs, and believed in immortality. It is a shame that the recent Nathan murder did not occur in the quaternary period, because paleontologists could have checked the many clues which are baffling contemporary detectives and could have solved the crime easily.

Twain's own conclusions are as follows. Primeval Man was an ass for breaking bones lengthwise instead of crosswise to get at the marrow. Primeval Man did not eat the bears whose bones are in those caves with human bones; it was the bears that ate the men. The Aurignac cave in which animal bones are mixed was not a graveyard but an ancient menagerie. Someone killed the animals and stole the cash box. Is it not missing? Ancient so-called flint knives were really files, and dull ones at that, while objects supposed to have been hatchets were really paperweights. Scientists are altogether too ready to present new theories which scoff at the equally silly old ones.

> Baker, Boggs, Ferguson, Von Hawkins, Herkimer, Hildebrand, Hooker, Howard, Hughes, [Alexander] Von Humboldt, Johnson, Jones, [Flavius] Josephus, Nathan, Perkins, Primeval Man, Von Rosenstein, Slocum, Thompson, Walker, de Warren.

["Breaking It Gently"] (LAIFI). See "Higgins."

"Brief Biographical Sketch of George Washington," 1866 (WG).

George Washington was born many years ago, on this date. As a boy he showed no promise. He could not even lie. Twain could lie before he could stand. Washington would have gone to sea as a boy but for the fact that doing so would have meant leaving home and mother. He was always a dutiful person. He became a surveyor, tried to free some English prisoners held by the Indians, defeated the French, led American revolutionary forces against the English, and became our first President. He would be the Father of his Country yet, if he had lived. He is an example which today's youth should strive to emulate, even though chances are against any kind of success.

> Governor Dinwiddie, George Washington.

"British Benevolence," 1873 (LAIFI).

Twain tells about witnessing a daring rescue at sea of the crew of a dismasted vessel called the *Charles Ward* by the *Batavia*, a Cunard ship commanded by Captain John E. Mouland. The Royal Humane Society of England voted medals and rewards for the brave men responsible. Twain wishes that the United States might establish a similar society and adds that the charitable instinct is unpretentious but deep in the British. The Cunard Company promptly promoted two officers for their heroism in connection with the rescue. Twain goes on to tell something about the history and professional philosophy of the company, and would add much more but for the thought that he really should not advertise the firm for nothing.

[Henry] Bergh, Burns, Burns, Sir Samuel Cunard K.C.B. or G.W.X., Third Officer D. Gillies, Judge "Sam Slick" Haliburton, Fourth Officer H. Kyle, MacIvor, MacIvor, Captain John E. Mouland, X.Y.Z.

"British Festivities (A Day at Niagara)." See "English Festivities."

'Brother Jonathan Abroad.' See 'The American Vandal Abroad.'

["The Brummel-Arabella Fragment"], 1967 (SB).

John Brummel enters, soliloquizing about his love for Arabella Webster. He remarks that he thinks of her name so often that he has even been known to put it by mistake into a newspaper account when he writes one. In her parlor, Arabella is thinking about Brummel, who she hopes will propose, and also about George Sherman, whom she does not especially like. Brummel enters and is about to propose when he hears a lynch mob shouting outside. He rushes out to cover the story. Sherman, who has just entered, sees all, remarks that he has no further reason to live, and departs. In a dark, lonely street early the following morning Sherman is discovered walking and muttering about poison. He dies. Brummel then saunters in, drunk, and soon encounters old Webster, a Mexican War colonel. The two chat briefly. Then Webster departs and Brummel discovers Sherman's body. He plans to write up an exclusive and mysterious murder story about it. But then he hears the town clock strike three. He will be too late to scoop the evening papers. So he takes the corpse to his cheap lodgings and tosses it

on Rogers, his sleeping roommate. The two quarrel until they hear
the police approaching. Then they put the body in a carpet sack
and rush off to the woods at dawn. Hoping to concoct a plan which
will save them from suspicion, Rogers climbs a telegraph pole, cuts
into the wire, and begins to send disarming messages.

> John Brummel, Gridley, Henry, George B. Howard, Maria,
> Mary, Rogers, Rough Scotty, George Sherman, [General
> Zachary] Taylor, J. Toodles, Arabella Webster, Colonel
> Webster.

"Buck Fanshaw's Funeral." From *Roughing It.*

The Burial of Sir Abner Gilstrap, Editor of the Bloomington *Republican*, 1853 (P).
   When we buried him, we used no drum, farewell shot, funeral
note, coffin, or even sheet or shirt. We wrapped the tory in a Hannibal *Journal.* The snorting railroad above him will be no disturbance.

> Sir Abner Gilstrap, Sir John Moore.

The Burial of Sir John Moore: And other parties, subsequently to
   the Destruction of the Sennacherib, 1866 (P).
   While the Assyrian comes down like a wolf, we turn the turf with
our bayonets, etc. There lies the wide-nostrilled steed where a
Briton has laid him, etc.

"A Burlesque Biography," 1871 (WMT 24).
   The author announces that since two or three people have said
that they would read his autobiography if he would write it and if
they had leisure, he will yield to public demand. The Twain house
is noble and stretches into antiquity. The earliest ancestor was an
eleventh-century man named Higgins, who lived in Aberdeen, Cork
County, England. Arthour Twain was a highway solicitor in the
time of William Rufus, went to a resort name Newgate, never returned, died suddenly. Augustus Twain was a humorist about 1160;
part of him was once put on a high place at Temple Bar. For the
next two centuries many Twains followed armies into battle and
preceded them out. In the fifteenth century Beau Twain wrote

beautifully, could imitate anyone's hand. John Morgan Twain sailed with Columbus in 1492, complaining all the while; when he was finally thrown overboard, he stole the anchor and sold it to savages, and then built a jail for some of the Indians and a gallows on which he elevated others. In the seventeenth century, a Twain called "the old Admiral" used to borrow loitering ships. Later in the same century, Charles Henry Twain became a distinguished missionary, and his South Sea flock pronounced him tender. A later Twain fought for General Braddock and even fired seventeen times, unsuccessfully, at Washington. There have been many other Twains, all of whom have hankered for notoriety but some of whom have taken the low way of going to jail instead of getting hanged. The author advises the would-be autobiographer to skip from his great-grandfather to himself. Twain's own parents were neither very poor nor especially honest. Almost every life history should be delayed until the subject has been hanged.

"The Admiral," General [William] Braddock, L.W.C , [Christopher] Columbus, D.F., [Jean] Froissart, B.G., Higgins, Nebuchadnezzar, Pah-go-to-wah-wah-pukketekeewis, Tom Pepper, O.M.R., George Francis Train, Ananias Twain, Arthour Twain, Augustus Twain, Beau Twain, Charles Henry Twain, John George Twain, John Morgan Twain, John Wentworth Twain, Richard Brinsley Twain, William Hogarth Twain, [General George] Washington.

"Burlesque Hamlet," 1967 (SB).
Basil Stockmar, a book agent with a canvassing company, reveals in a soliloquy that he was a farmer's baby and was nursed at the same humble breast with Hamlet twenty-three years ago. He has now come to the palace to try to get the Queen and Hamlet to sign up for copies of a new book. Their signatures would be excellent advertisements. Francisco, Bernardo, Horatio, and Marcellus then observe and try to talk with the ghost of Hamlet's father. Basil encounters it also, wants to sell it six copies of his book, but becomes frightened and offers it a presentation copy instead.

In the palace, Basil now sits slouching in the King's throne, smoking—until he realizes that cigars have not yet been introduced here. He feels obliged to get Hamlet to stay here and Laertes to return to France, and also to stop Hamlet's affair with Ophelia

Polonius, since the prince would soon break the girl's heart. In come the King, the Queen, Polonius, Hamlet, and others. They discuss Laertes's return to France, Hamlet's grief for his dead father, and the prince's obligation to remain at court a while longer. Alone again, Hamlet gives vent to his anguish. Then, when Horatio, Marcellus, and Bernardo enter and reveal that the ghost of Hamlet's father is abroad, the young man vows to speak with it this night. Basil meanwhile comments on the accuracy of the men's description of the ghost, which he says looks like a policeman. Basil then wonders if he might safely write down an order for a hundred books in the dead man's name.

Now Basil is in Polonius's house and speaks to himself critically of affected courtiers' unnatural talk. He adds that Hamlet is natural when the two are alone, that the Queen is considerate, and that Ophelia is really nice. All the same, Basil has been trying to separate Hamlet and Ophelia for political reasons. She and Laertes then enter. The two say goodbye. Polonius hurries his son away and then orders Ophelia to stop seeing Hamlet.

That night on the platform Hamlet, Horatio, and Marcellus wait for the ghost and then see it. Hamlet insists upon following it to talk, whereupon it reveals full details of the murder. Horatio and Marcellus follow, and while the three young men are talking of the need for secrecy, Basil reels in drunk, talking of a conundrum beginning "Boss" which he sprang on the King. While mumbling to himself, Basil, who swallowed a spool, pulls a couple of hundred yards of thread out of his busy mouth.

Next, it seems that Basil has discovered a plot to kill Hamlet, who is the only sane person in the palace. Ophelia and her father enter, and the girl reveals that Hamlet is behaving oddly toward her. Polonius concludes that the young man is insanely in love.

Back in the palace again, the King and Queen welcome Rosencrantz and Guildenstern, and ask them to draw their friend Hamlet out to learn what ails him. Polonius comes in with the theory that unrequited love for Ophelia is rendering Hamlet wild. All but Polonius then leave as Hamlet enters. He calls the old man a fishmonger and continues to harp on Ophelia . . .

> Bernardo, Francisco, Guildenstern, Hamlet, Hamlet, Horatio, the King, Laertes, Marcellus, Norway, Ophelia Polonius, Polonius, the Queen, Rosencrantz, Basil Stockmar, Mrs. Stockmar.

"Burlesque Il Trovatore," 1967 (SB).

Twenty-five live shrouds howl and break through a castle, which moves back to reveal a moonlit landscape. Two women approach and with no reason at all start singing. An odd bilk enters in doublet, plumed cap, and cloak, yells a while, but is then embraced by the chief woman. Another fellow comes in and starts a duel.

Some gory blacksmiths work on a poker but sing too much to get the job done. The knight and the woman enter and outstay the workers but soon have a misunderstanding. After a musical explanation, they rush off in glee. A bell rings two o'clock, and the hungry crowd surges in again looking for dinner. A young woman with a big cross stands up and sings. Then the knight does. Then some soldiers do. The curtain falls as a fight starts.

Those same ghosts sing in a row before some tents. The feathered chap sings and bothers the leading ghost. Some overgrown scrubs drag in the fat woman, unfairly. In the next scene, the knight and the woman with the cross go to a ratty country hotel to make love. He has lost his hat and approaches the footlights to express his consequent sorrow in a song.

At the same castle again, a woman dressed in black serenades herself. Then from the woods come men's stronger voices. But she has the last screech. The man with the feather leaves a house. Wanting to make up, the woman sings with him. He knows the song; so he helps her. Now we see a dungeon, and the fat woman is chained there. She sits on a viol case. The woman with the cross enters with a soldier and throws herself into the knight's embrace. Then they argue. The fat woman falls asleep and sings. The other woman kneels and covers the front of her low dress with her hands. The feathered chap returns, and then they all really carry on.

The Capt, Leonore, the X woman.

["Burlesque News Item"] (MTP).

Justice still prevails in at least one city. In a letter just received, it is reported that Maxwell said that in Elmira a stranger recently entered a factory, conversed with an old man blowing a whistle, and then shot him dead. The man with the gun was arrested. The people soon made up a purse for him, apologized, and acquitted him on the grounds of self-defense.

Maxwell.

["Burlesque Review of *Allen Bay*"] (MTP).

After reading S. Q. Stedman's *Allen Bay, A Story,* 1876, eight times, Twain must regard it as overrated in spite of certain published critical pronouncements on it with which he only partly agrees. He then analyzes the work thoroughly, with many quotations.

Hallet, Le Lisle, Lovejoy, Von Schlecter, S. Q. Stedman, Turner.

["Burlesque Sea Story"] (MTP).

In an impossibly described sea setting, an impossibly humble sailor implores Lady Gwendolen to let him worship her luminous beauty from afar, though of course hopelessly. That night, they meet and embrace, and the grumbling crew tumbles out of the scuttlebutts to wear ship during a barking dogwatch. The lovers compare their situation to that of a romantic novel. Suddenly they hear inexplicable laughter.

Albert, Lady Gwendolen.

"The Burning of the Clipper Ship 'Hornet.' " See *Letters from Honolulu* and "My Début as a Literary Person."

'Business,' 1901 (WMT 28).

Twain says that the commercial comments of the previous speaker, a man named Cannon, have furnished him with much to discuss. Cannon said that to be successful in business one should be loyal to his employer, diligent, and truthful. Twain believes, however, in being loyal to himself, in taking things easy while employers do the heavy work, and in covering up the truth. For example, he got a mail-delayed invitation to a dinner for the same night as the banquet at which he is now speaking. He wrote to decline and concealed his comments from his wife, who would only have been upset. He wrote to ask the sender of the other invitation to identify the express he had used. Twain added that he owed a friend a dozen chickens and wanted to send him a dozen eggs by the same slow express and let them develop on the way. Next Twain tells how he lost $40,000 supporting an invention, $56,000 when a publisher refused to let him withdraw a certain book, and $170,000 on a machine. However, he did make $140,000 in six months on

General Grant's book. Twain says that his motto is to succeed in business and avoid his example.

Bryant, Cannon, [Olivia Langdon Clemens], General [Ulysses S.] Grant, Southard.

"Busted, and Gone Abroad," 1866 (WG).
Most people are busted now, in California. When a big speculator sinks, you hear about it. But little people fail quietly. The mining nabobs of '63 are now sending their families east—to Europe or to their in-laws.

Blivens, Bloggs, Brown, Jones, Smith, Smithers.

"Byron and the Worm." See FW, 1869.

"A California Crow Story." See FW, 1870.

California Experience. See [A Forty-niner].

"The Californian's Tale," 1893 (WMT 24).
The narrator recalls an event of thirty-five years ago. He was prospecting without success on the Stanislaus, in a lovely, woodsy region near Tuttleton, where there are many pretty cottages, all abandoned, however, by miners who failed to strike it rich. In a few cases, ruder cabins are still occupied, but only by similar failures too proud or wasted to go back home. Suddenly, in the midst of all this loneliness is a strange man, about forty-five, in front of a well-kept little cottage, with a garden of flowers flourishing all about it. His name is Henry; and he invites the narrator in, shows him his immaculate place, and urges him to stay at least three days—until Saturday night—when his wife will be returning. Henry shows his guest her daguerrotype—she is girlishly beautiful—and explains that she is nineteen and has been visiting her parents about fifty miles away. The narrator decides to stay. Thursday night a miner named Tom drops in, asks about Henry's wife, and listens to a letter from her which the husband produces from his wallet. On Friday another miner, named Joe, appears and hears the same letter. Saturday at twilight still another miner, this one

called Charley, drops by. Soon Tom, Joe, and Charley get out a fiddle, banjo, and clarinet, and make music. They all drink. Suddenly Henry expresses fear for his wife; then while his friends are reassuring him he loses consciousness. Joe explains to the bewildered narrator that each year at precisely this time Henry imagines that his wife is returning. In reality, she has been missing for nineteen years, captured by Indians on her way back after visiting her parents. So Henry's friends drop in on the insane man, keep up the pretense, then drug him to sleep. When he awakens, he is always all right again for a time.

Charley, Henry, Joe, Jimmy Parrish, Tom.

[California's Dull], 1869 (probably by Twain) (P).

California has lost her Moguls and is therefore dull. But they will waggle home carrying their tails.

Mogul.

"Cannibalism in the Cars," 1868 (WMT 7).

The narrator is traveling toward St. Louis when a benevolent-looking gentleman boards the train at Terre Haute. He is forty-five or fifty years of age and speaks knowledgeably of Washington political life. Suddenly the man is reminded of a story, which he insists upon telling without interruption. It all began on December 19, 1853. He was one of twenty-four passengers, all male, bound from St. Louis to Chicago. On the prairie near the Jubilee Settlements a fierce snowstorm hopelessly blocked the tracks. For seven days and nights the group was marooned and grew ever more hungry. Finally Richard H. Gaston of Minnesota, tall and cadaverous, suggested that they determine which of them should die to furnish food for the rest. Elaborate nominations followed. After certain substitutions and in spite of natural objections, they ate underdone Lucius Harris of St. Louis, then Walker of Detroit, juicy Morgan of Alabama, scraggy Harvey Davis of Oregon, and numerous others. Blessed relief finally came one sunny morning. At this point, the mild gentleman stops his appalling narrative and disembarks. The narrator later learns from the conductor that the tale teller is a former member of Congress who was snowbound in the cars once and has been deranged ever since. The conductor adds that when the man speaks long enough he ends his story by explaining that he was at last the only man left, was elected to be eaten, but resigned and thus saved himself.

William R. Adams, Bailey, Baker, Baldwin, A. L. Bascom, Bell, Blake, Samuel A. Bowen, Buckminster, Harvey Davis, Doolittle, Dyer, George Ferguson, Richard H. Gaston, Grimes, Halliday, Lucius Harris, Mrs. Lucius Harris, Harris, Hawkins, Lucien Herrman, Holcomb, R. M. Howland, Charles J. Langdon, McElroy, W. Messick, Morgan, John Murphy, Penrod, Radway, Rogers, Rev. James Sawyer, Daniel Slote, Smith, Smith, John A. Van Rostrand Jr., Walker, Mrs. Walker, John J. Williams.

"The Canvasser's Tale," 1876 (WMT 19).

A canvasser enters the home of the narrator and tells him his story. He was once the presumed heir of a rich uncle, Ithuriel, who, however, began to collect things—cow-bells, bricks, hatchets, Aztec inscriptions, stuffed whales, and finally echoes. He always failed to amass a complete collection. While he was negotiating with Williamson Boliver Jarvis, who owned one hill producing a New York state echo, Ithuriel's rival echo-collector was buying the other hill, owned by Harbison J. Bledso. When litigation tied up the property, Ithuriel died in debt, and the canvasser was not permitted to marry a certain earl's lovely daughter Celestine. Although the narrator does not wish to do so, he relents and buys two echoes from the impoverished canvasser.

Harbison J. Bledso, Celestine, Ithuriel, Williamson Bolivar Jarvis, Earl.

"The Capitoline Venus," 1869 (WMT 7).

George Arnold, a sculptor in Rome, and Mary love each other; but her father refuses to give his consent to their marriage unless George produces $50,000 within six months. If he cannot, she must marry Simper. George says that the Hon. Bellamy Foodle of Arkansas regards George's statue of "America" as clever and noteworthy. But Mary's father is obdurate. What to do? George's boyhood friend John Smith gets the sculptor to submit to a plan without criticism and then strategically smashes parts of "America" with a hammer and takes it away. Six months pass. George's time will be up at two o'clock. Suddenly his creditors enter and mysteriously offer him further services and credit. Mary and her father then burst in, and he gives her to bewildered George. It seems that Smith buried the mutilated statue in a plot of Campagna land he bought and deeded to George, then exhumed it. Distinguished authorities have unanimously decided it is a third century B.C. sublimity, pay George five million francs in gold, and place "Venus" in the Capitol.

> George Arnold, Mrs. Mary Arnold, Arnold, the Barnum, the Princess Borghese, the Hon. Bellamy Foodle, the Pope, the Minister of Public Records, Simper, John Smith, Voices.

"Cap'n Simon Wheeler, the Amateur Detective: A Light Tragedy," 1967 (SB).

Charles Dexter and his cousin the poet Hugh Burnside enter. They see Captain Simon Wheeler hiding in a barrel, spying, and pretending to be a detective. So they decide to stage a quarrel to puzzle him. Then they leave, laughing. But Horace Griswold and his wife Matilda have seen the mock argument and are fooled by it into thinking that the cousins are quarreling over the will of their dead uncle, who evidently said he would leave all of his money to Charley. Griswold sits on Wheeler's barrel while he chats with his wife. It seems that Hugh loves the Griswolds' daughter Millicent, whom Griswold has ordered to stop seeing the penniless poet. The Griswolds leave. Hugh and Millicent then come in. Hugh sits on the barrel. When he accuses the girl of being cool toward him because of his poverty, she stamps out. The Griswolds, the widow Mrs. Higgins, and Wheeler's wife Jenny enter. Mrs. Higgins sits on the barrel. It is revealed that the uncle's money all went to Hugh, not Charley, after all. Millicent's parents are naturally annoyed. The Griswolds and Mrs. Higgins gossip about Wheeler's inept amateur detective work. Everyone but Wheeler leaves. Then Clara Burnside, Hugh's sister, enters with Charley. They sit on the barrel and talk about their suddenly discovered love for each other. Hugh will be glad and will celebrate the revelation in poetry. They leave. Then Lem Sackett, a telegraph operator, and his roommate Tom Hooker, a newspaper reporter, enter and

sit on the barrel. They kid each other, swear their eternal friendship, but then reveal that each has been pursuing Clara. They start
fighting. Wheeler emerges from his barrel and chases them offstage.
Because he has been unwittingly poked by people sitting on his
barrel and has also had tears, eggs, and ink spilled on him, he is a
ghastly sight to the Griswolds, Charley, Long the policeman, and
Mrs. Higgin when they enter.

By moonlight after midnight Hugh enters, under the influence
of a heavy sleeping drug. Speaking of a certain heartless one, he
then falls into a deathlike swoon. Wheeler enters, looking for clues
as to Hugh's whereabouts, sits down on his body, meditates on the
detective profession, and then wanders off. Tom the reporter then
enters, finds the "corpse," and takes it home to save it for an exclusive story. Hugh's mother, Mrs. Burnside, her daughter Clara, Mrs.
Higgins, and Long the policeman then come in, all looking for the
missing young man. Mrs. Higgins comforts Mrs. Burnside by explaining that her son Goliah similarly disappeared once but then
turned up merely drunk. Long finds Hugh's hat. Everyone departs
weeping. Tom and Lem, who room over at Mrs. Higgins's house,
enter with Hugh's "corpse." Blood is all over them from a fight. It
seems that Tom surprised Lem with his burden, and the two argued.
But now, feeling that they are bound to be arrested, convicted of
killing Hugh, and hanged, they pledge eternal friendship again
and then go home to straighten up their disordered room and pretend they never left it. At dawn Hugh returns, decides that he will
disappear a while to frighten Millicent, sees a ragged-looking
beggar with a hand-organ—he is actually Jack Belford, an escaped
desperado with a price of $1,000 on his head—and offers to exchange
clothing with him supposedly for a lark. They go into a nearby
thicket to make the switch. Wheeler and his wife come in. Jenny
admires his detective work. He theorizes that Hugh climbed a tree,
fell by accident on a left-handed man carrying lard, and was killed
by him. The Wheelers leave, just as Charley enters with a gun and
hunting for a wolf. He spies something in the thicket, fires, goes
after his quarry, and soon returns aghast. He thinks that he has
shot Clara's brother Hugh. He plunges into the thicket to hide the
evidence, just as Millicent enters. A newsboy then comes by selling
an extra reporting Hugh's murder. Millicent is grief-stricken.
Charles emerges to offer her some hypocritical consolation. As
they walk away together, Hugh comes out of the thicket disguised

as the organ-grinding beggar. Wheeler soon spots him, talks with him, and concluding that he is the murderer hires him to saw some wood for him, to keep the culprit under his eye.

Three weeks pass. Detectives Baxter, Billings, and Bullet are all now on the case. Wheeler enters with his wife and explains that it is tough to be in competition with three eminent New York sleuths but that he will solve the mystery. Then, in succession, he accuses Charley, Lem, and Tom; but they react so violently that Wheeler concludes that they must be innocent. He asks Tom about the suspicions of the three detectives, and learns that Baxter thinks Hugh's mother killed him with an axe, that Billings thinks it was the sister Clara with a stove-lid, and that Bullet thinks it was the sweetheart Millicent with a hymn book. Wheeler admires the ingenuity of his rivals and then terrifies Tom by boasting that he can identify the real murderer. Suddenly in comes the report that the body of the murder victim has been located. Tom and Lem feel lost. The professional detectives swagger. Hugh, still disguised as a tramp, is delighted at the grief he is causing. Long tells Mrs. Higgins to ask Mrs. Burnside to give him the reward, since he found the corpse. Charley and Clara enter, arguing about Jack Belford, the condemned desperado. He was supposed to be hanged but escaped. She thinks that Belford is the culprit and must now be far away. Wheeler continues to hover about, still suspicious of rag-clad Hugh. Griswold sarcastically wishes Charley happiness in his inheritance, since he will get it now that Hugh is gone. Millicent begins to play up to Charley. Bullet asks Hugh if he has seen a Plymouth hymn book, but the disguised young man pretends to be a deaf mute. Tom and Lem return and continue to voice their sense of hopelessness. The newsboy enters, hawking an extra reporting discovery of the body. Long attempts to whack the boy into silence, but Wheeler comes to his rescue. Baxter asks Wheeler about Mrs. Burnside, but Wheeler responds only with the cries of birds and animals, Billings then asks him about Clara, but Wheeler pretends to be a lunatic. Then Bullet queries him about Millicent, but Wheeler acts as though he were deaf. Now Tom and Lem return, having decided to scare off Wheeler by blowing up his little cottage. They put fuses into a powder keg, light them, and leave. Wheeler ambles up and sits down on the keg, finds one of the fuses, and theorizes verbosely as to its significance. Tom and Lem see him and, not wanting to add murder to "murder," toss a stone and thus warn him away just before the explosion.

Charley meets Clara and hopes for a kind word, but she snubs him. Millicent enters with her mother and father, who speaks sarcastically of the youth's going to Hugh's funeral. Hugh, still disguised as the tramp, sees Charley and Millicent together and is furious until he hears her reveal that she misses him and reveres his memory. A crowd of people come in, and Charley tries to use sign language with Hugh but fails to communicate. When Millicent gives the "tramp" some money, he kisses the hem of her dress. Tom and Lem lag behind, still worried that Wheeler seems to be always dogging them. Wheeler then enters, disguised as a Negro, and lectures on his sagacity to his complacently doting wife, whom he praises for always having faith in his brilliance. He tells her that his theory is this: Hugh bought some poison to kill himself, changed his mind, decided not to waste the poison, planned to go and kill his mother, but met the tramp, and—. But at this point Wheeler is interrupted by the advent of Hugh, still disguised as the tramp and returning from his own funeral, at which his virtues and talents were highly praised. Wheeler in Negro dialect urges the tramp, who he says must be tired thinking of his wood-sawing chores, to take a nap, during which Wheeler bends over him and says aloud that he heard him confess to being the murderer. Wheeler then disguises himself as an Irish woman, to surprise Hugh when he awakens.

Hugh stirs. Wheeler, disguised as a thick-tongued Irish woman, stands over him and tells him that the murderer is known. Hugh shivers and wonders how. Wheeler says that he talked in his sleep. Hugh tries to leave, but Wheeler collars him and accuses him of being the culprit. While Hugh is laughing up his sleeve, Wheeler boasts of his ability to follow clues but then takes pity on Hugh and offers to let him go. Hugh, however, confesses that he is the escaped desperado Belford and that he is tired of running. So Wheeler gets him to promise to reveal himself on signal, to make the arrest more drastic. Then the funeral procession enters, including the coffin. Everyone pauses, and even Wheeler is moved to tears. Hugh is beside himself with delight. Millicent tells Mrs. Burnside that she did not realize she loved Hugh until he was lost to her. The three professional detectives enter, each bearing the weapon he thinks was used to commit the murder. Baxter arrests Mrs. Burnside, whereupon Tom confesses. Billings drags in Millicent, whereupon Lem confesses. Bullet has Clara in charge, whereupon Charley confesses. Clara is thrilled, and Charley affirms her hope that he shot Hugh only by accident. But then in comes Hugh, still disguised as the tramp. Wheeler identifies him as Belford. Hugh then casts off his disguise and reveals himself for what he is. Millicent embraces him. Mrs. Burnside embraces him also. Clara apologizes to Charley and embraces him. Tom and Lem sigh with relief. Wheeler stoically laments his loss of reward and face, but his wife comforts him. Then Mrs. Burnside says that he restored her son to her and therefore deserves a reward of $1,000. Hugh gives him the tramp disguise, along with the hand organ. Charley then makes over the Belford reward of $1,000 to Wheeler, who feels all set up—and even more so when he is kissed by Clara, then Millicent, and finally even Mrs. Higgins. Wheeler suggests a jubilee for all.

Detective Baxter, Jack Belford, Detective Billings, Spence Buckner, Detective Bullet, Clara Burnside, Hugh Burnside, Mrs. James Burnside, Charles Dexter, Horace Griswold, Mrs. Matilda Griswold, Millicent Griswold, Goliah Higgins, Widow Higgins, Tom Hooker, Justice of the Peace, Puss Leathers, Jake Long, a Newsboy, Lem Sackett, Henry Savage, Hank Slocumb, Mrs. Hank Slocumb, Bub Stavely, Mrs. Jenny Wheeler, Captain Simon Wheeler, Bull Wilkerson.

"Captain Montgomery," 1866 (WG).
Twain fondly remembers Captain Ed Montgomery, who used to stop his passenger steamer near Grand Gulf, Mississippi, to buy worthless green wood from needy Mother Utterback at top prices. The woman was grateful when he visited with her, and she would shout to her six daughters to stir about and make him feel welcome.

Captain Ed Montgomery, Bets Utterback, 'Liza Jane Utterback, Mother Utterback, Sal Utterback, Miss Utterback.

"Captain Ned Wakeman." See RL.

"Captain Stormfield's Visit to Heaven," 1907-08, 1952.*
Twain begins with an introductory note to explain that he knew Captain Stormfield through having made three long voyages with

him. The man was rugged, tan, frank, and as honest and affectionate as a dog. Because of his mother, he was religious; he inherited from his father a propensity to swearing, which was augmented by his rough life at sea. At the age of sixty-five, he began to turn gray; but he was still essentially youthful, loving, and tough. Since he really believed that he had voyaged to heaven, Twain did not argue. Captain Ben (later Eli) Stormfield of Fairhaven and San Francisco explains that he now lies dying. The ship's doctor, the mate, and Chips the carpenter are discussing his case and his infernal destination after death. Just after eight bells he dies but then suddenly feels himself whizzing upward like a bird, into the sun, and beyond it. Later, in the dark again, he glows like a lightning bug. Suddenly Solomon Goldstein of New York drifts alongside, evidently bound—as Stormfield certainly knows he is—for hell. The two discuss their dreadful fate, and Goldstein begins to weep—because he will never again see his ten-year-old daughter Minnie, recently dead. The two men talk late, then sleep, then awaken again. Stormfield is thirsty and also wishes he had a smoke. They have voyaged at least 11,000,000 miles when a suicide named Bailey appears on their weather bow. It seems that his girl Candace Miller wrote him that she loved another. So he shot himself. Suddenly Tom Wilson sails alongside, sees disconsolate Bailey, and confesses that he sent the letter supposedly from Candace, who appeared too late to save Bailey and who wept so bitterly at his death that Tom also killed himself. Goldstein, full of grief himself, knows how to comfort the two men. After about a week of cruising, they pick up a Negro named Sam, cheerful, good-natured, and with tobacco. But in outer space it will not light. They know that it will burn in hell, though. More weeks pass. By the end of their first year, they have picked up all sorts of spirits, some so cantankerous that Stormfield orders them off as not up to standard.

Stormfield has been dead about thirty years, as he explains to his friend Peters, and here he is, still whizzing through space at a speed of about a million miles a minute. He overtakes a stupendously enormous comet, freighted with countless billions of souls and commanded by a wild captain. Stormfield makes the mistake of passing this celestial conflagration and insulting it as he does so. Therefore the rival captain dumps his vast Satan-bound cargo, pours on the brimstone, and quickly disappears, leaving Stormfield in his dark and silent wake. All the same, Stormfield soon arrives at a lovely, sunshiny, balmy region with gold walls and innumerable gates. He enters one, is quizzed by the head clerk, manages to explain that he has come from the Wart—as the earth is called up here—and is allowed to wander, even though veering after the comet so put him off course that he has entered the wrong gate. Correcting his mistake next day, he is told to stand on a wishing-carpet and wish himself to the appropriate gate, since being in the wrong celestial locale would only lead him to unhappiness. Gigantic sections of heaven correspond to geographical areas of the world. He is soon fitted with harp, hymn-book, wings, halo, palm branch, and cloud. But the harp-music and singing grow tedious almost at once, and Stormfield is happy to quit and start chatting with Sam Bartlett, an old friend, long dead, who explains that the viable section of their heaven is filled with work, suffering, pain (though not mortal), and enough other contrasts to make beatific happiness possible.

Some months pass. Stormfield knocks about heaven and then settles down in a pleasant region. He finds an old New Jersey friend named Sandy McWilliams, who explains several matters. In heaven people can will themselves to be any age they want, but mostly they settle on the age they were at death and stick at the place where their minds are at their best. Old souls often try being younger but soon grow discontent and age again. Some young people, however, even dead babies, continue to mature in heaven. One mother of limited intellect is sad in heaven for a time because she is seeking the soul of her baby, who after death elected to develop into a scientific thinker. But in due time the two will adjust to each other and be happy.

Stormfield has difficulty learning to fly with his wings and therefore soon gives up, preferring to wish himself where he wants to go. Sandy explains many divine things to him. Wings are best as regalia for receptions. Talmage, a Brooklyn preacher, wanted after death to weep upon Abraham; but he could not do so, because millions of more important souls have a greater claim upon the patriarch. Heaven is not democratic, since its King has divine authority. Heaven thus resembles Russia. This inequality only makes for more adoration. Certain souls unrecognized but having staggering potential greatness in life—both on earth and on more significant planets—outrank Shakespeare, Homer, Moses, and Napoleon in heaven. The universe's greatest poet is Edward J. Billings, a

Tennessee horse doctor treated ignominiously by his terrestrial associates but with a unique reputation in heaven. There are relatively few white angels in heaven but many red and mud-colored ones. Suddenly there is much stir: the soul of a New Jersey barkeeper is approaching. In a twinkling, vast grandstands fill with millions of beings, who have come to see the barkeeper but who are even more pleased by a glimpse of Moses and Esau as they pop out of tents near the place of honor.

Abel, Abraham, Adam, Alexander, Bailey, Sam Bartlett, Edward J. Billings, the Bishop, Bo, Caesar, Charles the Second, Chaucer, Chips, Confucius, Daniel, Sir Richard Duffer, Your Eminence, Esau, Ezekiel, Minnie Goldstein, Solomon Goldstein, Ham, Hannibal, Henry the Sixth, Henry the Eighth, Homer, Isaac, Jacob, Jeremiah, Job, Absalom Jones, Captain Kidd, Langland, Mahomet, Marais, Mary Ann, Sandy McWilliams, Candace Miller, Moses, Napoleon, Charles Peace, Peters, Richard the Lion-heartted, Saa, Sakka, Sam, Shakespeare, Soof, Captain Ben (Eli) Stormfield, Mrs. Ben (Eli) Stormfield, Talmage, Tom Wilson, Zoroaster.

*In *Report from Paradise,* ed. Dixon Wecter (New York: Harper, 1952).

"The Captain's Story" (WMT 22). Part of "Some Rambling Notes of an Idle Excursion."

"A Card from Mark Twain," 1866 (MTWY).
Twain thanks various Nevada officials for inviting him to lecture in Carson, promises to appear on November 3 at the theater and disgorge as much truth as possible without danger to himself, and apologizes for delaying his note of acceptance.

Governor H. G. Blasdel, O. A. F. Gilbert, A. Helm, H. F. Rice.

"Card to the Highwaymen," 1866 (MTWY).
Twain explains that, after his lecture at Gold Hill the night before, he and two friends were walking to Virginia when a party of highwaymen accosted them, robbed them of money and Twain's watch, ordered them to sit by the roadside for five minutes or risk

being shot, and strode away. Twain now writes a notice to the robbers: send his watch back and keep the money.

Judge Sandy Baldwin, Beauregard, the Captain, Stonewall Jackson, Mac, Theodore Winters.

'Carnegie the Benefactor,' 1909 (S).
Twain says that Carnegie has suffered from too many compliments tonight. If Dunfermline helped the United States by contributing Carnegie, what might have happened if all of Scotland appeared? Dr. McKelway said that Carnegie pays more taxes than he is charged. Richard Watson Gilder puffed his magazine and hinted at hiring Carnegie. Twain closes by saying that he has preserved his modesty past the age of seventy.

[Andrew] Carnegie, Richard Watson Gilder, Dr. [St. Clair] McKelway.

"The Case of George Fisher," 1870 (WMT 7).
This case is the truth, not an extravaganza like John Wilson Mackenzie's beef contract. The crops, herds, and houses of George Fisher were destroyed during the Creek War in Florida in September, 1813, perhaps partly by Indians and partly by United States troops pursuing them. In 1832 his widow, then remarried, sued for damages caused by the troops, but Congress denied her petition. In April, 1848, new Fisher heirs sued and collected $8,873 for destruction caused by the troops; in December of the same year an additional sum of $8,998 was paid, for interest since 1832, the date of the original petition. A year later Attorney-General [Isaac] Toucey awarded interest on the original $8,873 from 1813 to 1832— that is, an additional $10,005. The Fishers were content until 1854, when they unsuccessfully asked Secretary of the Treasury James Guthrie for more money. Then in 1858 Secretary of War John B. Floyd contended that the Indians had destroyed houses and contents but that the troops had destroyed all the corn, wheat, and livestock; Floyd paid the Fishers almost $40,000 more. In 1860 the Fishers wanted a review of all evidence and in spite of reports of forgeries therein were told by Floyd that all damages were the result of troop activity; accordingly they were informed that they

should be paid $65,520 on top of the $67,000 already received. Unfortunately, a new administration [that of Abraham Lincoln] came in, [President James] Buchanan and Floyd were out, and no further money was given to the Fishers. Next, the Fisher heirs fought in the Confederate army; then, in July, 1870, they began to beseech Congress through Garrett Davis for more damages. These are facts, which may be verified in H. R. Ex. Doc. No. 21, 36th Congress, 2d Session, and S. Ex. Doc. No. 106, 41st Congress, 2d Session. Is this a typical example of "hereditary fraud" against the Treasury of the United States?

The Auditor, [President James] Buchanan, Garrett Davis, George Fisher, Mrs. George Fisher, Fisher, John B. Floyd, James Guthrie, John Wilson Mackenzie, President [Abraham Lincoln], the Second Auditor, [Isaac] Toucey.

'Cats and Candy,' 1874 (S).

When Twain was fourteen, a seventeen-year-old lad named Jim Wolfe lived with the Clemens family. The two fellows slept together—virtuously. One winter night a candy-pulling party was going on downstairs. Cousin Mary and her friends were just setting several dishes of hot candy outside in the snow to cool. At the same time, the boys' sleep was being disturbed by a couple of cats yowling on a chimney just outside their room. Jim offered to crawl out and knock them away. Twain encouraged him. Finally Jim, dressed only in socks and short shirt, crept along the roof toward the chimney, but slipped on the ice out there, fell off with heels flying, and sat in the midst of Mary's party directly on the hot saucers. A stampede followed. Jim ran upstairs dropping broken china and dripping candy, burst back into the room, and announced while nursing his blisters that he had come close to catching the cats.

[Jane Lampton Clemens], [John Marshall Clemens], Cousin Mary, Jim Wolfe.

["A Cat-Tale"], 1959 (LFE).

The narrator is telling his little daughters Susy and Clara a story about cats. Catasauqua is a noble cat, a Manx and hence without a tail. She is the widow of Catullus. Her family includes Cattaraugus, white and pure of heart, and Cataline, young, black, and truculent. One day Catasauqua's house burns down; but because she has insurance and knows about catallactics, all is soon well again. She builds a catadrome with catkins and—in full leaf—a nice categorematic. The front garden is charming too. Since cats are packed with musical material often used by fiddle makers, the three cats sing well together, with Catasauqua doing the accompaniment on the catarrh. The narrator furnishes his children with a picture of the three cats and another showing the front half of a cat sleepy but its tail, the seat of passion, frisky. At one point, Cataline annoys his brother Cattaraugus by pretending to smoke his catpipe, which uses no tobacco since it is only a squeaking instrument used to signal disapproval at the theater. Cattaraugus calls Cataline a catapult; the two fight; but soon they make up and shake hands. Clara and Susy are impressed by their father's story but frequently interrupt to ask for the definition of some of the words used.

> Cataline, Catasauqua, Cattaraugus, Catullus, Clara [Clemens], Papa [Samuel Langhorne Clemens], Susy [Clemens], Rollo.

"The Cayote." From *Roughing It*.

"The Celebrated Jumping Frog of Calaveras County," 1865 (CJF).
   The narrator follows the request of a friend of his from the East, calls on Simon Wheeler in a bar of the old mining camp of Angel's, and asks about his Eastern friend's supposed friend Rev. Leonidas W. Smiley. Wheeler corners the narrator, admits that he does not remember any Leonidas Smiley, but recalls Jim Smiley well. Jim would bet on anything—on his apparently asthmatic mare, on his bull pup Andrew Jackson, even on whether Parson Walker's ailing wife would recover. But his favorite entry in contests was Dan'l Webster, his pet jumping frog, which could whirl through the air, catch flies off counters, and drop to the floor contentedly like a gob of mud. One day a stranger happened by and ventured to doubt that Dan'l had any virtues superior to those of other frogs. So Jim left Dan'l with the stranger and slopped through the swamp to catch a rival frog. Meanwhile, however, the stranger filled Dan'l full of quail shot up to his chin. So, when Jim returned with a frog for the stranger, Dan'l lost the contest. The stranger pocketed Jim's

$40, remarking again that Dan'l had no special points. Only later did Jim examine Dan'l, which belched out a double handful of shot. Jim sought but never found the stranger. Suddenly Wheeler is called out, and the narrator tries to leave; but the garrulous old man returns and offers to tell about Jim's one-eyed cow with a little tail like a banana. The narrator declines to stay.

In a later version ("The Jumping Frog . . . ," WMT 7), Mark Twain prints an execrable 1872 French translation, "La Grenouille Sauteuse du Comte de Calaveras," of his tale and then a literal translation of it.

> Jim Smiley, Rev. Leonidas W. Smiley, Mrs. Walker, Parson Walker, A[rtemus]. Ward, Simon Wheeler.

["Changing Definitions of 'Lady' and 'Gentleman'"] (MTP).

. . . Webster seems to be trying from the grave to keep the meaning of words from changing. But words insist on changing. Sunday-school lessons have for so long called any good, sappy person a lady or a gentleman that these words have lost their force. Originally the terms were restricted to persons of a certain high birth. One might as well have called a private a general, or a maid a duchess, as call just anyone a lady or a gentleman then. Really, these Sunday-school books have been lying, and the result is that in America ladies and gentlemen are merely female and male adults, and the lowest bartender in town would be insulted if he were told that he was not a gentleman.

"The Chapman Family," 1866 (WG).

Twain remembers the old Chapmans. They used to act with Dan Marble in New Orleans twenty-five years ago. They floated on the Ohio and the Mississippi Rivers, tying up at night and performing Shakespeare. Twain recently received a letter from the old lady telling about her current theatricals in Montana, where it is so cold that people chew their brandy.

> Chapman, Mrs. Chapman, Dan Marble.

"The Character of Man," 1973 (WIM).

Man is unique among creatures. He alone possesses malice, en-

joys inflicting pain, and has a nasty mind. Any sweetness he has is
shared with other animals. The following are all lies: that man is
independent, tolerant, heroic, and individual; that he has a conscience; and that he votes sincerely.

"Charade" (play) (MTP).
. . . Various people evidently are acting out an "inn" where
Mary serves. Mary must then "tell" what has happened. Then Adal-
bert Montmorency, shielding Mary, feels that he must "lie." Some
Pinkerton detective "gents" enter, and say that Arba Langton and
Trask are thieves. The final scene is the answer to the charade—an
"intelligence" office. Adal seems to be guilty. Vassar girls enter the
inn at one point.

> Bill, Hamersley, Gen. Hawley, Mrs. Hawley, Jim, Jim,
> Landlady, Arba Langton, Mary, Adalbert Montmorency,
> 6-fingered Smith, Trask, Davy Twichell, J[oseph]. H. Twi-
> chell, Warner.

'Charity and Actors,' 1907 (WMT 28).
Twain agrees with Frohman that charity reveals a multitude of
virtues. Actors have benefited everyone by lifting his weary spirits
and giving him a fresh impulse. The Actors' Fund Fair in New York
provides an opportunity for others to help those actors now.

> [Daniel] Frohman, President [Theodore Roosevelt].

Chassepot vs. Needle Gun, 1870 (probably by Twain) (P).
The little man with a needle gun cooks the Chassepot goose in
short order.

> Hi Slocum.

'China and the Philippines,' 1900 (S).
While introducing Winston Spencer Churchill to a New York
gathering, Twain boasts that for years he himself has been a self-
appointed agent to unify America and England. Both countries
have striven for open-door policies, even in China. England sinned

in South Africa; America sinned in the Philippines. Churchill is English through his father; his mother was an American. The blend is thus perfect. England and America are kin, and also kin in sin.

Winston Spencer Churchill.

["Chinese Labor &c 1870"]. See [*Mark Twain in Three Moods*].

"The Cholera Epidemic in Hamburg," 1923 (WMT 29).

In mid-August, 1892, a thunderbolt fell on Hamburg. People are dying like flies of something resembling cholera. The author is aghast because he is only twelve hours away but can obtain no reliable news. German daily papers are lethargic, and print only old and conflicting accounts. The numerous elaborate and formal German death notices lead one to conclude that the slaughter is not confined to poor, friendless victims. A letter coming to the city where the author is staying and written by a Hamburg physician gives a glimpse of the horror—sick people are being snatched from their homes and carted in wagons containing corpses. But official news is lacking. It is as though we were attending a play with the curtain down.

Rudolf Beck, Otto Steingoetter.

"The Christening Yarn" (MTP).

It is hard to tell a long story with a surprise ending, because sharp listeners can guess its conclusion. However, Bram Stoker used to tell the following such story well. In a humble village a baby is to be christened. The oratorical minister warms to his task, even though his audience seems to be glum. He says that we should not mind the fact that the baby is only a little fellow, since he will grow and may well turn into a great poet, an illustrious soldier, or the like. When the minister asks the name of the baby, Papa identifies it as Mary Ann.

Irving, Mary Ann, Papa, Bram Stoker.

"Christian Science and the Book of Mrs. Eddy." In *Christian Science*.

Christian Science with Notes Containing Corrections to Date, 1907 (WMT 25).
Book I. Writing in Vienna in 1899, the author says that during
the previous summer he fell and broke several bones. Some peasants
take him to a thatched farmhouse and bring a Christian Science
doctor who is from Boston and who is summering in the village.
Her name is Mrs. Fuller, and she and the author get into a verbose
discussion about her religion. The raw-boned lady assures him that
he feels no pain and would read to him from the Founder's *Science
and Health* but for the fact that she has forgotten her glasses. She
leaves the book, and the author is to read it while she gives him
absent treatment. He soon feels his fractures and dislocations knitting, grinding, and sucking back into place. All the same, he summons the village horse-doctor for additional aid. This pleasant,
aromatic man mixes his new patient a bucket of bran mash and a
drench of turpentine and grease, and says that frequent dosages of
the combination will quickly turn his stomach ache into the botts
and his head cold into the blind staggers. The author combines this
rumbling medicine with further reading of *Science and Health,* which
he pronounces both incomprehensible and conceited. He then expresses his respect for faith healers, who use the patient's own
imagination to effect cures. Some reputable physicians do the same.
But when Mrs. Fuller submits her bill of $234 for mending his
bones, he gets her to admit that nothing exists but mind and then
gives her an imaginary check. On the other hand, he happily pays
the horse-doctor for curing his stomach ache and cold.

It would help if we would all assume that everyone is partly insane. In most ways, most people are usually reasonable enough,
agreeing for example that water seeks its level, that the sun gives
light and heat, that eight plus seven is fifteen, and so on. But all
Mohammedans know that all Christians are insane, and vice versa.
In religion and politics we cannot convince each other. Christian
Scientists are picturesquely insane. Surely it is picturesque to
enshrine Mrs. Mary Baker G. Eddy as Mary the Matron over Mary
the Virgin. Christian Science is apt to become monstrously successful because it is a religion rather than merely a philosophy, it has
money and concentrated power, and it appeals to practically the
entire human race. Four-fifths of ailing mankind only imagine
their ills. In the *Christian Science Journal* are published many whopping
demonstrations of faith over "claims" of maladies. Further, one
lecturer on Christian Science affirmed that Mrs. Eddy and her

religion are foretold in *Revelations,* that, thus, Christian Science is
the second coming of Christ. But the real god of Mrs. Eddy's religion is the dollar. Its Mother Church in Boston does an enormous
business in Bible lessons, manuals, hymnals, histories, the Bible
Annex, the *Journal,* and other items. Its Massachusetts Metaphysical
College offers seven lessons in Christian Science healing, for $300
per student. By 1940 Christian Science will be the most formidable
political movement since the times of the Inquisition. It will divide
Christendom with the Catholic Church, which also has an effective
organization and centralization of power but lacks the cash. The
author asserts that Christian Science supports no charities. The
Christian Scientist may be likened to the railroad engineer; his
hand controls a source of power other than his own, and he is entitled to all the pay he can get. Critics of Christian Science are wrong
when they complacently say that since it appeals only to the unin-
telligent it will soon fade away. As with other religions, its strength
lies in its appeal to emotion rather than reason; and it is creating
an environment in which its teachings can spread by personal contact. Only when it is too late will conventional Christianity begin
to reckon with Christian Science.

Book II. Here Mark Twain begins by sketching the Man-Mystery,
a person ordinary in appearance, full of typical contradictions, vain,
mean-minded, deficient in education, but also courageous, ambitious, and fluent on the subject of the nebular theory. We agree,
Twain continues, to disagree as to Mrs. Eddy's motives. Some say
that she took her system from Quimby. But she turned it into a
Klondike and must now be regarded as more influential than anyone
else in the last thirteen hundred years. Her autobiography, like
most such works, is unconsciously revealing: it includes some of her
trivial alleged poetry and some ridiculous boasts about her ancestors. Further, it is full of grotesque errors and infelicities of diction,
syntax, grammar, imagery, and logic, as are all of her other non-
Christian Science writings. Yet the various editions of her *Science
and Health* are written almost perfectly. Does Mrs. Eddy employ an
old flintlock to hunt rabbits but an up-to-date Mauser for elephants?
It would seem so. Curiously, only the first forty pages of her autobiography are clumsily written.

Mrs. Eddy has said that she was inspired by God to write *Science
and Health,* and also to market her teaching and healing; she added
that God furnished all of her ideas and language. But when copy-

right questions arose, she quickly claimed authorship. In her auto-biography she lists three persons in a progression: the Virgin Mary, Jesus Christ, and herself. As Pastor Emeritus, she wants to be the only person in Christian Science to be officially called Mother. In his *Eddyism*, Frederick W. Peabody states that she is the successor to and the equal of Jesus; so the progression may well be 1. Jesus, 1. Mrs. Eddy, and 2. the Virgin Mary. Hard to draw though they are, these conclusions seem to emerge: Mrs. Eddy did not write *Science and Health*; God did or did not write it; and Mrs. Eddy thinks that she did, that she was inspired by God when she did, that she is a member of the Holy Family, and that She is equal to the head of it.

Other cultists have come and gone, and there will be more later. But ordinary cultists fail to organize effectively. Mrs. Eddy began to teach and heal, and to gather fervent, sincere converts to her religion. Then she organized an Association. She healed free for four years. Then, about 1880, she courageously but not recklessly aggrandized the Association to a church, with herself as pastor and with twenty-six charter members. She also started the Massa-chusetts Metaphysical College, with herself, husband, and foster son as faculty. In seven years she taught over four thousand stu-dents, who, since they paid $300 each, produced quite a revenue. Advanced students might take eighteen more lessons by paying $500 more. Some indigent students and some clergymen were permitted to attend at reduced rates or free. All payments in advance. Mrs. Eddy could expel at will. No invalids need apply!

The new church was brilliantly organized, by Mrs. Eddy, who wrote its by-laws, named herself Pastor Emeritus, controlled the establishment of the Board of Directors (including its President, Treasurer, and Clerk), constituted the Board of Trustees, had final power over the Readers (their election, the extent of their work, and even the quality of their English), and could limit church mem-bership. Her *Science and Health* is the sole source of doctrine. Her pronouncements are infallible, like those of "the other Pope." Mrs. Eddy gave land for the Mother Church, which was built at a cost of $250,000 and then given to her; she then gave it to the Board of Directors, but she is that Board. She has rewritten the Lord's Prayer a couple of times. She has listed unpardonable sins against her church, and the main one is working against the church. In *Christian Science History*, she explains that her spiritual sense can read the unspoken thoughts of malicious opponents. She has written three hymns and ordered them sung with specified frequency in church. She controls her Board of Education, teachers, Board of Lectureships, and missionaries. Mark Twain suggests that she ought to strike for a perpetual copyright on her *Science and Health*. She organized the Christian Science Publishing Association, relinquished control of the *Christian Science Journal* until it showed a profit, and then reclaimed it.

The author continues by criticizing Mrs. Eddy for combining hunger for money with a desire for both power and glory. The Mother Church is to be controlled by no other church, is to remain unique, and is to be the only Christian Science church to be described as "the" church. No branch churches are to have any so-called "first members," so as to resemble the aristocracy of the Mother Church. The Boston church has a museum of objects sacred through contact with Mrs. Eddy, including an oil portrait of a chair she sat in while composing her sacred writings. She has indirectly equated her *Science and Health* with the Holy Ghost, may be described as "the new Infallible," and urges her members to sell all the copies of her book they can under penalty of a kind of excommunication.

Twain pauses here to list the various functions of Mrs. Eddy, then insists that she is unstable and inconsistent in petty, human ways, but precise, ruthless, and confident in her professional actions. She was born with a far-seeing business eye, and merely had to wait for circumstance and opportunity. Time will test the claim of Christian Science that it can help the Spirit of God heal afflicted bodies and souls. Mrs. Eddy will maintain and extend her empire until her death, after which the President and Board of Directors will succeed her, and govern in accord with her by-laws.

The author now repeats and concludes. He thinks that it cannot be proved one way or another whether Mrs. Eddy took the Great Idea from Quimby, either in her head or in manuscript form. Twain regards it as unlikely that the Great Idea, if it ever independently struck her, would have interested her. It is obvious that she built a new religion on *Science and Health*. But he cannot believe that she ever wrote that book. He regards her as greedy, arrogant, and illiterate. Her followers regard her as unselfish, intelligent, and inspired. Her prefaces are so badly written that, in Twain's opinion, *Science and Health* must be "another person's book." That person did not protest when his book was published, because by then he was dead.

In six appendices, a note, and a conclusion, Mark Twain quotes extensive samples from the writings of Mrs. Eddy, accuses her of stylistic inconsistencies and a factual error—she wanted to be called "Mother" but said she did not—prints praise of Christian Science by Rev. Heber Newton, and challenges Christian Scientists to make honorable Christians out of privately honest but publicly dishonest politicians.

A, B, Bailey, Albert Baker, Grandfather Baker, Henry Ward Beecher, Big Metal, the Clerk, the Board of Directors, the Directors of the College, Early Subsequent Members, Rev. Mrs. Mary Baker G. Eddy, Dr. Eddy, First Members, Dr. Foster-Eddy, Mrs. Fuller, Furguson, Gordon, Judge Septimus J. Hanna, a Has Been, Sam Jones, General Henry Knox, Captain John Lovewell, General John Macneill, Sir John Macneill, the Man-Mystery, McCrackan, a Member, Hannah More, Rev. Heber Newton, Nixon, Number Two, the Official Reader, Frederick W. Peabody, the President, a Reader, the Scientist, Shadwell, Simpson, Smith, Dr. Edward Anthony Spitzka, a Student, a Subsequent Member, Dr. George Tomkins, the Treasurer, Sir William Wallace.

"The Christmas Fireside for Good Little Boys and Girls by Grandfather Twain: The Story of a Bad Little Boy That Bore a Charmed Life" (SS). See "The Story of the Bad Little Boy."

The Chronicle of Young Satan, 1969 (MSM).

Eseldorf, the Austrian village of the narrator, Theodor Fischer, in May of 1702 is wrapped in sleep and controlled intellectually by Father Adolf, who once drove the Hussite Frau Adler from the village, ordered the widow Gretel Marx to stop reading Hussite literature, and caused the Bishop to suspend nice old Father Peter, who therefore has gone deeper into debt for two years and now faces, with his lovely niece Marget, foreclosure and eviction by moneylender Solomon Isaacs.

Three boys are always together. They are Nikolaus Baumann, a local judge's son, whose nickname is Nicky; Seppi Wohlmeyer, an innkeeper's son; and Theodor, whose father is musician, tax collector, and sexton. The boys play in the castle park and thrill to ghost stories told by Felix Brandt, the serving-man there. One day a handsome young stranger appears before the boys, introduces himself as the angel Satan—the other Satan's nephew—and entertains them by telling stories of times cosmically long ago and by making out of nothing tiny creatures which he horrifies his witnesses by casually destroying. Telling the boys that they will be unable to say anything against him, Satan then causes himself to disappear as Father Peter comes doddering by. The old man then finds his lost wallet, stuffed miraculously by more than a thousand gold ducats, which he sorely needs.

Father Peter grows popular once again in town, and so does his niece Marget. They are grateful to the boys for supporting his story about the gold. But suddenly Father Adolf accuses Father Peter of stealing the gold from him and has the innocent man thrown into jail. Ursula, who is Peter's loyal servant and Marget's former nurse, is forced to take in washing for a little money, until she chances to meet Satan, who ecstatically delights Theodor by his sudden reappearance. Satan tells her that a weak stray kitten, which Ursula has found and which he miraculously energizes, should be called Agnes and will cause four pieces of silver to appear daily in her pocket. And so it happens! Theodor introduces Satan, as Philip Traum, to Marget, who likes him at once. He invites himself to dinner, and his hostesses are embarrassed until he miraculously provides more and more fish in the frying pan. Theodor is frightened when Satan hints that he would like to introduce Ursula to his lonely, princely uncle, who has a monopoly in the tropics and travels widely. The stranger enables Marget quietly to visit her uncle in jail and also gives Theodor a glimpse of its torture chamber. Then he provides an illustrated lecture on man's ineffective moral sense, which shows people the distinction between right and wrong, the latter being what they choose.

For a week Satan is gone. In this time, Ursula hires a servant, a dull, good-natured boy named Gottfried Narr, whose grandmother was burned as a witch. Ursula begins to show off by having parties, the food for which is provided by the magic cat. Father Adolf becomes suspicious, goes with forty other diners to Marget's house—which is tinglingly cheered by Satan's presence—and soon notices that a wine bottle refuses to run dry even though he pours and pours from it. But just as he is about to pronounce the house bewitched, Satan slips like a transparent film into the priest's body; then Father Adolf rushes into the street, juggles a circus performer's brass balls, skips along a tightrope, and behaves strangely in other ways. The three young boys' parents discuss the necessity of informing on Father Adolf to keep the whole town from suffering an interdict. Theodor goes to Marget's house and watches as her closest friend, the young and faithful lawyer Wilhelm Meidling, is defeated at chess by Satan, who smiles and sings captivatingly.

A few days later Theodor and his parents discuss Satan. It appears that the boy's sister, Lilly, has become infatuated with the stranger. She comes in and explains that the wonderful creature helped her with her embroidery, finishing a month's work in a few minutes. He wants, she adds, to codify Roman law. Joseph Fuchs, who is the twenty-one-year-old son of the rich brewer and is Lilly's close friend, enters and begins to relate town gossip about Philip Traum. Then Wilhelm enters despondently and eventually tells the group that his beloved Marget has fallen hopelessly in love with the stranger. When Satan sunnily enters, the young lawyer tries unsuccessfully to stab him; but he only laughs, hypnotizes the whole group, and soon is pleasantly chatting with Wilhelm about chess.

Theodor looks in on his sister Lilly in her bedroom and finds that she has been crying and is intensely critical of Marget. When he tells her that she is behaving toward Satan in the same way, the girl grows angry and sarcastic. So the boy goes to bed. In the dead of night, Satan visits him and whisks him off to China. Then they discuss cosmic perspective, the moral sense, and predestined sequences of events in human lives. Satan says that he can alter whole careers and sometimes does so for the good of the persons involved. For example, he has seen to it that Nicky twelve days hence will drown with sweet little Lisa Brandt instead of rescuing her, because if they lived Nicky would get scarlet fever and be paralyzed, deaf, dumb, and blind until he died at the age of sixty-two, while Lisa would grow depraved and be executed at the age of thirty-six. Theodor agrees that Satan is really kind. But when he tells Seppi, with Satan's permission, the two boys suffer anguish and give the happy, ignorant victim-to-be all kinds of presents.

Day after day Theodor and Seppi play with Nicky, knowing but unable to tell him that on the thirteenth of the month he will die. He is happy because his two chums are so kind to him. Finally, on the last night, they stay out too late and Nicky is whipped by his father and ordered to remain indoors the following day. Theodor and Seppi are delighted, but just before the time appointed for Nicky's death

Lisa's mother comes by and reports that her daughter is missing. Nicky's mother sends the boy out to look, and soon both children are drowned. Lisa's mother curses God; so when Theodor and Seppi ask Satan to alter her lot for the better, he gladly does so by having the weaver report her for blasphemy. She is therefore excommunicated, is burned at the stake, and—according to Satan—goes to heaven.

A few days later, the stranger reappears and shows Theodor and Seppi a pageant of civilization, beginning with the Garden of Eden, then Cain and Abel, the Flood, Sodom and Gomorrah, the Hebraic wars, Jael, and new wars following the advent of Christianity. He also predicts more wars in later centuries. He sarcastically offers to drink to civilization; but when the boys are distressed he offers them a toast with unearthly wine in opalesque goblets which soon escape back into the heavens. Seppi half-asks whether he will go to heaven himself one day, but Satan pretends not to hear. Then he explains that he likes animals much better than he does people, adding that to him animals never smell bad—not even skunks. Next he rescues some trapped animals; and when the game keepers catch him, he thwarts them all by threatening to expose their secret crimes to the authorities. Conrad Bart, the chief keeper, proving obdurate, Satan hints that the man let an innocent person go to the gallows for a murder which Bart committed. Just as Bart is about to shoot him, Satan turns the angry fellow into a stone statue. Converting himself into an image of Father Adolf, Satan then returns to town, is stoned by an irate mob, but only laughs. After a ridiculous coroner's inquest, during which a debate is held on the subject of God's intentions in the matter, the corpse's family takes the statue away and exhibits it for money. It finally winds up in the Pitti Palace in Florence.

Theodor resists asking Satan to give him a statement of his future because he wants to be surprised. His being told Seppi's future spoils their association for a little while. Satan gives each boy a book telling of the other's life. Then when the two friends grow up and are separated, they keep up with each other by reading their books. Back to their youths. They make a great deal of money by betting on events about to take place, as predicted by Satan secretly—how the church would be hit by lightning, how a certain man would break his leg, and the like. One day a "witch" who cures headaches by massage is caught and hanged. Theodor reluctantly throws a rock at her, since most of the other people are doing so. When Satan laughs, three workers ask why. He explains that it is amusing to see three cowards stoning a lady. When they threaten him, he predicts the imminent death of all three. One dies in a few moments, and the crowd panics. Then Satan takes Theodor to one side and lectures him on mob psychology, the tyranny of violent minorities, the dishonor of all wars, and the coming viciousness of British imperialism.

Satan disappears for a while; so Marget begins to forget him and encourages Wilhelm, who agrees to act as Father Peter's defense attorney. Evidence seems overwhelming against the kindly old suspended priest, who remains away in jail, until Satan suddenly appears—visible only to Theodor and Seppi. The stranger melts into the form of dejected Wilhelm, who suddenly announces that Father Adolf could not be telling the truth when he testified that he found the gold ducats two years earlier and that they had been stolen from him, because the coins were minted only a year before. An inspection of the coins verifies this statement, and Father Peter is acquitted. Satan, who once predicted that the old man would win the case and be happy, slips away and tells the prisoner that he lost. The priest goes permanently insane and begins to regard himself as the emperor, and Marget, Ursula, and Wilhelm as regal too. When Theodor ventures to upbraid Satan, the stranger explains that it is impossible to be both happy and sane. Then he lectures the boy on human stupidity, religion, love of aristocracy, papal infallibility, and the reluctance of people to laugh at humbug. Suddenly Satan transports Theodor to India, where, outdoing a magician, he causes a tree to shoot up from a cherry seed and produce oranges and other luscious fruits for the people. The foreign-born owner of the land tries to kick Satan off his property but is ordered to water the tree hourly; if he fails, he will die.

Then Satan goes into the Indian hills and discomfits a magician performing before a Rajah by taking the entertainer's apparently solid ivory ball and finding a diamond inside it . . .

> Frau Adler, Father Adolf, Conrad Bart, Nikolaus Baumann, Baumann, Frau Baumann, the Bishop, Felix Brandt, Lisa Brandt, Frau Brandt, Caspar, the Coroner, Lilly Fischer, Frau Marie Fischer, Rupert Fischer, Theodor Fischer, Fischer, the Foreman, Joseph Fuchs, Fuchs, Haas,

Hansel, Jacob Hein, Simon Hirsch, Solomon Isaacs, Johan, the Juryman, the King, Klein, Marie Lueger, Marget, Gretel Marx, Marx, Wilhelm Meidling, Müller, Gottfried Narr, Hans Oppert, Father Peter, Pfeiffer, Pope [Clement XI], the Prince, the Rajah, Satan, Satan, Siebold, Bartel Sperling, Ursula, the Wild Huntsman, Seppi Wohlmeyer, Wolhmeyer, Frau Wohlmeyer.

'Cigars and Tobacco,' 1910 (S).

Twain explains that he is a great smoker and has been ever since he was a lad who could expertly tuck quids under his tongue and cut plug tobacco for his pipe. When he was financially able, he bought choice Havanas, but they failed to please. He tried various other costly brands, but they all seemed deficient. So he sought out an honest tobacco merchant in New York, asked him to identity his worst cigar, experimented with one, was delighted, took a box, and has been a steady customer for them to this day.

"City Marshal Perry," c. 1863.*

Twain offers a humorous biography of John Van Buren Perry, the new marshal of Virginia City. He was born in Ireland, a descendant of a piece of property owned by Baalam and mentioned in the Bible. He came to the United States in 1792 and became a music teacher in New Jersey. His son, Martin Van Buren, became President of the United States; his grandson, also named Martin, a New York politician. While in New Jersey, John Perry became a naval commodore, fought on Lake Erie, and later turned into a whisky-drinking diplomat in Japan. Then he went to Rhode Island and invented a pain killer. Next he became a poet and wrote sentimental "Perry-Gorics," which were so criticized by the English that he had to take a rest at a retreat called Sing Sing. He has such large feet that he wears coffins instead of expensive leather shoes. When he put his feet on his desk in Congress he eclipsed the chaplain. He moved to San Francisco and starred as Old Pete in Dion Boucicault's *Octoroon*. As marshal in Virginia, Perry tried to persecute Twain, but our intrepid correspondent won the day and accepted six bits to hand Perry down to posterity in this biography.

Alderman, Baalam, Birdsall, Brokaw, Infant, Larkin,

Mother, Tom Peasley, Hon. Mr. John Van Buren Perry,
Speaker [of the House], Martin Farquhar Tupper, John
Van Buren, President Martin Van Buren.

*In *Wit and Humor of America*, ed. Kate M. Rabb, Vol. 5 (Indianapolis:
Bobbs-Merrill, 1907).

["City of Hartford"]. See "Misplaced Confidence."

"Clairvoyant," 1969 (HHT).

A young, brilliant-eyed Englishman named John H. Day comes
to the young narrator's home town of Hannibal and works in
Stevens's jewelry shop. For a year Day stays pretty much to himself, even to the extent of cooking and sleeping at the shop. He
has the curious habit of visiting with most villagers simply once
and also of looking into their ears ostensibly to report whether
they might go deaf later in life. The narrator is apprenticed to
Stevens, studies under Day, and even sleeps in his room with him.
The narrator likes his silent companion and enjoys watching him
late at night when the man thinks the boy is asleep. At these times
Day sits back and lets a parade of varying emotions flit across his
face as he evidently thinks of a variety of subjects. One summer
night he suddenly interrupts his musings to yell at the narrator
to rush to the Ratliffe house to warn the neighbors that crazy
Ratliffe is about to kill his mother with a knife. The narrator does
as he is told, though with tardy reluctance, and thus is instrumen-
tal in saving Mrs. Ratliffe's life. Day wants no credit for or even
mention of his part in the incident. The narrator does not betray
his confidence. On another occasion Day explains that G— killed
B— in a quarrel over some birds and still suffers remorse so agoniz-
ing that as soon as his mother dies he will commit suicide. It so
happens. Finally, Day correctly predicts that old E— will have an
attack of conscience and quickly return to Stevens's store to retrieve a bad bill he exchanged there.

B—, Brittingham, John H. Day, E—, G—, Ratliffe, Mrs.
Ratliffe, T. R. Selmes, Stevens.

[*Clemens of the Call: Mark Twain in San Francisco*], 1864.*
As a local reporter, Twain ranges far and wide. He analyzes San

Francisco earthquakes [1-5], street accidents [6-10], houses being moved through town [11-15], and miscellaneous items [16-21]. He discusses a temperance group, an anti-Negro Irishman, a Negro dance, a greenback controversy, vandalism at a hotel, a school parade and program, a minister's crayon portrait, the literary weekly *Californian,* a realistic painter, hotel breakfast quail, a shipping strike, and an orator who lamented the absence of the fireside spirit in California [21-33]. As for San Francisco's Chinese population, Twain reports on their opium, prostitution, a suicide, a knife fight, a kidnaper [34-41], a benevolent association's josh house, and a visit to another temple [42-45]. In his time off, Twain attends Fourth of July festivities [46-47], reports some horse races [48-49] and theatrical performances [50-54] and fairs [55-57], including the elaborate industrial one of the Mechanics' Institute [58-72]. He reports on the explosion of the steamer *Washoe,* which claimed a hundred lives, and on the death of a certain auctioneer [73-76]. Twain also includes miscellaneous descriptive and humorous sketches [77-81].

As a crime and police-court reporter, Twain files stories about street and calaboose drunkenness, especially in women [82-89]; a juvenile thief, drunken and wandering derelicts, and lost children [90-94]; and attempted suicides [95-98]. In addition, we have cases of assault and battery, some deadly [99-106]; swindling and harassment leading to a physician's suicide [107-115]; the corrupting of young girls [116-119]; a variety of robberies, some of which are solved by an evidently brilliant detective [120-128]; and serious sexual offenses, such as miscegenation, bigamy, and rape [129-136]. Twain also reports cases in circuit courts, mostly concerning abused sailors [137-141]. But his best talents emerge when he reports on sensational acts of murder and attempted murder: the bayoneting to death of one soldier by another, an attempt to kill a pawnbroker with a blackjack, and a wanted man's gory attempt to kill a detective pursuing him [142-149].

Twain is a critical and political reporter too. He criticizes litigants for stupidity and malice [150-152], witnesses for lying [153-155], and San Francisco's prosecuting attorney for incompetence [156-159]; but he does praise a couple of judges [160-161]. He also comments mildly on allegations that the police overstep their authority [162-164]. He castigates bureaucratic pettiness, negligence, irresponsibility, and cruelty—whether civic, especially at the mint [165-174]; business, especially at the mines [175-177]; or military, especially concerning censorship [178]. California, though far in the West, is influenced much, Twain notes, by the Civil War. He reports on the suggested fortification of San Francisco and the assembling there of a Union ironclad named the *Camanche* [179-184]; on efforts by the United States Sanitary Commission to collect funds in San Francisco for the relief of sick and wounded Union soldiers [185-187]; on allegedly treasonous violence, especially raids by supposedly secessionist guerrillas [188-194]; and on election campaigning in all of its feverish glory [195-198].

> [James J. Ayers, George E. Barnes, Henry W. Bellows, Beriah Brown, Martin J. Burke, Samuel Cowles, Albert S. Evans, Hubbard H. Kavanaugh, George W. Kidd, Thomas S. King, Davis Louderback Jr., Irvin McDowell, John C. Pelton, Clement T. Rice, Tod Robinson, George Rose, Philip W. Shepheard, Franklin Soulé, Robert B. Swain, Lewis P. Ward, William Wright].**

*Edited by Edgar M. Branch (Berkeley and Los Angeles: University of California Press, 1969).
**For further details concerning these twenty-one main characters, see Branch, ed., *Clemens of the Call, passim.* Branch's "Index," which is necessarily somewhat incomplete, names most of the 350 or more additional persons whom Twain mentions in his *Call* articles, all of whom are omitted in my sequence of characters below. I do, however, include the above twenty-one in my sequence. I hereby praise and thank Branch for his painstaking editorial work in *Clemens of the Call.*

"Clerks and Lady Shoppers." See FW, 1869.

'College Girls,' 1906 (S).

Twain tells an audience of female undergraduates that he is glad he has been fed, for he might be indiscreet on an empty stomach or mind. He will tell a story that he should have used before. Now it is too late. At Carnegie Hall later this month he will leave off formal speaking for pay. Hereafter, he will consent to address only non-paying young women students. Then he tells of escorting a girl to the theater while he was wearing unbearably tight shoes. He concludes by urging the girls to let his story be a lesson—of what sort, he does not know.

Miss Neron.

["Colloquy Between a Slum Child and a Moral Mentor"], 1972 (FM).
A religious man asks James, a slum boy, who made the grass. The
Chief of Police. No, God did. The boy accepts this. Who makes the
grass grow? The Chief. No, God. How does it grow? With a railing
around it. No, the Heavenly Father makes it grow. James uses so
much slang that the moral man warns him about going to the bad
place, where it is fiery. James replies that he would like to go there,
because he is always cold in winter and has only a shutter for a bed
covering. He uses bowling slang and puzzles the humbled mentor,
who asks what the boy would do if he were God and had made the
grass. James would roll in it. When the man explains that God
made James too, the boy says that he wishes God would fence him
in and care for him the way He does the grass in city parks. The
man says that God furnished James's bed even, at which the boy
expresses sorrow for Peanut Jim, who has no shutter to sleep under.

Cap, the Chief of Police, Higgins, James, Mike, Peanut
Jim.

"Colonel Sellers at Home." From *The Gilded Age.*

"Colored Typos." See FW, 1870.

"The Coming Man." 1871 (CG).
Twain has read in a newspaper that General Dewlap G. Lovel,
our ambassador to Hong-Wo, just resigned and is now being considered as the new minister to England. Twain wonders if the man
could possibly be his acquaintance Dunlap G. Lovel, a brigadier
general in the Nevada militia, who saw no service even in a July
Fourth parade, would never resign anything—not even duty in
tiny Hong-Wo—and was outclassed in the West by General P.
Edward O'Connor. All Dunlap ever did was permit the Nevada
desperado Thompson Billings's escape from jail once, appear in
uniform at a Carson City sanitary ball, help confirm the appointment of an illiterate named Captain Murphy as clerk of the Nevada
House of Representatives, and through political pull get sent to
Hong-Wo in place of the more deserving General O'Connor. It is
a pity that the candidate is Dewlap, not Twain's friend Dunlap.
If Dunlap should go to England, Twain would be content to die.

Thompson Billings, [President] Andrew Johnson, General Dunlap G. Lovel, [John Lothrop] Motley, Captain G. Murphy, the Governor [of Nevada], Captain John Nye, General P. Edward O'Connor, Brigham [Young].

"Commentary [on *English As She Is Taught*]." See "English As She Is Taught."

"Compiler's Apology," 1888.*

Twain explains that the selections in his *Library of Humor* which are from his own works were made by assistants and not by himself, which explains why there are not more of them.

*In *Mark Twain's Library of Humor* (New York: Webster, 1888).

"A Complaint about Correspondents," 1866 (CJF).

Twain complains that too many people in the East wrongly feel that once a person has been on the Pacific coast for six months he loses interest in everything back home. But the fault lies with letter writers. To keep emotional channels upon, they should discuss topics in which their readers take an interest. Twain's Aunt Nancy always writes about people he does not know and concerning events in the war he has read of weeks before her letters arrive; and she does not inform him about people he does know and cares for. Twain's mother sends the news by mailing him clippings and cryptic bits of gossip with people's initials, which unfortunately the lapse of years makes it hard for him to decipher. Children—for example, Twain's eight-year niece Annie—write the most informative and interesting letters: they tell the truth with brevity, and without abstractions or moral homilies.

> Johnny Anderson, Annie, J. B., Lottie Belden, Sam Bowen, Georgiana Brown, Hattie Caldwell, T. D., Miss Doosenberry, Mrs. Gabrick, L. P. J., B. K., Ben Kenfuron, Bill Kribben, W. L., Zeb Leavenworth, R. M., Rev. Mr. Macklin, Mrs. Macklin, Margaret, Sissy McElroy, McElroy, Mrs. McElroy, Aunt Nancy, Mary Anne Smith, Sowerby, Strother Wiley.

'Compliments and Degrees,' 1908 (WMT 28).

Twain begins by thanking the Lotos Club for its several hearty welcomes, past and present. He is grateful for compliments, but they always do embarrass people, even including Carnegie. All the same, Twain adds, he has collected compliments paid to him. Hamilton Mabie said that La Salle first voyaged on the Mississippi River but Twain first lighted it for the world. Albert Bigelow Paine said that Twain exemplifies all human strengths and weaknesses. Edison said that everyone loves his family and if he has any love left over loves Twain. The people at *Punch* once gave him a memorable dinner. Putting on his red gown from Oxford University, Twain next says that it makes ladies look dim by comparison. Twain then repeats, by invitation, his address at a farewell dinner, Liverpool, in July, 1907, during which he said that the honors accorded him made him think of a description by Richard Henry Dana, Jr., of a little ship hailing a gigantic Indiaman, which identified herself in booming tones and then demanded the name of the little ship. Her spokesman squeaked back that she was only the *Mary Ann* a few days out, with no cargo to speak of, and not bound far. In the night, Twain feels humble; but during the day, the warm approval of others makes him sail along like an Indiaman, now homeward bound.

[Thomas A.] Edison, the King of England, Queen [Victoria] of England, W[illiam]. D[ean] Howells, Frank B. Lawrence, Hamilton Mabie, Porter.

["Concerning a Bear"], 1917.*

Several men are assembled in a restaurant in Virginia City, Nevada, and are trying to decide on a vignette for the *Overland* magazine. When they choose a grizzly bear for the emblem, Nahl Bras. sketches one snarling over his shoulder; but it looks pointless until Bret Harte puts a couple of lines under it. Then it symbolizes California snarling at the advent of civilization coming west on railroad tracks.

Nahl Bras., Dan de Quille, Joseph T. Goodman, Bret Harte, Artemus Ward.

*In *Mark Twain's Letters,* ed. Albert B. Paine, 2 vols. (New York: Harper & Brothers, 1917), I, 184.

"Concerning a Reformed Pledge" (MTP).

Taking a pledge to reform is worse than useless. Afterwards, a man feels an instant wave of strength followed by uneasiness. If he keeps the pledge, it only proves that he is the sort who does not need a pledge. We should realize that all pledges are not the same, that too many people take pledges, and that the best way to improve is to study yourself. Twain admits taking pledges against smoking, chewing, swearing, and drinking, and then violating some of them. Tapering off is no answer. Catholics can fortunately be absolved of oaths, but Presbyterians cannot; so breaking oaths has pained Twain. Every time he lights a cigar, he breaks that old pledge. So he has stopped taking oaths, except in legal matters. We should say that we will try to curb a desire to drink, etc.; thus we would not try to fight two enemies, the mechanical habit and the desire, but only one enemy, the desire. Twain once started drinking scotch nightcaps to put himself to sleep during a rough voyage. The habit stayed with him, even ashore. But when he began to study German, he found that he needed no more nightcaps. Every few months, however, he still has a nightcap, just to show who is boss. And he will continue to smoke. His pastor says that he will smoke in the next world. Anyone can easily reform under Twain's improved method.

Cadet of Temperance, the Good Templars.

"Concerning a Rumor," 1871 (CG).

Twain wishes to scotch the unfortunate rumor that Agassiz's brain is softening. Twain recently read that the nationally known scientist has discovered ten thousand varieties of flies. Probably some fool spied on Agassiz snatching at flies, following them up walls, sitting on them to make their capture sure, and so on. The rumor probably has such a foundation.

[Louis] Agassiz.

"Concerning Chambermaids," 1866 (WMT 7).

The author launches the curse of bachelordom against all chambermaids. They put the pillows far from the gas burner so that it is hard to read in bed at night, push your trunk against the wall so the lid will not stay open, put the spittoon in unhandy positions, hide your boots under the bed so you will have to reach and curse, replace the matchbox with a glass object so when you grope you will break something, reverse the positions of rocking chair and slop bucket so you will come in and stumble over the former and sit on the latter, save scraps of paper you want destroyed and light fires with your manuscripts, steal your hair oil, offer to make your bed only when you are in it, and so on. The author plans to push a bill through the legislature abolishing chambermaids.

"Concerning Copyright: An Open Letter to the Register of Copyrights," 1905 (LAIFI).

In the form of a letter to Thorwald Stolberg, Register of Copyrights in Washington, Twain explains by a series of questions and answers his position concerning copyright laws. Five or six thousand books are copyrighted annually in the United States, for perhaps a total of 250,000 in the past century or so. Only five or ten books a year survive the present forty-two-year limit of copyright, or a total of fewer than a thousand American books. Therefore the present senseless system robs the orphans of only a handful of authors. The result is the reverse of Darwin's law: the fittest books are assassinated. Inventors and military defenders of our country are better protected, through royalties, commercial development, and pensions. When a book falls into the public domain, the public does not benefit. Publishers do. Imagine our President addressing and extolling a horde of illustrious inventors, soldiers and sailors, and authors, and then telling the authors that their widows and children can go to the poorhouse for all of him, after forty-two years. Twain suggests that a better way would be to require the owner of a copyright to keep in print a cheap edition of the book during and after its forty-second year. It might be priced at 25¢ for each 100,000 words. If the cheap edition were unavailable for as long as three months, the copyright would die. Twain says that under such a system his complete works would be available for about $7.50, and the cheap editions would advertise oncoming and more expensive new works of his. Publisher, binder, and middleman would make moderate profits per unit of cheap editions, but volume would be great. The exceptional author's family would thus be properly protected.

[George] Bancroft, [Alexander] Graham Bell, [William

Cullen] Bryant, Builder, Builder of its Material Greatness,
[Adna Romanza] Chaffee, [James Fenimore] Cooper, De-
fender, Defender of its Home and its Flag, [George] Dew-
ey, [Thomas A.] Edison, [Ralph Waldo] Emerson, [John]
Ericsson, [David G.] Farragut, [Andrew H.] Foote,
[Robert] Fulton, [Ulysses S.] Grant, [Nathaniel] Haw-
thorne, [Richard] Hoe, [Oliver Wendell] Holmes, [Oliver
O.] Howard, Immortal Three, Washington Irving, [An-
drew] Jackson, [John] Paul Jones, [Sylvester] Judd,
[Henry Wadsworth] Longfellow, [James Russell] Lowell,
[George B.] McClellan, [Nelson A.] Miles, [Samuel F. B.]
Morse, [Francis] Parkman, Patriot-Maker, [Edgar Allan]
Poe, Preserver, the President, the Promoter of its Fame
and Preserver of it, [William T.] Sampson, [Winfield
Scott] Schley, [Winfield] Scott, [Philip Henry] Sheridan,
[William Tecumseh] Sherman, [Daniel E.] Sickles,
Thorwald Stolberg, Mrs. Harriet Beecher Stowe, [Zachary]
Taylor, Teacher, [George] Washington, [George] Westing-
house, [Eli] Whitney, [John Greenleaf] Whittier, [John
L.] Worden.

"Concerning Dreams." See FW, 1869.

"Concerning 'Martyrs' Day,'" 1972 (FM).
    Twain has read of a proposal to establish a Martyrs' Day and to
make it a national holiday. He suggests instead a double plan—a
Martyrs' Day and a Monument Day. Let each worker in America
continue working on that day, contributing his day's earnings to
an ongoing monument year after year. Last year [1901] 52,264,534
workers in America earned wages amounting to $64,000,000 a day.
Each year the number of workers and the total of their daily wages
will increase. Twain proposes a circular monument a hundred miles
in diameter and nine miles tall, to be finished in a thousand years
at a cost of $700,000,000,000 worth of commercial mourning. His
plan will assure funds. It does not matter that we already have too
many holidays. In Italy there are 227 public holidays a year. Australia and New Zealand have three a week and would like to sell
us some.

    Contributor.

"Concerning Notaries," 1864 (MTWY).

At Carson City, Twain is approached by a would-be notary named Billson from Lander, with a petition yards in length. He asks Twain to use his influence with Governor Nye. Then another would-be notary who is named Boreas and is from Washoe approaches, asks Twain to use his influence, and buys him a drink. Next a polite fellow named J. Bidlecome Dusenberry of Esmeralda and New York City sidles up, gains a promise that Twain will use his influence, and gets him a drink. Twain drinks with another seventy or more would-be notaries and promises to use his influence. Back out on the street, he meets a stranger who surprises him by insisting that he does not wish to be a notary! Twain offers him a drink, after which the man feels that he should be a notary and tears down some wallpaper to write up his petition. Suddenly Twain himself feels that he should be a notary and prepares his own petition. Together, the two join the line forming near the Governor's office.

Ah Foo, Mayor [Rufus E.] Arick, John H. Atchinson, Sandy Baldwin, Billson, Boreas, Mrs. Boreas, the County Surveyor, J. Bidlecome Dusenberry, John O. Earl, Wells Fargo, Hong Wo, Bob Morrow, Judge North, Governor [James] Nye, Schemerhorn, William [M.] Stewart, Charley Strong, Chief Justice Turner, Jim Washoe, General Williams, John B. Winters.

"Concerning the American Language," 1882 (WMT 19).

When an Englishman on the train praises Twain for speaking English better than most Americans, Twain thanks him but says that he speaks American not English, then proceeds to distinguish between *cow* and *kaow*, *glass* and *glahs*, *hunting* and *'unting*, *here* and *h'yaah*, *dontchu* and *don't you*, *gods* and *gawds*, and also differences in the meanings of such words as *directly*, *clever*, *stout*, *lady*, and *gentleman*. The Englishman compliments Twain by saying that he can hardly follow. Twain likes him directly.

"Concerning the Interview" (MTP).

People do not like being interviewed; yet they succumb, because interviewers are courteous even when they come—all unconsciously—to destroy, like cyclones, which after all aim to cool hot villages and not to do harm. Interviewers, like cyclones, hate symmetry and prefer to scatter a person's remains. You want neither to be quoted nor to have what you have not said get into print; yet one or the other of these calamities follows every interview. Whatever is done, regret follows. So you speak evasively. The printed results are sickening. Does the interviewer tempt you to be humorous? You fail. So he invents some funninesses for you. They fail. Thus all interviews are mistakes.

"Concerning the Answer to That Conundrum," 1864 (SS). (See also "A Notable Conundrum" and "Still Further Concerning That Conundrum.")

The author goes out to see the whale, with an invalid friend named John William Skae. To cheer him up, the author talks pleasantly of cholera and consumption. When they get to the Cliff House, they enter but can see nothing except whiskey bottles. They stay a while, and within an hour or so John's speech has become thick. They look for the whale on the beach, but it turns into an ordinary stinking fish. Then John presents a conundrum: why is a whale like a certain blue-colored Western bird? Because it is a kingfisher. The author is so impressed that he makes John rest. However, the author notes to himself that you cannot present this riddle to a woman and then effectively say, "Because it is a king fish, madam." Oh, the author of the conundrum about Napoleon's resemblance to cheese has not yet come forward with the answer.

The Author, James Peterson, John William Skae, Skae, Mrs. Skae, Skae.

"Concerning the Jews," 1899 (WMT 22).

The author explains that he has had several letters from Jews in America in response to his incidental comments on Jews in a recent article ["Stirring Times in America"]. One such letter makes these points and asks these questions: Jews are generally well-behaved citizens. Can ignorance and fanaticism alone account for their unfair treatment? How can they improve the situation? Jews are non-partisan. Will persecution end? Where is the golden rule? The author instantly agrees that typically Jews are sober, orderly, home-loving, generous to their own indigent, and honest in business. There is, however, a small debit column. Some Jews have a reputation for petty cheating, making tricky arrangements, and avoidance of military duty. When Joseph cornered various markets in pre-Christian Egyptian times, he started the prejudice against Jews. Like the typical Yankee in the author's boyhood Mississippi Valley, the average Jew is sharper than the competition. The historical cure for Jewish success has been banishment. Such persecution is obviously commercial, not religious. Jews live by their brains rather than hands, know that money is universally worshipped, and go after it to be envied. The author then rebukes Jews everywhere for not uniting in a partisan way. They should get into politics in groups, like the Irish, and also into volunteer regiments. The author offers some statistics, attempts to explain a few possibly misleading population figures, and cautions against Jewish efforts to colonize Palestine—because such a concentration of brains would surely be opposed! He feels that racial and commercial prejudice against Jews will continue but that religious persecution will not. As for the golden rule, it is aired every Sunday but is otherwise regarded as irrelevant. The author concludes with praise of the Jewish people, who have contributed great names in various fields of endeavor far out of proportion to their relative numbers. The Jew must be immortal.

"Concerning the Scoundrel Edward H. House" (MTP).

Edward H. House has wet Twain with tears in public print once more. So Twain decides to offer fellow Hartfordians his side of the dispute. He first met House in 1867 when the man was on the Tribune and pleasantly reviewed Twain's Cooper Institute lecture. When House returned from Japan, he stayed briefly in Twain's Hartford home, read the manuscript of The Gilded Age, offered to write a review of it for the Tribune, then lied that the editor Whitelaw Reid had rejected the proposal and criticized Twain and Charles Dudley Warner for instigating it. Only years later did Twain learn the truth. In 1881 House again visited Twain, this time reading the manuscript of The Prince and the Pauper. House wrongly claimed that he first suggested that Twain dramatize it. Later House, again back from Japan and sick in New York, talked with Twain in general terms about the dramatization. Three years earlier, Twain and his friend Will Gillette also vaguely discussed dramatizing the novel, at which

time Gillette suggested having one actor play both leading roles—
an idea House later claimed was his. House said that in 1886
Twain wrote offering him half or two-thirds of the proceeds if
he would dramatize the work. House said that Twain often wrote
him about the project. Twain accuses the man of keeping a forged
diary of 1887 events which never occurred. When Twain again
entertained House as a guest, the man was busy writing *Yono Santo*
and scheming to invest in California property. Later he wrongly
claimed to have written an act of *The Prince and the Pauper* at this
time. Twain observes that there are no letters, contracts, proofs
of any kind of any understanding on his part. Why would House
wait a year and a half while Twain allegedly ignored a whole draft
which House says he sent in the summer of 1887? When Twain
put Mrs. Richardson under contract to dramatize the novel, House
wrote expressing surprise, and the two men met in New York. House
could produce no contract. Mrs. Richardson did not wish to withdraw. Now, Twain wonders, what could his motive be in supposedly
mistreating House? Money? But Twain had contracted to pay
Mrs. Richardson 50%. The actress Elsie Leslie? But House could
have gotten her as easily as Mrs. Richardson did. Mrs. Richardson's
greater fame? But the woman was not well known, and Twain had
even written her to ask House to help her with her writing. The
explanation is simple: Twain did not know that he was under contract with anybody. It cannot be shown that he has ever cheated
anyone.

> [Dion] Boucicault, Ejiro, Will Gillette, David Gray, Col.
> John Hay, Edward H. House, Miss House, Knox, Elsie Les-
> lie, Nordhoff, Whitelaw Reid, Mrs. [Abby S.] Richardson,
> Joseph H. Twichell, Charles Dudley Warner, Charles W.
> Webb, Sam Wilkinson, Mrs. Yost.

"Concerning Tobacco," 1917 (WMT 26).
    There are many foolish superstitions concerning tobacco. One
is that there is a standard governing tobacco. In reality, a man's
own preference is the only proper standard. Another myth is that
a man has a standard of his own. He really does not. You may palm
off a terrible cigar on him, and he will like it if he sees his label on
it. The only person who can tell you that a given cigar is enjoyable
is yourself. Twain likes cheap cigars; but his friends run when he

presents them some, that is, unless he first secretly places the red-and-gold labels of expensive brands on his offerings. Twain likes most cigars that other smokers do not and dislikes most brands regarded by others as good. He regularly smokes cigars which cost 27¢ a barrel but cannot abide those which friends say cost a dollar apiece. To him they seem to be made of dog hair. In a week he can happily smoke a hundred Italian cigars called Minghettis, for $3.60 per hundred. He also likes pipe tobacco used by Italian peasants. It is dry, black, and looks like tea grounds. When he burns it in his pipe, it expands, climbs, towers, and tumbles onto his vest.

["Congressional Poetry"]. See W 1868.

A Connecticut Yankee in King Arthur's Court, 1889 (WMT 14).

In a prefatory note, Mark Twain discusses the divine right of kings and explains that if the sixth century did not have all of the abuses included in the following story it had worse ones. While in Warwick Castle, the narrator meets an antique stranger who speaks oddly and says that he once put a hole, like a bullet hole, in a suit of armor pointed out by the cicerone. The narrator goes to his inn and reads in Malory about Sir Launcelot's rescue of damsels in distress and then of Sir Kay, who after Launcelot leaves uses that doughty warrior's armor advantageously. The aged stranger enters and tells the narrator how he was once employed in the famous Colt Arms Factory in Hartford, Connecticut, as a knowledgeable, inventive supervisor, got into an argument (in 1879) with a rival worker named Hercules, and was knocked senseless with a crowbar. When he awakened, a knight was standing over him, offered to joust, and took him prisoner not to Bridgeport but to Camelot. The stranger becomes drowsy, gives a manuscript account of his adventures to the narrator to read, and departs. The narrator sits by the fire and peruses the parchment.

Kay takes the Yankee to the castle at Camelot, past wretched, half-naked persons. In King Arthur's court, he meets a page, names him Clarence, enjoys the sights, but is appalled by the condition of his fellow-prisoners. Clarence tells him the date: June 19, 528! Courtiers scoff at Kay, whose prisoners have come in, until he admits that Launcelot wore his armor and did the fighting. Then aged Merlin rises and drones out a confusing tale of Arthur, the

Lady of the Lake, and the king's wondrous sword. Then Sir Dinadan the Humorist baits a dog cruelly, at which all the childish
people in the court laugh wildly. The authorities suddenly strip
their Yankee prisoner of his curious clothes, toss him into prison,
and soon reveal that he is to be burned at the stake next day at
noon. Clarence has become his timid confidant, and the Yankee
sends him to court with the threat that if burned he will blot out
the sun. As the execution is about to take place, sure enough, at
12:03 P.M., June 21, 528 (Clarence was wrong by a day), occurs the
eclipse, which the Yankee knew about. Arthur grants all of his
demands—to be named perpetual minister and executive, to retain
1% of what his services will earn the state, and to have some new
clothes. To diminish canny Merlin's remaining power, the Yankee
elaborately mines the magician's stone tower with blasting powder
and blows it up.

Gradually the dream becomes real. The Yankee is now called the
Boss, is an absolute benevolent power, but like the enormous
elephant is neither respected nor envied but simply feared. He
records his bitter opposition to the secular power of the Roman
Catholic church at this point, as well as his annoyance that inherited, unearned rank claims more respect in this sixth century
than do brains, which the Boss has in abundance. Soon a tournament is held, starring Sir Gareth. The Boss trains an intelligent
priest to report the jousts as training for a projected newspaper.
Unfortunately, just as Gareth is unhorsing Sir Sagramor, the Boss,
thinking of tedious Dinadan, says he hopes he dies. Sagramor
misinterprets the remark as an insult and challenges the Boss to a
duel, in three or four years, for Sagramor must go holy grailing first.

During the next four years, the Boss establishes efficient mines,
factories, schools, shops, tax collecting, and electric communica-
tion. He hopes quietly to undermine church authority. Clarence,
now twenty-two years old, is a splendid right-hand man who can
do anything, even write backwoods, nineteenth-century English.

It is now time for the Boss to go grailing. When a girl named
Alisande de Carteloise enters the court to plead for succor against
an ogre who has imprisoned forty-odd virgins, he decides to accept
the call to danger. The girl, whom he nicknames Sandy, leads him
through a beautiful, sylvan, autumnal setting; but he is increasingly
uncomfortable because he is so ridiculously encased in armor that
he cannot even scratch his nose. Also Sandy talks like a murmuring

millbrook, unceasingly. Soon they encounter a group of road menders called freemen. After he buys breakfast from them, the Boss harangues them on democracy and on the stupidity of the people for allowing themselves to be ruled by a few selfish aristocrats. One intelligent freeman is responsive; so the Boss sends him with a note to Clarence at the Man Factory. Obtaining flint and steel from the workers, the Boss astounds them all by puffing away on his pipe. Next day, charged by six knights, he blows smoke at them and they meekly surrender. Sandy now tells him a tedious story of Sir Marhaus and how Sir Gawaine fought him for hours before they became friends. Something suddenly reminds the Boss of Central, his ravishingly beautiful girl friend, aged fifteen, who works for the telephone company forward in the nineteenth century. She called him Hank.

The Boss and Sandy now enter the castle of Arthur's sister Morgan le Fay, the beautiful but unspeakably vicious wife of old King Uriens. A graceful young page accidentally jostles her at the lavish banquet she offers the Boss, and so she nonchalantly stabs the boy to death. (Later she offers to pay for him.) When the Boss mentions Arthur, whom she hates, she flies into a rage and would imprison her guests but for Sandy's timely warning that she should not threaten the dread Boss. To mollify her, the Boss tells her to execute everyone in the wretched musical band. Suddenly a scream pierces the castle. Morgan le Fay is happy to show the Boss its source. A brawny young man named Hugo is being tortured in the dungeon to make him confess that he killed a deer. Beside the man are his lovely wife and baby. The Boss clears the dungeon and persuades Hugo to tell him everything. The young man did kill the animal but hopes by not confessing to spare his meagre property for his widow and orphan. The Boss frees the three and sends them to his Factory. Pausing to praise a few kindly priests and also to complain that one's conscience does him about as much good as an anvil inside him, the Boss proceeds to empty his silky hostess's prison of its varyingly tortured inmates.

Two mornings later, the Boss and Sandy are off on more knight-errantry. She runs on again so tediously about Marhaus, who defeated the Duke of South Marches, that the Boss silences her by asking her age. Still on their way to the ogre's castle, they next encounter huge Sir Madok, whom the Boss has fitted with a sandwich board advertising toothpaste. At last they find the castle, which turns out to be a pigsty, with pigs for distressed damsels. To humor Sandy, the Boss goes along with her assumption that everything has been enchanted. He courteously frees the pigs, and soon he and Sandy encounter a troupe of pilgrims proceeding to the Valley of Holiness and its miraculous waters, which flow so long as no one desecrates the area by taking a bath. A slave trader and his manacled, wormy, efficiently whipped gang are a distressing sight; but the Boss decides not to interfere with the institution of slavery until he has the urgent backing of the entire population. Sir Ozana, whose sandwich board advertises gentlemen's furnishings, rides up to report that the waters have ceased to flow in the valley and that Merlin is already on the scene trying magic restoratives observed only by angels. The Boss refuses to replace Merlin but instead sends Ozana for some plumbing supplies, dines convivially with the neighborhood monks, visits a few hermits, privately inspects the well, and learns that it is simply leaking a bit. When Merlin's tiresome incantations fail, the Boss is given full sway: he and his assistants repair the well, run pump-driven pipes to the door of the chapel near the fountain, plant tubs of stupendous fireworks all about for show, prepare to fire them with battery-sparked wires, and wait to release the miracle until Sunday. When Sunday comes, the entire region is crawling with spectators. After a Latin chant, the Boss intones a few long German words, touches off tub after tub of fireworks, and then the special word "BGWJJ-ILLIGKKK!" releases the water. The Boss re-introduces bath-taking, finds a telephone operator named Ulfius nearby, learns from him that King Arthur and Queen Guenever are starting for the Valley of Holiness to pay homage to the restored waters, and returns to the abbey to discomfit a worthless rival magician.

Once Arthur arrives, the competition for royal commissions in the Boss's newly conceived standing army can take place; but his candidates, trained along modern lines at his recently established West Point, are disqualified because they are not of aristocratic stock traceable four generations back. The Boss counters with the idea of a royal army composed of paying noblemen, to be complemented by an army of commoners who can be trained at West Point. Arthur agrees. While the king is curing victims of scrofula by touching them, the Boss is handed a copy of his newly established newspaper. It gaudily reports his restoration of the well, along with court doings. Passing it about among the monks, he feels intensely flattered by their admiring murmurs.

The Boss and Arthur now disguise themselves as humble freemen to sample life among ordinary people. Arthur practices an
obsequious walk but succeeds only imperfectly, even though the
Boss drills him all day. When two knights come by and the king accidentally shouts some insults at them, the Boss for self-preserva-
tion has to dynamite them into drizzling fragments of flesh and
hardware. Next, Arthur and the Boss enter a hut where a woman
is dying of smallpox. Her husband is already dead. One daughter is
also, and another is dying. Her three sons are in the lord's dungeon
near the town of Abblasoure wrongly accused of cutting down his
fruit trees. Arthur behaves with genuine compassion, comforting
the woman and listening as, while dying, she explains that she
blasphemed the selfish church for its cruelty during her trouble
and was excommunicated for it. By midnight the hut holds only
corpses, denied Christian burial. The king and the Boss leave, soon
hear voices approaching, hide, and see the three sons of the dead
couple coming home. When Arthur realizes that they must have
escaped, his training compels him to want to aid in their recapture,
but the Boss persuades him to get out of the area at once. Soon
they come upon the lord's manor house, which is engulfed in
flames. When they ask food and shelter at the hut of a charcoal
burner (later named Marco), the Boss, who is both more astute and
more trustworthy than Arthur, learns that the escapees stabbed
their lord to death, set fire to his house, but then were pursued,
though ineffectively, by their own neighbors, who during the night
hanged eighteen peasants. Moreover, thirteen of the lord's prisoners died in the fire because it never occurred to anyone to try to
release them. When Marco privately admits to the Boss that he is
glad his lord is dead, the Boss happily concludes that there is hope
for the world since a man is a man essentially, regardless of contrary
appearances induced by protracted social injustice.

Strolling along with Marco to make the king think that they are
busy trying to warn the authorities about the murderers, the Boss
participates in the rescue of a child being hanged by other children,
then orders all kinds of furniture, table implements, and food for
a banquet he wants Marco to give for conceited Dowley the blacksmith, and the mason Dickon and the wheelwright Smug, Dowley's
fawning friends. The king, now being called Jones and identified
as a well-to-do farmer, is to supply new clothes to Marco and his
wife Phyllis. The party is such a huge success—especially when the
Boss showily pays the $3.91 bill—that Dowley is thoroughly out-

done. But then the Boss engages him in a long discussion on economics—mostly on apparent income vs. real purchasing power—and rouses the craftsmen's fear that he wants to expose them all for overpaying their workers. Arthur makes matters worse by discussing agriculture in lunatic terms. A fight ensues, and after a long chase the king and the Boss are captured, freed by an earl named Grip, but sold next morning as slaves in a town called Cambenet. Arthur fetches $7; the Boss, $9. Meanwhile, a speech on God-given liberties in Britain is in progress at the town square.

Several days pass, and the gang of slaves is driven through a variety of weather toward London. One night, in a snow storm, the driver allows a pursued witch to be burned in the center of a circle formed by his slaves, to keep them warm. Near London, a new mother, who was forced to steal after her husband was impressed and sent to sea, is hanged. A gentle priest vows to protect her orphaned child. The Boss and Arthur finally enter London and pass the king's palace; the Boss even sees Sandy from a distance. That night he picks his padlocks, frees himself, but lacks time to release Arthur before the master comes by to check. The Boss follows him out to attack him, planning to free all the slaves; but he pounces on the wrong man, and in the ensuing fight both are arrested and jailed. The Boss explains to the judge that he is Grip's slave and has come to town to find a doctor for his master, and is released. When he returns to the place where the slave gang was, he finds only the driver's battered corpse and then learns that the slaves have been captured and condemned to hang for the murder. The Boss traces a telephone wire to its source, rings up Clarence, begs for knightly help at once, but then, trying to parlay his rags into respectable Boss garb, is arrested as the one missing slave from the homocidal gang, and is taken to join the others on the gallows. Three slaves are quickly hanged before a cheering mob. Arthur, ranting but unrecognized, is to be next, when suddenly five hundred mailed and belted knights, with Launcelot at their head, roll into view on bicycles, charge into the discomfited constables, and rescue all.

Soon it is time for the Boss, now called Hank Morgan, to take on Sir Sagramor, recently returned from grailing—without the Grail—and determined upon revenge. Hating his scientifically magic rival, Merlin attempts to weave a protective veil about Sagramor so that he can safely lance the Boss into oblivion. But that resourceful fellow, clad only in circus tights and puffings, and mounted on a wiry little pony, is ready with cowboy lasso and dragoon revolver. With his snaky rope, he unhorses armor-encumbered Sagramor, then Sir Hervis, Sir Lamorak, Sir Galahad, and even Launcelot himself. When Merlin steals the lasso and Sagramor demands another bout, the Boss shoots his brash opponent dead and then challenges every remaining knight present. One after another they charge at him, only to be shot out of their saddles. Just before the Boss runs out of bullets, the remaining knights break and retreat. Merlin's stock is flat again. It would seem that knighthood is dead.

Three years quickly pass. Scientific progress, continued by the Boss, holds old-fashioned magic powerless. Commerce flourishes. There are railroads, machines, and electric-power plants; and the Boss has converted the Table Round into a stock exchange. Noblemen are now brokers, railroad conductors, and baseball players (the Bessemers vs. the Ulsters). The Boss longs to institute Protestantism and then, at the death of King Arthur, universal suffrage under a republican form of government. Sandy has become Mrs. Hank Morgan, and the rapturously happy couple has a daughter touchingly named Hello-Central by her mother. But one day the child comes down with the croup. After a long and anxious time, she rallies. On the orders of the doctor (later revealed to be in Merlin's pay), the Morgan family takes an extensive vacation in France. Gradually suspicious at the lack of news from home, the Boss returns alone to Dover, Canterbury, and finally London. He finds all electric lights shut off and the entire land languishing under the dark and ignorant church interdict.

Clarence reports to the Boss that Launcelot has split the realm, initially because of a railroad-stock venture which swindled Arthur's nephews Sir Agravaine and Sir Mordred, but also because Arthur finally grew suspicious of Guenever and Launcelot, and trapped them together. The queen was condemned to burn; but Launcelot rescued her, killing Sir Gawaine's brothers Sir Gaheris and Sir Gareth by accident in the process. In the dreadful conflict which followed, the flower of Arthurian knighthood perished, including Arthur, who killed Mordred, would-be usurper of the throne, before he died. Guenever has become a nun at Almesbury.

The Boss realizes that his goal of civilizing sixth-century England is unattainable now. Armed superstition is marching against him. But Clarence, anticipating much of what would follow, has mined and electrified a broad sand belt around Merlin's old cave. Fifty-two loyal lads, seventeen years old or younger, and hence untainted by religious superstition, soon man the dynamos, flood gates, and Gatling guns. While waiting for the battle to begin, the Boss writes his wife Sandy. Soon advancing hordes blanket the horizon. The first wave is destroyed by mines under the sand. Then the Boss pushes the buttons which touch off enormous charges under all of his factories, so that the enemy will not gain control of them. Rank after rank of advancing knights place sword or mailed hand on the deadly wires. Eleven thousand in all are electrocuted. Ten thousand more drown when the Boss's followers release the flood waters. It is a debacle.

In a postscript, loyal Clarence explains that when the Boss went out to tend the wounded, he was stabbed by Sir Meliagraunce, and that Merlin, disguised as an old goodwife, entered their encampment to cook for them, cast a sleep-inducing spell over the injured Boss, cackled in glee, but then leaned back into a fatal wire, and died laughing. Escape for the victors now seems impossible because of a plague caused by the heaps of corpses. Clarence will hide his entranced leader in a secret cave, along with his manuscript account. The sleep of centuries will then follow.

M. T. adds a final P.S.: the first narrator has finished reading the manuscript and, going to the stranger's room at the inn, finds the dazed man muttering in delirium about Sandy, Hello-Central, and a dream that he was of a later century returned to the sixth and then forward again in time. Soon he picks at his coverlet and, with a death rattle in his throat, shouts encouragement to his troops during their fight against the knights.

Sir Aglovale, Sir Agravaine, King Agwisance of Ireland, Annis, Sir Arnold, King Arthur Pendragon, Sir Bagdemagus, Sir Balmoral le Merveilleuse, Barker, Sir Bedivere, Sir Belias le Orgulous, Sir Bleobaris, Miss Angela Bohun, Sir Bors de Ganis, the Boss, Sir Brandiles, Sir Breuse Sance Pité, Sir Brian de les Isles, Brother, Bishop of Canterbury, King Carados of Scotland, Sir Carados, Central, Central, Sir Charolais of Gaul, Chief of the Herald's College, Clarence, Duke of Cornwall, Demoiselle Elaine Courtemains, [Sir Oliver] Cromwell, Sir Dalliance, Sir Damus, Demoiselle Irene Dewlap, Dickson, Sir Dinadan the Humorist,

Sir Dodinas le Savage, Dowley, Mrs. Dowley, Dowley, Sir Driant, Emperor of the East, Egglame, the Sultan of Egypt, Father, Puss Flanagan, King of France, Sir Gaheris, Sir Galahad, Sir Galahault, Sir Galihodin, Sir Galihud, Sir Gareth, Sir Gauter, Sir Gawaine, Sir Gillimer, Sir Griflet le Fils de Dieu, Earl Grip, Grummore Grummorsum, Queen Guenever, Hercules, Sir Herminde, Sir Hervis de Revel, Your Highness, Hugo, the Supreme Lord of Inde, Sir Kay the Seneschal, Sir Kay the Stranger, the Giant of the Knotted Bludgeon, King Labor, La Cote Male Taile, My Lady, King of the Lake, the Lady of the Lake, Sir Lambegus, Sir Lamorak de Galis, Sir Launcelot of the Lake, Sir Lionel, King of Little Britain, King Logris, King Lot of Lothian, Sir Lucan de Butlere, Emperor Lucius, Sir Madok de la Montaine, Mal-ease, Maledisant, Phyllis Marco, Marco, Marco, King Marhalt of Ireland, Sir Marhaus, Marinel, King Mark of Cornwall, King Marsil, Sir Meliagraunce, Meliganus, King Meliodas of Liones, Merlin, Sir Mordred, Hello-Central Morgan, Morgan le Fay, King Morganore, Mumble, King Nentres of Garlot, Princess Nerovens de Morganore, Norroy King-at-Arms, King of Northgalis, Sir Ossaise de Surluse, Sir Ozana le Cure Hardy, Sir Palamides the Saracen, King Pellam of Listengese, Sir Pellinore, Sir Percivale de Galis, Sir Perimones, Sir Persant of Inde, Sir Pertipole, Sir Pertipole, Sir Pertipole, Pertipole, Sir Pertolope, Peterson, Sir Priamus, the Knight of the Red Lawns, the King of the Remote Seas, Sir Reynolds, Sir Sagramor le Desirous, Sandy, Sir Segwarides, Smug, Duke of South Marches, Lord High Steward of the Palace, St. Stylite, the Sowdan of Syria, King Tolleme la Feintes, Sir Tor, Sir Turquine, M[ark]. T[wain]., Ulfius, Unknown, King Uriens of Gore, Sir Uwaine, Third Assistant Valet, Webster.

'Consistency,' 1884 (WMT 28).

We are continually warned to be consistent and are criticized when we depart from consistency. If a Jew becomes a Christian, other Jews sorrow over the change. So with Republicans and Democrats who change parties. Yet it is as natural to adopt new opinions as it is to grow physically and intellectually. Why are so-called turn-coats branded as traitors? If one remains consistent, he is often a traitor to himself. Saying that a person has deserted his political party implies that the party is like an army. But armies are composed of persons who are conscripted or who volunteer and pledge their loyalty. Members of political parties are neither forced to join nor obliged to pledge eternal loyalty. We praise our so-called freedoms—of conscience, opinion, speech, and action—and yet ridicule the turncoat. We are thus demanding that party members submit to servitude. When [James G.] Blaine was nominated for the Presidency, many of his former critics, whose opinions had been partly formed by adverse articles about him in the newspapers, irrationally reversed their opinions and so did those newspapers—all in the name of party loyalty. This is foolish consistency. Finally, we should remember that only the Mugwumps of this world have been its progressive reformers. They include Washington, Garrison, Galileo, Luther, and Christ. To be consistent is often to be fossilized.

[James G.] Blaine, Mulligan.

Contract with Mrs. T. K. Beecher, July 2, 1895 (P).

Twain says that if she is right and he is wrong, he will acknowledge the fact in frank language to her dear face a million years from now. But if he is right, he will be sorry, because there will be no trace of either of them.

Mrs. T[homas]. K. Beecher.

"Conversation, As It Was at the Social Fireside, in the Times of the Tudors." See "1601: Conversation, As It Was at the Social Fireside, in the Times of the Tudors."

"Conversation, As It Was by the Social Fireside." See "1601: Conversation, As It Was at the Social Fireside, in the Times of the Tudors."

"Cooper's Prose Style." See "Fenimore Cooper's Further Literary Offenses."

'Copyright,' 1906 (WMT 28).

Twain urges the Congressional copyright committee to support the bill proposing the extension of copyright life of a book to fifty years past the death of its author. Lawmakers speak with pride of our national literature and then discourage it. Why not extend copyright life to perpetuity? Real estate has no limit. When a book is no longer protected by copyright, any publisher can issue it, keep all the profits, and thus deprive the author's widow and children of their bread. Only one family per year in this country reaches a total of twenty-two children. Congress does not pass a law limiting families to twenty-two offspring. Only one author per year produces a book which can outlive the present forty-two-year limit. Why pass a law robbing that unusual author's survivors? Books contain ideas, and good ideas result in profit; so why not protect the originator? At his stage of life, Twain speaks mainly to protect others. Thus he is like the drunken sailor who, staggering home to an apparently weaving house, prayed for the safety of sailors out at sea on such a rough night.

[Clara Clemens], [Jean Clemens], Dr. [Edward Everett] Hale.

"Corn-Pone Opinions," 1923 (WMT 29).

Fifty years ago, when he was fifteen years old, Mark Twain was friendly with Jerry, an impudent, satirical young Negro slave who preached sermons from the top of a woodpile. In one of his sermons he argued that the source of one's corn pone is the source of his opinions, because people are not independent and therefore cannot afford views interfering with their sustenance. Twain now agrees in the main but feels, unlike Jerry, that one arrives at his beliefs less by calculation and intention than by an instinct to conform. Consider fashions in dress, wines, manners, art, and politics. In general, self-approval results from the approval of others.

Jerry, Jones, Smith.

"Correspondence," 1854.*

Signing himself W., Twain writes from Philadelphia to describe the cold weather of December, 1853, and then a recent fire, in which a fireman was injured and a policeman killed. Twain goes on about the markets, Germantown and its historic buildings, and then similar old houses in Philadelphia redolent of the past but falling into decay.

*In *Mark Twain's Letters in the Muscatine Journal,* ed. Edgar M. Branch (Chicago: The Mark Twain Association of America, 1942).

"Correspondence of the 'Journal,' " February, 1855.*

The author reports from St. Louis in mid-February that sales of valentines are brisk. When he sees a half-starved widow and her five needy children, on their way from Arkansas to Illinois, he is reminded that charity should begin at home and not with ignorant heathens half a world away. Then he discusses the passage of the first train from Washington through St. Louis on its way to the Pacific, some new newspapers, a fire in a livery stable, the ineptness of policemen, a production of *The Merchant of Venice,* and a course of Y.M.C.A. lectures.

Rev. Dr. Cox, "Jessica," the Sheriff, T. Turner.

*In *Mark Twain's Letters in the Muscatine Journal,* 1942.

"Correspondence of the 'Journal,' " March, 1855.*

The author reports from St. Louis in March that the weather is better, with no ice on the river. A drunken bookkeeper named James Reilly got into an argument with a German, shot him—not fatally—tried to escape, but was arrested. The O'Blennis murder case will be concluded soon. Many think that O'Blennis is guilty, but few expect him to be hanged. The author then reports on sickness in the city, theater news, the criminal-court docket, market quotations, and other news.

Hyde, Jackson, Jameison, O'Blennis, James Reilly, Sol Smith, Ward.

*In *Mark Twain's Letters in the Muscatine Journal,* 1942.

"The Countess Massiglia (Reality)" (MTP).

She is an odious and curious person, of humble Philadelphia birth, suspected of attracting shallow men from the start, and now conceited, industrious, and capable. She is comely but hard. She married and divorced in Philadelphia, then married again here, this time to Count Ribaudi-Massiglia, an Italian diplomat who took her to Turin, where she failed in society, and then to Florence, where she bought the Villa di Quarto for $29,500, started raising horses, and waved her husband off to a mission in the Orient. She evicted her peasants and replaced them with strange ones, in an act of unparalleled inconsideration. The Countess soon earned a reputation for meanness. Twain entered her life when through a lawyer he rented her villa for a year, starting late in 1903.

The Clemenses arrive in November from America, with Mrs. Clemens an invalid and in discomfort; but they are denied admittance, legally, because by the terms of the lease the renter must sign an inventory before taking possession. Then Mrs. Clemens is denied use of the best bedchamber because, according to the lease, an ailing person cannot enter such a room. The Countess makes trouble to gain time to remove the best furniture, all pre-inventoried, to an over-the-stable apartment for herself and her robust, handsome male "servant," who escorts her to the opera and is in reality her Master. Things go well for the Clemenses for a time, though the Countess is meddlesome and pseudo-solicitous. But suddenly she shuts off the water, and Twain must therefore buy water from the outside. A health problem persists, and Mrs. Clemens gets tonsilitis in December. Twain tries unsuccessfully to locate another villa, but in any event his wife could not be moved. The Countess gives oral permission for Twain to install a telephone but then nullifies her kindness when she says that permission must be in writing. She locks Mrs. Clemens's local doctors out. Twain threatens to sue the phone company and thus gets his instrument working again. The Countess must dream of skinning an innocent abroad.

> Dr. Grocco, Countess Massiglia, the Master, Dr. Nesti, Count Ribaudi-Massiglia, the King of Wurtenberg.

"The Countess Massiglia (Romance)" (MTP).

She is known in Florence, and is respected there for her benevolence. She is young, beautiful, intelligent, and brilliant in conversation. Since she is an American, from Philadelphia, she chooses not to occupy her vast Villa di Quarto and thus be pretentious and showy, but instead lives in her modest villino. Her title has not gone to her head.

Countess Massiglia.

"A Couple of Poems by Twain and Moore," 1875 (WMT 7).

Twain takes "Those Evening Bells" by Thomas Moore, about bells telling of youth and home, no longer heard by the dead, and to be heard by other bards when Moore is gone; and the humorist adapts it to "Those Annual Bills," a lament about goods consumed and now to be paid for, ending with a prediction that other bards will in their turn damn their bills with frantic quills.

"A Couple of Sad Experiences," 1870 (CRG).

When Twain recently announced that he was going to edit an agricultural column, he made his burlesque so broad that no one should have taken him seriously. But he was soon deluged with farming advice. It would seem, therefore, that it is hard to write a burlesque so wild that its purported facts will not be accepted at face value by somebody. Twain must be more careful not to obscure the nub of the travesty, nor to overwhelm the satire with extraneous interest.

'Courage,' 1908 (WMT 28).

In regard to courage, we all have our limits, even heroes, even Nelson. Twain is afraid to speak to an audience so arranged that some of his hearers are behind him. Therefore he will now sit down.

"The Coward's Revenge." See "An Extraordinary Case."

["Criticism of the Bible"] (MTP).

If the world's most intelligent and experienced man wrote a book, it would be full of common sense and credible statements. If God wrote the Bible, it would be also. But parts of the Bible are not. For example, it says both that we should be fruitful and multiply, and that few will pass through the narrow gate of heaven. Why produce children to fuel hell?

"Ye Cuban Patriot: A Calm Inspection of Him," 1869 (LAIFI).
We are all singing the praises of the Cuban patriot. Typically, he denounces his Spanish oppressor, is jailed, turns informer and spy, and watches his testimony cause the hideous execution of his former friends. We are half glad to hear that the authorities have destroyed a patriot, and yet we abuse them for their cruelty. Black slaves revolt and gently massacre innocent whites, in the name of patriotism. In truth, a majority on both sides of this conflict are ignorant, base, costumed bigots. They call their ghastly atrocities warfare. Both sides are so diabolical that our government should be pleased to recognize only their corpses.

Don Aguilar Jesus Maria Jose y John the Baptist, Señor Madre de Dios el Calderon Gewhillikins de Valladolid.

"A Cure for the Blues," 1893 (WMT 24).
Eight or ten years ago, Cable gave Twain a copy of a singular little pamphlet. It is called "The Enemy Conquered; or, Love Triumphant." Let us call its author G. Ragsdale McClintock. The charm of his writing, published by T. H. Pease, New Haven, 1845, lies in its total absence of wisdom, inventiveness, form, style, sane imagery, verisimilitude, credibility, or plot logic. McClintock wrote it in the vain hope that he would gain fame and money. Its eloquence is volcanic; its words, big and rumbling. No sense intrudes. It spews sentiment. It is constantly irrelevant and obscure. It begins with a eulogy to woman. The hero, twenty-two-year-old Major Elfonzo, has wandered long, returns home to see his father, and then starts going to a local school. By a series of surprises we learn that Elfonzo has long been in love with the sixteen-year-old heroine possessed of an incredible name, Ambulinia Valeer. Her father guards her with a crowbar. Elfonzo once lived among the Cherokees, has been in wars, and fiddles. There is a rival, one Leos. Ambulinia listens to the hero's plea, then beseeches her lover to go away, but then hides in an orchestra while he plays in it, and finally elopes with him. After his analysis, Twain prints the entire pamphlet.

[George Washington] Cable, G. Ragsdale McClintock,
T. H. Pease.

"Curing a Cold," 1863 (WMT 7).

The author wishes to write for his readers' instruction and tangible benefit. If he can help even one sufferer, he will feel rewarded, like a Christian who has done a good deed. When he lost in a Virginia City fire his house, happiness, constitution, and trunk, he was upset but only because of the last two losses. He had exerted himself getting ready to fight the fire but was too slow and thus caught cold unnecessarily. He took the following remedies, as advised by friends: hot bath, cold shower, big meal, starvation diet, quart of warm salt water, decoction of molasses and turpentine and other drugs, gin and then gin and molasses and then gin and molasses and onions, hunting-and-fishing expedition, cold sheet-bath, and finally in San Francisco half a gallon of whiskey a day. The reader with a cold should try this course of treatment, which if it does not cure cannot do more than kill.

Wilson.

"The Curious Book Complete." Not by Twain. See McClintock, G. Ragsdale, Twain's name for Samuel Watson Royston, author of *The Enemy Conquered: or, Love Triumphant*, New Haven, 1845. See also "A Cure for the Blues."

"A Curious Dream," 1870 (WMT 7).

In his dream the narrator is sitting on a doorstep in no particular city one balmy midnight, when a tall skeleton clacks by in a flapping shroud and with a worm-eaten coffin on its shoulder. Another walks past carrying an old headboard. Then comes a third, dragging a shabby coffin by a string and bending under a gravestone, which he asks the narrator to ease to the ground for him. The name on the stone is John Baxter Copmanhurst, and his death date is May, 1839. He explains that his pride has been hurt by the delapidated condition of the cemetery from which he and all of his friends are now emigrating. The burial plot was once in the flowery, breezy woods. But the descendants of the dead, though living comfortably on their inheritances, have allowed it to grow mouldy. The dead must even resort to filching shrouds from neighboring graveyards. They have decided to hoof it to New Jersey, if necessary, to find more respectable quarters, even though it is hard for some of the shades to recognize landmarks by which to travel. The narrator suggests to one shrouded wanderer that he would publish their distress but for the possible embarrassment it might cause their living relatives. The stately remnant assures the narrator that no community which tolerates neglect of its cemeteries would be sensitive enough to take offense. At this moment, a cock crows and the narrator awakens.

Bledsoe, Burling, John Baxter Copmanhurst, Barstow Dalhousie, Meredith Higgins, Anna Matilda Hotchkiss, Jarvis, Columbus Jones, Smith, Smithers.

"A Curious Experience," 1881 (WMT 15)

This is the story which the Major told the author. The time is the winter of 1862-1863. The place is Fort Trumbull, at New London, Connecticut. The Major is commandant, and garrison life is anything but dull, because it is wartime and also because recruits frequently disappear into the night. One day a lad about fourteen or fifteen years old enters, identifies himself as Robert Wicklow, and asks to enlist. He explains sadly that he and his father and aunt lived on a plantation near Baton Rouge. His father was a Union sympathizer, and so they were driven off when the war started. The aunt soon died. The father was caught and hanged. The boy made his way to an uncle, and the two went to New York. When the uncle deserted and went to Boston, young Wicklow followed and soon found himself at New London. The Major takes pity on the sensitive lad and enrolls him as a drummer. He soon arouses the suspicions of Sergeant John Rayburn, who notices that he is perpetually scribbling notes. With the aid of an officer named Webb and a clerk named Sterne, the Major collects some damning evidence: Wicklow has written cryptic messages about garrison armament, confederates on the post, and certain instructions from "the Master." Telegraphing the War Department for authority, the Major declares martial law in town, and arrests, interrogates, and even tortures Wicklow. The boy denies everything at first, then says that the messages are forgeries, but finally admits much though not all. The Major detains certain persons implicated by Wicklow, ineffectively raids a certain suspected room in the local hotel, and suddenly notices that the boy has eluded the men. Two soldiers find his trail and follow him to the home, twenty miles from the fort, of his frantic old parents. The boy wandered off, entered the post, made up his entire story, and enacted the role of spy for fun. Later the Major checks the author's written account of the experience and pronounces it substantially correct but for certain minor military details.

B. B., George Bristow, the Colonel, Congressman, Hyde, the Major, the Master, Sergeant John Rayburn, Sterne, W.W., the Secretary of War, General James Watson Webb, Webb, Robert Wicklow, Wicklow.

["Curious Legislation and Vinnie Ream"]. See W 1868.

"A Curious Pleasure Excursion," 1874 (WMT 7).

The editor of the New York *Herald* deems the following advertisement worthy of insertion in the reading columns. Mark Twain serves notice to the public that he and his partner Mr. Barnum have leased a comet from Mr. Coggia for a term of years and propose to fit it for interplanetary and interstellar travel. There will be a million staterooms, and also theaters, libraries, and a big driving park aboard. The comet will leave New York on the 20th inst. No dogs allowed. Mr. Hale of Maine is in charge of the postal service aboard. They anticipate no planetary hostility but will travel well armed and will promptly resent any insult. Missionaries will be aboard, and education will be compulsory. The comet will visit Mars, Mercury, Jupiter, Venus, and then Saturn. Not the Dog Star. The Great Bear, yes; and also the sun, moon, and Milky Way. They will seldom go more than 100,000,000 miles without stopping. First-class fare will be two dollars per 50,000,000 miles. They hope to get 40,000,000 miles daily out of this comet, which is unlike your regular old uninspected, ramshackle affair in the skies. Return to New York is scheduled for December 14, 1991. Passengers paying double fare will be entitled to share in any stellar and other discoveries made. Patent-medicine people and cremationists may wish to come along and do business. Since Mark Twain will be busy until departure time, he requests that for further particulars interested parties should apply not to him but to Barnum.

Barnum, General Butler, Coggia, Editor, Hale, Richardson, Shepherd, Mark Twain.

"Curious Relic for Sale," 1870 (CRG).

A recent *Herald* advertisement offered for sale by Daniel S. of William Street in New York an ancient Bedouin pipe procured in the city of Endor in Palestine and believed to have once been owned by the Witch of Endor. When he read the notice, Twain instantly saw before his mind's eye a scene just past Endor in the Holy Land, September, 1867. He and his mounted fellow travelers were pursued by ragged Arabs begging for bucksheesh. Suddenly a sickly-looking young beggar approached; but instead of giving him money, Twain bought his long, coarse pipe, which was so rank that it withered a nearby cactus. In English Twain asked if it were the Witch of Endor's pipe, and the youth answered yes in Arabic. For a while Twain rode along in the rear smoking the obscenity, but on the plain of Sharon he went to the head of the mule train with their Arab leader and wafted smoke behind him, to the detriment of the others, who fancied that the Arab leader was dying. The suffering group would have killed the Arab if they could have passed Twain on the way to him. Finally Twain furtively put out the evil pipe, and the whole group drank some water and made camp. Now Twain recalls that he gave that pipe to Dan for a keepsake and surely not to sell.

Birch, Church, Davis, Denny, Jack, Moult, Daniel S., the Witch of Endor.

"The Curious Republic of Gondour," 1875 (CRG).

As soon as the narrator learned their language, he became interested in the people of Gondour. That nation had tried universal suffrage but soon found that such a system delivered all power into the hands of ignorant non-tax-paying classes. They decided not to disenfranchise the stupid and unpropertied but to enlarge the suffrage by granting extra votes for education and wealth. Thus, a person with a high-school degree had four votes; one with

a university education, nine; and for each $50,000 a person added
to his property, he had one more vote. Gambling and speculation
almost ceased. People were honored and bowed to in accordance
with their voting power. Young people grew more ambitious to
become educated and financially successful. Political advancement
depended upon competitive examinations. Ignorance and incompetence lost their customary places in government. Official salaries
were high; so politicians were no longer tempted to steal. Judges
were appointed permanently during good behavior. The Grand
Caliph was elected for a twenty-year term, subject to impeachment
for misconduct. On two occasions women ably served as caliph.
Schools and colleges flourished. Everyone in Gondour was proud
of his country; and its national anthem dinned into the narrator's
ears so constantly that he was glad at last to return home, where
one never hears that kind of music.

The Grand Caliph.

"The Curse of McAllister" (MTP).
    McAllister seeks to emulate European aristocracy by creating an
imitation aristocracy of Four Hundred American families and is
cursed unprintably for his pains.

Four Hundred, [Samuel Ward] McAllister.

Cushion First, 1912 (P).
    When everything is dark and hopeless, and you haven't a shot in
sight, don't despair. Instead, step up, close your eyes, and take the
cushion first.

"The Czar's Soliloquy," 1905 (LAIFI).
    The Czar of Russia has just emerged from his morning bath and
meditates before dressing, as is his wont. The mirror shows him a
skinny libel on God's image, with a melon face, a dished chest, and
bony feet. Only his clothes and title, which are both artificial, render him impressive. Why should the meek Russian people for centuries allow the Romanoffs to rob, insult, torture, and kill them?
Such people are mere horses, with clothes and religion. It is curious

that moralists say royalty should not be killed, the Czar muses. Yet the Romanoffs are a family of cobras over a nation of 140,000,000 rabbits. The royal family are above the law, are hence outlaws, and should be shot. But the moralist protects them, saying that nothing good is ever achieved by violence. In truth, only violence achieves politically valuable ends. But then the Czar recalls that he violently destroyed the Constitution of Finland, had Bobrikov and Pleve assassinated, and massacred some innocent petitioners the other day. All of this has agitated the people. The ultimate result might be the establishment of popular patriotism and loyalty to the nation rather than to any royal family. Uneasily, the Czar then reads some clippings about his flogging innocent women, torturing prisoners, and holding up a religious ikon to bless the troops. It is grotesque that the vegetable he sees in his mirror is regarded as a deity but in reality is a devil. He must quickly put on his restorative clothes, to command the respect of his world, which is fading.

[Nikolai Ivanovich] Bobrikoff [Bobrikov], [Vyacheslav Konstantinovich] Plehve [Pleve], Romanoff, the Czar [of Russia].

'Daly Theatre,' 1887 (WMT 28).
Twain explains that he had an appointment to meet Daly by simply taking the train from Hartford to New York and entering the theater from Sixth Avenue. Twain was bored on the train and, beginning to read the newspapers, saw an advertisement of a dog show coming to New Haven with a St. Bernard weighing 145 pounds. Twain got to the theater and saw a huge St. Bernard in a back room and then a rough, fierce man at a door beyond it. He gruffly told Twain that he could not see busy Mr. Daly but then asked him what he wanted. In desperation, Twain said that he wanted to talk business about a New Haven dog show. The man beamed, mentioned his big dog, and ushered Twain into Daly's presence.

[Augustin] Daly.

["The Damned Human Race"] (LFE). See "Was the World Made for Man?", "In the Animals' Court," ["Zola's 'La Terre' "], ["The Intelligence of God"], and ["The Lowest Animal"].

"Dan Murphy" (CRG). See "The Widow's Protest."

"The Dandy Frightening the Squatter," 1852.*
The time is about thirteen years ago; the scene, Hannibal on the Mississippi. Hoping to impress them, a dandy announces to his fellow passengers aboard a steamboat that when they land he will frighten a brawny young woodsman on the river bank. The dandy then steps forward, armed with knife and pistols, and tells the fellow to say his prayers before getting drilled. The squatter calmly knocks the dandy into the water, and the young lady witnesses award the arms to the victor.

*In *Selected Shorter Writings of Mark Twain,* ed. Walter Blair (Boston: Houghton Mifflin, 1962).

"The Danger of Lying in Bed," 1871 (WMT 24).
When the man in the railroad ticket office asks whether the author wishes to buy an accident-insurance ticket, the reply is in the negative. The author has been figuring. In the last three years, he has traveled about sixty thousand miles, mostly by rail, without mishap. He often bought insurance but never could cash in. He concludes that the danger lies in staying home. American railroads move about two million passengers daily and yet kill only about three hundred annually. On the other hand, of the million Americans who die each year more than 987,000 die in bed. Beds are deadly. So the author's advice is not to stay home much, and when you must, to buy insurance and sit up all night.

"Daniel in the Lion's Den—and Out Again All Right," 1864 (SS).
The narrator confesses that he is not particular about his company and has in fact been associating lately with brokers. Really, though, they probably can be saved. Miracles do occur. San Francisco's Board of Brokers' hall is nicknamed the Den of the Forty Thieves and when in session is ruled over by the President, who bangs his gavel and shouts transactions in a lingo which is very hard to comprehend. The narrator goes one day with his own broker, who translates even while conducting business himself. At the consummation of every transaction, brokers untilt their chairs and pencil their notes furiously. Bulls and bears vie with one another. The narrator is running so short of foolscap, even though

he has reported only half what he might, that he quickly closes with the observation that in spite of the non-villainous appearance of brokers St. Peter would probably admit very few.

Ackerman, Adams, Atchison, Babcock, Badger, Bear, Billson, Bladders, Blitzen, Blivens, Bocock, Broker, William Brown, Bulger, Bull, Buncombe, Caxton, Chollar, Clutterback, Cobbler, Crowder, [Sam] Curry, Daney, Dashaway, Dilson, Dodson, Dummy, Gould, Guttersnipe, Hale, Higgins, Hogwash, Jiggers, John Jones, Norcross, St. Peter, Potosi, the President of the Board of Brokers, Uncle Sam, Savage, Simpson, Sladdery, Slushbuster, John Smith, Smithers, Snodgrass, Swiggins, Thief, Jonas White.

"A Daring Attempt at a Solution of It," 1870 (CG).

The Fenian invasion of Canada failed because it was not led by George Francis Train, a man of organizing ability, courage, and lunacy. But he sent a wild telegram from Chicago offering encouragement and money. Twain suggests that Train be marooned on some prominence, since he needs so much wind to keep going that his position would probably always be the center of a safe calm.

The Downtrodden People, George Francis Train.

"A Day at Niagara." See FW, 1869, and "Niagara."

'The Day We Celebrate,' 1899 (WMT 28).

Twain wonders why the audience applauded when Ambassador Choate said that one can be American or English but not both at once. Twain came here to the Fourth of July dinner in London to see that justice is done to the holiday, which has its commercial side. Yesterday an English Church dignitary took Twain's hat by mistake and lied all afternoon under its influence. Because of fireworks casualties, the Fourth is encouraged by surgeons, undertakers, and insurance companies. Twain closes by thanking other guests for referring to war matters, because that gives him a chance to mention that he was a Confederate soldier for two weeks.

Ambassador [Joseph Hodges] Choate.

"A Day's Work." From *The Adventures of Tom Sawyer*.

"De Coy's Moral Tonic." See FW, 1870.

"Deacon B. Criticizes 'The New Pilgrim's Progress.' " See FW, 1870.

"The Death Disk," 1901 (WMT 23).

In Oliver Cromwell's time, Colonel Mayfair, a young but sea-soned veteran, is home briefly, and in deep trouble. As the winter evening falls, he and his wife are talking. Their seven-year-old daughter Abby enters to say goodnight but first to ask for a story, preferably a scary one. So her father says that once upon a time three colonels got into trouble by exceeding their orders, and in-stead of feigning an attack to give Commonwealth forces a chance to retreat, turned feint into fact, carried the position and brought victory. General Cromwell praised their bravery but ordered them to London for trial. This very day, Colonel Mayfair concludes, the three colonels have been condemned to death for disobedience. Offered the chance to cast lots so that one would be shot for all, as an example, they refused. They are visiting their families for the last time. Abby's eyes dance in delight at the shivery story, but then some soldiers enter and march her father to the Tower. The next morning Mrs. Mayfair grows sick, and Abby goes out to play in the street and then, still not understanding, decides to go to the Tower to fetch her father home. A little later, when Crom-well is told that each man refuses to cast lots, arguing that such an act would really be a form of suicide, he sends for the nearest child in the street to have him take three disks, two white and one red— for death—and place one in the cupped hand, held behind him, of each of the three prisoners. It happens that Abby is ushered in, snuggles up to the grim Protector, and asks for a kiss, which he gives in memory of his daughter. He tells Abby that when his daughter commanded he obeyed and that he must therefore now do what Abby commands. Soon she places a disk in each hand, the red one in her unseeing father's hand, because the red one is the prettiest. The doomed man turns, sees his daughter, and embraces her fervently. The guards weep and begin to take Colonel May-fair away. Suddenly Abby darts out, returns with Cromwell, and tells him everything. He can do nothing, until she reminds him of his promise to do as she commands. Seeing it all as God's will, Cromwell obeys by freeing the prisoner.

The Colonel, General Oliver Cromwell, Miss Cromwell, Abby Mayfair, Colonel Mayfair, Mrs. Mayfair.

["Death of a Princess"]. See LSI.

"The Death of Jean," 1911 (WMT 26).

On December 24, 1909, Twain records that his daughter Jean, an epileptic, has just died. Their servant Katy reported the calamity without warning. Just last night the girl and Twain walked happily hand in hand in their home. Thirteen years ago Twain and his wife Livy were stabbed with the news that another daughter, Susy, had died. Now Twain must send word to their one surviving daughter, Clara, in Berlin with her sick husband. Livy died five years ago, in Florence. Others close to Twain have recently died. The house is full of Christmas preparations. Livy used to wear herself out preparing for Christmas, and Jean more recently did so as well. She was so full of energy that she frequently overtaxed herself. She rode horses, superintended their Connecticut farm, played billiards, and acted as her father's secretary. Twain would not recall her to life, if he had the magic power. Life's most precious gift is death. He remembers family life in their Hartford home. Jean's German dog prowls the house in mute misery now. Jean had a kind heart, loved all animals and birds, replied to all mail, and spoke Italian and French and German well. Telegrams of sympathy pour in. On Christmas Day Twain records that he looked again upon the face of his dead child. In death it resembled Livy's, long ago in Italy. He also looked into Jean's closet and found a big globe, her undelivered Christmas gift to him. On Christmas night Twain records that others have taken Jean's corpse away, and it has begun to snow. Jean loved the snow. On December 26 Twain records that it continued to snow and then stormed. In the afternoon the funeral was taking place far from him, in Elmira, New York. In his mind's eye he could picture the scene. At last Twain says that he and Jean were a blessed little family upon his recent return from Bermuda, but for only two days. May God rest her spirit.

[Clara Clemens], Jean [Clemens], Langdon [Clemens], Livy [Olivia Clemens], Susy [Susan Clemens], [Ossip Gabrilowitsch], George, [Richard Watson] Gilder, Jervis, [William M.] Laffan, Katy [Leary], [Albert Bigelow] Paine, George Robinson, [Henry Huttleston] Rogers, Charles Dudley Warner.

"Death—Robbery," 1863 (MTWY).

Twain reports from Carson that Charles Potter, a Constitutional Convention member, has died, that a teamster was murdered and robbed between Carson and Virginia, and that the police plan to investigate the case next week.

Hon. Charles S. Potter.

"The Death Wafer" (play) (MTP).

Minnie gives her father the Colonel the red paper, when Cromwell asks her to distribute one red and two white pieces. Her father is thus condemned to execution. The Colonel's wife enters and falls upon his corpse as Minnie is dancing about, happy that she gave her father the bright color.

Captain, Colonel, [Oliver] Cromwell, Major, Mamma, Minnie, Soldier.

"The Death-Wafer" (play) (MTP).

Colonel Mayfair and two fellow officers disobediently turned a feint into a victorious charge, thus incurring General Cromwell's wrath. The Lord Protector orders the men to draw lots, so that one of them may be executed; but they refuse, saying that doing so would be tantamount to the act of committing suicide. So Cromwell asks Abby, Mayfair's lovely little daughter, to give one man a red wafer and his two fortunate comrades white ones. Earlier, Abby so reminded Cromwell of his own daughter that he promised to obey any command of hers. So after she innocently gives her father the red wafer and then learns that it would mean his death, she commands Cromwell to issue a pardon, which he fervently does— to the intense relief of Barbara, her mother.

A Chaplain, the Court Martial, General [Oliver] Cromwell, Abby Mayfair, Mrs. Barbara Mayfair, Colonel Mayfair, Officer, Spokesman.

"A Deception." See "How the Author Was Sold in Newark."

'Dedication Speech,' 1908 (S).
Twain tells the audience at the College of the City of New York that Choate could use some higher education, since he is poor in statistics and mathematics. Twain has failed all his long life to acquire that higher education which gives a person modesty. Further, Ambassador Bryce when he referred to his alma mater Oxford should have mentioned Twain, since he has a degree from there also. He ends by hoping that Oxford will last seven more ages.
Ambassador [James] Bryce, [Joseph Hodges] Choate.

["Defeat of the Impeachment Project"]. See W 1868.

"A Defence of General Funston," 1902 (LAIFI).
Washington was born with a certain disposition, as permanent as a rock, on which training, associations, and circumstances built his moral character. Since he did not create any of this, he is really not entitled to any credit for it. All the same, we worship his memory; and we should, because he is a wonderful influence upon our nation's patriotism. Similarly, General Funston did not create either his own disposition or the outside circumstances working upon it. So it is relatively easy to defend him for his dastardly capture in 1901 of Aguinaldo, the defeated chief of the Filipino insurgents. Funston persuaded a rebel courier to betray his hidden leader, then disguised himself and his soldiers, used forgery and other treachery, and accepted the welcome of Aguinaldo only to shoot several of his guards and capture him. At one point, while approaching Aguinaldo's mountain refuge, Funston and his forces were so close to starvation that they had to ask their unsuspecting enemy for food, which he gave. Such a betrayal of a benefactor should have branded Funston forever. Yet he has been acclaimed an American hero. He is not to blame. His disposition and the

circumstances of his training are responsible. But we must expose him so that he will cease to be a hero to Americans, who ought instead to continue to revere Washington.

[Emilio] Aguinaldo, [Leon Czolgosz], Dare Devil, General [Frederick] Funston, [Ulysses S.] Grant, [Abraham] Lincoln, President [William McKinley], Patriot, President [Theodore Roosevelt], General [Jacob] Smith, Traitor, Major [L. W. T.] Waller, [George] Washington, [Valeriano] Weyler [y Nicolau].

"A Defense of Royalty & Nobility" (MTP).

Americans are warped when they think that monarchy is simply bad. American writers wrongly condemn Europeans for accepting baronies. Do Americans refuse postmasterships? Do we not cringe before millionaires? People wipe their feet on inferiors, who enjoy it. The whole situation makes the nobleman content with his position. People revere aristocrats. Witness the Four Hundred, a circle which is impregnable to virtue, fame, money, intelligence, and political pressures, and in which only Dutch backgrounds count . . .

The Derelict, c. 1935 (P).

The dying derelict mutters that he was once a proud, towering ship whose thunder presaged heroic acts. But then his freight included soap and hay. Then he carried swine, as both cargo and crew. Now he awaits a watery death.

Admiral, Almshouse Attendant.

"The Dervish and the Offensive Stranger," 1923 (WMT 29).

When the Dervish begins to talk about good deeds, the Offensive Stranger interrupts to explain that there is no such thing but that instead there are good and evil impulses, and further that good intentions can have evil results, just as evil intentions can have good results. The Dervish sputters briefly, but the Offensive Stranger silences him and then explains that the white man's useful river dam causes Indian lands to turn arid and fruitless. Also Columbus's good discovery of America caused emigrants to rob the aborigines, the French Revolution killed millions but brought liberty to later generations, we have freed but are now mistreating the Filipinos, and England morally uplifted the Boers but few of them have survived. As for China, thousands of natives have now embraced Christianity but fortunately other millions there have escaped it.

The Dervish, Indian Chief, the Offensive Stranger, the White Chief.

["Dialogue on the Philippines"] (MTP).

In a dialogue between an Old Person and a Young Person, it develops that Y.P. after investigating the facts refused to fight in support of his family against some neighbors when he had concluded that his own family was both wrong and also safe. But he did fight in its support when it was in danger from other neighbors even though it was again wrong. Then O.P. badgers Y.P. into admitting that he has an opinion concerning the Philippine episode even though he has not investigated the facts. And yet O.P. finds it impossible to get Y.P. to see that national honor is no different from family honor and that people of other nations are no different from people in one's neighborhood. Y.P. confesses that he does not keep himself informed about world events through reading newspapers. Still, he feels that one should support one's country, regardless; otherwise one would be a traitor. Finally Y.P. sees O.P.'s drift and admits that a nation is simply an enlarged group of families with different opinions, and that it is not traitorous to hold a minority view. O.P. adds, however, that when a nation is invaded everyone should shoulder his musket in its defense, just as Y.P. defended his family against those powerful neighbors. Meanwhile, though, leading children to pledge blind allegiance to one's flag—right or wrong—is the same as teaching treason.

Jones, Old Person, Smith, Young Person.

"Dick Baker's Cat." In *Roughing It.*

"Did Not Hurt the Mule," 1902.*

Squire Johnson has a concealed grudge against Jim Boggs. One morning, while he is riding his jumpy mule named Jervey to town and he sees Jim, who likes to bet, he recognizes his chance. He tells Jim that Jervey can kick a fly off a man without its hurting him. Willing to wager $5, Jim stands up, points to a fly on his shoulder, and is promptly kicked through the air like a flying bird. He demands his money, but Johnson points out that kicking the fly off did indeed not hurt the mule.

Jim Boggs, Squire Johnson.

*In *Masterpieces of Wit and Humor,* ed. Robert J. Burdette (n.p., 1902).

"Dining with a Cannibal . . ." See FW, 1870.

'Dinner to Hamilton W. Mabie,' 1901 (WMT 28).

Twain compliments Hamilton W. Mabie, the editor of *The Outlook,* for behaving gloriously in his position as chief guest of the banquet. *The Outlook* is frank in delinquencies, outspoken in departures from fact, and vigorous in mistaken criticism of men like Twain. But a man is always better than the editorials he writes, just as a man has more virtues than does his portrait. In private, Mabie is as clean as Twain.

[James W.] Alexander, Hamilton W. Mabie.

'The Dinner to Mr. Choate,' 1901 (WMT 28).

Twain says that America's greatness may be explained by two anecdotes. One concerns Washington and his hatchet, and accounts for our moral greatness. The other, more commercial, concerns Choate. He and a Jewish colleague were skinning a client. When the Jew suggested writing a bill for $500, Choate said that he would handle matters. Next day he did so and soon thereafter gave his colleague $5,000 as half the loot. The Jew said that he was almost persuaded to become a Christian. Important people heard about the event and made Choate a diplomat, and he has been advancing the American cause ever since, on the diplomatic principle of give and take—give one and take ten.

Joseph H[odges]. Choate.

'Dinner to Mr. Jerome,' 1909 (S).

Twain is happy to add his expression of confidence in [New

York District Attorney] Jerome. Choate and Shepard have already praised him. Twain adds his voice and would vote for the man except that Twain now resides in Connecticut, where he is the first farmer to be able to grow two blades of grass where three used to grow.

[Joseph Hodges] Choate, [New York District Attorney] Jerome, Shepard.

'Dinner to Whitelaw Reid,' 1908 (WMT 28).

Twain recalls his overwhelming pleasure at recently visiting Oxford University and being honored there. Then he says that he is glad we are about to restore the motto "In God We Trust" to our coins, now that Pierpont Morgan has stepped in and prevented a national financial crisis. Then Twain rambles about Reid and Choate and John Hay; the three of them and Twain all came from the dregs of society but had talents and the tolerant country used them well. Years ago Twain came to New York, looked in on Horace Greeley of the *Tribune*, was asked what in hell he wanted, and left.

[Joseph Hodges] Choate, Horace Greeley, John Hay, Bishop Lawrence, [J.] Pierpont Morgan, [Whitelaw] Reid.

"Diplomatic Pay and Clothes," 1899 (WMT 23).

The author notes from Vienna, January 5, that the morning news reports two American members of the Peace Commission to have received $100,000 each for six weeks' work in Paris. The author is delighted, because the pay may set a precedent which will help improve the financial plight of American ambassadors and ministers. We have shabbily paid them and have also clothed them in unbecoming black swallow-tails. We have hypocritically tried thus to project an image of Republican simplicity. [Benjamin] Franklin probably started this mock modesty. We inconsistently allow diplomats to appear in military uniforms if they were once generals or admirals. We should now confer such ranks, temporarily, on diplomats who have always been civilians. We should also try to match the fine salaries which the canny, commercially minded British government pays its ambassadors. To do so would enable our representatives abroad to be properly hospitable instead of repaying game and champagne with ham and lemonade at official functions. Experienced salesmen know the value of luxurious entertaining. Fathers know that when their daughters grow up it costs more to house and outfit them. Well, our republic has come of age! The author adds a postscript dated January 10 to the effect that, according to the morning news, he is not to be the new ambassador in Vienna after all. He is not really upset. He will never accept any ambassadorship at an annual salary less than $75,000. Back home, insurance presidents and railway lawyers make almost that sum; abroad, our government is a humbug.

'Disappearance of Literature,' 1900 (WMT 28).

Twain begins with the boast that he has been trying to reform the German language, which inhumanly separates verb parts. Then he says that we need not be alarmed that literature is disappearing. It will be no great loss if certain modern novels do not outlast those of [Sir] Walter Scott. Nobody reads *Paradise Lost,* which is a classic—that is, a book everyone wants to have read but nobody wants to read. As for Scott, one can read *Ivanhoe* happily at the age of eighteen but ought to wait until he is ninety to read some of the rest.

Professor [William P.] Trent, Professor Winchester.

"Discovery of Anesthetics" (MTP).

When Dr. Riggs and Dr. Wells, Hartford dentists, saw Colton's sideshow, which featured laughing gas in 1844, the event was momentous. A colonel named Sam Cooley took a whiff of the gas, began to rant and break furniture, cut his shin, but when he calmed down said that he had felt no pain. Wells had an idea, and he and Riggs discussed it, Wells enthusiastically, Riggs coolly. When Wells suggested gassing a drunk for experimental purposes, Riggs vetoed the idea; so Wells volunteered to gas himself. He administered a dose to himself, and Riggs pulled one of his infected teeth—without evidence of pain. When he came to, Wells was thrilled but could not persuade established surgeons to adopt the painkilling method. Then a couple of young doctors, Ellsworth and Marcy by name, tried it. Next, a couple of Hartford *Courant* printers had teeth pulled painlessly after taking gas. But then a Boston doctor named Morton smouched the discovery and claimed the fame it brought, both here and abroad. Wells tried but failed to establish prior claims and later grew freakish and committed suicide. Earlier, Wells journeyed to Boston, talked with a former pupil of his—Morton by name, and a dentist—and through him was allowed to demonstrate his discovery to illustrious Dr. Warren's class in medical school. Wells worked too hastily, however, and the patient claimed that he felt the extraction. Wells was hooted out of town. Later Morton visited Hartford and learned from Wells everything about the gas, returned to Boston, hired a chemist named Dr. Jackson to produce laughing gas for him, and obtained a Massachusetts patent for anesthesia. Massachusetts began to claim credit for the discovery. Jackson forced Morton to go into partnership with him, and the two journeyed to Washington, D.C., to demand $200,000 in back royalties. Congress became involved, with Senator Truman Smith of Connecticut, jealous of Massachusetts, encouraging Wells to testify. When he successfully did so, Morton and Jackson were thereafter unable to get those royalties.

> Colton, Colonel Sam Cooley, Dr. Ellsworth, Havens, Dr. Jackson, Major General—, Dr. Marcy, Dr. Riggs, Dr. Warren, Dr. [Horace] Wells.

"Disgraceful Persecution of a Boy," 1870 (WMT 7).

A San Francisco newspaper reports that a well-dressed boy on his way to Sunday-school was arrested for stoning Chinamen. But wait. What taught the boy to act this way? It was the daily papers, which report that Chinese pay a mining tax but Celts need not, taxes are collected from Chinese, at the mines Chinese robbers are hanged but other kinds of robbers are merely driven out, Chinese are arrested by vigilant city policemen while genuine rascals go uncaptured, Chinese immigrants must pay $10 to be vaccinated at the wharf although city doctors would do the job for fifty cents, and so on. Therefore the well-informed Sunday-school lad felt it a duty to God to persecute Chinamen. Butchers who set their dogs on Chinese laundrymen and knock their teeth out for fun are surely setting examples for the young. How curious it is that Pacific coast police are diligent in arresting boys who assault Chinamen.

> John, Tommy Jones, Patrick, So-and-so, Such-and-such-a-one.

"Dr. Loeb's Incredible Discovery," 1923 (WMT 29).

The New York *Times* reports that scientists are likely to greet skeptically the announcement that Dr. Jacques Loeb of the University of California has created life by a chemical process. The article adds that the consensus of biologists is probably that Loeb has more imagination than accuracy. The author, however, opines that a typical consensus examines new things with feelings rather than mind, and is guided by prejudice. History tells us that whatever new thing a consensus bets against the smart money should bet on. Examples include steam engines, inventions called toys, medical discoveries, and especially pasteurization. The author himself was prejudiced enough to bet against the linotype and cyanide gold-processing. Imitate the disciple Thomas, who did not accept or reject on trust, but examined and determined for himself. Don't be like God's consensus as described in Adam's diary: they sat around for six days doubting that the world could be made out of nothing, then got up and looked out the window at it.

   Adam, Dr. Funk, Dr. Jacques Loeb, Old-Man-Afraid-of-the-Consensus.

'Dr. Mark Twain, Farmeopath,' 1909 (S).

Twain begins by telling his audience of physicians that he used to be a sharpshooter but has recently joined their profession, which is equally deadly. A short time ago his house was robbed, but he was grateful to the burglars since they scared off all his servants. He considers the Children's Theatre and the Post-Graduate Medical School to be the country's two best institutions. He has been practicing his new profession in ever-more thinly populated Connecticut. He works in conjunction with a horse doctor named Jim Ruggles, a sexton, and the Redding undertaker, Bill Ferguson. Twain consulted his farmacopia and is now a farmeopath. Their one big disease up there is race suicide, a rational malady. Twain treated a sailor for his rolling gait and never saw a patient more serene at death. Later Twain's dog treed an African; they operated for appendicitis, found only darkness within, and diagnosed their patient's sickness as infidelity. Twain's paramount rule is to bleed the patient.

   Bill Ferguson, Jim Ruggles.

"Dr. Van Dyke as a Man and as a Fisherman" (MTP).

Twain likes Dr. Van Dyke, even though he is a clergyman and a professor. One day Twain reads an item by Van Dyke in a magazine and clips it out. The next day he happens to meet Van Dyke in front of the Roman Catholic cathedral on Fifth Avenue. Van Dyke argues that people have fine qualities, such as bravery, loyalty, a sense of justice, pity, and generosity. Further, he insists that he knows hundreds of such virtuous people. Twain replies that he knows a good, high-class Christian with none of those virtues; in fact, Twain adds, that same Christian has been cowardly, deceptive, and even murderous toward a child. At this point, Twain hands Van Dyke the clipping from his own writing, asks him to substitute *child* for *fish*, and lets him read his own description of how he caught a brave, fighting, land-locked salmon. Twain concludes by remarking that Van Dyke's specialty is literature, not human nature.

A Cardinal, Dr. [Henry] Van Dyke.

"Does the Race of Man Love a Lord?" 1902 (WMT 24).

A British friend of the author decides to query the old saying that an Englishman dearly loves a lord by adding, "How about the Americans?" It is curious how sayings can gain currency. For example, it is said that Americans adore the almighty dollar and that rich American women buy European titles and husbands. But in truth, everyone loves money and envies those who have it, and all women buy their husbands—with or without titles. Not merely do the English love a lord; everyone does. Why? The author suggests that we envy an important person's power and conspicuousness. Each social group, whether it is all of China with its emperor or only a group of profane sailors, has its potent, conspicuous leader. Each of us likes attention from the person above us in our group. The author remembers yet the surge of pride he felt four years ago when some Viennese police let him through a crowd being kept back from the emperor. He was Herr Mark Twain! How often we have heard someone say that he was close enough to such-and-such a celebrity to touch him. And how frequently we see envy and meanness in the eyes of others when we boast of having stood near greatness. Chambermaids sold loose strands of the Prince of Wales's hair, and lynch ropes go for two dollars an inch. People crane to get their faces into photographs, and resolve to buy the paper next morning. People like titles. Fail to call an ex-governor "Governor" or a senator "Senator" and watch the reaction. Of course everyone loves a lord, that is, the head of any group large or small. We delight in looking upon power and conspicuousness. The author even knows a cat in the Jardin des Plantes that is vain of its friendship with an elephant there.

A Congressman, the Emperor, the ex-Congressman, Prince Henry, His Majesty, His Majesty, His Imperial Majesty, the Queen of Roumania, Sylva.

"A Dog in Church." From *The Adventures of Tom Sawyer.*

"A Dog Story." See FW, 1870.

"Dogberry in Washington," 1870 (authorship uncertain) (CG).

One might think that the Post Office Department decision to let authors' manuscripts through at newspaper rates was made to save writers a little money. But it is not so. Postal authorities have decided that an author's manuscript must be intended for a book, and not for a pamphlet, article, or column. Thus the modest saving per author is rendered most negligible. The Buffalo postmaster told Twain about the interpretation but could cite no written proof. If the officious fellow had been out in California, he would have been derided for such reasoning.

Old Smarty.

"Doggerel," 1871 (CG).

A correspondent from Minnesota has just written Twain to report that he and a friend named S. went up the Missouri to Sioux City. While there, S. contracted to buy a white Eskimo dog from an expected litter to be owned by W. The travelers returned in three months but could not buy the puppy, because, as W. explained, a horse stepped on it. The correspondent adds that while up the river he heard a fellow tell a story about a dog that chased a beaver up a tree. The beaver had to climb because the dog was crowding it.

S., W.

"A Dog's Tale," 1903 (WMT 24).

A Presbyterian dog named Aileen Mavourneen, daughter of a St. Bernard and a collie, is telling the story. Her mother was very wordy and liked to toss around for effect such jaw-breakers as "unintellectual," "synonymous," "supererogation," and "intramural incandescence." But she was kind, gentle, and brave, never held a grudge, and taught Aileen by example as well as words. When the inevitable sad day of farewell forever came, she urged Aileen not to mind being undeserving of man's heaven but to find her own reward in living for the good of others and in being unselfishly brave. Aileen then went to the home of the Grays. Mr. Gray was a tall, handsome, renowned scientist of thirty-eight. His thirty-year-old wife was sweet and lovely. They had a daughter named Sadie, aged ten, and a little baby. Aileen could never understand Gray's complicated laboratory, although she was sure her mother would have been able to. A handsome neighborhood dog was Robin Adair, also a Presbyterian. When Aileen had a cuddly puppy by and by, her happiness was complete. One winter night, while she was asleep beside the baby and its nurse was momentarily out of the room, a spark from the fire set the crib ablaze. Aileen began to scamper for the doorway; but then, thinking of her mother's words about unselfish courage, she returned and at the cost of some burns dragged the baby to the safety of the hall. At that moment, Gray came rushing up and began to strike furiously at Aileen with his cane. But the nurse then appeared and shouted "Fire!", the master rushed to the nursery, and Aileen crawled to the safety of the dark garret, in terrible pain from a crushed foreleg. She hid for days, until Sadie finally found her and brought her back to the grateful and shamed family. Soon Mrs. Gray and the children went on vacation. Gray met in his laboratory with some fellow scientists and lectured to the effect that Aileen's brave, misunderstood act was above instinct, was in fact the result of reason. Next the men discussed optics and whether a certain kind of brain injury would produce blindness. Such talk bored Aileen. But then, for an experiment, they deliberately cut part of the velvety head of Aileen's puppy, which—sure enough—went blind in proof of Gray's theory. Aileen was happy when her puppy died and the footman buried it in the garden, not only because it was asleep and hence out of pain but also because she knew from observation that seeds when planted grew into nice flowers and she hoped that her puppy would come up a handsome dog like Robin

Adair. But she watched at the grave two weeks, and the puppy never came up. Still she would not leave but waited patiently, then fearfully. She grew weaker and weaker, finally could not stand on her three sound feet, but refused all food which the kind servants brought. Then one of them incomprehensibly but chillingly said at twilight of a certain day that the family would come back in the morning and never understand that the brave dog had gone where the beasts go that perish.

Sadie Gray, Gray, Mrs. Gray, Gray, Aileen Mavourneen.

"Don't Let It." See FW, 1869.

["Doré Gallery"] (MTP).

Twain loves the Doré Gallery in London. He goes again and again, most recently with a friend. While they are there standing before Doré's sublimely pathetic picture of Christ about to take up the Cross, an old stranger comes up and urges Twain to buy an engraving of it. Then the old fellow offers an explanation of the whole picture, and even identifies Christ, Judas, and others for Twain, who, however, silences him by saying that he ordered such an engraving a year ago and goes off with his friend to view a smaller painting. The elderly salesman rushes forward to offer an engraving of this one as well. Twain hurries his friend off to another picture, at which point a bearded salesman offers to put them down for engraved copies of what they are now inspecting. Twain and his friend leave the gallery by leaping out the window. Twain falls on a sandwichman advertising the gallery. His dying words are to the effect that an engraving will be made of his demise.

"A Dose of Pain Killer." From *The Adventures of Tom Sawyer.*

"A Double Barrelled Detective Story," 1902 (WMT 23).

In Virginia, in 1880, Jacob Fuller, aged twenty-six, an emigrant from Sedgemoor, has just married a spirited, nineteen-year-old beauty, against her father's wishes. The next morning her sullen husband explains that since her father repeatedly insulted him he intends to be revenged. For three months he heaps miseries upon the uncomplaining young woman; then, when these tactics fail to break her spirit, he ties her to a tree, has his bloodhounds tear her clothes off, and bids her farewell. Farmers release the pregnant woman, and she returns to her dying father's house, which she sells in due time. In 1886 in a New England village we find her again, calling herself Mrs. Stillman and her young son Archy. The boy has the nose of a bloodhound and can follow any track. She tells him that his destiny is to pursue his vile father, who broke her heart. He agrees, and when he is sixteen years old he sets out with unlimited funds, great love for his mother, and determination to hound Jacob Fuller, a quartz-miner in Denver; for the mother has discovered that the miner is her vicious husband. Archy goes to Denver, posts a notice that a certain man in town shamed his wife back east in 1880, details the manner, and offers $10,000 for his whereabouts. Then Archy privately writes Fuller advising him to escape or suffer the consequences. In this manner Archy intends to hunt him from place to place, and make him suffer. To get the man's scent, Archy rooms for a time in the hotel he occupies. Archy follows him out to Silver Gulch, then back to Denver, only to discover that he is guilty Jacob Fuller's innocent younger cousin. The hounded fellow disappears; and Archy, anxious to make amends, follows him to California, Australia, India, Mexico, and back to California. Archy rests up and gets his bearings back at Silver Gulch, then hits the trail again to Hope Canyon, California, and begins to room there with young Sammy Hillyer. Sammy is kind to a kinsman of his, a coarse miner named Flint Buckner, whom kind Sammy says trouble has made misanthropic and aloof.

One crisp morning in October, 1900, while the lilacs form a bridge for wingless creatures in the trees and a solitary esophagus sleeps on motionless wing in the empty sky, the action resumes. Buckner is abusing his sixteen- or seventeen-year-old English apprentice, Fetlock Jones, so badly that other miners want to step in; but Fetlock meekly begs them to leave things as they are. He is secretly nursing a plan to murder Buckner. A couple of days later, the miners are discussing Buckner and Fetlock; they agree that the two are most puzzling, but an even greater mystery is Archy Stillman, whose tracking ability is unearthly. Just as they are marveling over this talent, Mrs. Hogan bursts in and calls for Archy, since her little daughter is missing and only he can search her out. He arrives, sniffs about, and soon leads the excited crowd of miners to Injun Billy's wickieup, where the child is located, brought there for her safety out of the sage brush by the friendly Indian. Next afternoon Fetlock's distinguished uncle arrives in camp. He is Sherlock Holmes, famous detective immortalized in fine literature. Several miners argue that he undoubtedly could have ascertained the Hogan girl's whereabouts without leaving the tavern, merely by consulting clues. In the evening Sherlock and Fetlock take a stroll and then return to the others, whom the extraordinary man treats to drinks. But while the tavern is gay with song, a violent explosion rocks the gorge. The crowd spills out and soon finds Buckner's mangled body, where it was tossed by blasting powder set near the man's leveled cabin. The men call an inquest, decide that Buckner died by his own hand or that of person or persons unknown, and conclude that news of the explosion will raise the price of claims all about. Back at the tavern, Sherlock, who has collected innumerable irrelevant clues, lectures the rapt miners, exonerates his nephew Fetlock—who was with the others at the time of the deadly explosion—and names Sammy Hillyer as the murderer, since his face is scratched—obviously by a piece of flying wood. Sherlock even exhibits a fragment of wood with blood on it. Sammy denies everything, and it is Archy's turn to step into the limelight. That human bloodhound quickly summarizes his findings. Fetlock, knowing that his victim never shared drinks with anyone at the tavern, mined the man's cabin, stepped momentarily away from Uncle Sherlock during their evening walk, lighted a candle which was set to burn down to a fuse in five hours, and soon rejoined both uncle and then crowd. With a sob, Fetlock confesses all and surrenders to the constable.

Next morning Archy and Sammy are burying Buckner when a melancholy stranger comes by. By his smell Archy recognizes the innocent Jacob Fuller, whom he wrongly hounded around the world. Seeing Archy, the old man insanely calls him Sherlock Holmes and then babbles that he himself is innocent. The sentimental miners adopt poor Fuller and comfort him with the lie that Sherlock Holmes was hanged by mistake a week ago in San Bernardino. Fuller tells everyone that he was mistaken in Denver three and a half years ago for his cousin—who had the same name—and was closely pursued. One night voices told him that redoubtable Sherlock Holmes was the one after him; so he redoubled his efforts to flee—to California, Australia, India, and so on. Now here he is, innocent but broken. Next morning rumor has it that, since Sherlock Holmes was responsible for harassing poor Fuller, a mob intends to lynch him. But Sheriff Jack Fairfax is quietly sent for and arrives in the nick of time, just as smiling Sherlock is about to be burned alive. He receives the sheriff's impassioned apology. The mob melts away. News comes that Fetlock has escaped and disappeared. Let his uncle track him! Ten days later Archy writes his mother that innocent Jacob Fuller is feeling better and that, according to Sammy, Flint Buckner, now dead and buried, was guilty Jacob Fuller.

Coward of Rapaho, Daly, Sheriff Jack Fairfax, Wells-Fargo Ferguson, Jacob Fuller, Jacob Fuller, Mrs. Jacob Fuller, Constable Harris, Peter Hawes, Shadbelly Higgins, Sammy Hillyer, Mrs. Hillyer, Hogan, Mrs. Hogan, Miss Hogan, Sherlock Holmes, Injun Billy, Tom Jeffries, Fetlock Jones, Jake Parker, Peterson, Pat Riley, Ham Sandwich, Sandy, Billy Stevens, Archy Stillman, Mrs. Stillman.

["Doughface"], 1969 (HHT).

Deacon Kyle gives the narrator [Huck Finn] a hymnbook for pulling his daughter out of the water. The boy parlays the unwanted item into a bullfrog, then a cat, and finally a hideous false face which he loans to Tom Sawyer, who loans it to Rowena Fuller. That vivacious young lady puts it on for a prank and scares old Miss Wormly. Unfortunately the old spinster goes insane. Miss Rowena's life is spoiled too.

[Huck Finn], Rowena Fuller, Deacon Kyle, Miss Kyle, Tom Sawyer, Miss Wormly.

"Down among the Dead Men." See "Among the Spirits."

"Down the Rhône," 1923 (WMT 29).

August, 1891, and the author plans to go down the Rhône River with a boatman and a courier. On a Saturday he proceeds from Geneva by train to the Castle of Chillon on Lake Bourget near Aix-les-Bains. Peasant girls carry his luggage up a winding road to the castle, where he spends the night. In the morning he looks down through green leaves to the blue lake, shining in the sun. After an outdoor breakfast, he hears a horn blast, which announces the arrival of their roomy, long, shaded flatboat. The boatman is an expert named Joseph Rougier. The narrator nicknames him the Admiral. They are off, past families strolling in their Sunday best and then by bold precipices. The author stops at Chanaz to get some stamps in a miniature store. They eat some fried fish and then clear out again. The current begins to roar. The river widens and grows very deep. They pass little villages, go under suspension bridges, see a couple of ferries and a few fortifications, and glide across reposefully calm waters. There are many statues to the Virgin and several ruined Roman towers. They step ashore at St.-Genix, put up at the hotel, walk in the dark, and are scared by phantoms whirring by on bicycles. In the morning it is raining; so the narrator has a delightful breakfast in bed. By 1:00 P.M. it clears, and they are off again, past loftly highlands, around flat islands, and into L'Eau Morte. The author sees a woman paddling across, and she reminds him of the "Mona Lisa," which in turn reminds him that when he first saw that painting he was indifferent to it, which in turn reminds him of the Flagg brothers, who until they studied art in Paris thought they were artists. By mid-afternoon it is raining again; so they take shelter at a stone inn at Port de Groslee, where rough natives are drinking red wine and guffawing. The travelers have hot fish and coffee in a dripping garden shed. Later in the afternoon they leave, pass quarries, see a fleecy sunset, and step ashore near the Hôtel du Rhône Moine. The author enjoys observing peasant life during the evening and prepares for bed early. He is happy that the landlady has left the family jewelry and a silver watch in his room, since she therefore obviously trusts him. He is reminded of the time he went to Hopkinson Smith's New York apartment to borrow an overcoat from the man's housekeeper because it was getting chilly, and the woman trusted him with it. Later Smith told him that she recognized him by his drawl. Suddenly, back near the Rhône, he is startled by the landlady, who comes into his room, beams, and snatches away both jewelry and watch. On Tuesday, September 22, they breakfast in the open air, and the narrator gets lost walking through some woods toward the shore; so a sturdy old female poacher leads him out and walks with him over a fearful little precipice to the boat. The incident reminds him that some people, including himself, are afraid of heights, whereas others are afraid of dentists, which he is not; he even has a theory that the alleged pain dentists cause is in reality exquisite pleasure. Next, they approach the Falls of the Rhône, and the author gets out and walks to the Villebois bridge to avoid the boiling rapids. Next, the Château de la Salette, then St.-Etienne. Floods of rain. He observes a varied group of women patiently washing clothes in the river during the storm, while a hearty man shelters himself with an umbrella and supervises. Wednesday, it is still pouring. The fields are drenched and lonely looking.

Dr. Horace Bushnell, Noel Flagg, Joseph Rougier, [F.] Hopkinson Smith, Mrs. [F.] Hopkinson Smith.

'The Dress of Civilized Woman,' 1910 (S).

Civilized women are charming partly because of their dress, which can be beautiful and expensive. Their accoutrements come from all over the world. Even their hair does. But try this. Pick up a hairpin from the carpet of a Pullman car, and you will find that no woman present will admit that it is hers.

'Dress Reform and Copyright,' 1908 (S).

Twain explains that he likes to wear light-colored clothes and is no longer afraid of being criticized for doing so. The vivid clothes women wear to the opera are pleasant, but the formal black attire men wear makes them about as inspiring as a flock of crows. Clothes are supposed to enhance the wearer's dignity and comfort. The best-dressed fellow Twain ever saw was a Hawaiian wearing only a pair of spectacles. Plug hats are terribly silly. When Howells wore one yesterday, he looked ashamed of himself. Twain has retired from work, now that he is past the age of seventy, and is merely dictating his long autobiography, which is so caustic and diabolical that it can be published only after he is thoroughly dead. Shyness prevents his naming some of the people exposed in it.

[William Dean] Howells.

"The Drinking and Smoking Habits Cured" (MTP).

Twain wishes to cure people of drinking and smoking. He will charge a fee, because free things are accorded no value. His patients must live with him and follow directions. He will accept no customers who have taken pernicious pledges. He likes to see people slip because doing so gives them strength. Twain's method appeals to the intellect, not the will. Twain likes to chew, smoke, and drink hot scotch punches; but he can do without these habits when he wishes, by using his reason rather than his will. You can learn to stop swearing, fingering your moustache, or teasing animals, simply by killing your desire to do these things. When a desire dies, the habit easily follows. Rid yourself of the desire for drink, at first merely by watching that desire and not letting it gain the upper hand.

A, B.

"Dueling," 1923 (WMT 29).

Dueling is a common pastime in Austria and France; but, whereas it is dangerous and tragic in Austria, it is only monkeyshines in France. In France the adversaries end by hugging and kissing, but in Austria they fight until one man is dead or disabled. The author has kept a scrapbook of Viennese accounts of duels, which involve military men, journalists, students, doctors, lawyers, legislators, cabinet officers, judges, and policemen. Although dueling is forbidden by law, the police intervene only when police duelists are involved. The undertaker is opposed to such interference. One duel concerned an incident at a card game; another was between a prince and a major; another, between a sturdy newspaperman and a feeble opponent, who died; another, between a student and a military officer who thought that the student was staring at him and who therefore challenged and killed the lad. The author laments the needless anguish suffered by the mothers, wives, and children of duelists, whose families are thus the real principals. Think of the torture inflicted upon the mother of a fellow who awakens her at three in the morning to report that he has been insulted and will therefore be dueling in the afternoon. On the other hand, a newspaper account from Paris explains that a certain duel was stopped when one adversary was scratched in the forearm and elbow. In Italy the deadly Austrian form of dueling is still in vogue.

Count Badeni, Cavalotti, Lieutenant Colonel Henry, Colonel Picquart, Senator Ranc, Representative Wolf, X.

[The Duke's Version of Hamlet's Soliloquy] (P). In *Adventures of Huckleberry Finn.*

"Duncan of the *Quaker City*," 1877 (LAIFI).

Twain writes the editor of the *World* to express amused indignation that Duncan, who was degraded from his position as captain of the *Quaker City* and made head waiter as soon as she sailed ten years ago for the Holy Land with the innocents aboard, should be lecturing about passenger Samuel Clemens, and criticizing his drinking, his inability to distinguish tea from coffee, and the like. Twain will not name the man, who—he thinks—hopes for some kind of free publicity. Then, a couple of days later, Twain adds a postscript to the effect that he has just learned that three years ago Duncan mishandled Shipowners' Association fees and also cheated the Seamen's Association, of which he was president. Twain closes by branding the man as hypocritical, cowardly, and dishonorable.

Bunsley, [Charles C.] Duncan, Edward H. House, Leary.

"Duncan Once More," 1877 (LAIFI).

Twain writes the editor of the *World* again, to complain further against Charles C. Duncan, the Shipping Commissioner, who under "An Act for the Further Protection of Seamen" has been systematically robbing sailors and the federal government. A firm of New York lawyers has examined the act and reported as follows. Sailors' grievances have been transferred from equity to law courts, at higher expense; the act takes some of their rights away and gives them no new rights; shipping and discharging of sailors now cost fees, to be paid by the sailors; deputies of the Commissioner act for him in valid and binding ways; sailors can no longer be given credit; they can be shanghaied without legal redress; and they are encouraged to desert and thus forfeit their pay. The whole act has sixty sections to protect the Commissioner but none to protect the sailor. It creates unnecessary federal jobs for hirelings of the Commissioner, who has pocketed $160,000 in four years while hypocritically mouthing Sunday-school pieties. Such is Duncan.

Charles C. Duncan, Jack, Kidnapper, [Henry Wadsworth] Longfellow, Morris, Officer, Wilder.

"The Dutch Nick Massacre." See "The Latest Sensation."

"Early Rising as Regards Excursions to the Cliff House," 1864
(MTWY).
   Twain quotes Benjamin Franklin on early to bed and early to
rise making a person healthy, wealthy, and wise. Then he quotes
George Washington, who said he disagreed. Twain has tried getting up early and getting up late, and only the latter suits him.
Why should the bird be early to catch the worm, if it does not
want any worms? Well, Twain and his friend Harry arise before
dawn one morning, in order to have the road to the Cliff House
unencumbered with traffic and free of dust, to see the glorious
sunrise, to smell the dewy flowers, and to have a vision of white
sails out at sea. They hitch up a horse, whose harness soon breaks.
Harry fixes it while Twain shivers under a smelly horse blanket.
The wind is numbing and soon bears a three-cornered stone into
Twain's eye. The road is bumpy. They observe some sportive seals
on the rocks but no sails anywhere. The beach is lonely. At the
Ocean House they feel like human icicles until a glum waiter
brings them some hot coffee. Then everything brightens. Twain
and Harry have cigars and drive into town. The horse kicks, and
the axle breaks; but these are minor accidents, the unimportant
consequences of their having gotten up before dawn, like fools.
In the future, Twain wants no bracing atmosphere, no perfumy
flowers, dust rather than gravel for his eyes, lots of traffic to share
the road bumps, and no morning-glory sunshine so that when he
fails to see it he will not be disappointed. He is neither healthier
nor wealthier for his trip but is now wise enough not to repeat
the experiment. He does recommend the Cliff House after dawn.
   Harry, the Unreliable.

The Earth Invoketh the Sun (to Livy, November 27, 1892), 1960 (P).
   You are my rich source, my warm ray, my dear light.

"Earthquake Almanac" (WG). See "A Page from a California Almanac."

"The Echo That Didn't Answer." See "The Canvasser's Tale."

"The Eclipse." See FW, 1869.

"The Editorial Office Bore" (CG). See "The Office Bore."

'Edmund Burke on Croker and Tammany,' 1901 (S).

Addressing a political group interested in breaking up Tammany rule, Twain explains that when the great British orator Edmund Burke inveighed against Warren Hastings, corrupt and autocratic governor of the East India Company, with headquarters in Calcutta, he was saying things which could be applied exactly to Richard Croker, Tammany boss in New York City. Later Twain remarks that since Tammany is dead there is no use in vilifying him. Twain also recalled that a dying man was once advised by a clergyman to consider heaven for its climate but hell for its society.

Edmund Burke, the Calcutta Great Council, [Robert] Clive, the Court of Directors, Richard Croker, Warren Hastings.

'Educating Theatre-Goers,' 1907 (WMT 28).

Twain begins by thanking the children of the Educational Alliance for its pleasant performance of *The Prince and the Pauper,* recalls his family's production of it twenty-two years ago—he played Miles Hendon—and explains that his not knowing earlier about the Alliance is a little like a Buffalo resident being unaware of nearby Niagara Falls. He praises the theatrical group for furnishing decent plays and says that the city would be a better place with forty more such establishments.

[Clara Clemens], [Jean Clemens], [Olivia Langdon Clemens], [Susan Clemens], [Patrick McAleer].

'Education and Citizenship,' 1908 (WMT 28).

Twain suggests that the College of the City of New York ought to establish a chair for a professor to teach good citizenship. Plenty of bad citizenship is taught in colleges today, including a type of citizenship called patriotism, which is taught by loud scoundrels. Our coins say we trust in God; and leaving out gamblers, burglars, and plumbers, perhaps we do put some trust in God. But we should not leap to conclusions. Consider the story told Twain by Bram Stoker, about the eloquent little clergyman who at a christening foretold a great future for the potato-like little baby in his arms. Perhaps he would become a fine poet or famous warrior. Then the preacher asked the father the name of his little son. "Mary Ann" was the answer.

Mary Ann, Bram Stoker.

'The Educational Theatre,' 1907, 1908 (WMT 28).

Twain thanks the officials of the Children's Theatre for asking him to invite many important people of New York to come and watch a performance. He is glad that children are turning their backs on Bowery theaters to come here instead for purer entertainment. He offers to tell his guests about Miss Herts, who conceived the idea of a theatrical group for children. Some months later Twain addresses another audience at the same theater, explaining that he is happy to be its honorary president and hence be merely ornamental. He is much moved that children should sacrifice candy money to buy tickets and cheer for the villain to get his bullet.

Miss Herts, Sally.

"Edward Mills and George Benton: A Tale," 1880 (WMT 24).

While still babies, Edward Mills and George Benton, who are distantly related—perhaps seventh cousins—are adopted by the childless Brants. They tell the infants that if they are honest and industrious they will be successful and will never lack friends. Edward is a good child, but George cries and thus gets his way. Edward is a source of comfort to the Brants; but George is disobedient, tells lies, and has to be bribed to behave. When the two are old enough to work, Edward quickly advances through apprenticeship to partnership with his master; but George runs away from his master, steals, and causes the Brants great inconvenience. Edward interests himself in church work, charities, and other uplifting movements. George takes to drink. When the Brants die, their will requires Edward to buy out his partner and take George into the firm as a new partner. Then George becomes a real tippler and even marries Edward's fiancée, who wants to reform George. Edward marries elsewhere and prospers until George develops a fondness for gambling, borrows on the firm's credit, and loses everything. Edward becomes a hod carrier, is suspended from the various charitable organizations to which he has belonged, but later becomes a trusted bank cashier. Meanwhile George temporarily reforms, is coddled by temperance and other societies, falls again, and is rescued and coddled some more. At one time he even lectures with great success as a reformed drunkard. Later he becomes a forger, is caught and jailed for two years, but when released is aided by the Prisoner's Friend Society. One winter night George and some confederates try to rob the bank where Edward works. When the good man resists, they kill him. George is caught, tried, and condemned to death, and in spite of petitions by various persons and organizations is hanged. On his tombstone appears this: "He has fought the good fight." Edward's widow and children, it is true, receive a sum of $500 collected by grateful banks; but his own bank tries without success to prove that his accounts were juggled and that he committed suicide with a club. On his tombstone appears this: "Be pure . . . and you will never—" His family is soon destitute, but the people eventually collect $42,000 and build a memorial church with the sum.

George Benton, Mrs. Mary Benton, Benton, Benton, Brant, Mrs. Brant, the Governor, Edward Mills, Mrs. Edward Mills, Mills.

"Electricity—With the Modern Improvement." See FW, 1869.

["The Emperor-God Satire"], 1972 (FM).
The Emperor of the island is not simply honored but worshipped. He is said to be a century old in his present form and to practice metempsychosis, moving from body to body—with his hundreds and hundreds of used forms embalmed in a mausoleum. The civilized cities are in the interior. Close to the sea are many tribes of savages, a half dozen of which reside in the Unyumi Valley. The Emperor never visits the cities but lavishes his solicitude only upon the Unyumians. Priests in the cities sacrifice to him, and to him are lifted many prayers there, mostly by women but also by

men in hard times. The city priests send gifts and written prayers to the Emperor, whose priests enjoy the gifts but who, however, orders the prayers burned because he will not alter his inflexible and just laws—he says. Yet in Unyumi the Emperor constantly interferes, aiding and slaughtering princes whimsically, and meddling in tribal law, temple services, and even intimate domestic affairs. At one time, the interior region is blighted with drought and its priests beg the Emperor to set aside his laws and bring some rain; but he refuses. However, when a priest in the interior refuses to order his tribe to vacate some land and give it over to the Unyumians, the Emperor waxes wrathful and makes the moon back up; the resulting tide drowns thousands of innocent persons far from the eviction area. The survivors of the flood fancy that they are being punished for neglecting the Emperor.

The Emperor.

"The Enchanted Sea-Wilderness," 1967 (WWD).

Scattered in our oceans are big patches where compasses do not work. One of the worst of these spots lies between the Cape of Good Hope and the South Pole. Around this area, five hundred miles in diameter, race hideous circular winds along what is called the Devil's Race-Track; in the center is a deathly calm region, about fifty miles across, called the Everlasting Sunday. A bronzed old sailor tells about this area.

It is December, 1853. The narrator is a young sailor of twenty-three, aboard the *Mabel Thorpe,* commanded by tough Elliott Cable and now becalmed far in southern waters. The sailors' pet is a huge, friendly St. Bernard which appeared just before sailing time two months earlier. One night the ship catches fire, the dog alerts Cable, and the men are able to launch a lifeboat. Cable praises the dog but ties him to the mast, since he would be an encumbrance. As the boat pulls away, fire swallows up the howling animal. They are now in the Indian Ocean five hundred miles south of Port Natal and therefore strike north by the stars. At daybreak they run across the *Adelaide* bound for Australia, as the *Mabel* was. Since Captain Moseley of the *Adelaide* died a month earlier, Cable takes over but after an eighteen-day gale discovers that they are half-way between Kerguelan's Land and the Antarctic Circle, heading for the Devil's Race-Track, which in due time they hit. Next comes the Everlasting Sunday, into the deathly stillness of which they drift after a week. The compass whizzes madly like a soul in hell. The weather grows still and frosty. After seven dreadful months, during which they inch ever closer to the very center of the Everlasting Sunday, the spiritless men sight another vessel, then several more. But when they explore them, they find nothing but frosty corpses. The log of one ship reveals that it was trapped there six years ago. Another vessel has been becalmed there for 130 years. Dry, cold weather is a great preserver . . .

Captain Elliot Cable, Captain Moseley, Mrs. Moseley, Miss Moseley, Robert, Admiral Sir John Thurlow.

"An Encounter with an Interviewer," 1875 (WMT 19).
A dapper journalist from the *Daily Thunderstorm* comes to interview the narrator, who first pretends not to know what "interview" means, then says that he is nineteen years old but was born in 1836 (later he says it was Monday, October 31, 1693), that he was drowned once and not his twin brother, and that the most remarkable man he ever met was Aaron Burr—because he sat up with the driver of his own funeral hearse. The nonplussed interviewer reverently withdraws.

Aaron Burr, Bill.

"The Enemy Conquered; Or, Love Triumphant." (WMT 24). See "A Cure for the Blues."

["Engagement Rings"], 1870 (CG).
Twain is delighted to read that diamond engagement rings are becoming less fashionable than rings with emeralds or opals. Soon matrimony will be within reach of all.

"English As She Is Taught," 1887 (WMT 26).
First Twain recounts an anecdote about Samuel Johnson, who

was distressed that a school child could recite Cato's soliloquy but did not know how many pence in sixpence. Then Twain repeats some difficult questions asked in geography tests. Finally he gives a great number of boners compiled by a teacher and her assistants, put into a hilarious manuscript, and submitted to him with a request that he tell whether it is worth publishing. He thinks so, emphatically. The boners deal with fifteen general subjects, from etymology and grammar to oratory and metaphysics. Sometimes key words mislead the little scholars. Sometimes secret truths are expressed unknowingly. Geography gets jumbled. The year 1492 is overworked. History is curiously treated. Facts blend into curious mosaics. One should not laugh, however, at pupil or teacher but rather at examining boards. It is obvious that immature minds are ruthlessly crammed.

["English Phone and Postal Service"] (MTP).
Returning to London late in 1899, Twain notes that England is still conservative. Telephone service continues to be slow. Twain is now residing in Dollis Hill House, which lacks a phone. He must rely on getting his supplies from Whiteley, whose lack of a phone is inconvenient. He wants to move in eighteen days and cannot summon packers except by letter, which he does, though with delays. Suddenly Twain turns to a criticism of the London address system, which must cost many cabbies their sanity every year. Also the English do not know how to pronounce the name Cromwell.

> The Admiral, [William] Gladstone, Harrod, the Head of the Ecclesiastical Department, the Head of the Ham Department, Whiteley, the World-Provider.

"English Festivities." Part of "A Day at Niagara."

"Enigma," 1865 (SS).
The author offers his own particular puzzle. It has sixteen or seventeen letters. Some letters mean something; others mean certain other things; still others mean much else. Twain hopes that somebody can decipher this enigma, because, though stunned by his brilliance in devising it, he cannot solve it. Enigmas sometimes amuse and cannot do more than cause insanity or murder.

["Enigma"], 1870 (CG).

Twain offers a puzzle. It is a word of thirteen letters. Some are a European village; some, a kind of dog; others, a kind of stuff; some, a Russian philosopher's middle name; and others, a nice bug. To any diligent person solving the puzzle will go a gold pen or a cheap sewing machine. Twain later explains that he is not certain of the answer.

"An Entertaining Article," 1870 (WMT 24).

Twain begins by printing a paragraph from the Boston *Advertiser* in which it is reported that his *Innocents Abroad* has been criticized in the London *Saturday Review* for October 8 [1869]. He then takes the liberty of reproducing the whole *Saturday Review* article. In this critical essay, *The Innocents Abroad* is called more than curious, and then its author is taken to task in detail for lying about Europe, for his innocence, and for his ignorance. The pernicious book is praised only for giving the reader some interesting facts about life in America.

Twain then reports receiving letters and reading newspaper paragraphs about the London review. Before reprinting some of the comments, he confesses that he wrote the so-called London *Saturday Review* essay on *The Innocents Abroad* and had it published in the December *Galaxy*. One comment on the spurious review was that it is as funny as Twain's own "Jumping Frog." Another also praised the humor of the review. Still another observed that the supposedly British reviewer was only pretending to shake his head with owlish density. Next, Twain confesses that what inspired him to write the fake review of his own travel book was his reading in the Boston *Advertiser* a note to the effect that the *Saturday Review* had published a criticism of his book. He adds that he never saw the real review until after he had written and mailed his burlesque. He offers to bet, at twenty to one, any person who doubts these facts. In a postscript, Twain adds that the Cincinnati *Enquirer* later reported that he had been taken in by the humorous British review and that he thereafter had ingeniously but dishonestly pretended that he had written it. Twain flatly calls this statement a falsehood and offers to pay $500 to any person who can produce a copy of the London *Saturday Review* for October 8 containing the critical essay which he insists he wrote and which first saw light in the

Galaxy, to which he sent it for publication. He orders the *Enquirer* people to swallow their lie or send an agent to the *Galaxy* offices. He concludes by remarking that the *Enquirer* must be edited by children.

   Sheldon.

"Entertaining History of the Scriptural Panoramist." See "The Spiritual Panoramist."

"An Epidemic." See "The Approaching Epidemic."

"An Epistle from Mark Twain," 1866 (MTWY).
   Twain reports the arrival in San Francisco of Queen Emma, who was greeted courteously by a cutter which fired a salute, by the pleasant Hawaiian Consul, and by crowds of the curious. Twain next describes visiting the fair of the State Agricultural Society, where John Quincy Adams Warren exhibited thousands of types of lava, worms, and vegetables from Hawaii. Finally Twain explains that he will soon head for Honolulu to claim revenge upon Whitney, the editor of the *Commercial Advertiser,* for not being able to distinguish between Twain's straight writing and his burlesques.

   C. W. Brooks, Queen Emma [of Hawaii], Hitchcock, Jerome Leland, Charles L. Richards, John Quincy Adams Warren, Commodore Watson, Whitney.

["Equestrian Excursions"]. See LSI.

Ye Equinoctial Storm, 1884 (P).
   At three bells of the middle watch one calm night, Middleton and Bleydenburg throw a riotous party aboard ship. They sing and roar and drink. When Captain Cox and other virtuous persons endeavor to remonstrate, the villains say that it is warm, they have been quiet, and an equinoctial storm is causing the noise.

   Bleydenburg, Captain Cox, Dickinson, Field, Lake, Middleton, Captain Queen, the "Rajah," Dr. Shorb, Marcus Twain.

"The Esquimau Maiden's Romance," 1893 (WMT 23).
    Lasca, the lovely, slightly plump Esquimo girl, tells Mr. Twain
that she will explain anything about her life that he wants to know.
The two have been companions for a week, fishing and sealing together. The Northern Lights flame over their sofa—a block of ice—
as she begins. Her rich father's home is the pride of the tribe. Its
icy parlor and sleeping benches, Twain agrees, have no equal in the
finest American homes. And not even Vanderbilt, a very rich man,
can boast of slop tubs in his drawing room. Lasca dreamily gnaws
a candle end as she says that when soap was first introduced in her
region the people were reluctant to eat it, but now they do not
mind. Then she turns to the story of her romance. She wanted to
be loved for herself and not because her father was the envied owner
of twenty-two fish hooks made of iron. One day a stranger named
Kalula came by and soon announced his love for her. He rejoiced
when he saw her father's home, all lighted with rag lamps for the
betrothal feast, during which her father ostentatiously showed off
his fish hooks. He tossed them about as though unaware of their
value. In the night, Lasca saw a shadowy form drift toward the hiding
place of the hooks. Then she fell asleep. Soon, however, she heard
her father accuse Kalula of stealing a hook, since one was missing.
Although he protested his innocence, Lasca could find the hook
nowhere and the lover was placed on trial for his life. The method
was simple: an accused person would be thrown into the water; if
he sank and drowned, he would be adjudged innocent, but if he
swam away he would be pronounced guilty, pursued, and killed.
Kalula swam away; so his accusers caught him and set him on an
iceberg drifting south to the ocean. Nine months later, as the Annual
Sacrifice approached, it was time for Lasca to comb her hair. In it
she found the missing fish hook. She will never smile again!

    Kalula, Lasca, [Mark] Twain.

'Eulogy of the Fair Sex.' See 'Woman.

"European Diet." From *A Tramp Abroad.*

"The European War," 1870 (CRG).
    The first day's headlines announce the European war, with hos-

tilities imminent and Austria arming. Headlines on the second day say that fighting is imminent, Russia sides with Prussia, England remains neutral, and Austria is not arming. The third day, and no battle yet; however, Prussia and France are allegedly invading each other. On the fourth day it is announced that bitter strife is imminent, all invaders are safe, Russia supports both sides, and England will fight both. Twain, who has been reporting from Berlin and Paris, writes from London that he is returning home to wait until the fighting starts.

The Emperor, Field Marshal Mike McMahon.

"Eve Speaks," 1923 (WMT 29).

Eve explains that the fierce cherubim drove them from Eden. It is all so unfair. She and Adam meant no harm. They simply did not understand. No mother would punish her child for disobeying an incomprehensible command. Adam says that Eve has become wicked, but she replies that she is what she is and is not to blame, since she did not create herself. They bitterly understand such things as hunger, cold, pain, hate, and remorse now. They dream of Eden sometimes, but when they wake up it is gone. Yes, they know right from wrong too, because they now have the moral sense. The animals are not degraded with such a sense. But Adam and Eve do not know death. Adam now enters and says that Abel is still sleeping. Adam and Eve found Abel covered with blood. He said that quick-tempered Cain had struck him down; then Abel fell asleep. His parents happily watch him rest; but when he turns pale and cold, and does not awaken, they grow terrified. Is it that long sleep called death? Will he wake no more? Satan adds a postscript to the effect that one day these creatures will cease to think ill of death.

Abel, Adam, Cain, Eve, Satan.

"Eve's Diary," 1905 (WMT 24).

Eve records her age as one whole day. She feels like an experiment. In the rush of finishing up the world, the mountains were left ragged; still the whole place is majestic and beautiful. There are too many stars, to be sure, and the moon got loose and slid away last night, unfortunately. Eve wishes that she could get some stars to put into her hair. She went to the horizon with a basket to gather some but got tired and hurt her feet. Then she nestled with some tigers, which have sweet breath from eating strawberries. She follows the other experiment about. It is evidently a man but looks like a reptile or some architecture. It does not want her tagging along after it. It rests much of the time. Later she records that the moon returned last night. Why does the other experiment pay no attention to her? She threw some clods at it, and it used language back at her. Is it a he? He avoids her, even though she has taken the work of naming all things off his hands. She can name everything instantly. Thursday, and he is still avoiding her. She feels lonely when he is not around. He is always busy building his shelter now, but when she tried to enter he put her out in the rain. She tried to get him some apples but could not throw straight. He is not very bright, but that is of no consequence. The true values lie in the heart. She enjoys looking in the pool at the lovely white body painted in it. It is her sister. Oh, how beautiful the flowers are! Eve had apples for lunch. She wished he would come, but he did not. She rubbed a stick in a hole in another stick, and a blue film rose. Then there was delicate pink dust, which hurt her fingers when she felt it. She calls it fire. She told him, but he was not interested. Apples left in the fire taste better. Fire has given her a new passion—fear! Now she does not want him to go over the falls, as he likes to do.

Adam records in his diary that she is young, possessed of infinite curiosity, and loves flowers. She is graceful, even beautiful in certain positions. She wanted to use the brontosaurus for a bridge, but Adam was afraid that it would sit on the house and mash it.

Eve now records that she dislikes loneliness and loves the company of animals and birds. She is curious about everything. How does the water get back uphill in the night? It must, for the pool never runs dry. When she solves this puzzle, water will be less interesting. There are other little problems. For example, she has learned that wood and other objects can swim in water; so stones should, but oddly they do not. She thanks the Giver of all for making such a wonderful world. After the Fall she is sad, because the Garden, when one looks back on it, was a marvelous dream and now is lost. But he loves her. Why does she love him? Not because of his brightness, consideration and delicacy, education, or chivalry (after all, he told on her). It is because he is masculine and is hers. Love simply comes. There is no use reasoning about it. Forty years pass, and Eve prays that they may die together or that if one must go first it be she, for he is stronger. She could not live without him. Later, at her grave, Adam says that wherever she was, there was Eden.

    Adam, Eve.

"The Evidence in the Case of Smith vs Jones," 1864 (WG).

    Here in the rough California police court we see a pulpit where the gray-haired judge sits, a table at the left for reporters, a nest of lawyers in the center, some pine benches on the right for prisoners and witnesses, and a guard by the door. A holy calm is all about. The case of Smith vs Jones begins. Alfred Sowerby testifies that Jones started an argument with Smith by hitting him in the nose. McWilliamson deposes that Jones tried first off to shoot Smith in a bar. Washington Billings swears that the altercation occurred when Smith and Jones bumped into each other in the muddy street. Jeremiah Driscoll testifies that the two men blackguarded each other in the town square and started fighting simultaneously; under cross examination, he allows that slingshots and grenades might have been involved, but then he decides that he saw a different fight entirely. Other witnesses offer other versions. At another trial, two witnesses have to check some writing on cards to be able to say who they are. Should Smith or Jones be awarded the damages? Let the people decide.

    Washington Billings, Jeremiah Driscoll, James Johnson, Jones, McWilliamson, Judge Shepherd, Smith, Sophronia, Alfred Sowerby, John Ward.

"Experience of the McWilliamses with Membranous Croup," 1875 (WMT 7).

    Mortimer McWilliams tells Mark Twain, when the two meet by chance on a journey, of the following experience. Seeing their child Penelope chewing a pine stick, Mortimer suggests to his wife Caroline that she put a stop to it. The wife therefore says there is no harm. After dinner, Caroline reports that Georgie Gordon has membranous croup. When a nurse brings in Penelope and she coughs over her prayer, Caroline grows terrified, wants the child's crib placed in her bedroom and Mortimer's, then moves all sleeping arrangements into a room adjoining the nursery to be near their second baby, then sends the coachmen for the doctor only to learn that he is sick, then plies Penelope with medicines which the physician sent by the coachman, then orders Mortimer to turn the heat register on, then tells him to heat some goose grease and massage it into Penelope, and then urges him to prepare a flax-seed poultice. Mortimer stumbles about a good deal, catches a few winks of sleep, but is roused suddenly in the morning. Caroline shouts that Penelope is sweating and orders Mortimer to fetch the doctor, who reluctantly comes and after examining the child explains that the cough was not due to membranous croup but to some pine splinters lodged in her throat.

Georgie Gordon, Baby McWilliams, Caroline McWilliams, Mortimer McWilliams, Penelope McWilliams, Maria, Mark Twain.

"Extract from Captain Stormfield's Visit to Heaven," 1907-08 (WMT 27—incomplete). See "Captain Stormfield's Visit to Heaven."

"Extracts from Adam's Diary," 1893 (WMT 24).

Adam says that the new creature, which calls itself Eve, gets in his way and talks too much. He is not used to company. She keeps naming things; for example, she calls their estate Niagara Falls Park. Adam builds himself a shelter against the rain, but the new creature intrudes and talks, and when he objects she sheds water out of the holes she looks with. She eats too much fruit and on one dull Sunday tries to get some apples out of the forbidden tree. When he goes down Niagara Falls to cool off, she shudders; when he tries to escape her, she follows and sheds more water. She wonders how the lions and tigers can live on a diet of grass, since their teeth are obviously for eating each other; also the buzzard seems an oddity, since it is intended to live on decayed flesh, which is non-existent. When Eve gets friendly with a snake, Adam foresees trouble and emigrates. A few days later, the animals suddenly begin to tear at each other! Adam knows Eve has eaten the forbidden fruit and thus brought death to the world. He gets hungry out on the plain, and Eve brings him some apples, which he eats. She titters and blushes. They creep to a place where an animal battle occurred, get skins, and make some suits for themselves. Later she accuses Adam of causing their disaster: the serpent assured her that the forbidden fruit was chestnuts and that chestnuts were stale jokes. Adam turns pale, knowing that he has made poor jokes. The first chestnut was his quip that Niagara Falls would be more spectacular if they tumbled upwards. The following year, while Adam is away trapping on the north shore, Eve catches Cain in the timber near their dugout. Is Cain a fish? a kangaroo? a bear which will eventually grow dangerous teeth? Months pass; and while he is hunting near Buffalo, Eve catches another one, which she names Abel. By now Cain is talking. Is he a parrot? Ten years later, Adam records the observation that Cain and Abel are boys. He knows now that it is better to be with Eve outside the Garden of Eden than inside it without her. Blessed be chestnuts.

Abel, Adam, Cain, Eve.

"An Extraordinary Case" (MTP).

While studying in a foreign land, Morris Hart is stricken with bad news from his widowed mother: his sister Agnes, loved but then abandoned by Arnold Holliday, who has married Alice Major, has committed suicide and the mother intends to do the same deed to herself. After two days of grief, Hart begins to lament the fact that he is too cowardly to take revenge. He remembers wrongs done him and also his never avenging any of them. He returns home in disguise, learns that Holliday is living in Philadelphia, goes there, and takes rooms. In disguise he goes to Holliday's house, rings the bell, but runs away before being admitted. That evening he upbraids himself and rushes with a knife to his enemy's house. When Holliday opens the door, Hart quakes, stammers an excuse, and stumbles into the night. He begins to reason that he was created by God as a joke—with the ability to hate but not the courage to act. Admitting his cowardice to himself, he now plans to wait fifty years if necessary for revenge, and meanwhile he openly returns home and affects surprise at news of the death of his mother and sister. He tells an old friend, Wesley Hallet, the bearer of the sad news, that he will pray for Holliday. Hallet calls Hart a dirt-eater, slaps him, and leaves. Other villagers insult and cut him, for a year, after which, having settled his mother's estate, Hart gives out the information that he is returning to Europe forever. Once back in Philadelphia, he learns that the Hollidays now have a baby girl named Millie. Hart tells the old couple with whom he rooms that he is a private detective and soon becomes adept at disguises, complete with voice changes. He grows in boldness and hires himself as an old Irishwoman to wash windows in Holliday's house and also as her Irish brother to saw wood there. After a year or so, Hart hits upon the idea of revenge against Holliday through his daughter. Hart plans to kidnap little Millie and wring her father's heart with letters mysteriously posted from fictitious addresses.

Wesley Hallet, Agnes Hart, Morris Hart, Mrs. Hart, Mrs. Alice Holliday, Arnold Holliday, Millie Holliday, William Rogers.

"A Fable," 1909 (WMT 27).

An artist paints a small and beautiful picture, places it so that he can see it in a mirror, and pronounces it twice as beautiful through greater distance and a softening effect. The animals hear of all this, through an intelligent cat. But the ass ventures to doubt, goes to the mirror, and sees himself. The other animals, even the mighty elephant, do the same. Moral: you can find what you bring to a text, if you stand between it and the mirror of your imagination.

"The Fable of the Yellow Terror," 1972 (FM).

The time is long ago. The Butterflies hold vast flowery, fragrant lands. The Butterflies are colorfully dressed, and are highly civilized and proud of it. They send missionaries to pagan insects to make them unafraid of death and to learn how to stage expensive funerals. The Butterflies have two unique techniques: making honey and using their stings. These processes enable them to conquer the world, except for the empire of the Bees. So the Butterflies go after them. But the Bees courteously refuse to have Butterfly civilization and processes shown them. So the Butterflies argue far and wide that the Bees constitute a Yellow Peril. That sounds so shuddery that every Butterfly tribe sends a missionary into Beeland. The Bees object, and Butterfly civilization rolls into enemy territory irresistibly. The Bees submit. Peace is established. God is thanked. And the Bees soon learn to love honey, which they buy in huge quantities from Butterfly merchants. Next, one tribe of Bees wants to learn the civilized art of stinging, and does learn. The world rejoices, until a sober old Grasshopper tells a Butterfly leader that trouble will ensue. One Bee tribe will show brother tribes how to wield their stings. All the Bees will develop local honey industries, corner the world market, develop their own army, and force the Butterflies out. Bee merchants may actually go land-grabbing over the frontiers into Europe. The Yellow Peril should never have been invented. Then the Grasshopper asks the Butter-fly leader for a passport.

Bee, Butterfly, Grasshopper.

"Facts Concerning the Late Senatorial Secretaryship" (CG). See "My Late Senatorial Secretaryship."

"The Facts Concerning the Recent Carnival of Crime in Connecti-cut," 1876 (WMT 19).

The narrator eagerly anticipates a visit from his favorite Aunt Mary, even though she sometimes bothers his conscience by asking him to stop smoking. Suddenly a mouldy little dwarf, who oddly looks like the narrator, enters, seizes his pipe and starts smoking it, insolently imitates his drawl, and then annoyingly accuses him of lying and being selfish and mean. Discovering the dwarf to be his conscience, the narrator tries to kill him but fails. They declare a truce and talk. The dwarf explains that one's conscience, invisible to others, nags him not to improve him but because it is commanded to do so and enjoys it. The dwarf gleefully agrees when the narra-tor says that a person's conscience often bothers him whether he lies or tells the brutal truth. The dwarf then says that he was seven feet tall when the narrator was a boy but that tussling with the nar-rator has shrunk him a bit here and there. He refuses to show the narrator his friends' consciences but does tell him that Aunt Mary's is gigantic and that of a certain thieving publisher is sub-micro-scopic. Aunt Mary suddenly comes in. Soon she is reminding the narrator of his broken promises and other misdeeds. All this in-sufferable weight causes the dwarf to fall to the floor. The narrator strangles him, telling puzzled Aunt Mary that his strange behavior is owing to tobacco. She beseeches him anew to stop smoking. The narrator throws the dwarf into the fire as a burnt offering. Then he shrieks that he is a man without a conscience, and Aunt Mary flees. Now he can kill, burn, and swindle consciencelessly.

Aunt Mary, Robinson, Hugh Thompson, Tom Smith.

"The Facts Concerning the Recent Resignation," 1868 (WMT 7).

Mark Twain, Clerk of the Senate Committee on Conchology, has resigned and now wishes to explain why. He could no longer hold office and retain his self-respect. He suffered outrages. He had no one to play billiards with. When he offered suggestions to heads of departments, he was neither thanked nor obeyed. He told the Secretary of the Navy to order Admiral Farragut home from Europe, advised the Secretary of War to massacre the Indians with soap and education, offered to improve the Secretary of the Treasury's report; then he attended a cabinet meeting, met the President, but was gently bid farewell by the Secretary of State. When one of the Senators on the Conchological Committee wanted a copy of a report on bomb, egg, and clam shells, Twain thought the demand unfair and quit, submitting his bill, in the sum of $2,986, for services rendered—including transportation to and from Jerusalem via Egypt. But only his $6 a day—that is, $36—was allowed. It is odd the hard work some federal clerks do. Some paste as many as ten scraps daily in scrapbooks. Others fight documents valiantly for only a few thousand dollars a year. There are not half enough clerks working for our national government, and they get too little pay.

Admiral [David G.] Farragut, General [Robert E.] Lee, the Secretary of the Navy, the President, the Senator, the Secretary of State, the Secretary of the Treasury, Mark Twain, the Secretary of War.

"The Facts Concerning the Recent Trouble between Mr. Mark Twain and Mr. John William Skae of Virginia City—Wherein It Is Attempted to Be Proved That the Former Was Not to Blame in the Matter" (SS). See "Mr. Bloke's Item." (See also Colfax, Schuyler; G., E. B., General; G., Miss; Murry; and Stiggers. These characters from the former item are not in the latter.)

"The Facts in the Case of George Fisher, Deceased" (CG). See "The Case of George Fisher."

"The Facts in the Case of the Great Beef Contract," 1870 (WMT 7). The narrator has the facts concerning the notorious beef contract. John Wilson Mackenzie of New Jersey contracted with the government on October 10, 1861, to furnish General Sherman with thirty barrels of beef. Mackenzie followed Sherman from Washington to Tennessee to Atlanta, but never caught up with him. Learning that Sherman was going by the *Quaker City* to the Holy Land, Mackenzie went to Jerusalem with his beef but discovered that Sherman was way out west fighting the Indians. Mackenzie followed but was killed and scalped. Sherman's army got one barrel of beef, but the Indians made off with the rest. One after another, many were left the contract but could not collect. One after another, they all died prematurely, until the contract falls into the hands of the narrator, who goes from the President of the United States through various cabinet officials, auditors, and comptrollers to a clerk of the Commissioner of Odds and Ends. This young man tells the narrator that to be paid he must produce the Indian and the tomahawk that killed Mackenzie. At this point, the narrator makes a gift of the contract to the clerk, who follows the pattern and dies.

> Barker J. Allen, Chief of the [Odds and Ends] Bureau, the Commissioner of Odds and Ends, the Commissioner of the Patent Office, the First Auditor of the Treasury, First Comptroller of the Corn-Beef Division, Fourth Assistant Junior Clerk, Vengeance Hopkins, Bethlehem Hubbard, Illustrious Vagrant, the Secretary of the Interior, O-be-joyful Johnson, Bartholomew W. Mackenzie, John Wilson Mackenzie, William J. Martin, the Secretary of the Navy, the Ninth Auditor, the Postmaster-General, the President of the United States, Anson G. Rogers, the Second Auditor [of the Treasury], the Second Comptroller of the Corn-Beef Division, General [William T.] Sherman, the Sixth Comptroller [of the Corn-Beef Division], the Speaker of the House of Representatives, the Secretary of State, the Third [Auditor of the Treasury], the Third [Comptroller of the Corn-Beef Division], the First Lord of the Treasury, the Twelfth Auditor.

"The Facts in the Case of the Senate Doorkeeper," 1867 (LAIFI).
The Doorkeeper of the United States Senate wishes to set the record straight. He charged senators 50¢ each for admission to the Senate, voted on various questions, rose frequently to points of order and attempted to recite a poem beginning "Woman! Oh, woman," sought to discuss female suffrage while the senators were voting to honor General Garibaldi, and finally was the cause of a little rebellion on the floor. For these few reasons, he was impeached. Rock-firm, he now awaits the verdict.

The Doorkeeper of the Senate, General [Giuseppe] Garibaldi, [President Andrew] Johnson, Senator, Senator, Senator, the Sergeant-at-Arms, his Majesty King Theodorus, Benjamain F. Wade.

"The Facts in the Great Landslide Case." See "The Great Landslide Case." (See also Brayton, Hal; and Sides, Richard [D.].)

"A Falsehood" (CG). See the third third of "An Entertaining Article."

"A Fashion Item," 1871 (WMT 7).
The most fashionably dressed lady at General G—'s reception is Mrs. G. C., who wears a pink satin dress with train, white bodice with Pompadour sleeves, pearl necklace, and hair frizzled in front but plaited in back in a stumpy pony tail. She has a beautiful complexion, most of which rubs off on the reporter as she squeezes past him at the door.

Mrs. G. C., General G—.

"Fashions," 1866 (WG).
Except for bonnets and shoes, it is hard for Twain to tell ladies back in Nevada what is orthodox in California fashions. Certainly women of all types wear their hair in all styles. And it is difficult to say what is acceptable in the matter of hoops. Perhaps the best way to judge the new tent-shaped hoop is to look furtively up at one above you on a hill. What handsome garters!

"The Fashions."—See "Fashions."

"Favors from Correspondents," 1870 (CG).
A reader from Cleveland sends Twain a sample of sentimental prose by Lucretia which tells how the angels brought a new baby to a joyful home in New Haven. He ventures to doubt this procedure as a method of acquiring offspring. A reader from New York reports that a friend read Twain's burlesque called "[The Facts in the Case of the Great] Beef Contract" as a libel on our government. Lame satires are usually interpreted literally by certain thick readers. Other correspondents send Twain other items, some of which are funereal in nature.
Later, a New Yorker sends Twain a poem by William L. and Mary G. Burt, lamenting the death of their daughter Etta A. Burt, who is quoted as saying that she was going to a different shore to give it a whirl. The trouble with most obituary verse is that it is not bad enough to be good. A Bostonian, who liked Twain's "Johnny Skae's Item" ["Mr. Bloke's Item"], sends a copy of a wretchedly written piece—which Twain prints—telling how Cornelius Kickham was fatally injured trying to stop a runaway horse. Twain then appends his own description of William Schuyler's accident and invites his present readers to decide which—the Boston clipping or his item—is a burlesque. Next, a reader sends a Cambridge, New York, clipping which Lucretia's essay, reprinted earlier, resembled; the same reader then offers a poem which concludes with the suggestion that Saint Peter should not be blamed when couples have children. A Missouri friend then reports that when an old man was once blown sky-high in a steamboat accident, he remarked to a fellow victim, also ascending fast, "How is this for high?" Twain promises more funereal literature later.
Next, Twain prints a Nevada lawyer's poem about the heirs and assigns of vernal birds in leafy nests. Twain then urges a reader who has objected to itinerant book agents to regard vendors of *The Innocents Abroad* as indispensable. A reader complains humorously about the stupidity and pomposity of some ministers she has known. Twain tells of a congregation which was afraid that a dead man would not get a proper eulogy from their dour minister. So they prepared a list of topics which they wanted him to touch on. Instead, he read the list, then said that only a fool would add a comment, and closed with an invitation to prayer. Twain prints a

lugubrious poem by M. A. Glaze on the death of some of Samuel and Catharine Belknap's children (see "Post Mortem Poetry").

Finally, Twain reports that a reader wrote him about a traveling salesman who tried to induce a Massachusetts minister to buy a copy of *The Innocents Abroad*. But when the man noticed an illustration showing Twain crying at Adam's tomb, he pronounced the author a sniveling calf and refused to buy. Twain then reports that a fast Iowa colt has been named after him. This is humorous, because the only thing slower than Twain is a corpse. Next, he writes about a retired Hawaiian editor named Henry M. Whitney, who used to be a cannibal. He and Twain ate heartily in those old days—lived off the fat of the land, so to speak. Next, Twain quotes a Mormon wedding announcement: Brigham Young marries Martin, Pendergast, Jenickson, etc. Then an advertisement about quick divorces. Then more tombstone verse. A correspondent sends Twain a humorous account of a stupid reader of Twain's "Map of Paris" who could not keep track of the directions west and east, along with the longitudinal lines. Next, Twain reports that the Yale College *Courant* recently promised to give a copy of his Parisian map to any group of a hundred new subscribers who would pay the expected $400. Twain closes with a promise to publish his portrait of King William of Prussia in an early issue.

Addie, Rev. Dr. B., Rev. T. K. Beecher, Mrs. Catharine Belknap, Samuel Belknap, Belknap, Etta A. Burt, Mrs. Mary G. Burt, William L. Burt, Susie P. Cleveland, Frances, a Friend, S.S.G., M.A. Glaze, S.J., Mrs. R.M. Jenickson, [President] Andrew Johnson, Cornelius Kickham, John Kickham, Lucretia, M., Emily P. Martin, Mrs. J. R. Martin, Solomon N., Miss L. M. Pendergast, Saint Peter, Quizquiz, William Schuyler, Johnny Skae, Senator Stewart, a Subscriber, Henry M. Whitney, King William III of Prussia, Elder Brigham Young.

"Fearful Domestic Tragedy." See FW, 1870.

"Female Suffrage: A Volley from the Downtrodden," 1867 (LAIFI).

Mark Twain writes to the editors of the Missouri *Democrat* to protest petitions favoring female suffrage, on the grounds that women belong at home and are already busy enough there and on nonpolitical committees. Mrs. Mark Twain then writes the editors to criticize them for publishing her idiotic husband's drivel and to announce her support of female suffrage. Mrs. Zeb Leavenworth also writes in to criticize Twain, who is wrongly allowed to vote while women far more intelligent then he are denied the privilege. Next Augusta Maitland writes in, saying that she collects trinkets for faraway savages and yet cannot vote. Then Cousin Jennie writes Twain a private letter to scold him gently; she says that in secret he surely must favor the cause of women, who often are wise and can work hard. A. L. takes up the cudgels, with a letter to the editors saying that men are not superior to their wives but instead browbeat them for such petty dereliction of duty as not sewing on buttons. Then Twain privately writes Cousin Jennie to explain the difference between justice and expediency. Some women would vote better than many illiterate male immigrants and could discharge public offices better than the third-rate male pettifoggers who are now there and who get elected because the pay is too poor to attract more talented candidates. But good women would vote the same way as their good husbands, and so with bad couples; therefore, the same people would win the elections anyway. Moreover, good women might stay home and not vote at all, whereas foolish women might go to the polls in great numbers. Some women would be reluctant to vote, because they would first have to declare their ages. Also, women if given the vote would pass laws regulating men's hours, drinking and smoking habits, and property rights. Twain adds that his goose of a wife is going to have a suffragette meeting in their back parlor, which will be unfortunate, because he is planning to blow up that section of the house. At the end, A.L. chips in with the comment that although a man's brain typically weighs more than a woman's, everyone knows that gold is more valuable than lead.

> Miss A., Cousin Jennie, Mrs. Jones, A.L., Mrs. Zeb Leavenworth, Augusta Josephine Maitland, Judy McGinnis, President Dorcas Society, President Ladies' Union Prayer Meeting, President of Ladies' Society for Dissemination of Belles Lettres among the Shoshones, President Pawnee Educational Society, Sallie Robbins, Maria Sanders, Smith, State Crinoline Directress, State Hair Oil Inspectress, State Milliner, State Superintendent of Waterfalls, Mrs. Treasurer, Mrs. Mark Twain.

"The Feminine Grand Jury." See FW, 1870.

"Fenimore Cooper's Further Literary Offenses," 1946 (LFE).

Twain quotes a passage from *The Last of the Mohicans*, ridicules its poor diction and its redundancies, criticizes its flat style, and rewrites it more simply. Then he takes another passage from the same novel and notes its inexactnesses. Finally he quotes a section from *The Deerslayer*, italicizing the unnecessary words in it, and ends up by rewriting it with a third omitted. Here and there he cites composition rules [from his 1895 essay "Fenimore Cooper's Literary Offenses"] violated in the selections quoted here.

    [James] Fenimore Cooper.

"Fenimore Cooper's Literary Offenses," 1895 (WMT 22).

After quoting in displeasure Professors [Thomas Raynesford] Lounsbury and Brander Matthews and novelist Wilkie Collins, who praise [James] Fenimore Cooper's Leatherstocking tales, Mark Twain says that these persons should have read Cooper before delivering opinions on him and adds that the novelist has violated eighteen of the nineteen (some say twenty-two) rules governing literary art. Cooper's *Deerslayer* accomplishes nothing and arrives nowhere, is loosely episodic, has inconsistent dialogue, and involves woodsman stupidities and miraculous events, fuzzily defined heroes and villains, and varieties of poor style. Cooper lacked inventiveness and overworked the broken twig in his plots. A particularly annoying episode in *The Deerslayer* concerns a settler's scow in a circuitous stream. Another is the shooting contest in *The Pathfinder*. Wretched dialogue is exemplified by the Scotch officer who in stilted language commands his troops to hold their fire and to use cold steel against the enemy instead so as to avoid killing his daughters [in *The Last of the Mohicans*]. Finally, Twain accuses Cooper of having a dull word-sense, of producing literary sharps and flats. If one ignores the objections specified, he may conclude that Cooper produced art.

    Wilkie Collins, [James] Fenimore Cooper, [Thomas Raynesford] Lounsbury, Brander Matthews.

"A Fine Old Man," 1869 (WMT 7).

John Wagner is the oldest man in Buffalo. He is 104 years old, walked five blocks in the rain last November, voted for Grant, has a new wig and a new set of false teeth, and plans next week to wed a girl aged 102. The couple has been engaged for eighty years. Their parents withheld consent until recently. John drinks no liquor—except whiskey.

John Wagner.

"The Finished Book," 1923 (WMT 29).
After finishing a book, as the author did his *Joan of Arc* in Paris in 1895, it is a shock to return to your study and find it all tidy and repellent. It is like visiting a sick room at your regular hour and finding the medicine gone, the bed stripped, the furniture pushed back, and the place stark and vacant. All the author can do is bring in another patient, nurse it through, and send it out for the last rites. And he will.

"First Interview with Artemus Ward," 1871 (WMT 7).
The author has never seen Artemus Ward before. But now they meet and plan to have breakfast together, with Hingston present. In the silver-mining region, it is almost a religion to precede such a meal with whiskey cocktails. Even though the author tries to resist on the grounds that alcohol goes to his head, Artemus gently insists. Sure enough, the author soon feels cloudy. Artemus begins to describe his novice notions of silver lodes in plausible but totally incomprehensible terms. When the author, admitting to befuddlement, asks him to repeat, Artemus becomes even more verbose. Finally Hingston collapses behind his newspaper in laughter. And Artemus Ward has been criticized for not being fluent in conversation.

Hingston, Artemus Ward.

"The First Writing-Machines," 1905 (WMT 24).
A correspondent sends Clemens a typewritten letter, dated in 1875 from Hartford over the signature of Mark Twain and stating that the undersigned owns a typewriter but does not wish to receive requests to describe it and has therefore stopped using it. Is

the letter genuine? Clemens replies to the effect that his best answer is contained in a chapter from his unpublished autobiography, from Florence in 1904. The chapter reports the following: Clemens saw his first typewriter in Boston in 1873 when he was lecturing there with Nasby. Clemens bought one for $125, practiced on it, dictated to a typist using it, hired a girl to copy part of *The Adventures of Tom Sawyer* on it in 1874, but decided after a year or two that the machine was degrading his character and therefore gave it to Howells. But Howells found that his morals worsened because of the machine and therefore returned it to Clemens, who gave it to his coachman, who later traded it for a side saddle.

Edward Bok, [William Dean] Howells, Patrick McAleer, [Petroleum V.] Nasby.

"Fitz Smythe's Horse," 1866 (WG).
Fitz Smythe's horse feeds on newspapers, as the narrator has just seen. Then a boy tells him that his father plans to kill the horse because it also eats puppies, Bibles, tracts, and cats, in fact anything it can get into its mouth. Smythe rides it stiffly.

General Macdowl, Fitz Smythe.

"The Five Boons of Life," 1902 (WMT 24).
In the morning of life a fairy offers a youth one gift among the following five: fame, love, riches, pleasure, and death. She warns him that only one is valuable. He chooses pleasure but in a few years feels mocked. She returns, and he chooses love but after many years sits by a coffin in an empty home in sorrow. He then takes the gift of fame from her, but after a time laments that fame causes envy, hate, and finally pity. She asks him to choose again, and he takes wealth but after three years calls his money gilded lies and begs for death. But now the fairy says that she gave death away to a child who was sensible enough to let her make the choice. Now the man must endure the insult of old age.

["Flies and Russians"], 1972 (FM).
His Majesty is so fascinated by what he is reading that he stops

dressing. He reads that rabbits were created to cower, mollusks to sleep, idiots to live in dull dreamland, and bees to make honey for robbers to enjoy. What are Russians for? To suffer their work to enrich a robber family. It is a puzzle, like the creation of the fly. The making of flies and Russians must have been a mistake. Yet when it made other errors, for example, saurians and pterodactyls, nature abolished them. In a few million more years, nature will probably notice that flies and Russians were mistakes and will accordingly obliterate them. It is also comforting to realize that it took nature eons to evolve from a dog-like and then a calf-like creature the noble horse that we know today. Perhaps, in the fulness of time, flies and Russians will evolve into something less enigmatic. Even now, Russians could be converted into something useful with the injection of intelligence. See how well they fight in Manchuria. They should use the energy that they expend in keeping their regal chipmunk on his throne to destroy both him and it.

    His Majesty [the Czar of Russia].

Following the Equator: A Journey around the World, 1897 (WMT 20, 21).

    In mid-summer, Twain with two members of his family goes from New York to British Columbia to start a lecture tour. After forty days they take a steamer for a three-week Pacific voyage. The captain is handsome but dislikes tobacco smoke. The purser is an iron-willed invalid. One passenger is a Canadian alcoholic. All of this occasions an essay by Twain on the need of a would-be self-reformer to destroy desire rather than a given habit. A lady acquaintance of Twain's had no bad habits; so when she got sick, she had nothing to give up and hence pined away. The ship gets into hot weather, and the passengers amuse each other by accounts of prodigious memories. Then they play at story-completing, the best incomplete tale being about kind, shy John Brown, who leaves his buggy and undresses to wade in some water to retrieve his hat, only to have his horse walk off. He catches the buggy, dresses except for his trousers, then flings a lap-robe over himself just as his fiancée Mary Taylor and her somewhat disapproving mother appear on the road. Mary wants to borrow the robe—.

    Seeing Honolulu through his port-hole reminds Twain of his

visit to Hawaii twenty-nine years before, but cholera ashore keeps everyone from landing, even a lecturer. So Twain dilates on matters Hawaiian: Kamehemeha I, Liholiho, taboos, the old pagan church, Kamehameha V, and Christian missionaries. From his memories, from talks with passengers whose home is Honolulu, and from such authorities as Mrs. Krout, he pieces together contrasting pictures of Hawaii past and present, then concludes by discussing leprosy and Father Damien. In diary form Twain describes crossing the equator, which some passengers photographed. He plays in a shuffleboard tournament and loses impressively. The crew wash down the decks and paint the ship in such a way as to slop the passengers. They all cross the International Date Line and move from Sunday, September 8, to Tuesday, September 10, which causes many jokes on time. When the passengers discuss the Scotch pronunciation of *three*, Twain dis honestly settles the matter by making up a couplet from revered Robert Burns. He then criticizes the Southern Cross, which is out of shape. Going through the Horne (Hoorn) Island group reminds him of his reading about New Caledonia and Queensland slave trade in the area. He quotes from three authorities: Captain Wawn, a mercenary slave-recruiting shipmaster; Rev. Mr. William Gray, a humane missionary; and Right Rev. M. Russell, an idealistic im perialist. At Suva, in the Fijis, the passengers see an American ship, from Duluth, and when ashore sample the torrid midwinter weather. Twain meets with some officials, looks about, and dis cusses Fijian history and notions of immortality. Next he chats aboard ship with a cultivated, fluent Englishman who is a resident in New Zealand and an expert on Australian fauna—kangaroos, dingos, wombats, moas, sundowners (tramps), and the fabulous ornithorhyncus—to which he wrote an "Invocation." Approaching Sydney at night, Twain sees phosphorescent por poises and then recalls the tragedy of the *Duncan Dunbar*, ship wrecked at the false opening near Sydney Heads and killing two hundred wives and children returning home. Next he discusses the Australian climate, quoting Sturt and Gane on the withering heat and the dust storms of the interior. Now follows a violent castiga tion of England for its shipping of convicts to Australia at the end of the eighteenth century, for its inhumane punishment of those convicts there, and for its brutal New South Wales Corps of militia men with their monopoly on rum, etc. Twain discusses Australian hospitality, accents, and manners, partly in comparison to those of America. When Twain tells a missionary named Mr. X. about a cosmic pantheistic dream he had in Sydney, the missionary comments on it and then explains that Hindus prefer their gods and religious heroes to those of Christians because theirs are stronger—for example, Samson carried only city gates on his shoulders (and they are gone), whereas Hanuman carried part of the Himalayas and the evidence is still visible. Twain writes next about buildings and gardens in Australia, then high society there, the governor's functions, the Admiralty House, and finally bounty-fishing for dangerous sharks. This leads him to present the story of how Cecil Rhodes cornered the Australian wool-market—by reading in a ten-day-old London newspaper which he took from a shark's stomach in Sydney news of the declaration of war by France against Germany, and consequently interesting a rich broker in buying the crop deliverable in sixty days.

On the way by usually comfortable rail to Melbourne, capital of Victoria, Twain inveighs against the two gages of jealous railroads (which occasion car-changing) and railroad coffee (so bad that sheep-dip improves it). Passing the town of Wagga-Wagga makes him think of Arthur Orton, who once lived in that town and who claimed to be Sir Roger Tichborne. Twain explains how a titled Englishman whom he will call Henry Bascom invited him to his estate several times in the 1870s and later wrote from Melbourne to Twain's wife expressing his condolences following Twain's death during his lecture tour in Melbourne. (Twain dramatically promises to take up this topic later.) Melbourne at last. Twain sketches the unique excitement of the annual Melbourne Cup horse-races, the sociable larrikin (friendly loafer), the hospitality, the temperate war-talk, the ducal palace grounds, and the place of convicts in Australian history. Pausing to note that the British Empire is a fourth larger than the Russian Empire and further that the average Australian produces forty times what the average Indian does, Twain rushes off to Adelaide, capital of South Australia, seventeen hours by train across the scrub—so convenient for Australian novelists anxious to lose a heroine—and then through lovely hill country with bewitching trees and startling gorse and broom. On the train, Twain meets first a man who arrived in South Australia with thirty-six shillings and made millions in a copper strike and then an American who has unique charge of the kangaroo-skin trade. Twain summarizes Adelaide's panics and booms, then praises its religious tolerance. Next come comments on the laughing jackass, dingo, telegraph line epically stretched from Adelaide to Port Darwin (thus linking South Australia to Java and hence India and London), and then the happy, childlike, deaf innocence of the Old Settlers, one of whom praises the aborigines for the boomerang and the weet-weet (a springy toy thrown underhand and made to bounce along the ground) and much else. Now an "intermezzo" on a fox-hunt: Twain recalls how he met the Earl of C. He asked Twain, who was watching a fox-hunt in England, where the fox went, and Twain answered, "Which fox?" Quoting Mrs. Campbell Praed, Twain now satirically castigates the white man for savagely decimating the aborigines, whose contradictory nature he describes and whose cleverness at dodging, leaping, digging, observing, stalking, and drawing he praises. Then he quotes accounts by Henry N. Wolloston of phenomenal stoicism among the natives. Next a few words about expressive Australian slang.

In mid-October, Twain goes on to Horsham, seeing cottonwoods, pepper trees, and birds (including magpies) on the way. He visits the Horsham agricultural college and then goes to Stawell, noting its mined gold, fine wines, and melancholy gum trees. The party proceeds to Ballarat, locale of a prodigious gold-strike in 1851, of the labor strike against the government mining license, and of supposedly pure, Ballarat English, like "Q" and "Km" for "Thank you" and "You are welcome." Late in October, on to Bendigo, where Twain meets Blank, founder and sole member of the Mark Twain Club of Corrigan Castle, Ireland. Blank confesses that he wrote the letter (purportedly by Bascom) to Twain's wife telling of Twain's death in Melbourne. Going over toward New Zealand reminds Twain of Professor X. of Yale, who, when he had to attend a dinner for a New Zealand visitor, did research on New Zealand until he knew more about it than the New Zealander. Passing near Tasmania inspires Twain (citing Bonwick as authority) to recount the incredible story of George Augustus Robinson, the Conciliator, who went unarmed into the stronghold of Tasmanian aborigines and persuaded them to accept fatal resettlement. Robinson's appearance in answer to fate's call reminds Twain of Commodore Vanderbilt's Memphis tobacco assistant Ed Jackson; he was given for a practical joke a letter of introduction to Vanderbilt, who saw through it but hired Jackson anyway. Stopping only briefly at the neat city of Hobart in Tasmania, Twain comments on its setting, museum with marsupials and skeep-killing parrots, arrow-heads made by aborigines of bottle fragments, and old folks' home (here Twain inveighs against the miseries of old age).

At last, New Zealand, early in November. They land at Bluff, where Twain comments on the rabbit-plague there, then Dr. Hockin's collection of curiosities (including a lignified caterpillar), and finally the public-spirited Society of Artists. The efficient New Zealand train reminds Twain of the wretched one at Maryborough, Australia, and a conversation about it he had with an amusingly irate fellow passenger. Twain goes to Christchurch through an area that looks like Junior England. At the museum he sees native carvings, jade, and a ten-foot moa skeleton. He sketches the Maori briefly, then discusses the good effects of woman suffrage in New Zealand. He goes by a foul, overloaded cattle-scow from Lyttleton to the first way-port, disembarks fast in nauseating disgust at the parsimonious Union Company (owner of the scow), and gets a better little boat to Nelson, scene of the gory 1866 murder by Burgess (whose icy confession Twain quotes), Sullivan, Levy, and Kelley, of Kempthorne, Mathieu, Dudley, and De Pontius. New Plymouth, then Auckland (which produces Kauri gum by the ton), in late November. Rotorua—the Carlsbad of Australasia—with hot lakes, geysers, and thermal baths, is nearby, but Twain is sick and therefore cannot visit it. Gisborne (Twain mentions transferring passengers by yard-arm basket-chairs and the good work of the Salvation Army). Napier to Hastings early in December (he describes lush vegetation). Then he tells how at lunch in Waitukurai, thinking incorrectly that a certain picture on the wall was of Napoleon III's son, he started talking of him, only to have his wife (who had not seen the picture) do the same—telepathy of an error. While at Wanganui, he learns of Maori intelligence, tabus, love of war as a pastime, and patriotism. So to Wellington early in December. While at sea Twain reads Julia A. Moore's unbelievably sentimental doggerel. In Sydney he writes a ridiculous poem using weird Australian place-names like Mullengudgery and Woolloomooloo.

In the second volume Twain leaves Sydney on December 23, 1895, bound for Ceylon. He likes his Lascar crew but is glad to get to Hotel Bristol in Colombo, where the fiery-colored native costumes are a thrill and put hypocritical European clothes to shame. In Bombay late in January, Twain is delirious with joy at seeing India at last. A troupe of serious bellhops carries his belongings in. When the German hotel-manager cuffs an Indian servant for a misdemeanor, Twain suddenly thinks abashedly of his boyhood observation of slaves. A cough sends him to bed early, and he listens to an incredible combination of wild noises outside his room. Next he describes the sinful, talkative Indian crow. Twain delights in stories of Indian gods and peasants suddenly elevated to nobility but deplores stories of poverty in India.

He hires a lazy servant—Manuel X—but releases him in favor of Mousa, whom he renames Satan and who introduces him to a worshipped friend named God. Twain is delighted when God learnedly discusses Huck Finn with him. After visiting a native prince named Kumar Schri Samatsinhji Bahadur, Twain goes to the Parsee Towers of Silence, where in the presence of a ceremonial dog the dead are reverently fed to vultures and their bones are then sun-dried and thrown into the tower wells. Twain goes to witness an Indian prince's reception of a deputation of the Jain community to thank the prince for reforms which have earned him a knighthood from Queen Victoria. Suddenly Twain digresses to compare white and dark complexions; he gives the highest praise to the rich blacksatin Zulu skin. Later the same evening Twain drives through the city, whose street-sleepers look like plague-smitten corpses (a year later the plague did hit Bombay) to attend a jewel-studded betrothal party of an aged twelve-year-old bride. Next he quotes at great length the newspaper account of a recent grisly and bungled murder of a twelve-year-old Hindu girl named Cassi. This leads him to comment on Indian perjury, swindling, forgery, plagues, suttee, famine, gods, poverty, temples, castes, and finally Thugs.

Late in January, aided by Satan and another servant, named Barney, Twain and his group go in first-class railroad-cars to Baroda, carrying all their bedding with them. Twain is met, breakfasted, and driven through the ancient town. Then he rides on a trained elephant, with howdah and mahout. On the train going back from Baroda, he sees a long, low dog with parenthetical legs; this reminds him of how he guessed the dimensions of a huge St. Bernard dog, the pet of Augustin Daly's Irish doorman, whom he thus got past. Following Eugène Sue, Meadows Taylor, Captain

Vallencey, but mostly Major Sleeman (who was charged with the task of ridding India of Thuggee), Twain discusses Thugs at great length. We are all modified Thugs, he says, and enjoy the sport of killing in many forms. Next he digresses on the subject of curious Indian train customs and then the dreadful but beautiful suttee (citing Sleeman as authority).

A two-day train ride takes Twain to Allahabad, through mud villages which cause him to ponder the meaningless cycles of life. He also comments on Indian midwives, astrologers, trade unions (of sweepers), stoical servants, and finally the sacred Ganges, which meets the Jumna River at Allahabad. Next to the intensely holy city of Benares nearby. Twain goes to a bungalow-like hotel, comments on trees, baths, and the stinking dorian fruit, and then suggests that the unchanging devotion of Hindus to Benares means that their religion will probably last a while. Twain details a mordant, satirical itinerary for devout Hindus to follow to purge themselves and get to heaven; then he suggests that they should instead hope to return to earth as asses and thus avoid their gods, priests, fakirs, hell, and heaven. The nasty Ganges waters kill cholera germs, Twain reports seriously, and he goes on to describe joyous bathing there and then cremation-boats, idols, and minarets. Next he ambivalently praises Warren Hastings, the hardy British soldier who forcefully rescued India from oppression. Still in Benares, Twain now has an interview with a living deity, Sri 108 Matparamahansaparivrajakacharyaswamibhaskaranandasaraswati, and voices his sincere reverence of him; this occasions a violent denunciation of an instance of universal irreverence—British and probably also American desecration of the lovely Taj Mahal.

Now to Calcutta, with its lingam-like monument to Ochterlony, its Black Hole (which the British were foolish not to preserve as an angry monument), its intriguing museum, and its cool February weather (during which door-knobs are only made mushy, not melted). Then Darjeeling in the Himalayas, on the way to which Twain thankfully sees no women toiling in the fields, as they do in Europe, but does see jungles, plains, Ghurkas, and from the Darjeeling Club windows the lofty peak of Kinchinjunga and also some Thibetans. Then he goes by railroad hand-car thirty-five miles thrillingly down past cliffs and banyans and various birds to the plains, for what he calls his most enjoyable day on earth. Next he provides statistics on deaths in India by wild animals and snakes,

and then astronomical figures on governmental killing of dangerous animals and snakes.

Next, northwest from Calcutta to Muzaffurapore, near Dinapore,
then on to Benares and Lucknow. This last location reminds Twain
of the Great Mutiny of 1857—including the ferocious siege of
Lucknow—which he writes about in detail (quoting G. O. Trevel-
yan). When Twain sees the ruins of the Lucknow Residency, Cawn-
pore, and the memorial to its dead nearby, he is reminded of the
Taj Mahal. So he quotes several passages from travel literature
describing this matchless edifice, then says that they all err in
stressing its gem-like quality. He compares it to trees after an ice-
storm, when the sun has come out. Twain goes on to Lahore and
rides an elephant, proceeds to the Afghanistan frontier, then on to
Delphi and Jeypore. He recalls that his servant Satan, who was fast
and likeable, got drunk once too often at Agra and was therefore
released. His successor is Sahadat Mohammed Khan. Suddenly
Twain launches into a criticism of American and Indian educational methods, which are too demanding upon the young. He quotes
letters to him in inaccurate Indian English, then quotes American
pupils' boners (as published by Caroline B. Le Bow). He says that we
should gage teaching to students' ability, the way Miss Sullivan
taught the miraculous Helen Keller.

From Calcutta by water at the end of March to Madras, and then
a long voyage to Mauritius. The captain of the ship is doubted when
he tells the truth, whereas a Scottish passenger credibly tells
whoppers—for example, he once had a pet flying-fish which caught
rats in neighboring fields. Twain adds that in his own writings he
resembles both men. He revels in the charm of lazy voyaging, and
on a ship with no copy in its library of *The Vicar of Wakefield* or
Jane Austen. He docks at Port Louis in Mauritius in mid-April and
proceeds by slow train to Curepipe. Then he pretends to quote an
English citizen on the subject of Mauritius: its relationship with
England, its population, newspapers, sugar crop, cyclones, and
Paul and Virginia. Twain goes on to expatiate on rapacious European colonial policies but then adds that the English rule of India
is representative of government generally preferable to previous
despotisms. Next come comments on native foods (camaron, palm-
iste), monkeys, the landscape (pretty but not riotous), and, again,
the cyclone of 1892. At sea again, and soon into Delagoa Bay in
Mozambique early in May. The Second Class Passenger tells Twain

how [P. T.] Barnum offered to buy the neglected birthplace of Shakespeare, aroused a public outcry, took back his payment, and settled for Jumbo the celebrated British elephant instead (the last part of the story, Twain adds, is untrue).

From the comfortable Royal Hotel in Durban, South Africa, Twain observes muscular Zulu 'rikisha-pullers and the fly-catching chameleon, then drives over the Berea and notes the dazzling flowers and curious trees there, and then visits an impossibly but admirably ascetic Trappist monastery. Next comes a long sketch of the tangled politics (including the British-Boer War of 1881) leading to Jameson's Raid (January, 1896), with Cecil Rhodes coming in for bitter criticism as a villainous British imperialist and Jameson summarized as a hero in England, a pirate in Pretoria, and an indiscreet ass in Johannesburg. Twain wrote most of this sketch a year after he left South Africa, he explains, and used information from books by F. Reginald Statham, Garrett, Mrs. John Hays Hammons, and Russell, as well as details from persons with whom he stayed briefly in South Africa. He sarcastically concludes, on the basis of British vs Boer casualty figures, that Jameson needed 240,000 soldiers, should have emulated Boer tactics, and should have fired something less than 100,000 rounds per enemy dead. Next Twain briefly discusses South African gold-mining, calls Rhodes a highwayman (later a convulsion of nature), and gloomily predicts (on historical precedent) the ruin of the black races in South Africa. Suddenly he begins to praise Cape Colony trains, the rolling veldt, and the liquid voices of African Negro women. Then he criticizes the ugliness and slovenliness of Boer farmers, and the cruelty of Boer jail guards to Negro prisoners. Now for diamonds: Twain tells about the geological formation of the Kimberley diamond crater, the history of the discovery of diamonds in South Africa, the formation of the De Beers Company, mining and processing the blue rock containing the diamonds, sorting, and values— $70,000 mined daily. On to Cape Town in mid-July. Twain looks about briefly. He inveighs violently against Cecil Rhodes, half archangel, half Satan. He tells the story of Dr. James Barry, a wild but capable Cape Town military surgeon who on dying was discovered to have been a woman. And so to England, completing the circumnavigation of the globe in thirteen months.

Kumar Schri Samatsinhji Bahadur, Barclay, Barnard, Barney, [P. T.] Barnum, Dr. James Barry, Henry Bascom,

Blank, Blank, Mrs. Blank, Blind Tom, Brompy, John
Brown, Nusserwanjee Byramjee, B., P. C. B., Earl of C.,
Miss C., Calder, Dr. Campbell, Captain, Captain, Chase,
C. [Clara Clemens], [Olivia Clemens], Colonel, Connor,
Coomber, Mrs. D., Augustin Daly, Davies, Sarah Enderby,
F., Alfred Fairchild, Charley Fairchild, Forbes, G., Gaik-
war of Baroda, Julia Glossop, God, General U. S. Grant,
Hanuman, Major Carter Harrison, Rev. Mr. Haweis, Dr.
Hockin, [Thomas Hughes], Hunter, Mrs. I., Ed Jackson,
Jamrach, Sahadat Mohammed Khan, Kinsey, Professor
Lawson, Jimmy Lewis, Lewis, Maharajah of Mysore, Manu-
el X., Milligan, Sri 108Matparamahansaparivrajakacharya-
swamibhaskaranandasaraswati, Mortimer, Moseley, Mousa,
Dr. Murray, Naylor, Norris, Arthur Orton, Palmer, Rao Ba-
hadur Baskirao Balinkanje Pitale, Polly, Major [J. B.]
Pond, Professor of Theological Engineering, Pugh, Purser,
Mina Bahadur Rana, Cecil Rhodes, Roper, Satan, Second
Class Passenger, S. C. P., Lieutenant General [Philip H.]
Sheridan, Smith, Carlyle Smythe, Professor S., Mrs. T.,
Mary Taylor, Nancy Taylor, Taylor, Thomas, Sir Roger
Tichborne, Commodore Vanderbilt, Viceroy of India,
Pudd'nhead Wilson, Dr. X., Mrs. X., Mrs. X., Professor X.,
X., Z.

["For Free Silver"] (MTP).

In November, 1900, Bryan is elected, in spite of prophecies that
the free-silver law, to go into effect three years hence, would cause
fiscal and other desolations without parallel in America. The
world waits uneasily. Europe sells American securities to Americans. Americans import a little less from abroad. Once in a while
a foreign vessel leaves America not to return. America's export
ships diminish in business and number. Passenger ships disappear.
The United States becomes isolated. Customs houses shut up shop.
The expected Fourth of July arrives, after which free silver begins
to operate officially. No problem. To avoid paying double the free
rate for goods produced abroad, Americans invest in American
factories and home demand rises. Europeans begin to buy in
America, because silver dollars are as good as gold ones. American
factories need more laborers, and ships are built to bring over
foreign-born workers to fill the need. Wages are exemplary. Silver

circulates freely and equitably. Monetary values become stable. Now Europe has a problem. Cheap silver is no longer so readily available. Its price, in fact, rises practically to that of gold. The only thing European leaders can do to discourage the American monopoly of world trade is to adopt a policy of free silver also.

"For the Journal: Washington Correspondence," 1854.*

Signing himself W., Twain describes a recent messy snowstorm in Washington, and his pleasure at seeing various buildings, statues, and monuments. He especially likes the Capitol, activities in Congress, and the Smithsonian Institute—with its museum curiosities, especially Franklin's antiquated printing press.

Park Benjamin, Senator [Thomas H.] Benton, Senator [Lewis] Cass, Mr. Chairman, Senator [Stephen A.] Douglas, [Edwin] Forrest, [Richard March] Hoe, Senator, Senator [William Henry] Seward.

*In Mark Twain's Letters in the Muscatine Journal, 1942.

["Foraging for Food"]. See LSI.

"The Force of 'Suggestion'" (MTP).

When people read about a lurid crime, some of them are tempted to go out and duplicate it. Reports of rape beget repetitions of that crime, and families often hush it up through reluctance to air their embarrassment in court. When alcoholics and gamblers try to reform, we cooperate by putting their bottles and cards out of sight. Yet newspapers repeat salacious stories and thus tempt certain readers to re-enact the terrible deeds reported. The current high crime rate is directly due to open courts and irresponsible journalism. If lurid crimes were tried in secret and not reported to the public, the crime wave might subside.

[The Forgotten Writings of Mark Twain], 1869, 1870, 1871 (FW).*

In 1869 Twain reasons that ballet dancers, such as DeRosa and Bonfanti, are really automatons. Recently he saw an immodestly dressed gymnast who swung by a foot from a trapeze and held first her husband in her teeth and then other men by their hair. Twain

proclaims himself a noble fellow from Tennessee, surprised that
upon his arrival in Buffalo there was no "ovashun." He got a room
in a smelly boardinghouse by giving as a letter of recommendation
a prescription written by a doctor who had treated him for dys-
pepsia. Twain offers a recipe for hash, composed partly of hair and
dish water. He expatiates on women's rights: man is immutably
"the guvnor." Twain hopes that Buffalo will keep its waterworks
intact, since with the solid matter in the water he has already filled
a gulley near his house and intends to build on it; moreover, his
new moustache can act as a filter. In "Vanderbilt—Mark Twain
Sends an Open Letter to the Commodore," Twain inveighs against
the capitalist for profitably allowing an illegal excess of passengers
on his vessels. Twain explains that he has been imitating Vanderbilt by denying charity to others, but still no one gives him
publicity for his pettiness. As a member of the "Society for the
Confusion of Intelligence," Twain writes about raising hogs, adding
that Noah must have liked them a lot since he named his son Ham.
"What He Really Said" tells of a minister named Charles Chasuble,
who supposedly told a deaf deacon to go to hell. What he really
wanted was for the man to go to the vestibule, but a reporter
printed the comment as "go to —," which only shows what trouble
a dash can get one into. Twain then offers another "Society for the
Confusion of Intelligence" item, about the Greek orator Demosthenes, who has been lecturing the Fenians on the Negro question.
"How I Made a Fool of Myself" recounts the narrator Tom's visit
to his Uncle Jeremy's estate in Warwickshire before his departure
from England. Tom confers with his brother Fred about the danger
of getting married, but when Tom arrives at Marston Hall he quickly falls in love with his lovely, independent cousin Agnes. He
intentionally falls from a horse, lounges around recuperating,
and proposes to the laughing, agreeable girl. "Another View of the
Great Jubilee" burlesques the Boston peace jubilee: the music is
so loud that the arrangements committee passes out cotton for the
ears, there is a jews-harp opera in French celebrating Bunker Hill,
a foreigner criticizes John Brown and almost gets mobbed, and a
performance of "Hail Columbia" is so loud that it blows off the
coliseum roof and rattles Boston crockery to pieces. In "Benjamin
Franklin," Twain spoofs Boston—the city of the hero's birth—tells
his story, then signs the effort Hy Slocum. The same man is the
reputed author of "Venerubel Fogee," in which Hy and his rustic

wife Nance are accosted by a women's righter, who criticizes Nance so abusively that she wants Hy to defend her; when he does not, she begins to pound him. "Andy on Grant" reports Andrew Johnson's supposed criticism of President Grant, whom Andy reviles as soulless and timid. In a "Letter to Nasby," Twain commiserates with his friend for losing the postmastership at Confederate X rodes and confesses that he himself is no longer postmaster at Snobby's Corners, Noo York. After a number of brief items we have "Local Notes Taken on the Run," about rains so heavy in Buffalo that one farmer wants an underwater reaper, and about the soapy taste of Niagara water—owing no doubt to bathers on the spot. "Legend of a Musket" is about an old gun which is loaded with handfuls of powder and unseats the old man who fires it. Humorous one-liners follow, about Vanderbilt, Brigham Young, John Chinaman, and Susan B. "The Eclipse" reveals Twain's delight in unusual natural phenomena; some cronies prepare for the eclipse by collecting smoked glasses to look through. After several additional minor items, we have "Olive Burnett—a Tale Told out of School," about a peppy schoolboy disciplined but liked by his teacher, whom years later he comes back to and marries. In "He Wrestles with Prohibition, and Discovers Why Boston Is Called 'The Hub,' " Twain describes trying to find a drink on Sunday in Boston, failing, and concluding that the statue-dotted city is called the hub because it is the slowest part of the wheel. More brief items follow, including a section on "People and Things," about the Civil War, Siamese twins, a rich woman's will, a spiritualist, an immoral French dentist, a petrifaction hoax, California Chinese, the high price of coal, dull preachers, and developed and latent heat. "Public Lecturing" offers a recipe for failing. The original half of "A Day at Niagara" reports that the hack fares are higher than the Falls and that prohibitory signs are all about the much-visited region. In "Girl's Brothers," Twain suggests that the suitors of a girl can judge her family by observing her brothers. "Professor Jenkins" is a bespangled cyclist who crosses the Niagara River. In "Hamerica vs Hingland," Twain contrasts the two countries chauvinistically. After additional minor items, Twain in "The Prodigal Son Returns" tells readers that some California pioneers are returning East and should be honored. In "A New Theory of Gravitation" he spoofs scientists. "The Arkansas Traveler Comes to Light" recounts the bravery of a mobbed but plucky Arkansan.

Then, at considerable length, Twain criticizes Byron in "Lady Byron—Mrs. Stowe's Revelations," by having bright Mrs. Peasely and stupid Miss Grace De Griddle gossip about the poet's affairs. More minor items precede "Microscopic Meanness," about deadbeats, a piece about ready Irish wit, and comments about Brigham Young, Andrew Johnson, Vanderbilt, and a farmer who generously gave several pecks of apples to some urchins. "The Judge's 'Spirited Woman' " puns on how a girl dismissed her lover because he gave her father some spirits. "Rev. H. W. Beecher" satirizes the divine's agricultural efforts. Twain gets a letter from readers of his "Last Words of Great Men," to the effect that men who are married never have the last word. "Electricity—With the Modern Improvements" jokes that both electricity and itinerant preachers travel in circuits, and also discusses electricity and Byron. More miscellaneous topics follow, about fashions, royal politics, and then Twain himself: his favorite tree?—any bearing forbidden fruit; his favorite gem?—Jack of Diamonds; prose author?—Noah Webster; person he would most like to be?—the Wandering Jew with an annuity; what he most dreads?—exposure; etc. Then some jokes at the expense of the British; for example, to the visiting cockney who asked if there is the "hentail" in America, a native said no but we like cocktails. In a "Letter to the Editor" from "A Lady," in "Forlorn Creature," and in "Clerks and Lady Shoppers," Twain criticizes shoppers who take clerks' time without any intention of buying. Brief items make humor out of undertakers, printers, stupidity and pretentiousness, spiritualism, medical quacks, Horace Greeley's handwriting, male dry-goods clerks, cattle rustlers, teachers, Mormons, baptism, dull preachers, gossip, music, stupid store signs, and death. In "Concerning Dreams," Twain says that Shakespeare thought that dreams were made of stuff, whereas we know that they are made by stuffing—stuffing ourselves with food. The ghost of Hamlet's father was armed "cap a pie," meaning night cap and mince pie. Dreaming is better than being awake. The meanest dream is more exciting than Plutarch. We all dream covetously. Some dream books are inaccurate; for example, no dream should be interpreted to mean that Twain will become a grandmother. Various items discuss hens, French maids, Byron, fashions, and coins. Twain in "Another Fossil" offers a new petrifaction story: a clay-covered creature found near Syracuse turns out to be a drunken Irishman. Minor columns concern death, puns, morals, and money. "A Loving Swain" is about a fellow at the theater who is more anxious to kiss his girl friend than to watch the play. "Wanted Them Sorted Again" tells of a carriage driver getting a bunch of drunks mixed up and asking their friend to sort them out again so that he can deposit them at their right destinations. Accounts of chicanery are followed by "Don't Let It," which tells how Tom Penjolin, a writer, moves from London to Paris to work. While he is there, a medical quack gets into Tom's house, advertises, and begins to receive patients. Meanwhile, a friend named Kramme writes Tom offering him a chance to write a book on war. So Tom returns to London, is mistaken for the quack by a series of doddering patients, seeking nostrums, gets into trouble with the mother of his fiancée Lucy, but straightens everything out at last. We have an item called "Appendix Concerning Dreams," some columns on spiritualism, words, dirt, death, Mormonism, photography, cloister scandals, and Negroes on the subject of comets, and then "A Rural Lesson in Rhetoric," which contrasts artificial diction and rural directness. After a poetic parody in praise of marriage, comments on tall Missouri trees, and a cat that drowned in a can of milk—it was all right, because the owner later strained the milk—Twain launches into a discussion of the uselessness of all kinds of dogs, especially the yellow variety—in an essay called "Yaller Dogs"—from Noah's time on down. The next item of note is "Back from 'Yurrup,' " a piece satirizing the superciliousness of Americans recently returned from Europe, with its counts and fashions. "About Signs" jokes about a variety of signs on store fronts and elsewhere. Then, calling himself Little Red Riding Hood, he writes about his *Innocents Abroad* and how the girl sought its author. "Aladdin, or the Wonderful Scamp" tells of a rascal in Tartary who manipulates stocks like a modern swindler. Twain offers an eight-chapter story called "Byron and the Worm": in 1815, a year or so before their separation, Byron and his wife are living quietly in Newstead Abbey, which has a secret entrance under an ancient oak, beneath which is an illicit still. Byron needs money; so his faithful servant Thomas Blokes agrees to manufacture a quick hundred gallons of whisky for his indigent master to sell. But Timpkins, Mumpsey, and Dickson follow Blokes's little boy, who is bringing food from home for his busy father, and confiscate the still in the name of the law.

In 1870 Twain offers "A New Year's Story," which features an attorney named Arthur Playne, who loves Eva Selby in the city of Dashington but grows disconsolate when Eva's jealous cousin Margaret Danton intercepts his love letter to Eva and returns a forged rejection. Arthur's friend John Darrell, a young surgeon, calls on Eva to rebuke her for spurning his friend, who has gone off to Boston. When John later tells him that Eva lied, Arthur grows suspicious, guesses that Margaret has been the wrongdoer, returns to Eva, and all is joy. The narrator of "Affecting" tells of a stranger leaning against a tombstone and evidently talking to his departed Jenny. The narrator offers comfort with a sketch of the hereafter, and the stranger turns and explains that the lost one made superb potpies. In a couple of pieces called "What I Don't Know of Farming," Hy Slocum chides Horace Greeley for his lack of agricultural knowledge and points out that most amateur farmers lose money, and further that even regular farmers must not be well off financially since they tell the tax collectors that they are not. "Dining with a Cannibal . . ." concerns the King of Easter Island, in the Pacific, who tells the narrator his recipes not only for poi flavored with grasshopper and angleworm but also for yam-seasoned dog, explains how tasty a certain missionary named Johnson was, complains that a missionary named Williams wrote back to America complaining about the King, and then offers the narrator some tempting cooked Frenchman named Gaultier. Suddenly the King faints. He has been eating his own brother. It seems that Gaultier's native fiancée effected a timely switch and escaped with her lover. Twain's "Romance of the XVIth Amendment" tells of Zenobia De Vere, a poor but honest lawyer—really a lawyess—who falls in love with Clarence Fitz Howard, proposes to the faintly moustached, fainting fellow, starts to elope with him by carrying his limp form from his boudoir down a ladder, but runs into his mother, a stern woman who rebukes the daring Zenobia for being an unprincipled kidnappess. Twain satirizes stoicism: most stoics pretend indifference to death but quail in due time, the bravest Indian (for example, the Dirty-foot Grin-and-bear-it) can be scared to death by the sight of a bar of soap, and in the face of pain today's stoic is often aided by ether. After minor items about cannibalism and American justice against the Chinese, Twain offers "Japan," in which he argues that the Japanese are contrary but manly. Between minor items is a French account of the temptation and fall, with M. Adam, Madame Iv, and ze snake in ze garden. "Servant-

Girlism" tells of Turvey Drop's difficulty in obtaining an Irish maid, even with bribes of tobacco and wine, and a promise that his family and others will aid in the work. Soon we have "The Feminine Grand Jury," which points out that with the advent of female juries lawyers must now be handsome. A Wyoming jury of women recently acquitted Handsome Charley Lyndon of the charge of abducting Minnie Hoyle against her will, on the grounds that the alleged kidnaper was romantic and dashing; but the same jury condemned little George Snoop for assaulting Roxana, his 180-pound virago of a wife, when all she did was demand two new hats a month and kick him convulsively when he protested. In "A Big Thing" Twain exposes the probable dishonesty of an item in a Kentucky newspaper in which a respectable physician reports that he has mysteriously discovered a rich silver mine. After a few other minor items, Twain offers "Another Big Thing," in which he pretends to offer the public an opportunity to buy stock in his Behring's Strait and Baffin's Bay Railroad Company. Some punning follows, and then we have "Colored Typos," about competent and valued Negro printers in governmental offices in Washington. More nonsense, and then "Police Court" reports various types of criminals confessing, denying, and sentenced in rhyme. In "Orthographic Retrenchment" Twain estimates the amount of money the British lose by spelling *Labour* with a "u" and explains that Americans might save untold sums by learning to spell by ear, like Nasby and Billings. "Some Life Insurance" tells about mutual insurance companies, dice-throwing actuaries, rewards of neckties to persons reaching the age of 110, and typical questions insurance agents ask: are you in the habit of committing suicide? do you wash your feet much? were your parents related? etc. In a piece called "Personal," Twain answers criticism directed at him for censuring the Rev. Dr. T. De Witt Talmage for writing in a published essay that some laborers offend their fellow church-goers by their smell. Twain says that perhaps Talmage was being ironical, but then quotes his comments in detail and criticizes their atrocious style. "Biography A La Mode" details the life of Robert Kidd, Pirate, who as a child was tough, was apprenticed to a lawyer, then got a boat and went cruising for clients, pillaged them, but was finally caught and suspended. "A Strange Story" concerns an Indian squaw who predicts the San Francisco earthquake. "Fearful Domestic Tragedy" retells the story of Jefferson

Davis Othello, his wife Desdemona (daughter of Senator George W.
Brabantio and niece of Deacon Ebenezer Gratiano), Jim "Honest
Iago" Crow and his wife Emilia, Major Mike Cassio, Billy Roderigo,
Detective Lodovico, and Ex-Commissioner Montano of the Frontier
Police. After his arrest, Iago Crow retains O'Baldwin Graham as
counsel. "One of the 'Polite Circle': The Prize Ring" details the
prize fight of Mace and Allen, who for the benefit of an elite crowd
which includes some clergymen exchange thirty blows, any one of
which ought to have been more effective than the single celebrated
blow in the Cain-and-Abel match. In "Deacon B. Criticizes 'The
New Pilgrim's Progress,' " a reporter identified as Ralph 5 interviews a deacon who purchased The Innocents Abroad from a ped-
dler for $4, read it twice, found it blasphemous, and sold it to
Ralph 5 for $3.75 on condition he could come over and read it
again in case he ever wanted to go through with his plan to preach
against it." 'Lo' at the Capitol" concerns the visit to Washington
of Indians named Red Cloud, Red Dog, Spotted Tail, and He-that-
scratches-his-head, and their retinues. When an annoying bootblack offers to shine the mocassins of Red Cloud, he tomahawks
and scalps the lad. The Indians quiver with delight at the sight
of fashionable chignons among Congressional visitors. Red Cloud
complains to Secretary Cox that the hobbies of horse-stealing and
emigrant-massacring are hard to pursue in the West at this time.
An Indian suffragette is called the woman without any bend.
"A Spicy Correspondence" concerns the narrator's efforts to invite
a group of distinguished people, from Horace Greeley to Louis
Napoleon, to a liquorless soirée, and their various responses. "A
California Crow Story" tells how a big crow built a bar to sell
whiskey-soaked corn to lesser crows, get them drunk, and make
them easier to shoot. "A Dog Story" tells about a naval officer who
owned a faithful double-nosed pointer which stayed pointing at a
covey of partridges while the officer was suddenly called to the
Mediterranean fleet; not only did the pointer die in his tracks,
as the owner learned after mustering out three years later and returning home, but so did the galvinized birds. After minor items,
Twain in "A Severe Stab at Women's Rights" criticizes a Niagara
husband who demanded the right to supervise his washerwoman
wife's orders. In "The Trotting Season" Twain suggests that human
beings should be bred as carefully as horses and offers comments
on some people's betting instincts; a fellow was dozing in church

when he heard a reference by the preacher to Siloam's pool and leaped up to place a bet in it. Minor items follow; then comes "John Chinaman in New York: The John Question," which praises the Chinese for frugality but ridicules their imitativeness and awful music. More tiny items, including one-liners, give way to poetry critical of Napoleon and the inroads Old Time makes on all things but friendship. Minor items, including "Moguldom" and "An Honorable Gentleman"; then comes "Jim Todd: A Sketch in Crude Oil," about a stupid Pennsylvania farmer who strikes oil and becomes conceited as though he deliberately selected the family homestead he was born on. "His Official Thrift and Prosperous Remorse" describes a petty politician named Tom Smith, who wields bribes and embezzles $500,000; when located, he agrees to repay fifty cents on the dollar and thereafter lives well, on the remnant, to a hoary old age. "The Bathing Tutor" tells about the fun a brawny man has in helping young ladies learn to swim at the beach; he hates ugly squealers but loves to slosh clinging beauties. Next appears a correspondent named Ab. O'Riginee, who writes from Aspinwall, Panama, about political instability down there and a statue of Columbus sent from France and impatient to be set up. Brief items, some of them featuring puns, precede "The Upper Mississippi," in which C, an occasional Correspondent, describes Western and Southern types on the river, and some of the intricacies of piloting. Ab. offers "Life on the Isthmus," with comments on overweight Panamanians, a Negro robber, the death of Sam Curry, a Negro-murdering policeman, and cock fighting. "De Coy's Moral Tonic" is a satirical piece about the dramatically beneficent effects of Professor De Coy's popular truth syrup: lying, stealing, and hypocrisy are all on the wane. Silly items are followed by "The Hawkeye State," concerning Iowa's distinguished Civil War record and the legendary hospitality of early Iowans. Soon we have "Agricultural Twaddle at the Institute Farmer's Club," in which Carl Byng reports on gentleman farmers, including Greeley, and their inefficient efforts to grow things. "Jenkins at Wilhelmshohe" recounts an interview with Napoleon, who reveals a few things about his background and Eugénie, then leaves a relic from his nose on the reporter's shirt. Items about drunks, beggars, and bedbugs precede "Three Aces: Jim Todd's Episode in Social Euchre," which tells of Jim Todd's defeat at cards aboard the *Natchez Ranger*. Ab. O'Rig Inee then continues his report from Panama: Columbus's statue is up, and local citizens playfully duel with skyrockets. "War and 'Wittles' " reports that, what with the Franco-Prussian War still raging, the ingenious French have devised enticing new dishes, including minced cat and shoulder of dog. "Some Unpublished Literature of Paten Mecine " includes five testimonials by persons disenchanted with nostrums. In "Review of Holiday Literature," Twain offers a multi-paragraph analysis of "Hey, diddle, diddle!", a poem by the celebrated authoress Mother Goose. In "Advice to Parents" he suggests that the only fool-proof way to bring up children is by their hair, and follows that sketch first by describing his father's disciplinary power and second by advising parents to tell inquisitive children to shut up.

Early in 1871 Twain offers "That Book Agent," about a door-to-door canvasser so persistent that Twain buys many useless volumes, and finally brains and burns the salesman, and sells his ashes to the potash man.

Abednego, Monsieur Adam, Agnes, Ah Song Hi, Ah Why, Aladdin, Allen, Angelina, Susan B. Anthony, the Appointment Clerk, Archbishop, Prince Arthur, Modesto Arze, Augusta, Aunt, Aurusta, Deacon B., Agag Solomon David B., Bailey, Mrs. Bailey, [Phineas T.] Barnum, Barstowe, Baz, Rev. H. W. Beecher, Sally Benjamin, Josh Billings, Mrs. Birney, Tom Blennerhasset, Blennerhasset, Master Blodgett, Bobby Blokes, Thomas Blokes, Mrs. Thomas Blokes, M. Blot, James Bly, Bonfanti, Boreas, [Dion] Bouc-cicault [Boucicault], Josh Bowers, Mrs. Josh Bowers, Bowers, Bowery, B'Hoy, Senator George W. Brabantio, [Mary E.] Bradden [Braddon], Brady, Dick Brand, Bridget, Brief, Sy Brown, Brown, Brown, Brown, Brown, Brown, T. Browne, Buckwheat, Johnny Bull, Ned Buntline, Olive Burnett, Robert Burns, General [Benjamin F.] Butler, Lady Byron, Lord G. Gordon Byron, Byron, Mrs. Byron, Carl Byng, Cabinet Minister, the Cacique of Coín, Cain, California Pioneer, Canard, Canard, Cap, Cap, a Captain, William Carter, Count Caskowhisky, Major Mike Cassio, Cato, Chang, Charles, Sir Charles, [Charles Albert], Charlie, [Salmon P.] Chase, Rev. Charles Chasuble, Choy-Chow, City Father, Mr. Clerk, John Close, Mrs. John Close, Lady Cockledoodledoo, Christopher Columbus,

Confucius, the Congressional Printer, Consul, Coroner, President Correoseo, Correspondent, [Thomas] Corwin, Count, [Jacob D.] Cox, Mrs. Emilia Crow, Jim Crow, Sam Curry, Cy, Dan El Dru, Margaret Danton, John Darrell, Dead Beat, Professor De Coy, Grace De Griddle, C. E. De Long, Demosthenes, Great Uncle Dent, De Rosa, Zenobia De Vere, Charles Dickens, Anna Dickinson, Dickson, Director, Doc, Thomas Dodd, Tommy Dodd, Dr. Dosemwell, Fred Douglass, William Douglass, Douglass, Columbine Drop, Turvey Drop, Mrs. Turvey Drop, Dry Goods Clerk, the King of Easter Island, an Elder, Elihu, Eng, Empress Eugénie, Farceur, James Fisk Jr., Fisk, Clarence Fitz Howard, Mrs. Fitz Howard, Augustus Fitzmaurice, Florence, Forlorn Creature, Emperor Francis II, Benjamin Franklin, Fred, [Robert] Fulton, Gaultier, Genii, Good Templar, Mother Goose, Gossip Five, Gossip Four, Gossip One, Gossip Two, O'Baldwin Graham Esq., Grandma, Grange, President [Ulysses S.] Grant, Grant, Deacon Ebenezer Gratiano, Miss Gray, Great Father, the Hon. Horace Greeley, Grin-and-bear-it, Gustavius, General Halleck, Ham, Bob Hamilton, Hannah, James Hannay, Aunt Hanner, Harpalus, Hawk, Herrings, He-that-scratches-his-head, Sam Hilderbrand, Hiram, His Honor, Hopkins, Hornet, Mrs. Hornet, G. Howard, [Elias] Howe, Minnie Hoyle, Hoyle, Victor Hugo, an Inquiring Texan, Madame Iv, Jaghoole, Janet, Professor Jenkins, Jenkins, Jenny, Jeremy, Joe, Joe, Count Johannes, John, John Chinaman, John Chinaman, President Andrew Johnson, John Johnson, Johnson, Jonah, Buck Jones, J. Jones, Jones, Jones, Jones, Jones, Mrs. Jones, Jones, Josh, Joshua, Her Honor the Judge, K., Ka-besh-co-da-way, Kenukel, Andrew Jackson Kidd, Mrs. Betsey Kidd, Robert Kidd, the Knight of the Strop, Koopmanschap, Koopmanschoop, Kraft, Kramme, L., L., a Lady, the Lamented, Lashetschriskoff, Layman, Mark Lemon, Leonard, Levi, Little Red Riding Hood, Detective Lodovico, Lucy, Judge Lynch, Charles Lyndon, M. F. Mabie, Mace, Mace, Mary, Mary, Johnny McGrade, Mellowhead, Metternich, the Mexican Minister to the United States, M'Gilp, Military Governor,

Miss Milldam, Moker, Ex-Commissioner Montano, Edward Moon, the Moral Phenomenon, Mr.—, Mudie, Mrs. Mulrooney, Bill Mumpsey, Dr. My Gosh, Napoleon, Louis Napoleon [III], Petroleum V. Nasby, Nathan, Mr. Negro, Sir Isaac Newton, Noah, Oberon, an Occasional Correspondent, Oliver, Ab. O'Riginee, Mrs. Desdemona Othello, Jefferson Davis Othello, Paddy, Mrs. Partington, Parton, Mrs. Parton, a Partridge, Patrick, Mrs. Peasely, Tom Penjolin, Professor Pepper, Charles S. Pierce, Pilkins, Arthur N. Playne, Timothy Porter, Mrs. Timothy Porter, Postmaster, the President, Privateer, Professor, Mrs. Pry, Ex-Constable Quinn, Sir Ralph, Reporter Ralph 5, the Reading Committee, Red Cloud, Red Dog, the Red Ink Deputy, Redpath, Regular, Robinson, Billy Roderigo, a Roman Augur, Romero, Jerry Ross, Rossini, Mrs. Rossini, the Russian Minister in America, Saengerbund, Saint-Beuve, Sally, Sam, Sam, North Adams Sampson, Jules Sandeau, Eva Selby, Selby, Senator, Western Senator, Seventeenth, [William H.] Seward, Shadrach, George W. Shanks, General [Philip H.] Sheridan, General [William T.] Sherman, Sing-Man, Dr. Sixhammers, Dr. Skinner, H. Y. Slocum, Hy Slocum, Mrs. Nance Slocum, Slocum, Dr. Slow, Dr. Sluable, Henry T. Smith, John Smith, John Smith, John Smith, John Smith, the Hon. Thomas Smith, Aunt Smith, Dr. Smith, Smith, Smith, Smith, Mrs. Smith, Smith, Smith, Smith, Smith, Mrs. Smith, Smith, Smith, Smith, Mrs. Smith, George Snoop, Mrs. George Snoop, Jake Snoop, Solon, Somefellow, Sorosis, Sorosis, Souchong, General Spinner, Spotted Tail, Squire, the State Auditor of Missouri, [George] Stephenson, Stephenson, Mrs. Stew, Stockjawber, Stoic, Mrs. [Harriet Beecher] Stowe, Subscriber, the Sultan, Hugo de Swagger, Talcott, Rev. Dr. T De Witt Talmage, William Tell, Tell, Tim, Time, Timpkins, Titanis, Jim Todd, Mrs. Jim Todd, Tom, Tom, a Tombs Shyster, George Francis Train, Hans Twaddles, Frau Hans Twaddles, [William M.] Bill Tweed, Commodore [Cornelius] Vanderbilt, Rip Van Winkle, [King] Victor Emmanuel [II], Queen Victoria, W , the Prince of Wales, Dr. Warren, George Washington, Webster, Gideon Welles, Fridden

Werm, Wheelock, [John Greenleaf] Whittier, Widow, King William, Williams, Mrs. Winslow, Ned Wright, Yellow Bear, Brigham Young, Young, Father Youngman, Zeno.

*Mark Twain's Buffalo *Express* items. See *The Forgotten Writings of Mark Twain*, ed. Henry Duskis (New York: Philosophical Library, 1963). Many items in this unreliable book are of doubtful authenticity. The titles of individual items in this book are not listed in my Chronology above but are interspersed through this alphabetized sequence of summaries for reference.

"Forlorn Creature." See FW, 1869.

"Fortifications of Paris." See "Map of Paris."

[A Forty-niner], 1871 (CG).
A Forty-niner has just sent Twain a poem which was written years ago in Stockton, California, and which is called "The Miner's Lament." In it, an unsuccessful miner gripes about his poor food and ragged clothes.

A Forty-niner, Kean.

"Forty-Three Days in an Open Boat." See "My Début as a Literary Person."

"Foster's Case" (LAIFI). See "Mark Twain on Foster."

"Fragments of Prussian History" (MTP).
The time is January, 1732. The scene is wintry and desolate. Plodding along are several carriages, bearing Prince Henry, heir to margraveship of Bayreuth, and Henry's spirited little bride, Wilhelmina, the daughter of the King and Queen of Prussia, and their retinue. Wilhelmina breaks her boredom by telling her maid that she has been dreaming again about the old prophecy that she is destined to bear four crowns. She almost married into English royalty. True, she will have a Bayreuth crown; but London would have been so nice, and what of the other crowns? The procession enters ugly little Bayreuth, and Governor Dabenek gives such a stirring speech of welcome, and the crowds seem so sincere, that Wilhelmina is almost happy for a moment. Court life here seems

too frowsy, however, after her gilded dreams. All the same, the humor of the situation eases her predicament. At last they enter what passes for the local castle, a dull square box of stone. She is greeted graciously by the Margrave himself, who in scrawniness and affected manners gives a fair imitation of Louis XIV, his idol. The royal family takes Wilhelmina upstairs to her rooms, which are lofty but dingy. Of its tapestry depicting the Children of Israel in the Wilderness, only the Wilderness remains. The bride is appalled but when asked describes everything as *wunderschön* . . . [Notes follow.]

The Margrave of Bayreuth, Baron von Burstell, Chief Maid of Honor, Governor von Dabenek, Escort, Prince Henry, King of Prussia, Queen of Prussia, Baron von Reitzenstein, Royal Court, Princess Wilhelmina.

"Francis Lightfoot Lee," 1877 (LAIFI).

Francis Lightfoot Lee is conspicuous to historians only because he signed the Declaration of Independence. But it may be appropriately added that he came from an honorable family, was accustomed to wealth, was well educated, loved his library, managed his estate admirably, was a dedicated justice of the peace, and was a gentleman. He worked diligently in the provincial legislature, labored patriotically in the Continental Congress, answered the call to duty in the state legislature, and finally was allowed to retire to his beloved home, family, and friends. What a contrast between Lee and the typical congressman today!

Francis Lightfoot Lee.

["The French and the Comanches"], 1962 (LFC).

The love of cruel, savage massacre grows out of a people's social system. It is hard to say whether the French or the Comanches are superior in this love, although the latter's refusal to fight among themselves probably means that they rank higher than the former. The French may not really be more cruel than the Comanches, but they are surely more ingenious. Look at what the French nobility did to their docile people for a thousand years: riding down crops, punishing poachers, bizarre executions, and of course *le droit du seigneur*. The French are unique in dramatizing the spirit of massacre. Consider the St. Bartholomew's Day massacre back in 1572. During two days and three nights some seventy thousand people lost their lives. Why? Because of French docility. But beware when the typical Frenchman doffs his rabbit skin and dons that of the tiger. The foreigner is a boon to France. For example, Napoleon certainly gave his meek subjects glory. The French love that, and parties, lots of brag, *vive* to this and that, hurrahs, hearses, and other such inexpensive grandeurs. The tiger within the French, when combined with their enormous vanity, results in mighty soldiers. Well, then, we can agree that in some ways the French are superior to the Chinese and in fact are hardly inferior to the Comanches after all. America must help the French perfect themselves. How? By sending trained squads of lay missionaries to France, to lift its citizens, those links between apes and men, up to brotherhood with the rest of mankind.

Queen Mother [Catherine de' Medici] of France, King [Charles IX] of France, Napoleon, Napoleon III.

"The Jumping Frog." See "The Celebrated Jumping Frog of Calaveras County."

[From an Article in a Police Court Column] (P). See "Police Court," in FW, 1870.

["From an English Notebook"], 1962 (LFE).

Twain describes his feelings when he drives through Hyde Park and sees the Albert Memorial. It is a huge jewel in a battered, blackened city. At the four corners of the memorial are statuary groups representing Asia, Europe, America, and Africa. Its enclosure has a frieze of statues of great artists and writers. It seems incredible that this noble building should all be in glorification of Prince Albert, a foreign gentleman essentially mediocre and commonplace. The International Exhibition honors him too. England frequently immortalizes the deserving Nelson and Wellington. But why Albert?

Turning next to old St. Paul's, the author confesses to profound emotions, even when he considers its back yard, the pavement of which was designed by Morgan Jones and the railings of which were built by Ralph Benson. Some of Benson's tools are preserved in the British Museum. Twain gives details as to dimensions of the railings and adds that there is no charge for looking through or climbing over them. The stone pediment beneath the railings was erected by William Marlow, pupil of Hugh Miller, and combines Pre-Raphaelite and Renaissance architectural modes. Incidentally, tone and feeling are everything: you need an expert to tell you how to respond to the tone and the feeling of venerable art objects. The front yard of St. Paul's resembles the back but in addition has a statue of a regal-looking black woman. The rest of St. Paul's has so often been described that Twain feels he need not concern himself with it here.

Finally, the British Museum is especially impressive to Twain, who learns from a friend there that ministers come in droves on Saturdays to copy sermons. Another acquaintance enables him to see the eighteen miles of tall bookcases in the museum. He also visits the impressive reading room, and elsewhere is shown necklaces, death casts, old vases, prehistoric relics, and mummies. He almost cries upon one mummy's chignon but does wonder how mummies ever walked with all those bandages on.

Ralph Benson, [King] George III, Morgan Jones, Lee, William Marlow, Queen Mary, Hugh Miller, Vandal, Woodward.

["From an Unfinished Burlesque of Books on Etiquette"], 1962 (LFE).

At a funeral do not criticize the main guest, or his casket or flowers. Listen with seeming attentiveness to the boasts made about him. Be moved to the right degree, based on closeness to him. Avoid bringing your dog.

If you are ever in a position to rescue a strange young lady from a fire, apologize for not having been introduced to her, remark that a fiery doom overshadows her with its crimson wing, say "Permit me" when you touch her, and bow and smile politely. Avoid brusqueries while rescuing chambermaids. Carry to safety persons caught in boardinghouse fires according to a priority list, which begins with fiancées, sisters, and cousins, goes down to invalids and unclassified females, and ends with clergymen, servants, firemen, furniture, and finally mothers-in-law. Do not let the confusion force you into a breach of etiquette. Use certain modes of address. Do not propose marriage during an actual rescue. Rescues at sea or from destruction occasioned by hurricanes, earthquakes, or railroad crashes should be consummated in accordance with specified modifications of the above.

The proper leaving of visiting cards is an earnest of one's cultured seriousness. The texture of the card, its style of engraving, and the hour of leaving it are all telling. Use linen cards, never a greasy or second-hand deck. Have your name engraved on the back of face cards and on the front of other cards. Do not leave a card before breakfast, since it might be construed as a plea for some food. Never leave a card after bedtime, because you might get shot. Remember that card suits speak a language of their own. Diamonds symbolize one's independence of means; hearts, love; clubs, fashion; and spades are noncommittal. Go straight in, without being too friendly with the servants, and leave your chosen card. The denomination of the diamond hints at the degree of your wealth, from three meaning $300,000 to king meaning $20,000,000. An ace means that you own a monopoly. Later switch suits and continue leaving cards. Start low, outplay rivals, and eventually propose by pasteboard. Mind you, when you propose, be in evening dress— or in uniform, but without revolver or spurs. The lady should wear unripe orange buds, and other clothes too, of course. The two parties should follow the appended sample conversation. If rejected, demand a new deal or junk your hand. If accepted, give flowers daily and let their red hue gradually deepen in intensity. Better still, give a handkerchief, then a napkin, then a towel, and so on to a big blanket on the wedding day.

Second Lieutenant Baggs, Mrs. 2d-Lieut.-Co.-B.,-42d-Regt.-N.Y.-Mounted-Militia Baggs, Hooligan, Mrs. Clerk-of-the-Board-of-Aldermen Hooligan, Jones, Mrs. Superintendent-of-Public-Instruction Jones, Madmoselle, Mary, Miss, Lady Portsmouth, Reginald, Spinster, Strange Young Gentleman, Strange Young Lady, Thomas, William, Young Gentleman.

From "Home and Mrs. Byron" (Supposedly Written by Lord Byron to His Aged Sister), 1869 (probably by Twain) (P).

Lord Byron expresses love for his sister Aurusta and then alludes to a certain story in the *Atlantic Monthly*.

Aurusta, Lord Byron.

"From My Unpublished Autobiography." See "The First Writing-Machines."

[From "The Entertainment Yesterday"], 1870 (probably by Twain) (P).

Squire Vanderpool rules on John Deming, convicted of beating John Greiner; Peter Eberhardt, accused of beating Jim Green; Patrick Horan, convicted of stealing; and Henry T. Smith, indicted for cheating his landlord.

Dick Dalton, John Deming, Peter Eberhardt, Charley Fellen, Jim Green, John Greiner, Patrick Horan, Henry T. Smith, Squire Vanderpool.

"From the 'London Times' of 1904," 1898 (WMT 22).

Mark Twain is in Chicago, April 1, 1904, and resumes his report to the *London Times* about Captain John Clayton. The writer should first explain that in Vienna back in March, 1898, at the house of Lieutenant Hillyer, the American military attaché, Clayton (then an army lieutenant) and the brilliant inventor Szczepanik argued about the latter's telelectroscope, then not yet released, and even came to blows. The scene shifts to Chicago in the fall of 1901. The telelectroscope was developed by that time; in addition, it had been successfully connected with the telephone systems of the world, and it thus became possible simultaneously to see and talk with persons anywhere on the globe. Clayton, assigned to the Chicago area, and Szczepanik happened to meet again, and soon they renewed their terrible quarrel. On December 29 a corpse, identified as that of Szczepanik, was found in Clayton's basement. The officer was arrested for murder, tried, convicted, and sentenced to hang. Clayton's wife was the governor's niece, and she was able to get stays of execution through 1902 and 1903; but the man was finally scheduled to hang March 31, 1904. He was given every comfort, including a telelectroscope with an international-telephone hook-up. He loved to call Yedo, Hong-Kong, Melbourne, and so on. As Clayton was led to the gallows, his wife in widow's weeds beside him, Twain, who loyally stood by in the prisoner's comfortable quarters, happened to tune in Peking, saw the coronation of the new Czar, and observed Szczepanik in the procession. Twain shouted from the window, and Clayton was released. But then in April, 1904, as the reporter's final dispatch reveals, it was decided before the Supreme Court of the United States, which since the constitutional amendment of 1899 has jurisdiction over retrials, that, on the French precedent concerning Dreyfus, Clayton's pardon was invalid because although Szczepanik was not murdered, a murdered corpse had been found in his basement, and that therefore the accused, proved in court to have killed Szczepanik, must hang. So poor Clayton was hanged. America deplores this example of French justice.

Captain John Clayton, Mrs. John Clayton, Miss Clayton, Mr. Justice Crawford, the Czar, the Governor of Illinois, Mr. Justice Halleck, Lieutenant Hillyer, K., Chief Justice Lemaître, General Merritt, Szczepanik, Mark Twain, W., Mr. Justice Wadsworth.

"A Full and Reliable Account of the Extraordinary Meteoric Shower of Last Saturday Night," 1864 (SS).

The narrator writes Professor B. Silliman, Jr., of San Francisco, to describe details of the meteor shower. The narrator took copious notes and expects the good professor to honor his promise to publish these observations in the *American Journal of Science.* Anyway, last Saturday night the narrator got two tumblers to use as telescopes, rinsed them with Veuve Cliquot, elevated them to a 90° angle, and looked through them out his window. But no stars. After the third wash, he thought that he saw some stars shoot around and Jupiter fall on a watchman. The man said, "By Jupiter"; so it must have been that star. More rinses, and the narrator saw more stars, one of which fell onto an American flag flying in the Plaza, thus predicting the elevation of Nevada to statehood. Soon the narrator went into the street, bumped into the actor Charles Kean, and watched that star fall. Next the narrator was hit in the stomach by a whizzing star made of a pasteboard cylinder and a thin pine stick. Later he got into a fight with a fellow who ducked a left and threw a right cross to the head. Many more stars. Another star at once appeared and shone with a police number on it. The narrator's punster friend John William Skae soon showed up, spoke of his Susan, and said that he was going to meteor by moonlight. In closing, the narrator says that he hopes Professor Silliman will print the above observations, with suitable illustrations.

Dick, the Governor of Nevada, the Governor of the Third House, Charles Kean, Professor B. Silliman, Jr., John William Skae, Susan.

'Fulton Day, Jamestown,' 1907 (WMT 28).

Twain says that he and his friends are here to celebrate the anniversary of an historical application of steam by Robert Fulton. It is an American holiday, unlike the Fourth of July, which was an event managed by English residents in America. Twain turns to Admiral Harrington for details about Fulton's little boat to relay to their audience. The boat was ten feet long and two hundred feet broad, and first voyaged from Jersey City via Albany to Chicago. Twain will not compliment Harrington, the next speaker, because praise always embarrasses people and makes them tongue-tied. But he will say that he and Harrington arranged to have Pocahontas save Smith as a publicity stunt to advertise Jamestown, and further that he and Harrington have been mistaken for each other because they have the same high qualities.

Robert Fulton, Admiral Harrington, Pocahontas, Powhatan, Smith.

"The Funeral of 'Buck' Fanshaw." From *Roughing It.*

"Further Concerning That Conundrum" (SS). See "Still Further Concerning That Conundrum."

"Further Correspondence of Mark Twain Concerning the Occupancy of Grace Cathedral" (SS). See "Further of Mr. Mark Twain's Important Correspondence."

"Further of Mr. Mark Twain's Important Correspondence," 1865
(SS). (See also "Important Correspondence . . .")
Although he promised to publish his correspondence with Rev.
Phillips Brooks of Philadelphia and Rev. Dr. Cummings of Chicago, relative to inviting them to consider coming to occupy Grace
Cathedral in San Francisco, the narrator now wishes to decline.
The two ministers wrote him that he was stupid, was ruining the
clerical image, and should accept some money from them to keep
quiet. He will not repeat their words but will instead simply say
that each man is earning more than $7,000 a year and is also profit-
ably involved in the stock market—Brooks in oil and Cummings
in grain. The narrator is sad. He merely tried to help the church.
Now he is swarmed over by hungry backwoods preachers who are
eating him out of house and home, and his housekeeper is on the
verge of rebelling.

    Rev. Phillips Brooks, T. St. Matthew Brown, Rev. Dr. Cum-
mings, [Rev. Bishop] Hawks, Mike MacSwain, Mick Twine.

'Galveston Orphan Bazaar,' 1900 (WMT 28).
    Twain laments the fact that the Governor of Texas neglected
to show up and speak, and thus say something which would provide Twain a text. He has been in New York only a few days and
is all talked out from having tried to regulate the moral and political situation of the planet. Some years ago a man approached
Twain and said that he looked like Mark Twain. Twain humored
him by saying that he had dressed to look like that excellent man.
The stranger replied that Twain resembled the great man on the
outside but probably was different inside. Twain closes with the
hope that sufferers will be sympathetically helped. In this hope
he is not playing a part.

    The Governor of Texas.

'General Grant's English.' See 'A Rejoinder by Mark Twain.'

'General Grant's Grammar,' 1886 [1887] (WMT 28). See 'A Rejoinder
by Mark Twain.'

'General Miles and the Dog,' 1907 (S).

Twain begins by observing that it is so hard to speak after a complimentary introduction that once when he had to introduce a speaker he thought he would jokingly put him on the defensive by accusing him in the introduction of all kinds of impossible things. But a silence followed. Twain had been telling the man's life history. A person should keep up his character; earn it if possible, assume it if necessary. Last spring Twain saw General Miles, who remarked that it was strange the two men had never met while they were both in Washington years and years before. To keep up his own character, Twain did not remind him that they had indeed met there. It seems that Twain was then penniless, was writing *The Innocents Abroad*, and was living with another poor fellow, a Scot named William Davidson. At one point they desperately needed $3, and Twain found himself exhausted from looking for the sum and resting in a hotel lobby. Up came a beautiful, lonely dog, which Twain promptly patted. General Miles entered, admired the dog, and asked Twain to price it. Twain suggested $3, and the general gave over the sum and carried the dog to his room. Soon the owner came in, asked around concerning his missing pet, and offered Twain $3 if he could find it. Twain got it back from the general, returned his $3, and gave the dog back to its owner for the reward.

William Davidson, General [Nelson A.] Miles.

"A General Reply," 1870 (CG).

Twain observes that when he was about seventeen years old he wrote some essays, took them to a local newspaper office intending to offer them for publication, but got cold feet and retreated without showing them off. Now that he is a man of letters, he receives numerous requests from would-be writers asking him to help them find employment in the crowded field and also to read samples of their work. Twain offers a general reply. Literature is not overpopulated with talented persons, although plenty of idlers rationalize to this effect; he will not offer opinions on samples of writing, for fear of encouraging a bore or stifling a potential Dickens; and he suggests that budding authors write for three years without pay, since apprentices in most fields work in just that way. Why should young people think that they have the right to wield the pen, that mightiest of weapons, without serving an arduous apprenticeship first? If one's writings are worthy, people will soon know it.

"General Washington's Negro Body-Servant," 1868 (WMT 24).
The stirring part of this celebrated Negro's life begins with his first death. His name was George, and he helped lay to rest his illustrious master General Washington, and then he himself first died ten years later—that is, in 1809—in Richmond, Virginia, at the age of ninety-five. His death was again reported, this time in Macon, Georgia, in 1825. But then he appeared at Fourth of July festivities in the 1830's. In 1840 he died again, this time in St. Louis. He appeared again on a few Fourths of July, then died once more, in 1855, this time in California. He died for the last time—or at least the latest—in Detroit, still ninety-five years old. Each newspaper account indicates that George's memory was unimpaired to the end. In fact, the latest bulletin reports that he could remember not only Cornwallis and Bunker Hill but the Boston Tea Party and the landing of the Pilgrims. By the time he dies again, he may recollect the discovery of America. Each account mentions his age as ninety-five at the time of his death; his age, however, never kept pace with his recollections, and he must in reality have been more than two centuries old when he last died. In a postscript, the author reports that George has just died again, this time in Arkansas. Too many communities have had to bury this man, who, let us hope, will stay dead at last.

> [General Edward] Braddock, [General Charles] Cornwallis, George, Patrick Henry, John Leavenworth, General and President [George] Washington.

"A Genuine Mexican Plug." From *Roughing It.*

"George Wakeman," 1870 (CG).
George Wakeman died late in March. He was a talented, versatile, energetic journalist, who took shorthand well, and wrote gracefully, rapidly, and with humor. He was a good, gentle, loyal friend. He had no enemies and will be greatly missed.

George Wakeman.

"The German Chicago," 1892 (WMT 15).
The author begins by comparing Berlin to Chicago, which though young seems more venerable. In Berlin the streets are wide, straight, and well lighted. The city is on a level, and its buildings are stately and beautiful. The city government is superb. Taxes and duties are levied fairly and collected patiently. Berlin policemen are courteous and persistent. The fire department is run in an effortless way. Newspapers are abundant. Theater advertising is skillfully managed, by small posters on tall, thick pillars. Horse cars are clean and comfortable, but they meander oddly all over town. Cabs are orderly. The streets are cleaned sensibly and not by talk, as in New York. But the naming of streets and the numbering of houses on them are chaotic and perhaps contribute to the high suicide rate in Berlin. The author attended with great pleasure a recent civic celebration in honor of the seventieth birthdays of Professors Virchow and Helmholtz, the renowned scientists. A thousand vividly costumed and armed students attended, among others, in a huge, long hall with galleries. The author was honored to sit at the table with the principal guests. Applause in the form of swords slammed on tables was deafening when the revered classical scholar Mommsen walked in. The author concludes by noting that Berlin is well managed because, partly, Virchow is a non-paid alderman in its government.

[Hermann Ludwig Ferdinand von] Helmholtz, [Theodor] Mommsen, [Rudolf] Virchow.

'German for the Hungarians,' 1899 (WMT 28).
Twain offers to help apportion taxes between Hungary and Austria. Those who are celebrating the emancipation of the Hungarian press can act for Hungary. He will speak for Austria. He will let grain come in free and even pay the freight. As for the Gegenseitigengeldbeitragendenverhältnismässigkeiten, he will let Hungary off at 25%. In return, he will take anything within reason. This ausgleich has kept him awake for anderthalbjahr. He could never handle it before, because of a big doorman at the Foreign Office in Vienna.

["German Servant 'Wuthering Heights' "]. See "Kaltenleutgeben."

["Getting Technicals Right"] (MTP).
A writer who describes details of an unfamiliar process will always make mistakes. Thus, Alice Kegan Rice's *Mr. Orr* and a ballad by John Hay treat steamboats inaccurately, and Bret Harte's "Heathen Chinee" has a mistake in it. Twain has an impossible bugle call in his own "Horse's Tale," but to an army bugler who writes him about it he confesses his indifference and then tells the fellow about his plan to describe a thrilling but technically impossible fall at sea—from the garboard strake.

> Bret Harte, John Hay, Alice Kegan Rice.

["Ghost Life on the Mississippi"], 1948.*
Joseph Millard was a St. Louis and New Orleans packet pilot, and a truthful man, according to the narrator. When Millard lay dying, he decided to reveal the following story. On a snowy, rainy night years ago, the captain of the *Boreas* said to William Jones, his pilot, that it would be too dangerous to try to run a narrow bend near Goose Island. But Jones replied that he would take her through if the devil seized him five minutes later, successfully navigated the passage, boasted that he was "The King of Pilots," then went below, but soon disappeared. There was blood on the starboard guard, and a fireman said that a man had fallen from above, hit his head there, and toppled overboard. But no one was sure, and many laughed at the story. When the *Boreas* arrived at St. Louis, she was sold, lay idle until the following winter, and then headed for New Orleans with Millard and Ben Reubens as pilots. Above Goose Island, it started to snow and Millard stopped the engines, preparing to wait until daylight. Suddenly he was conscious of the bloody, dripping presence of dead Jones in the locked pilot house. Millard stared, frozen in horror as he watched Jones turn the wheel and signal by pulling the bell lines. The ghost pilot steered the *Boreas* through Egyptian darkness, then passed through the bolted door, and disappeared. Ben rushed up, was let in, and told Millard that he was a better pilot then even the legendary Jones. But Millard in a quaking voice swore Ben to secrecy and told him what had happened. Then the two men noticed something on the floor and found a silver watch with its crystal broken. On the back was the name "William Jones."

> The Captain, William Jones, Joseph Millard, Ben Reubens.

*In the *Pacific Coast Spectator*, II (Autumn, 1948), 485-490.

"A Ghost Story," 1870 (WMT 7).

The narrator takes a large room far up on Broadway in a lonely, dusty, silent building. The first night, he climbs the dark stairs, gropes his way through cobwebs, and enters his room with its cheery fire in the grate. For two hours he sits there dreaming of the past, then retires, and sleeps profoundly until he suddenly wakes up with a start. His bedclothes are being tugged off him! Terrified, he hears a terribly heavy step moving away. The sound passes through the locked door. He convinces himself that it has all been a hideous dream, gets up, lights his pipe, and sits before the fire again, when suddenly he notices a gigantic footprint in the ashes on his hearth. Then he hears grating noises and chains being dragged, sees floating phosphorescent lights, and feels a blood-like liquid spattering on his face. The same heavy tread approaches and passes through the door toward him. A pale glow stands beside him and focuses into the Cardiff Giant. The gas light flickers brighter in sympathetic relief. The narrator greets the creature amiably, until he begins to sit all over the furniture, smashing everything and even beginning to scatter bits of his plaster-like thighs on the floor. When the narrator voices a rebuke, the Giant weeps and says that he has not sat down for a century. The narrator tosses a blanket over his big guest and puts an inverted sitz-bath on his head for a helmet. The two chat. The Giant confesses that he is the spirit of the Petrified Man in the museum across the street. As a ghost, he can have no rest until the authorities bury that Cardiff Giant again. The ghost haunted the museum and even enlisted some fellow spirits, but to no avail. So they came over to the building in which the narrator has his residence. Attracted by his light, they immediately renewed their haunting to gain attention. The narrator scoffingly tells the Giant that he has been haunting a plaster cast of his original self, since the real Cardiff Giant is in Albany. The ghost is floored, then expresses his sense of outrage that the Petrified Man, having cheated everyone else, has ended up fooling his own ghost. He slowly tramps out, carrying the narrator's blanket and tub with him.

The Cardiff Giant, Newell.

"A Ghost Story." See "The Golden Arm," part of "How to Tell a Story."

The Gilded Age: A Tale of To-Day, 1873 (WMT 5, 6).

Squire Si Hawkins of Bedstown, in eastern Tennessee, where he owns 75,000 acres, receives a letter from his friend Beriah Sellers, urging him to move with his family to Missouri, a land of great opportunity. Hawkins wastes little more time at his rural store in talking with his tobacco-chewing customers but instead shares the news with his faithful wife Nancy, and soon they are off.

After three days, Hawkins, Nancy, their two little children— George Washington and Emily—and their Negro servants Dan'l and his wife Jinny stop at a log cabin in the woods, find a boy named Clay, about ten years old, whose widowed mother's burial is about to take place, and adopt him when the neighbors admit that they lack the means to do so. A few days later the party reaches the Mississippi River and that night sees a mighty, fiery steamboat, which Dan'l mistakes for a vengeful lord and prays to for deliverance. Soon they all board the *Boreas* headed for Missouri, on the way to which her captain and the pilots George Davis and Jim decide to race the *Amaranth,* which has just picked up Wash Hastings, a pilot of legendary skill. But soon the *Amaranth* explodes with dreadful loss of life. And the official verdict? Nobody to blame! The Hawkins family adopts a five-year-old girl named Laura Van Brunt, orphaned by the explosion. Soon the *Boreas* arrives at smoky St. Louis, and the group goes on a smaller vessel 130 miles north to a tumble-down Missouri village, where they arrive in October twilight. Then two days by team and wagon, and upon them bursts "Colonel" Sellers with a voluble welcome. Within a couple of weeks the children are in school and "Judge" Hawkins is established in a village store. (The town is later identified as Murpheysburg.)

Ten years pass. The Hawkinses now have eight children, including Clay and Laura. Sellers also has eight children and has moved on to Hawkeye in search of greener pastures. Hawkins has made and lost a couple of fortunes, and is now in poor shape financially. Suddenly a stranger comes and offers him $10,000 for his mineral-rich Tennessee lands; but Hawkins demands $15,000 and a half-interest in the stranger's profits, and so he loses out. Clay returns home from work elsewhere, and his $200 savings help. Laura, now a ravishing beauty on the verge of womanhood but also as cold as an iceberg, offers to go to work; but the idea strikes horror in weak, spiritless Hawkins's heart. His wife Nancy is despondent but loyal. They send their son Washington, a dreamy, ineffectual inventor in his early twenties, on to Hawkeye, where he soon arrives and puts up with ebullient Sellers, who is surrounded by children and schemes, but who can warm his chilly abode only by putting a candle in a stove—to give the appearance of heat, which is enough, he insists. Sellers makes Washington's head spin with wonderful talk about hog and corn speculation, bank manipulating, and manufacturing medicine for sore eyes; then he takes the young man to General Boswell, dignified and reserved, for whom he is to clerk and with whose family he is to room and board. He hardly has time to meet and fall hopelessly in love with Boswell's seventeen-year-old daughter Louise and begin to wish again that Sellers would bring him a scheme to make money before he is called home by the mortal sickness of his father. Laura rebukes Clay for not calling her promptly to sit beside her "father." When the old man dies mumbling about his Tennessee lands, the family gives away to frenzied grief.

Now Laura finds out that she is not the Hawkinses' real daughter. It seems that Major Lackland was exposed as a corrupt congressman, returned to Missouri, and died shortly after Hawkins did. Incomplete correspondence between the two men hints that Laura is not a Hawkins. She pries into the matter, gains an imperfect image of her father—evidently injured and somewhat demented by the steamboat explosion—but decides to forget it all and remain with Nancy Hawkins, until village gossip causes her gentleman friend Ned Thurston to jilt her. Within two months the whole Hawkins family has moved to Hawkeye. One day Washington, temporarily neglected by Louise, calls on Sellers to have dinner and finds that the entire repast is turnips and water, the virtues of which the Colonel extols: the combination can prevent the plague.

Suddenly the scene shifts to New York. Young Philip Sterling, a tall, handsome Yale man who is not succeeding as a writer, meets former classmate Henry Brierly, who talks him into joining him in a railroading expedition to Missouri under the aegis of Henry's rich railroader uncle. Philip agrees, writes his mother, his uncle, and Ruth Bolton of Philadelphia, and is off next day—a pleasant spring one. The leaders of the commercial enterprise are Duff Brown, a bluff, heavy-jawed contractor from Boston, and Rodney Schaick, a slick New York broker. The group goes by railroad through Chicago to Alton and then by steamboat to free and easy St. Louis, where Henry pretends to be laying out engineering drawings at the hotel while Philip looks around. The two encounter oily Sellers, who chats with them and then sponges a drink and a cigar.

Meanwhile, in Philadelphia restless Miss Bolton reads Philip's letter and then disputatiously tells her placid Quaker mother Margaret that she wants to break out of the mould and attend medical school. That evening she talks with her father, ex-Quaker Eli Bolton, about Philip's hopes for a western fortune. Ruth's parents discuss her professional ambition, and Eli decides to let the girl try. That night he brings home Bigler, a dishonest, influence-buying railroad contractor of the firm of Pennybacker, Bigler & Small, which wants money for a scheme. Ruth trips him up with embarrassing questions. Soon she begins work in medical school, where one night she and another female student are silently reproached by a "new" Negro corpse in the dissecting room.

Back to St. Louis. Philip and Ruth exchange letters, and although he is uneasy about her medical plans he would defend her decision against anyone. Ruth disapproves of Sellers, she writes, and of his type, which is common in Philadelphia. Sellers windily advises Philip and Henry to speculate in land around Stone's Landing, which he urges them to persuade divisional engineer Jeff Thompson to develop. Their money low, the two young men journey to Magnolia and report at hearty Thompson's camp. The group moves steadily on to Stone's Landing, a tiny town of few buildings and much mud. The natives share Thompson's whiskey, and Sellers arrives to lecture on the future city there—which he names Napoleon—and on the need for federally financed dredging of Goose Run—to be known as Columbus River in the future. Henry, Sellers, and Thompson spin plans; but Philip does not sign for any shares because he doubts that he could fulfill any pledge. Henry and Sellers repair to Hawkeye.

The Civil War has come and gone. The eight years between 1860, the year of Si Hawkins's death, and the present, when Henry arrives in Hawkeye, have seen momentous historical changes. Sellers was a home-guard captain and defended Stone's Landing from an absent enemy. Washington Hawkins joined the Confederate army, was captured, but was released by his Union captors in the hope that he would further injure the Southern cause by returning to his regiment. Clay has continued to support the Hawkins family. Laura forgot Murpheysburg gossip once she arrived at Hawkeye, but during the war she was rendered shiningly beautiful by knowledge of evil: Confederate Colonel George Selby commanded the Hawkeye district, promised marriage to Laura, lured her to southwestern Missouri, and seduced her there and then left her with a sneer.

Henry now greatly admires Laura, whom he quickly meets· at Hawkeye through Sellers, with whom he is now making elaborate plans for Napoleon. Laura, who has been rendered hard and unscrupulous by sadness and also by too much reading of romances which exaggerate women's influence, enflames and frustrates poor Henry. The young man suggests that she ought to go to Washington, D.C., perhaps being escorted there by Sellers, and adds that she would be the rage there. When Philip rides into Hawkeye from the railroad camp, Henry introduces him to Laura, who measures him accurately and who would profoundly interest him but for Ruth. Pompous, windy, grasping, and successful Senator Abner Dilworthy (later identified as representing the state of Happy-Land-of-Canaan, with its capital at Saint's Rest) visits General Boswell of Hawkeye. Sellers squires him around, getting him interested in the Napoleon project and also in Laura, whom he invites to Washington. He also hires Washington Hawkins to be his secretary. Henry leaves for the engineers' camp in a jealous rage.

Ruth tires of medical school and goes to a little New England college at Fallkill. She begins to live with the happy, prosperous, cultured Montague family, on the recommendation of Philip, who was once acquainted with Alice, one of the five Montague children. Ruth does not excel as a student there but enjoys the mild social life of the region. In the middle of the next winter, Philip and Henry arrive at Fallkill, stay at the local hotel, see the Montagues and Ruth every evening, and have a pleasant week. But Philip grows uneasy: Henry's New York uncle seems slow in giving financial support to their plan to link the Salt Lick Extension railroad to the Pacific line, and in addition Henry is entirely too successful at impressing cool Ruth with his romantic western tales. So the two men separate. Philip studies engineering in New York, publishes some technical papers, and gains professional respect, while Henry reports to Dilworthy. Ah, Washington, D.C., with its railroad, hotels, varied climate, costly capitol, art works, Washington Monument, Treasury Building, White House, boardinghouses, dishonest congressmen, job-grabbers, and federal loafers! Washington Hawkins is here as the senator's secretary. After much struggling, the appropriation to dredge the Columbus River near Napoleon is passed, partly because of Henry's honest lobbying. Washington Hawkins writes delightedly to Louise, telling her the good news and also reporting that a stranger has offered $40,000 for the Tennessee land. Henry writes Sellers that hard talk, not bribery, enabled the bill to pass. The two men soon meet again at Stone's Landing, sell a few lots as feelers, and hire a horde of laborers to begin rerouting the river and digging a canal. But when no money flows from Washington, the workers chase Henry out and would hang Sellers but for his silvery tongue.

Ruth returns to Philadelphia but soon grows bored in her parents' fine old house, until her father tells her that Philip is going to survey some land he has generously but impractically taken as collateral on shaky business deals with unsavory Bigler and Small. He praises Philip, who writes Ruth about the Napoleon debacle and also mentions Henry's friendship with beautiful Laura.

Meanwhile, back in Hawkeye, Polly, the uncomplaining wife of Sellers, begins to worry about the future until he spins off a summary of new railroad routes and plans. She is then content again. But soon comes a letter from Henry, prompted by his visit in New York to the president of the Columbus River Slackwater Navigation Company, who stupefies Henry with the news that the $200,000 appropriation is all gone—in bribes and printing bills—and further that Henry owes the company a 10% assessment on his capital share: He and Sellers supposedly also owe the Napoleon workmen their back pay. Louise also has a letter: Washington confesses that he refused the $40,000 offer for the Tennessee lands, wanting $150,000 and therefore getting nothing. The final calamity: Hawkeye has subscribed enough money to get the railroad to come straight to it rather than curve over to Napoleon, and therefore Stone's Landing is again tenanted only by tadpoles, bullfrogs, and turtles.

On his surveying mission for Bolton, Philip takes a train for Ilium, Pennsylvania. On the way there he tries to rescue a lady in distress and is hurled off the train. He walks the rest of the way, stops at P. Dusenheimer's wretched hotel, and pushes on to establish camp before winter hits the mountainous tract, which he is soon convinced contains coal.

Good news. Washington Hawkins writes Louise that Dilworthy is selling the Tennessee land to the federal government, is sending two free railroad tickets and is advancing $2,000 for Laura to buy a wardrobe in New York and come to Washington. Laura persuades Sellers to be her escort. In November the two arrive in the nation's capital. Philip returns for the winter to Philadelphia. Henry drops in and decides to tarry at the Boltons' house. Alice comes down from Fallkill to see Ruth, who is now occasionally attending lectures in town. Philip does not know where he stands with Ruth but confides morosely in Alice. Henry is so smitten by Ruth that he seems to have forgotten Laura. One night Philip, Ruth, Alice, and Henry go to a concert. When a sudden cry of fire causes a panic, Philip fights to protect the girls and sustains a broken arm, which Ruth grimly helps a physician to set.

Soon after Henry finally gets down to Washington, he runs into Laura at a vivid evening party, escorted there by Dilworthy and causing such a furor by her dazzling beauty that for once Henry is speechless and feels that he may have missed out by not wooing her earlier. Dilworthy wants to use Laura to promote his scheme to sell the Tennessee lands of the Hawkins, ostensibly to aid needy Negroes. Laura quickly begins to succeed in attracting two of the three main types of high-society Washingtonians. Antique aristocrats like Mrs. Major-General Fulke-Fulkerson and her daughter leave their cards, as do parvenus like the Higgins, Oreillé, and Gashly ladies; but stolid middlegrounders between these two types do not. Laura is especially amused by Mrs. Patrique Oreillé, whose husband was born in Ireland but came to America and got rich on political graft with William W. Weed in New York and who thereafter took his family to Paris and became Frenchified. Laura, who remains a bit unrefined in spite of much home reading, trades sarcasms with Mrs. Oreillé.

Laura becomes the center of wild rumors. She is a lobbyist. She is pursued by men, whom she fascinates but then depresses by telling she will remain single. She wants revenge on men for what Selby did to her. The government wants to purchase her ancestral lands, but—it is said—Dilworthy is blocking things by insisting that Negroes be aided by the land and that no votes be obtained through the sale. Meanwhile, Laura's brother Washington is impatient to get his hands on some of the money, so that he can build a lavish house, marry Louise, and die worth $12,000,000. While Laura, who effectively notes everything that is going on, talks frankly to Dilworthy about lobbying for the land bill, Sellers whiles away his time chatting with newspapermen about congressmen who frank their clothes home through the mail and who do other slightly dishonest things.

Laura goes to a bookstore, seductively but also sarcastically bewilders a callow young clerk for a while there, and then steps back into the street precisely in time—she thinks—to meet Representative Buckstone. But he is not there, as he would have been in most novels. So she sends him a note, and he calls upon her for a couple of hours that evening. He is a shrewd, observant widower; and Laura, who fancies that she is making another conquest, may not succeed with him.

One day at fashionable, respected Mrs. Schoonmaker's home, Laura and her awkward brother meet fellow guests Blanche Leavitt and Grace Medlar, among others. Suddenly Laura sees Colonel Selby. She goes home to Dilworthy's residence, gets a raving headache, is sick—and is gossiped about for a few days—and then arms herself with a pistol, because, as she explains, she heard a prowler. Obtaining his address, she then writes an anonymous letter to Selby, and he reports to Dilworthy's house and finds her. She plans to revile him. But he admits his guilt smoothly, and soon they are planning to resume their liaison—in spite of his admission that his wife is with him, out at Georgetown.

Sellers continues to lobby in Washington, now has the ear of President Grant himself, and gives the journalists some of their best tips. Washington Hawkins is willing to sell half of his Tennessee land to the government for $2,000,000, but Dilworthy professes to want the government to obtain control of the region in order to improve the lot of Negroes and to build an industrial college there. Henry sees that Laura is rather thick with Selby and is jealous, wanting to get out of the town soon, to go and help Philip mine Bolton's coal. Laura alternately loves and rages at Selby, suggesting that with money they might skip to Europe together. He mollifies his wife by saying that Laura will help him get federal money for his war-damaged cotton. When news of Selby's philandering reaches Henry's ears, that young man, hopelessly in love, warns Laura, who continues both to entice and scorn him. He also writes Philip about the affair. That young man, convalescing at the Boltons' home, is soothed by calm, nice Alice but excited by attractive Ruth. Suspecting that Pennybacker is cheating Bolton, Philip plans to run down to Washington soon and investigate.

Like most other men who meet Laura, Buckstone is soon in her camp trying to influence others in Congress to vote for the Tennessee land bill and also its Knobs Industrial University provision for Negroes. But one congressman, Trollop by name, wants to make trouble. So Laura persuades Buckstone to write a speech for Trollop, copies it herself but omits a page, and then when he reads it in Congress and stumbles noticeably calls him to her and threatens to expose him as one who must rely on ghost writers. She also has other evidence of improprieties with which to bring him around to a promise of active support. When various newspapers begin to attack the bill, Laura is distressed until Dilworthy explains that the publicity will help their cause.

As soon as Philip arrives in Washington, he learns from Henry of that hopeless young man's passion for Laura, then goes to her, confronts her with the local gossip about her affair with Selby, and obtains from the hardening girl a statement that she must live her life as it is fated to be and that she has no pity for moth-like Henry. Suddenly the Tennessee land bill is maneuvered by Buckstone onto the agenda of the House of Representatives, where, after an all-night wearing down of the opposition, its proponents force a vote and it passes. Washington Hawkins is to receive $3,000,000 for all but ten thousand acres of his father's long-held land, if the Senate will only concur. Washington rushes to Dilworthy's home to tell Laura, who, however, has gone to New York with Henry, according to a note in that dandy's room. Philip hastens after them but reads in a Jersey City newspaper that Laura has shot and killed Selby in a New York hotel and that Henry is also being held. It seems that Selby was about to embark with his family for England when Laura caught up with him. Philip immediately gets Henry out on bond and persuades him to aid Bolton and his Ilium coalfield development. Sellers, Dilworthy, Washington Hawkins, and especially poor old Nancy Hawkins all arrive to provide what comfort they can for Laura, who soon has three distinguished New York criminal lawyers preparing her defense. Meanwhile, the newspapers play up the lurid story.

Bigler, annoyed that recent elections have results in no pay-offs for him, obtains still more money from worried but pliant Bolton, to his placid wife's mild displeasure. Philip, still without arriving at any understanding with cool Ruth, returns to Bolton's mountain, this time with buoyant Henry as consulting engineer. They sink a tunnel in search of coal, but without success. Henry is recalled to New York for Laura's trial, but it is postponed. One night Philip is awakened by a shout that the miners have found coal. But it turns out to be only a short vein. Bolton, momentarily encouraged by Philip's report, is soon forced to sell all his property, including his house, to cover debts caused by Bigler's swindler. In the fall, Philip buys the Ilium tract, convinced that coal is in it, then goes to Fallkill to visit the Montagues. Patient Alice delights him by saying that Ruth loves him. Squire Montague agrees to invest in the Ilium tract, reasoning that the timber on it is sufficient collateral. In the spring Philip travels to Philadelphia, and during a tender moment at the modest new residence of the Boltons Ruth whispers that he means everything to her.

Back in Washington, Washington Hawkins has been growing despondent, and Sellers is obliged to muster all of his eloquence to renew the young man's confidence that the land bill will go through the Senate and further that Laura will be acquitted. Dilworthy is also helpful, taking Washington around to temperance lectures, religious meetings, and various discussions promoting the cause of Negroes and Indians, and thus enlisting the forces of morality on the side of the land bill. Persuaded that his scheme is safe, Dilworthy takes a quick trip to his home state, where he attends temperance and religious meetings, preaches at the Cattleville Sunday-school, and buys the ostensible support of an enemy named Noble.

On February 15 the trial of Laura Hawkins for the murder of Colonel Selby begins, only eleven months after the crime was committed. The selection of the jury takes four weary days, with Laura's senior attorney, a man named Braham, objecting to people who can read or who favor capital punishment for capital crimes. McFlinn, the district attorney, promises to prove cold-blooded, premeditated murder and calls various witnesses to the stand. Henry, Washington Hawkins, the physician who heard Selby's last words, and Dilworthy's servant all reveal damaging evidence. But then Braham paints a picture of Laura's background and queries old Mrs. Hawkins, who effectively describes Laura's background and early maturity at great length. Sellers then takes the witness stand and irrelevantly meanders on the subject of Laura's missing father while the judge and the lawyers argue technical points. Medical experts expensively differ as to the accused's insanity. After the trial has continued for two weeks, Braham sums up brilliantly and emotionally; McFlinn then delivers his summation, with equal skill but without touching the jurors' feelings. The jury then begins to deliberate.

Back in Washington, Sellers and Washington Hawkins soon begin to receive telegrams from Braham telling them that the jury is still out. They also learn that Noble, back at Saint's Rest, has exposed the bribe attempt of Dilworthy, whose land bill is therefore defeated in the Senate. Sellers and Hawkins are flattened until they receive a wire telling them that Laura has been found not guilty and is free. Oily J. Adolphe Griller quickly offers her $12,000 for thirty performances on a lecture circuit. Henry goes to the Pacific coast, to try a new scheme. When spring comes, Philip returns to the Ilium mine, fortified by Montague funds and certain religious convictions. Poor old Mrs. Hawkins says farewell to Laura, knowing that the gap between them will widen.

Unshaken by Noble's charges, Dilworthy accuses his enemy of keeping money which Dilworthy gave him to loan to a mutual friend to start a bank with. After extensive deliberation, a senatorial investigating committee exonerates Dilworthy and decides not to prosecute Noble for attempting to corrupt a senator. Later Dilworthy tries to get his $7,000 back but fails. Meanwhile, Laura experiences a variety of emotions and then decides to lecture. Griller arranges all details; but on opening night only forty coarse people show up, and they hiss her off the stage. She reels home, prays for forgiveness, dreams of her childhood, and dies of a heart attack.

Clay Hawkins, for years a successful merchant in Melbourne, Australia, learns of his sister Laura's trial, sells out at a loss, rushes to San Francisco and then Hawkeye, where news greets him of her death. Meanwhile, Sellers and Washington decide to quit the nation's capital, since Louise has obtained her commercially humbled father's permission to marry. Ridding himself of the accursed Tennessee lands by refusing to pay $180 in taxes now due, Washington plans to practice law back home. Sellers agrees to do so as well, figuring that eventually he will become a Supreme Court justice.

Philip and his men continue digging through the summer in their Ilium tunnel for coal but find none. He pays and discharges them, but they work free for a while longer. Then, all alone but refusing to quit before giving the mine one final blast, Philip uncovers a rich vein of coal. His soaring spirits are soon dashed, however, by news that Ruth, who has been overworking in a hospital, is gravely ill. He immediately takes a slow train through the hot August countryside to Philadelphia, where his strength and love draw Ruth back to health. He gives Bolton back his interest in the mine. Soon Philip and Ruth are blissfully happy at Fallkill, unaware that Alice's letter of love to them emanates from a heart aching with love too.

In an appendix the authors apologize for not being able to locate the real father of Laura Hawkins.

Mrs. A., Cousin Abner, Admiral, Senator Atchison, B., Mrs. B., Rev. Orson Balaam, Senator Balloon, Batters, Beverly, Blacque Bey, Bigler, the Black Swan, Miss Blank, Senator Blank, Bobbett, Eli Bolton, Eli Bolton [Jr.], Mrs. Margaret Bolton, Ruth Bolton, Miss Bolton, Louise Boswell, General Boswell, Mrs. Boswell, [George S.] Boutwell, Braham, Henry Brierly, Brierly, Duff Brown, Mrs. Buckner, Representative Buckstone, Mrs. Buckstone, Burton, Canada Joe, Chairman, Clawson, Committeeman, Congressman, Patrick Coughlin, Coughlin, Susan Cullum, Damrell, Uncle Dan'l, George Davis, Jeff[erson] Davis, Senator Abner Dilworthy, Mrs. Abner Dilworthy, Ethan Dobb, Dr. Dobb, Dobson, P. Dusenheimer, Mrs. P. Dusenheimer, Eph, Fairoaks, Fanshaw, Fluke, Foreman, Count Fugier, Major-General Fulke-Fulkerson, Mrs. Fulke-Fulkerson, Emmeline, Peter Gashly, Mrs. Peter Gashly, Gashly, Miss Gashly, General, Mrs. Gloverson, Dr. Golightly, Gonderil, Sir George Gore, Governor—, [President Ulysses S.] Grant, Grayson, J. Adolphe Griller, Gringo, Hadley, Governor Hager, Hanks, Harry, Wash Hastings, Emily Hawkins, Franky Hawkins, George Washington Hawkins, Henry Clay Hawkins, Laura Van Brunt Hawkins, Nancy Hawkins, Squire Si Hawkins, Hawkins, Avery Hicks, Hicks, Drake Higgins, Mam Higgins, Oliver Higgins, Mrs. Oliver Higgins, Si Higgins, Mrs. Si Higgins, Widow Hopkins, Hopperson, Huffy, Cousin Hulda, Dr. Jackson, Jake, Jerry, Jex, Jim, Jim, Aunt Jinny, Johnny, Johnson, Judge—, Major Lackland, Dennis Laflin, Michael Lanigan, Dr. Leathers, Blanche Leavitt, General Leffenwell, Dr. Longstreet, Mrs. McCarter, Dr. McDowells, General McFingal,

Mrs. McFingal, McFlinn, Maria, Grace Medlar, Millie, Alice Montague, Mrs. Oliver Montague, Squire Oliver Montague, Montague, Montague, Montague, Russ Mosely, Murphy, Murphy, Noble, O'Keefe, Bridget Oreillé, Patrique Oreillé, Mrs. Patrique Oreillé, Judge O'Shaunnessy, Larry O'Toole, Pennybacker, Pete, Johnny Peterson, Brother Plum, Plum, Plumly, Baron Poniatowski, Mrs. Poplin, the President [of the United States], Puffer, Quiggle, Roberts, Rodney Schaick, Jake Schmidt, Mrs. Schoonmaker, Representative Schoonmaker, Colonel George Selby, Mrs. George Selby, Selby, Colonel Beriah Sellers, George Sellers, James Fitz-James Sellers, Lafayette Sellers, Marie Antoinette Sellers, Polly Sellers, Roderick Dhu Sellers, [Sarah] Sellers, Sis Sellers, Sellers, Senator, Senator, Senator, Senator, Senator, Senator, the Sergeant-at-arms, Governor Shackleby, Shepley, the Sheriff, Hannah Shoecraft, Dr. Shovel, Simon, Simons, Conductor Slum, Small, Mrs. Small, Miss Small, J. W. Smith, the Speaker, the Speaker [of the House of Representatives], Splurge, Dr. Spooner, Dr. Sprague, Philip Sterling, Mrs. Sterling, General Sutler, Jim Terry, Jeff Thompson, Senator Thompson, Ned Thurston, Tim, Tom, Trollop, J[ames]. Hammond Trumbull, Tubbs, Van Brunt, Mrs. Van Brunt, the Vice-President [of the United States], William M. Weed, Henry Worley, Mrs. Worley, Mrs. X, Senator X.

'Girls,' n.d. (S).
Twain recently received a manuscript from a teacher who had collected her pupils' boners. Example: an equestrian is a person who asks questions. A sample of a boy's composition observes that girls are stuck up, like to play with dolls, are afraid of violence, like church, and know their lessons better than boys do.

"Girl's Brothers." See FW, 1869.

"Glances at History." See "Papers of the Adam Family."

["God"]. See ["Intelligence of God"].

"The Golden Arm." Part of "How to Tell a Story."

"Goldsmith's Friend Abroad Again," 1870-1871 (CRG).

From Shanghai, Ah Song Hi writes his friend Ching-Foo that he is leaving his oppressed land for employment in America, the home of freedom and bravery. America welcomes everyone. Next Ah Song Hi writes while at sea. Although an American employer had summoned him, Ah Song Hi had to pay his own passage, in steerage. He and many other Chinese were very crowded; but the white authorities explained that in steerage they would be safe from temperature changes and air drafts. Next Ah Song Hi writes Ching-Foo from San Francisco. When they disembarked, he and a Chinese friend named Hong-Wo were kicked by some policemen and then searched. The authorities found Hong-Wo's opium in his queue; so he was arrested, and the baggage of both men was confiscated. Next Ah Song Hi had to be expensively vaccinated for smallpox, which disease he had already had. His money was all gone; but he was still hopeful, because he would surely be able to work and save and soon bring his wife and children over to join him in California. But in his next letter Ah Song Hi explains that his original employer discharged him, and as he was walking along the street some ruffians for sport set a vicious dog after him. He was bitten and torn badly, and two Irish policemen came by, arrested him, booked him, and threw him into jail. Ah Song Hi was surprised: he thought that America being free had no need of despotic prisons. In the large cell were many different types of people, drunken, quarrelsome, loving, obscene, and injured. One prisoner died of head injuries just before dawn, in spite of a tardily summoned physician. Ah Song Hi's final letter describes his trial. Chinese are not allowed to testify. The arresting officers asserted that Ah Song Hi had created a disturbance, and he was quickly given five dollars or ten days.

> Ah Song Hi, Ching-Foo, Hong-Wo, Mother Leonard, Mickey, Officer O'Flaherty, Officer O'Flannigan, Stiggers.

Good Bye, 1867 (P).

Now that the fleet has finished its voyage, the ships go their separate ways. One will dance on tropical seas in eternal June. Another will sink under a northern blast. One thing is sure: the ships will never meet again in sisterly concord.

[Good-by, Good-by], 1853 (P).
It is hard to say farewell, but I must bend to destiny.

[Ann Virginia Ruffner].

[Goodnight, Sweetheart, Goodnight], 1931 (P).
Goodnight, my love. The stars shine; the snow is white; light
fails; night falls fast. All is well. Sleep.

Sweetheart.

"Goose Fable," 1972 (FM).
Flying north with the other geese, young Snowflake and her
mother discuss religion. The mother senses that she may soon die
and wants first to impress on her offspring the belief that the
divine Human Race is righteous, merciful, just even though seemingly not so at times, and adorable though now and then apparently
cruel. Geese have the duty to worship human beings always. Finally
the mother urges Snowflake to resist temptations and go to the
cow for advice in times of trouble.

The Human Race, Snowflake.

["The Gorky Incident"], 1944 (LFE).
Seventy-five years ago York Minster, a native from Tierra del
Fuego, was taken by a British warship to England and was later
invited to appear at the King's ball in St. James's palace. York decided to appear in native dress, that is, nude save for a piece of
untanned skin on his back. Though the innocent fellow meant no
harm, there was an outcry, because his conduct went against custom. Laws are coldly rational, but customs—for example, the wearing of long hair by women—develop organically and must not be
transgressed. Gorky should have known about York.

[Maxim] Gorky, York Minster.

"Government by Article 14" (MTP).
Twain criticizes the 1896 reform of the Austrian Parliament for
being so slight that it amounts not to a Boon but only a boon.

Hungary is not represented. Future reforms will be slight, because Article 14 of the Austrian Constitution forbids permanent major changes in governance.

"The Governor Who Talked Nonsense" (MTP).

On a certain solemn occasion, Twain suddenly almost laughs, because he has begun to think about Gov.—, who, though educated, cultivated, and excellent, loved to talk sheer nonsense in front of strangers. He would take to beaming courteously at an innocent newcomer and spouting solemn lunacies. He did the same thing to rural deputations coming to ask him for impossible governmental favors.

Gov.—.

"Graceful Compliment." See MTSF.

"The Great Alliance" (MTP).

Twain begins by praising Isidor Straus's Educational Alliance for its fine work on the East Side, especially its superb Children's Theatre. The theater charges only a dime a ticket, has seven hundred seats, and is always filled. It produces only clean, realistic, elevating plays. It started with Miss Minnie Herts, four years ago. Soon such theaters will be as common in this country as prisons. The idea must spread, because children are natural mimics. The managers draw on volunteer stagehands, electricians, and the like. Scene shifts are especially adept. During a recent performance of *The Prince and the Pauper*, the kids themselves changed a set with the curtain up, and the audience loved the spectacle. Before a Shakespeare play is performed here, the children study a thousand copies of a cheap edition of it; the result is that those kids know Shakespeare better than most New York adults do. Would you believe that persons with foreign names like Leah Hirshman and Meyer Brownstein could play Shakespeare? They do, and well; their English is splendid, thanks to the Educational Alliance. Watching children enjoying a play is a thrilling sight. To a child, drama is real. One autumn night Twain invited a group of adults to a performance. The response was so hearty that he concludes that his potential guests knew much about the Children's Theatre.

Illustrious people accepted the invitation and were moved by the performance.

John Bigelow, Ray Bomzon, Meyer Brownstein, Philip Brownstein, Jacob Delmonte, Harry Dukelsky, Sylvia Eisenberg, Morris Fein, David Friedman, Miss Fry, Miriam Gerson, Henry Ginsberg, Joseph Ginsberg, the Governor of the State, Abraham Grosstein, Minnie Herts, Leah Hirshman, Amelia Kramer, Morris Le Dene, Charles Ludwig, Solomon Neuwirth, the President of Harvard, Rhoda Rosenbloom, Frances Rosenthal, Samuel Sachs, Flora Schwartzberg, Louis Scott, Millicent Shamforoff, William Singerman, Anna Sirowitz, Joseph Siskind, Isidor Straus, Francis Verdi, Philip Yentes.

"The Great Beef-Contract." See "The Facts in the Case of the Great Beef Contract."

["The Great Dark"], 1967 (WWD).

Alice Edwards explains that her family was not prepared for the dreadful occurrence. She and her husband Henry have two daughters, Jessie, aged eight, and Bessie, six. It was Jessie's birthday, and Henry had been romping with the girls all day before the guests were due at the party. He had been showing them wonders in a drop of water when seen under a powerful microscope, one of the presents. He lay down to catch forty winks and asked Alice to add a tiny touch of Scotch whisky to the drop of water. She did so, and later when she returned she saw him at his desk writing.

Henry now narrates events. They look through the microscope at a fly's eye and then at creatures plowing through a drop of water. When he lies down, the Superintendent of Dreams visits him and agrees to provide a whaling vessel and crew, with accommodations for the whole Edwards family during their voyage of discovery. Half a minute later Henry hears a hoarse voice bawling orders in a terrific storm at sea. They have been voyaging for ten frightful days. Turner, the second mate, chats confidentially with him about their whereabouts. They have been heading for Greenland but cannot find it. Turner has seen a hairy-legged whale and other impossible creatures, which he blames on drink. The wind continues to rage, but the sea is now as level as a table. The two seek the comfort of Henry's parlor, where Turner accepts some coffee. Henry notices the cloaked Superintendent of Dreams, but Turner does not and sits down right through him. Turner reminisces about Captain Jimmy Starkweather and his ill-fated pledge to avoid liquor on a three-year voyage. Meanwhile, the Superintendent plays tricks with Turner's coffee, to the man's intense discomfiture. The mate is dismayed at their crazy nautical progress, the constant dark, the disappearance of the Gulf Stream, the absence of sun, moons, and stars, and other inexplicable phenomena. After he leaves, Henry chides the giggling Superintendent so severely that the spectral being darkly explains that the miscroscope above them is causing the perpetual dark and that they may be voyaging in a huge circle. Then he hints that perhaps Henry's former life was a dream and this trip the only reality. With a mocking smile he fades away into mist. Now Henry hardly knows which is the dream, his former land life or this present voyage. He wonders how he can conceal his worries from Alice, whom he quickly decides to awaken and consult. She brings her crocheting and a kitten. They talk, and soon it appears that in her view Henry only thinks they once went to Europe: in reality, she tactfully insists, this voyage—partly with a different crew—has been their entire life. When he reminisces about their experiences in London and Edinburgh, she recalls them as dreams without substance in reality. When he speaks of their home in Springport, she accuses him of dreaming again. When she tells about their past life aboard the ship, he begins to recall little episodes, but only as dream incidents at first. She mentions the time long ago when they were on the edge of a great white glare. Then she apologizes for neglecting him these last ten days while she indulged herself in grief over old shipmates; now, she adds, it is time for him to take some needed exercise with George, their Negro servant, who enters, and boxes and fences with Henry. Oddly, Henry did not think he could box and fence effectively, but as he begins it dawns on him that he is an expert. Then the Edwardses, including their daughters, go down for the evening meal in the main saloon. They sit with Captain Davis, Phillips the purser, his sweetheart Lucy (the captain's daughter), her little sister Connie, the surgeon, a naturalist, and the chief mate. George and Germania, servants of the Edwards family, aid at supper. A morose stranger sits beside Henry, who keeps silent because he believes that the others think he should know the troubled fellow. Davis and Phillips argue over the ship's position, and the pleasant meal ends in confusion. Henry sits for a long time smoking and drinking coffee. Gradually ship life seems more real than his former land life. He retires at six bells, awakens later, and already his old life is still more faded and remote. Henry continues his narrative. They have all been voyaging for twelve years now. Their baby, Harry, was born about three months after they shipped with the present crew, who think they are bound for the South Pole. For a while Alice's memories do not correspond with Henry's, but gradually the husband prods the wife's memory until it all comes back. They even recover their children's land life, and also the servants'. So they all have double pasts. One black day, while Henry and Alice are discussing the appearance of a spider-squid a dozen years before, the ship heels over, in the grip of a gigantic octopus. The crew shoots bullets into its eyes from gatling guns until it releases the vessel, which then rocks and plunges crazily. The children are missing! Alice soon abandons hope and grows hysterical, but then Turner profanely shouts the welcome news that they have been found deep in the hold. Captain Davis next discovers that his crew, terrified by recent developments and in ignorance as to their location, have begun a mutiny, led by Stephen Bradshaw the wily carpenter. Davis braves his challenge and dares him to fire his revolver, which the captain knows is not loaded. Other mutineers try to shoot him with gatling guns, but they too are harmless. At this point Davis exhorts his men to be obedient, telling them that they are all in the hands of God together.

Arnold Blake, Stephen Bradshaw, Dr. John Brown, Connecticut Davis, Lucy Davis, Captain Davis, Delia, Mrs. Alice Edwards, Bessie Edwards, Harry Edwards, Henry Edwards, Jessie Edwards, George, Germania, Robert Hall, Captain Hall, Father Matthew, Captain Moreland, Rush Phillips, Harvey Pratt, Captain Jimmy Starkweather, Storrs, Sturgis, the Superintendent of Dreams, Turner, Veitch, Williams.

"The Great Journalist Interviewed" (MTP).
As soon as Joseph Pultizer, the new editor of the New York *World*, arrives at his hotel, a *Gazette* reporter interviews him. Pultizer is big, graceful, frank, and sharp. When asked about recent floods

in his native Mississippi Valley, the great editor theorizes that they were caused by too much water and proposes a series of dams and floodgates from Keokuk to New Orleans. In support of his position, he quotes Hamlet, who said "dam'd be he . . ." The interviewer asks his opinion on Shakespeare, whereupon Pultizer reminisces about meeting Byron, author of "Lay of the Last Minstrel," when he visited America with Lafayette. On a boat cruising the Mississippi River, Byron recited his "Boy Stood on the Burning Deck" and caused tears to start in Lafayette's eyes. Then Tom Moore stepped up and sang the poem to the air of "The Last Rose of Summer." When the interviewer ventures to doubt that the poem could be sung to that song, Pultizer renders it himself. Then, confessing that he poetizes himself, he recites his own "Kiss me, darling, I am dying . . ." in several faultless but confusing stanzas. Pultizer then explicates his poem ingeniously, in a voice mounting to such a pitch that other hotel guests burst in to object. The two men then discuss journalism, and Pultizer offers a suggestion for improving the art of the interview: reporters should write their interviews at home without conducting any dull real-life question-and-answer sessions. Pultizer adds that he interviewed Mark Twain recently in that manner, but the trouble is that the resulting write-up was so funny that it must be published in book form. Pultizer starts to read it to the interviewer but soon begins to rattle in a laughing convulsion.

Byron, Lafayette, Tom Moore, Joseph Pultizer, Your Reporter.

"The Great Landslide Case."* Part of *Roughing It*.

*See Mark Twain, *The Great Landslide Case*, ed. Frederick Anderson and Edgar M. Branch (Berkeley: The Friends of the Bancroft Library, University of California, 1972).

"The Great Prize Fight," 1863 (WG).

For a month the sporting world has been eagerly awaiting the prize fight for a purse of $100,000 at Seal Rock Point between Leland Stanford, Governor of California, and F. F. Low, Governor-elect. Their seconds, or rather bottle holders, are respectively William M. Stewart and Judge Field of the Supreme Court. The two principals train hard for six weeks. At last the fated Sunday arrives. The narrator leaves a message to be called early and gets on his rented horse, a spirited Morgan which bucks all the way to the appointed spot and then nibbles at children. At 10:05 the referee General Wright starts the bout. The two contestants soon get furiously angry, smash each other mercilessly, break heads and jaws, pull out lungs, remove limbs, and so on. At last Wright announces a draw, and the crowd screams. But then the narrator admits in a postscript that he did not actually attend the bout. Instead, a knave named Frank Lawler falsely described it to the narrator, who believed him and wrote up his colorful account as though he had been there. When confronted with the truth, Lawler lamely excused himself on the grounds that he had received his information from John B. Winters, who plans to represent Washoe in Congress and hence was regarded as reliable.

Barry, Judge [Stephen J.] Field, Augustus Maltravers Jackson, Hon. J. Belvidere Jackson, Frank Lawler, Governor-elect F. F. Low, Patten, Governor Leland Stanford, William M. Stewart, John B. Winters, Brigadier General Wright.

"The Great Revolution in Pitcairn," 1879 (WMT 15).

Nearly a century ago the crew of the British ship *Bounty* mutinied, set captain and officers adrift, sailed the ship south, got wives at Tahiti, and established a tiny colony on Pitcairn's Island in mid-Pacific. In 1808 a ship was surprised to find the island occupied by twenty-seven persons, led by chief magistrate John Adams, who was to become governor and patriarch. Now the population is ninety. The island is three-quarters of a mile long and a half mile wide. There is small livestock. The leader owes allegiance to the Queen of England. Occupations are farming and fishing. The only recreation is religious service. Last September Admiral de Horsey of the British fleet visited the island, did a little trading, and officially described the place, mentioning the fact that Adams had died in 1829, that Church of England services were conducted by Simon Young, and that an American had settled at Pitcairn. Here are the °facts, as obtained by Captain Ormsby of the American ship *Hornet*. The American settler was Butterworth Stavely, a troublemaker. He threw himself into religious work and soon created factions, moved to impeach the chief magistrate James Russell Nickoy by fomenting trouble following the simple trespass case of Thursday October Christian against Elizabeth Young, and got himself elected magistrate, whereupon he poisoned the people against England, declared the island's independence, established martial law, built up an army and a navy, levied taxes, but was finally ousted.

> John Adams, the Marquis of Ararat, the Duke of Bethany, the Archbishop of Bethlehem, Viscount Canaan, Fletcher Christian, Thursday October Christian, Admiral de Horsey, Emmeline, the Grand Duke of Galilee, the Countess of Jericho, John Mills, James Russell Nickoy, Captain Ormsby, a Social Democrat, Butterworth Staveley, Mrs. Nancy Peters Stavely, Elizabeth Young, Simon Young.

"Greetings to Artemus Ward" (WG). See "Artemus Ward Announces His Coming to Washoe . . ."

"Hamerica vs. Hingland." See FW, 1869.

"Happy Memories of the Dental Chair" (MTP).*

Dentists are now better talkers than barbers. But let's get to the point. Twain never needed to visit a dentist until one chances to see him laughing wider than usual and advises him to report to Dr. Riggs, since Twain clearly has Riggs's Disease, a decay in tooth roots accompanied by gum infection. So Twain goes to Riggs—an old grayhead with steel bodkins and the ability to bear the pain of others. Poised to scrape, Riggs pauses to lecture on the disease, then rakes chips off the damaged area. Twain's contribution to the talk is "Um." At first it seems painful; but then Twain realizes that it is merely disagreeable to have bones near your ears dug at. Sniffing a little chloroform makes the pain less personal and the dentist's voice muffled. Riggs tells how he performed the first painless operation in the world, back in 1835, by means of laughing gas. After two days with Riggs, Twain's teeth are all scraped nicely, but they tingle in the open air for a time. When Riggs offers to fill some little cavities, Twain decides to wait a few years.

[Sam] Cooley, Dr. [John M.] Riggs.

*Incompletely published in Sheldon Baumrind, "Mark Twain Visits the Dentist," *The Journal: California Dental Association*, XL (December, 1964), 493-496, 562.

"Hartford." See RL.

"Have We Appropriated France's Civilization?" (MTP).
   Twain objects to Paul Bourget's statement that America has
taken the best and worst of French civilization. Twain would not
have minded if the Frenchman had said art rather than civilization, because civilization covers quite a lot. Modern civilization
has been a long time in the making. The following go into it:
political liberty, religious liberty, the reduction of capital offenses,
equality for each person before the law, woman's rights, anesthesia in surgery, the development of patents, the cotton gin, and so
on. All of these civilizing aids were invented or advanced in
America. Twain lists about a hundred additional American inventions, then gives the British their due, by listing thirty or more
developments for which their country may take credit. Then he
kids the French for their few inventions, which include uniquely
perfect cooking, to be sure, but also the guillotine and Lourdes.
Germany, Italy, China, Spain, and Russia come off badly at the end.
   Paul Bourget.

["Hawaiian Legislature"]. See LSI.

"The Hawkeye State." See FW, 1870.

He Done His Level Best, 1865 (P).
   No matter whether he was mining, working, preaching, saving
sinners, cursing, lying, or stealing, he always done his best. (In
"Answers to Correspondents.")
   Simon Wheeler.

"He Wrestles with Prohibition, and Discovers Why Boston Is
   Called the 'Hub.'" See FW, 1869.

The Heart's Lament: To Bettie W—e, of Tennessee, 1853 (P).
   Rambler knows that Bettie W—e of Tennessee will forget him,

not listen to his expression of love, but concern herself with more gifted persons crowding about her.

Rambler, Bettie W—e.

"Helen Keller the Wonderful" (MTP).

Twain describes his thrill at meeting Helen Keller and summarizes her painfully acquired education—learning to spell, read, and speak.

Helen Keller, Miss [Annie Sullivan].

"Hellfire Hotchkiss," 1967 (SB).

James Carpenter, who is a county judge living at Dawson's Landing, and his Presbyterian wife Sarah are discussing their son Oscar, nicknamed Thug. She has been most indulgent and pathetically regards her son as brilliant. Carpenter, however, has coldly noted alarming vacillation in the boy and has grown so indifferent to him that he now thinks the only solution is to send him off to St. Louis so that he can become an apprentice under a printer named Underwood. The Carpenters dispute mildly about religion; but when the Judge voices his belief that the only thing Oscar might do well is to become a creed-changing minister, Sarah quivers with anger. Before she can speak, however, distant shouts indicate that Thug has become marooned on some ice floating in the Mississippi River and is in danger of drowning.

As the Carpenters rush into the street and toward the river, they see a black horse galloping past, bearing a trim young girl. She is Rachel "Hellfire" Hotchkiss, to the rescue. While the adults all stand around helplessly, she ranges along the shore to the point nearest the huge block of ice bearing terrified Thug to some deadly snags. Taking a life preserver which she has brought along, and a bottle of whiskey from a well-wisher, she plunges into the freezing water, swims over to Thug, gives him a drink of "milk" from her flask, and helps him into the preserver. Back they go to the cheering crowd.

Hellfire is like Vesuvius—isolated, conspicuous, well-formed, beautiful in repose, but subject to fiery eruptions. Her mother, now dead, was an invalid. Her father is a dreamy preacher. From the start, Hellfire was mild, preferring the rough companionship of boys to the dolls and tears of little girls. Hellfire once beat up a bully named Shad Stover, although he was five years older than she. She broke horses for a pastime, once switched a circus elephant she disliked, and joined the firemen in several daring rescues. Later, Shad and his older brother, Hal, are threatening a stranger on the street with revolvers. Hellfire happens by from a baseball game and lays out both ruffians with her bat. In revenge, they begin to spread stories, untrue but scandalous, about the girl. An old family friend, Betsy Davis, gently warns the girl that people may soon start believing the filth and advises her to change her tomboyish ways. She gives it some very serious thought.

. . . Thug Carpenter has now left Dawson's Landing and is apprenticed to Ustick the printer, whose other employees call the lad Parson Snivel. Thug regularly writes his mother, who is devoted to him, reasonably religious, and incredibly eloquent in her quiet way. His latest fad is to conduct his daily life in imitation of Benjamin Franklin's abstemious, studious example.

Mrs. Buckner, Judge James Carpenter, Oscar Carpenter, Mrs. Sarah Carpenter, Betsy Davis, Ed, Miss Hepworth, Rachel "Hellfire" Hotchkiss, Rev. Mr. Hotchkiss, Mrs. Hotchkiss, Peter Jones, Martha, Miss Rector, Miss Roper, Rev. Mr. Rucker, Uncle Benny Stimson, Hal Stover, Shad Stover, Jake Thompson, Underwood, Ustick, Pudd'nhead Wilson.

"A Helpless Situation," 1905 (WMT 24).

S. L. Clemens explains that once or twice a year he gets a certain type of letter. And one, from California in 1879 by a woman now dead, is typical. She wrote that she was a girl of fourteen living near the Humboldt mines sixteen years ago. She reminded Clemens of certain details and said that he knew her Uncle Simmons though not the man she later married. She then asked a favor: she wanted him to use his influence to get her book published. Clemens knows that such letters are terribly common. An established author is hard put to decline without offending. This is how he set up an answer. Perhaps he sent the woman a copy of it. At any rate, he found its original pigeonholed with her letter. The reply is in the form of an imaginary conversation between H. the publisher and

Clemens, in which it is revealed that Clemens was asked to use his influence, does not remember either the woman or her uncle, and has not read the book in question. H., whose company is in business to examine any manuscript sent in, is bewildered. Clemens concludes by commenting that publishers are eager to receive manuscripts but despise influence.

Clagett, Hal Clayton, Mrs. [Jane Lampton] Clemens, S[amuel]. L[anghorne]. Clemens, Dixon, H., Oliver, Parker, Uncle Simmons, Smith, Tillou.

'Henry Irving,' 1900 (WMT 28).
Twain says that the greatest of all arts is the ability to write plays. He has written hundreds. Well, really the highest talent is getting those plays accepted. He lacks that ability. He asked a friend to check into the rarity of a dramatic formula of his, which was the play in the form of a dream. The friend sent lists of such plays to Twain and even traced several back almost to the Flood. Twain confesses that he has furnished Sir Henry Irving with many plays and thus has contributed to his success. Pinero will now follow Twain as speaker. Twain has written more plays than Pinero, but Pinero has worked off more plays on his managers. Together the two men are at the head of the profession.

Sir Henry Irving, [Sir Arthur Wing] Pinero.

'Henry M. Stanley,' 1886 (WMT 28).
Because he happened to be around and was asked, Twain will introduce Henry M[orton]. Stanley. He really needs no introduction. His achievements when compared even to those of Columbus are staggering. All Columbus had to do was point his ship west and let America discover itself. But since Dr. [David] Livingstone was scattered all over Africa, Stanley had to wander far and wide to find him. Stanley is indestructibly American.

Dr. [David] Livingstone, Stanley M[orton]. Stanley.

"Hey, diddle, diddle!" See FW, 1870.

"Higgins," 1870 (CG).

When Judge Bagley falls down the courthouse stairs, breaks his neck, and dies, simple Higgins is asked to take the body in his wagon to the judge's home and break the news gently to his wife. Higgins gets there, shouts out for Widow Bagley, and tells her that only an inquest will comfort the judge now.

Judge Bagley, Mrs. Bagley, Higgins, Maltby.

"His Official Thrift and Prosperous Remorse." See FW, 1870.

["History 1,000 Years from Now"], 1972 (FM).

As the twenty-ninth century draws to a close, everyone concentrates his thoughts and dreams upon the past. Today people are reading many historical books, which may be condensed into the following sketchy synopsis. A thousand years ago a series of accidents rescued our country from the cruel bondage of democracy and established a monarchy. The first event was the seizure by our government of the Vanishington Archipelago during the reign here of President George (or was it Archibald?) Vashington. Thus our vast empire began to emerge. It was not always called the Filipino Empire. In fact, the islands taken may once have been called the Filipino Archipelago. During our struggle against democracy, historical records were destroyed. But we know enough to conclude that the whole conquest was grand. In fact, at the outset the Filipino nation had a population of 260,000,000, was civilized, and was advanced in the arts of war and manufacture.

Dawes, Hawkshaw, President George Vashington.

["History and Legend"]. See LSI.

"'History Repeats Itself,'" 1870 (WMT 7).

A Sandwich Island paper reports that the Hon. T. H. Benton did not use tobacco, gamble, or drink liquor, because his mother urged him not to do so. The author notes a curious coincidence. His grandmother told him not to chew tobacco before breakfast, whispered to him at one point to put up his cards because the other fellow had a flush, and successfully encouraged him to stop drinking—water.

"'Hogwash,'" 1870 (CG).
For five years Twain has treasured a sample of imbecilic, sickly bathos, published in a California newspaper. When he falls into melancholy, reading this sentimental tripe cheers him. It is called "A Touching Incident" and depicts an apparently happy mother on a mansion verandah in a big city holding an infant, then bursting into hot tears, and then preparing to go within.

"The Holy Children," 1972 (FM).
The time is seventy years ago; the place, the narrator's village. People come from hundreds of miles around to see little Hope and Mary, and their young stepsister Cecilia. The girls rise at dawn, read the Bible aloud, and pray away, even for their cursing father, who soon dies. Once they become perfect, the Holy Children learn to pray successfully. In a time of drought, they pray for rain; it comes in floods, and a calamity follows. When they pray for cold to assuage a sick man's fever, the ensuing frost ruins many crops. They pray to save a dying man; he gets well, commits murder, and is hanged. A man dies, and the Society for the Encouragement of Missions inherits his property; when a friend of his returns and gets the Holy Children to raise the Lazarus to life again, horrible litigation follows. The popularity of the children wanes. A vicious brute of a man, named Marvin, is about to die, to the relief of almost everyone. But the children pray him back to robust health. So the citizens hold a meeting and resolve that no one shall ask in the expectation of receiving, that health and peace and rain must not be prayed for, that persons so praying shall be executed, and that the official town prayer henceforth will be only for God's will to be done. Well and good, but then the Holy Children pray for the sun and moon to stand still, to help a posse exterminate some tramps. The resulting tidal wave drowns millions of people, and the Holy Children are hunted down and shot.

Cecilia, the Governor, Hope, Lazarus, Marvin, Mary.

"L'Homme Qui Rit (Translated from Victor Hugo)," 1967 (SB).
The tailor boy Gwynplaine starts up a hill during a night of
terrifying storm. It is snowing. Snow always falls in flakes. Hail is
something else. Likewise sleet and rain. The boy comes upon a
gallows, from which hangs a decaying party, labeled "African
Slave Trade." Then the boy encounters a corpse. It is that of a
woman. In her arms is a baby girl. Gwynplaine calls the baby Dea—
for Democracy. The two go to the next town, stay with a gentleman
and a wolf—itinerant actors—join their troupe, and play in many
places. Meanwhile, the ark called *African Slavery* is wallowing in
an awful storm. Overboard with everything, including the baggage. A stranger aboard, a man named Confederacy, puts a parchment concerning Gwynplaine into a well-emptied brandy bottle,
seals it, and throws it into the sea. Down goes the ship, without
insurance. Twenty years later an heir is being sought for Lord
Clancharlie, an exile who sought discomfort in Southwark. Gwynplaine, with his beloved but blind Dea, performs so well there that
he is jailed. But then the bottle washes ashore; and when the
people discover the truth about Gwynplaine they release him and
make him an earl. He quickly contracts the vertigo. Now, vertigo
whirls one up, and also down, in an unreal manner. Gwynplaine
seeks vengeance. He forsakes his Democracy. He mounts the wind,
rides the whirlwind, swings the circle, goes to the mighty people,
tells them how he has played many parts, and leaves with them
the Constitution and the flag with thirty-six stars. Then he deserts
and returns to his Dea. They sail away. When she dies, he throws
himself overboard. (Mark Twain explains in a postscript that part
of his story comes verbatim from Victor Hugo's *L'Homme qui rit*.)

Lord Clancharlie, Confederacy, Democracy, Gwynplaine,
Victor Hugo.

"An Honorable Gentleman." See FW, 1870.

"Honored as a Curiosity," 1866 (WMT 7).
If you get into conversation with a stranger in Honolulu, he is
likely to be a sea captain, a minister, or a high officer in the Hawaiian government. The rest are common Kanakas and mercantile

foreigners. One day a solemn fellow accosts the narrator, calls him
"your reverence" and then "captain" and then tries political titles
on him. All in vain. The narrator explains that he is merely a private American citizen, whereupon his auditor announces that he
has waited for sixteen years to see such a rarity, then swoons in
gratitude. The narrator picks his pockets and leaves.

"Honored as a Curiosity in Honolulu." See "Honored as a Curiosity."

'The Horrors of the German Language,' 1897 (WMT 28).
    Twain tells the Vienna Press Club in German, of which he pro-
vides a stiff literal translation, that it has him deeply touched
here hospitably received to be. His spoken German is poor, but he
here writes like an angel. He has long wished to give a speech in
German, but permission has been hard to obtain. He protests that
he does not wish to hurt the language but only to effect a few
changes. He wants to compress the parenthetical construction and
bring the verb closer to its subject, so that will they an elegant
language possess. Pötzl thinks that Twain has come to Vienna to
clog the bridges, but in truth he is using them only to string out
noble German sentences the bridge railing along his contents with
one glance to overlook. Twain has forgotten his conclusion; so
again proffers he them his heartiest thanks. (The German version
is entitled "Die Schrecken der Deutschen Sprache.")
        Schiller, Pötzl.

"Hors de Combat," 1864 (WG).
    Twain reports that his friend Dan de Quille was galloping back
from American City [to Virginia City] on a spirited Spanish horse
when he ran into another horse standing in a corner of the road.
Dan was thrown three hundred yards, was split wide open, and
had his head caved in, his legs broken into bamboo-like joints, and
his spine twisted like a rail fence. He wrote his will and repudiated
his bills, but he is now recovering. Dan then gives his version. He
merely sprained his knee. He adds that Twain pretended to go
into mourning but really tried to obtain legal permission to administer Dan's estate. He also took Dan's shirt, socks, cane, and
toothbrush. Later Dan reports that he has forgiven Twain, because

the poor fellow took a boxing lesson and had his nose so smashed that it resembled a piece of tripe spouting streams of claret and that it must be amputated and replaced with a quarter of veal. Marshall Cooke, Dan de Quille.

"A Horse's Tale," 1906 (WMT 27).

Part of this story is told by Soldier Boy, Buffalo Bill's horse, the son of a Kentucky bluegrass aristocrat mare and a bronco of long lineage—back to fossils. Boy admires handsome BB and is strong and tough, though not large. He is knowledgeable and observant. When he returns to Fort Paxton, he gets all the gossip from Potter, the general's dog, and Shekels, a cavalry hound. It seems that General Thomas Alison, an old bachelor, is about to receive his young brother George's nine-year-old daughter Catherine, whose parents have just died in Spain.

Now sick Mercedes writes her brother-in-law General Alison about her dead sister's daughter Cathy, who is kind, firm, multilingual, and in love with all animals. General Alison writes his mother that Cathy conquered the fort in forty-eight hours, with her gaiety and vivid temper. The Indians have named her Lightning Bug. When Buffalo Bill galloped in, she charmed him too, and he set her in triumph on his enormous shoulder. Cathy soon falls in love with his horse Soldier Boy. She writes her aunt about her delight in the wild, vast country hereabouts, and how BB took her on shiny black Boy to visit two Indian camps. General Alison now writes to Mercedes, in Spain, about Cathy and her Negro mammy, named Dorcas, a servant of the Alison family for years. Cathy is learning to ride fearlessly, is an honorary officer in the cavalry and the dragoons, beat up an Indian boy who was torturing a raven once, mentions the Cid when other camp children speak of George Washington, and pursues her studies only now and then.

Boy is talking with a Mexican plug named Mongrel and tells him all about Cathy. She recently won a race, riding another horse, not Boy, and defeating all the other fort children. She has taught the others to ride in various cavalry formations, and they sweep about in grand style. She taught Boy to salute with his right hoof, in order to apologize to soldiers if he ever does anything wrong. She can summon Boy with a special call on her silver bugle. Suddenly he hears the call and gallops off. Later, talking to the dog Shekels,

Boy praises Mongrel for his big vocabulary and then reveals that Mongrel has hinted that some human renegades are planning an ambush for BB, because he once ran them out of Medicine Bow and took their stolen horses away from them. The ambush occurred, sure enough. Boy tells Shekels that BB and another scout named Thorndike were on their way to Fort Clayton. Cathy rode Boy part way, as honor guard; then, when they heard that the men had been wounded, they tried to rescue them. But Cathy grew tired, fell off Boy, and broke her arm. Boy guarded her against the wolves until she was found by some soldiers. BB, though wounded, caught her in his arms and then gave loyal Boy to her. Boy is delighted.

Back at the fort, Cathy is still recovering. General Alison and Dorcas discuss the girl, whose honorary rank is greater than that of her doctor. She is annoyed that the surgeon fails to salute her; and she wants the general to avoid embarrassing her sentries, to preside over a court martial of two of her child-officers who have fought over a doll, and to shake hands with disconsolate Boy.

Some months later, Thorndike and a Spanish cowboy named Antonio are out on scout duty, and they talk of General Alison's imminent retirement and Cathy's desire to see Spain, where her aunt lives. Antonio says that he has been in the area, and then he glowingly describes the first bull fight he ever saw. It was glorious, with the bull goring various horses, being beautifully tortured himself, and finally being dispatched after he had furnished the gay crowd all the amusement possible. Thorndike's plug, Mongrel, and Antonio's mount, whose name is Sage-Brush, discuss the talk of their riders. They conclude that man cannot help being brutal, because it is his nature and also because his religion occasionally excites him.

General Alison writes his mother about his retirement, turning over the fort to his replacement, General Burnby, the musical military farewell given popular little Cathy, and their trip east through the Rockies, the Black Hills, and the plains to the railroad. Now they are in Spain, perhaps for the remainder of their lives. In a postscript he reports the dreadful news that Soldier Boy, brought along to Spain by Cathy, has been stolen. Five months or so pass; and Boy is traded down and down, as he explains in a soliloquy, and now he lives in a shabby stable. He wishes that Cathy would call him with her silver bugle. The other horses have told him that soon they may be sold to the bull ring. He does not mind dying but wants to see Cathy again. General Alison writes his mother again. He says that he does not know how Cathy found Boy, but one day she saw him at a bull fight, a blindfolded wreck but with his military bearing intact. He was gored mortally. Cathy leaped into the ring and kissed him. But then the bull charged and killed her.

Catherine Alison, George Alison, Mrs. George Alison, General Thomas Alison, Mrs. Alison, Antonio, Buffalo Bill, General Burnaby, Hank Butters, the Chaplain, the Colonel, Professor Cope, Dorcas, Tommy Drake, Colonel Drake, Mrs. Drake, Agnes Frisbie, Major Fuller, Blake Haskins, Fanny Marsh, Captain Marsh, Mrs. Marsh, Professor Marsh, Mercedes, Mongrel, Sage-Brush, Shekels, Jimmy Slade, Soldier Boy, Thorndike, Thunder-Bird, White Cloud.

"The House That Jack Built: With New & Beautiful Handmaid Illustrations from the Pencil of the Celebrated Water-Color Chiropodist Mark Twain: Favorite Pupil of Sargeant, E. A. Abbey, & John Alexander" (MTP).
Twain offers sketches of himself and of various items in a new story about the house (Knickerbocker) that Jack built (deposited money in), and also about malt (money), rats (Lawyers), a cat (Satterlee), a dog (another Lawyer), cows (Depositors), a forlorn maiden (Permanent Receiver), a tattered man (an influential minority of Depositors), a bald Priest (Public Opinion), and a cock (the morning newspaper).

E. A. Abbey, John Alexander, the Artist, Depositor, Depositors' Committee Lawyer, Lawyer, Permanent Receiver, Public Opinion, Sargeant, Satterlee.

["Housekeeping"] [1] (MTP).
To start keeping house can be maddening. The narrator knows nothing about it. And his wife is no better. She told the cook recently to go buy a yard of beefsteak.

["Housekeeping"] [2] (MTP).
The narrator, who has boarded since he was thirteen years old,

really likes housekeeping now that he is trying it. He knows all about it, as if by instinct. But the servants need to be managed with firmness.

"How for Instance." See "An Inquiry about Insurance."

"How I Edited an Agricultural Paper," 1870 (WMT 7).

Needing the money, the narrator temporarily replaces the vacationing editor of an agricultural paper. The narrator works hard for a week, and his first issue appears. It makes a stir. Individuals stare at him in wonder, and two men leap through a window as he returns next morning to his office. Then an old farmer comes in, demands that the narrator read aloud his editorial on shaking the turnip tree to avoid bruising the crop. The outraged old fellow shouts and leaves, banging the door. Next comes another rustic reader, to whom the narrator is happy to read his advice on rearing the guano bird, setting out corn stalks, gander spawning, and the like. Finally the editor returns, having cut his vacation short in perplexity. He brands the narrator a celebrity all right, but a lunatic as well, and demands his resignation. At this point, the narrator explains that critics write drama notices without knowing how to act, reviewers cannot write books themselves, and therefore it is fitting that, knowing nothing about agriculture, he should write well on the subject. He has increased circulation. Farmers would not long read his agricultural editorials, but another class of readers would. Therefore the editor is the loser.

Pie-plant.

"How I Escaped Being Killed in a Duel," 1872.*

Twain claims that the following story is true and adds that its moral at the end is there to curry favor with religious readers. After reporting for a couple of years on the *Daily Enterprise* of Virginia City, Nevada, he became editor-in-chief. He soon made trouble for a man named Lord, the editor of the rival newspaper. So, to liven his own paper, Twain called Lord some bad names in print. Lord replied in kind, and Twain challenged him to a duel. Twain's friends were furious when Lord declined. Twain sent another challenge, and his friends were exultant—though Twain was not—at the ensuing acceptance. Next, Twain practiced firing unsuccessfully at a barn door with a navy six-shooter. He and his second, Steve Gillis, heard Lord firing practice rounds in the next ravine. Twain feared that Lord's spies would sneak by and notice that he could hit nothing. Suddenly a bird lit on a sage bush thirty yards away. Gillis whipped out his revolver and killed it. Sure enough, some of Lord's spies then approached, and Gillis nonchalantly remarked that Twain had shot the bird's head off at thirty paces. An hour later, Lord declined to duel. Twain closes with the moral that dueling is immoral but adds that if a man challenged him now, he would lead him to a secluded room and kill him.

Steve Gillis, Lord.

*In *Tom Hood's Comic Annual for 1873* (London: Fun Office, 80 Fleet Street, [1872]).

"How I Made a Fool of Myself." See FW, 1869.

"How I Went to the Great Race between Lodi and Norfolk," 1865 (MTWY).

Twain is anxious to see the *Norfolk* race the *Lodi* but cannot find transportation out to the San Francisco coast. A crippled dray horse rents for $240 a day. He refuses to rent the neck of another horse for $19 and ride with six others on the poor beast. Then he meets Benj. W. Homestead of the Incidental Hotel. Homestead says that he has a vacancy and begs Twain to accompany him. Twain is ecstatic, but when he arrives punctually at the hotel the morning of the race to join Homestead he finds more than a hundred others, all waiting to ride with Homestead. That smirking gentleman soon emerges to announce that they can all walk together.

Brimstone, Buncombe, Benj. W. Homestead, Smith.

["How Is This for High?"], 1870.*

As a gentleman was being blown up in a Mississippi steamboat explosion, he looked just below at another person also ascending and said, "Say, friend, how is that for high?" (In FW, 1870.)

*In the *Galaxy*, October, 1870.

"How Mark Twain Was Sold in Newark." See "How the Author Was Sold in Newark."

[How Sleep the Brave . . ?], 1862 (P).
How do brave soldiers sleep, far from the battlefield, with ease and repast but no sun?

"How the Author Was Sold in Newark," 1872 (WMT 7).
The author is to lecture in the evening to the Clayonian Society. In the afternoon a young member comes to explain that his uncle has grown bereft of all emotion and only wishes that the man could laugh, or even weep, again. The author suggests that the uncle come to his lecture and offers to hurl some formidable jokes at him. He will surely laugh at them, or perhaps cry. The nephew is most grateful. Lecture time comes, and the young man places his uncle in the second row. But the speaker, though he rants and sweats, simply cannot make the man respond. Only afterwards does he learn that the sober old fellow is deaf, dumb, and blind.

"How to Make History Dates Stick," 1914 (WMT 26).
Twain says that he wants to tell children how to learn historical dates. Pictures help, particularly if you make them yourself. Twain recalls how confused he got when he first started lecturing, until he transformed his topical notes into pictures. Sixteen years ago his children were trying to memorize the dates of the thirty-seven English monarchs from William the Conqueror on down. The governess was making little progress; so Twain decided to pictorialize it all in the yard of the family farm. He measured off the pathway from porch to lower fence to carriage road up the hill, assigned a foot for each of the 817 years of English history, and marked the start of individual reigns with wooden stakes. Although he is at present in a Swedish village, he can still visualize the segments of that marked path, on which the family also indicated events in European and American history. For example, he now always associates Edward I with a small pear bush and green fruit. An indoor equivalent would be a series of pictures on two-inch squares of different-colored papers pinned on the parlor wall, one square for each year of a given king's reign, thus: William I,

whale, white paper, twenty-one years; William II, whale, blue, thirteen years; the Henrys, hens; the Richards, lions; the Edwards, editors; and so on, each king with different numbers of colored papers, to assist the memory.

[Clara Clemens], [Jean Clemens], [Susan Clemens].

"How to Tell a Story," 1895 (WMT 24).

Mark Twain contrasts the humorous story (American), comic story (English), and witty story (French). The humorous story, which depends on the manner of telling, is lengthy, wandering, and aimless. Comic and witty stories, which depend on matter not manner, are brief and pointed. The humorous story involves artistry and must be told gravely. The teller of a comic story announces beforehand that it is funny and often repeats his nub pathetically. The teller of a humorous story may finish with a snapper, but you must be alert to get it, because he often pretends ignorance of its meaning. Here is an example of a comic story: A soldier whose leg has been shot off is being carried to safety but then has his head taken off by a cannon ball. When the plodding would-be rescuer tells his officer that the man has lost a leg and is rebukingly told that he means a head, the rescuer looks for himself and then says that the casualty said it was HIS LEG!!!! When a humorist like James Whitcomb Riley presents this story, it is recited as though told by a witless farmer and is dragged out for ten minutes, with confusions and irrelevant details, quaking inner laughter, and apparent unconsciousness of the art displayed. The true humorist—for example, Artemus Ward—slurs his main point, drops studied remarks with seeming inadvertence and as if thinking aloud, and pauses with perfect timing. Twain then offers as a type of the humorous story requiring the well-timed pause the Negro ghost story called "The Golden Arm." When the golden-armed wife of a mean man died, he buried her in the prairie but later returned to retrieve the valuable arm, only to hear while trudging home through the snow a wind-like voice asking over and over, "Who got my golden arm?" At last, the teller must pause and then shout at the most frightened little girl in his audience, "*You've* got It!"

"Huck Finn." See ["Doughface"].

"Huck Finn and Tom Sawyer a nong the Indians," 1968 (HHT).

Huckleberry Finn explains ｝ ｨ t after Jim's rescue on the Arkansas farm of Tom Sawyer's aunt Sally and uncle Silas, she took them all home to Missouri and then across the state to visit some of her relatives on a hemp farm. It was dull there. Tom gets depressed and proposes to go farther west for some adventures in Indian country. When Huck and Jim hang fire, Tom lectures persuasively on Indians, their sense of honor, generosity, courage, strength, eloquence, physical attractiveness, keen eyesight and sense of smell, and hospitality. Tom, Huck, and Jim prepare to go. They assemble much equipment, buy some mules, and—once Tom has written his aunt Polly not to worry—move out one moonlit night. After about five days of travel, they come upon a Missouri family migrating by wagon to Oregon and are invited to accompany them. The family includes a fifty-five-year-old man named Mills, his wife, their strapping sons Buck, Bill, and Sam, and their daughters Peggy and little Flaxy. Peggy has book learning, and is beautiful and sweet. The Mills boys teach Tom, Huck, and Jim to lasso, shoot, and ride. After a couple of weeks of travel, with the United States far behind them now, they come upon an Indian camp by the Platte River.

They rest here, because the Mills family has arranged to wait at this spot for Peggy's twenty-six-year-old fiancé, Brace Johnson, said to be a big, brave man who has lived among the Indians and is to join the Mills party soon. A group of Indians comes up in a friendly fashion. They include Hog Face, Blue Fox, and Man-afraid-of-his-Mother-in-law. They eat with the Millses, have friendly wrestling matches with the Mills boys, and trade for items—for example, a flint for an old gun. Tom is tremendously impressed with their nobility and wants to go hunting with them. The Indians agree, but the night before the hunt they cleverly separate the white people. Tom grows curious and walks with Huck away from the wagon on the pretext of fetching water but really in order to go behind some trees to discuss his suspicions. Thoroughly worried, Tom goes to alert the Mills sons, now at Hog Face's camp. But then Huck sees some of the Indians shoot and scalp old Mills, tomahawk and scalp Mrs. Mills, grab and tie Jim, seize the two girls, and take off with them, and Jim, and also with all the livestock and supplies. Huck runs for his life and passes a miserable, long night. At dawn he returns to the burned wagon and finds Tom, who says that Buck, Bill, and Sam have been butchered. Tom suggests waiting nearby for Brace Johnson. Two or three days pass. They catch snakes, and roast and eat them. At one point Huck asks where Tom acquired his notions of Indian nobility. "Cooper's novels" is the sullen reply.

Brace finally turns up, is aghast at what happened, and questions the boys. They tell him almost everything, even that Huck exaggerated to the effect that the Millses were waiting for Brace as part of a group of seven white men. But when Brace wonders whether Peggy had a dirk he gave her to kill herself with if taken by Indians, Huck does not reveal that she loaned it to Blue Fox and may not have gotten it back again. Brace is left to assume that she had it and used it. He tells Huck exactly why he hopes that his Peggy is now dead. Huck later finds the dirk and hides it in his jacket lining. They bury the bodies of Mills, his wife, and their sons, camp there that night, and in the morning begin to pursue the Indian party in order to find Peggy's body— Brace thinks— and to rescue Jim and Flaxy, who, in Brace's expert opinion, will not be hurt in any way. After two days of hard riding, they come upon remains of the Indians' camp. Brace sends Huck and Tom ahead to find and bury Peggy's body. An instinct tells Huck to insist that they lie about it; so the boys wait a while and then return to Brace, and lead him to believe that it is all over and done right. He is profoundly relieved and grateful.

After four more days, Brace, Huck, and Tom begin to gain on the Indians, who by this time seem to be no longer afraid of pursuit. One day Brace kills an antelope, speaks tenderly of it, and then cooks it for their meal. The boys admire the tall, handsome, strong, immaculate hunter. He lectures them on Indian religion, with its sensible notion of a Good God and a Bad God. When they are talking about their plans that evening, it comes out that Brace thought it was Saturday. Learning, however, that it is Friday, he glumly announces that they are in for bad luck because it has long been his habit to perpetuate (Tom thought he said "propitiate," but Huck knows better) the Bad God by abstaining from meat on Fridays and Sundays. Sure enough, next morning a fog rolls in and Tom gets lost. Brace and Huck wait until it clears, then Brace tells the boy to feed a fire with green grass for a smoke signal while he circles in search of their missing companion. An hour later Brace returns, not with Tom but with a half-starved man, whom he found crazed and crawling on the prairie. Huck cares for him through the long, dreary day; but in the night, while the boy chases their straying mules, the man awakens, gorges himself on meat and bread, and dies. Lightning, thunder, and rain further discomfit the boy, who is delighted at sun-up to see Brace come back with Tom. The boy explains that he got off his mule in the fog to cinch up, was frightened by a rattlesnake, and ran in fright.

The three continue following the Indians and camp late in the afternoon in a beautiful valley. Tom stays behind while the other two seek water. Just after Brace goes down to look for puddles by the river's edge, two horse thieves ride up to Huck, but he fools them into following him to the camp of his fictitious sick pap, his aunt, and his sister. Suspicious too late, they start shooting at him; but Brace kills them both, one with his lariat, the other with his pistol. That night, the three seek and find the gang of thieves from which the two dead men came, decide to leave them alone and ride back along the river, when suddenly Brace senses the swift approach of a devastating waterspout. It chases them up a hill, where they are safe from the terrifying deluge which accompanies it. For eight days they are marooned on their hill, with a waste of water all about them.

Finally they resume their pursuit of the Indians. One morning later, they encounter evidence of a huge, recently used Indian camp. Brace finds an arrow with blue silk which he recognizes as Peggy's. Huck finds a piece of her dress, which he promptly hides from Brace's sight. Meanwhile Brace runs across the print of a white woman's shoe. Seeing that it is Peggy's, the boys surreptitiously stamp it out before the young man can return to examine it more closely. Tom rationalizes that leading Brace to believe his fiancée is dead is really a kindness, under these circumstances. Huck enormously admires Tom's reasoning.

Fearing that general trouble must have broken out between the whites and the Indians, Brace now decorates his bucksin coat with dried bugs, butterflies, and lizards, so that any Indians they encounter will regard him as insane and hence inviolable. The three follow the trail almost straight north, then more westerly . . .

Bill, Blue Fox, Brulé, Mrs. Douglas, Huckleberry Finn, Gin'l Gaines, Hog Face, Jack, Jim, Brace Johnson, Man-afraid-of-his-Mother-in-law, Mary, Mary, Bill Mills, Buck

Mills, Flaxy Mills, Peggy Mills, Sam Mills, Mills, Mrs. Mills, Sally [Phelps], Silas [Phelps], Polly, Roubidou, Tom Sawyer, Sid, Archibald Thompson, Mary Thompson, Thompson, Vaskiss, Miss Watson.

"A Human Bloodhound," 1969 (HHT).

Harbison's case is interesting to his older brother, Edward, less so to his other brother, Alfred, who is sick. The Corpse and Johnson are very friendly toward Harbison. Everyone talks about him; so the narrator, who can keep confidences, learns details. Harbison was five or six years old before he learned that he was not like other children, that his ability to identify hundreds of items in the dark simply by their smell was unique. Then he began to be sought out as a curiosity so much that he grew ashamed and reclusive. Now grown up and big, with his three purple birthmark stripes across his face, and his gloomy unagingness, he is most impressive. His sense of smell enables him to identify individual books and bricks, and of course people and animals. His smell-memory is uncanny. He regularly finds lost children—for example, Billy Clark—for distraught parents. He once saved Henry Blake, an ordinary loafer and thief but no killer, from being lynched for the murder of the Aldrich widow. Harbison took off briskly on the track of the real killer over a fence, through a field, and toward the river into a fog . . .

Godkin could seem to be looking through a thick wall and identify an object behind it—by the smell . . .

Mrs. Aldrich, Black, Henry Blake, Billy Clark, Clark, Mrs. Clark, Jack Collins, the Corpse, Godkin, Alfred Harbison, Edward Harbison, Harbison, Johnson, Deacon West, White.

["Human Destiny"] (MTP).

The Angel of Destiny ponders, marks on a scroll, and ponders again until all seems correct. The scroll shows one line moving to the right and dividing into two lines, each of which moves to the right but one upward and the other down. The Angel summons Arafel, reveals the diagram, and explains that it shows the course of human life—simple until an individual is seven years old; then it becomes a matter of choosing good or evil. The Angel tells Arafel that even now a young child is starting life and orders Arafel to see that he chooses good not evil, and that he avoids the path leading to military, political, or commercial renown.

The Angel of Destiny, Arafel, Elis.

"Human Nature," 1870.*

Some people are reluctant to call a bad deed a bad deed without first inquiring into the political background or the nationality of the offender. When a Feejee Islander was told that Cain was a Feejee Islander himself, the native began to abuse Abel.

Abel, Cain.

*In *Mark Twain's Sketches* (London: Routledge, 1872).

"A Humane Word from Satan," 1905 (WMT 24).

Satan writes a letter to the Editor of *Harper's Weekly* explaining that since the American Board accepts contributions every year from Satan it should stop calling Rockefeller's contribution tainted and accept it too. Satan says that three-fourths of the support of charities is conscience money. Why uniquely criticize Rockefeller? Every rich man perjures himself annually before the tax board. Money given to the American Board is diverted from taxes and hence is the wages of sin; therefore it is Satan who gives it. (In a note, the Editor explains that although the message is signed by Satan it is probably from Mark Twain's pen.)

The Editor, [John D.] Rockefeller, Satan.

"Hunting the Deceitful Turkey," 1906 (WMT 27).

When he was a boy, the author used to go hunting with his uncle and cousins. The youngest boy was Fred. He and the author shared a light shotgun. The older hunters were such fine marksmen that they could stun a squirrel by hitting the branch he was on: he would then fall, and the dogs would kill him. The author once stalked a stately wild turkey, which pretended she was lame to lead him away from her invisible children. The author followed diligently, got close, but never close enough to grab her and bring her home alive. She led him over a good deal of geography, finally flew into a tree, and then smiled down on him. On his way back, he found a deserted garden full of tomatoes and ate so many that he does not like tomatoes now.

> Fred.

[I Never Played at "Vingt et Un"], 1870 (probably by Twain) (P).
Ab. O'Rig Inee complains that he is unlucky at cards, in fights, and even at auction . . .

> Ab. O'Rig Inee.

'An Ideal French Address,' 1882 (S).
Twain explains that French sermons are like French speeches. They identify historical events only by date. A typical French speech might praise January 21 for breaking chains, criticize the 18th Brumaire, curse the man of December 2, and so on. In an oddly eloquent French sermon, we might be cautioned to remember January 13 with sorrow and also the consequent event of November 30; however, it all resulted in blessed December 25. Partial translation: Adam and Eve ate the forbidden fruit and were expelled from Eden. Twain advises churchgoers in France to take along annotated almanacs.

"If I Could Be There" (MTP).
If Twain could hide and listen, he would hear conversation of interest. For example: a Stranger reports to the Lord that a certain man died in sin and should therefore be punished. But the Lord replies that he is as indifferent to that tiny creature's fate as the Stranger is to that of a microbe. The Lord tells the Stranger that as many microbes are born and die in one person's body in ten days as there are people in the world today, and each person exists to feed those microbes—much, in fact, as the Stranger thinks God created the creatures of the field and ocean to feed men. The Lord starts to tell the Stranger that microbes think as well as men do—which isn't saying much. Neither can man build moons and halt the sun, strangely enough, though it is simple when you know how . . .

> The Lord, a Stranger.

["The Illinois State Association"]. See W 1868.

["Imaginary Dialogue with the President"] (MTP).

In order to vent his feeling about the most awful phrase in any language, Twain imagines a dialogue between the President of the United States and an Ignorant Citizen. I.C. tells the President that he wished to kill a certain neighbor boy but had to wait until the lad turned sixteen and gave his consent. The President expresses his opinion that I.C. is insane, until I.C. explains that he was only making up the story. However, he adds, the law is insane to let the seducer of a young woman go free if the young woman was of age and consented—consented, that is, to multiple murders, her own in essence, her mother's, her father's, etc.

An Ignorant Citizen, the President of the United States.

"An Imaginary Interview" (MTP).

In the form of a dialogue between a Lady and himself, Twain opines that the religion of a daughter is that of her mother, as he has discovered by talking with lots of girls. But boys as well as girls inherit from their fathers the martial spirit and loyalty to political dogmas which the children do not really understand well. In fifty years, women have done much to improve their rights. The superiority of women over men in ability to follow national leaders is owing to women's faith, sincerity, and sureness of purpose. Women have let men do the governing because their mothers trained them to do so. They train children to "honor" all women, as though those women were weak and could not take care of themselves. But women who cook, scrub, and wash work harder than their men. The average woman is often her husband's mental superior. Most married couples are mismated intellectually. To remedy this situation, mothers should start teaching children to respect women's capacities, for a change. This can be accomplished, by training, especially if started in the nursery. Middle-aged and old mothers cannot be depended upon to help in this regard. New mothers must start this conspiracy if it is to win. Universal suffrage would be a mistake: it brought Tammany and Pennsylvania politics. The remedy is a restricted woman's suffrage. If unrestricted, women's votes would get submerged in the major political parties and enlarge the total number of ballots cast. Only educated women should be allowed to vote; this would restrict the total number and give an impetus to education. That formidable block of sensible women's votes would scare bad politicians and inspire proper ones. That block would be like a volcano, not erupting often but always scary.

Lady.

["The Importance of the Hawaiian Trade"]. See *Letters from Honolulu.*

"Important Correspondence between Mr. Mark Twain of San Francisco, and Rev. Bishop Hawks, D.D., of New York, Rev. Phillips Brooks of Philadelphia, and Rev. Dr. Cummings of Chicago, Concerning the Occupancy of Grace Cathedral," 1865 (SS). (See also "Further of Mr. Mark Twain's Important Correspondence.")

Long desirous of helping the Grace Cathedral in San Francisco even though he is not a member of its congregation, the narrator decides to second its vestry's invitation to Rev. Bishop Hawks of New York to come to its pulpit by writing directly to the man himself. The narrator begins his letter by explaining that the salary of $7,000 is subject to negotiation and that he can get the bishop two or three times that sum. In addition, Hawks need not write any new sermons; instead, he can bring his old ones and also rely on the narrator to write some, as he has done most effectively for Episcopalian, Methodist, Unitarian, and other ministers here. All Hawks would have to do is learn to sing the litany. He can save money, too, by living with the narrator and even sharing his shirts like a twin. Hawks replies most gratefully but in the negative, explaining that he has just taken an uptown church for $10,000 a year and also that he has some cotton investments which require close watching. The narrator is touched but thinks that he detects a whiff of irony in Hawks's windy letter. Still, the minister said that he would pray for the narrator, who admits that he probably qualifies as a sinner at large and hence gets prayed for only after all other groups of sinners have been treated. He promises to publish next week his correspondence with Rev. Phillips Brooks and Rev. Dr. Cummings on the occupancy of Grace Church.

Rev. Phillips Brooks, Rev. Dr. Cummings, Rev. Dr. Bishop

Hawks, Bishop Kip, Rev. Mr. Stebbins, Rev. Mr. Thomas, Martin Farquhar Tupper, Rev. Dr. [Charles] Wadsworth.

"An Impression of Pelée." See "St. Pierre."

'In Aid of the Blind,' 1906 (WMT 28).

Twain explains that he is new at presiding over meetings but that he always does the best he can at things. That was the way an inept country band was once described in a local newspaper: it done the best it could. Twain is speaking now in aid of a New York association to promote the interests of the blind. The blind lead cheerless lives but can be greatly helped if they can be trained to use their hands in various industries. The association needs $15,000. The best way to raise such a sum is to get people to promise regular contributions, not gigantic lump sums. Twain helped obtain pledges for $2,400 annually to aid Helen Keller and her teacher Miss Sullivan in the late 1890s. Twain once knew what it was like to be blind. He and Joseph Twichell were traveling in Germany, stopped at a Heidelberg inn, and were assigned to an incredibly large bedroom. In the night Twain became restless, got up without a light in the inky darkness, sought his clothes to dress and go sit by the fountain in the square, but got lost. Next Twain introduces Mr. Choate, a man so handsome and generous that Twain would say anything about him that would help, even if it were not true.

[Andrew] Carnegie, [Joseph Hodges] Choate, Hutton, Helen Keller, Miss Sullivan, Rev. Joseph [H.] Twichell.

"In Carson City," c. 1863.*

Twain describes his sitting up all night in Virginia [City], so as to catch the stagecoach for Carson early the next morning. All his traveling companion Joseph T. Goodman does is swear at the weather. That evening Twain goes to a party held at Governor J. Neely Johnson's beautiful home. A man named Horace Smith stares into a mirror there until it breaks. Later the Unreliable enters, looking hungry and vicious. He and Twain guard a punch-bowl until its contents apparently evaporate. After that, the dancers are all a hazy whirl. The Unreliable eats his way through mountains of fancy food. The party breaks up late; and Twain, having been awake forty-eight hours, sleeps the next forty-eight.

Joseph T. Goodman, Governor J. Neely Johnson, Colonel [John J.] Musser, Horace Smith Esq., the Unreliable.

*In *Wit and Humor of America,* ed. Kate M. Rabb, Vol. 5 (Indianapolis: Bobbs-Merrill, 1907).

"In Defense of Harriet Shelley," 1894 (WMT 22).

Mark Twain takes umbrage at [Edward] Dowden's *Life of Shelley,* which is critical of the poet's wife Harriet. The book has a style reminding one of a Negro cake-walk in its lack of ordinary motion. The book is like a mindless Frankenstein, like a mountain hidden by fog. We are asked to believe that Harriet was at fault for Shelley's act of deserting her and taking up with another woman. When the poet first met Harriet, he was nineteen, had just been expelled from college for writing an atheistic pamphlet, and was between affairs; Harriet was sixteen and quickly fell for him. They were soon married [in 1811], lived happily in Edinburgh on little money, read together, then moved to York to be with [Thomas Jefferson] Hogg, and had a daughter—named Ianthe—in June, 1813. Shelley wrote endearing poems to mother and child. Then he met Maimuna Boinville of Bracknell, and also her daughter Mrs. Cornelia Turner, with whom he studied Italian poetry to Harriet's distress and the neglect of her Latin. In October, the Shelleys returned to Edinburgh, and Dowden foolishly says that Harriet's manifest joy was due to Ianthe's bearing the trip well! It is known that [Thomas Love] Peacock, their companion at this point, ridiculed the Boinville menagerie. In December, the Shelleys went back south, to London and then Windsor, where the poet was unhappy—according to Dowden—because an old friend of his there had died. But there were Bracknell, Cornelia, and Italian poetry for solace.

Early in 1814 Shelley began to live in the Boinville house. Probably Harriet was not invited. Mrs. Boinville wrote Hogg that the poet needed rest of mind and body. Why does Dowden not explain, or let Harriet explain, her feelings? She must remain silent. The conclusion seems inescapable that Shelley, who wrote uneasily to

Hogg, was conscience-stricken and ashamed for deserting Harriet and consorting with Mrs. Boinville and Mrs. Turner. Dowden tries to explain that the desertion was due to Harriet's demanding a carriage, discontinuing her reading aloud and studying, walking with Hogg to shops, hiring a wet nurse, watching an operation on Ianthe without blenching, and continuing to allow her unmarried older sister Eliza Westbrook to stay with her. Twain then demolishes these flimsy arguments one by one, concluding that in spite of Dowden's whitewashing attempts Shelley behaved unfaithfully because of his love for Cornelia Turner and the luxury which life at Bracknell provided.

By March, 1814, mischief had been wrought. Shelley was in the Boinville paradise, and Harriet was husbandless. Her letters have disappeared, but she must have been ashamed and resentful. Dowden piously refuses to heap blame on her! But Twain is willing to heap plenty on Shelley, whose wife, according to Mrs. [William] Godwin, told her that Shelley had fallen in love with Mrs. Turner and also should be denied access to young Mary Godwin. Meanwhile, it is a fact that Shelley and Harriet were remarried according to English Church rites! About the same time Harriet was walking her floor, trying, according to Twain, to memorize a charming poem by her husband eulogizing her as uniquely virtuous and gentle, he was falling in love with tough, no-nonsense Mary Godwin. It seems that by summer he had become a welcome visitor at Godwin's London book shop and his peculiar household above it. Harriet was so much in the dark that in July she wrote her husband's publisher to try to ascertain his whereabouts. At this point, Twain bitterly rebukes Dowden for insinuating that poor Harriet was anything but pure and faithful, and adduces evidence against the biased biographer. Soon Shelley ran off briefly to the Continent with Mary Godwin; Harriet bore his child in November, and Mary had one by him a couple of months later. Shelley got some of his money from Harriet to support Mary, who later was critical in her diary of "nasty" Harriet for sending creditors to her husband. Harriet bore her wretchedness more than two years and then drowned herself. Three weeks after her body was found, Shelley married his mistress Mary. Yet Dowden, the prejudiced, evidence-juggling "fabulist," concludes that no act of Shelley's caused Harriet's suicide.

[William] Baxter, Allegra [Byron], [Alfred] Boinville,

Mrs. Maimuna Boinville, Lord Byron, Jane Claire Clairmont, [Edward] Dowden, [John] Gisborne, Mrs. [John] Gisborne, Fanny Godwin, Mary Godwin, [William] Godwin, Mrs. [William] Godwin, Harriet Grove, Miss Hitchener, [Thomas Jefferson] Hogg, Hookham, Thornton Hunt, Dr. [James] Lind, [John Frank] Newton, Mrs. [John Frank] Newton, [Thomas Love] Peacock, Cornelia Robinson, [Charles Bysshe] Shelley, Harriet Westbrook Shelley, Ianthe Shelley, Mary Godwin Shelley, Percy Bysshe Shelley, [William] Shelley, Miss Shelley, [Edward John] Trelawney, Mrs. Cornelia Turner, Turner, Eliza Westbrook.

In Dim & Fitful Visions They Flit across the Distances, 1966 (P).

A poor old lady tells the narrator that twenty-five years ago her curly-headed baby daughter was lost or stolen from her. Then sixteen years ago another child, a lovely daughter about ten, wandered off, while being punished by being ignored, and was never seen again. But the woman had another daughter; this one when just sixteen was in a school play and then simply vanished. Ten years have passed since that time, but the woman had a final loss to bear: the shadows of death closed around the delight of her eye, her last daughter. The narrator expresses his heart-felt pity; but when the grieving woman leaves, a friend approaches and explains that the woman was not bereft of four children, since she had but one. The narrator closes with the opinion that it is possible for one child to seem to die often, since our visions of little forms fade and we know one changing child as successively lost.

Goddess of the Flowers.

In Memoriam: Olivia Susan Clemens: Died August 18, 1896; Aged 24, 1897 (WMT 22).

The poet remembers a fair valley from long ago. Near it stood a temple, within which dwelt a spirit made all of light. The priests were devoted to the light, but a disaster suddenly struck: the light passed away and left only a vacancy. Surely the light will return.

Olivia Susan Clemens.

["In My Bitterness"], 1972 (FM).

   Twain is glad that she [Susan Clemens] is dead and thus set free
from life's insults. She was not freed through pity but instead so
that God might knife him once more. God never does kindnesses;
He only sets traps. Riches and health and love are given only so
that they may be withdrawn. But since she is now at peace, God
can never really hurt Twain again.

   [Susan Clemens].

[In Sorrow I Sorrow], 1867 (P).

   I am grief-stricken and urge women to rise. But demons drown
my voice in blasphemies. Let me die, a martyr to suffrage.

   Demon, Secretary of the Society for the Dissemination
   of Poetry among the Pawnees, Woman.

"In the Animals' Court," 1962 (LFE).

   In court, the Rabbit is being tried for cowardice and army desertion, pleads that he was merely following a law higher than
the military—namely, God's law which denies courage to rabbits—
but is found guilty and sentenced to be hanged. The Lion is given a
dukedom and fame for his courage. The Fox is sentenced to life
imprisonment for stealing, even though he pleads that he has
followed divine law in doing what he did. The Horse is praised
for not submitting to temptation while he was locked up in the
paddock with some hens. The Wolf is sentenced to death for killing, even though he pleads that it is his nature to kill. The Sheep
is extolled for resisting the temptation to commit massacre. Finally,
the Machine is tried for turning when it should go straight and
for speeding through crowds and laying down a stench wherever
it goes. The Machine pleads that it is a slave to its maker and that
its powers are set into motion by forces beyond its control. The
Court is persuaded and releases the prisoner.

   The Court, the Fox, the Horse, the Lion, the Machine, the
   Rabbit, the Sheep, the Wolf.

"In the Metropolis," 1864 (WG).

   The reporter is happy to say that to the Washoe miner, who has long breathed dust and eaten cheese, the Occidental Hotel in San Francisco is a veritable heaven. If you do not breakfast until noon, lunch until 3:00, dine until 7:30, take tea until 9:00, and then sup until midnight, the landlord will be offended and will move your trunks out. The Opera House, the Metropolitan theater, and the traveling circus also offer splendors. In fact, everything in town—birds, flowers, Chinamen, winds, and sunshine—is joyous. Yet the natives complain about the wind and the dust. One even criticized the painting of Samson and Delilah at the Bank Exchange because the scissors depicted were too modern.

Harry Courtaine, [Sam] Curry, Dan, Fred Franks, Gould, Julia Dean Hayne, Annette Ince, Emily Jordan, Mrs. Judah, Frank Lawlor, Maguire, Caroline Richings, James H. Taylor, Ella Zoyara.

"The Income-Tax Man." See "A Mysterious Visit."

'Independence Day,' 1907 (WMT 28).

Instead of celebrating, Twain says, he has to defend his character. Sir Mortimer Durand will not believe that Twain did not steal the Ascot cup. So he might as well confess he took it. Twain recalls that he got himself placed third on the list of speakers before a society of Britishers in New York a couple of years ago, so that he could catch an early train and get home. But a famous English clergyman, also listed to speak, persuaded Twain to switch places with him so that he could catch a train and thus not break the Sabbath. The result was that Twain broke the Sabbath and has not kept it since. The trouble with our Fourth of July is that too many people shoot off fireworks and cause serious accidents. One of Twain's many uncles caught a rocket in his open mouth and was scattered over forty-five states. Twain now praises the English for giving us many Independence Days. The first was the day of the Magna Carta; the second, the day of the Bill of Rights; next, the day of no taxation without representation. The Fourth of July, 1776, was an English affair too. Every man who signed the Declaration of Independence was British. The only Americans in 1776 were the Indians out on the plains. Our latest—and the only uniquely American—Independence Day was the day Abraham Lincoln emancipated the slaves and thereby their masters as well.

Ambassador [Joseph Hodges Choate], Sir Mortimer Durand.

"Indiantown," 1967 (WWD).

Time: June, seventy years ago. Scene: Indiantown, on the west side of the Mississippi River. The town boasts 1,500 God-fearing inhabitants. The Indian River curves down from the north, empties into the mighty river, and occasionally contributes to terrifying floods which can eat up part of the town in a single day. Most buildings are of wood and have red-brick sidewalks in front. There is dust or mud, depending. There is no local newspaper. A typical old gentleman is Dr. Stevens. Burt Higgins has his blacksmith shop at the north of town. Beyond are the mansions of rich cotton farmers Squire Charles Fairfax, Andrew Harrison, and Orrin Lloyd Godkin, all of whose holdings extend on both sides of the swirling river.

The population divides itself into grades. At the top of the quality is Squire Fairfax, a resolute planter from Maryland, aged thirty-five, who once interfered when a visiting desperado named Jim Tyler was abusing a boy. When Tyler tried to make trouble, Fairfax broke his jaw, disarmed him, and ordered him never to return to Indiantown. Fairfax is married to a charming but sickly Virginia lady, and they have a little daughter named Helen. Old Andrew Harrison is all business. His humble, idealistic son George helps him, but under limitations. George's wife has just died. So has the husband of his sister Mrs. Wilkinson, who is an obsequious hypochondriac. O. Lloyd Godkin, whose name provides the villagers a mild line of profanity, is a forty-year-old bachelor, so funereal in appearance that his nickname is the Corpse, which he rather likes. He is courteous and graceful, and would be handsome but for his waxy pallor and his wistful black eyes. Next come the Bateses and the Gridleys. Judge Bates is handsome, amiable, but a trifle too dainty; his wife is like him but for the touch of poison in her flattery. Rev. Mr. Bailey is manifestly genuine and friendly, and so is his wife.

David Gridley is a split personality. He is naturally profane, untidy, inartistic, anti-social, and anxious to shock. His lovely, educated, deeply religious wife Susan is the very reverse, undertakes to reform David, whom she secretly regards as an incipient arch-angel, but once is saddened when she hears him swearing power-fully on the occasion of his noticing that buttons are missing on some of his shirts. She repeats one of his naughty words but cannot help laughing when he snickers at her. Over the years, their daugh-ters have enjoyed watching Susy's efforts at reformation but are only half persuaded that their father is ever really improved.

Rev. Mr. Bailey, Mrs. Bailey, Judge Bates, Mrs. Bates, Dr. Bradshaw, Squire Charles Fairfax, Mrs. Charles Fairfax, Helen Fairfax, Fairfax, Fairfax, Gilbert, Orrin Lloyd God-kin, David Gridley, Mrs. Susan Gridley, Miss Gridley, Andrew Harrison, George Harrison, Mrs. George Harrison, Tom Harrison, Burt Higgins, Professor Mahaffey, Marsh, the Widow Pilgrim, Randall, Dr. Stevens, Jim Tyler, Mrs. Jim Tyler, Tyler, Wilkinson, the Widow Wilkinson, Wil-kinson.

"The Indignity Put upon the Remains of George Holland by the Rev. Mr. Sabine," 1871 (CG).

The Rev. Mr. Sabine refused dead George Holland the privileges of his church, because Holland was an actor and in Sabine's opinion the theater does not sufficiently inculcate morals. Outraged, Twain calls Sabine a spiritual pygmy and a slimy, self-righteous reptile, and wonders why his soul does not ooze through the pores of his body along with its other waste matter. In Twain's opinion, *King Lear* unforgettably teaches filial gratitude, *Othello* the dangers of jealousy, William Tell plays heroic patriotism, and innumerable novels the best of Christianity. Christ is the seed, but should we therefore worry overmuch about the cut of the sower's garment? Twain makes it clear that he approves of the work of most men of God, but he adds that the theater and the newspaper are more influential through having mankind's atten-tion more of the time. And too often the pulpit bores, chloro-forms, and stupefies its audience. Let it be remembered that clergy-men are by no means the only servants of God on earth.

Black Crook, Cook, George Holland, [Isaac S.] Kalloch, Rev. Mr. Sabine.

"Information about Westminster Abbey" (MTP).

It is twenty years ago, and the narrator is on a Cunarder from England to America. He is chatting with two fellow passengers in the smoking cabin. One is a dull, rural clergyman; the other, a Scotch farm lad. When talk gets around to London, the boy asks if the narrator was at Westminster Abbey. He says no, that he stayed instead at the Langham. Told that the Abbey is not a hotel, the narrator asks why he should go there. Because it is a church, but unlike other churches. The narrator asks what is wrong with it. Nothing, but it has tombs of England's great dead. How savage, says the narrator, to bury fat people so publicly. The boy explains that by great dead he meant illustrious dead, and adds that they are buried right in the church. The narrator is aghast and wonders if live people go and sit on the tombs. No, on chairs. In a graveyard? The narrator professes outrage, whereupon the rural minister assures him that the lad has been telling the strict truth. The matter thus being settled, the narrator gives up the game.

"Information for the Million," 1864 (CJF).

To William, a Missourian who has written for information about Nevada, Twain happily replies as follows. He could give a full history in about five hundred pages but will resist and be brief instead. The territory became Nevada in 1861. Silver was recently discovered. The seasons are irregular. The soil is sandy except for a few fertile ranches. The place is healthy enough, although people die of conical balls, cold steel, erysipelas, and intoxication. A discontented person should not leave Missouri for Nevada unless he can be happy earning more or less than he earned back there. Do not plan to sell tracts here. Twain does not know William's friend Joel H. Smith, now in Nevada, and suspects that the man must really be John Smith, to whom Twain sold an interest in an unproductive mine. He offers William an interest also in a mine or two. He hopes to hear from William soon and advises him to accept the facts in this Nevada report but not its bantering tone.

> [Sam] Curry, Gould, Grosch, [Franklin S.] Rising, Joel H. Smith, John Smith, William.

"Information Wanted," 1868 (WMT 7).

The author writes to ask the government for information on any islands it plans to purchase. It seems that his uncle, who is industrious, honest, and anxious for quiet, tried to settle on the new island of St. Thomas. But he was robbed, caught seven kinds of fever and nearly died, had a farm washed out there, bought a mountain but lost it in an earthquake, started a brick factory which was destroyed by a volcano, and therefore is looking elsewhere. The author wonders whether the government plans to buy Porto Rico.

"Information Wanted about Silver Land." See "Information for the Million."

"Ingomar over the Mountains," 1863 (MTWY).
Mrs. Claughley urges her daughter Parthenia to marry Polydor and save her father Myron Claughley from debt. The Comanches, led by Ingomar, capture Myron for ransom. Polydor sneers and refuses Parthenia any aid. She goes to the Indian camp and offers herself as hostage for Myron. She and Ingomar fall in love, and Ingomar turns into a tame citizen of Silver City. Polydor demands payment of his old debt; but some Comanches, now under Thorne, their chief, snatch him bald instead. Timarch, the police chief of Silver City, effects a treaty with the Indians. Ingomar becomes mayor. All is well.

Myron Claughley, Mrs. Myron Claughley, Parthenia Claughley, Ingomar, Polydor, Thorne, Timarch, Wright.

The Innocents Abroad: Or the New Pilgrims' Progress, 1869 (WMT 1,2).
Mark Twain is happy to be accepted as one of about sixty passengers aboard the Quaker City on its voyage to Europe and the Holy Land. After a month, they start in a rain early in June, 1867. Twain feels superior for not being seasick but is soon abashed to notice many captains aboard the ship. The passengers learn nautical language, play deck games, start journals, briefly enjoy magic-lantern exhibitions and charades, and sing. After ten days they land at Fayal, a filthy island in the Azores, and young Blucher gives a banquet for nine fellow passengers which seems expensive until the bill of thousands of Azores reis is translated into $21.70. Next they take donkeys and scamper along the smooth roads of Fayal.

After a week of tempestuous weather the ship docks at Gibraltar, where the passengers are thrilled by the sight of a Yankee clipper with stars and stripes flying. We are treated to much geographical and historical information on Gibraltar, which resembles a gob of mud on the end of a shingle. Twain, Dan, and the doctor go to Tangier, where Twain is sold a pair of shabby gloves by a pretty lady clerk. The antiquity and vivid color of Tangier are evoked. Blucher almost rides his ass into a sacred Moorish mosque, which nonbelievers are never permitted to enter. Twain describes executions and other punishments for crimes committed in Tangier, tells about the Moorish cats there, indicates how bored the lonely American consul-general is, and then prepares to leave Gibraltar. Shortly after a stirring Fourth of July celebration at sea, the ship steams into Marseilles; and Twain and a couple of his friends go ashore, mangle their French in ordering supper, and then inefficiently find their way to the noisy, humorless Grand Casino. They register at the Grand Hotel du Louvre et de la Paix and soon get used to French hotel life—except for no soap. They are embarrassed by a noisy American who orders wine with the dishonest boast that he never dines without it. They drive in the Prado, visit the Chateau Borély, then the zoological gardens—which have an entertainingly solemn crane—and finally the melancholy Castle d'If—where Dumas's Monte Cristo and the Man in the Iron Mask were imprisoned.

Next they go five hundred miles by rail through pleasant France to Paris. Twain states his preference for the American stage-coach over the tight little compartments on French railroads. A nice slow dinner at Dijon. City after city, and then magnificent Paris. They go from the efficient station to the Grand Hotel du Louvre, then have dinner and a ruinous French shave. A game of billiards proves frustrating again, since the European table is faulty, as usual. Twain and his two cronies hire as guide A. Billfinger, whom they rename Ferguson. He eats prodigiously at their expense and sidetracks them to silk shops instead of taking them quickly to the Louvre and the International Exposition. They see and contrast energetic Napoleon III, Emperor of France, and sleepy Abdul Aziz, Sultan of Turkey. They inspect Notre Dame—rich with history—the gloomy Morgue, some public gardens (in one of which a Cancan is presented), then the laden Louvre, and finally the extensive Bois de Boulogne. Visits to the famous cemeteries of St. Denis and

Père la Chaise inspire Twain to present a burlesque history of dastardly Abelard, pure-souled Heloise, and her uncle Fulbert the canon (or howitzer). Next Twain ridicules the French for advertising that they can speak English in their shops and can serve American drinks in their bars, when they cannot. He adds that the grisettes are so ugly that to call them immoral would be flattery. Versailles is inordinately impressive, with its park, galleries of statues and paintings, and stables, until one returns to the slums of the Faubourg St. Antoine in Paris.

At sea again. But some of their friends are still scattered on different European tours. The Quaker City goes to Genoa, with its thick-walled palaces, its innumerable churches (some with too many relics), its crooked streets which are so narrow that the buildings above them seem like cave walls, and its vast cemetery. Rushing from Genoa by train past the battlefield of Marengo, Twain and his cronies arrive at Milan and first see the incomparable cathedral by moonlight. In the morning they explore the cathedral, the princeliest creation of man, and then see the bejeweled tomb of good St. Charles Borromeo, and many relics in a treasure room nearby. Their ill-speaking guide takes them to La Scala, the Ambrosian Library (where they see a Virgilian manuscript annotated by Petrarch, which causes Twain to register sympathy for Mr. Laura, husband of Petrarch's inamorata), a Roman amphitheater, and elsewhere. The three men enjoy their baths in a public house until they notice an absence of soap. Twain visits Da Vinci's "Last Supper" and fancies that the copies are better. (This leads him into an essay on aesthetics.) For a franc the doctor is allowed to kiss a pretty girl who then demonstrates a remarkable echo for the group.

At Como and Bellagio, after being fumigated, Twain has a chance to make a comparison between celebrated Lake Como (with its pretty setting) and matchless Lake Tahoe back home. A steamer takes the party down the Lago di Lecco to Lecco, and then a carriage carries them past indolent Italian towns toward Bergamo. The driver tells them about the legend of Count Luigi's fortress with an iron hook projecting from a wall. The travelers drive on past Padua and Verona to shimmering Venice, thoroughly described as to its gondolas, the canals by moonlight and daylight, the music, back streets, crowds, palaces, bridges, and former oligarchical tyranny. Then Twain tells how a Venetian smuggled the bones of St. Mark in lard vessels to Venice to build the cathedral on. Twain tours through Venice at leisure, observing the pretty promenaders and despising affected Americans, and seeing so many tombs and religious paintings that he must honestly speak out against saints pictured with their trademarks (St. Sebastian with arrows, etc.) and voice his preference for Renaissance realism. Dan and the doctor pretend to relish an Italian shave; so Twain volunteers and is hacked bloodily too.

The group is joined by other wandering travelers from the *Quaker City*, and soon they go to Florence, which has weary miles of picture galleries, laboriously made mosaics, Dante's tomb (at Santa Croce) but not his body, and soldiers so ignorant that they cannot help Twain find his hotel when he gets lost. At Pisa they see the Leaning Tower, the Duomo, and the Baptistry (with Galileo's lamp and a curious echo). Then they proceed to their ship at Leghorn. While in dull Civita Vecchia—a nest of dirt, vermin, and ignorance —Twain praises the Italian railroad system but reviles the whole priest-ridden country for being a museum of magnificence on the one hand and misery on the other. He criticizes the old masters for serving such despots as the Medicis. Next he despairs of being a discoverer of anything in Rome, all of whose treasures are well known now. If only he were a slothful, superstitious, ignorant Roman, he would go to America on a voyage of discovery, and find there democracy, literacy, milk, windows, fire-engines, clean clothes, spectacles and false teeth, books and newspapers, religious tolerance, moderate taxes, high mountains and long rivers, and farm machinery. Twain is tremendously impressed by the size of St. Peter's and the view from its dome. He and his friends go to various places and buildings in Rome, including the Coliseum, a symbol of grandeur and decay. Twain imagines a playbill in gladiatorial Rome and then a report of the show in next day's *Roman Daily Battle-Axe*. The expression "butchered to make a Roman holiday" is so tiresome that Twain is reminded by it of his western friend Judge Oliver, who on a mining trip patiently submitted to an adverse fate until at last he said that it was monotonous. This memory in turn reminds Twain that Michael Angelo is praised for doing so much in Italy that it is monotonous now to hear his name. In Rome the group bedevils the guide by asking if Michael Angelo built the Roman Forum and certain Egyptian obelisks. (Here Twain is reminded of the doctor's response on being shown a sample of the handwriting of Columbus in Genoa—"Is he dead?") In the Vatican Museum they wonder whether the Egyptian mummies are dead. Finally Twain visits the catacombs in Rome and presumes to doubt certain early Christian legends.

The second volume begins with a sardonic description of the grisly Capuchin Convent in Rome, with its subterranean vaults decorated with monkish bones. Twain likes only Raphael's "Transfiguration" in the Vatican and seriously deplores the fact that too many Italian paintings are devoted to religion and too few to history. A trip to St. John Lateran inspires him to rank holy personages as follows: the Virgin Mary, God, Peter, several Popes, and then Christ.

Twain and his friends go by rail to Naples, thus escaping the quarantine of their vessel. They go to restful Ischia, delight in the Blue Grotto at Capri, deplore the Neapolitans' jeering of Frezzolini (a faded singer at the San Carlo opera house), ridicule the ceremony of showing St. Januarius's periodically liquifying blood, observe the filth and glitter of Naples, and finally ascend Vesuvius with its theatrical fires and its matchless view. Pompeii fascinates Twain: its streets, low buildings, obscenities, skeletons of victims, and so on. Twain ponders the evanescence of fame.

With all passengers aboard and well, the *Quaker City* steams from Naples past Stromboli, through the Straits of Messina (where a passenger called the Oracle mistakes Scylla and Charybdis for Sodom and Gomorrah), to Piraeus, where they are told that because of quarantine laws they cannot briefly visit Athens. So Twain, Denny, Dr. Birch, and Jackson sneak ashore by moonlight in a small boat. They see the Acropolis, the Parthenon, Mars Hill, and much else. They steal grapes. And they are chased back to their boat by brigands and policemen. The islands of Greece are desolate, and Twain adversely compares present-day Greece with its illustrious past.

Soon they cast anchor in the Golden Horn and visit Constantinople. It is like a dream: shops, streets, geese, dwarfs and human monsters, St. Sophia, dervishes, the Thousand and One Columns, the mausoleum of the Sultan Mahmoud, the bazar, etc. Next Twain discusses the Turkish slave market, the prevalence of cheating in Turkey, its flea-bitten and lazy dogs, its frequently suppressed newspapers, a certain filthy lunch-room, and his disillusion with Turkish baths and narghili and coffee.

They go through the Bosporus into the Black Sea and visit war-shattered Sebastopol and its dread battle sites—Malakoff, Redan, Inkerman, Balaklava. Twain's watch becomes so confused with time changes that it stops. The ship goes for coal to Odessa, a thoroughly American-looking city blessedly without objects worth seeing. The Americans are treated so courteously in Russia that they go on to Yalta for an audience with the Emperor. The American consul at Odessa lectures the party on how to behave, and all goes smoothly. They are amicably received at the Emperor's residence, and the Empress and grand dukes and duchesses are there. They all go over to Grand Duke Michael's palace a mile away and have a kind of informal indoor picnic. Twain closes this section by listing the visitors the ship has recently had; but now, he says, the travelers must be more particular since they have associated with an emperor.

On the way from Constantinople (which they briefly visit again) through the Dardanelles to Smyrna, the crew entertains the passengers by burlesquing their audience with the Czar. Smyrna inspires Twain to inveigh tiresomely against conveniently narrow interpretations of vague biblical prophecies (specifically those concerning Smyrna and Ephesus). Then he praises the cleanliness and attractiveness of the Christian Armenians in Smyrna. He is puzzled to see three veins of oyster-shells high in a hill exposed by a road-cut and theorizes amusingly on their origin. An odd Oriental train takes the party and a load of donkeys to Ephesus, the history and beauty and desolation of which Twain discusses in guide-book terms. Next comes a comic redaction of "The Legend of the Seven Sleepers." Seven young Christians leave Ephesus to avoid being persecuted by King Maximilianus. They drink in a cave, sleep, and awake two centuries later. When they descend to a changed Ephesus, they learn the truth and lie down to die. At Ephesus the American travelers are searched and forced to return pilfered fragments of sculpture. On ship they overhaul their gear for the Holy Land.

At brightly beautiful Beirout Twain and seven other hardy men hire Abraham, a dragoman, for a three- or four-week pack-train trip through Syria and down Palestine to Jaffa. In the Valley of Lebanon Twain is amused by the camels, is frightened by his horse Jericho, recalls the history of Joshua, and visits Noah's tomb. He is intrigued by the massive architectural ruins at Baalbec and then outraged that three of this party insist on pushing their mounts so as to avoid traveling on the Sabbath. After cruel riding they get to Damascus by twilight on Saturday, trot in, and are treated to fine hotel-rooms but also anti-Christian looks to such an extent that Twain again voices the hope that Russia will soon soundly defeat Turkeydom. He recalls the story of St. Paul's conversion near Damascus. Twain drinks from Ananias's well. Later he has a brief attack of cholera.

Then the travelers leave on horses and with green glasses and umbrellas to go through many squalid Syrian villages, one of which they christen Jonesborough and another of which—Banias—has a decayed castle. Dr. Birch treats numerous sore-eyed infants at Banias. Trading Jericho for a new horse (called Baalbec after the other ruin), Twain debunks the notion that Arabs care for their horses tenderly. At Dan, in the north of Palestine, Twain pauses to contrast short Holy Land distances with vast ones in the United States. When the dragoman orders camps made early out of Dan, Twain sneers at the rumor of fierce Arabs nearby and ridicules the author William C. Grimes for his accounts of hairbreadth escapes from the Bedouins. The area may have seen slaughter in the times of Joshua and Jael, but now it is quietly desolate. Jack gets a sunstroke listening vainly for the voice of the turtle. Twain sincerely praises and retells the story of Joseph, then lauds Esau.

The travelers swim in the Sea of Galilee, bargain there for a boat to take them to Magdala but lose the chance through their stinginess, and have to ride on. Twain is immensely impressed by the fact that Christ's life was spent in a geographically restricted area. The group proceeds from Capernaum to Magdala, which is frescoed with camel-dung and alive with vermin. After visiting the house of Magdalene and the walls of Tiberius, Twain debunks romantic descriptions (including W. C. Grimes's) of the Sea of Galilee (which is smaller than Lake Tahoe and is in a wasteland environment) and ridicules pilgrims who bring preconceived notions to it. Scorning the services of a lavishly but rustily armed guard, the group rides up to Mount Tabor (scene of Christ's Transfiguration), where Twain recalls accounts of battles during the Crusades. They go on to Nazareth and visit Mary's fountain and the spot traditionally marked as that of the Annunciation. Twain when elsewhere could imagine the actual angelic visitation better than he can now. Next he inveighs against bogus grottoes and Nazarene girls who are not

Madonna-like but are said to be so by many writers, including
W. C. Grimes, whose *Nomadic Life in Palestine* Twain now ridicules
in detail. Thinking of apocryphal legends of Christ, Twain with
the others leaves Nazareth, which clings like a wasp's nest to its
hills. And so to the Plain of Esdraelon and the towns of Endor,
Naim, and Shunem (where Samuel was born), Jezreel (where Ahab
lived), Jenin, and Samaria. They are not attacked by any of Grimes's
Bedouins.

Then they go past Shechem (with its archives), Joseph's tomb,
Jacob's well, Shiloh, and so to Jerusalem on its eternal hills. The
town is small, with crooked streets and ragged filth. Twain discusses the Holy Sepulcher and Calvary seriously but then ironically
treats legends of the true cross, the sword of Godfrey of Bouillon,
the ability of St. Helen to find anything she looked for, Melchi-
sedek's tomb, the tomb of Adam, and the present-day disunity of
Christian churches. Twain follows some of the stages of Christ's
progress to the cross, and then partly burlesques the tale of the
Wandering Jew. They see the Mosque of Omar with its huge rock,
the Place of Wailing, the pool of Bethesda, the Mount of Olives,
the Garden of Gethsemane, and much else. The pilgrims are sur-
feited, and in addition beggars spoil the sights.

For a change of scene, some of the travelers exhaustingly go
through a hot region rumored to be full of hostile Bedouins to
Bethany (where they see Lazarus's tomb) and on to ancient Jericho,
then early next morning to the crooked little Jordan River (which
they wade across before dawn) and thence to the Dead Sea (which
they float in). Then to hot Mars Saba, where they spend the night
at a hospitable Catholic convent (which Twain sincerely praises).
Bethlehem is next. Back in Jerusalem, they are thoroughly glad to
make plans to leave. They go to Jaffa and see animated rags there.
Twain comprehensively brands Palestine as dismal and heartbroken.

At sea again, all feel relief. They see the sights of Alexandria.
The souvenir-hunters chop vainly at the Egyptian granite. Then
Twain and his friends go by train to Cairo and wretched Shepherd's Hotel, then past the Nilometer and out to climb the Pyramids. For a dollar an Arab runs down Cheops, ascends Cephren,
and returns to the top of Cheops. Twain repeatedly bets Dan's
dollars that the Arab will fall to his death. The Pyramids remind
Twain of smaller Holliday's Hill back home, down which he and
a friend almost disastrously rolled a huge boulder once. The

Sphinx is earnest, lonely, and impressive in size and hardness, and resists American souvenir-hunters' efforts to hack at it. Twain now says that he will not tell of Egyptian legends about birds, horses, granaries, and the like, or of other scenes observed. The passengers settle down for the long voyage home. From the ship they see Malta, Algiers, Sardinia, Malaga, and Gibraltar. Then Twain and three other men run a quarantine blockade to spend a week in Seville, Cordova, and Cadiz. A few days later, Bermuda, then—ever more homesick—on for New York and customs. Twain is now an unprovincial Hadji: he has made the pilgrimage. He has glowing memories of the trip and would willingly go again, on the same ship and with the same sinful passengers.

Abbot of St. Denis, Abdul Aziz, Abelard, Abraham, Adams, Mrs. Adams, Ah-ah Foo-foo, William L. Ainsworth, Albert, Brother Alexander, Alexander II Emperor of Russia, Brother Anselmo, William G. Astrolabe, Emperor Aurelius, J. Ellsworth Baker, Moses S. Beach, Rev. Mr. Henry Ward Beecher, A. Billfinger, Dr. Birch, Blondin, Blucher, Captain Bursley, Marshal [François Certain] Canrobert of France, Brother Carlo, Alexis du Caulaincourt, Charley, Armand de la Chartreuse, Church, Claudia, the U.S. Consul at Beirut, the U.S. Consul at Odessa, the U.S. Consul-General at Jaffa, C. W. C—, Dan, Denny, Diodorus, Julie di Diomede, Prince Dolgorouki, Captain Charles C. Duncan, the Enthusiast, Far-away Moses, Ferguson, Ferguson, Ferguson, Ferguson, Ferguson, Colonel J. Heron Foster, Frezzolini, George W. Fulbert, the Game, General [Giuseppe] Garibaldi, Isabel di Genova, Leonardo di Genova, Countess Lucretia di Genova, Count Luigi Gennaro Guido Alphonso di Genova, George, Gift, Gordon, the Grand Duchess, Uriah S. (or Z.) Graunt, R. R. G—, Alphonse Henry Gustave de Hauteville, Heloise, Herbert, Hercules, High, J. T. H—, the Interrogation Point, Jack, Jack, Jackson, Captain Jones, Laertius, Hadji Mohammed Lamarty, Low, Captain L—, Malchus, Grand Duchess Marie, King Maximilianus, Mehemet Ali Ben Sancom, Grand Duke Michael, Mohammed, Henri de Montmorency, George P. Morton, Moult, Napoleon III Emperor of France, Old Travelers, Judge Oliver, the Oracle, the Pilgrim, the Poet, Roderigo Gonzales Michael Angelo, the Empress of Russia, Sally

Maria, Scharkspyre, Lieutenant-General [William T.] Sherman, Smith, Johannes Smithianus, Susan, Captain W. W. S—, Brother Thomas, General Todleben, Trumps, Baron Ungern-Sternberg, Marcus Marcellus Valerian, John P. Whitcomb, Lloyd B. Williams, Baron Wrangel, the Young Achilles.

"An Inquiry about Insurances," 1866.*

Coming down from Sacramento, Twain finds a pamphlet in the steam saloon explaining that a certain accident insurance company offers especially wide coverage—everything, in fact, from dog bite to earthquake. Twain has a few questions: can you be insured for one thing and not another, does an earthquake cost a policy holder more in San Francisco than elsewhere, why is it that so few of the company's customers get killed? Etc.

Smith.

*In *The Celebrated Jumping Frog* (New York: Webb, 1867).

"Instructions in Art (With Illustrations by the Author)," 1903 (WMT 29).

The author explains that painters can get mixed up when they do a number of portraits at once and forget to label them by subject. Is a given painting a picture of Howells or Depew? Edward VII or Cromwell? The author had the most trouble when he painted the head on one canvas and the bust on another. It was even hard to tell whether the bust was upsidedown or not. But still he has had success. In one day he got orders from sixty-two people not to be painted. First he simply throws off a study and does not know himself who it is going to be. Genre pictures differ from the encaustic and other schools in ways too complicated to explain. Still-life painting is so called because it is fanciful only. One of the author's paintings looks like a Botticelli because of its limbfulness. The author did a marine picture of Joseph Jefferson, using perspective and foreshortening. He also did a sketch of an animal, but its front end went around a corner before he could get to it. He started a Raphael-like portrait of Queen Elizabeth, but because of difficulty with her lace he turned her into Pocahontas and then Eve. To

encourage yourself, you should carefully watch your progress in
painting: save your works, date them, and thus measure your strides.
Practice is the secret. The author paints from three to seven hours
daily.

The Cabinet, the President.

["The Intelligence of God"], 1962 (LFE).
God made everything and then pronounced it good. With our
mouths we judiciously praise God's handiwork. But our acts sometimes belie our words, for example, when we swat a fly. We also hunt
out fleas, rats, snakes, and microbes. Yet He pronounced all of them
good. We should rephrase our laudatory prayers.

"International Copyright," 1886 (LAIFI).
Twain favors an international copyright because it would prevent the inundation of America by cheap, immoral novels—like
those of Zola—which weaken the morals and democratic thinking
of our young people.

[Émile] Zola.

"The International Lightning Trust. A Kind of a Love Story," 1972
(FM).
Jasper Hackett and Stephen Spaulding sit broodiug in their
cheap boardinghouse room, their rent overdue, the landlady Mrs.
Maloney full of insults, and their pipes smoked out. Just as Steve
expresses a wish that he were dead, Jasper lets out a whoop and
announces that he has thought of a scheme which will make their
fortunes. He orders Steve to get $100 from the laborers living
with them, by promising them 1000% profit. While Steve is gone,
Jasper writes out an advertisement: for $1 a person can purchase
from the International Lightning Trust a lifetime policy which
will pay $5,000 if the client is killed by lightning; for $5, $35,000;
and for $10, $100,000. Steve returns weary but laden with $200.
Jasper reads him the circular, and Steve is tremendously impressed.
They discuss its implications. People are almost never hit by
lightning, but everyone from kings on down fear it. The odds will

appeal to the average person. Jasper and Steve will print tickets by series, with Series A for the red dollar ones, B for the blue fives, and C for the yellow tens, and each series starting with #21021 to make the public think that the trust is a going establishment. If an inquest establishes death by lightning, the dead ticket-holder's estate can collect. The more ticket-carrying lightning victims the better, because payoffs will advertise the trust widely. Only twenty-eight people are killed in America annually. Yet millions will invest, from chambermaids and mechanics to sailors and professors. At this point Mrs. Maloney enters and is about to deliver an ultimatum concerning the rent when she sees Steve's pile of greenbacks, whereupon she sweetly invites the two men down to dinner. They hope to be served there by her daughters, Kitty, who has recently preferred a local plumber to Steve, and Molly, who seems to like a carpenter more than Jasper. The girls appear only briefly, on their way out with the two male rivals. In the morning the four return, married.

Two months pass. Jasper and Steve are at their office in Fordham Court, raking in so much money that they decide to hire as clerks both Kitty and Molly, now deserted by their husbands, who have gone west to seek their fortunes. The lightning-trust experts are grateful to Providence for providing success but become so uneasy at lying in their advertisements that they decide to hire a liar to handle that phase of the business in the future. Next day a wild thunderstorm scours the city, and in the evening lightning kills a blacksmith named Saugatuck J. Skidmore in Connecticut. Jasper prepares a $5,000 lightning ticket, journeys to Connecticut, hides the ticket in the dead man's vest pocket, attends the inquest, and pays the delighted widow in new fifty-dollar bills. The audience cheers, and the news story receives national coverage. Jasper and Steve design a seal for their trust, showing a blacksmith cracked by lightning and a motto reading "In Providence We Trust." They decide to rename their venture the International Christian Lightning Trust to improve its image. They pay back their creditors with 100% interest, give them some stock, and send them abroad as agents to drum up foreign business.

Two years later we find Jasper and Steve rolling in money in palatial offices. They buy and sell railroads, steel companies, oil interests, and aristocratic titles. Molly and Kitty have thousands of clerks under them. But the men are unhappy. The girls, being staunch Catholics, will not hear of divorce and if set free by the death of their absent husbands would probably not wed the young billionaires for fear of being called fortune hunters. All the same, Jasper and Steve feel that Providence, which has provided so well up to now, will come through in the end. Soon thereafter, Jasper is drawn by a mysterious impulse to Arkansas Flats along the shimmering Mississippi River. One Sunday out there two men are breaking the Sabbath by fishing. They almost drown. They are saved and grow so repentant that they rush off to church but are killed there by lightning. Jasper sees all. They are the husbands of Kitty and Molly. So he equips their corpses with $100,000 lightning tickets, the proceeds of which Kitty and Molly can decorously inherit. All ends well, because Steve and Jasper have been humble, virtuous, and self-sacrificing.

Dick Adams, Count Alibi, Countess Alibi, Jim Bailey, Mrs. [Mary G. Baker] Eddy, Jasper Hackett, Kitty Maloney, Molly Maloney, Mrs. Maloney, Maria, Pr [esident?], Quimby, Saugatuck J. Skidmore, Mrs. Saugatuck J. Skidmore, Skidmore, Stephen Spaulding.

"Interviewing the Interviewer" (MTP).

Identifying himself as a novice journalist, Twain asks Charles A. Dana, a genius and the editor of the New York *Sun*, for a drop of wisdom from the fountainhead of American newspaperdom. Flattered, Dana reveals the secret of his success: let every edition include a sensation, vilify the unpopular, praise what is in vogue, libel all you can, glorify the wealthy, attack all competition, and rage indignantly. When reporters begin to stream in with erroneous accounts, Dana orders them to write up Gen[eral]. Grant's drunkenness and Mark Twain's death. When Twain identifies himself, Dana replies that he is hardly responsible for Twain's eccentricities and adds that an offensive obituary is already in the works. Between other comments, Dana has been urging Twain to imitate the friendless Ishmael, cackle noisy opinions, rejoice in filth, and make up interviews without troubling to visit the subjects of them.

Charles A. Dana, Gen[eral]. Grant Greely, Mark Twain, Gen[eral]. W., Mrs. W.

'Introducing Doctor Van Dyke,' 1906 (WMT 28).

Twain says that the Rev. Dr. Van Dyke, Princeton author of delicious books, needs no introduction. So Twain will say just a few words and give Van Dyke a chance to reflect on his speech and decide whether he should give it. A month or so ago a citizen of Missouri left $10,000 for the dissemination of Twain's idea of a gentleman. But what is it? Someone said that a man had to go to college in order to qualify as a gentleman. Twain thinks that lets too many out, including himself. A New York journalist recently tried to interview Twain to get his notions on gentleman, but Twain had bronchitis and was excused. Then the reporter faked the interview—on gentlemanliness! What is an American gentleman? He must be courteous and of good character. But Americans are generally not courteous, as we know when we return from courtesies abroad and hear American customs officials and trolley conductors bawl at us. Some might wonder why Twain does not improve his own manners. The answer is that it is nobler to teach others—and less trouble.

Simon Hanks, Rev. Dr. [Henry] Van Dyke.

'Introducing Riley and Nye,' 1888 (S).

Twain expresses his pleasure at being asked to introduce James Whitcomb Riley and Edgar W. ("Bill") Nye, who are going to give readings here in Boston. Twain last saw the pair when Barnum, who had gotten them from Siam, was showing them off. Since then, one got into trouble, and the sheriff required that their ligature be cut. Riley is really Chang, and Nye is Eng. They were once so close that when one dined the other digested, and when one was asleep the other snored. In morals, Chang Riley is the dynamo and Eng Nye is merely the motor. But in intellectual affairs, Eng Nye is the dynamo and Chang Riley the motor. When they work together, they are superb. Twain hopes that the audience will better understand their readings now that he has provided this little vivisection of them.

[Phineas T.] Barnum, [Edgar W. "Bill"] Nye, James Whitcomb Riley.

"Introduction to 'The New Guide of the Conversation in Portuguese and English,'" 1883 (WMT 24).

The author delights in the unconscious ridiculousness and enchanting naïveté of Pedro Carolino's little book of sample conversations. It has been criticized and allowed to go out of print; but forth it issues again, wafted along by the wind of laughter. It was indubitably written by a serious, honest, upright idiot. It could not be the result of pretended ignorance. For one example among many, consider the following from Dialogue 16: "The streets are very layed out by line and too paved."

Pedro Carolino.

"Introductory to 'Memoranda,'" 1870 (CRG).

In burdening himself with the editing of the "Memoranda" department of the *Galaxy*, Twain has been actuated by a feeling that he was needed in this field. Too much attention has been given to poetry and romance, and not enough to statistics. He intends to condense reports from the Patent Office, excerpt from political-economy dissertations, and give market reports and farming instructions. He has not sold out his interest in the Buffalo *Express*, will not be humorous here, recommends the plainness of his title "Memoranda," and will avoid puns.

"The Invalid's Story," 1882 (WMT 22).

The narrator is a bachelor of forty-one, but he seems sixty and married. He wants to explain why. Two years ago, on a wintry night, he received news in Cleveland, Ohio, that his dear friend John B. Hackett had died and that he must honor the dying man's request to accompany his corpse by train at once to Bethlehem, Wisconsin. The narrator agreed, arrived at the station, tacked an address card on a pine box described to him, went out for sandwiches and cigars, and when he returned found a man tacking a card to an identical box. Only later did the narrator realize that an accidental switch had occurred, that he got a box of guns, and that the other person shipped the corpse to Peoria, Illinois. Suddenly the conductor called "All aboard," and the narrator had to travel in the express car with the "corpse." At that moment, a stranger put a package of Limburger cheese on the gun box for shipment, and skipped out. Thompson, the old expressman, went breezily about his work until suddenly he noticed the smell. He and the narrator attributed it to the corpse. They broke a window, took turns sniffing fresh air, went to the platform but nearly froze, sprinkled the car with carbolic acid, and burned chicken feathers; but nothing helped matters. The narrator was eventually taken from the platform unconscious, went into a fever, and has been an invalid ever since.

Cap, John B. Hackett, Deacon Levi Hackett, Mrs. Levi Hackett, Thompson.

Invocation, 1897 (P).

Twain invokes the Ornithorhyncus to emerge from its oozy couch—misplaced bones and flesh, odd fin and tail, kangaroo legs, and all—and explain why it is not yet a fossil like all of its friends.

"Is he dead?" (MTP).

In Paris about 1845 Jean François Millet loves Marie Leroux, but she is being sought by André Bastien, to whom Millet owes money. André would ruin him except that Agamemnon Buckner, nicknamed Chicago, decides to create a demand for Millet's paintings, especially *The Angelus,* by circulating the story that the artist is dead.

His friends persuade Millet to pretend that he is dying offstage, assume the identity of his widowed sister Daisy Tillou, and paint furiously. Chicago and his crony, Hans von Bismarck, nicknamed Dutchy, get rich Australian Jared Walker to buy *The Sowers* for 90,000 francs. Daisy then pays André, who, however, learning the value of the "dead" artist's paintings, tears up the check and vows to collar the art work.

André falls in love with Daisy, who forces him to burn a contract which he forged and by which he could claim all of Millet's productions. Marie, thinking that Millet is Daisy, beseeches "her" to marry André. Millet's funeral is almost spoiled when a priest wants to see the corpse; but Dutchy puts some Limberger cheese in the brickfilled coffin, and all is well. An American is distraught because after buying *The Angelus* for 500,000 francs he was obliged by the French government to give it up for 550,000 francs. Later some of the other opulent gullible customers buy Daisy's imitations of Millet. Suddenly Marie enters, see Daisy dancing about her studio, and is shocked to think she can do so while her brother's funeral is in progress. Daisy explains it all as hysterics. Next, Daisy, seeing André lurking near, pretends that she is bald and decrepit, and is making herself beautiful just for him—with false eye, wig, artificial leg, etc. Finally, all are assembled for Millet's wake. Marie is uncontrollable, until Daisy explains that her place will be taken by a rich, disguised stranger named Placide Duval—Marie has heard the key name before. Then Millet reveals himself to his ecstatic sweetheart and says that France through pride will never publicly admit the artistic humbug.

—an—, Alfonso de Alcantara 'y Salvador de Toledo, Madame Audrienne, the Emperor of Austria, André Bastien, Madame Bathilde, the King of Bavaria, Hans von Bismarck, Boy, Agamemnon Buckner, Madame Caron, Charles Everest, Sandy Ferguson, Flandreau, King [of France], Juggernaut Jamboree, Cecile Leroux, Marie Leroux, Papa Pierre Leroux, Mother Leroux, Li-Hung-Chang, Jean François Millet, Mohammed Ali ben Omar, Phelim O'Shaughnessy, Page, Pal, Henry Parker, Reporter, the Emperor of Russia, Basil Thorpe, the Sultan of Turkey, Jared Walker.

"Is He Living or Is He Dead?", 1893 (WMT 23).

The author is spending March of 1892 in Mentone, on the Riviera. One day a rich man—call him Smith—comes to the hotel and strikes up an acquaintance with the author. At breakfast Smith points out an old man about to leave and explains that he is a wealthy, retired silk manufacturer from Lyons named Théophile Magnan. Then Smith alludes briefly to a Hans [Christian] Andersen story, for children, about a caged song bird which is neglected and dies, only then to be given an elaborate little funeral. In the evening, the author sees Smith again and accepts his invitation to have a smoke and some scotch. Soon Smith begins to reminisce about his youth as an artist. He and two other wandering painters, named Claude Frère and Carl Boulanger, ran out of money in Breton and were saved from starving by François Millet, who was then as unknown as they. When it became evident that they must do something desperate, Carl made the brilliant suggestion that they draw straws and that the winner furiously paint a stack of fragments to go with his completed pictures and then pretend to die. Since artists have only posthumous fame, his works would then command fantastic prices. Millet was elected. While he painted madly, the others spread out over France to sell his completed works and also to start rumors about both his ability and his frail condition. Soon the four stage his death and funeral. Now his reputation is staggering, and his fragments command top prices. When the author wonders whatever became of Millet, Smith reveals that Magnan the silk manufacturer is really Millet.

Carl Boulanger, Claude Frère, François Millet, Smith.

Is Shakespeare Dead?, 1909 (WMT 26).

No matter how foolish their arguments are, claimants of any sort can attract a following. Look at Satan, Louis XVII, Mary Baker Eddy, and William Shakespeare. It is so because their stories are clothed in mystery. A friend recently sent the author a new book from England called *The Shakespeare Problem Restated*. Delia Bacon's book back about 1856 or 1857 started the controversy. At that time Mark Twain was an apprentice steamboat pilot aboard the *Pennsylvania* under George Ealer, who read Shakespeare to him by the hour and interlarded the text with nautical commands. Ealer was fiercely loyal to Shakespeare and was so opposed to the Baconians that for argument's sake the author took the other side, winding up convincing himself. To prove it all to Ealer, he wrote out a passage from Shakespeare mixed with steamboat orders, had Ealer read it, and asked him to admit that no landlubber could write such a passage, any more than Shakespeare could have written the works attributed to Shakespeare, since they are filled with similarly expert lawyer talk. Ealer promptly lost his temper and told Twain that he was an idiot. Ealer played the flute well, and when the *Pennsylvania* blew up, killing the author's brother Henry, he saved not only himself but also his flute.

When Twain was a Sunday-school scholar more than sixty years ago, he asked his teacher Mr. Barclay the stonemason for facts about Satan and explained that he wanted to write his biography. Barclay reluctantly told him many standard conjectures concerning Satan but few facts and then urged the boy to put away his pen. It is curious that there is a similar poverty of facts concerning Shakespeare's life. Twain then lists the few known facts and stresses Shakespeare's will, in which, curiously, the man does not mention books or his granddaughter's education. Twain also points out that Shakespeare's death made no stir in his native Stratford. So far as anyone can prove, the Stratford Shakespeare never wrote a play, a letter, or any poem other than the poor one on his tomb. All the same, biographers and historians conjecture that he attended school in Stratford, butchered with his father, poached upon Sir Thomas Lucy's deer preserves, clerked in a Stratford court, abandoned his Warwickshire dialect to learn London English, got up facts about law and war and courtly life by reading and listening, held horses in front of London theaters, traveled extensively though briefly and thus learned several foreign languages, began to write and to act in the early 1590s, and soon thereafter became a stockholder in two theaters.

Three cults have sprung up concerning the Shakespeare controversy. One group knows that Shakespeare wrote the works. Another knows that Francis Bacon did. A third group is sure that Shakespeare did not but only suspects that Bacon did. Those thugs favoring Shakespeare add 2, 8, 7, and 14, and get 165. Baconians take the same figures and usually arrive at 31, and never more than 45. Here is an illustration. Put a rugged old tomcat, an inexperienced kitten, and a mouse in a small room with no exit. After half an hour, look in. The mouse is missing. The Shakespearites will reason that the kitten might have gotten some training, studied catology in a garret, learned some cat court-talk, and gone cat soldiering; then they will conclude that it ate the mouse. The Baconian verdict is otherwise.

It is curious that when Shakespeare died in 1616, no one in Stratford seemed aware that a great writer had departed. Seven years later, the quarto was published, and Ben Jonson shook off his indifference and sang a song of praise. Sixty more years passed, and only then were inquiries made in Stratford about Shakespeare; questions, however, were not asked of those who had been Stratfordians in Shakespeare's day. Twain considers his own case, reports the facts about his youthful life in Hannibal, Missouri, along the Mississippi River, and then out west, and comments that sixty years later several of his schoolmates, fellow pilots, and newspaper reporters are still alive and willing to tell tales about him.

If the author had to decide officially whether Shakespeare wrote the plays, he would simply ask the investigators whether Shakespeare had ever been a practicing lawyer. The plays have accurate

law talk but not good war or sea lingo. Richard H. Dana writes of
the sea like one who was there. Twain knows mining in various
phases and can therefore spot a person, for example, Bret Harte,
who gets his mining talk from books and from listening to miners
rather than from first-hand experience. The same with printers'
phrasing. Returning to the question of the playwright, Twain
quotes extensively from a chapter called "Shakespeare as a Lawyer"
from *The Shakespeare Problem Restated,* in which evidence is
presented which should lead to the conclusion that the author of
the plays had such intimate knowledge of law and lawyers that he
must have been a lawyer and could not have been the Stratford
Shakespeare.

Did Francis Bacon write Shakespeare's plays? Nobody knows.
We can infer, to use a type of reasoning abused by the Shakespearites, that Bacon is a good candidate. His father was a Lord Chancellor; his mother, a distinguished linguist and theologian. Young
Bacon spent three years at the university, then three in Paris with
the English ambassador there. At the same time, Shakespeare was
supposedly at school in Stratford and then a butcher's apprentice.
Next, young Bacon studied law, was in daily contact with lawyers
and judges, and gradually worked his way by brilliance to the Lord
Chancellorship. When scholars praise Shakespeare for his knowledge of the law, their words seem to be describing Bacon. The
author of Shakespeare's works had intellect, wisdom, imagination,
and humor. Ben Jonson and Macaulay praise Bacon's oratory,
overwhelming intelligence, energy, and capacity for prodigious
work; his essays are superb, his wit dangerously powerful, and his
Novum Organum a veritable revolution. He could have written the
best of Shakespeare. He would not have stooped to compose the
doggerel on Shakespeare's tomb.

Twain refuses to try to convince anyone that he should abandon
his indefensible notion that Shakespeare wrote the works. Twain
knows how well prejudices are engrained. We all thrive on fetishes.
We are made that way. Perhaps by the year 2209 Shakespeare will
be off his pedestal. However, it must be added that the Stratford-
olaters are wrongly irreverent when they discuss the opposition.
They should not compel others to hold their Shakespeare sacred.
When you think of it, is it not really odd that of all the great and
celebrated people of the past, only Shakespeare is a mystery? Even
race horses' biographies are better known than his, because he had

no history to record. Recently the Hannibal *Courier-Post* reported that S. L. Clemens made the little Missouri town so famous that natives reminisce about him. A few days ago Becca Blankenship, Huck Finn's real-life sister, died in Hannibal at the age of seventy-two. Mark Twain remembers her vividly. And she never forgot him. Yet everyone in Stratford quickly forgot Shakespeare, although he lived there half his life.

Ambassador, Delia Bacon, [Sir] Francis Bacon, [Sir Nicholas] Bacon, Mrs. [Nicholas] Bacon, Barclay, [Horace] Bixby, Becca Blankenship, Brown, Lord Campbell, Henry [Clemens], [Jane Lampton Clemens], [John Marshall Clemens], Richard H[enry]. Dana [Jr.], William Dickason, George Ealer, Mary Baker G. Thompson Eddy, Huck Finn, Jimmy Finn, General Gaines, Bret Harte, Injun Joe, Bishop Jewell, Ben Jonson, Captain Klinefelter, [King] Louis XVII, Sir Thomas Lucy, [Thomas Babington] Macaulay, Arthur Orton, Professor Osborn, Archbishop Parker, Lord Penzance, [Sir Walter] Raleigh, Satan, Anne Hathaway Shakespeare, [Hamnet] Shakespeare, [John] Shakespeare, [Judith] Shakespeare, [Mary Arden] Shakespeare, Susanna Shakespeare, William Shakespeare, Lambert Simnel, [Edmund] Spenser, Tichborne, the Veiled Prophet of Khorassan, Percy Warbeck, Anne Whateley.

["The Island by Night"]. See LSI.

"Italian with Grammar," 1904 (WMT 24).

The author remarks that an intelligent person can learn Italian without a dictionary but that a grammar is occasionally useful. The trouble lies mainly with the verbs. Regular verbs have tail-like suffixes. Catch them by the tail, and you can tame them. Irregular verbs—those born out of wedlock, so to speak—are another matter and must not be used in the presence of the author. He gets help from a servant, whom he calls the Facchino-Doctor-Brigadier because he is a former horse doctor, now a doorman, who can command verbs like a military officer. There seem to be fifty-seven ways of saying "I love" in Italian. Since this is too difficult, the Brigadier orders the forms of "have" to pass in review. But to have what? Dog? It frightens the peasants. Chicken? That is better.

The squad of definite past verbs comes forward: "Ebbi polli," "Avesti polli," etc. But when the author learns that the indefinite past forms are approaching, he countermands the order. Fortunately, the noon gun booms in Florence at this point, and everything stops, including verbs.

Facchino-Doctor-Brigadier.

"Italian without a Master," 1904 (WMT 24).
The author has been living for two weeks in a medieval villa outside Florence. He cannot speak Italian, and the servants cannot speak English. So no harm is done, and everyone is happy. From the newspaper he picks up Italian words and phrases, without learning their precise meaning. Then he uses his new words while they are fresh, for they do not keep in the climate here. Yesterday's word was "avanti," which probably carries the Shakespearean meaning of "avaunt" or "get out." It is fun to read of Florentine scandals, because the participants are neighbors and hence practically friends. He can translate pretty easily. For example, "Inaugurazione della Chiesa Russa" concerns the inauguration of a Russian cheese—admittedly a little puzzling. Another account deals with a "disgrazia" (disgrace) on the Ponte Vecchio. The slight uncertainty as to precise meaning only lends charm and mystery to the author's daily reading. He delights in the account of a "Revolverate in teatro" (revolveration in theater) in Wallace, Indiana, in which a "spettatore" was "spalleggiato" by his friends. Since the word "spalleggiato" has "egg" in it, it must mean that the man was "egged on" by his friends during the revolveration. If the author had a phrase book, it would not help him with words to use if he should fall and skin his leg.

"An Item Which the Editor Himself Couldn't Understand." See "Mr. Bloke's Item."

"James Hammond Trumbull," 1897 (LAIFI).
News has just reached Twain in Switzerland of the death of Dr. James Hammond Trumbull of Hartford. Twain praises the man for his intelligence and for his generosity in sharing it. Twain once had an idea for a play but decided first to write Trumbull to learn

if it were original. The answer took the form of six pages of titles of works from ancient China to the present in which the idea had been used. A needy descendant of Audubon once sold a copy of his *Birds* for $100 to a scholar, who then resold it for $1,000 and praised his own shrewdness. On the other hand, when a poor woman once offered Trumbull a copy of Eliot's Indian Bible for $100, he proposed that he should sell it to the British Museum for $1,000. She accepted; he did so and sent the entire sum to her.

[John James] Audubon, Dr. James Hammond Trumbull.

"Jane Austen" (MTP).

Twain says that when he starts reading *Pride and Prejudice* or *Sense and Sensibility*, he feels like a bartender entering a Presbyterian heaven—not superior to the people there but indifferent since they are simply not to his taste. So what does the bartender do? Quit and go to hell? No. He wanders off a while, then comes back and tries again to associate with those Presbyterians. But it always fails. It is all a matter of taste. As for Jane Austen, she draws characters well only when they are odious; all others in her fiction are mere wax figures or shadows.

Jane Austen.

"Jane Lampton Clemens," 1969 (HHT).

The author reminisces about his mother Jane Lampton Clemens, who died at the age of eighty-seven in October, 1890. His first memory of her was of her kneeling before his brother's corpse. She was interested in everything, sought the best in everyone, and once even suggested praying for Satan. She stopped a Corsican from whipping his daughter and another man from beating his horse. She befriended the homeless, including numerous cats. She was privately proud of her aristocratic Earl of Durham ancestors back in England. She never criticized the institution of slavery, because she had never heard it criticized and had indeed heard it defended from many pulpits. Cruelty to slaves was rare in the author's youth. His father was humane. He once took a trip south on the Mississippi River to collect a debt; he voluntarily reduced the amount owed and yet during the same trip sold a slave. Jane Clemens danced in her eighties, but toward the end her memory failed—

though never her intellect or her ability to be humorous with a straight face. She was always beautiful.

> Mr. B., Charles I, Charley [Benjamin] Clemens, Mrs. Jane Lampton Clemens, [John Marshall] Clemens, [Samuel Langhorne] Clemens, Clement, the Earl of Durham, the Earl of Durham, Lambton, Lambton, Mrs. Lambton, Lampton, Lampton, Sandy, Colonel [Mulberry] Sellers.

"Japan." See FW, 1870.

"Jenkins at Wilhelmshohe." See FW, 1870.

"Jim Baker's Bluejay Yarn." From *A Tramp Abroad*.

"Jim Todd: A Sketch in Crude Oil." See FW, 1870.

"Jim Wolfe and the Cats." See 'Cats and Candy.'

"Jim Wolfe and the Tom Cats." See 'Cats and Candy.'

Joan of Arc. See *Personal Recollections of Joan of Arc*.

'Joan of Arc,' 1905 (WMT 28).

Twain explains that he studied the history and character of Joan of Arc for twelve years. She was marvelously intelligent, nobly spirited, and pure. Illustrators always depict Joan as a fish woman, a cropped peasant, with a face like a ham. Beard excellently illustrated Twain's *Connecticut Yankee in King Arthur's Court*, thus helping to make the book a sardonic laugh at human trivialities, and at priestly and monarchical insolence. Williams illustrated *The Innocents Abroad*, but the publisher spoiled things by hiring a cheap wood engraver. Twain had trouble explaining to Williams the combination of Bowery coarseness and innocence in Jack Van Nostrand, one of the innocents who went abroad. Jack was the youth who said that Ben Halliday, the stagecoach manager out west, could have transported Moses's people faster than Moses did. Jack was a consumptive and died when he was only about twenty years old. It was just as well, because he had seen the aspects of life which are valuable and soon would have lost his illusions; and illusions are the only element in life making it worthwhile.

[Dan] Beard, [Andrew] Carnegie, Ben Halliday, Joan of Arc, Sir Purdon-Clarke, Jack Van Nostrand, Williams.

"John Camden Hotten," 1872 (LAIFI).

Twain writes to the editor of the London *Spectator* to complain that brainless John Camden Hotten is pirating his works, adds chapters to them, retitles them, gives Twain the false pen name of Carl Byng, and pays him no royalties. George Routledge and Sons are his authorized British publisher.

Carl Byng, John Camden Hotten, George Routledge, Routledge.

"John Chinaman in New York," 1870 (WMT 7).

The narrator passes a big tea store in New York and sees a Chinaman sitting out front as a sign and dressed in Chinese peaked hat, frogged silk blouse, tight blue pants, and cork-soled shoes. Is the poor Oriental dreaming of rice fields back home in China? He looks so degraded that the narrator taps him on the shoulder and sympathetically tells him that it is merely one citizen who is heartlessly exploiting him and that good Americans will raise a purse to send him back to China. At this, the seated man explains that he makes four dollars a week but that the "furrin clothes" are "expinsive." New York tea merchants are not likely to run out of such Chinamen.

John Chinaman.

"John Chinaman in New York: The John Question." See FW, 1870.

"John Hay and the Ballads," 1905 (LAIFI).

Twain mentions an article in which Howells wonders whether John Hay's *Pike County Ballads* were written before Bret Harte's similar ballads. Twain says that Hay told him about 1870 that he had published them earlier in some obscure Western journals. Hay later felt that those ballads had blocked his progress in politics for a while. Pretty much the same thing happened to Harte, whose "Heathen Chinee" was so popular that the public preferred its sort to Harte's more serious local-color fiction. It was through Hay that Twain met Horace Greeley, into whose sanctum he stumbled by mistake while seeking Hay in the New York *Tribune* offices. Greeley glared at Twain, and with firm mouth and virile interest asked him what the hell he wanted.

Horace Greeley, Bret Harte, John Hay, [William Dean] Howells.

"Johnny Greer," 1870 (WMT 7).

The Sunday-school superintendent recalls the stillness in church that Sabbath, the small coffin there with the corpse of the little black boy, and the eloquence of the pastor in describing the heroism of young Johnny Greer in preventing the drowned body from being swept into the depths and forever from the agonized parents. At this point a ragged urchin asked Johnny for details and when he learned that no one paid him any reward blurted out that he should have anchored the corpse in midstream and demanded five dollars for it.

Johnny Greer.

"Johnny Greer's Way." See "Johnny Greer."

"Journalism in Tennessee," 1869 (WMT 7).

Informed by his physician that he should go south to improve his health, the author repairs to Tennessee and takes a position as associate editor of the *Morning Glory and Johnson County War-Whoop*. The editor tells him to write a condensation of news from various Tennessee newspapers sent to the office on exchange. He does so, in polite prose; but the editor grabs it, calls it gruel, and is rewriting it with a scraping pen when Smith, a rival journalist, shoots at him through the window. Our editor fires back. In the melee, the author is wounded in the thigh and loses a finger. Next, a grenade comes down the stove-pipe, explodes, and a fragment knocks out a couple of the author's teeth. The editor shows his associate the rewritten column, which is now full of proper vitriol. Next a brick crashes through the window, jolts the author in the back, and presages the appearance of Colonel Blatherskite Tecumseh, who duels explosively with the editor. In the fracas, the author catches a bullet in the arm and also suffers a chipped knuckle. The duelists beg him not to move, since he is not really in their way. As he leaves, the Colonel politely asks directions to the undertaker. The editor tells the author to take care of Jones, Gillespie, and Ferguson, all of whom are expected in the office soon, and then departs for dinner. Gillespie, Jones, and Thompson sally in and toss through the window, cowhide, and disrobe the author. The editor returns and assures the author that he will like the place when he grows used to it. But the author verbosely denies as much and courteously announces his plan to return north.

John W. Blossom, Buchner, Ferguson, Gillispie, Jones, Lancet, Smith, Colonel Blatherskite Tecumseh, Thompson, Van Werter.

"The Judge's 'Spirited Woman,'" 1870 (WMT 7).
The judge tells the story. He was holding court on a tedious, hot summer day. They were trying a Spanish desperado for killing the beloved husband of a pretty Mexican woman. The men had their coats off, were lolling about, sweating, smoking, and whittling. The customary verdict of not guilty was expected, and it came. The widow asked the judge whether the law was finished with the smirking defendant, who had murdered her husband before her very eyes. Yes. At that, she pulled a revolver and killed the murderer. The judge adds that they all put their coats on, took up a collection, and sent the spirited wench over the mountains to her friends.

"The Jumping Frog. In English. Then in French. Then Clawed Back into a Civilized Language Once More by Patient, Unremunerated Toil" (WMT 7). See "The Celebrated Jumping Frog of Calaveras County."

"The Jumping Frog of Calaveras County" (SS). See "The Celebrated Jumping Frog of Calaveras County."

"The Jungle Discusses Man" (MTP).

Reynard the fox returns from visiting the regions of man, and lectures about his discoveries and answers questions from his fellow animals. His book of pictures arouses much interest. The first picture is of an armed soldier followed by a missionary with a book. Then Reynard shows a picture of people with clothes—skin-like things they wear even when they don't have to, and keep on in hot weather through shame of nakedness. Why be ashamed of nudity before one another when God can see them stripped bare?

The King, Reynard.

["Kalamazoo"]. See W 1868.

["The Kalihi Valley"]. See LSI.

"Kaltenleutgeben" (MTP).

The narrator and his family have been in Kaltenleutgeben for two weeks, keeping house. It is hard to get used to their four local servants. They are all fine, to be sure; yet the cook talks perpetually, like an Austrian parliament. She cooks marvelously, however. Charlotte, the maid, is strong and quiet. The other maid is called Wuthering Heights and is about forty years old, active, alert, and so talkative that she will surely speak after death. W. H. domineers everything, which the narrator likes even though it bothers his family. She freshens his whole life. His wife, the Executive, tries without immediate success to reconstruct W. H. One morning, his wife tells the maid that she talks too much, and W. H. apologizes in hundreds of words, including some profane ones. The Executive says that her husband also dislikes the verbal torrent and that the other servants object to W. H.'s bossing them. And why did W. H. not allow Madame Blank to see the narrator yesterday? W. H. verbosely replies that he was writing and would not have wanted to be disturbed. After more talk, W. H. rationalizes it all away on the grounds of being Viennese.

Madame Blank, Sorel Blqwrczlzbzockowicz, Charlotte, the Executive, Princess Tzwzfzhopowic, Wuthering Heights.

["Kealakekua to Kau"]. See LSI.

"The Kearny Street Ghost Story," 1866 (MTWY).

The house of Albert Krum on Kearny Street has been the locale of disembodied spirits. The family can no longer keep servants. One night Bridget had no sooner gone to bed and blown out her light than a wailing ghost came in, placed nine bloody little kittens on her pillow, and moaned off again. What would you do if a ghost had kittens in your bed?

Bridget, Albert Krum.

Kiditchin, 1912 (P).

Lieb' Kiditchin, braying like a Chinese gong, is bewitching and will feast well if it behaves.

James.

["The Kilauea Volcano"]. See LSI.

"The Killing of Julius Caesar 'Localized,'" 1864 (WMT 7).

A reporter likes best of all things to gather details of a murder, write them up, and scoop the other newspapers. The author was not present at the assassination of Julius Caesar; all the same, he can offer us this translation of an account of the event from the original Latin of the Rome *Daily Evening Fasces*. Yesterday was a quiet day in Rome, until it was thrown into excitement by the murder of J. Caesar, Emperor-elect. When Caesar's majority was declared, Casca of the Tenth Ward and other opposition hirelings began contemptuous whisperings. The Senate was in a passion. Caesar approached via Demosthenes and Thucydides's drug store, and refused to read suits from Artemidorus and Decius Brutus. Near the capitol, Papilius Lena murmured something about an enterprise to George W. Cassius, and Marcus Brutus heard him. Cassius said he thought their purpose had been discovered. A crowd closed around doomed Caesar, who fought them off valiantly with his fists until he saw Marcus Brutus approach with his dagger. Then Caesar stopped fighting, covered his head with his mantle, and took the final treacherous blow. While the coroner was summoning a jury, Mark Antony and other friends of deceased lugged his body to the Forum, where some speeches have led the chief of police to predict a riot.

Mark Antony, Artemidorus, Decius Brutus, Marcus Brutus, Julius Caesar, Casca, George W. Cassius, Metellus Cimber, Publius Cimber, Cinna, Demosthenes Caius Legarius, Papilius Lena, Thucydides, Billy Trebonius.

'A Kind-Hearted Druggist,' 1890 (LAIFI).

Twain tells a convention of druggists that he and three friends long ago back home tried to scare a foolish, fish-eyed person named Nicodemus Dodge when he first came to town. They borrowed a skeleton from a druggist, who had ordered it for $50 for the local doctor. The boys put it in Dodge's bed while their victim was in town. He returned home. Silence followed. In sudden fear, the boys peeped at Dodge through his window and found that he had sold the skeleton—for $5—had bought candy and toys, and was immensely pleased. The druggist agreed to let the boys go on condition they would will their skeletons to him. But then one of the four drowned, another disappeared in a balloon, and a third was blown to pieces in a dynamite explosion. The druggist then watched Twain carefully and only recently asked if he might have part payment now. Twain calls the gesture typical of all generous druggists.

Nicodemus Dodge.

King Leopold's Soliloquy: A Defense of His Congo Rule, 1905 (LAIFI).

King Leopold II is excited. He scatters the pamphlets which he has been reading, pounds on his table, swears, and then kisses a crucifix hanging from his neck. He speaks.

I have squandered millions on religion and art, and to muzzle the press. But leaks still occur. And slander too. All I wanted was to have the Congo under my control so that I could bring light to 25,000,000 gentle blacks. America and thirteen European countries agreed to let me Christianize the place. I made officials out of my pals and pimps. I fooled one American president. Then others. Let them go ahead and tell how I trampled native rights underfoot and brought swag only to myself. My critics are only pests. They should have kept silent. Imagine exposing my sacred person. God seems to approve of my conduct. Why must my enemies tell how I enforce tax collecting in the Congo? True, I use unfriendly black soldiers against the Congolese, and each shilling here means a rape or a murder there. My hand-picked missionaries are active; yet my critics say nothing of the efforts of those ecclesiasts. My critics irrelevantly rake up old stories of my abusive treatment of my wife and daughters. Anyway, I was too shrewd even for my tardy Yankee critics. Too late America realized that it had lent its influence to my establishment of an absolute monarchy in the Congo. Meddling foreign missionaries count the hands of natives chopped off, the skulls of natives shot, and the number of men castrated as punishment for not producing enough rubber. I tried to encourage the story that we were merely following the custom of natives to behead and otherwise mutilate each other, but my critics refused to be silenced thus. Why must they say that I only take from the natives and do not give? My missionaries offer them eternal salvation. I do not approve of the practice of cannibalism among my native troops; yet my detractors say that I am responsible simply because I have absolute power in the Congo. They claim that I have reduced the Congolese population to 15,000,000. Some even suggest that I should marry Death's daughter and reorganize the family business, and that for my mausoleum should be built a pyramid of my victims' skulls. What diseased imaginations. It does seem too bad to kill a laughing baby or let female hostages starve in jail. However, business is business. We should not have crucified those native women, though, since doing so seems to profane the Cross; moreover, skinning them would have answered. One thing I want clearly understood: I seek no respect from common men. I am superior. All kings feel this way. The masses are stupid to grant us homage and continued power. True, some poets— for example, Swilburne, Thomas Bailey Eldridge, and Colonel Richard Waterson Gilder—yelp against the Czar, but their bite is really nothing. If my critics get too eloquent, I will buy up or otherwise suppress the journals in which they are published. One thing I do fear, however, is the camera. It is impossible to bribe or suppress that eyewitness to atrocities. At least I am glad that most people who look at what I have done shudder and turn away. In that gesture lies hope for my continued success.

In a supplementary section, Twain reports that a truly admirable Belgian commission has corroborated the implications of the foregoing. Its findings were at first suppressed, but then were edited and released. Leopold's claim to the Congo should now be questioned. Petitions to this end have now been sent to the President and the Congress of the United States. Twain includes excerpts from reports by official American and Belgian spokesmen. He concludes by reprinting W. T. Stead's 1905 *English Review of Reviews* essay "Ought King Leopold to Be Hanged?"

Lyman Abbott, President [Chester Arthur], [Andrew] Carnegie, Casement, the Czar, Thomas Bailey Eldridge, Colonel Richard Waterson Gilder, David Starr Jordan, King Leopold II of Belgium, Queen [Marie Henriette] of Belgium, Morel, John Morley, Rev. W. M. Morrison, Lord Aberdeen Norbury, Sir Gilbert Parker, President [Theodore Roosevelt], Rev. A. E. Scrivener, W. H. Sheppard, Swilburne, Henry Van Dyke, John Wanamaker.

"Labouchere's 'Legal Pillory'" (MTP).

Americans show their British origin in all aspects of their behavior except that they do not beat their women. America is the only nation which avoids beating women. Each national type has a certain trait. For example, Germans are sluggish. The main American trait is bad manners. Every nation detests a particular crime. For example, the English loathe crimes against the farthing. Judging by Labouchère's *Legal Pillory,* if that farthing is in the form of a game bird it would be better for a man to take up rape as a hobby than mess with that game bird. The poacher is the worst criminal in England. Such offenders are tried by magistrates descended from rich men with no experience in hunger; hence they are less lenient toward poachers than toward wife-beaters.

[Henry du Pré] Labouchere [Labouchère].

'The Ladies,' 1872 (WMT 28).

Twain says that he is proud to reply to the toast "the Ladies," although a better word might be "women." The Bible never calls Eve a lady. Two of Twain's favorite poems begin "Woman! O woman! . . ." and "Alas!—alas! . . . ," and concern ladies, but Twain cannot remember the remaining lines. He always thrills when he thinks how Joan of Arc fell at Waterloo, when he recalls Sappho the singer of Israel, and when he muses on other famous women. Women are gentle and generous. We all remember our wives and mothers.

Lucretia Borgia, Cleopatra, Eve, George III, Joan of Arc, Sappho.

"Ladies' Toilettes." See "All About the Fashions."

"Lady Byron—Mrs. Stowe's Revelations." See FW, 1869.

["Lady Franklin"], 1870 (CG).
  Twain praises Lady Franklin for having devotion enough to the memory of her dead husband, Sir John, to undertake at the age of eighty a voyage halfway around the world. She wishes to obtain a scrap of his writing in the possession of a man who will deliver it only into her hands.
  Lady [Jane] Franklin, Sir John Franklin.

'The Last Lotos Club Speech.' See 'Compliments and Degrees.'

[The Last Word], 1869 (probably by Twain) (P).
  Some Little Women write Twain to express relief. His article "Last Words of Great Men" leads them to doubt the statement that a married man never has the last word.
  Little Woman.

"Last Words of Great Men," 1869 (CRG).
  Last words of famous people are often plagiarized and often reflect little credit upon the utterers. A person should rehearse his last words. Otherwise, when the time and the relatives come the speaker might be embarrassed. Daniel Webster did not plan carefully, and all he could say was "I still live." John Quincy Adams spoke about the last of earth. But more earth is still left. He should have said, "Adam was the first and Adams is the last of earth." Napoleon and Marshal Neil spoke pointlessly about the army. Next-to-last words might furnish us with better material to fashion last words out of. Lord Chesterfield wittily pretended that death was a gentleman calling on him and asked his servant to fetch a chair. Benjamin Franklin was so great at axiom-building that when death approached he idiotically said, "None but the brave deserve the fair." Byron spoke of Augusta, Lady Byron, and Harriet Beecher Stowe; Joan of Arc, about boys marching; and Alexander the Great, about drinks. One man asked permission to recite the unabridged

dictionary. And so on. Rather neatly, Seward said, "Alas!-ka."
Twain closes by lamenting that no illustrator can picture people's
last words.

John Quincy Adams, Alexander the Great, [Henry] Bergh,
Lady Byron, [Lord] Byron, Lord Chesterfield, Cleopatra,
Garret Davis, Queen Elizabeth, Benjamin Franklin, H. G.,
[Ulysses S.] Grant, Joan of Arc, John, Andrew Johnson,
Empress Josephine, Augusta [Leigh], Louis Napoleon,
Napoleon, Marshal Neil, Sir Walter Raleigh, Red Jacket,
[William Henry] Seward, [William] Shakespeare, John
Smith, Harriet Beecher Stowe, Daniel Webster.

"The Late Benjamin Franklin," 1870 (WMT 7).
Benjamin Franklin was twins: two different houses in Boston
claim to be his place of birth. He was vicious, and he prostituted
his talents to the invention of aphorisms which now torture the
young. He would lead us to believe that he worked all day and
studied algebra by firelight in the evening. His sayings make boys
feel guilty when they spend a little money or avoid a little work.
If the author had followed Franklin's advice, he would probably
be a respectable storekeeper somewhere now. Franklin flew a kite
on Sunday and pretended to be experimenting. He could always
justify his actions by ripping off maxims. His stove would smoke
your head off. Anyone could have entered Philadelphia with
nothing but a few rolls under his arm. Franklin's sayings are
clichés. His eccentricity was evidence of genius, not the creator
of it.

Benjamin Franklin.

"The Late Reliable Contraband," 1869 (LAIFI).
Since Twain is busy with a new book, he cannot appear before the
New York Press Club and deliver an extemporaneous speech. So
he sends it instead. In it he praises the Reliable Contraband, that
is, the unimpeachable source of imaginative misinformation repeated by journalists. The Reliable Contraband was born of the
recent war, flourished in it as a rumor monger, and died with the
advent of peace.

The Reliable Contraband.

"The Latest Sensation," 1863 (MTWY).

Abram Curry reports a frightful massacre at the log house of Philip Hopkins, between Empire City and Dutch Nick's. Hopkins galloped into Carson with the bloody scalp of his wife in his hands, and his own throat cut. He soon died. Sheriff Gasherie headed a posse which rushed to the house, where they found the wife's scalpless corpse, seven of the nine Hopkins children butchered, and the other two bludgeoned but alive. It seems that Hopkins had been a steady miner but had recently lost heavily through investing in an unreliable San Francisco water company. The next day, Twain takes back the entire story.

Abram Curry, Sheriff [D. J.] Gasherie, Emma Hopkins, Julia Hopkins, Mary Hopkins, Philip Hopkins, Mrs. Philip Hopkins, Tommy Hopkins, Hopkins, Miss Hopkins.

"The Launch of the Steamer Capital." See "The Scriptural Panorima mist."

"Lawn Whist" (MTP).

The Knight of the Black King tells Twain about a chess game with people for chessmen but adds that the spectacle was spiritless because the game was slow. So Twain describes a better game— lawn whist, complete with dukes and duchesses as players, and ladies and gentlemen in different costumes for the suits and denominations dancing on the lawn when the master of ceremonies—the Joker, of course—calls the leads and plays, and when the players assemble their tricks.

The Black King, the Knight.

'Layman's Sermon,' 1906 (WMT 28).

Twain begins by reminding his audience that since the people created the police they are responsible for the police and should therefore pause before criticizing them. Twain recalls picking out a stateroom on a train, because he could smoke in it. The conductor soon said that there has been some mistake and tried to order him out, but Twain refused. In the morning Twain saw an importantlooking man eating broiled chicken in the dining car, ordered the same, was told that there was none, insisted, and got it when the same conductor came by. Someone once wanted Twain to define a gentleman. He thinks that a gentleman must be a person with merciful and kindly instincts. Patrick recently died. He was Twain's coachman, had been with the family for thirty-six years, guided the children, was all honor and honesty and affection, and remained handsome and upright all his life. An ideal gentleman? Patrick McAleer.

[Clara Clemens], [Jean Clemens], [Olivia Langdon Clemens], [Susan Clemens], William Dean Howells, Patrick McAleer, Osgood.

"Legend of a Musket." See FW, 1869.

"Legend of Sagenfeld, in Germany." See "Legend of the Sagenfeld, in Germany."

"Legend of the Capitoline Venus." See "The Capitoline Venus."

"The Legend of the Musket." In *Mark Twain's Travels with Mr. Brown.*

"Legend of the Sagenfeld, in Germany," 1882 (WMT 19).

A thousand years ago in Sagenfeld, soothsayers predicted that little King Hubert would be saved in his fourteenth year by an animal whose singing would sound sweetest to him. Sagenfeld should always honor this animal. So, when he was thirteen, Hubert listened to linnets and thrushes and other warblers. Suddenly a little peasant maid interrupted by bringing her donkey, whose "Waw . . . . . . he!" she thought sweetest. She and her ass were whipped out of court, and Hubert finally chose the nightingale. A year later while out riding, he was thrown into a declivity and his leg was broken. Then the birds sounded succorless, and he longed to die. Suddenly the peasant girl's donkey brayed singingly, wandered up, and saved Hubert, who proclaimed the ass's song the finest and married the girl when she turned fifteen. This explains why asses are in most royal cabinets to this day.

King Hubert.

"Letter from Mark Twain to the Editor of the *Californian*." See "The Moral Phenomenon."

"A Letter from the Comet," 1972 (FM).

A Comet writes to explain that he visits the earth once every seventy-one years. Time after time as he whizzed by, he used to enjoy seeing Adam—fine fellow, handsome, worked in a garden, raised an enormous family with his wife. What was her maiden name? Well, on his fourteenth swing around the earth, the Comet failed to see Adam. Will someone send his new address? Moreover, the Comet has not observed Methuselah or Noah in five or seven hundred years. On the other hand, he has not missed a friendly face on Sirius in the past thirty million years.

Adam, Comet, [Eve], Methuselah, Noah.

"Letter from the Recording Angel," 1946.*

The Recording Angel writes Abner Scofield, a wealthy Buffalo coal dealer, about his recent act of benevolence and self-sacrifice, and also about his public prayers and private supplications. Granted are his secret prayers for bad weather to advance hard-coal prices, for an influx of laborers to depress wages, and for a break in rival soft-coal prices. Certain other private prayers must be redirected, taken under advisement, and reserved for later consideration because of conflicts. His secret supplications get first attention. His public and family prayers are usually denied because of conflicts with his more sincere secret ones. Thus his public prayers for milder weather, better times, and more plentiful food for the poor are all refused. Most of his public prayers count for wind only and will be bunched into storms to retard the ships of improper persons. His good deeds count for much more in heaven than those of a better man because of the strain on Scofield. For example, when he was worth $100,000 and sent $2 to a poor widowed cousin, there was applause in Sheol. Even more impressive was his recent gift of $15 to a certain widow who wrote begging for $50 to get to a far village to teach school. When they heard of Scofield's generosity, Abraham and Peter actually wept.

Abraham, Peter, the Recording Angel, Abner Scofield, John Wanamaker.

*In *Report from Paradise*, ed. Dixon Wecter (New York: Harper, 1952).

"Letter Read at a Dinner of the Knights of St. Patrick," 1876 (WMT 19).
Twain praises St. Patrick for combatting evil in the prosperous republic of Ireland. He killed corrupt political officials, for example, the bribe-taking secretary of war and also the secretary of the interior, who neglected the Indians. He also massacred godless congressmen. Would that St. Patrick were here now, to improve us for the upcoming centennial.

St. Patrick.

["Letter to Governor Francis"], 1904 (LAIFI).
Twain writes Governor Francis to send his regrets. Circumstances beyond his control oblige him to remain at Villa di Quarto, in Florence, much as he would like to exhibit himself at the World's Fair in St. Louis. However, he will be represented there by a portrait of him by Professor Gelli. Twain closes with words of praise for the Fair.

Governor Francis, Professor Gelli.

["Letter to Jules Hart"], 1972.*
Twain says that anything becomes possible when politics and municipal government mix. He is appalled to learn that nine hundred out of a thousand die at the Blackwell's Island orphanage. The rate is worse than in any war, famine, or pestilence. By contrast, the death rate of forty out of a thousand at the Hebrew Infant Asylum is heavenly. Twain urges that the survivors be sent to "civilize" China.

*In *A Pen Warmed-up in Hell: Mark Twain in Protest,* ed. Frederick Anderson (New York: Harper & Row, 1972).

"Letter to Nasby." See FW, 1869.

["Letter to Sylvester Baxter"], 1917.*
Twain expresses joy that the Brazilians have overthrown their monarch [Emperor Dom Pedro II], and then scoffs at anyone who still respects kings and stolen titles. He invites his reader to compare

the state paper announcing the fall of the Brazilian throne and his own Connecticut Yankee's announcement of the dissolution of Arthur's kingdom. He hints at perversion among English nobility and predicts that ousted kings will soon be on our police forces and otherwise crowding the ranks of unskilled labor. He closes by inviting Baxter to pretend that the Brazilian statesmen plagiarized from his novel about the Connecticut Yankee.

[Sylvester] Baxter.

*In *A Pen Warmed-up in Hell: Mark Twain in Protest,* ed. Frederick Anderson (New York: Harper & Row, 1972). The letter was originally published in Albert Bigelow Paine, ed., *Mark Twain's Letters* (New York and London: Harper and Brothers, 1917).

["Letter to the Earth"] (LTE). See "Letter from the Recording Angel."

"Letter to the Editor." Se FW, 1869.

["Letter to the Editor of *Free Russia*"], 1972.*
    Twain is glad for the opportunity to talk about conditions in Russia. He deplores the half-way measures of some would-be liberators. You have simply to kill rattlesnakes, dynamite run-away fires, shotgun to death bloody maniacs loose in your house and after your loved ones. Despotism is cured only by bloodshed—never by mere petition. The throne of Russia must be kept vacant by explosives until all candidates refuse to sit on it. Victims of orders to go to Siberia must be avenged by masses of outraged mourners.

    *In *A Pen Warmed-up in Hell: Mark Twain in Protest,* ed. Frederick Anderson (New York: Harper & Row, 1972).

"Letter to the Editor of the *Californian*" (SS). See "The Moral Phenomenon."

"A Letter to the Secretary of the Treasury," 1906 (WMT 24).
    Mark Twain writes from Riverdale-on-the Hudson to the Secretary of the Treasury in Washington, D.C., on October 13, 1902, explaining that since the price of fuel has risen out of reach of im-

pecunious authors, he wishes to order some government bonds, early greenbacks, and seasoned old postal currency for his furnace and stove. If these items are sent promptly, he will pay cash and vote right.

The Secretary of the Treasury.

["Letter to William T. Stead"], 1917.*

Twain advocates peace by compulsion. Given human nature, peace by persuasion is not possible. He favors improving the chances for peace by urging four big powers to reduce their armaments by 10% a year, then having them coerce smaller powers. Modern weapons are so deadly that 2,800 men could now fight the equivalent of the Battle of Waterloo. This method guarantees a saving of money and also makes war so cheap that anyone can afford one.

*In *A Pen Warmed-up in Hell: Mark Twain in Protest*, ed. Frederick Anderson (New York: Harper and Row, 1972). The letter was originally published in Albert Bigelow Paine, ed., *Mark Twain's Letters* (New York and London: Harper and Brothers, 1917).

"Letters from a Dog to Another Dog Explaining & Accounting for Man: Translated from the Original Doggerel" (MTP).

The writer addresses a letter to dear St. Bernard, asking him to pretend that he is a puppy again and accept the truth that a man is as good as a dog and that it is only his environment which is against him. A dog in his place might behave as ridiculously. You see, man lacks freedom of conscience, speech, and action, all of which dogs have. Moreover, men are slaves from birth and must always be on the alert, which makes them selfish and cruel. Yet man thinks that he has ascended from lower creatures. Further, only man among the animals shows malice, envy, lust, cruelty, immodesty, and the ability to enslave and torture. Only men and dogs are bootlickers. Only man has invented a heaven, from which he excludes all animals but himself. Nevertheless, with patience man might yet attain the moral heights achieved by the better animals. Men divide themselves into different races, which they fancy have specific doglike tendencies. But what human race could resemble the St. Bernard?

Bull Wilkerson thinks that the French resemble black-and-tan terriers and that the British are like pugs. Yet surely the British are wrong to compare themselves to bulldogs like Bull, who smiles all the time unless provoked, is not demeaned by Bull Tanner (who was born in the State House), and once rescued Puss Wilkerson's four kittens. Would an Englishman behave that way? Look at the way Russians bow down to their Czar. Yet a Russian would prefer not to be a dog. So says a Russian terrier whom the letter-writer knows. A ruler has to keep a standing army, the real purpose of which is to protect him from the people. America needs no such standing army. In times of danger, the people rise.

Boss, Bull Tanner, Bull Wilkerson, Grand Lama, Pip Lapierre, Lapierre, Pope, Priest, Puss Wilkerson, the Czar of Russia, St. Bernard, Tige Lathrop.

[Letters from Honolulu], 1866.*

["The Burning of the Clipper Ship 'Hornet' "]—See "My Début as a Literary Person." Only in the original version are the following; Allen, Ferguson, Samuel Hardy, William Lang, Lang, Antonio Passene, Captain Spencer, John S. Thomas, [General Van Valkenburgh], Walker, and George Washington (all of which see).

["The Sugar Industry"]—Twain presents statistics on the increasing production of sugar in the Sandwich Island; compares it to Louisiana suger crops; discusses prices, expenses, and profits; describes a typical Hawaiian plantation and the process there of converting the cane into fine sugar; praises cheap Chinese labor and recommends its increased use in California; and closes with a rhapsodic prediction as to the future commercial greatness of California.

"The Whaling Trade"—Twain presents statistics on whaling vessels operating out of Honolulu, describes different types of whales, and explains that since 1853 the industry has been temporarily declining. Then he urges San Francisco to do its utmost to become the main whaling port of the Pacific.

["The Importance of the Hawaiian Trade"]—Twain gives figures to show the importance to the United States of encouraging trade with Hawaii. Then he suggests first that Congress should lower duties and second that the American population in the islands should be built up, by establishing a regular steamer service there instead of relying on necessarily inefficient China steamers.

Allen, Captain, Superintendent, Swift.

*Edited by Thomas Nickerson (Chicago: Lakeside Press, 1939). The titles of individual items in this book are not listed in my Chronology above but are interspersed through this alphabetized sequence of summaries for reference.

["Letters from the Earth"], 1962 (LFE).
God gazes into space and with a gesture creates whole universes. When the Grand Council disperses, Satan voices doubt that the establishment of automatic, self-regulating natural laws will prove worthwhile. Michael and Gabriel are also worried. Eons pass. Then a messenger announces that God is now making animals, as an experiment in morals and conduct. The animals prey on each other. The masterpiece is man, with good and bad traits, and with his home on a new globe called the earth. Satan gets sarcastic; so he is exiled into space, flaps around a while, and then decides to visit the earth and check on the human experiment.

Satan's first private letter back to Michael and Gabriel reports that everyone on earth is insane, that man is a sarcasm thinking itself the noblest effort of God, Who he thinks is proud of Man and to Whom—get this—he offers flattering prayers. People even think that they are destined to go to heaven.

In his second letter Satan reports that mankind has invented a curious heaven. On earth people delight in sexual intercourse, dislike singing and playing musical instruments and going to church and hearing loud noises, look down on those fancied to be inferior (for example, Negroes and Jews), and enjoy intellectual exercise. But in man's peculiar heaven, intercourse is omitted, everybody loudly sings and prays and plays the harp, all nations, regardless of color, are jumbled together, and no intellectual activity takes place.

Letter III reports that hundreds of religions have been invented and discarded on earth. A principal one is called Christianity, and its Bible is full of poetry, fables, gory history, morals, obscenity, and lies. Two things in this Bible which are not found in earlier bibles are hell and heaven. Curiously this Bible says that God took five days to build the tiny earth but then only one more day to light it with stupendous stars. God warned Adam and Eve not to eat a certain fruit about which they knew nothing. Then a serpent came along and persuaded them to do so. Thus they gained knowledge of good and evil, acquired a moral sense which should have placed them below all clean-minded animals, discovered intercourse, and became unnaturally modest. Shouldn't God have given Adam and Eve another chance instead of assassinating them and also their innocent children? Yet mankind calls God righteous and loving.

In his fourth letter, Satan reports that after the expulsion Adam and Eve followed orders and had children, with lots of wild results. God turned discontent and decided to abolish the human race, almost. Since creating it was the master crime in the first place, He should have destroyed them all; but instead he ordered Noah, a farmer, to build an ark, which was necessarily inadequate, and let mankind and the animals start over again.

Letter V says that it must have taken Noah a long time to collect his species for saving, since it later cost the Romans years to gather relatively smaller numbers of fighting quadrupeds for arena amusements. Noah missed countless types of creatures on the far side of the earth which neither he nor God knew anything about. One event which made Noah sail off fast was the rumor that a parade of saurians was approaching to be saved: they would have eaten all the rest, including the menagerie managers. Noah lost time through shipping millions of different kinds of flies and tons of filth for them to eat. Before they drowned, the people left behind prayed to their all-pitying God.

In his sixth letter, Satan explains that when Noah discovered that a certain fly had been left behind, he returned, got it, and thus guaranteed the infection of the new race of mankind with typhoid. It was so ordained, by Providence, from the beginning of time. The biblical God is a curious combination of goody-goody verbal morality and active malignities, all motivated by simple jealousy. At first God said that he was a jealous God, then that people should have no other gods before Him, but finally that He is the only God. He became irrationally jealous of Adam and Eve once they gained wisdom. To attack every part of that delicate mechanism called man, there is a special disease, and God is commander-in-chief of that army of maladies. Yet people blandly call Him Father.

Letter VII: Noah's family was loaded with microbes, in order to infect mankind in its future millions. The ark was clouded with disease-bearing flies, the greatest scourge of man. In addition, Shem carried hookworms, one of God's most ingenious inventions to make people wretched, and Ham carried sleeping-sickness bugs. Only recently have scientists discovered the nature of diseases, but then pious folk give God the credit for medical advances. Once there was a man who asked a priest how to be worthy of his newly acquired religion. When he was advised to imitate our Father in heaven, the man proceeded to break his wife's back, betray his brother, give his children diseases, and act as a pander.

Letter VIII: Man is such a fool that his every law is aimed at defeating one or more of God's natural laws. For example, there is a law against committing adultery, and yet it is according to the God-given nature of all men between the ages of sixteen and sixty-six, and of all women from seven to their graves, to wish to copulate like goats (not tortoises) as often as possible—and for females that is really often. Man therefore concludes that God smiles upon monogamy.

Letter IX: Well, the ark floated through dreadful rains, but not so bad as those of other so-called universal floods in previous history, and then settled on Ararat, after which Noah and the others got out. He raised grapes and got drunk. He was a poor specimen of new humanity; so only a tiny fraction of his descendants merited salvation by a crucified divinity. If God foresaw all this—and pulpits say so—then He must be a moral pauper.

Letter X: The Old Testament God was concerned with life, blood, sensuality, and death; the New Testament one, with fire, salvation, and hell. At first death was enough, but then God in the form of Christ brought salvation and with it eternal punishment too. Divine sentences are too severe for the crime. For example, the Midianites, all of whom merely behaved according to nature, got indiscriminately exterminated because a few of them violated book law.

Finally, in Letter XI Satan remarks that although the Church is cruel, history is even more cruel. The God-sanctioned selling of virgins into slavery was an act repeated in the unspeakable atrocities committed by unendurably oppressed Minnesota Indians in 1862. Examples could be multiplied. The Bible says that the merciful are blessed. One should read Numbers and Deuteronomy from the pulpit when one reads the Beatitudes, just for the record.

Abel, Adam, Baasha, Cain, David, Eve, the Family, Gabriel, God, the Grand Council, Ham, Père Hyacinth, Jeroboam, Jesus Christ, Leviticus, Man, Messenger-Angel, Michael,

Noah, Onan, [Saint] Paul, [John D.] Rockefeller, Satan, Shem, Solomon, Dr. Charles Wardell Stiles, Symmachus, Titus.

[*Letters from the Sandwich Islands*], 1866 (LSI).*

["On Board Steamer *Ajax*"]—Twain and his fellow passengers, including Brown, leave San Francisco aboard the *Ajax* on March 7, 1866. Captain Godfrey sings out orders beautifully. Twenty-two passengers are violently seasick for the first several days. Twain and six or seven others feel fine, although it is hard to avoid spilling things because of the ship's rolling.

["The Old Nor'west Swell"]—Twain discusses the trade winds and equatorial calms. He thinks that Balboa misnamed the Pacific, since it is stormy two-thirds of the time. Americans will have to develop efficient steamer service between California and the Sandwich Islands, or they will lose commercially there to the French and English. Time hangs so heavily on the passengers' hands that even the antics and fate of livestock aboard seems noteworthy. Old whalers on the *Ajax* play euchre noisily.

["The Steamship *Ajax*"]—The *Ajax* is two thousand tons, is heavily timbered, can accommodate sixty cabin passengers and bunk forty more, has excellent officers, and a fine chief engineer (with a crew of eighteen men). Twain advises young men to forget the romantic notion of running off to sea and becoming steamer firemen. They shovel coal four hours at a stretch, below the water line, with the temperature at 148°.

["Arrival at Honolulu"]—The *Ajax* sights rugged Oahu and homely Molokai on March 18. The passengers see the Hawaiian flag, fire a salute, and observe the natives. Their costumes are vivid. The women are usually adept on horseback. Twain finds dry land too quiet and steady for comfort at first; but the more he visits parts of Honolulu the better he likes the city, especially when compared to ugly parts of San Francisco. Brown, however, waxes critical of Hawaiian "santipedes," mosquitoes, and spiders.

["Living Conditions"]—Twain discusses the comfortable American Hotel in Honolulu and then his cottage accommodations in the center of town. His next topics include the algeraba and mango trees, the way the native women do laundry, local water, fruits, cigars, and wines and liquors. When you meet a stranger here, assume that he is a sea captain or a preacher, and you will usually be right.

["Equestrian Excursions"]—Twain rents a decrepit horse, which he names Oahu, from a typically disreputable native dealer and tours the area, finding a beautiful cocoanut grove a mile from town, then an ancient temple in ruins, where the chiefs used to offer human sacrifices to harsh gods. The missionaries have changed all this, and the natives now work and have consciences, unfortunately.

["The Island by Night"]—Twain canters up to a party on horseback that he wishes to overtake, and they ride on and on, until sunset finds them up a hill along an alleged shortcut. A native guides them down again through the fragrant darkness and into an old battlefield thickly strewn with human bones, perhaps the remnants of some enemies of King Kamehameha I, or perhaps the result of the 1804 pestilence. When they get back to town, Twain cavorts on his horse in front of a comely girl, who tells his companion that she thinks Twain must be drunk.

["Saturday in Honolulu"]—On Saturday Twain mounts a new steed, this one named Hawaii, to see the market place, with its colorfully dressed girls, tatooed visitors from the South Seas, and poi and *awa*-root merchants. Saturdays used to be more spectacular here, with frenzied horse races and *hula* dancers. Twain inspects the clean and efficient government prison, and talks with a couple of demented inmates—Captain Tait, who reads the Bible assiduously, and a Virginia Negro called General George Washington, who though old is immensely strong and who talks dreamily of the Blue Ridge and Richmond.

["Mrs. Jollopson's 'Gam' "]—Twain meets Mrs. Captain Jollopson on the street. She explains in sailors' lingo that while she was shopping for her hungry husband a drunk bumped into her and sent her reeling. Twain then translates her salty speech and adds a few words about mining slang in California and Washoe.

["The Kalihi Valley"]—Twain visits the Kalihi Valley. The beauty of its mountain walls, ridges, clefts, vivid foliage, stream, bushes, and vines is enchanting. Not far away is a handsome, costly palace, built at a cost of about $30,000 by Shillaber, then sold to Sam Brannan, and now falling into picturesque decay. By comparison, the nearby palace of the king is neat and tidy. But the monarch usually resides at Waikiki. At the palace one may see old Kamehameha I's war cloak of rare feathers and barbaric splendors of other native warriors.

["Hawaiian Legislature"]—The government of Hawaii has a king, nobles, and representatives. The king backs the nobles, who though outnumbered get things done. Twain visits the legislature, which has about six white men and thirty or more natives. Its president is M. Kekuanaoa, the king's father, a tough old man of eighty who fought beside Kamehameha I and later married his daughter. Kekuanaoa calls the typically wooden-headed legislature to order, and a bilingual half-breed named Bill Ragsdale translates proceedings.

["The Solons at Work"]—Twain observes the legislature in action. Bills are introduced, and are hotly and irrelevantly debated. Harris, the Minister of Finance, is especially ugly and dull. Dr. Hutchinson, the Minister of the Interior, is not much better, but at least he does not speak much. Once outside again, Twain and Brown are sad that they just missed seeing the king.

["Death of a Princess"] Princess Victoria Kamamalu Kaahumanu dies late in May, and Twain hopes that he may observe native mourning habits. Victoria was in her late twenties and had been betrothed to Prince William. She was well educated, was a fine musician, sang in the church choir, had many estates, and was loved by her people. Before the missionaries came, funerals of royalty were horrible saturnalias. Twain discusses the hold which Americans have on native commerce, agriculture, and fishing; the arrival of Anson Burlingame, our Minister to China, and several others; and then the story of the shipwrecked *Hornet*, the crew of which after forty-three days in an open boat were about to draw straws, to see who would be eaten first, when they sighted land.

["A Month of Mourning"]—One night Twain and a few other Americans are invited to sit on Dr. Hutchinson's verandah and watch the natives, who are still mourning Princess Victoria. The natives are packed on the royal grounds, in torchlight, swaying and yelling, chanting, shouting speeches, pounding dull drums, and doing the lascivious *hula*. Twain next contrasts the efficient, nononsense Puritan missionaries from America, the showy Episcopal efforts of tactless Bishop Staley from England, and the reliable French Roman Catholicism of Bishop Louis Maigret.

["A Royal Funeral"]—On the morning of June 30 Twain witnesses the elaborate funeral procession of Princess Victoria. Notable are the many soldiers and mourners, the catafalque, the vivid kahilis—feathered symbols of sorrow—and the protocol of it all. This funeral contrasts with the death and bone-burial of Kamehameha I, the history of which Twain quotes at great length.

["At Sea Again"]—Twain takes an inter-island schooner named the Boomerang from Honolulu. The trip is marred by rats, cockroaches, a crowing rooster, and cramped quarters, but is improved by Captain Kangaroo's efforts at kindness and some spectacular scenes by moonlight. Brown is sick, but Twain fails in his effort to please him through his recitation of a poetic rendition of Polonius's advice to his son. The travelers see some mountains at Hawaii, go on the Kailua, and then Kealakekua Bay, where coffee and oranges are big crops.

["Story of Captain Cook"]—After disgressing on Hawaiian sugar and then lava, Twain recounts the story of Captain James Cook, and how he abused native hospitality and was killed.

["Foraging for Food"]—Twain and Brown wander around Kealakekua Bay. They inspect the very spot where Cook was killed. They read inscriptions left there in his memory by later British sailors. And they try to dislodge some cocoanuts from some palm trees—Brown throws chunks of lava and Twain prepares to collect the nuts—but without success. So they hire a native boy to run up a tree and get some. The milk is delicious. Soon the rain is gone, The Boomerang works into the bay by moonlight, and they get aboard.

["History and Legend"]—Twain recounts the story of Charlton, former British consul at Honolulu, and of Lord George Paulet, who tried to force King Kamehameha III to pay Charlton an undeserved sum of money but was frustrated by the honesty of British Rear Admiral Thomas. Then Twain describes nearby native temples, tells about a lachrymose Christian convert named Obookia, explains how the author watched some native girls swimming, and finally says that he prevented Brown from carting off as a souvenir a monument to Cook.

["Voyage by Canoe"]—Twain summarizes the legend of Lono the god who killed his divine wife Kaikilani Alii and whom Cook later impersonated. Then Twain tells how King Liholiho got drunk, ate against custom with Kaahumanu, the dowager queen, and thus broke the tabu. Twain and Brown hire a sweaty native to take them in his outrigger canoe to the ruins at Honaunau, where they see the City of Refuge, the expertly built temple walls, a well-engineered road, and a petrified Niagara of cooled lava with tunnels and caves behind it.

["Kealakekua to Kau"]—Twain and Brown examine a big hole in a wall of the City of Refuge and find it filled with human bones— perhaps regal—and a canoe. Then they see more pretty girls bathing. Captain Crane's *Emmeline* picks the men up, and they sail through stormy seas and winds to Kau. Brown gets so seasick that Twain recites some more of his poetry, whereupon Brown vomits and soon feels better. Ashore again, they hire horses and trot through gorgeous scenery toward the awesome volcano of Kilauea.

["The Kilauea Volcano"]—When Twain first sees the volcano, it seems small, but gradually its titanic dimensions grow on him. He and Brown go to the fine Volcano House for supper, then return in inky darkness to the rim, beneath which they view the hellish sight again. It is a boiling, hissing, sulphurous cauldron a continent in width.

John Adams, Thomas Jefferson, John Quincy Adams, J[ames]. J. Ayres, Bacon, Baxter, Mrs. Bishop, Miss Blank, Mrs. Blank, Miss Boone, Sam Brannan, Brown, Dr. A. C. Buffum, Anson Burlingame, the Captain, the Chaplain, the Chaplain, Consul Charlton, Chief, Chief Clerk, Clerk, the Collector, the Collector, the United States Consul, Captain James Cook, Captain Crane, Captain Cuttle, Desnoyers, Captain Fish, Captain Fitch, the Minister of Foreign Affairs, Frank, Captain Godfrey, Captain Gordon, W. L. Green, [C. C.] Harris, the Prince of Hawaii, the Queen of Hawaii, High Chief, Hite, Dr. Hutchinson, Honorable John Ii, John, Captain Jollopson, Mrs. Jollopson, Judge Jones, Jones, Jones, Mrs. Jones, Dr. A. F. Judd, the Judge, Queen Kaahumanu, Kaikilani Alii, Major General Kalaimoku, Colonel David Kalakaua, King Kamehameha I, King Kamehameha III, King Kamehameha IV, King Kamehameha V, Captain Kangaroo, William Kanui, M. Kekuanaoa, Kekuokalani, King Keoua, Honorable Kiawawhoo, Honorable Kowkow, Honorable Ku, Honorable Kulaui, Laller, Leland, Lewers, King Liholiho, Lono, Prince William C. Lunalilo, Mackie, Bishop Louis [D.] Maigret, the Sheriff of Maui, James McBride, McCook, Henry McFarlane, McIntyre, Minister, Minister of State, the American Missionaries, Captain [Josiah A. Mitchell], Noble, the Governor of Oahu, the King of Oahu, Obookia,

the Bishop of Oxford, Page, Marshal W. C. Parke,
Rev. Mr. Parker, Lord George Paulet, Captain Phelps,
Captain Phillips, the Dowager Queen, Bill Ragsdale,
Representative, Vice President Rhodes, Rev. Franklin S.
Rising, Rev. Mr. Rowell, Sanford, the Sergeant-at-Arms,
Shillaber, Acting Consul Simpson, Skinner, J. Smith, Smith,
Smith, the Speaker, Lord Bishop [T. N.] Staley, Susy,
Captain Tait, Mrs. Tait, Tait, Tallant, Jack Tar, Rear
Admiral Thomas, King Umi, [George] Vancouver, General
Van Valkenburgh, M. De Varigny, Princess Victoria
Kamamalu Kaahumanu, General George Washington,
Whartenby, Prince William, Horse Williams, Wyllie.

*Ed. G. Ezra Dane (San Francisco: Grabhorn Press, 1937). The titles of
individual items in this book are not listed in my Chronology above but are
interspersed through this alphabetized sequence of summaries for reference.

*The Letters of Quintus Curtius Snodgrass.**

*Not by Twain. See Allan Bates, "The Quintus Curtius Snodgrass Letters:
A Clarification of the Mark Twain Canon," *American Literature*, XXXVI
(March, 1964), 31-37.

"Letters to Satan," 1923 (WMT 29).

The author regretfully requests that Satan pay full postage on
the letters he sends up and then expresses the hope that His Grace
will return to earth for a pleasure tour instead of handling matters
by proxy through him. Satan would have a great welcome in all
the major cities of the world. He could name his own figure if he
would go on the lecture platform. The author then reports that
he and his family saw the Queen's Jubilee, broke up housekeeping,
moved to an expensive but inconvenient English hotel, and fortunately used Thomas Cook & Sons [sic] when planning their visit
to Switzerland. They proceeded to Queenboro by train and over
to Flushing by slow steamer. Near Flushing they stayed at the
Grand Hôtel des Bains. The only grand thing was the price, especially of scotch. The Dutch railroad was bumpy, but when they
got into Germany everything went smoothly. In closing, the author
explains that Cecil Rhodes will serve Satan without being bribed.
The European Concert will do so as well. In fact, all the foreign
offices in Europe are under His Grace's sovereignty.

[John M.] Cook, Thomas Cook, Queen [Victoria], Cecil
Rhodes, Satan, Joseph Very.

'License of the Press,' 1873 (WMT 28).
   The press scoffs at religion and defends official criminals. Our
free press in America is licensed to print infamous things. In England one can sue libelous papers, but trying to do so in America only
increases the circulation of the abuse. Thirty or forty years ago,
newspapers in America were champions of right and morality. Not
so today. Failures at ditching and shoemaking fetch up in journalism on their way to the poorhouse. Most reporters are liars.
Papers here ridiculed Stanley of African fame when he lectured
badly. They did the same with Bret Harte when he had to write
something fast for money and did it ineffectively. Twain has been
reported dishonestly as an indecent lecturer and as a wife-beater.
He does not dare to sue. He closes by saying that newspapers
have obvious virtues but that he will let other people discuss
them.

   "Black Crook," Colfax, [William] Foster, the Governor of
   New York, Bret Harte, Charles Reade, Rozensweig, [Sir
   Henry Morton] Stanley.

"The Lick House Ball," 1863 (WG)
   The author receives a long letter from a Washoe girl named
Oenone, who asks for a description of San Francisco fashions. He is
happy to tell her about a recent ball at the Lick House, given him
by a number of friends in an effort to induce him to play billiards
more gently with them. At the ball were the Duke of Benicia, the
Countess of San Jose, and other titled personages. The ladies
were dressed in mohair or horsehair, arastras or asters, a tasteful
tarantula in jet, a gold beetle, fresh radishes, string-bean epaul-
ettes, zero velvet, goffered flounces, Raphael blouses, and the like.
They were lovely. The narrator could write more but for the fact
that the Lick House children are romping outside his door again
and the chambermaid's tread is also audible. He must abandon his
writing desk at once.

   Miss B., Mrs. A. W. B., Barron, the Duke of Benicia, Billy
   Birch, Lord Blessyou, Brooks, Charley Creed, Erickson,

the Empress Eugénie, Mrs. F., Lord Geeminy, Brigadier General, the Duchess of Goat Island, Jonesy, Mrs. F. F. L., Mason, the Emperor Norton, Oenone, Capt[ain]. Pease, Jerome Rice, Mrs. W[illia]m, M. S., the Countess of San Jose, the Queen of the Shoshones, Mrs. J. B. W., John B. Winters.

'The Life and Sayings of Artemus Ward.' See 'Artemus Ward.'

"Life as I Find It," 1874 (LAIFI).

A man tells his nephew a story about a person who when young and poor picked up pins outside a bank, thus attracted the rich banker from inside, and was made a partner and married the banker's daughter and is now rich. The nephew tries the same maneuver in front of another bank but is chased away.

"Life on the Isthmus." See FW, 1870.

Life on the Mississippi, 1883 (WMT 12).

Mark Twain begins by suggesting the vastness of the Mississippi River and its valley. He discusses the crookedness of the river, its depth at the mouth, its disposition to make cuts, and the fact that after DeSoto saw it more than a century passed before La Salle, deciding to explore it, surpassed the efforts of Joliet and Marquette and went all the way to the Gulf of Mexico. More than a century passed before an extensive white population and commerce appeared. Barges, keelboats, steamboats, coal flats, and rafts plied the river. In a novel which Twain is writing, Huck Finn, escaping from a persecuting father and with the runaway slave Jim, climbs aboard a keelboat near Cairo to learn their location; while there he overhears a series of keelboatman boasts, sees a fight between little Davy on one side and Bob and the Pet Child of Calamity on the other, and is detected but is saved by Davy from Bob, who wants to paint him and heave him overboard.

When Twain was a boy, the one ambition which he and his friends had was to be steamboatmen. The arrival of boats at Hannibal, Missouri, was a vivid event. A hated rival became an apprentice engineer and strutted until his boat blew up, but then after all he unfortunately recovered and reappeared—a bandaged hero. Twain longed for a pilot's salary, which was six times that of a preacher, but could make no headway toward his ambition, until finally, when away from home and in Cincinnati, he read that the Amazon River had not been completely explored. He took passage on an ancient tub called the *Paul Jones* for New Orleans, relished floating down the Ohio River and then the Mississippi, tried to make friends with the crew but succeeded only with the gin-drinking, ungrammatical night watchman, who confessed that he was the unwanted son of an English nobleman. In New Orleans at last, Twain decided that his funds were too low to permit him to wait for passage to South America; so he laid siege to Horace Bixby, pilot, and finally persuaded him to teach him the river from there up to St. Louis for $500.

The lessons began. The *Paul Jones* moved north, with Bixby lecturing on points which the cub promptly forgot, until catechized and profanely ridiculed. At St. Louis, Bixby and his cub transferred for the return trip to a big, gaudy steamer with tall pilothouse, cuspidores, chandeliers, and the like. A number of idle pilots were aboard, to refresh their knowledge of the ever-changing river. One night Bixby heroically negotiated the dangerous Hat Island crossing, and the onlookers shouted their praise. Bixby continued catechizing his cub, who began to make intermittent progress. One inky midnight, Bixby did not tell his partner, W., where they were, because W. reported ten minutes late. This was another lesson to Twain, who naively tried to stay awake in the pilothouse to help W. When Bixby explained that a pilot had to recognize changing shore-shapes and varying water-depths, his pupil grew melancholy again. One day Bixby let Twain handle the boat alone. The cocky cub bowled along happily until he mistook a wind reef for a bluff reef and seemingly was headed for catastrophe, when out stepped his mentor to correct him. He told the novice that he must learn to read the changing face of the water in every mood and season. Twain gradually learned but concluded that much of the beautiful romance of the river disappears from the vision of one who, like a doctor, must read features for symptoms of danger.

Months passed, and Twain seemed to be learning. So Bixby quizzed him on changing heights of bluffs and then explained that when the water rises a boat can go inside chutes which would be dry at low water. They encountered timber rafts, coal barges, and trading scows, which they sometimes maimed in the night, happily. Small-fry craft often came to a larger vessel to ask for newspapers, and when they were tossed religious tracts the profanity which ensued was incredible. The river was picturesque but dangerous when refuse from sugar plantations was burned along a hundred miles of shoreline. One night X., who was George Ealer's partner, came up and offered to steer through Helena crossing; he did so brilliantly, but George then learned that X. was a somnambulist and was asleep during the feat. At times of low water, the sounding boat was sent ahead to determine the depth and lay lighted buoys to guide the steamboat. Once, Tom G., Twain's hated rival cub, by a strategem went sounding instead of Twain and by accident was run over by the steamboat but unfortunately emerged limp, drenched, and heroic in the eyes of all passengers, including a pretty sixteen-year-old girl, whom Twain thereafter loathed. Next, to illustrate the fact that good pilots have fine memories, he tells of Mr. Brown, who unfortunately remembered everything, undiscriminatingly. In addition to memory, pilots need judgment and courage. One day Bixby let Twain steer the ship through an almost bottomless crossing but shook his confidence by asking whether he was sure of its depth. Soon Twain became scared. The leadsmen, in on the joke, called the wrong figures. Twain soon made a fool of himself, through lack of confidence.

To illustrate the rank and dignity of piloting, Twain now tells about Stephen W., a happy-go-lucky pilot who when out of work was hired by Captain Y. at half-pay, but who independently piloted the vessel up the middle of the raging Mississippi until raised to full pay, whereupon he professionally steered through time-saving chutes near shore. Next is explained in great detail the gradual evolution of the Pilots' Benevolent Association, which ultimately raised wages, improved service, went into insurance-policy writing, and created a monopoly until it was wrecked by the advent of the railroad, by war, and by steamer cargoes pulled by tugs.

Twain turns to a discussion of celebrated steamboat races, most dramatically from New Orleans to St. Louis, and then to devastating cut-offs of the rampaging river. Next comes the story of Stephen, who borrowed money from everyone, including Young Yates, whom Stephen depressed when he reported that he was planning to repay all creditors in alphabetical order. Twain then turns to his memory of Brown, under whom he served as pilot aboard the *Pennsylvania*. Brown was vicious and deaf, and delighted in setting tasks which his apprentice could not do well, and then criticizing him. But once when he abused Twain's little brother Henry [Clemens], then an under-clerk on the vessel, and called the boy a liar, Twain knocked Brown down with a stool, to Captain Klinefelter's necessarily secret delight. But Twain had to transfer to the *A. T. Lacey* from the *Pennsylvania*, which a few days later sustained a dreadful boiler explosion and fire, with consequent great loss of life, including those of Brown and young Henry.

After twenty-one years, Twain returns to the Mississippi. As he travels west of New York, whiskers, hands in pockets, chewing tobacco, and boots become the fashion again. St. Louis is sadly changed: its new houses are better spaced, and there are fine parks and public buildings; but smog blankets the city, and its shipping has been ruined by railroads and towboats. Twain takes passage on an Anchor Line packet named the *Gold Dust* bound for Memphis and notes many changes in shipping and the river. The pilot, Robert Styles, lies to Twain about government boats which dredge for alligators, then when pinned down calls his visitor by name and lets him gratefully steer a while. As the boat moves from St. Louis to Cairo and then Hickman, Twain chats with garrulous old Uncle Mumford, the first mate. Conversation turns to the subject of the Civil War, and the pilot reminisces about his war experience: his steamboat, the *R. H. W. Hill*, took Confederate troops to a combat area, and when his pilothouse was fired at he hid but was later commended for gallantry. Then they discuss the Darnell-Watson feud in Kentucky and Tennessee, and then the devastating 1882 flood.

Twain quotes from several travelers and historians—including Captain Basil Hall, Mrs. Trollope, Charles Augustus Murray, Captain Marryat, Alexander Mackay, and Ernst von Hesse-Wartegg—who have described the Mississippi. Then Twain discusses numerous changes for safety—torches, charts, pilings, jetties, and snag boats—introduced by the federal government and the many theories under consideration for "improving" the wild river. The next topic is the rapacious Murel [John A. Murrell] gang, which specialized in stealing Negro slaves or enticing them to run away to the gang, which sold and resold them and finally murdered them, along with other victims. Immediately thereafter Twain discusses the recent Memphis yellow-fever plague which killed three-fourths of the population. Below Memphis Twain observes impoverished migrating Negro families, recalls an argument between A and B over flooded fence rails, has fun letting a passenger from Wisconsin lecture him incorrectly on boat parts and then discover him at the wheel piloting, glories in sunrise over the river, and comments on the growth and industry of Helena, Arkansas.

When they arrive at Napoleon, Arkansas, Twain tells his companions that they must all disembark for a while, because he has a mission to perform. It seems that when he was living in Munich, Germany, he visited the municipal house of death, whose watchman, Karl Ritter, told him that years before, in Arkansas, Private Franz Adler, a member of Captain Blakely's cavalry company, had, in the presence of a merciful soldier named Private Kruger, murdered Ritter's wife and daughter. Ritter followed them but killed innocent Kruger by mistake. Years later he discovered the murderer, Adler, prematurely placed in the charnel house and gloatingly withheld essential brandy from him and watched him die. Later dying himself, Ritter begged Twain to make restitution to Kruger's son Adam of Mannheim, Germany, by locating and giving to Adam a treasure secreted in a certain building in Napoleon, Arkansas, which Kruger had told Ritter about. Twain and his cronies— Thompson, Rogers, and the poet—decide against sending the treasure to Adam, because sudden wealth would ruin him. They plan to keep the money but are soon told by Captain McCord of the *Gold Dust* that Napoleon was entirely destroyed years ago by a titanic flood!

Twain now discusses shifting boundary lines in Mississippi River waters, the financial problems of a cotton-growing syndicate in Arkansas called the Calhoun Company, problems involving planters and Jewish merchants and former slaves, and the absence of drinking aboard Mississippi steamboats. Next he summarizes stories concerning ferocious mosquitoes from Lake Providence, Louisiana, as told to him by H., a Sunflower River packet mate riding as a passenger aboard the *Gold Dust*. Moving past Vicksburg reminds Twain of the famous 1863 siege there, about which he talked with a man who with his wife Maria survived it by living in a cave. Suddenly the story of a college professor is presented: when the man long ago was on a ship from Acapulco to San Francisco, on his way to a surveying job in California, a stranger named John Backus, apparently an Ohio cattleman, got into a card game with some gamblers and frustrated their unsavory plans, because he was a professional cardsharp himself. Twain now announces that the *Gold Dust* has ended its trip. Three months later, she blew up, killing Lem Gray, pilot, and sixteen others, and injuring forty-seven. Twain now turns to a variety of subjects. He describes the typical Southern "house beautiful," its library, piano, pictures, bric-à-brac, and furniture; then a typical dirty Cincinnati steamboat; the city of Natchez, so adored by Mrs. Trollope in 1827; its ice factory and yarn mills; river drummers of oleomargarine and cotton-seed oil flavored to resemble olive oil; the elegant capitol building at Baton Rouge, with architecture reflecting the Southern mania for the medieval romances of Sir Walter Scott; Southern feuds; and finally the nonsense told gullible British travelers by fun-loving Southerners. And now New Orleans. Twain discusses its levees, warehouses, wharves, streets and gutters, architecture, progressive spirit, and burial customs. He quotes authorities on the dangers of inhumation in time of plague, because of rising corpse gas. Then he turns to a discussion of J. B., an oldish acquaintance whom he now encounters and who appears young and blithe, because he has become an undertaker and can, for example, easily talk Mrs. O'Flaherty into having as expensive a funeral for her husband as Mrs. O'Shaughnessy had for hers. Next come discussions of New Orleans iron lace, [George Washington] Cable's literary talent, the dirty-looking St. Louis Hotel, the cathedral, swamps and canals and Lake Pontchartrain, New Orleans cooking, the Washington Artillery Building, and the Southern accent, diction (including the word "lagniappe"), and speech patterns. Southern sports include talk about the Civil War, cockfights, and mule racing. Twain finds that Southern reporters are generally accurate, until they write romantically like Scott about women. Next comes a brief account of the romantic Mardi Gras, then more criticism of Scott for perpetuating silly medieval chivalry, even in the face of the effects of the satirical *Don Quixote*.

In New Orleans Twain and Cable welcome Joel Chandler Harris one morning; but, though they read from their books to show how easy it is, they cannot persuade shy, red-haired little "Uncle Remus" to entertain some visitors by reading from his works. Twain then tells how he and [Charles Dudley] Warner got into trouble with the name of Eschol Sellers in their novel *The Gilded Age:* a man of the same name turned up and threatened to sue them unless they altered the name to Beriah Sellers.

One day on a street in New Orleans Twain sees Horace Bixby again. He is unchanged in twenty-one years and is now captain of the steamer the *City of Baton Rouge*. Twain, Bixby, and some others become guests of Major Wood and visit the vast sugar plantation of ex-Governor Warmoth. The process of steam-plowing, cultivating cane, and making sugar is most complex. On the way back to New Orleans, Twain is annoyed by the ship's hoarse and vulgar parrot. During a conversation with some other passengers, Twain learns that a former pilot under whom he once steered has become an opulent spiritualist, which fact stimulates Twain to voice his criticism of spiritualism.

Twain tells us that ex-pilots often become unsuccessful farmers, that pilots are uniformly brave in sacrificing themselves to save passengers' lives, that Thornburg's cub set a bear loose aboard ship once, and that a clerk whom he once knew—and whom he will call George Johnson—lost out on a fortune by lying that he was married to a rich old man's servant girl (really only Johnson's mistress), whereupon the old man left his money to "Mrs. George Johnson," then legally non-existent.

Suddenly Twain remembers Captain Isaiah Sellers, a tall, raven-haired, stately old patriarch—the ancient mariner of the Mississippi—who started piloting back in 1811. On his entrance, bald-headed pilots would stop trying to impress neophytes with their stories. Sellers wrote informative, reminiscent paragraphs for the New Orleans *Picayune* under the pseudonym of "Mark Twain," which Samuel Langhorne Clemens once unfortunately burlesqued for the New Orleans *True Delta*, thus earning Sellers' bitter and unique hatred. After Sellers' death, Clemens took his pen name and has tried ever since to honor it.

Twain and his friends board the *Baton Rouge* for St. Louis, on the way to which there is a rousing storm. He recalls a boyhood friend who might have become a good blacksmith but instead saw an amateur Shakespearean show and became a Roman soldier in *Julius Caesar* for more than thirty years. In St. Louis Twain encounters a man with whom he was a militiaman during the riots until Twain handed him his musket and deserted—to get a drink, as he explained. All at once Twain tells the story of "Charlie Williams," clergyman's son, Harvard graduate, and convicted burglar serving a nine-year sentence in prison. He wrote himself a letter and signed it "Jack Hunt," a man purporting to be a former fellow-prisoner converted to Christianity by Williams and then released. Hunt said that he had prayed and after rescuing two children in a runaway carriage had obtained a job through the grateful father, Mr. Brown. Hunt was writing Williams to thank him and casually mentioned Williams' consumptive and bleeding lungs. The letter circulated widely, but before Williams could be released the fraud was exposed.

Twain sees Alton, Illinois; then Louisiana, Missouri, near which he maneuvered while in the rebel army in 1861; and then Hannibal, his boyhood hometown. Twenty-nine years have changed all the people in it but not lovely nature about it. Twain recalls the fate of two childhood friends of his. Lem Hackett drowned one Sunday, and the juvenile survivors all quaked through a thunder and-lightning storm that night in fear that the venegeance of God would fall upon them next. And Dutchy, who could recite three thousand verses from the Bible, also drowned; again a storm made Twain uneasily repentant and temporarily determined to lead a better life. Now he goes to a couple of Hannibal Sunday-schools and admires the young people, although he still recalls the Model Boy of his day with loathing. All is changed, especially the girls whom he once knew and who are now mothers and grandmothers. He remembers a saddler named John Stavely who used to rush out ostentatiously when steamboats arrived, to pretend that they were bringing him business. He also remembers a lying carpenter who related in a whisper the story of his killing thirty or sixty people all named Lynch, because his fiancée had been killed by Archibald Lynch. Twain regrets lacking time to go to a cave a mile or two below Hannibal, where the corpse of a girl is (or was) preserved in an alcohol-filled copper cylinder. Next Twain recalls giving matches to a vagrant drunkard with a pipe—he was not Jimmy Finn, as one Hannibal resident wrongly remarked—only to be aroused in the night by crowds going to a fire in the calaboose to see the stranger burning to death. Twain uneasily talked in his sleep about the incident, was terrified when his little brother aroused him, but was relieved when his brother reported that Twain said while asleep that Ben Coontz gave the man the matches. The boys then agreed not to betray Ben to the authorities but to watch him instead. Twain's next topic, once they pass Marion City, Quincy, La Grange, Canton, and

Keokuk, is an angelic orator named Henry Clay Dean, who once spellbound an initially hostile audience at Keokuk. Into view come Burlington and Muscatine, scenes of spectacular sunsets.

Twain praises city after city on the Upper Mississippi—Davenport, Rock Island, Moline, Clinton, Lyons, Dubuque, Prairie du Chien, and La Crosse, among other places—none of which has been visited by foreign tourist-writers. The scenery is gorgeous, but the railroads are taking business away from the steamboats. One pasenger among several new ones added at La Cross is a former tourist-guide who lectures verbosely on the beauty of the shoreline and the virtues of new towns along the river to the north. He and Twain also discuss Indian legends. When the man recommends Schoolcraft's book on Indians, Twain looks it up and tells us the allegory of Peboan (Winter) and Seegwun (Spring): Peboan is an old man who explains that his breath freezes rivers and his frosty locks shed snow; the younger man, Seegwun, replies that birds and flowers spring up in his path. Twain relegates the Indian tale of "The Undying Head" to an appendix. Finally the group reaches St. Paul. It is a fast-growing city, Twain observes. Newspapers never tire of comparing the balmy weather of New Orleans to simultaneous cold weather in St. Paul. Of the many lakes about, White-bear Lake is the best. It has a curious legend, involving the rescue by the young warrior Kis-se-me-pa of the chief's daughter Ka-go-ka from a fierce white bear.

At last Twain and his friends return home, through Chicago, which changes faster than prophecies about it, and then aboard the Pennsylvania railroad to New York—last stop on a uniquely enjoyable five-thousand-mile journey.

Several appendices follow. Appendix A tells of the voyage of a relief boat sponsored by the New Orleans *Times-Democrat* in 1882 through flooded regions. Appendix B is Edward Atkinson's 1882 report on the need for federally funded Mississippi River controls. Appendix C concerns the reception in this sensitive country of Captain Basil Hall's *Travels in North America*, 1829. Appendix D records the Indian tale of "The Undying Head"; it concerns Iamo, whose head is severed but still works miracles and is restored to Iamo's resurrected body in due time; Iamoqua, Iamo's devoted sister; Mudjikewis, one of ten brothers who seek some precious bear-guarded wampum; and Nemesho, an old Indian who aids Mudjikewis.

A, Private Franz Adler, Charles William Allbright, Dick Allbright, B, J. B., John Backus, Captain Tom Ballou, Squire Bell, Bill, Horace Bixby, George Black, Captain Blakely, Bob, Bogart, Jim Brady, Thomas Brown, Brown, Brown, Brown, Burgess, [George Washington] Cable, Colonel Calhoun, Captain —, General Cheatham, Claggett, Claggett, Henry [Clemens], [John Marshall Clemens], Ben Coontz, Crenshaw, Fraulein Dahlweiner, Darnell, Darnell, Mrs. Darnell, Davy, Henry Clay Dean, [Hernando] DeSoto, Major Downing, Dutchy, Captain Eads, George Ealer, Ed, [Admiral David G.] Farragut, Huck Finn, Jimmy Finn, Pap Finn, Senator Frye, Tom G., Billy Gordon, the Governor of Missouri, [General Ulysses S.] Grant, Lem Gray, H., Lem Hackett, Hamlet, Captain Asa Hardy, Mrs. Asa Hardy, Jane Hardy, John Hardy, Joel Chandler Harris, Harry, Dr. J. G. Holland, Tom Holmes, Aleck James Hopkins, Jack Hunt, Iamo, Iamoqua, Jesse James, Jesse Jamieson, Jim, Jim, Jimmy, John, George Johnson, Mrs. George Johnson, [Louis] Joliet, Beck Jolly, John Jones, John Jones, Jones, Ka-go-ka, Dick Kennet, Kis-se-me-pa, Captain Klinefelter, Adam Kruger, Private Kruger, Kruger, [Sieur de] La Salle, Louis [XIV] the Putrid, Archibald Lynch, Lynch, Mack, Manchester, Mayor, Captain McCord, Maria, [Père Jacques] Marquette, Windy Marshall, Mary Ann, Miss —, the Model Boy, Commodore Montgomery, Mudjikewis, Uncle Mumford, [John A.] Murel [Murrell], the Mysterious Avenger, Nemesho, Pat O'Flaherty, Mrs. Pat O'Flaherty, Bridget, O'Shaughnessy, Dennis O'Shaughnessy, Brother Page, Peboan, General Pemberton, the Pet Child of Calamity, Dr. Peyton, General Ev. Mr. —, Rex, George Ritchie, Karl Ritter, Mrs. Karl Ritter, Miss Ritter, Rogers, I. S., Seegwun, Beriah Sellers, Eschol Sellers, Captain Isaiah Sellers, Seymour, Jim Smith, John Smith, Smith, Smith, John Stavely, Stephen, John Stevenson, Stewart, Robert Styles, Thompson, Ben Thornburg, Thornburg, Henri de Tonty, Lorenzo Tonti, Triangle, Jonas Turner, Stephen W., W, Governor Warmoth, [Charles Dudley] Warner, Watson, We-no-na, Hank Wiley, Charlie Williams, Jim Wilson, Major Wood, Wood, X., Captain Y., Young Yates, Billy Youngblood.

"Lionizing Murderers," 1872 (WMT 7).

The author has heard so much about Madame —, the fortune-teller, that he goes to consult her. She has a dark complexion, greasy hair, bits of snuff in her moustache, and garlic on her breath. She tells him at once that his great-grandfather was hanged and that he will murder several members of the Brown family in New Hampshire, will be caught, tried, and condemned to hang, will be converted, will have hymns sung in his prison cell by dewy maidens, and will be swung to Paradise in front of a weeping crowd. What a splendid fate! The author facetiously thanks the fortuneteller, and then seriously deplores glorifying confessed murderers and weeping over them.

  Brown, Madame —, Pike.

"A Literary Nightmare." See "Punch, Brothers, Punch."

"A Literary 'Old Offender,'" 1870 (CG).

Twain says that he recently published "The Story of the Good Little Boy," in which his juvenile hero sits in some nytroglycerine, is spanked, and explodes. Twain explained at the time that he took the idea from an item in a California newspaper. Shortly after his sketch appeared, Twain received a letter from a certain disreputable author claiming that he wrote the original work. But Twain, who refuses to masculinize the rogue by calling him a literary pirate, denies that the fellow could have written the story and beseeches the real author to step forward—with evidence.

'Literature,' 1900 (WMT 28).

Twain praises the mildness of the previous speaker [Anthony] Hope's statements but adds that exaggeration in order to approximate truth is his own style. He is about to leave London to return to America and run for President. He favors everything anybody else wants; thus, he will be a whole President, not half a one. Christendom had fifty thousand new authors last year. It will be up to the Literary Fund to support them, sooner or later.

  [Anthony] Hope.

"Literature in the Dry Diggings." See "An Unbiased Criticism."

"A Littery Episode—Speech." See "The Story of a Speech."

"Little Bessie," 1972 (FM).

Thoughtful little Bessie, about three years of age, asks her mother what sadness and pain are for. Her mother replies that God thus disciplines us and makes us better. So she was taught. Bessie wonders why Billy Norris caught typhus. To make him good. But he died. Then it was to discipline his parents or perhaps to punish them for some sin. But Bessie reminds her mother that it was Billy who died and asks whether that was right. Yes, everything God does is right. Even killing the stranger who was trying to save an old woman from a fire? Letting a drunk man stab Mrs. Welch's baby with a pitchfork? Having lightning hit the church? The mother grows weary and suggests that Bessie go out and play. But the child rambles on, telling her mother that Mr. Hollister says every bug, fish, bird, and reptile has an enemy that eats it, to discipline it and make it religious. For example, spiders sting flies and suck their blood, and wasps eat spiders alive. Bessie's mother criticizes Hollister for his scandalous thought. When the child suggests that her brother Eddie needs to be disciplined—by diphtheria or bone-rot?—the mother faints. Later, Bessie tells her mother that Hollister told her that people can no more help their nature than animals can. We would not punish a cat for torturing a mouse, but God punishes us for simply being what we are. Moreover, God created houseflies, which breed wildly and kill millions of people every year. God commands us not to kill but then lets the flies go. Still later, Bessie queries her mother about virgins. When she is told that a girl ceases to be a virgin before she can have a baby, Bessie replies that Sally Brooks has a baby and says she is a virgin. When Bessie says that Hollister regards the Virgin Mary as properly an ex-virgin since she had five children after the unique One, the girl's mother brands Hollister as an unbelieving miscreant and orders her daughter to get to the nursery. Finally, Bessie and her mother discuss aspects of the Trinity and the immorality of pre-Christian gods. Bessie says that Hollister wishes he were such a god, because he would make virgins scarce. At this point, the girl's mother yells for Mary Ann to come get the child.

Bessie, Sally Brooks, Burgess, Burlap, Eddie, a Has Been, Hollister, Uncle Jonas, Jones, Mary Ann, Billy Norris, Smith, Welch, Mrs. Welch, Williams.

"Little Nelly Tells a Story Out of Her Own Head," 1972 (FM).

The time is twenty-two or twenty-three years ago, at the Fairbanks mansion in Cleveland. Mother Fairbanks was one of the innocents abroad. She and Twain reminisce, and then one day a group of children plans to present a little drama based on *The Prince and the Pauper*. The girl assigned the part of Edward VI is delayed; and to fill the interval, Nelly, a charming little girl aged nine, tells a story, while her twin sister sits on stage beaming smiles at her. Once there were two ladies, twins named Mary and Olivia Scott. They lived together but had no children. They prayed for a baby, and— sure enough—one came. It could not eat, since it had only gums and no teeth. The twins prayed some more, and a woman with lots of children came and showed Mary and Olivia what to do. They were so happy that they prayed for more children, and a total of thirteen came by fall. Nelly ends her story with the statement that persons who trust in God will have heaps of rewards. The audience of about a hundred and fifty people, including many adults, roars with appreciation until tears of laughter and relief come.

[Abel W.] Fairbanks, [Mary M.] Fairbanks, Mary Scott, Olivia Scott, Scott, Mrs. Scott, Severance, Mrs. Severance.

"A Little Note to M. Paul Bourget," 1896 (WMT 22).

The author assumes that a rejoinder, called "Mark Twain and Paul Bourget" by Max O'Rell, to his essay "What Paul Bourget Thinks of Us" was really dictated by Bourget to an amanuensis. Bourget had every right to dictate his reply, of course, but his lack of skill at dictating is evident in the article's lack of purpose and logic. The author admits that for a moment he was tempted to think that someone else wrote the rejoinder, but he soon dismissed the notion because no outsider would have the impertinence to meddle in a literary dispute between two friends. Then the author complains that he stuck to the subject and therefore Bourget should have done the same; however, the published rejoinder reads like a deaf person's irrelevant replies to a shouter. Moreover, it alters Twain's remarks when quoting them. The rejoinder says that France can teach America plenty? Twain agrees that she could help us improve our government, tax system, and fine arts. But then he objects to being called nasty, insulting, and unrefined, and comments at length on Bourget's rudeness to a certain New York hostess at one time. He thanks the author of the rejoinder for recommending certain French writers and next turns to the grandfather joke, suggesting as a way out that he and Bourget swap the anecdotes since Frenchmen can trace their lineage way back and since Americans have no difficulty in identifying their fathers.

Paul Bourget, the Deaf Person, A Fault-Finder, Max O'Rell, the Shouter, Wetherby.

["Living Conditions"]. See LSI.

"'Lo' at the Capitol." See FW, 1870.

[Lo! the Poor Indian . . .], 1862 (P).
The untutored Indian doubles the pot until he goes busted.

"Local Notes Taken on the Run." Se FW, 1869.

["The Lost Ear-ring"], 1972 (FM).
The time is June, 1878. The author is staying at a little house on the Königsstuhl. Suddenly Fräulein Marie steps into the living room, utterly disconsolate. She has lost part of a pretty though inexpensive earring. Her mother, her two sisters, and an old woman who knits stockings register intense sorrow and hope to God that it may be found. If not, they must bow to God's blow. The author expresses his sympathy in irregular German and then while the others go and search everywhere for it retires to his room to write. After three hours he takes a stroll in the nearby beech grove. The aged knitter is there, and when she sees his canvas shoes she shrieks with delight and says, "In God's name, cloth!" She explains that they all looked for the earring in the house, the road, and the forest, but to no avail. Then Marie rushes up with radiant face and explains that she found it in her apron pocket, where it evidently fell while she happened to tilt her head in a certain way. The old crone thanks God and says that His ways are wondrous.

Fräulein Marie.

"Lost in the Snow." From *Roughing It.*

"The Lost Napoleon," 1923 (WMT 29).

The Lost Napoleon is part of a mountain range, about six miles in length, which shows the military leader sleeping on his back with an arm folded on his chest. The author discovered the view himself while floating down the Rhône River ten or eleven years ago. He had gone by train from Geneva to Lake Bourget, then down the Rhône for ten lazy days to Arles. About the eighth day, when perhaps half a mile above a little village [Beauchastel], he discovered Napoleon on the left, shaped by the distant mountain. If advertised, it could become a great tourist attraction.

'Lotos Club Dinner in Honor of Mark Twain,' 1893 (WMT 28).

Twain, recently back from Europe, responds to a flattering introduction by saying that he has seldom heard compliments so nicely phrased or so well deserved. He should take warning from the prodigal son, who in the presence of his brothers David and Goliath foolishly spoke of all his failings. Twain adds that in Europe he saw lots of Americans, all of whom were proud of their country except one old lady who had forgotten her native land and was glorifying monarchical institutions. He told her that she should admit that, unlike China, America had the merit of allowing citizens who were tired of the country to leave, then thanked God that America did not restrict such people's movements.

[Charles A.] Dana, David, Goliath, [Seth] Low, McKelway.

[Love Came at Dawn], 1966 (P).

In the morning, Love came and said that it was life. It came again in the evening and said that it was rest.

Love Concealed: To Miss Katie of H—l, 1853 (P).

Rambler says that Miss Katie of H—l will never know how love and friendship for her battled in his heart. But she loves another. Katie, Rambler.

"Love on the Rail—A Rehearsal" (MTP).

S and C, the latter being a girl, decide that since they cannot learn the parts they are rehearsing they will pantomime the action instead. Hence, "Love on the Rail—A Comedietta in Four Acts" will be billed as "Love on the Rail—Tableaux Vivants." So, reversing roles, they pantomime love at first sight in a railway car. They happily agree that acting is easier without bothering with words. Then they pantomime a bridal trip: they enter with C loaded down with satchels and assisting "his" self-conscious bride affectionately. Then C pretends to fall asleep on S's shoulder as fellow passengers stare. Next they pantomime boarding the train after three months of marriage, this time with the wife carrying the baggage; they appear to argue, and when she nods sleepily he pushes her away, whereupon C seeks the smoking car.

C, Mary, S.

Love Song, 1892 (LAIFI).

I do not ask whether your hope is still pure and your love still warm, but rather how's your liver.

"The Loves of Alonzo Fitz Clarence and Rosannah Ethelton," 1878 (WMT 19).

It is cold in snowy Eastport, Maine. Alonzo Fitz Clarence, a handsome, rich young bachelor, is so bored that after a sumptuous breakfast he goes to his desk and, talking as though to the floor, chats with his aunt, Susan Howland, who tells him that all is rainy in the balmy December where she is. Alonzo looks out at driving snow, then hears a sweet voice singing "In the Sweet By-and-By," and returns to his desk to ask his absent aunt who is singing. Her cheerful voice introduces the singer. She is Miss Rosannah Ethelton. Alonzo bows and motions the disembodied voice to a chair. Let us now flit to the luxurious home of a certain refined lady. It is tastefully appointed. Beside the piano sits a delicately beautiful young girl of snowy complexion, with soft blue eyes, and with golden tresses. Her dress is divine. She is Rosannah. She and Alonzo talk for nearly two magical hours. They adjust their evidently erratic clocks. When they break off their conversation, Alonzo sighs and confesses to himself that his heart is now in San Francisco. Meanwhile, Rosannah is favorably comparing him to empty-headed Sidney Algernon Burley, whose one talent is the ability to mimic.

Four weeks pass. Burley, the cast in his eye working ominously, is in the drawing room of Aunt Susan's sumptuous San Francisco house on Telegraph Hill. He has been brilliantly mimicking the illustrious of the city but now asks the mistress of the place a question, is told to wait in a room upstairs, and goes to do so. But on the way there, he passes a private parlor and hears Rosannah exchanging endearments with an unseen male and evidently showering him with kisses. Then each speaks rapturously of the wondrous photograph of the other. Alonzo's mother rushes to congratulate her son. Simultaneously, a continent away, Susan congratulates her ward Rosannah. Meanwhile, Burley has learned his rival's name and address, since Rosannah murmured them in her ecstasy. Gnashing his teeth, Burley vows to spoil their planned wedding.

Two weeks pass. Burley goes to Alonzo in Eastport and introduces himself as a retired Cincinnati minister named Rev. Melton Hargrave. He has an invention which can tap long-distance telephone lines to hear intimate talk. Seeking to protect his telephonic whisperings with Rosannah, Alonzo encourages "Hargrave," who one day gains access to Alonzo's phone and, mimicking its owner, insults Rosannah's flat rendition of "Sweet By-and-By." Hearing Alonzo coming, Burley hides behind the curtain. Alonzo picks up the phone, but the girl breaks off her engagement with him. He tries to call her back. At sunset in San Francisco, and three and a half hours after dark in Eastport, he gets through, only to learn from Aunt Susan that the distraught girl has packed and fled. Alonzo and his mother find the card of Burley, San Francisco, behind the curtain and quickly guess the truth about Rev. Hargrave.

Almost two months transpire. No word from Rosannah. Alonzo has packed a portable telephone, wanders far and wide, climbs telephone poles, and cuts into lines in a vain effort to hear his love render "By-and-By," which he knows she frequently sings when sad. No luck. In March he is confined to a New York asylum. He proves to be a tractable patient. But then one evening he chances to hear the flattened strains of "By-and-By." He crawls to a corner, discovers a telephone, and shouts into it the truth about cruel Burley, his mimicking rival. Rosannah whispers her forgiveness and then reveals that she is staying with her uncle Rev. Nathan Hays, a retired missionary in Honolulu. She and Alonzo agree to marry at 8:00 A.M. on April 1. They ring off. Then Burley drops in on Rosannah again. She now seemingly succumbs to his repeated importunities, agrees to marry him on April first at eight o'clock in the morning—if he will avoid her presence until then. Off he capers, triumphantly. On April 1, according to the newspapers, with her uncle officiating, Rosannah is telephonically married in Honolulu to Alonzo in New York. She goes by yacht to Lahaina and Kaleakala for her honeymoon. He goes with his parents to the aquarium for his little wedding trip, since he is still too sick to do more. In time, Rosannah crosses the continent, meets her husband face to face for the first time, and is happy with him. As for Burley? He is annoyed at being thwarted and later tries to kill a crippled artist but falls into some boiling oil and dies.

Alfred, Sidney Algernon Burley, Rev. Nathaniel Davis, Alonzo Fitz Clarence, Fitz Clarence, Mrs. Fitz Clarence, Captain Hawthorne, Rev. Nathan Hays, Mrs. Nathan Hays, Susan Howland.

"A Loving Swain." See FW, 1869.

["The Lowest Animal"], 1962 (LFE).
Man is the lowest animal in creation. Look at the St. Bartholomew Day's massacre, the persecution of heretics, the slaughter and enslaving of neighbors, sins, villainies in the name of patriotism, and discrimination according to sex. A British earl in the western part of the United States once slaughtered seventy-two buffalo, ate part of one, and left the rest to rot. But when Twain offered seven calves to an anaconda in the London zoo, it ate one and left the others. Men gather excess millions of dollars; but not even squirrels, bees, birds, or ants horde more than one winter's supply of food. Roosters enjoy harems, but the hens consent; human harems are different. Animals are never obscene. Man has good reason to blush, uniquely among the animals. Atrocities are only human. Look at war, robbery, slavery, patriotism, and religion. Obviously, man is an unreasoning animal. History is one long story of lunatics. Man is separated from the higher animals only by his moral sense, which enables him to distinguish between right and wrong so as to do wrong. Rabies is an innocent malady; the moral sense, a guilty one. We human beings are at the bottom of the evolutionary scale; only the French are below us, with their immoral sense. The human body

is a basket of diseases and physical nuisances. Look at the teeth, tonsils, appendixes, male nipples and beards and bald heads, the inaccuracy of human sensory organs compared to those of the higher animals, and the horrors of menstruation, pregnancy, and childbirth. What is supposedly supreme in man? His intellect. Yet he leaves intellectual joys out of his vision of heaven.

"Luck," 1891 (WMT 15).

At a banquet in London honoring a highly decorated military leader—let us call him Lieutenant-General Lord Arthur Scoresby, Y.C., K.C.B., etc.—the author is suddenly told by a reliable clergyman friend that Scoresby is an absolute fool. The Reverend explains that forty years ago when he was an instructor at the military academy at Woolwich he took pity on sweet, guileless, stupid Scoresby and coached him concerning stock questions on Caesar and phases of mathematics. Surprisingly, the lad took first prize. The Crimean War broke out; and Scoresby was promoted to captain, blundered through various engagements, replaced the colonel when he was killed, and through sheer ignorance fell forward to the left when ordered to fall back to the right. His regiment stumbled into the Russians, who flew into a wild retreat. Marshal Canrobert decorated inept Scoresby on the spot. So he is now a shining soldier to a generation, but still a fool.

Marshal [François Certain] Canrobert, the Reverend, Lieutenant-General Lord Arthur Scoresby.

"Lucretia Smith's Soldier," 1864 (CJF).

It is May, 1861, in the village of Bluemass, Massachusetts. Reginald de Whittaker, a clerk for a drygoods and grocery store, has just enlisted in the army. But moments before he is to break the news to his girl friend, Lucretia Borgia Smith, that imperious creature spurns him, telling him that she cannot love a malingerer. She slams the door. Stunned, he turns away. The next day a neighbor tells Lucretia what Reginald did and adds that the young man marched off glumly. The girl dissolves in tears and suppressed curses, and later reads that R. D. Whittaker has been gravely wounded. She rushes to the side of the heavily bandaged soldier, whose jaw has been shot away and who is recovering in a Washington hospital. After she has sobbed over him for three weeks, the doctors remove the bandages of—Richard Dilworthy Whittaker of Wisconsin. He is Eugenie Le Mulligan's soldier, not Lucretia's. The other Whittaker has not yet reappeared.

Bushrod, Director of the Overland Telegraph Company, Ferguson, Eugenie Le Mulligan, Lucretia Borgia Smith, Smith, Reginald de Whittaker, Richard Dilworthy Whittaker.

["Macfarlane"], 1973 (WIM).

When Twain was twenty years old, he lived in a Cincinnati boardinghouse which was filled with bustling, good-natured, but dull people—except for Macfarlane, a forty-year-old Scotchman. He and Twain used to talk early in the evening. Macfarlane worked from six to six at an unnamed job, then returned to his room, and read two or three hours late in bed. He was tall, thin, sincere, humorless, and impersonal. He knew the Bible and the dictionary thoroughly. In his 1856 conversation he anticipated some of Darwin's discoveries. Macfarlane thought that life ascended from a divinely planted microscopic seed until ruinous man emerged. Macfarlane regarded man as uniquely malicious, filthy, patriotic, and oppressive of others. He felt that man's intellect was the brutalizing addition to his nature.

Macfarlane.

"The McWilliamses and the Burglar Alarm," 1882 (WMT 27).

Their conversation has drifted from weather to crops to scandal to religion and thence to burglar alarms, about which McWilliams tells Mr. Twain. After they built their house, McWilliams wanted to contribute some leftover money to charity, but his wife wanted a burglar alarm. So they compromised and bought the alarm. An expert installed it; but about a month later McWilliams smelled smoke one night, investigated, and found a second-story man smoking his pipe. McWilliams bought back the loot and in the morning called for the expert, who wired the second floor. Then one night McWilliams found a burglar in the third story, redeemed his property, and called for the expert again. The annunciator grew and grew. All might have been well but for the fact that the cook kept tripping the alarm when she entered the kitchen early in the morning. And the alarm hurled the McWilliamses all the way across their bedroom and thus cost them much sleep. Various newly installed switches only complicated matters, and repair bills mounted. The McWilliamses eventually learned simply to disconnect room from alarm on the annunciator. But then burglars came and stole the entire alarm system. The expert then installed a patented clock which could be set to turn on the new alarm at night but not in the daylight; but the clock soon reversed the twelve-hour cycles. Eventually burglars came and occupied the house, as the safest place in town; furthermore, they refused to share expenses for the alarm. So McWilliams took it out, traded it for a dog, and shot the dog. He then bids Mr. Twain goodbye and gets off [the train].

McWilliams, Mrs. McWilliams, Thomas, Twain.

"A Majestic Literary Fossil," 1890 (WMT 22).

We have advanced intellectually in the past fifty years mainly because, for a change, certain progressive thinkers believe that a new idea may occasionally have merit. This was not always so. Formerly there was reverence for old ideas and hostility to new ones. A realm of great recent change is medicine. A *Dictionary of Medicine* by Dr. James of London, published in 1745, details classical remedies in ways which should make a pro-modern out of any reader of it. According to this book, bleeding used to be regularly prescribed for all ailments, spiders were to be feared, and bites from spiders should be treated with applications of incredibly messy concoctions. We should all thank homeopathy.

'Major Perry and the Monitor *Camanche*,' 1864.*

Twain asks Major Perry to accept a beautiful cane, fashioned by a host of local aborigines. The red men whom the speaker represents, though they abhor soap and water, admire the major's unblemished integrity. Perry sports no necklace of human bones and wears no scalps at his belt, and yet they know that he is brave and can see him even now in their imagination back at Bull's Run and Antietam. If he will visit the Indians, they will happily feed him crickets and grasshoppers, and let him bed down on coyote skins. The cane's head shows a hand grasping a fish, symbolic of the major's unflinching grip, which enabled the intrepid man to raise the sunken *Aquila*. Twain salutes him in the name of various chiefs, all standing here, thirsty.

> Buckskin Joe, Buffalo Jim, [General George B.] McClellan, Captain [J. J.] Merritt, Major [Edward C.] Perry, Sioux-Sioux, Washakie, Winnemucca.

*In *American Literature*, XXXIX (May, 1967), 176-177.

[Mammoth Cod], c. 1920.*

The poet thanks God for the bull's cod, which works to give us meat; for the ram's cod, whose work produces our mutton; and for the boar's cod, which labors for our pork. It is odd that of all the creatures of God only man plays with his cod. (In a note, Twain explains that he wrote this poem to teach children that the instinct of animals is superior to the reason of man. The poem is intended for Sunday schools and for a pretty children's song.)

*Printed for the Hammer & Chisel Club. 2nd ed., 19 copies, 1937.

["Man Kills Wife"] (MTP).

The narrator dislikes his wife, who tries to be endearing but grows depressed. He considers a separation, but that would leave him penniless. Then he thinks of suicide and finally murder. When he happens to see Mary Matthews, he falls hopelessly in love with her and determines to act. Mary is briefly visiting his city and soon returns to her town of X—, six hundred miles away. He follows her, assumes a different name, and courts and wins her. They plan to marry in four months. He hopes that in a short while his other wife's failing health will free him. But one night his wife asks who Mary is. He has been talking in his sleep. He is vague, and when his wife falls asleep he kills her with a wire through her armpit. He is momentarily nonplussed when their bedroom door swings ajar but soon falls asleep. The family doctor, when summoned, is not suspicious. The narrator writes his late wife's devoted brother, a resident in faraway St. Petersburg. After the funeral the narrator announces his intention to travel abroad but veers off to X— and lovely Mary. In his obscure hotel room one night, he finds a note telling him that this is not foreign travel. He covers his tracks, visits Mary again, and goes to a new inn. But another devastating note awaits him. He tries without success to find his persecutor, to beg mercy or bribe him. When he returns from seeing Mary again, he finds another note, this one ending with a threat. Suppose an enemy wishes to expose him to the Matthewses. He will admit that he courted Mary before his wife's death. That was no crime. Mary will come around. The narrator sleeps but wakes up thinking of the threat at the end of the last note. He must hide his tracks completely. He buys an oilskin from a seedy stranger, walks circuitously through the rain, and checks into a shabby boardinghouse. That night he asks Mary to marry him early; but she declines, explaining that many guests have been invited for the specific date. Then she and her parents wonder why his guests are evidently not coming. He explains that his proud family was annoyed at his marrying for love rather than for riches or a title. The Matthewses are pleased. While romping with Mary and some other young people, the narrator sprains his ankle and must stay in the Matthewses' guest room. He momentarily worries about his luggage but is then delighted, because his pursuer will surely not come here . . .

Mary Matthews, Matthews, Mrs. Matthews.

"The Man That Corrupted Hadleyburg," 1899 (WMT 23).

The town of Hadleyburg for years has proudly enjoyed its reputation for honesty. Its citizens keep temptation from its youth. But one dark night a mysterious stranger, offended some time before by the virtuous town and therefore determined upon revenge, delivers a heavy sack to the home of Edward Richards, the aged bank cashier, and his old wife Mary. With the sack is a note explaining that the contents, 160 pounds of gold, are to go to the kind Hadleyburg resident who a year or two earlier helped the stranger, then a ruined gambler, by giving him $20, with which he ultimately made his fortune by gambling some more. The benefactor may identify himself by reciting the kind remark he made to the stranger, which words are in a sealed envelope inside the sack. Honest Richards is to inquire privately or, if he prefers, to advertise in the local paper and ask the candidate for the reward to present his sealed remark to Burgess, formerly the town minister, if he is willing to conduct the affair. The stranger further suggests a public meeting at the town hall thirty days hence at 8:00 P.M. Richards and his wife joke for a moment that they might simply keep the money, but soon he hurries off to place the notice in the paper, whose editor-proprietor Cox is willing to rush the matter into print. Home again, Richards talks with his wife; and they agree that Barclay Goodson, now dead, was the only Hadleyburg citizen ever capable of aiding the stranger in this manner. Goodson was hated for his honest opinion of the self-righteous town—more hated than anyone else, except for Burgess, who became disliked and was removed as minister by the townspeople but was secretly warned of the trouble and thus saved from danger by Richards, who, however, has a troubled conscience because—as he now confesses to Mary—he had proof that Burgess was totally innocent but concealed it. The Richardses ramble on a while; and then suddenly, stricken by the same thought Mary has, Richards rushes out to try to stop Cox from printing the notice. But he is too late, and both he and Cox are angry that they did not simply split the gold in silence. Home again, Richards commiserates with his wife, and they agree that all events are ordained and that Hadleyburg citizens are trained to be honest, unfortunately. Suddenly they both wonder if they might possibly be able to guess what the remark was that Goodson made to the thankful stranger. Meanwhile, the foreman of Cox's paper has alerted the Associated Press to the curious happenings, and Hadleyburg wakes up famous.

Hadleyburg's nineteen leading citizens are beaming. The town will become a symbol of incorruptibility. Crowds gather. The sack of gold is on display at Pinkerton's bank. But within a week a change begins to occur. Jack Halliday, the irreverent town critic, notices that the nineteen seem sad and then sick. They are secretly wondering what Goodson could have said to the stranger. Three weeks pass. Then Richards receives a letter from a stranger who signs his message as Howard L. Stephenson and explains that Goodson told him that Richards—was it Richards?—did him a favor, the value of which Richards probably never knew, and further that Goodson wanted to leave him a fortune, if he had had one. The letter suggests that if Richards agrees that he really deserves the money, he may freely claim it. The message to Goodson was this: "You are far from a bad man; go, and reform." Mary rejoices; but when she asks Richards to explain the favor he did Goodman, her husband untruthfully says that he cannot because he promised not to tell. That night, while Mary dreamily spends vast sums, Richards cudgels his brains to remember what favor he ever did Goodson and finally thinks that is must have been his warning that Nancy Hewitt, the man's fiancée, was part Negro. Stephenson sends the other eighteen leading citizens letters identical to the one he sent Richards, and all of the men try hard to recollect imagined favors while their wives think of ways to spend the reward. Halliday notices a peaceful, holy happiness in town. Burgess is surprised as he gradually collects nineteen envelopes, all furtively handed to him, to be opened on the long-anticipated Friday evening in the town hall.

The big room looks fine, and especially the flag-draped platform, where the sack of gold rests. Burgess addresses the huge throng of citizens on the subject of Hadleyburg's purity. Then he reads Deacon John Wharton Billson's statement of the message to the stranger: "You are very far from being a bad man; go, and reform." But when he reads lawyer Thurlow G. Wilson's message, it proves to be identical but without the word *very*, a difference which Thompson the hatter points out. So Burgess decides to open the stranger's letter of explanation to see whether *very* is in it. The word is not there, but the message concludes thus: "Go, and reform—or, mark my words—some day, for your sins, you will die and go to hell or Hadleyburg—try and make it the former." The crowd is stunned but then explodes in laughter. Wilson recovers rapidly, rises, and confesses not only that he said all of those words to the stranger but that in addition he saw Billson near his desk, where his letter to Burgess was lying, and must conclude that Billson took a hasty look at it but remembered the text imperfectly. Billson protests vehemently but is silenced. Now, however, Burgess proceeds to read off message after message from all of the remaining incorruptible nineteen leading citizens—with the exception of Richards. That old man whispers to his agitated wife that perhaps they should confess, but they decide not to do so since they seem spared by a miracle. Burgess next reads the stranger's postscript to the deliriously sarcastic townspeople. It says that there was no generosity but instead an insult, which the stranger decided to avenge in this fashion, by hurting the smug town in its precious vanity. Burgess finally rips open the sack and finds only gilded disks of lead. The town saddler suggests that Halliday auction the slugs and give the proceeds to Richards, the only virtuous citizen of note in Hadleyburg. A strange-looking man, who resembles a detective posing as an earl and who observed the proceedings with quiet contentment until it became apparent that Richards's name was not to be read, enters the bidding, purchases the disks for $1,282, and announces that he intends to stamp the names of the eighteen corrupt citizens on them and thus create rarities. The audience roars its approval; but "Dr." Clay Harkness, a wealthy patent-medicine manufacturer and also a candidate for the legislature opposing Pinkerton, whispers to the stranger an offer to purchase the lead pieces and reluctantly agrees to pay $40,000 for them. Each candidate hopes to be elected and then influence the legislature to vote a new railroad through his property. Somewhat earlier the stranger has publicly announced his intention to reward Richards to the tune of $10,000. This news upsets the old couple; but they resist the urge to confess that they too sent Burgess a message, especially when the stranger hands them three $500 bills as partial payment.

The Richardses go home and conclude that their windfall was ordered by fate. Next morning the stranger picks up the sack of slugs, sells them to Harkness for $40,000, obtains several checks from him drawn to "Bearer," and quietly delivers an envelope to the Richardses' home. Mrs. Richards thinks that the disappearing man is the stranger who brought the accursed sack that night. Her husband decides that he must be Stephenson then. The old couple are delighted when they see that he has given them not the rest of the promised $10,000 but a total of $38,500 in checks signed by Harkness. An accompanying note in Stephenson's hand explains that he is disappointed not to have proved all nineteen leaders corrupt but that honest Richards deserves the whole pot. Next comes a note from Burgess explaining that since Richards helped him once when he was accused and almost universally condemned, he has willingly lied now for his benefactor. Richards and his wife only wish that they deserved all of these complimentary words. Harkness stamps Pinkerton's name and statement about going and reforming on the lead slugs and thus easily defeats his political rival in the election. But soon the Richardses are tortured by oppressed consciences. They suspect next Sunday's sermon of ironically pointing at them, imagine that Burgess is avoiding them, and think that their servant Sarah must have overheard them talking about the gold. They grow mortally sick, rave deliriously about their guilt and innocent Burgess's concealment of it, thus complete the discrediting of once-glorious Hadleyburg, and die. Officials remove the word

"not" from the town motto, which now reads "Lead Us into Temptation."

> John Wharton Billson, Rev. Mr. Burgess, Cox, Mrs. Cox,
> Barclay Goodson, Jack Halliday, "Dr." Clay Harkness,
> Mrs. Clay Harkness, Nancy Hewitt, Johnny, Parsons,
> Pinkerton, Edward Richards, Mrs. Mary Richards, Sarah,
> L. Ingoldsby Sargent, Sawlsberry, Howard L. Stephenson,
> the Tanner, Thompson, Robert J. Titmarsh, Voices, Eli-
> phalet Weeks, Nicolas Whitworth, Archibald Wilcox, Mrs.
> Archibald Wilcox, Oscar B. Wilder, Thurlow G. Wilson,
> Mrs. Thurlow G. Wilson, Wingate, Gregory Yates.

["Man's Place in the Animal World"], 1973 (WIM).

For centuries religions have caused wars and persecution. On
Sundays we are beseeched to be brotherly; yet patriotism urges
the opposite. Twain has studied man and the higher animals in the
London Zoological Gardens and has come to these conclusions. Man
is uniquely cruel, miserly, vengeful, sensual, subject to shame,
bellicose, thieving, nationalistic, religious, and rational (though
also unreasoning). Man is separated from the higher animals by
having the moral sense, which enables him to do wrong. We have
descended from simpler forms of life: first come the animals, then
human beings, and at the bottom the French, who have the immoral
sense. Compared to animals, human beings are rickety, have poor
teeth, useless tonsils and appendices, and are afflicted with countless diseases. Compare a man to a Bengal tiger, with its grace,
beauty, physique, and majesty. Man has the enormous superiority
of his intellect, with which he has imagined a heaven in which there
will be no intellectual pleasures. Is this not a confession that perhaps heaven is reserved for the higher animals?

"Map of Paris," 1870 (WMT 19).

Twain is happy to reproduce his Buffalo *Express* "Map of the
Fortifications of Paris" here in the *Galaxy*. The map has been much
admired, although some strangers connot understand it. The Prussian forces are shown to be situated both at a farm house and also
at Podunk. Von Moltke may merely take a raft down the Seine to
Paris, which has never been in such danger as on the present map.

Prince Frederick William, General [Ulysses S.] Grant, [Count Helmuth] von Moltke, Napoleon [III], General [William T.] Sherman, King William [I].

"Marienbad—A Health Factory," 1892 (WMT 29).

Getting from Aix to Geneva, Zurich, Stuttgart, Nuremberg, through Bavaria, and finally into Bohemia, where Marienbad—Mary's Bath—is located, takes thirty hours by train through wonderfully varied scenery. Houses at Marienbad are all creamy in color, trimmed in white and dim red. Few people are in uniform here. The crowds are fashionably dressed. The cure takers are routed out at 5:30 in the morning, drink foul water, take baths in tubs of water or in mud, walk, and eat sparingly and only what they do not like. The author did not come here for treatment but soon got talked into it. He feels that a person without diseases and bad habits has a dull life. The whole place is cold and wet most of the time. It is dreary to walk through its silent forests. People talk only about their ailments—overweight, lack of weight, and especially bad livers. At Marienbad, sidewalk manners are rude, women pull carts, and a despondent man once poisoned his own whiskey to commit suicide but was beaten up by an evil tramp who took the whiskey and drank it and died and thus made the would-be suicide a hero who became a successful policeman.

"Marjorie Fleming, the Wonder Child," 1909 (WMT 29).

The author intensely praises Marjorie Fleming, who has been dead a century now. She was vividly alive once, and wise, loving, and interesting. And she died toward the end of her ninth year. She was a Scot, and the author first heard of her in conversation with her biographer Dr. John Brown, author also of *Rab and His Friends*. At the age of six Marjorie started a journal, which she kept intermittently the rest of her short life. Sir Walter Scott revered her and immensely enjoyed hearing her recite poetry. She read widely and especially liked Shakespeare. She was very friendly with her cousin Isabella Keith, to whom she wrote letters. Her handwriting was bold, her spelling and punctuation atrocious; and she hated the multiplication tables. She disliked a certain fat person named Miss Potune, whom the author therefore has also despised. In her

journal, Marjorie changed her subjects rapidly. She was fond of
writing about love but often tried to discontinue doing so. She even
wrote once of being proposed to by handsome fellows. She relished
visiting nearby Braehead, a delightful place owned by "Mrs.
Crraford" [Crauford]. Marjorie often expressed regret at having a
violent temper. Isa Keith wisely refused to chastise the unusual
child. When she was good, Marjorie was given small sums of money,
which she spent in imagination on gifts for friends, especially Isa.
Marjorie wrote a little verse, once about the death of some young
turkeys. She began her first journal in January, 1809, and her last one
late in 1810; its final entry is dated July, 1811. She died five months
later. Shortly before her death, she recited some melancholy poetry
by Robert Burns most movingly to her distraught and adoring
father. Fifty years later, her sister remembered the touching scene
and also Marjorie's death, of a dire malady then called water in the
head.

> Aunt, Charles Balfour, John Balfour, Mrs. John Balfour,
> Dr. John Brown, Cay, Miss Craford [Crauford], Miss
> Craford [Crauford], George Crakey [Cragie], Crakey, Mrs.
> Crraford [Crauford], Marjorie Fleming, Fleming, Mrs.
> Fleming, Miss Fleming, Jobson, Dr. Johnstone, Isabella
> Keith, James Keith, John Keith, William Keith, King, King,
> James Macary, Mary, Miss Potune, Tommy, Harry Watson,
> William.

"Mark in Mormonland." From *Roughing It*.

"Mark Interviews Himself." See "The Yacht Races."

"Mark Twain a Committee Man," 1866 (WG).
    Mrs. Foye asks the crowded San Francisco audience to name
some respectable men to come onstage to supervise her séance.
Twain is immediately nominated, which is natural because he made
some friends promise to name him. Others are also selected. They
write names of dead people and collect slips from the audience with
more such names. Then a few names are chosen apparently at random, and answers to questions concerning them are rapped out.
A German named Ollendorf comes onstage, asks questions about a

supposedly dead friend, then hoots derisively at the answers and explains that the name given is that of a living person. But Ollendorf is driven offstage when Mrs. Foye grandly objects to having her religious beliefs toyed with—partly by spirits—in such an unseemly manner. Another German comes up, asks questions in his own tongue, and receives evidently satisfactory answers. T. J. Smith is identified as a deceased teacher of religion and for about an hour answers numerous questions about matters in the next world. Twain asserts that the foregoing description is entirely accurate, that he does not know how the rapping was produced, and that the answers all seemed inexplicably intelligent. He intends to pursue his study of spiritualism unless he goes insane first.

J. M. Cooke, Captain Cuttle, Fraulein Eruback, Mrs. [Ada Hoyt] Foye, William Nelson, Ollendorf, Owfter, George Purnell, Sesostris, G. L. Smith, T. J. Smith, Wallenstein, Whiting.

Mark Twain Able Yachtsman Interviews Himself on Why Lipton Failed to Lift the Cup. See "The Yacht Races."

"Mark Twain among the Spirits." See "Among the Spirits."

"Mark Twain and Copyright." See "Petition Concerning Copyright."

"Mark Twain and the Mental Photograph Album." See "Mental Photographs."

["Mark Twain and the Question of Carl Byng—and Literary Pirates"]. See "John Camden Hotten."

[*Mark Twain in Three Moods: Three New Items of Twainiana*], 1948.*
"Scenery." Twain recently [1868] went by horse-drawn sleigh through the Sierras to Donner Lake, then on by hack a few miles to invigorating Lake Tahoe, which is surrounded by snow peaks, is very deep and blue, and has remarkably transparent water. It is a joy to sleep in the cold air under three blankets, with the sociable

ants. In the morning you can fish or try to hunt the elusive mountain sheep. The region is lonely and seems divine. Sunset is a feast of beauty.

["Chinese Labor &c 1870"]. Twain quotes a news item about the President of the Southern Pacific Railroad, who assures white workers of San Francisco that if the company gets a million-dollar subsidy all of it will be used to pay white labor, not Chinese. Twain then comments sarcastically on the prejudice and chicanery implied in the President's position. At the end, Twain notes that the measure narrowly passed, mainly because white paupers with no tax money to lose voted yes.

[Third item not by Twain.]

The Governor of California, the President of the Southern Pacific Railroad.

*Edited by Dixon Wecter (San Marino, California: Friends of the Huntington Library, 1948).

"Mark Twain Interviewed" (MTP).

In response to the interviewer's questions about significant national issues, Twain rambles inanely about bronchitis and real estate, including his Hartford residence. Then he offers the journalist a Porto Rican cigar and rambles about his house at Tarrytown. When the reporter tries to leave, Twain tempts him by promising to speak frankly. He explains that he has been deliberately wasting the young man's time because the young man intended to waste Twain's time. Twain says that he gets paid for words and not ideas, and he has already given the interviewer $400 worth of words.

Mark Twain, Young Interviewer.

"Mark Twain Mystified" (MTSF). See "Mark Twain's Interior Notes."

[Mark Twain of the Enterprise], 1862-64.*

[1.] (December, 1862) Twain informs his readers that the Nevada Supreme Court will meet soon to consider a case which has just been written up in words which he cannot understand. He comments on Colonel William's road map, which resembles bird tracks in wet sand or fly slime on white paper.

[2.] (December, [1862]) This report concerns an eighteen-pound turnip, a candy pull and a spirited dance, and the new engine of the Empire City fire company.

[3.] (December, 1862—January, 1863) A stock reporter goes to a wedding, gets drunk, and mixes stock and wedding news. A storm wrecks some Virginia City structures. Twain reports seeing a ghost in the street one night. But the big item of news is the sanitary ball, to which Twain invites a dozen or so young girls, in the hope that one or so will accept; but they refuse in a body and insultingly, then urge him to invite a thousand. The dance is a success, especially the Virginia reel.

[4.] [January, 1863] Twain goes on a trip to Carson City with Joseph T. Goodman, who frosts his nose on the way and turns silent. While there, Twain attends a fancy party at J. Neely Johnson's home, which glows with beautiful objects. Twain's curious journalist friend the Unreliable enters, uninvited and dressed partly in clothes from Twain's wardrobe. He and Twain demolish the contents of the punch bowl, and the Unreliable puts quantities of food in his cavernous, slant-toothed mouth, then sings offensively. Other guests sing beautifully.

[5.] [February, 1863] When the Unreliable reports in his newspaper that Twain stole some things from him, Twain angrily challenges him to a duel with bootjacks. The Unreliable snivels and grows sick. To cheer him up, Twain gives him a coffin. Twain reports the Carson City wedding of James Sturtevant and Emma Curry. The fiddle-playing and dancing bewilder Twain, as does the champagne which others drink all about him.

[6.] [February, 1863] At Carson City, Dr. J. H. Wayman and Mrs. M. A. Ormsby surprise everyone and get married. The dance which follows is marred by the presence of the Unreliable, who crashes it in borrowed clothes, stands in the dancers' way eating sauerkraut from his hat, and even tries to steal some silver spoons. The acting governor decides against calling an extra session of the legislature, which, Twain avers, is composed of many honest, righteous persons. Twain must leave now for Virginia City, in spite of a petition signed by numerous wise and pretty ladies begging him to remain.

[7.] (May, 1863) Twain reports that he is now in San Francisco, with the Unreliable, who commandeers rooms, ignores bills, and even persuades Twain to go to a disreputable concert. They buy pit tickets and then climb into private boxes. Twain summarizes wedding and travel news, and gives some mine-stock prices.

[8.] [August, 1863] Twain has a bad cold but still writes from Steamboat Springs to rebuke the *Enterprise* editor for publishing a biography of Jack Perry, about whom Twain could set everyone straight. He mentions his recent vacation at Lake Bigler [Tahoe], and summarizes a dispute between miners and farmers over water rights along Steamboat Creek.

[9.] (August, 1863) Twain is still at Steamboat Springs. The hotel is handsome and friendly. The nearby hospital, managed by Dr. Joseph Ellis, has given life back to persons afflicted with rheumatism, erysipelas, and venereal diseases. The baths provide a lively combination of cold showers and steam closets. But the most moving treatment is what is called "Wake-up Jake," a stinking emetic which scours you clean.

[10.] (September, 1863) Twain takes a wild stagecoach trip from Virginia City to Carson City and on to Sacramento. He sits beside the talkative driver and behind a crack team of horses. He goes on to San Francisco, attends a performance of *Mazeppa* starring [Adah Isaacs] Menken, and is impressed by her lithe movements in the ridiculous play.

[11.] (October, 1863) Twain reports on the first annual fair of the Washoe farming, mechanical, and mining society, held in Carson City: prize-winning animals parade, an entertaining pantomime of an orator is offered, and there are horse races. Twain suggests that water be piped from the nearby Sierras into the center of town for a park and fountain. He concludes that the fair was a very pretty success, and a financial one too.

[12.] (November, 1863) A convention, which includes numerous important persons, is now in session in Carson City to draft a constitution. Few people can find Washoe on the map, but Nevada will make them sit up. The territorial government should vote the convention a little spending money; otherwise its work may be delayed.

[13.] (November, 1863) From Carson City, Twain rebukes the *Enterprise* editor for printing the biographical sketches of convention delegates, compiled by William M. Gillespie, without giving that busy man any credit. Twain responds to criticism of his recently published hoax about a massacre in Empire City by reporting that a certain fellow named Samson beat up some critics with an ass's jawbone; Twain concludes by voicing the hope that the San Francisco *Evening Journal* editor will be stupid enough to state in print that this story about Samson is another hoax.

[14.] (December, 1863) The local theater was recently the scene of a performance given for the benefit of the new Carson City church. To pacify [L. O.] Sterns, who begged the convention reporters to report his speeches verbatim or not at all, Twain offers an exact transcription of one of the orator's recent effusions, redundant verbosities and all.

[15.] (December, 1863) Twain praises the Logan Hotel at Lake Bigler. He explains that Bill Stewart seeks to avoid a tax on mines by defending a mine as a hole where digging is done, then having miners blast instead of digging; hence their holes could not be defined as mines. Next Twain discusses the office of state printer, among other subjects.

[16.] (December, 1863) Twain describes a rowdy meeting of the Third House, a burlesque, in a saloon, of the Nevada state constitutional convention. The Third House meets, suspends rules, dispenses with prayer, and elects Twain president. Certain officers swear that they have not had and do not wish to have anything to do with duels. Taking charge, Twain rebukes a stammering speaker, silences a man who wants to oppose taxing mines, interrupts a man spewing quartz-mill statistics, ridicules a proposal to build a railroad, and misinterprets a vote concerning the proceedings in general. He asks for cold medicine for himself—a little molasses and a gallon of gin. Later, the Third House transacts some business—concerning open doors, married women, board and fines, and arrests.

[17.] (December, 1863) The author explains that he recently received a box of Christmas presents from Carson City. They include a toy rabbit, a toy Pi-Ute Indian made of raisins, and a watchman's rattle. An accompanying letter explains that after a pleasant Christmas party at a children's school it was decided to send the things to Twain in Virginia City.

[18.] (December, 1863) The author reports a recent meeting of a number of citizens of Storey County. They have decided to bolt the state constitutional convention and elect their own delegates. The author satirizes their inefficient parliamentary proceedings.

[19.] (December, 1863) The author proposes to expose a would-be swindle. Read & Co., Philadelphia, have advertised for investors in a projected Nevada mining operation. The author explains that the advertisement betrays lack of knowledge of local mining terms and details, and says that unsuspecting speculators will lose everything if they subscribe to the scheme.

[20.] (January, 1864) Twain says that as soon as the constitutional convention had drafted a constitution, a state nominating convention proposed a slate of state officials. But since the constitution proposes a tax on mines, the defeat of the document is certain, which means that the nominees will be unemployed. Twain offers the individuals for sale or rent. He is glad that the constitution will be voted down, because territorial governor Nye illegally filled in blanks—having to do with dates, memberships, and money— before he signed it.

[21.] (January, 1864) Twain briefly reports opposing a Virginia City man who wanted the state capital moved out of Carson City; then offers employment, political entertainment, juridical, and other news; and finally quotes part of a letter he received from Artemus Ward.

[22.] (January, 1864) Twain reports that there is some doubt as to whether citizens of Carson City will vote in favor of the constitution, even though doing so would help to bring a federal mint and consequent prosperity to the region.

[23.] (January, 1864) Twain reports on [R. G.] Marsh's troupe of traveling juvenile actors; then on a friend who jammed his leg into a post hole, could not get it loose until some coyotes came by and scared him, and then pulled his limb out and brought the hole up too; and finally about the first meetings of the House of Representatives.

[24.] (January, 1864) Twain tells about Miss [Hannah K.] Clapp's Carson City school, with its systematic classes in spelling, poetry recitation, and composition.

[25.] (January, 1864) Twain and the Unreliable report on legislative proceedings—offering resolutions, the doings of clerks, and certain general orders concerning notaries.

[26.] (January, 1864) Twain boasts about giving his first speech. It seems that he agreed to deliver his address as governor of the Third House [for a church benefit] and conferred wisdom generously, except that people in the rear could not hear him. He hopes to receive a $200 watch for a prize, and plans to print his speech in 300,000 copies and several languages.

[27.] (February, 1864) Twain praises the beauty of Theodore Winters' expensive but suitably furnished new home in Washoe Valley; extols the unique skill of [William B.] Lawlor, who is such a brilliant schoolteacher that he could teach anyone except certain nearby prosecuting attorneys; and excoriates the local mercenary undertaker, who makes a thousand dollars a week on other people's desolation.

[28.] (February, 1864) Here are reports on a variety of topics: an attempt by a telegraph company to corner the Nevada market, the sleepiness of representatives voting "aye," their rising to take exception, Twain's pet bills coming in and going out, laws on fishing, the difficulty of rhyming Bigler with any other word, an attempted holdup in a Carson City street, and the irresponsibility of some representatives whose bills are up for vote.

[29.] (February, 1864) Twain violently attacks the editor of the Carson City Independent for criticizing his abuse of the local money-mad undertaker. He then says that the rival journalist may verify the account by doing a little professional investigating for a change and concludes that the undertaker surely has his death-seeking eye on the Independent. Twain also criticizes the rival's response to his Empire City massacre hoax.

[30.] (February, 1864) Twain details a number of shady legis-lative deals—voting money to relieve [Sheriff] D. J. Gasherie, building a private seminary at public expense, legislators voting for measures which will profit them personally, etc.—none of which, he says, could ever take place if the capital were in Virginia City under the vigilant eye of a free press, which Carson City lacks.

[31.] (February, 1864) Twain reports in detail five legislative sessions, during most of which the members discussed moving the capital to Virginia City. Exact votes are recorded, and procedures for summoning absent members and listening to their excuses and fining them are given. On the last day, it was voted to present [William H.] Clagett, a wild-haired member, with a comb, which he can give to an uglier person, if he can find one. At midnight the house adjourned, whereupon some men repaired to the governor's residence for drinks and then went on to serenade the speaker.

[32.] [April, 1864] Twain presents brief comments on the condi-tion of the fine road between Virginia City and Carson City, where he now is; on a couple of local murderers; on acting governor [Orion] Clemens's troubles in getting office space; on festivals planned by ladies' groups, to benefit a church fund and a fair; and on the exorbitant rates the local telegraph monopoly is charging.

[33.] (May, 1864) Twain tells how the citizens of Virginia City raised $13,000 in a few hours for the St. Louis sanitary fair, by auctioning a sack of flour repeatedly.

[35.] (May, 1864) Clemens demands that James Laird, editor of the Virginia City *Union*, which has published insults against him, print a retraction or give him satisfaction. Clemens regards Laird as the proper party to demand these alternatives of, since his newspaper has stated that its proprietors are solely responsible for all comments therein and he has the most seniority among the proprietors. Laird turns the challenge over to the author of the insulting lines, one J. W. Wilmington, a former Union army officer. Wilmington writes Clemens that he penned the comments and has nothing to retract. Clemens writes Laird again, says that Wilmington has nothing to do with the affair, and demands satisfaction peremptorily. Laird replies that *Union* proprietors are responsible for editorials, but as for communications the proprietors merely stand ready to provide names of authors. He declines to meet Clemens but adds that if Clemens declines to meet Wilmington then Clemens is a puppy, liar, and poltroon. Clemens accuses Laird of trying to shield his carcass behind an outsider, repeats his charges and challenge, and threatens to post Laird as a coward. Meanwhile, Clemen's friend S. E. Gillis writes Wilmington to mind his own business or call upon Gillis. Wilmington privately replies that he seeks no quarrel. Laird writes Clemens briefly to recapitulate and state his plan to stay out. Clemens closes the matter with a final letter branding Laird an unmitigated lair and an abject coward. [Twain then published the entire correspondence in the *Enterprise* on May 24, 1864.]

[36.] (May, 1864) The author remarks that according to rumor some of the money collected at a fancy ball held in Carson City for the benefit of the sanitary fund was diverted to aid a miscegenation [a freedman's relief] fund. The author refuses to quarrel with any ladies concerned with the ball and offers an apology for any impoliteness.

[34, 39, 40, and 41 are personal letters by Twain. 37, 38, and 42 are not by Twain.]

[Rufus E. Arick, Alexander W. Baldwin, Cornelius M. Brosnan, K. B. Brown, W. H. Brumfield, Samuel A. Chapin, William H. Clagett, Hannah K. Clapp, Hal Clayton, Orion

Clemens, Abraham V. Z. Curry, Mrs. W. K. Cutler, Rollin
M. Daggett, E. C. Dixson, Thomas Fitch, William M.
Gillespie, Stephen E. Gillis, Joseph T. Goodman, Peter
Hopkins, J. Neely Johnson, James L. Laird, Marcus D.
Larrowe, John K. Lovejoy, Miles N. Mitchell, Gordon N.
Mott, John L. Musser, John W. North, James W. Nye,
John Van Buren Perry, Clement T. Rice, James W. Small,
James Stark, L. O. Sterns, William M. Stewart, James H.
Sturtevant, John K. Trumbo, Warren Wasson, Theodore
Winters, William Wright, Samuel Youngs.]**

*Edited by Henry Nash Smith (Berkley and Los Angeles: University of
California Press, 1957).

**For further details concerning these forty main characters, see "Bio-
graphical Directory," by Smith, ed., *Mark Twain of the Enterprise*, pp. 225-231.
Smith's admittedly somewhat incomplete "Index" names most of the other
two hundred or more additional persons whom Twain mentions in his *Enterprise* articles, all of whom are omitted in my sequence of characters above.
Following Smith, I do, however, include the above forty in my sequence. I
hereby praise and thank Smith and his associate Frederick Anderson for
their painstaking editorial work in *Mark Twain of the Enterprise*.

"Mark Twain on Foster," 1873 (LAIFI).

Twain writes the editor of the *Tribune* to object to petitions to
commute the death sentence of the convicted murderer William Foster. The arguments of the man's lawyers are nothing: they would
plead for Judas, who to Twain's mind was little more than a premature congressman. The attitude of the jury means little, because
our jury system is a joke and most jurors are intellectual vacuums.
But how can Foster's friends rationally depict the man as sweet and
temperate, when he committed murder with a car-hook? If it takes
twelve people on a jury to convict in the first degree, it should take
twelve more to vote for commutation. Why put it all on the
governor?

[William] Foster, the Judge.

"Mark Twain on Juvenile Pugilists." See "Train Up a Child and
Away He Goes."

"Mark Twain on Notaries." See "Concerning Notaries."

"Mark Twain on the Ballad Infliction," 1865 (MTWY).

A year ago everyone was singing "Johnny Came Marching Home." Then we were tortured with "You'll Not Forget Me, Mother," and "When We Were Marching through Georgia." Soon San Francisco must endure "Wearing of the Green," which, especially when accompanied by wretched accordions, will drive us to misery and perhaps suicide.

Wheatleigh.

"Mark Twain on the Mental Photograph Album." See "Mental Photographs."

"Mark Twain on the New Wild Cat Religion," 1866 (MTWY).

Still another spiritualism investigator, a fellow named G. C. De Merritt, has been shipped of to the asylum. But why should people be upset with spiritualism? In Twain's youth, Methodist and Campbellite camp meetings caused a good bit of insanity, and no one complained. Why blame this new wildcat religion called spiritualism? Yet his old Presbyterian upbringing compels Twain to suggest that we stick to safe old religions. No Presbyterians go insane over religion. The old faiths are safer than wildcat ones.

G. C. DeMerritt, Friend of Progress.

"Mark Twain on the Signal Corps." See "The Signal Corps."

"Mark Twain on the Spiritual Insanity." See "Spiritual Insanity."

'Mark Twain on the Weather.' See 'The Weather' (WMT 28).

"'Mark Twain' Overpowered," 1865 (SS).

Twain is so affected by a sentimental news item which recently appeared in the *Enterprise* that he offers a similar one and calls it "Uncle Lige." The narrator strolls into the suburbs and encounters a tear-starting sight. A little girl and a blind old man are seated on a bank—an old faro bank. Her left hand (the one with warts) is resting on his right shoulder (the left one is missing). She is gazing

at Indian graves on Lone Mountain. He is listening to some nearby
carriages. She introduces blind-drunk Uncle Lige. He raises his
gin-blossomy face, belches, and spits on his shirt. She says that he
tells her wonderful stories. Two tears start in his eyes but, noting the
cheeky terrain below, retreat again. He praises our flag and belches
again. The narrator bursts into tears and departs.

Addie, Dan, Uncle Henry, Uncle Lige, Robert.

"Mark Twain's Amusing Sequels to Several Anecdotes." See "About
Magnanimous-Incident Literature."

Mark Twain's (Burlesque) Autobiography and First Romance. See "A Burlesque Biography."

"Mark Twain's Cats," 1904.*
    Twain explains that his undistinguished cats died early, probably
because their names were too heavy. They were Sour Mash, Apollin-
aris, Zoroaster, and Blatherskite, and were so named to give the
children practice in pronouncing big words.

    *In M. H. Carter, *Cat Stories Retold* (New York: Century, 1904).

"Mark Twain's Description of the Azore Islands." From *The Innocents
Abroad.*

"Mark Twain's Duel." See "How I Escaped Being Killed in a Duel."

'Mark Twain's Explanation.' See 'Unconscious Plagiarism.'

'"Mark Twain's" Farewell,' 1866 (MTWY).
    Leaving San Francisco for travel which may take him around the
world, Twain bids farewell to his friends and fellow citizens. He
expresses his gratitude for California kindness and cordiality, commends the Western press for being composed of good fellows, expresses fear that his home—to which he is now returning—will be
terribly changed, and ends with a prophecy. San Francisco—and
California in general—will soon become a luxurious crossroads of

international trade and travel, and the center of immense factory and mining activity.

Fellow-Citizen, Friend.

'"Mark Twain's First Appearance,"' 1906 (WMT 28).
Twain voices his sympathy for persons who have stage fright. He remembers his first lecture, in San Francisco. He was terribly nervous. He had hired big friends with clubs to attend, laugh, and pound the floor. He also placed the Governor's wife in an upper box and got her to promise something: when he would glance up at her, she was to deliver a gubernatorial laugh. Well, in the middle of a pathetic, sentimental part of his speech, he caught her eye by mistake, she laughed, and the audience broke up. Twain concludes by thanking the present audience for its kindness toward his daughter, who just presented her first recital as a contralto.

[Clara Clemens], the Governor of California.

["Mark Twain's General Reply"], 1882.*
Twain observes that every editor is asked to judge manuscripts written by novices. He himself has been asked so often that he now wishes to issue a general reply. Literature, like all other professions and occupations, is hindered because there are too few good people working in it and too many shirkers in it. He will not pass judgment on any proffered writing: if he praises something poorly written, it might be inflicted upon the public; if he criticizes something done by a genius, the world might be robbed of another Dickens or Shakespeare. The best thing for an ambitious young writer to do is write for three years without expectation of pay, in a kind of self-imposed apprenticeship, and then see if anyone will buy his later writing. Tinners, mechanics, lawyers, doctors, and others have to undergo tedious apprenticeships. So should a young person planning to wield the pen, which after all can overthrow dynasties and change religions.

*In *Authors and Authorship,* ed. William Shepherd (New York: Putnam, 1882).

"Mark Twain's Interior Notes," 1866 (MTWY).
Twain writes about several California towns: beautiful Sacra-

mento has tilted sidewalks to offer its citizens the possibility of some stimulating exercise; pleasant Marysville's trade is being sapped by the railroads; Grass Valley is a quartz-mining locale, and its leading mines are the profitable Eureka, the Ophir Hill, and the Ione. Nevada also has good mines. Twain once went from the Valley to Nevada to deliver a letter of introduction to Hon. A. A. S—, but as a stupid practical joke a fellow named Duell pretended that he was S— and took the letter. Twain plans to get even.

After going by horseback to the Red Dog mining camp, Twain takes a stage to Meadow Lake, a beautiful spot but with too many houses, given the modest mining operations in the region. Then he is off to Virginia aboard a stage drawn by progressively uglier little horses. He sees few changes in Nevada since he was there last. Gold Hill and other mines, especially around Washoe City, are doing better. Twain was robbed one night recently—by his friends, they later said, returning his property; but the culprits looked professional enough at the time.

Twain praises San Jose for its being out of debt, its admirable Academy of Notre Dame, and its burgeoning silk industry, whose presiding genius is an unselfish man named Prevost. Next, Twain complains about the incomprehensibility of certain telegraphic dispatches—for example, the one about Gen. Wxgrclvtkrvw's opinion of General Sedgwick and Col. T. G. Perkins near Matamoras on the 24th ult.

Blaze, Abraham Curry, Duell, Hale, Norcross, the Orphan, Col. T. G. Perkins, Prevost, Honorable A. A. S—, General Sedgwick, Gen. Wxgrclvtkrvw.

"Mark Twain's Kearny Street Ghost Story" (MTWY). See "The Kearny Street Ghost Story."

Mark Twain's Letter to the California Pioneers. See "To the California Pioneers."

"Mark Twain's Love Song." See "Marienbad—A Health Factory."

"Mark Twain's Map of Paris" (CG). See "Map of Paris."

[*Mark Twain's Margins on Thackeray's "Swift"*], 1935.*

Twain dismisses Thackeray's essays on other eighteenth-century writers as dull, calls his portrait of Johnson's grudging admiration of Swift neat, and suggests that some phrenologists may have developed their opinions of Swift by examining the wrong skull. Twain doubts Thackeray's sincerity when the man writes that he would willingly have been Shakespeare's bootblack but applauds his depiction of Swift's servility before patrons. Twain admires Sir William Temple's smooth style and sympathizes with Stella. He writes at some length about the contradictions in Swift's nature and praises Thackeray's description of them. Twain finds an aptness in Swift's account of Gulliver's kissing the horse's hoof in the *Travels*. But he loathes the dean for praising Vanessa's cleanliness and moderate competency, and brands him as Abelard to her Heloise. Then Twain parodies Swift's poems to his Stellakins and rebukes his sighing for Stella after her death, as a satiated cat might grieve for an eaten mouse. Did Swift not keep her love letters because he used them for shaving paper? Twain disagrees when Thackeray calls Stella witty, saying that she was really only coarse. But Twain sympathizes with neglected Vanessa and criticizes Stella for her treatment of the woman after her death. He praises Thackeray for calling Swift's fall like that of an empire; agrees with Voltaire that Swift is Rabelaisian if less bestial; and concludes by calling Swift icy, glittering, and inhuman.

Stellakins, [William Makepeace] Thackeray.

*By Colin B. Taylor (New York: Gotham House, 1935; Folcroft, Pennsylvania: Folcroft, 1969).

"Mark Twain's New Year's Day." See "New Year's Day."

["Mark Twain's Own Account"].* See "A Visit to the Savage Club."

*In Aaron Watson, *The Savage Club* (London: Unwin, 1907).

"Mark Twain's Remarkable Gold Mines." See "Remarkable Gold Mines."

[*Mark Twain's San Francisco*], 1863, 1864, 1865, 1866.*

After minor items appearing in book form elsewhere, Twain

in 1865 includes in "Answers to Correspondents" a reply to an upset True Son of the Union by printing a New England Mechanic's
query as to why our flag is not flying from the Custom House on
the anniversary of our greatest day, the Battle of Bunker Hill. Next
Twain prints a complaint from a Sentinel Agriculturalist upon the
National Watchtower to the effect that alcoholic John Doe remained sober on Bunker Hill Day; Twain offers words of praise
for John Doe, who unselfishly and patriotically stayed sober ex-
pressly to celebrate. "Smith Brown Jones" (also "S. Browne Jones")
tells how the editors of the *Golden Era* have secured the services of
vacationing S. Browne Jones, the brilliant foreign writer. Even if
he writes only half a column a week, they will happily pay him
$2.50 each time. First off, he writes about arriving with his friend
the Hon. John C—s by steamer at San Francisco and getting mixed
up with the geography and the hack drivers. In the next installment
of this piece it is reported that Mark Twain, editor of the *Bohemian*,
wrote the confusing letter previously issued as though by Jones,
who tells the *Golden Era* editors that one Marcus Twain or Swain
called on him and overheard him talking to his friend Conness, who
introduced Jones to Pixley, an aspirant for the Senate; Twain then
persuaded Jones to write an essay on "Death, Hell, and the Grave"
for his *Bohemian*. Learning that his magazine is not what Twain
passed it off as being, Jones now intends to prosecute. The final
installment summarizes the testimony in the court case against
Twain, who is defended by Delos Freshwater. Jones testifies that
the defendant overheard his conversation with Conness and Pixley
about the *Golden Era* offer. One of its editors then testifies that
Twain once worked for him but displayed a morbid love of obituaries. Conness and Pixley testify. When Twain's friend C. H. W[ebb].
Inigo describes the defendant as a generous man and a superb
poker player, the defense attorney throws his client on the court's
mercy. In consideration of his tender years, Twain is sentenced to
only forty-eight hours in the city jail. Minor items follow, in which
Twain reports a buggy accident, a divorce action, some Addisonian
lectures, theatrical news, the impending arrival of a concert pianist
named George F. Benkert, C. H. Webb's play *Arrah-na-Pogue*, and a
girl molester named John Summerville. In "Graceful Compliment"
Twain sarcastically thanks the Internal Revenue people of California for complimenting him as a man of goods and chattels before
levying an income tax of $31 for 1864; he satirizes the penalty
feature by suggesting that he can liquidate the national debt by

waiting a hundred thousand years and then being penalized a billion dollars. Next come comments on a rival reporter named Fitz Smythe [né Albert S. Evans, of the *Alta*], Rev. O. P. Fitzgerald's *Christian Spectator*, uppity saloon "ladies," the tidy grass of the new Portsmouth Square plaza, Chief [Martin J.] Burke's lazy police force, an *Alta* editorial on Christmas (which Twain reprints as blank verse), the pleasure a reporter feels in entertaining his readers with stories of crime and misery, and the police court (which is a boring, smelly black hole).

In 1866, " 'White Man Mighty Onsartain' " tells how Aleck Badlam, in partnership with Samuel Brannan, constructs a huge swimming pool on Third Street, and then hires some Italian fishermen to bring up a shark from Mexico, harpoon him in the Bay, and exhibit him —then other sharks—to discourage Bay swimming and promote his private pool. Minor items follow and concern embezzlement at the mint, Calaveras opals and Idaho diamonds and Esmeralda agates, New Year's Day weather and festivities, Fitz Smythe's voracious horse, the recent overuse of the word *neodamode*, and James Linen's poem "I Feel I'm Growing Old" and how its untranslatable phraseology inspires imitations. "More Cemeterial Ghastliness" vilifies the mercenary nature of some undertakers. Next we have brief comments on a fine minister named Rev. Richard F. Putnam, changes in ladies' fashions, Chief Burke's theatrical police commissioners' board, Sacramento's numerous saloons, and a passenger aboard the *Ajax* who when ordered to "Bear a hand aft, there" thought the message was "The bears are after you there." Finally, Twain satirizes insurance agents who write policies on various types of accidents and then say "So long."

> Alcatraz, Aleck Badlam, George F. Benkert, Samuel Brannan, Broderick, Chief [Martin J.] Burke, Cap'n Hon. Schuyler Colfax, the Collector, Senator John Conness, John Doe, John W. Dwindle, John H. Dwinelle, Edward Everett, Fitz Smythe, Fitzgerald, Delos Freshwater, Gridley, Smith Browne Jones, James Linen, [Davis] Louderback [Jr.], Governor [Frederick F.] Low, George Marshall, Hall McCannister, McDougall, Meiggs, a New England Mechanic, Postmaster Perkins, Pixley, Prosecuting Attorney, Rev. Richard F. Putnam, Sargent, a Sentinel Agriculturalist upon the National Watchtower, John Summerville, True Son of the Union, Charles H. Webb, Samuel M. Williamson.**

*Edited by Bernard Taper (New York: McGraw-Hill, 1963). Considered here are only those items not appearing in book form elsewhere, namely, in SS, MTWY, WG, Mark Twain of the Enterprise, and Clemens of the Call. The titles of individual items which appear in this book and which I summarize here are not listed in my Chronology above but are interspersed through this alphabetized sequence of summaries for reference. Some of such items may not be by Twain.

**Only the more important characters appearing in Taper's unindexed Mark Twain's San Francisco are included here and in my sequence of characters below.

'Mark Twain's Speech on Accident Insurance.' See 'Accident Insurance.'

"Mark Twain's Steed Oahu." From Roughing It.

[Mark Twain's Travels with Mr. Brown], 1867.*
[Letter I] Jones, Smith, and Thompson say goodbye dramatically and often to various friends, while fruit hurtles through the air from dock to ship as others bid other friends farewell. The America (later called the Columbia) is off in mid-December, 1866, with Twain and his hearty friend Brown among the passengers. By nightfall a hurricane is lashing the ship, and passengers pray, cower, and vomit. A fifteen-year-old girl has eloped aboard the ship with her lover, even though her father and a policeman tried to prevent the act. When doughty Captain Wakeman (later called Waxman) learns that the couple are not married, he wants to marry them, in spite of remonstrances from some passengers that the two should be left alone.
[II] The weather grows better. Unctuous Isaac, one of the passengers, draws and sells elaborate little cards for a living. Captain Waxman, a gruff, salty man, marries the runaway couple and then lectures them in nautical terms about the benefits of getting spliced and weathering life's storms together. Brown interrupts Twain's writing to report on the incorrigible gossip Miss Slimmens, a correspondent.
[III] While waiting for the appearance of a choir which a few of the passengers have organized, Waxman tells about the uncanny knowledge of rats, which desert doomed ships. A group of rats once rigged a hammock and slung out of a doomed Indiaman in Liverpool a consumptive comrade rat.
[IV] On Christmas Day a baby dies aboard ship and is buried at

sea. Isaac falls from grace by selling what he claimed was his dead wife's jewelry. The captain tells about offering years ago to save what appeared to be a burning whaler, only to be told that the fire was harmless and that the whaling men were cooking doughnuts. Late in December the ship docks at San Juan del Sur, at the Isthmus, which the passengers cross grotesquely in wagons pulled by abused little mules toward Greytown and their waiting steamer.

[V] On the way to the northern coast, Twain pauses to admire twin volcanoes in Lake Nicaragua, then an ancient castle, and next some local monkeys and parrots and the lush vegetation. He reports some statistics on Nicaragua, the population of its towns, and its mining production, exports, tariffs, and local wages. He is happy when an insufferable bore, who has been asking the names of trees in the region, is silenced when Brown begins to lecture him tediously in proof that alligators cannot climb trees.

[VI] Under way again, aboard the *San Francisco* now, the passengers sing more hymns and wretched songs like "Dog Tray." Brown and Smith, Twain's roommates, concoct a drink of brandy and fruit juices which they christen the West-sou'-wester. A passenger who bought a little gray monkey in Greytown puts it into the bed of a sleeping woman, with startling results. Some of the men ridicule Miss Slimmens in a poem they call "Auld Lang Syne." Early in January, off the coast of Cuba and then Florida, cholera breaks out and rages aboard ship, and in five days five people die, including the lovable Episcopal minister Rev. Fackler.

[VII] Twain tells about Key West—its appearance, health officers, cigars, Negro section, roads, and Episcopal church. When the party gets to sea again, the cholera seems to be left behind and hilarity reigns once more. A passenger named Kingdom tells "The Legend of the Musket," about an overloaded Queen Anne's musket, and then "The Tale of the 'Bird of a New Specie,' " about two boys who shot some birds and put a crow's tail into a chicken hawk's rear end and annoyed the father of one of the boys. Next Twain summarizes statistics about the Gulf Stream, filches some nonsense from Brown's journal, and reports the arrival of the ship at New York.

[VIII] New York is an overgrown city with busy people and confusing streets. Its theaters are spectacular; especially notable is Niblo's gorgeous display of barely clad actresses. Ladies' walking dresses in New York are hard to describe. The Century Club is very respectable, and has a limited membership and lots of brilliant men of letters waiting to get in.

[IX] Twain commends the police of New York for size and courtesy to pretty girls crossing busy intersections. The most entertaining thing to do on Sundays, since liquor laws are so rigid, is to attend church, preferably one in which Henry Ward eloquently preaches, in which Bishop Southgate's chorus chants, or in which the surpliced boys of St. Alban's sing like ringing bugles. Twain's companion Brown disguises himself as a policeman to escort pretty ladies. Twain reports with a thrill the invention of a Californian: a revolving wheel of type which casts print in plaster with great rapidity.

[X] Twain describes his going to a Russian bath in the depths of winter and being scalded, iced, and pommeled. Then he comments on the famous feminist Anna Dickinson, whose sarcastic eloquence he admires but whose rhetorical timing is off, he says. Finally he says that New York is growing more expensive and its natives more insolent.

[XI] Twain summarizes the itinerary and other plans of a grand European pleasure voyage of prominent Brooklyn residents. He goes to apply with a *Tribune* friend, who introduces him as Rev. Mr. Twain. Next he criticizes Barnum's museum. Then he tells of a woman who prayed for children and when she got triplets thought she would do God a return favor and put some money on the coffin of a grieving and impecunious woman's husband, only to return for her misplaced gloves and find the corpse sitting up counting the greenbacks. Finally Twain describes the discomfort he felt when he attended the Academy of Music costume ball.

[XII] Twain happily goes west on a New Jersey Central train in the middle of a March snowstorm. Gradually the discomforts of the ride weigh on him, as he and Brown encounter the rudeness of the conductor, pass through sooty Pittsburgh, and lurch on amid frequent dull stops. But the luxury of a berth is a delightful compensation for inconvenience. Covering 1,100 miles in fifty-two hours, they arrive in St. Louis. Twain tells about old friends, relays anecdotes, and describes such local pastimes as sociables and stag euchre parties.

[XIII] Twain writes from St. Louis that he is home again. The city and its suburbs are bigger now, some of his friends are dead, but—more startling to him—others are mature and married and have children. The steamboat business is changing. Missouri women are agitating for the vote. Twain reports that he went to church and preached his story of the jumping frog, without a moral, to an applauding audience. St. Louis is badly governed, and its mayor and commissioners are feuding over the responsibility for burying cholera victims, potholes in the streets, and negligent policemen. Twain closes with words of praise for the local school system.

[XIV] Twain discusses speech habits of people in St. Louis and minor items about the city, then tells about the lack of prosperity in Hannibal, Missouri, and Keokuk, Iowa (both of which towns have been hurt by railroads going elsewhere), about bustling Quincy, Illinois, and about wealthy General Singleton near Quincy.

[XV] Twain comments on a rift in the Mormon ranks, with the Joe Smith faction trying to oust Brigham Young. Twain criticizes the villainous Heming House of Keokuk, with its dinginess and paucity of reading matter. He and Brown take an express train through big towns they never heard of, on their way back to New York, where C. H. Webb has announced plans to publish Twain's "Celebrated Jumping Frog" in book form. Twain will definitely sail aboard the *Quaker City* for Europe and the Holy Land, leaving New York on June 8.

[XVI] Twain praises the Society for the Prevention of Cruelty to Animals and also has a good word for the Midnight Mission's efforts to rehabilitate New York prostitutes. He expresses surprise that so few crippled Civil War veterans are visible, comments on an old humbug named Washington II, puffs his newly published book, and announces that the *Quaker City* will definitely sail on June 8.

[XVII] Twain says that he saw Jefferson Davis meekly enter New York and go out again, without attracting any notice one way or the other. Billy Fall and Harry Newton, both of California, got into an argument, shot at each other on Broad Street, and annoyed the police. Adah Isaacs Menken, the celebrated actress, is gaining notoriety by posing for photographs with the mulatto French novelist Alexandre Dumas. Nantucket has grown so neutral that one article of its military constitution requires its militia to disband in time of war. Twain voices annoyance that the actress Ristori, who chatters on stage in Italian, should attract such publicity and make so much money. Rev. Dr. Chapin is a powerful, sincere preacher, whose eloquence is as irrestible as an avalanche. Various San Francisco entertainers have recently succeeded in New York and include the San Francisco Minstrels, Tom Maguire's Japanese Jugglers, the Worrell sisters, and Miss Lotta [Crabtree]. Twain reports that he enjoyed a very pretty success lecturing at the Cooper Institute the other night.

[XVIII] Brown is upset because his wardrobe is getting tattered and yet everyone tells him to wait and buy his clothes in Paris. Twain notes that New York is quieter now that an excise law has been passed controlling late-hour drinking, but Hoboken is riotous since thirsty people cross over there from Manhattan. He likes the dignified Travellers' Club and recommends that San Francisco start a similar one. He comments on the iron bridge over Broadway and Fulton Street. Finally he describes his night in a seamy, sordid jail: he and a friend tried to stop a brawl, were arrested, and were held overnight.

[XIX] The California wine business is growing in New York. So many Americans are going to Paris this summer that when Brown finds a man in New York who says that he is not, Brown cannot believe him. New York weather is uncertain: Twain is frequently caught in sudden rains without his umbrella, but such unpredictable changes add spice to life. The New York *Herald* personal columns are fun to read: Robert asks Caroline to be sure to wear a white rose in her hair, a lady left a glove at the bust-elevator establishment, her mother begs Mary to come home please, etc. Twain doubts figures about California exports, praises certain New York hotels for adopting the European plan, and declines all invitations to lecture since he has to get ready to leave for Europe soon.

[XX] Twain describes his visit to the enormous Bible House, which has printed millions of Bibles in dozens of languages. In the same building are housed the headquarters of the American Church Missionary Society, the Evangelical Knowledge Society, and the Children's American Church Missionary Society, about each of which he has something to say.

[XXI] Twain recounts his visit to the Blind Asylum, where he observed more than a hundred blind boys and girls weaving, making brooms and baskets, knitting, learning to read, playing with puzzles, and practicing on the piano. Then he discusses the new word *fraud*, Sut Lovingood's book, and the preternaturally canny New York bootblacks—especially those crowding the pit at the Old Bowery Theatre.

[XXII] Women are impolitely treated on New York streetcars.

Men rarely give their seats even to pretty white girls and never to sinfully homely old women. C. C. Harris of Honolulu has come lobbying to New York, whose officials should be warned against cooperating with the tricky, gobbling fellow. The *Santiago de Cuba*, under the command of Captain Behm, with whom Twain traveled aboard the *San Francisco* from Greytown to New York, was beached through an error in seamanship; and the captain, whom Twain found to be conscientious and sober, is now in trouble. Twain explains that there is so terribly much violence in New York—for example, demented Bridget Durgan stands accused of murdering her employer Mrs. Corriell of Jersey—that he can hardly enjoy his breakfast unless it is accompanied by newspaper accounts of assassination, murder, suicide, and prize fights. He adds some words about the inevitability of an outbreak of cholera in New York's teeming tenements.

[XXIII] Twain criticizes the Academy of Design art show and also the ugly building in which it was housed. He argues that the editor Greeley should not have gone surety for Jeff Davis, after castigating him in the *Tribune* during the Civil War. Twain reports that a Massachusetts school teacher has been criticized for flogging a pupil; times were different when Twain was little. He offers some adverse comments on Stewart's mausoleum-like marble mansion which defaces Fifth Avenue. Finally he reports that General Sherman is not going on the *Quaker City* but that the actress Maggie Mitchell is. [She did not.]

[XXIV] Twain notes that Bierstadt's painting called "The Domes of Yosemite" is accurate as to outlines but has an unrealistically romantic atmosphere. He summarizes some of the curious apochryphal stories about Christ and also about the phoenix which he read in a spurious 1621 New Testament in New York. He then discusses local street vendors who sell puzzles, whistles, and toys on rubber strings. He also tells about a retired sailor named Captain Summers who wanted to bombard some South-Sea islanders when a missionary said that they were interrupting his sacerdotal exercises: Summers thought that the churchman meant the natives were stopping the man's grog. Finally Twain reports that Artemus Ward's body has been returned from England for burial in Maine.

[XXV] Twain complains that New York is a place of lonely crowds, unnaturally busy people, and confusing traffic and house-numbering systems. Bridget Durgan was convicted and has hinted that she will confess she is innocent but saw the murder committed. The Travellers' Club invited reporters to a dinner honoring General Sutter on June 1 but then secretly held the banquet the night before to avoid publicity. Twain satirizes the ignorance of some people about America by describing a woman who thought that San Francisco was part of Idaho. Finally he ridicules the drunkenness displayed by the Good Templars at their temperance picnic.

[XXVI] Twain goes to Harry Hill's sleazy tavern, thinking that it is a meeting place of intellectuals. He fancies that he sees such luminaries as Professor Agassiz, though he is puzzled for a while when the genius's female companion wants Twain to buy her a few drinks and take her home. The ship will leave tomorrow for the Holy Land. Some bill collectors call on Twain, and a passenger is upset when General Sherman announces that his party will not be going along. At long last, Twain concludes by summarizing his various New York activities, which have abundantly satisfied his curiosity, and then announces that the *Alta* will publish his travel letters from abroad.

Adam, Father Agapius, Professor [Louis] Agassiz, W. de Angelo, Mrs. B., Johnny B., Tommy B., Backus, Baker, [George] Bancroft, a Bank Note Reporter, [Phineas T.] Barnum, Baxter, [Moses S.] Beach, Miss Beach, Rev. Mr. Henry Ward Beecher, Captain [T. W.] Behm, Dr. Bellows, Belmayne, [Henry] Bergh, Bernard, [Albert] Bierstadt, Bilgewater, Bill, Birch, Bladder-nose Jake, Bob, Edwin Booth, June [Junius Brutus] Booth, a Bore, Elias Boudinot, W[illia]m. Brown, Gen[eral Benjamin F.]. Butler, George Butler, Cadet of Temperance, Captain, Caroline, Rev. Dr. [Edwin H.] Chapin, [King] Charles II, the Chief of Police, Chipman, Colonel, General Connor, Jay Cook, [Frederick Coombs], J[ames]. Fenimore Cooper, Peter Cooper, Dr. Corriell, Mrs. Corriell, Corriell, Lotta [Crabtree], Rev. Mr. Damon, Davenport, Jefferson Davis, Dick, Anna Dickinson, Director, Doctor, Justice Dowling, Joe Dudding, Duke, Alexandre Dumas, Captain [Charles C.] Duncan, Admiral Dupont, Bridget Durgan, Rev. Dr. Dyer, Elbridge, Elder, Emperor, Ericsson, Rev. Mr. Fackler, W[illia]m. C. Fall, Jimmy Finn, Fitzgerald, Edwin Forrest, Mrs. Edwin Forrest, Mose

Franklin, Frohling, Good Templar, Dr. Grant, Grau,
Horace Greeley, H., Professor Hagenbaum, Harold, C. C.
Harris, George [Washington] Harris, ["Benecia Boy"]
Heenan, Henry, Hercules, Harry Hill, Sallie Hinckley,
Hingston, Hosmer, an Inspector, the Secretary of the In-
terior, Isaac, Italian Knight, Japanese Juggler, Jim,
Jimmy, Joan of Arc, Joe, Johnny, Johnson, Jones, Joseph-
us, the Judge, Kendall, Orpheus C. Kerr, King, Kingdom,
Kohler, Godfrey de Langley, W[illia]m. F. Lawler, Bishop
Lee, James Lennox, Lewis, Martin Luther, Tom Maguire,
Manager, Max Maretzek, [William E.] Marshall, Mary,
Lieutenant Laury, [Ferdinand] Maximilian [Joseph],
the Mayor, Felix McClusky, McDevitt, Adah Isaacs Men-
ken, Captain Mikes, Mrs. Mills, the Minister, the Gover-
nor of Missouri, Maggie Mitchell, Geo[rge]. D. Morgan,
Professor [Samuel F. B.] Morse, Mother, the Secretary of
the Navy, Harry Newton, Dr. Norton, Governor [James W.]
Nye, R. L. Ogden, One-Eyed Bill, Mrs. O'Shaughnessy,
O'Shaughnessy, Perkins, Aggy Perry, Peterson, Phelan,
Police Commissioner, President, [Joseph] Proctor, the Pur-
sar, the Pursar, the Queen of the Fairies, Franklin S.
Rising, [Adelaide] Ristori, Robert, Saint, San Francisco
Minstrel, [William Henry] Seward, Cha[rle]s. Dawson
Shanley, "Shape," the Sheriff, General [William T.]
Sherman, Miss Sherman, General [James W.] Singleton,
Johnny Skae, Sleet, Miss Slimmens, [Joseph] Smith [III],
Smith, Smith, Frank Soulé, Bishop [Horatio] Southgate,
Bishop [T. N.] Staley, Stern, [Alexander T.] Stewart, the
Street Inspector, Stribling, Captain Summers, the Super-
intendent, the Surgeon, General [Johann A.] Sutter, Sweet
Kate, Thayer, Thompson, Jim Townsend, Dr. Tyng, Rev.
Dr. Van Dyck, Emma Francis W., Wambold, the Wander-
ing Jew, Lionel Warburton, Artemus Ward, Captain
Waxman, C[harles]. H. Webb, S. R. Weed, White, Ben
Wilson, Witherspoon, [Irene] Worrell, [Jennie] Worrell,
[Sophie] Worrell, Brigham Young, Young People.

*Being Heretofore Uncollected Sketches by Mark Twain for the San Francisco Alta
California in 1866 & 1867 . . . , ed. Franklin Walker and G. Ezra Dane (New
York: Knopf, 1940).

'Mark Twain's War Experiences,' 1877.*

Twain thanks the Ancient and Honorable Artillery Company of Massachusetts for inviting him to dine and speak [at Hartford]. He too was a soldier. Early in the Civil War, he joined a detachment of rebels under Gen. Tom Harris out of Hannibal, Missouri. Col. Ralls swore them in—to uphold the Constitution of the United States and also to fight against Yankee invaders who were trying to do the same thing. Twain's men developed no discipline. They made Ben Tupper their orderly sergeant. His ears were so big that they cast a shadow like a newspaper. The men slept in corn cribs with the rats. When Twain repeatedly tried to order Ben to shut up or do picket duty, the ignorant fellow refused. When it rained, Twain borrowed umbrellas from the local farmers for his men. Once, it was rumored that the enemy was planning to advance; so Twain and his followers appealed to Harris to assign them to a more peaceful district. When Harris threatened to hang them if they moved, they disbanded and tramped on home. Twain closes by offering a toast to his forgotten cohorts, who were first in war, first in peace, and busy in between.

Brigadier Gen[eral]. [Thomas H.] Harris, the Putnam Phalanx, Col[onel]. Ralls, Ben Tupper.

*In *Dick's Recitations and Readings, No. 6,* ed. William B. Dick (New York: Dick, 1877).

Married in Podunk on the 3rd ultimo, by the Rev. D. Willis, Mr. H. Hoe and Miss Anne Handle, all of that city, 1853 (P).

A Handle without a Hoe is useless, and vice versa. Here Hoe and Handle are joined and will smooth their life together until they are hoed under by death.

Anne Handle, H. Hoe, Rev. D. Willis.

"Marvellous 'Bloody Massacre.'" See "My Bloody Massacre."

"Mean People," 1871 (CG).

Doesticks, a friend of Twain's in New York, submits a report about Asa T. Mann, the mean captain of an unpretentious schooner.

Once, when he was sailing from Perth Amboy down to Virginia, his little son fell overboard and a sailor named Jones leaped over and rescued him. Mann clapped Jones in irons for leaving the ship without permission. Twain has a better story about a mean man. When C. got married, S., who was quite rich, sold a wedding present C. had given him and bought C. a present with the proceeds.

> C., Mrs. C., Doesticks, Jones, Captain Asa T. Mann, Mrs. Asa T. Mann, Mann, S., Mrs. S.

"A Medieval Romance," 1870 (WMT 7).

It is the year 1222. The scene is the feudal castle of Klugenstein, whose crusty lord tells his only child, a daughter dressed always like a man, named Conrad, and twenty-eight years old now, that it is time to explain the mystery. His dead father had two sons, Ulrich the Duke of Brandenburgh and Baron Klugenstein. According to the dead father's will, succession to the Duchy of Brandenburgh should pass to the son who has a son, and if neither provides one, then to the son who has a stainless daughter, with Ulrich's daughter outranking Klugenstein's. Now, Conrad is a woman, but since everyone attending her birth was hanged, no outsider knows. Ulrich has a daughter named Lady Constance. Conrad, who expresses great reluctance to cheat his cousin Constance, must now go, accompanied by an array of knights, to Brandenburgh, avoid the capital offense of sitting in the ducal chair until he is crowned duke, and get the title. After his departure, his father Klugenstein silences his complaining wife by telling her that he has dispatched devilish Count Detzin on a mission to dishonor Constance; so all should go well. Six days later, while the loyal people at the Duchy of Brandenburgh welcome handsome Conrad, Constance is weeping. It seems that she has loved villainous Detzin, who has now fled, only too well. Will she go mad? A few months pass. Conrad pleases everyone; and his old uncle, Ulrich, soon turns everything over to his control. But meanwhile Constance falls in love with Conrad, throws herself in his path, declares her love, is spurned by the groaning female Conrad, and therefore begins to hate him. More time passes. Constance and Conrad are not seen together any more. Conrad regains his health and governs well. But suddenly Constance has a baby. When he hears the news, Klugenstein is delighted and promises to reward

sneaky Detzin. Stained Constance must stand trial, which Klugenstein attends in secret glee. Conrad as the Premier must sit in
judgment over Constance. It develops that the only thing that can
save Constance is for Conrad to ascend the ducal throne, which
an uncrowned man but not an uncrowned woman can do, and pronounce this judgment: Constance will be freed if she names her
guilty lover and delivers him to execution. Conrad so ascends, sits,
and pronounces, whereupon Constance names Conrad as the father
of her child! What to do? If Conrad proves that he is a woman,
she will be executed for sitting on the ducal throne. Conrad and
Klugenstein swoon away. At this point the author interrupts the
narrative to confess that he does not know how to unwind his
plot.

> Duke Ulrich of Brandenburgh, Conrad, Lady Constance,
> Count Detzin, Baron Klugenstein, Baroness Klugenstein,
> the Lord Chief Justice.

"Meisterschaft: In Three Acts," 1888 (WMT 15).

In a footnote the author explains that his play is a valuable invention for learning languages. One may substitute French or any
other tongue for the German in it.

Margaret Stephenson is alone and laments being cooped up
with her sister Annie in a private home in a village, required by
her father to speak and hear only German. Three weeks have passed,
and she must stay here three months. Between complaints, she
recites her German lessons, from Meisterschaft primers. Annie
enters, reciting model sentences also. Seeing her sister, Annie reports that their boy friends—George Franklin for Margaret, and
William Jackson for Annie—have arrived at this very village, to
learn German. Since the young men must speak only German in
the girls' presence, they will cram Meisterschafts until day after
tomorrow and then report. As the girls leave, Mrs. Blumenthal
the landlady enters, expresses to herself some sympathy for the
poor girls' plight, and then welcomes their father. She tells
Stephenson that she learned German in order to speak with her
intended, who was German. Stephenson plans for his daughters to
keep away from their two pursuers as well as learn a foreign
language. Mrs. Blumenthal reports that they are making little
progress and suggests that she ought to pretend she is sick in bed,

since the girls insist on replying to her in English. In this way, they will be compelled to communicate with the talkative maid Gretchen, who speaks only German. Stephenson commends the idea highly.

A couple of days later, Annie and Margaret may be seen still practicing with their primers. They speak to each other in irrelevant sentences. Suddenly Gretchen announces the arrival of two frantic young men. The girls quickly leave, to make themselves more presentable. The two men have been practicing sentences from their grammars in front of the maid, who thinks that they must have a screw loose. They enter and grumble at Gretchen's volubility, practice more sentences, and when the girls return recite their memorized phrases solemnly and meaninglessly. When the foreign conversation lags, William by prearranged plan signals a change of subject by the word "umsteigen" [change trains]. Thinking the whole quartet insane, Gretchen slips into the room with a gun; but the two men bribe her into silence, and the four young people proceed to conjugate "haben."

Three weeks later we see Gretchen smartly dressed, dusting, and fondling her silver coins happily. Then she leaves, and Mrs. Blumenthal enters, remarking that Stephenson's train has just arrived. He enters. She tells him that their plan has worked perfectly. Gretchen has crammed the girls with German and even bullied them to church. As they leave, George and Margaret enter, whispering sentimental German and kissing each other. George offers her an original poem, entitled "Du bist wie eine Blume!" They leave. Annie and Will soon saunter in, and he presents the same poem—as his. The other couple returns. The four go through a little dumb-show of love-quarreling and are exchanging sweet nothings in German as Stephenson and the landlady return. They listen and then reveal themselves. The girls embrace their father enthusiastically. After a moment's hesitation, George and Will follow suit. The father forgives all, even Gretchen.

> Mrs. Blumenthal, George Franklin, Gretchen, William Jackson, Annie Stephenson, Margaret Stephenson, Stephenson.

"The Memorable Assassination," 1917 (WMT 26).

Of all large events—assassination, the ruin of a city, destruction of innumerable people by plague—the assassination of an empress is the largest. No such murder had occurred for two thousand years until the Empress of Austria was assassinated in 1898. News used to travel slowly; but now, with the advent of the telegraph, this shocking report girdled the globe almost instantly. Who was the perpetrator? A mangy Italian idler, with no morals or talent or charm. All of our minds are diseased to some extent, some for love, others for fame. In five minutes the Empress's assassin outstripped all other seekers of notoriety. Before the event, no one would have considered knowing him to be of any importance. Now it is a distinction for everyone from the highest officer under whom he might have served down to his landlady's small son. Twain witnessed the Empress's funeral from his window in the Krantz Hotel, in Vienna. It was a vivid spectacle: mourning garb, pictures of the gracious dead woman, the simple church, files of infantry, court personages, military officers, knights, the religious cortege, cavalry, soldiers, and the coffin with its glittering guard. When all was over, the pageantry crumbled like a ruined rainbow, and three ragged little girls capered in the empty square. The Empress entered Vienna in state on two occasions; once when she was a bride of seventeen, in 1854, and again today. For ordinary people, she was serene, like an Alpine height.

> [Elizabeth] the Empress of Austria, the Captain, the Colonel, the Commander, the General, Hungarian Guard, Johnny, Knight of Malta, the Landlady, [Luigi Lucceni], of Austria, the Sergeant.

"A Memorable Midnight Experience," 1874 (WMT 29).

Late one night the narrator is rushed out of his bedroom by a friend who takes him in a cab through mysterious London streets to a great black edifice. They enter, and Wright meets them with a lantern, to show them around Westminster Abbey. They walk past many tombs and effigies. Wright tells them about Sebert the Saxon, Thomas Parr, Ben Jonson and many other poets, royalty, and nobility. A kitten enters and rests on the feet of a statue of Queen Elizabeth. The narrator reads the carved name of William West, tomb shower, 1698, and ponders on the slow sweep of historic time. The clock on the Parliament House tower chimes midnight. The moon lights the windows.

William West, Wright.

"Memoranda," 1872.*

As a prefatory note to his department called "Memoranda" for the *Galaxy*, Twain explains that his columns will not be humorous exclusively and by definition. He reserves the right to discuss serious matters, for example, Homer or international law, even if the reader should not survive. But Twain will not pun.

* In *Mark Twain's Sketches* (London: Routledge, 1872).

"A Memory," 1870 (CRG).

The narrator and his austere father were always on distant terms with each other. When their neutrality was broken, suffering followed; but everything was always impartial—that is, the father did the breaking, and the boy did the suffering. For example, his father liked only one poem, and that was *Hiawatha*. One day he read part of it and then announced that in a certain warranty deed, which he took out of his pocket, there was more pure poetry than in all of the tradition of all the savages alive. The narrator volunteered to compose the poem behind the deed, which was to property given on November 10, 1856, to his half-brother Orrin Johnson by Joanna and Philip Gray, whose lives Orrin had heroically saved. The father handed the boy the document but warned him to stick to the truth and avoid fancy. The boy could not resist: he cast into *Hiawatha* meters the deed itself rather than the act of heroism which occasioned it. He entitled the poem "The Story of a Gallant Deed," and it began thus: "This indenture, made the tenth . . ." He hurried into his father's presence to recite his efforts, but soon he was dodging a bootjack hurled at him and leaving the room.

Mrs. Joanna S. E. Gray, Philip Gray, Orrin B. Johnson.

"Mental Photographs," 1869.*

To a page of questions which he recently received Twain answers that he dislikes the dun color, likes the forbidden-fruit tree, the gem known as the Jack of Diamonds, lying as an occupation, etc. He most dreads exposure, and he feels that the words "Dust unto dust" are the saddest words.

*In *Mark Twain's Sketches* (London: Routledge, 1872).

"Mental Telegraphy," 1891 (WMT 15).

The author explains in a note that he made his discovery about "mental telegraphy" sixteen or seventeen years ago, that he wrote part of the following essay in 1878 for *A Tramp Abroad* but did not incorporate it into that book, and that eight or ten years ago he sought to publish it in the *North American Review* but was refused because it dealt with "coincidences." But since then the world has grown more receptive, partly because of the work of the English Society for Psychical Research.

In 1878 the author wrote a friend, after delaying about six weeks, at precisely the same time the friend was writing him. They must have read each other's minds. Earlier, back home, just as the author was going to mail a letter complaining about some defective electrical work in his house, a technician came to make the necessary repairs. The previous summer, the author took a walk late one rainy night in Washington [D.C.], sensed that he was about to bump into his friend O—, and did so. We wrongly say "Speak of the devil" and consider such grave phenomena accidents. Two or three years earlier, the author was suddenly struck with the inspiration for a book about a Nevada silver-mine bonanza. He wrote a Nevada friend of his, with whom he had not been in touch for years, outlining his plan; but then he pigeon-holed the letter, only to receive an almost identical one from his friend seven days later. The author concludes that he read the man's mind. Have original ideas been thus stolen unconsciously by other "inventors"? There are instances of such plagiarism in literature. At one time, the author was approached in Venice by a woman who urged him to comfort a distraught American couple, worried about not hearing from their son in eight months; a day after the author suggested that they cable him—feeling certain that this procedure would bring a message from him—the couple received a letter from him. The author then details other incidents, in which members of his family correctly completed his sentences, then suggests that a good invention would be the *phrenophone*, summarizes the Darwin-Wallace "coincidence," quotes a clipping about a casual visitor to a Hartford house who was able to supply a long-sought roll of unusual wall paper for the place, and concludes with comments on waking visions—including a curious one of his own.

[Louisa May] Alcott, Brown, Will Carleton, [Mrs. Jane Lampton Clemens], Anna M. Crane, the Earl of Durham, George, [William Dean] Howells, Lambton, Lambton, Metcalf, Frank Millet, O—, William H. Wright.

"Mental Telegraphy Again," 1895 (WMT 22).

Clemens wants to add some incidents under the heading of "Mental Telegraphy," which was written seventeen years ago. While lecturing with George W[ashington]. Cable in Montreal, he was honored with an early afternoon reception in a hotel. Far back in the line he saw Mrs. R., a friend from Carson City, Nevada, whom he had not heard of for twenty years. She did not approach and shake his hand but instead disappeared. That evening she was in the lecture-hall waiting room and spoke to him. When he said that he had seen her at the reception, she denied it and reported that she had arrived from Quebec less than an hour before. Clemens next tells of writing R. S. Smythe of Australia about lecturing there, only to receive a letter on the subject from him written six weeks earlier. Next Clemens says that shortly after he was thinking at one time that it would be nice to be made an honorary member of the Lotos Club in New York, he received a letter on the very subject. Finally, he reports that immediately after telling his friend Joseph H. Twichell about an incident in Milan—Lieutenant H. lost his letter of credit and borrowed money from a stranger whose daughter Clemens met the next day—Clemens saw the daughter again at a school in which one of Twichell's daughters was a fellow pupil. Are these events only coincidences?

> George W[ashington]. Cable, [Samuel Langhorne] Clemens, Mrs. Clemens, John Elderskin, Archibald Forbes, Lieutenant H., Miss Porter, Mrs. R., R. S. Smythe, Henry M. Stanley, Joseph H. Twichell, Miss Twichell, John Brisben Walker, [Charles Dudley] Warner, F. G. Whitmore.

"Microscopic Meanness." See FW, 1869.

["Milliners"] (MTP).

Milliners never keep their word. The first fig-leaf apron was delayed five days after delivery date, but the first skinsuits were on time. Since Eve was responsible for the apron (Adam handled the suits), it was also her fault that the thing did not fit, that trimmings, lining, hooks and eyes, gathers, and pullstring were all awry. Present-day milliners are true daughters of Eve.

> Adam, Eve.

"The £1,000,000 Bank-Note," 1893 (WMT 23).

The narrator, Henry Adams, explains that he is twenty-seven years old, a San Francisco mining-broker's clerk, and a stock expert, alone in the world but armed with wit and a clean reputation. One Saturday afternoon he sails in the Bay too far, nightfall overtakes him at sea, and he might have drowned but for a passing brig bound for London. He has to work his passage across without pay, and when he arrives he is ragged, shabby, and broke. About ten o'clock one morning he sees a partly eaten pear in the gutter and is stooping for it when a gentleman at a nearby window orders him into the house. He is confused by two eccentric brothers—A and B—who have made a bet as to whether an honest, intelligent, and impoverished stranger in London could survive there with nothing but a million-pound note. After they interview Adams but without telling him any of these details, they thrust an envelope upon him with the extremely unusual bank certificate, force him out of the house, and then disappear themselves. Adams is in the cold again before he looks inside the envelope, and then what he first sees he thinks is simply some paper money. So he goes to a cheap eating house, examines the monstrous bank note, observes the obsequiousness of Harris the proprietor, and with dramatic carelessness asks for change. Unable to provide it, Harris begs him to eat his fill now and pay later. Adams returns to the mansion where he was given the envelope, to demand an explanation; but the servants tell him that the rich brothers will not be back for a full month. Only then does Adams read the letter which accompanies the money, and it tells him that the two men have made a bet and that if the writer of the letter wins, Adams may have any position within the benefactor's power to grant.

Adams ponders his situation. If he goes to a bank for change and tells the truth, he will land in an asylum; if he lies, he will be arrested. If he loses or destroys the million-pound note, its owners will simply stop payment. Still pondering, he walks past a tailor shop, enters to ask for some cast-off togs, is treated rather shabbily by an employee, and has a sudden inspiration. He flashes his big bill. The employee's liquid smile turns to frozen lava. The owner bustles up, quickly bows and scrapes, and begs Adams to try on some princely raiments which fortuitously happen to be in the establishment at this very time. Payment may be deferred indefinitely, even eternally. Within a week Adams is sumptuously equipped at a luxurious hotel, continues for old times' sake to eat with Harris (who presses loans of money on him), and soon finds himself written up regularly in the newspapers as the vest-pocket million-pounder. If he does not have fame, he certainly has notoriety, especially when *Punch* caricatures him dickering with a beefeater to purchase the Tower of London.

After ten days of this, Adams quietly pays his respects to the American ambassador, who turns out to have been a friend of Adams's father at Yale and who invites him to a fancy dinner that evening. Adams feels that he is in too deep to disburden himself to the official; so he accepts, reasoning that all may be well if out of the salary for his future job with the eccentric brother he is able to repay his various debts. At any rate, the party is lovely. Fourteen persons are there, including some nobility and a beautiful English girl of twenty-two, named Portia Langham, who is visiting the daughter of the ambassador and his wife, and with whom Adams falls instantly in love. And she with him, as he can easily tell. Another guest is Lloyd Hastings, a friend from San Francisco. Lloyd is in trouble, having come to London to sell Gould and Curry Extension stock but failing utterly to do so thus far. Dinner is marred by some silly arguments over precedence but is livened by lovely Portia, who exchanges words of love with Adams. He explains in full the circumstances of his getting the million-pound note, at which she laughs wildly. Later he and Lloyd walk to Adam's luxurious rooms, have a drink, and talk about the Gould and Curry stock. If Lloyd allows his option to run out at the end of the month, he will be ruined. Adams suggests that they spread the word that he approves of the investment, at which innumerable British investors will swarm into the market and Lloyd will be saved. He and Adams can share the profits.

And so it happens. Meanwhile, Adams and Portia spend all their time together at the ambassador's place, talking about love and Adams's financial prospects with the eccentric brother. At the end of his month, Adams has a million dollars to his credit in a London bank and decides to tease Portia by asking her to accompany him for moral support when he returns to the eccentric brothers. He calls upon them and evidently startles them with his gorgeous fiancee Portia. He produces the million-pound note intact. The winning brother shouts in glee and collars the £20,000 bet. Adams then gloats by showing his deposit certificate for £200,000, amassed by his harmless thirty days' use of the note. Portia is now surprised and wonders why he has been fibbing to her about their

possibly penurious future. One brother then asks whether Adams
wants a situation provided for him, but he declines with thanks.
Then Portia upbraids him for not thanking the brothers properly
and to remedy the defect promptly sits on the lap of one and plants
a big kiss on his mouth. Then the two gentlemen roar with enjoyment. The kissed one is Portia's dear step-father; the other,
her Uncle Abel. At this, Adams demands a situation after all, that
of son-in-law. Granted. And he and Portia live happily ever after in
London, with the cancelled million-pound note framed as a memorable wedding present.

Abel, Adam, Henry Adams, Adams, Lady Anne-Grace-
Eleanor-Celeste-and-so-forth-and-so-forth-de-Bohun,
Lady Blatherskite, Lord Blatherskite, Brother B. Viscount
Cheapside, His Serene Highness the Hospodor of Hali-
fax, Harris, Lloyd Hastings, Blake Hopkins, Portia Lang-
ham, the Countess of Newgate, the Earl of Newgate, the
Duchess of Shoreditch, the Duke of Shoreditch, Tod.

The Miner's Lament (P). See [A Forty-niner].

"Miseries of Washoe Men," 1866 (WG).
Do not fancy that if you owe money at the Russ House you can
register with impunity at the Occidental. Hardenburgh, formerly employed at the former, is now at the latter. A fellow who used to work
at the Brooklyn is now employed at the What Cheer. And so on. The
whole town is spoiled.
Amiraux, Childs, Hardenburgh, Olmstead, Smith.

"Misplaced Confidence," 1870.*
As the Sunday-school superintendent walks to church one late
winter Sabbath, he notices that the City of Hartford has cut through
the ice and is at the pier. He feels a pang, because he knows that
his little pupils will all be playing hookey. But there they are, in
church. Gratefully, he starts to thank them for preferring Sunday
school to a close view of the ship. They spring up and vanish. It was
he who broke the news to them!

*In Mark Twain's Sketches (London: Routledge, 1872).

Miss Slimmens, 1867 (P).

Trim Miss Slimmens wears a broken-down dress and has a malicious tongue. She accuses the ladies of being partial toward Jeff, gives Truman and Brown a hard time, battles White and Thayer, devastates Smith, makes Lewis promise to buy the newspaper she writes for, and insults charming Baker. Take a hint, Miss Slimmens, and be silent.

> Baker, Brown, Jeff, Lewis, Miss Slimmens, Smith, Thayer, Truman, White.

'Missouri University Speech,' 1902 (S).

Upon returning to his boyhood home in Hannibal, Twain explains, he was emotionally strained. Seeing old faces which were young fifty years ago is profoundly moving. Now he wishes to refute the oft-printed charge that he stole fruit when he was a boy. He did take a watermelon once from a farmer who was not looking, but he discovered that it was green and returned it for an apology and a better specimen.

> [Gardiner Lathrop].

["Mrs. Jollopson's 'Gam'"]. See LSI.

"Mrs. McWilliams and the Lightning," 1880 (WMT 15).

Mortimer McWilliams is explaining to Mr. Twain how afraid of lightning some women are. One night his wife Evangeline, who was hiding in a closet, woke him up and upbraided him for sleeping while a storm raged. Between flashes and concussions from outside, she told him not to strike a match, not to stand near the chimney or the window or a wall, and not to open the door or turn on the water. She wanted him to hide in the closet with her, but it was too small. So she read precautions from a German authority on lightning and made Mortimer put on his metal fireman's hat, saber, and spurs, stand on a chair, and ring a bell. At this point, some neighbors looked in through the window and reported that there was no storm, that a cannon was flashing and booming in celebration of news that [James A.] Garfield had been nominated. McWilliams then gets off the train and leaves Twain.

> Evangeline McWilliams, Mortimer McWilliams, McWilliams, [Mark] Twain.

"Mrs. Mark Twain's Shoe," 1871 (authorship uncertain).*
   Mr. and Mrs. Twain are arguing about her wanting to learn to skate. He says that skating is a pastime only for pretty, trim young ladies who like to skim over the ice and flirt. When she tries to interrupt, he remarks that she is fat, awkward, and waddles like an overstuffed buzzard. Twain then confesses that he recently tried skating, fell and cracked the ice, and was fined for damaging the owner's pond. Twain next hints that his wife would not wish to skate and thus expose her feet if she knew what the cobbler said about her shoe when Twain took it to him to be mended. Mrs. Twain demands to hear the insult; so Twain says that the cobbler took one look at the shoe and burst into tears because it reminded him of his sainted grandmother's coffin.

   The Irish Giant, Mark Twain, Mrs. Mark Twain.

   *In The Dime Dialogues, No. 10 (New York: Beadle, 1871)

'Mistaken Identity,' 1881 (WMT 28).
   Twain begins his address to members of a Boston club by re-marking that years ago he was in a position identical to the one he is in right now. He had to change railroad cars at Salamanca, New York, one evening while traveling east. He joined a confused, dusty, and softly profane crowd rushing toward a sleeper, and could not be accommodated. He muttered to his companion that the authorities obviously did not know who he was. Suddenly a Negro porter spied Twain, whispered to the conductor, and the celebrated passenger was given the red-carpet treatment. Twain tipped the porter lavishly and beamingly asked him who he thought Twain was. "Jenuel McClellan" was the answer. Twain's companion asked what he had to say now. Twain was speechless then—and now.

   "Jenuel" [George B.] McClellan, Tom.

"Mr. Beecher and the Clergy," 1869 (WIM).
   The Ministerial Union of Elmira, New York, has voted to discon-tinue cooperating with Rev. T. K. Beecher in his immensely popular Sunday sermons at the Opera House. No matter, now, that he re-vivified the Union. Let him be directly responsible to God without having the advantage of the Union's mediation.

Rev. T[homas]. K. Beecher, Alderman Jones, Jones, S'cat,
Smith.

"Mr. Bloke's Item," 1865 (WMT 7).

John William Bloke, the esteemed friend of the author, who is
a sub-editor in Virginia City, walks into the newspaper office
one evening with a distressing news item, all written out. Bloke
places it on a desk, mutters something about a friend of his and
how sad it all is, bursts into tears, and leaves. The sub-editor
stops the presses and sends the item off to the head editor, who
quickly storms in. Only then does the sub-editor read the item. It
starts to tell about William Schuyler but gets off the subject in mid-
sentence, mentions Schuyler's wife's mother's death, and hints at the
dangers of drink. The sub-editor re-reads the item several times but
can make no sense out of it.

John William Bloke, William Schuyler, Mrs. William Schuyler.

["Mr. Justice Field"]. See W 1868.

["Mock Marriage"], 1972 (FM).

The Four Hundred devises an ingenious scheme to raise $2,000
for the Decayed Ladies' Retreat, one of its favorite charities. Four
hundred tickets are sold at $50 apiece for a ball, supper, and multi-
ple mock-marriage entertainment. The cost of the affair will be
$18,000, and hence the profit will come to the desired $2,000. All
unmarried ticket holders will arrive masked and in costumes, and
they will draw lots. Thirteen male and thirteen female winners will
draw again, the males drawing letters A through M, the females,
N through Z. In a mock ceremony, A will then be wed to N, B to O,
C to P, etc. Then the new couples will waltz and then unmask;
and everyone present, especially the onlookers, will have fun.
At the proper time, a clergyman advances to gay music and con-
ducts the ceremonies, complete with rings. Suddenly a voice shouts
out that all the marriages are real. The newly and irrevocably
married persons scatter and flee in panic, without unmasking.

We are concerned with only one such separated couple. They
are Schuyler van Bleecker and his new, beautiful wife Edith Depuyster-Breevort. They really love each other, but they did not

recognize each other when masked. Edith's parents are talking late the night of the party, about which they know nothing in detail. They agree that Schuyler is of good family, of the right Dutch Reformed religion, and of impeccable character. The trouble is, his annual income is only a quarter of a million. With a sigh, they agree to support the couple. But at this moment in bursts Edith with the shocking news that she is married to a masked partner in what she erroneously thought was only a mock ceremony. Her stoical parents agree that, given her character, she will indeed regard herself as indissolubly wed, though of course she will never associate with the masked stranger. Then in comes Minna, Colonel Depuyster-Brevoort's maiden sister. Lighting a cigar and helping herself to her brother's drink, Minna tells the ineffective old fellow to stop passively regarding this event as a seeming calamity which may be good luck in disguise. Instead, they must act. She advises their secretly advertising for the absent masked groom, having a look at his photograph, and taking the matter from there. They should meet fate halfway. Tacitly the parents approve of Minna's scheme.

Meanwhile, young Schuyler van Bleecker is rushing back to mama. He reports that he not only did not see his lovely Edith, of whom the mother thoroughly approves, at the ball but is now resolved for his own reasons never to marry. He may explain later, but not now. Hoping that she and Colonel Depuyster-Breevort may work on Schuyler to change his mind again, Mrs. Van Bleecker leaves the room. Alone, Schuyler starts thinking practically about his plight. A sudden flash! He decides to advertise. Perhaps masked E, his fatal partner for life, may prove endurable. He begins to write, at precisely the moment Minna is doing so in the Depuyster-Brevoort household. Mental telegraphy accomplishes the rest.

A, B, Schuyler van Bleecker, Mrs. Van Bleecker, C, D, Colonel Derrick Depuyster-Brevoort, Edith Depuyster-Brevoort, Mrs. Louise Depuyster-Brevoort, Minna Depuyster-Brevoort, E, F, G, H, I, J, K, L, M, N, O, P, Q, R, S, T, U, V, W, X, Y, Z.

"Moguldom." See FW, 1870.

["A Month of Mourning"]. See LSI.

"A Monument to Adam," 1912 (WMT 24).

Some person has revealed to the *Tribune* that the author once suggested to the Rev. Mrs. Thomas K. Beecher of Elmira, New York, that a monument to Adam should be erected. The plan started as a joke but nearly came to fruition. It all began thirty long years ago, just after Darwin had initiated the process of Adam's degradation. But then two Elmira bankers saw the commercial advantages of the monument, proposed an indestructible statue to advertise Elmira, and began to collect money. The author even framed a humorous petition to Congress and got the support of General Joseph R. Hawley of the House of Representatives, but he backed out on the grounds that Congress might take it all seriously.

Rev. Mr. Thomas K. Beecher, General Joseph R. Hawley.

"A Monument to Adam Petition." See "A Monument to Adam."

"Moral and Intellectual Man" (MTP).

Man is the only witness to the assertion that man has morals. Thoughtless people believe that man is superior to animals because man says so. Proof that mankind is fiendish is contained in such evidence as the Westminster Catechism. Man is above the animals only in intellect. With his mind he can invent things which enable him to outdo animals in speed, strength, and vision. But in morals man is a pauper compared to the meanest beast.

"The Moral Phenomenon," 1866 (SS).

Twain writes the publishers of the *Californian* to suggest that they should hire him as editor if they wish to improve the moral tone of their newspaper. He was a missionary in Hawaii and so impressed the natives with the dizzy altitude of his morality that they called him the Moral Phenomenon. The *Californian* has printed too many sentimental, witty, humorous, and elevating tales. What it needs is Twain's direct moral line.

The Moral Phenomenon, Serious Family.

'Morals and Memory.' 1906 (WMT 28).

Twain is happy to address the young ladies of Barnard College and to be their affectionate brother. He is aware that everyone has morals. He would rather teach morals than practice them. One's memory is like a certain California bird which picks up and hoards useless items, but passes by items which would be helpful to it. The following illustrative memories probably have morals in them somewhere. Late in her life Twain visited his failing mother, who fancied that he was still a boy in school. When to humor her he said that he stood first in the class, her old fire returned and she snapped at him that she would like to know what the other boys were like. When Twain was young he stole a watermelon, broke it open, discovered that it was green, and returned it indignantly to the farmer, who was properly apologetic. When Twain was seventeen, he took a peach of a sixteen-year-old girl to the theater, secretly removed his terribly tight boots during the show, could not put them back on again later, and was embarrassed to have to carry them home before a laughing crowd. Twain closes with the hope that the morals imbedded in these little memories will help the Barnard girls, who have given him a better time today that he had with that peach fifty-three years ago.

[Jane Lampton Clemens].

'The Morals Lecture,' 1895-1896.*

Twain has decided to lecture on morals, starting with illustrations and following with general principles. You should treasure the crimes you commit, because they teach you unforgettable lessons. The more crimes you commit of the total of 462 possible ones, therefore, the more nearly perfect your moral edifice will become. Twain suggests that his procedure is a kind of moral vaccination. When he was a boy, he stole a watermelon, broke it open at his convenience, found it to be green, began to reform, made restitution of the farmer's property, and demanded a ripe watermelon of the man. Here is another thought: whatever you do, do it with all your might. Jim Baker of California could translate into English the sophisticated talk of the bluejay, which is smarter and more articulate than the cat and also likes scandal the way human beings do. Philosophical Simon Wheeler of California argued that almost every human event could inculcate a moral lesson. Twain then tells Wheeler's story about Jim Smiley and his jumping frog. Speaking of Adam and the apple, Twain observes that since what is forbidden is desirable the serpent should have been forbidden. Then

Twain tells of playing hookey one day and planning to sleep that night in his father's office, which he discovered contained the corpse of a man. Next Twain tells how Tom Sawyer informed Huck Finn and the middle-aged slave Jim that crusades are great to keep people from feeling the effects of passing time. Finally, Twain says that he has been sick for weeks and feels too shaky to stand here and talk much longer, so he will close by telling about the minister who sang the praises of a tiny baby at christening time and said that he might grow up and be a Napoleon or a Caesar, then asked what name to use. Mary Ann was the answer.

Jim Baker, Huck Finn, Jim, Mary Ann, Tom Sawyer, Jim Smiley, Simon Wheeler.

*In Fred W. Lorch, *The Trouble Begins at Eight: Mark Twain's Lecture Tour*, 1968.

"More Cemeterial Ghastliness." See MTSF.

"More Distinction." See "To Raise Poultry."

"More Spiritual Investigations," 1866 (WG).

Twain investigates spiritualism once again, this time with two old gentlemen and a middle-aged couple. They set a heavy table in the middle of a room, place their hands on it, and watch it tilt. As it does so, the pointer on a dial which is on the table and which is fitted with letters spells out messages. Twain has no idea what causes the table to move. Messages are from a dead man named Thomas Tilson, who says that he reads Mark Twain's *Territorial Enterprise* essays through a living affinity named Mac Crellish; from William Thompson, who says that he knows Twain now but never did on earth; from one of the irrepressible Smiths, who humorously tells the group to sit right there until he returns with some whiskey; and finally from Wentworth, who spells out a graceful essay on losing friends.

Mac Crellish, Smith, William Thompson, Thomas Tilson, Wentworth.

'Municipal Corruption.' 1901 (WMT 28).

Twain says that the Bishop [Potter] has just commented on the lust for gain as the force behind corruption. Twain adds that forty-nine people out of fifty are honest but that the dishonest minority is organized. When he was a boy he and his friends had an organization which elected officers. Unfortunately, votes were purchased, with doughnuts. So Twain organized an Anti-Doughnut party, put up candidates, and lost. This taught him the strategy of threatening to defeat poor candidates of either party, which forced both parties to nominate good people. We need an active Anti-Doughnut party now. It is called the Mugwump party today but is not active. Twain refused to cast his vote for Bryan, because he was weak on finances, or for McKinley, because he was wrong on the Philippines. Twain's vote is still unused but clean.

[William Jennings] Bryan, [William] McKinley, Bishop [Potter].

'Municipal Government,' 1900 (WMT 28).

Twain says he is grateful that Bishop Potter of the Diocese of New York and Dr. Mackay of the St. Nicholas Society have commended him for his contributions to theology. He is back in New York after an absence of nine years. The place looks better. The skyscrapers might impress foreigners by daylight as ugly like old teeth or tombstones, but at night they are enchanting. Our elevators are better than European ones. New York has a fine system of street railways, clean and well-lighted streets, and excellent laws, manners, ideals, customs, and government. It is such a well-regulated city that the very angels are envious.

Dr. Mackay, Bishop Potter.

["Murphy"] (CG). See "The Widow's Protest."

["Music Box"] (MTP).*

Since every tourist who goes to Geneva buys a music box, Twain ascertains that Samuel Troll has the best music-box establishment in town and reports there. The salesman assumes that Twain is not really interested, and little progress is made at first. After humming in accompaniment to various little boxes, the salesman shows Twain a music box the size of a trunk. Its music is a celestial combination of flutes and violins. Twain orders one; and when it arrives, back in America, Twain eagerly cranks it up. Its music is as discordant as a shivaree. Twain cannot keep it around, because its noise might kill a guest. It would be extravagant to store it. If left in the cellar, it might go off and injure the house. Twain still has it. He would exchange it for an elephant, or have it challenge an elephant to a duel.

Samuel Troll.

*A rejected chapter from *A Tramp Abroad.*

"My Bloody Massacre," 1870 (WMT 7).

The author tries a satire on stock manipulation which backfires through the habit of readers of taking the wrong things seriously. Since various San Francisco newspapers have made an outcry about the practice by a silver-mining company of declaring a false dividend to inflate stock prices, the author publishes an account of how a certain citizen murdered his wife and nine children, and then committed suicide, through melancholy brought on by his buying falsely inflated mining stock and thus losing every cent he had. In his newspaper account, the author stresses impossibly gory and otherwise untrue details, and buries his exposé of the mining company in a note at the end. Then at breakfast he watches a couple of innocent, rustic-looking miners, who sit down to eat but whose bug-eyed reading about the multiple murders causes them to lose their appetite. They never get to the point of the satire. The author's moral is that we rarely read the dull explanatory parts surrounding fabulous accounts we are not suspicious of.

Dan, Jim.

"My Boyhood Dreams," 1900 (WMT 23).

Mark Twain says that his boyhood dreams have not been realized. Disappointment is the automatic result for anyone whose early dreams do not come true. Regardless of the dream, if it fails then the dreamer is sad. Long ago, back in 1830, the author met with some friends in Boston, and under the seal of confidence they revealed their boyhood dreams to each other. Howells had wanted to be an auctioneer; Hays, a steamboat mate; Aldrich, a horse doctor;

Brander Matthews, a cowboy; Stockton, a barkeeper; Cable, a circus ring-master; and Uncle Remus, a buccaneer. All were disappointed. Twain then salutes these old friends in a [Rubaiyat-like] poem, not only lamenting the loss of youth, the misery of thoughts about what might have been, and the coming of sicknesses, but also expressing gratitude that death follows all. In a note, the Editor explains that the men whose supposed dreams are here revealed have denied everything, even the alleged Boston meeting. Twain counters by saying that his friends write well but lack his ability to handle the truth.

[Thomas Bailey] Aldrich, [George Washington] Cable, Editor, [James T.] Fields, [John] Hay, [William Dean] Howells, Ralph Keeler, Brander Matthews, Boyle O'Reilly, [James R.] Osgood, [Frank] Stockton, Uncle Remus.

"My Début as a Literary Person," 1899 (WMT 23).

In his early days the author published only his "Jumping Frog" story but had more sizable ambitions; so he was gratified when his article on the clipper ship the *Hornet* appeared in a New York magazine in December, 1866, signed "Mark Twain." He was now a literary person. The *Hornet* burned on May 3, 1866, at 112° 10' W. long., 2° N. lat. Of the thirty-one men on board, fifteen made it to Honolulu after forty three days in an open boat, across four thousand miles of water, on ten days' rations of food, under the command of resolute Captain Josiah Mitchell. The author, then on the islands writing for the Sacramento *Union*, was sick but was aided in gathering material for his report by Anson Burlingame, then on his way to China. The report was mailed to San Francisco, was telegraphed to New York, and earned the author $300.

Captain Mitchell's *Hornet*, bound from New York to San Francisco, is carrying two passengers. From Stamford, Connecticut, they are Samuel Ferguson, aged twenty-eight, whose lung trouble is to be fatally aggravated by the shipwreck and consequent exposure, and his brother Henry, aged eighteen. On May 3, a sailor goes into the booby-hatch with an open light and causes a fire. Of three lifeboats launched, two become damaged. The men have little time to load provisions. The laconic captain keeps a diary. So do the Ferguson brothers, of whom Samuel keeps the fuller one. Next day the men, hovering near the doomed ship hoping to be res-

cued, see her suddenly sink. They decide not to go east to the Gala-
pagos or northeast to Mexico, but slightly west of north to Hawaii.
They suffer from drenching rains, very little food—eked out by
occasional catches of fish—blazing heat, loss of sleep, weird
snatches of broken dreams, an evidently thieving "Portyghee" sailor, the doldrums, and the like. On May 19 the captain reluctantly
decides to stop towing one of the two damaged quarter-boats. Three
days later they must cast off the remaining boat. (Neither of them
is heard of again.) Most of the men are steady in their prayers. They
are soon reduced to a diet of crumbs and mouthfuls of water. Some
of the men begin to criticize the captain, and others speak tentatively of eating the first available corpse. The last five days they
have absolutely no food. So they gnaw ham bones, leather straps,
and chips from the butter cask. Finally they see their first rainbow,
and next day land! They are soon rescued and fed. They have survived only because of the character and intelligence of Captain
Mitchell. The diaries quoted are eloquent beyond any art.

B—, Anson Burlingame, Cash, Charley, Cox, Henry Fer-
guson, Samuel Ferguson, Joe, Jones, Captain Josiah [A.]
Mitchell, Miss Mitchell, Peter, the Portyghee, Mark
Twain.

My Dog Burns, 1884 (P).
    No longer will my beautiful dog scamper through storms. She
lives quietly in Hartford. Dear because dead, she was trusty like a
good author.

"My Famous 'Bloody Massacre' " (CG) See "My Bloody Massacre."

"My First Interview with Artemus Ward." See "First Interview
    with Artemus Ward."

"My First Lie, and How I Got Out of It," 1899 (WMT 23).
    The author cannot remember his first lie but does his second: he
was nine days old and cried, pretending that a pin was sticking
him. We all tell lies, but the lie of silent assertion is the worst.
America silently lied to excuse slavery. The French did, during

the Dreyfus affair. And Chamberlain did, to manufacture war in South Africa. Why worry about trifling personal lies in the face of such monstrous national ones? The English will not tell spoken lies but commit the other kind. The author once argued with an old British friend on the subject. He rebuked the author for saying that he was of the same family (the human family) as the Prince of Wales, just to get out of trouble; yet the Britisher then acted a lie by pretending to know a stranger and also boasted that he once lied to prevent a dead person's family from learning that the man was no good. The author rebukes Bryant, for his bravado lie that truth crushed to earth rises, and then Carlyle, for his ecstatic lie that lies shall not live. He also criticizes George Washington for following his true confession about the cherry tree with the lie that he could not tell a lie. Anyway, the mere spoken lie is nothing compared to that of silent assertion. Oh, the author remembers getting spanked for that second lie.

G—.

"My First Literary Venture," 1871 (WMT 7).

The author recalls that when he was thirteen years old and precocious, he was a printer's devil on his uncle's newspaper, the *Weekly Hannibal Journal*. When the man left town for a week, he put the boy in charge. The boy decided to rival local journalism by illustrating the abortive suicide attempt of Higgins, who was a jilted rival newspaperman, and by satirizing and lampooning a neighboring editor, and two local citizens and a ladies' man poet-tailor named Runnels. The various victims dropped in to maim or kill the perpetrator but took pity on his age. When he returned, the boy's uncle was annoyed until he looked at the list of new subscribers.

Fahnestock, Higgins, Mary, Sir John Moore, J. Gordon Runnels.

My Last Thought, 1966 (P).

I always intended to serve my country well. Some think that my heart has changed. It has, though not to turn hard. Now it bleeds, for widows, orphans, the ruin of freedom, broken faith, fraudulently seized lands. May God forgive me for being a weak atom in that seat which only men like Lincoln fill well. I only meant to serve my country. I freed the Pearl of the Antilles and was myself in doing so. But soon thereafter evil advisers assailed me, and I sought to become a world power. Then I committed the treason of selling out a nation. Our flag, once colored like snow and flame, is now blood-red and black, and with skull and bones instead of stars. Death comes. Let it, and let me sleep. Let flowers blooming out of my grave offer this message to people who might seek me: you can learn nothing here; forgive and forget him.

"My Late Senatorial Secretaryship," 1868 (WMT 7).

Mark Twain is the private secretary of General James W. N—, U.S. Senator. One morning Twain is ordered to appear before his boss, who is in a rage at certain letters sent out to persons asking favors. He told Twain to persuade people at Baldwin's Ranch that there was little need for the post office they wanted. So Twain wrote them that they could not read and would also steal money from mail passing through out there. To people in Nevada wanting to incorporate the Methodist Episcopal Church, Senator N— told Twain to write that, given the weakness of religion out that way, the church was probably not essential. So Twain wrote to tell them that they were feeble in intellect, morality, and piety. N— ordered a non-committal letter sent to aldermen of San Francisco wanting Congress to establish city rights to water lots; so Twain wrote them about certain selected nursery rhymes. People from Humboldt wanted N— to help run a post route in a certain way; but when he asked Twain to be both deft and dubious in handling such a delicate question, the idiot wrote incomprehensibly. Failing to justify his letters, Twain is told to get out forever and ever. The secretary takes the hint and resigns.

> Biter-of-the-Clouds, Dilapidated-Vengeance, Rev. Mr. John Halifax, Jones, Senator (General) James W. N—, Perkins, Smith, Mark Twain, Wagner.

"My Massacre." See "My Bloody Massacre."

"My Military Campaign." See "The Private History of a Campaign That Failed."

[My Name It Was "Old Chris"], 1870 (probably by Twain) (P).
Ab O'Riginee writes about Old Chris, who tells of sailing in quest of the New World and of his subsequent mistreatment at the hands of the cruel King of Spain. (In FW, 1870.)

Old Chris, Ab O'Riginee, King of Spain.

"My Platonic Sweetheart," 1912 (WMT 27).
In his dream, the author is seventeen years old and she is fifteen. They are in a Missouri village, walking past the blacksmith's lonely shop in a Sabbath stillness. He gives her a kiss, and she welcomes it. He is George, and she is Alice. They enter a log house with food steaming on the table. They go on to a cemetery. He awakens and finds himself in real life in Philadelphia, and nineteen years old. Ten years later, he is seventeen again in his dream, and she is still fifteen. They are in twilit Natchez, in a magnolia forest. She is darker now and is called Helen. His name is Jack. She removes her summer hat so that he can kiss her more easily. He carries her across a stream. Her words make dream sense but are virtually inexplicable in waking life. He carries her to her plantation house. A Negro servant enters. It grows dark. Moonlight floods the place. He is suddenly crossing a frozen lake, alone. He awakens in a San Francisco newspaper office and is twenty-nine. He has two fleeting dreams of her in 1865 and 1866. Then in New York, in January, 1867, he dreams of failing as a lecturer, and then she approaches and calls him Robert. She is Agnes. Suddenly they are in a valley in Hawaii speaking words which cannot be easily translated. A man-of-war-bird lights on her shoulder, turns into a kitten, then a tarantula, and finally a star-fish. She lifts a stone which flies away as a bat. A white-headed old native comes by with a curious gun which shoots arrows. He fires one high into the air, and when it finally falls it hits and kills the girl. The author awakens and is actually in New York crossing Bond Street with a friend. He goes to his quarters and experiences another lightning-swift dream: he is in Athens with Agnes, who is still fifteen but now in a Greek costume. Every detail of the house

they are in is etched in the consciousness of the author, who concludes that dreams are true, their occupants immortal, their details sharp and real. A week ago, in India, going on sixty-three years of age, the author saw his sweetheart again. She is still fifteen; he, only seventeen.

Alice, George, Socrates.

My Ranch, 1865 (P).

I have an extensive ranch, with turnips, oats, a few stones and clods, and a lovable sow. It's all mine. (In "Real Estate Versus Imaginary Possessions, Poetically Considered: My Ranch" [SS].)

"My Return to Virginia City." See RL.

"My Trip on the Henry Chauncey." See RL.

"My Watch: An Instructive Little Tale," 1870 (WMT 7).

The author explains that his beautiful new watch ran perfectly for eighteen months; then he accidentally let it run down, had to set it by guess, and stopped next day at a jeweler's to set it exactly. It was four minutes slow. The jeweler took it out of his hands and insisted upon adjusting its regulator. Thereafter it ran furiously fast. The author took it to a watchmaker, who insisted upon cleaning and oiling it. Then it ran slow. Another watchmaker looked at and reduced its barrel. Then it wheezed. Another repairman replaced its king-bolt; another called the hair-trigger bad; still another found fault with the crystal and mainspring. Finally a former steamboat engineer said it made too much steam. The author's uncle William used to say that a horse was good until it once ran away and a watch worked until repairmen looked at it.

William.

"The Mysterious Chamber" (MTP).

Out of rust from a treasure-chest bolt, Carlo de Piacenza makes some ink and starts his diary, on October 4, 1742. He is is twenty-five years old, is from an illustrious family in southern Italy, was used to idle luxuries, was highly accomplished, killed Count Rinalducci in a duel, and was quite a ladies' man. Now this is how his story goes. He wooes Maria Odescalchi, who prefers him to young de Rimini. The happy couple walks in the woods and comes close to the Haunted Castle, when Maria refuses to proceed. The place curses those who venture too near. But Carlo urges her onward; so, removing her engagement ring, lest spirits enchant it, she advances with him but soon drops her ring down a deep hole. They retreat, but later Carlo is discussing with an old servant the possibility of retrieving the ring when he learns that Maria's father, the Count Odescalchi, would rather let her enter the Mysterious Chamber than venture near the Haunted Castle. His curiosity stirred, Carlo asks Maria about the Mysterious Chamber. She turns sober and explains that her grandfather sealed the room fifty-five years ago, wasted away, died, and left some kind of family parchment which is supposed to specify a date when the room may be reopened. (Four days later, Carlo continues his diary.) Maria and Carlo are to be married on May 30. Shortly before that date, he goes hawking, his horse takes fright, and the young man is obliged to return to the Odescalchi castle on foot. He enters by the postern to avoid being teased for being thrown, goes privately to his room, tries on his wedding costume, and walks out arrayed like a peacock through remote corridors for his private pre-nuptial delectation. He passes a cobwebby door to what he concludes is the Mysterious Chamber. (October 9, Carlo writes more.) He notices a spider anchoring a web to a bolt head which, when the man chances to examine it, seems quite different from the thousand others all about it. He presses it, and the door groans ajar. Who could resist? Checking the corridor to make sure that he is unobserved, Carlo enters the colossal, windowless vault of ponderous stone. [Extensive notes follow, telling of Carlo's imprisonment, his managing to learn household news by listening at a kitchen drain, his survival by eating slops culled from a subterranean river, his learning of Maria's bereavement but subsequent marriage, and finally his rescue when the Mysterious Chamber is officially opened—twenty years later.]

Maria Odescalchi, Count Odescalchi, Count Odescalchi, Carlo de Piacenza, de Rimini.

The Mysterious Chinaman, 1947 (P).

I hear a gentle rapping, tapping at my chamber door, which I mistake for that of Maim or perhaps Fannie. But then in walks sad-faced Ah Chang from the kitchen. When I tell him to leave my door, he says, "No shabby 'door.'"

Ah Chang, Fannie, Maim.

"Mysterious Newspaper Man," 1866 (WG).

Colonel Conway has appointed newspaperman Brian McAllister to be his secretary. It is well to have a journalist on the expedition. But a word of caution is necessary. The group will be cramped as it travels. Will the dried salmon hold out? If the trip were over water, an extra ship—. But do you understand?

Colonel Conway, Brian McAllister.

The Mysterious Stranger, 1916 (WMT 27—inaccurate version). See *The Chronicle of Young Satan*, "Schoolhouse Hill," and *No. 44, the Mysterious Stranger*.

"A Mysterious Visit," 1870 (WMT 7).

The author has hardly settled into his new role of dignified houseowner when a stranger, introducing himself enigmatically as a U.S. Internal Revenue Department assessor, comes to pay a pleasant social call. Since the fellow seems reluctant to discuss his own affairs, the author decides to boast in order to charm his guest into doing the same. So the author talks and talks, and the assessor laughs and laughs. The author asserts that he earned $14,750 by lecturing last winter and spring, got $4,000 as four-months' income from the *Daily Warwhoop*, and almost $200,000 in recent royalties from his book, *The Innocents Abroad*. As the visitor departs, he leaves an envelope containing what he calls an advertisement about his business. It proves to be a wicked tax-return form, full of detailed, impertinent questions. The author figures that he must pay $10,650 income tax. But then he goes to a friend of his, an opulent man of enviable reputation, who smoothly explains tax deductions, losses, payments, and other things, and says that he uses such devices to avoid being beggared to support our tyrannical

government. The author is soon able to figure his income tax at
$250. And why not? The most respected men in America do it this
way.

Marie.

"A Mystery Cleared Up," 1869 (LAIFI).
The Associated Press reports that Ex-Secretary Stanton had an
interview with Secretary Fish and probably discussed the Alabama
question. But the author says that he was present and can report
that they really talked about methods of removing warts.

> The Attorney General, Brown, Secretary [of State Hamil-
> ton] Fish, the Secretary of the Interior, Jones, the Presi-
> dent, Smith, Ex-Secretary [of War Edwin M.] Stanton.

"A Nabob's Visit to New York." From *Roughing It*.

Napoleon after Hagenau, 1870 (probably by Twain) (P).
The chap has learned that Rhine water is not to his taste and
that sauerkraut is bad for a Nap.

> Nap[oleon], Hi Slocum.

"Nasr-ed-Din, The Shah of Persia." See "O'Shah."

"Nevada Nabobs in New York." From *Roughing It*.

"Nevada Sketches." See "Advice to the Unreliable on Church-
   Going," "City Marshal Perry," "In Carson City," "Ye Sentimental Law Student," "A Sunday in Carson," and "The Unreliable."

"A New Beecher Church," 1871.*
If an ordinary minister were to build a new church, we could
trust that it would be ordinary. But the Rev. Thomas K. Beecher
is planning such an unusual, eccentric, and individual church that
it must be referred to as a new Beecher church. Twain explains that
a known humorist is so seldom trusted that he must make a solemn

oath that what he is about to reveal is strictly true. This new Beecher church will really be three buildings. The main building will contain a lofty circular auditorium with graduated tiers enough to seat a thousand people. The second building will be attached to the first, and will have Sunday-school rooms and a playroom. The third building, also attached to the main one, will have parlors for social gatherings, a free circulating library, bathrooms for indigent members of the congregation, second-story rooms for live-in employees and also an infirmary, and a third-story kitchen. Beecher's idea is to weld his parishioners into a family. He mailed confidential requests for pledges of money to his church members and quickly raised the required $50,000. All materials to be used will be sound; and the hope is that the workers, hired by the day at full pay, will be honest. Elmira is buzzing with talk about the new church.

Rev. Thomas K. Beecher, Beecher, Beecher.

*In *Mark Twain's Sketches* (London: Routledge, 1872).

New Cock Robin, 1872 (P).

Who is to be the new editor of the *Tribune*? Schuyler Colfax, whose pen slaughters like an axe, wants the job. So does Georgius William Curtis, though his pen inert is. Whitelaw Reid fights against Tweed and all of his breed and might succeed. Speaker Blaine, who has slain Democratic foes and would raise Cain with the Locofocos, wants the assignment. But so does Mark Twain, since the office would be his castle in Spain.

Speaker [James G.] Blaine, Schuyler Colfax, Georgius William Curtis, Whitelaw Reid, George Francis Train, [William M.] Tweed.

"A New Crime," 1870 (WMT 7).

In the last thirty or forty years, the United States has produced some remarkable cases of insanity. A quarrelsome Ohioan named Baldwin shot to death a man who had two days earlier knocked him down for insulting a crippled person; Baldwin was acquitted as temporarily insane, killed two other people later, and got off again through influence and money. A Pennsylvanian named Lynch Hackett attacked Bemis Feldner, who so pommeled him with his fists that Hackett two weeks later stabbed him to death, only to be acquitted as insane. In New Jersey recently, a servant named Bridget Durgin stabbed her mistress to death, dismembered and burned her body, carried the dead woman's baby to the house of some neighbors, and afterwards confessed everything; there was no motive—neither revenge nor robbery—so, in spite of the fact that she ought to have pleaded insanity, she was hanged. A lad in Pennsylvania shot at the cheek of a pretty girl to disfigure her and thus keep her from getting married, but he aimed badly and killed her; the idiot was hanged. Insanity is on the increase, and crime is dying out. If a murderer either before or after the crime seems ill at ease, he is adjudged temporarily insane and acquitted. What we need is a law against insanity.

Baldwin, Baldwin, Bridget Durgin, Bemis Feldner, Mrs. Bemis Feldner, Lynch Hackett, Mrs. Lynch Hackett.

"The New Dictionary-Word" (MTP).

A new dictionary is advertised as uniquely keeping abreast of the changing times. For example, it has the new word *Depew-Binder* in it. This word means a legal document binding a person to pay another, and then when he does not, nothing happens; in short, a binder that does not bind.

A, D, E, Student.

'A New German Word,' 1899 (S).

Twain explains to his Austrian audience that his collection of long German words is still incomplete. If, however, he could have put on his tombstone a word like *Personaleinkommensteuerschätzungskommissionsmitgliedsreisekostenrechnungsergänzungsrevisionsfund* he would sleep in peace.

"New Ideas on Farming," 1902.*

First Twain says that he would like to retire to a quiet farm, then adds that he likes cows except when they refuse to let people decide which side they will sit on while milking them, then praises

sheep (even black sheep), and next calls horses the noblest of all.
When he was a boy, Twain wrote a composition explaining that you
cannot farm well and keep your clothes clean, that early birds ought
to prefer cherries to worms, and that hired men have no right to
complain about the quality of the cooking of farmers' wives.

    Stephen.

*In *Masterpieces of Wit and Humor*, ed. Robert J. Burdette (n.p., 1902).

"The New Planet," 1909 (WMT 29).

    The author quotes a notice that perturbations in the orbit of the
planet Neptune have led Harvard astronomers to wonder whether
there is a planet beyond Neptune. Then he reminds us that Neptune
itself was discovered in the summer of 1846 because it caused
perturbations in the orbital movement of Uranus. During that very
summer the author began perturbating when farmers used dogs in
their watermelon patches, for there is nothing—not even a planet—
like a dog to make one perturbate. When September, 1846, rolled
around, the author stopped perturbating—because Neptune was
discovered. Recently he has been perturbating again, up here on his
Connecticut farm. Since you cannot raise watermelons on his farm
even with a derrick, the author's present perturbation must be due
to the existence of a planet beyond Neptune. The author hopes
that it will be named after him, especially if he cannot have a con-
stellation.

"A New Specimen." See "The Tale of the 'Bird of a New Specie.' "

"A New Theory of Gravitation." See FW, 1869.

"The New Wildcat Religion" (WG). See "Mark Twain on the New
    Wild Cat Religion."

"New Year's Day," 1866 (WG).

    Twain pays social calls on New Year's Day. It is fun to drop
in on your friends. But it is awkward when Smith appears and
drags you off to meet his friends. Twain takes wine at one house,
fruit at another, and finally corrals some breakfast. Many ladies

are vividly dressed—as Faith and Charity, Cleopatra and Hebe, and so on. They give kisses, either the kind you can bite or the kind you can merely taste. In strange homes, you grow tired, especially when people you do not know pile in and start to reminisce with each other. If you explode a joke, you are apt to have a creepy feeling, as though you were caught whistling at a funeral. The best tables are set not by fancy hostesses but by their maids in the basement. The Biddies in town all ransack their employers' brandy closets.

Beecher, Biddy, Bridget, Brown, Charity, Faith, Hope, Jones, Murphy, Smith.

"A New Year's Story." See FW, 1870.

'The New York Press Club Dinner,' 1900 (S).
Twain is always tempted to shoot chairmen who introduce him with compliments. Now here is Colonel Brown, tonight's chairman, who has done the same thing; so Twain will claim the privilege of complimenting him in return. Brown is very old. His features show a man apparently dead to honor and bear traces of all known crimes. Yet he has actually spent much time in Sunday-school and now spends all of his time there. His private character is virtuous, but his appearance belies the fact. He practices his virtues secretly

Colonel [William L.] Brown.

"Newhouse's Jew Story," 1972 (FM).
Twain explains that George Newhouse, an ancient pilot aboard the *Alonzo Child* in 1860, rebuked a passenger one day for making a scurrilous comment on Jews. Then Newhouse explained that he reveres all Jews because of a certain event. Back in 1845 a cruel gambler named Jackson was defeating at cards a rich old Louisiana planter named Mason. Jackson had won his victim's ready money and two of his slaves, and was about to win the lovely mulatto servant of his daughter. The crowd of timid onlookers gathered closer. When Jackson won that prize too, Miss Mason burst into the gaming hall, wept, and pleaded, but to no avail. Not knowing that it was Jackson's habit to goad his victims into challenging

him so that he could choose the weapons—bowie knives—and stab them to death, Mason was about to challenge the insulting desperado when a young Jewish fellow, who knew all about Jackson and who had been watching, anticipated Mason's rash move by reaching over and slapping Jackson. The gambler sneered and challenged him, whereupon the Jew named pistols as the weapons this time, went ashore, and killed Jackson. Newhouse concluded his story to Twain with great satisfaction.

Jackson, Mason, Miss Mason, George Newhouse.

"Niagara," 1869 (WMT 7).

The author finds Niagara enjoyable for its splendid hotels and reasonable prices. And the fishing is not equaled elsewhere: it is uniformly bad for five miles along the river. One can descend a staircase a hundred and fifty feet down, to the water's edge. But why do so? The guide tells how *Maid of the Mist*, the little steamer, lived through the fearful rapids at one time. Then you can drive over the Suspension Bridge, stand for photographers, and pose like an insignificant worm before nature's majesty. The author gets into waterproofs and walks under the precipice below the river's level and past the American cataract, and visits an Indian group by the bridge to Luna Island. He addresses one as Speckled Thunder, who, however, identifies himself as Dennis Hooligan and threatens to destroy him. The author then calls a maiden Laughing Tadpole, but she says she is Biddy Malone. He makes a final attempt at conversation but is mobbed, beaten, and thrown over the Falls into the eddy, from which a policeman finally plucks him.

> Beneficent Polecat, Bub, Bully Boy with a Glass eye, Devourer of Mountains, Gobbler-of-the-Lightnings, Hole in the Day, Dennis Hooligan, Johnny, Biddy Malone, the Pride of the Forest, Red Jacket, Roaring Thundergust, Sis, Whoopdedoodledo.

"Nicodemus Dodge—Printer." From *A Tramp Abroad*.

["No Poets at Pittsfield"] (MTP).

To prove that Pittsfield cannot produce a poet, Twain went over the area with a surveyor and a mining engineer. The following requisite formations were lacking: gneiss, hornblende, etc.; further, the following items absent where poets grow were there: Silurian conglomerates, etc. Yet, the same year this study was undertaken, Pittsfield ground bore a native poet. It all goes to show that science fails occasionally.

"The Noble Red Man," 1870 (CG).

In books, the Indian is tall, handsome, magnificently garbed, eagle-eyed, poetic, true, and devoted to women. In reality, he is scrawny, ugly, filthy, untruthful, cowardly, treacherous, and lazy compared to his women. Humanitarians are wrong to weep at his extermination.

> The Noble Aborigine, the Noble Red Man, the Noble Son of the Forest, the Noble Son of the Plains, the Son of the Forest.

"A Notable Conundrum" 1864 (SS). (See also "Concerning the Answer to That Conundrum" and "Still Further Concerning That Conundrum.")

Twain says that the Fair continues and is a compliment to its planners whether they make any profit or not. Lovers meet there. Twain picked up a soap salesman's business card on which Arabella had written a note to her boy friend, who must have been confused as to whether to meet her at the beach or the soap factory, since both were mentioned. The art gallery at the Fair is nice. A woman from Arkansas described one portrait there as sad and thinkful. Weller's bust at the Fair was smashed, and one fellow said that it was Weller when a bust but the reverse when busted. Twain likes the game called Muggins. You shout "Muggins!" when a person makes a mistake of any kind. Twain shouted it when a policeman arrested him as he was crawling into his own window, but the policeman merely shouted back. Oh, the conundrum? How is Napoleon in the Alps like cheese at the Fair? Unfortunately, the inventor of the riddle did not give Twain the answer.

> Arabella, the Author, John Smith.

["Note on Mark Twain"] (SS). Part of "Wicked Mark Twain," which see.

"The Notorious Jumping Frog." See "The Celebrated Jumping Frog of Calaveras County."

"Novel Entertainment." See RL.

"A Novel: Who Was He?", 1967 (SB).
The author will now keep his promise and write a novelette. Gillifat is a man. Two men are talking. The *Enfant*, a croupier, lies at anchor. Storms rise under certain atmospheric conditions, even when Columbus sailed. Well, in a burning house we see the agonized face of beautiful Demaschette. Did you know that the round human eye protrudes from but cannot fall out of its socket? Suddenly, with all of this action converging, Victor Hugo emerges reading from one of his books. The climaxes do not come. Things scatter. V is Victor still! (At this point, the author, his brain reeling, quits and surrenders his contract. He made the mistake of reading the first part of *The Toilers of the Sea*.)

Demaschette, Gillifat, Victor Hugo.

No. 44, the Mysterious Stranger, 1969 (MSM).
In 1490 Eseldorf, Austria, is sleepy. Father Adolf warns Frau Gretel Marx, chases Frau Adler away, discomfits the Devil, and lies to the Bishop about Father Peter, who therefore is about to be evicted—with his niece Gretchen—by Solomon Isaacs.

The narrator is August Feldner, a sixteen-year-old apprentice to Heinrich Stein, about fifty-five, a printer living and working in a corner of the mouldy old Rosenfeld castle which hangs over the river. With Stein are his lean, devilish wife, the former widow Maria Vogel, whose vicious, seventeen-year-old daughter Maria Vogel is her favorite; an astrologer-magician Balthasar Hoffman, whom Frau Stein likes; seventeen-year-old Marget Regen, Stein's niece; his sister Frau Regen, the lovely girl's paralyzed mother; Katrina, sixty-year-old cook; her wenches Sara and Duffles; man-servant Jacob; and porter Fritz. Stein's printing force includes a surly bachelor named Adam Binks, sixty; Hans Katzenyammer, a drunk red-head, thirty-six; Moses Haas, twenty-eight, sometimes critical; Barty Langbein, a sunny, fifteen-year-old cripple; Ernest Wasserman, a cruel, underhanded, seventeen-year-old apprentice; and August himself.

Stein's family and his workers all live together in the castle. After supper they gather for conversational battles. One cold day after the noon meal a stranger about sixteen or seventeen appears, ragged and hungry. Frau Stein wants to toss him out; but kind, gruff Katrina and Stein prevail, and the lad is offered room and board in return for hard, menial work. When his new master queries him, he says that his name is Number 44, New Series 864, 962. Moses calls it a jail number, and the boy distresses Stein by not denying it. Forty-four begins to carry enormous logs upstairs to the fireplace. Hoping to see him injured, Frau Stein orders 44 to walk their vicious dog. The dog turns gentle and trots happily out with the lad. Frau Stein decides that Balthasar must have enchanted 44. Balthasar simpers, pretends agreement, and coyly leaves. Egged on by Moses, Ernest challenges 44 to a fight, but the lad only holds his puffing adversary's wrists until the bully surrenders.

Since 44 did not deny being a jailbird and also failed to drub Ernest, he is ridiculed by several and befriended only by Katrina. August likes 44 but is afraid to help him. When 44 does prodigious feats, such as gently ordering the dog to bow before Balthasar as though in the presence of royalty, the magician takes the credit. Forty-four is kind, reads August's mind and answers his unspoken questions, gives the boy several magically appearing glasses of mulled claret for a fancied chill, and lets him go swiftly back to bed.

In the morning, August feels fine, but he thinks that the previous evening was all a dream until 44 meets him and beams his gratitude. He explains that August cannot inform against him even if he should want to do so. After breakfast, Stein announces that he will be 44's friend, since the boy has worked faithfully, and that he will also make him a printer's apprentice. The other workers turn sullen, try to make trouble for 44 in the shop, but are unsuccessful because August telepathically briefs the strange lad on the processes he should follow. The others suspect him of being a runaway printer's apprentice. Binks sarcastically quizzes him on his alleged ability in Latin and Greek, but he passes gloriously. August is delighted, except for two facts: while masterminding 44's training, he did his own work in the shop badly and was punished; and Ernest—though earlier promising to keep matters confidential—reveals that August and 44 are friends. So August hides, spends a cold, hungry, and wretched night, and in the morning gets breakfast from Katrina and decides to pay the Sisters of Perpetual Adoration to pray for him. During the day, the men in the shop make life miserable for both 44 and August. Wednesday is just as bad, but 44 endures. So the men announce a strike, to be continued until 44 is fired. If Stein does not complete a certain special printing job of two hundred Bibles for the University of Prague within a couple of days, he will be ruined.

August goes to Katrina, and they decide to get the sisters to pray for Doangivadam, a handsome, learned, but unstable wandering printer, to return and save them. They also ask Balthasar to intercede, but he says that the battle is between titanic cosmic forces and that he really should not interfere. Sunday dawns, and the villagers come over to attend chapel in the castle. The organ plays, and kindly Father Peter preaches on the subject of miracles and asks for money to repair the convent. Suddenly lightning harmlessly strikes the chapel, even though the sky is clear. Is this a miracle? August hopes desperately that Doangivadam will arrive, and on Monday morning he does! He sees from the sullen attitude of the idle workers that something is amiss. August boldly starts to tell him, but 44 interrupts and efficiently explains all. The men start a fight with Donagivadam, but he disarms all but Katzenyammer and Binks, both of whom 44 gently chokes into unconsciousness. Doangivadam is trying to reason matters through to a solution when Ernest, who ducked out during the fight, reports that something monstrously odd is going on in the shop. They all rush to it and see type, paper, ink, and presses flying like lightning and rain in incredible activity, all manned by invisible, cold, ghostly workers. Chuckles are then heard, and the men gather in their beer-and-chess room to talk. They want to denounce Balthasar to the Church authorities and have him burned, but he cravenly denies everything. When Moses wonders whether the printing has been done correctly, 44 investigates and reports that the contract is saved.

Marget rushes to tell her disconsolate uncle, and the news makes Stein well again. Then the men vote to continue the strike until he agrees to pay their wages while they were waiting. He refuses. What to do about loading the finished printing job? The gentlemen will soon be here to take delivery. Doangivadam promises that all will be done. Forty-four offers to help carry, but Katrina thinks that he is in enough trouble already. All of a sudden, when Doangivadam has laboriously packed five enormous boxes, they see Katzenyammer, Binks, Moses, Gustav, and finally Ernest staggering under their weight and walking along. The contract is saved. But in the morning the five men deny ever touching the boxes. When Stein says that he has been paid and that the delivery wagon is gone, the men blame Balthasar, who, to save his hide, "confesses" that he taught 44 some little tricks which he must have used to effect the miracle. The men force the charlatan to put a spell on 44 which will cause him to crumble into ashes if he ever tries any more tricks. Katrina is terrified, and even Frau Stein and her daughter Maria act more kindly toward the strange boy.

August goes timidly to his room with 44 to pray for him, but 44 confesses that he is indifferent toward religious matters. August is shocked but then realizes in a transfixing rush of emotion that he wants to devote his life to 44. The stranger takes some spiders— odd for February—from August's neck and then says that he is in a different century, gets out a jew's-harp, plays it, and simultaneously spins through the air. August then notices that they are in 44's room. The stranger explains that he is preparing a trick which will enhance Balthasar's reputation, and further that he is master of tricks of which the so-called magician is totally ignorant. He teaches August a secret word which will render him invisible whenever he wishes, so that he will be afraid no longer.

Forty-four now presents himself to the other workers in the dainty outfit of a bejeweled gentleman. When they shout derisive insults, he seems hurt and says that Balthasar provided his costume. Katzenyammer slaps 44 and taunts the magician to do anything about it. Forty-four bows, says that Balthasar wants him to do something, and soon proceeds to create duplicates of all the workmen, who begin to fight their other selves—but to no avail. It is soon apparent that the duplicates will act as scabs and work free in the shop. The originals order Balthasar to destroy 44 as he promised. Forty-four promptly shimmers before them, suddenly flashes into fire, and crumbles to ashes.

August is sad; so he makes himself invisible and floats around the house observing. Katrina is inconsolable. The workers are timorous now, while their duplicates remain industrious. Word spreads through the village that 44 was destroyed by supernatural fire. His ashes are buried in unconsecrated ground not far from the castle; but when August returns to his room, there is 44! He explains that he really died—as he has done several times before—but is alive and well again now. He provides some tasty food for the two of them from an undiscovered place called America, terrifies August by smoking, and then explains that the duplicates are only apparent though when they begin to use their imaginations—ah! Forty-four created them to enhance Balthasar's fame. He then tells August that everyone is split into a workaday self and a dreamy, flitting self.

Days go by. Father Adolf tries without success to find Balthasar, to punish him, and does stake out all the duplicates to burn them; but they keep disappearing back to the shop. They also start making love to the local girls, to the annoyance of the originals. Meanwhile, revealing to August that he does not belong to the human race, 44 fills the boy's head with a flash, the result of which is much instruction but with it some envy. Saying that he finds humanity pitiful but amusing, 44 disappears for a week, then returns, and takes August on a flying trip to show him Johann Brinker, who thirty years earlier was a brilliant young painter until he rescued Father Adolf from freezing water but became paralyzed, deaf, dumb, and blind. In the morning 44 whisks August off to an open space behind the monastery, where feeble old Frau Brinker, who babbles insanely of her son the artist, is about to be burned at the stake as a witch. When she complains of the cold, 44 obligingly sets fire to some of the nearby fagots. A burly official tries to hit 44 to stop him, but he crushes the man's fist. Others rush up and put 44, whom they regard as Balthasar because of his costume, in a dungeon, from which he soon secretly escapes. Meanwhile, Father Adolf orders Frau Brinker burned. Blessedly, she dies fast. When he learns that "Balthasar" is captured, Father Adolf orders him to the stake; but he cannot be found. Then he appears, is chained for burning, but laughs and disappears. Forty-four has thus augmented Balthasar's fame still more.

August is suddenly back in his room, and 44 brings breakfast from faraway places not yet discovered and lectures about time, man's dismal animal nature, and the origin of material things in divine thought. Then he remarks indifferently that old Frau Brinker is in hell, gives August a billowing glimpse, and disappears. And now August feels again the love which he has long known for lovely, lithe Marget. So he floats invisibly along a corridor to watch her. She seems to sense his nearness. To make sure, he materializes, touches her arm, and begins to whisper endearments; but she rebukes him, goes on alone, and yet still seems to long for him. He rushes forward and while still immaterial kisses her passionately. Calling herself Elizabeth von Arnim, she returns his kisses and addresses him as Martin von Giesbach. They drift to her door. His duplicate appears, expresses jealousy, and is boxed on the jaw by August, who floats back invisibly to his room to sort out his thoughts. In her dreams, Marget becomes Lisbet and seeks Martin, her dream notion of the waking August. Each person has a waking self, a dream self, and also a soul, which is immortal. Next August thinks of his duplicate, his dream self made flesh by 44 and called Emil Schwarz. Through having the intensities of a dream, Emil is August's superior. Next morning after mass, August disembodies himself and follows Marget, who keeps a tryst with Emil, covers him with kisses, sleeps in his arms, but in her dream rebukes Emil and finds Martin. The two enact their marriage, but then Emil's footsteps disturb them by awakening her. When Emil apologizes, Marget kisses him. August is so upset that when Doangivadam, thinking that the lad is grieving for supposedly burned 44, suggests a drink, he agrees and soon gets tipsy and careless. He goes off to Marget's room to peep at her but forgets to make himself invisible. She, her mother, and her maid all see him. He dematerializes and flies to his room, where Stein soon comes to report that he thinks the culprit must have been August's duplicate. But when August agrees—this is a lie—Stein says that the duplicate will marry his niece this day! What can August do? He wishes that 44 would return. But instead a Negro minstrel-singer materializes before his eyes, sings "Way down upon de Swanee river" with intense and moving emotion, and then becomes 44, who suggests that the two have a feast. August is soon feeling better, until 44 offers to solve his problem by killing both Marget's maid and August's duplicate Emil. August objects; so 44 turns the maid into a cat, which enters and explains in cat language that she is genuinely delighted to be finished doing chores. Forty-four promises that the cat can stay with August and have leftovers from his mysterious meals.

After a 44-induced nap, August is refreshed and is next visited by Emil, whom he examines and pronounces fraternally handsome but who reproaches his host for letting 44 clothe him in flesh and bind him to Marget. Emil longs for freedom to wander the eternities again. August promises to plead for him. While Emil rests, the maid-turned-cat—now named Mary Florence Fortescue Baker

G. Nightingale—enters, sniffs through the room, and admits to confusion as to which is August and which is his duplicate. When August recites a poem which 44 taught him, she believes that he is his duplicate, and then takes a cat nap—in the dressing-room, for modesty. August awakens Emil, who lectures him poetically about his trips through both universe and time, and upon the entrance of 44—disguised still as the magician—pleads to be released from linkage with August. Forty-four agrees, and Emil—first clothes, then skin, then bones—melts and disappears like a soap bubble. Mary, the cat, re-enters, curtseys to 44, who she thinks is Balthasar, and asks for supper. Forty-four lectures on the use of Joseph-dreams, which are faster than telegrams, and on Mary Baker G. Eddy's puzzling June 27, 1905, request in Christian Silence dialect, printed in a Boston newspaper, that prayers for peace must cease. The cat returns to report that all hell is breaking loose in the printing shop. Forty-four is ecstatic and explains that he has stopped predicting the future for now so that he too can enjoy some surprises, like mortals. August wonders again where 44 came from but is debarred, as usual, from asking. The cat says that Katrina intends to kill 44, thinking that he is Balthasar and that he burned 44. The striking originals intend to murder their duplicates.

Forty-four rushes downstairs, with August tagging along invisibly behind, creates an eclipse, and then appears before Katrina as himself, bathed in celestial light. She kisses his feet; he pats her shoulder, kisses her gray hair, and disappears. August returns to his room to nap and eat, and the cat glides in to tell him, what he already knows, that the magician is alive and well. Then they read in a Boston newspaper for June 28, 1905, that an uncivilized fleet has scored an immense victory. Forty-four, still disguised as Balthasar, comes in and complains that those whom he has invited to his celebration—including Eve and Nero—are pleading insufficient time; so he will make time go backwards to accommodate all. This marvel will be the world's most staggering one. He and August amuse themselves by watching previous events reel off again in reverse—Katrina seeing 44, then funerals, battles, and sailing vessels with scared crews. Forty-four hopes that the miracle will gain Balthasar such a reputation that he will be burned.

The gigantic Assembly of the Dead, called by 44, begins in darkness gradually illuminated by a half dawn. He has enlarged the castle hall enormously. Biblical, regal, and ordinary sufferers file by, their bones clacking. Suddenly 44 waves his hands, and he and August stand in an empty, soundless world. Forty-four must bid his young friend farewell forever and now tells him that everything is a vision, a dream. Nothing exists, not even capricious-seeming God; and 44—only a creature of August's imagination—is perishing. He vanishes; and August, only a vagrant, useless, homeless thought, knows the truth.

Adam, Frau Adler, Father Adolf, King Arthur, Beelzebub, Bishop Belsune, Adam Binks, the Bishop, Cunnel Bludso, Johann Brinker, Frau Brinker, Fraulein Brinker, Robert Bruce, Caesar, Charlemagne, Cleopatra, Dagobert, David, Dr. DeLort, Doangivadam, Düffles, Eve, August Feldner, Gustav Fischer, 44, Fritz, Goliah, Gretchen, Moses Haas, [King] Henry I, Balthasar Hoffman, Hummel, Solomon Isaacs, Jacob, Katrina, Hans Katzenyammer, Barty Langbein, Bishop Louis, Flora Mc-Flimsey, Gretel Marx, Marx, Wilhelm Meidling, the Missing Link, Nero, Mary Florence Fortescue Baker G. Nightingale, Noah, Father Peter, Pharoah, the Prince, Marget Regen, Frau Regen, Prince Rosenfeld, Sara, Satan, Emil Schwarz, Heinrich Stein, Maria Stein, Fraulein Maria Vogel, Ernest Wasserman, Frau Wasserman.

Nursery Rhyme, 1865 (P).

Poor battered Macdougall, what can make you forget your torn clothes, bruised throat, and swollen nose? No court action, surely. You must pick your time and pommel Tom Maguire to get even.

W. J. Macdougall, Tom Maguire.

'Obituary Poetry,' 1895 (S).

Hemming and hawing, Twain tells his Philadelphia audience that he often has been wrongly accused of writing obituary verses for the *Ledger*. He does admit that years ago when he was a compositor for the *Ledger* he set up some such poetry. But he did not write it, at least not all of it.

[Ode to Stephen Dowling Bots, Dec'd] (P). In *Adventures of Huckleberry Finn*.

"The Office Bore," 1870. (WMT 7).

The office bore arrives regularly at nine o'clock in the morning, lights an office pipe, lolls about, grunts with mangy enjoyment, sighs, talks with his comrades about politics and more general subjects, interrupts the busy editor and thus robs him of his time, then droops some more. You get so that imagining his funeral ceases to soothe.

Smith.

["Official Report to the I.I.A.S."], 1962 (LAIFI).

H. J. Walker, secretary of the Indianapolis Institute of Applied Science, reports on his inquiry into the alleged discovery of the North Pole by Dr. Frederick Cook in 1909. Walker consulted Professor Hiram Bledso, an authority in comparative science and theology, who advised that if Cook claimed a miracle any proof would suffice but that if he claimed a fact more detailed proof would be necessary—for example, testimony from two Eskimo caddies for a fact, but only one for a miracle. Historically, miracles bear no resemblance to facts. The difference between the two is like the difference between a mermaid and a seal, back in Henry Hudson's time.

Dr. Asher, Professor Hiram Bledso, Henry Hudson, Janvier, H. J. Walker.

"Old Age," 1972 (FM).

People who have not arrived at the age of seventy may be interested to know that it is neither novel nor thrilling. It looks like age sixty-nine, just the way sixty-nine looked like sixty-eight, and so on. The reason for this is that growing old is like dragging across a continent behind oxen. But once you have crossed the hot equator and climbed the icy summit, you can look back down with a more devastating perspective: the temple is empty, the idols are broken, the worshippers are gone, and you see that you are the dead end of a dream so ingenious that it seemed real at the time. Gaze back across the stages of your journey and then ask yourself whether you would do it over again.

["The Old Nor'west Swell"]. See LSI.

Old Time and I, 1870 (probably by Twain) (P).
The poet Mark Lemon drinks with old Time not to riches and
hope but to friendship and rest.

Mark Lemon, Time.

"Old Times on the Mississippi." In *Life on the Mississippi.*

'The Old-Fashioned Printer,' 1886 (WMT 28).
The reminiscence by others about Gutenberg has caused Twain
to remember old times too. He worked for printers thirty-five
years ago, did their chores, delivered their papers, and got bitten
by all the dogs in town. Subscribers paid in groceries and wood.
One customer paid in cash but reserved the right to alter editorials
and write articles. Printers in the old days used to make filler out
of handy galleys of philosophical stuff nobody read. Twain remembers the horse bills on the printing-office walls, the candle
tallow in the boxes of type, and the tramping jour printer. But
perhaps what Twain is saying seems unfamiliar; so he will stop.

Junius.

"Oleomargerine" (MTP).
A widow, dying, gives Johnny some seeds obtained from a fairy.
Johnny is to plant the seeds in the spring, water them, and eat the
resulting flower. Johnny is cuffed about by neighbors that lonely
winter. In the spring he does as he was told; eats the pink, gold,
and pale blue flowers; and stumbles into the wilderness, where
suddenly a kangaroo offers comfort, chats with him, and explains
that the boy must have eaten some of the juju flowers. Other animals gather and befriend Johnny. They have a perpetual arcadian
picnic until one day the boy finds a handbill offering a reward for
anyone who can locate missing Prince Oleomargerine, who has
been kidnapped by giants. The animals offer to help Johnny
collect the reward, if the King promises to protect all witnesses.
Johnny goes to the palace, obtains the promise, and returns to his
animal friends, who escort him with great ceremony back through
the streets to the palace. Johnny introduces his menagerie of witnesses to the King: the tiger saw two giants go down a precipice
with Prince Oleomargerine, the eagle followed till dark, the owl

pursued the group to the sea, the gull watched them enter a marsh, the alligator tracked them to the desert, the snake trailed them to the plain, where the antelope took over until relieved by the reindeer, who saw them go into a cave, where the bat says he saw the Prince charmed to sleep and then guarded by two dragons.

Johnny, the King, Prince Oleomargerine.

"Olive Burnett—a Tale Told out of School." See FW, 1869.

["The Omitted Chapter of *The Prince and the Pauper*"], 1880 (LAIFI).

The whipping-boy is telling his youthful king about a painful experience which befell him last summer. Imagine a drowsy Sunday back in Bilton parish. The boy's father, Sir Humphrey, has placed his prize-winning masque costume in a closet, with herbs to protect it from bugs and rot. While the pious man is in a forest a mile away, praying the devil out of Gammer Hooker and surrounded by impressed onlookers, the boy takes out the costume for a forbidden look. The hose shine green. There are red buskins with long spurs. The robe is jeweled crimson. Included are belt, sword, and capacious helmet with plumes. The boy cannot resist donning the gorgeous apparel, after which he walks outside, sees a bull, and seizing the hell-sent opportunity leaps aboard him for a ride, which quickly takes him everywhere. At one point, the enraged bull kicks into a beehive, and the infuriated insects swarm after rider and mount. Then the bull really travels and soon tears into the woods where Sir Humphrey is exorcising the devil. When the zealot sees a scarlet rider on a maniacal animal, he thinks that his prayers have borne fruit, until he recognizes his son, whose memory of what followed is still painful.

[King Edward VI], [Princess] Elizabeth, [King Henry VIII], Gammer Hooker, Sir Humphrey [Marlow], [Humphrey Marlow].

["On Achievement"] (MTP).

What is an achievement to one person is little to another. For example, San Juan Hill was an achievement to the Soldier of One

Battle, whereas to illustrious generals it would be forgotten. Big-time generals even avoid garrulity about enormous victories, for example, Waterloo.

The Soldier of One Battle.

'On Adam,' c. 1880 (WMT 28).
Twain happily drinks in silence to the royal family or the President. Most toasts are tiresome, stale, even rancid. But one is not offered, and that is to Adam. Yet the world owes him a lot. Twain once tried to erect a monument to him, but Congress proved uncooperative. Adam gave us life and death, two most precious gifts. Adam was a good citizen, a fine husband before he was married, and a good father in spite of never having been young himself. He could have been governor, speaker of the house, anything. Twain's praise of him is not due to their being related.

Adam.

'On After-Dinner Speaking,' 1880 (WMT 28).
Twain reports that in giving this speech welcoming the Quebec poet Frechette he is breaking a weatherbeaten old vow of eleven years' standing, which is that he would never give another after-dinner speech. But he has already broken that vow in sixty-four places. It is simply impossible to resist the temptation to hear oneself speak, especially in pleasant surroundings. The trouble is that when one reads his speech in the newspaper next morning, it looks so corpse-like that it should be buried at once. Frechette was honored by the Academy of France and later given another boost when Twain translated his poems into English, making the pathetic ones funny and the funny ones sad.

[Louis Honoré] Frechette.

["On Board Steamer *Ajax*"]. See LSI.

"On Boot-Blacks," 1866 (WG).
The great numbers of boot-blacking facilities in Sacramento attest to the former prevalence of dust and mud there. The best boot-blackers are Negroes. Chinamen do not know the art.

"On California Critics," 1866 (WG).

Twain informs the distinguished actor Edwin Forrest that if he comes to San Francisco to perform, the western critics will review him adversely, telling him superciliously that he should not think western audiences are unrefined.

Bandman, Boniface, Edwin Forrest, Heron, Frank Mayo, [Adah Isaacs] Menken, Vestvali.

"On Children." See "Advice to Parents" and "Train Up a Child and Away He Goes."

"On Fashions." See "Fashions."

'On Foreign Critics,' c. 1889 (WMT 28).

Twain says that he looks harried because he is worrying about foreign critics. They refuse to concede that America has a real civilization. Sir Lepel Griffin says that he would hate to live in America or Russia. But Twain wonders what civilization really is. Surely it is any system without slavery, despotic government, inequality, a brutal penal code, superstition, ignorance, and almost universal poverty and dirt. No country was civilized more than a century ago. Liberty and intelligence started civilization, and they first became effective with the American Revolution. Then, when we got rid of slavery, we truly became civilized. Before our revolution, France, Germany, Scotland, and England, for example, had oppressive governments and miserable living conditions for the masses. It took our revolution to start modern newspapers and to encourage other peoples to rise and strike for freedom. We invented civilization.

Sir Lepel Griffin.

"On Letter Writing." See "One of Mankind's Bores."

'On Lincoln's Birthday' (WMT 28). See 'Watterson and Twain as Rebels.'

"On Linden," 1866 (SS).

Twain has a theory that as California legislators go north up the river to Sacramento, they lose their intellects. Last Saturday night, he and some friends went north on Captain Poole's *Antelope*. To amuse themselves, one recited the first line of "Hohenlinden"— "On Linden, when the sun was low." The next man had to give the next line. And so on. Any mistake would cost its reciter drinks all around. They arrived with enfeebled intellects, which proves Twain's theory.

Lieutenant Ellis, John Paul, Captain Poole, Bill Stevenson, Texas.

"On Murders," 1863 (WG).

If a man tries to kill someone in Virginia City, the judge has him arrested, advises with him, and suggests that he get out of the territory—all to no avail. If a man commits murder, he is not convicted.

Police Judge.

'On Poetry, Veracity, and Suicide,' 1909 (S).

Twain reminisces about a poet named Butter whom he knew during his reporter days. Butter once confided to him that he was going to kill himself, since he could not express himself poetically. Twain said that it was a good idea and that he hoped to write up the event for his newspaper. Butter was interrupted at the water's edge by the sight of a life preserver, which he pawned for a revolver with which he shot a tunnel straight through his head. After that, he could write poetry. Twain complains that of late he has been receiving letters urging him to tell the truth for a change. Young John D. Rockefeller may teach his Bible class about veracity, all right; but Twain, at the age of seventy, knows twice as much about veracity as Rockefeller. When George Washington told his father that he had chopped down the cherry tree, his veracity should not have been praised so much as his sagacity: the little boy, only seven years old, was already bright enough to realize that his father could tell from the size of the wood chips that only a boy's hatchet could have done the job. The trouble with the whole story is that it discourages people who have the ability to tell lies.

> Butter, John D. Rockefeller, George Washington, George Washington.

"On Postage Rates" (MTP).

Idiots in Congress write bills out of ignorance, pass them into law, and when confusion results have other governmental idiots issue "interpretations." An instance of current lunacy is the copyright law. Another is the story of book-rate postage in America. An "interpretation" in January, 1882, obliged authors sending manuscripts to leave the package open at both ends and be accompanied by proofsheets. How can the manuscript of an as-yet unprinted book be accompanied by its proofs?

> Postmaster General [Marshall] Jewell.

["On Progress, Civilization, Monarchy, etc."] (MTP).

Every government is imperfect, but changes are best when they give the common citizen advantages and take them from royalty, priests, and aristocrats. The best form of government is the one under which there are only commoners, unenslaved and worthy of respect because of their own accomplishments. We should respect people, not institutions. If Twain were king, he would laugh at his stupid subjects for respecting him rather than their own manhood. We would laugh at a dynasty of plumbers—plumbers by divine right, so to speak—because they would work badly. Is it different for czars? To be sure, a monarch's symbol of office is a scepter rather than a soldering iron. Truly, progress should be measured by the diminution of oppressors' comforts.

'On Speech-Making Reform,' c. 1884 (WMT 28).

Twain has occasionally resolved not to make any more speeches, under a money penalty. He will not break his vow often. He advises genuine impromptu speakers not to despair but to promise to quit public speeches also. The fellow who practices his supposedly impromptu effects can never be induced to reform, however, nor can the person who rehearses a one- or two-sentence response but then carries on embarrassingly for several more minutes.

General Smith.

'On Stanley and Livingstone,' 1872 (WMT 28).

Twain thanks the group in London for its kindness to him and says that what he has done for England and civilization he has performed without thought of reward. He is proud that he found Dr. Livingstone after hunting all over a hundred African parishes for him. When Twain found him at Ujiji, Livingstone had eaten his last elephant and was wearing only an old naval suit. Twain told him that Stanley would be along soon. Then he surveyed the whole region and has been feasting on honors ever since.

Dr. [David] Livingstone, [Henry Morton] Stanley.

"On the Decay of the Art of Lying," 1882 (WMT 19).

Addressing the Historical and Antiquarian Club of Hartford, the speaker begins by observing that the virtuous custom of lying has not decayed. As long as the Club survives, there will be liars. But the art of lying has decayed. Lying is really a necessity. Everyone lies, every day. Many say "How do you do?" to persons but do not care how they do. The silent lie is also common. The speaker recalls reminding a particularly virtuous person that she lied when she left blank parts of a form she was asked to fill in to report the conduct of a nurse who actually slept on the job. Later that nurse had the life of sick little Willie Jones in her incompetent hands. We all lie, and must. But we should lie with head erect, not haltingly. It is necessary to examine what sorts of lies are best and most wholesome. The Hartford Club could be trusted to provide experts for such a study.

Johnny, Willie Jones, Jones, Per—.

"On the Philosophy of Shaving," 1880 (LAIFI).

Nine out of ten men today shave or are shaved, and all for vanity, since the custom is not universal. Some shaves are better than others, and some are more difficult than others. Barbers should charge accordingly.

["On the Proportions of God"] (MTP).

The biblical God is to the present-day God as a grain of sand is to the ocean. The old God presided over a small globe, but we have astronomical discoveries to reckon with now. The old God was unfair and also proud of his invention, man. Then He thought better, swept all of mankind away in a flood, but let a few escape in an inadequate ark. The old God did not know about America, or many other things. His Bible, which He wrote to convince everyone, is really not persuasive. On the other hand, the modern God, who really constructed the heavens, deserves our trust because of His sweep. He has promised nothing, but is changelessly beneficent and loyal to his unwritten natural laws, and will be steadfast in the hereafter if He has ordained one. We should require no more assurance than that.

"On Training Children," 1885 (LAIFI).

To the editor of the *Christian Union,* which ran an article about a surly boy whose parents were distressed, Twain offers to tell what those parents should have done. It seems that the child took a letter from his father's hands, burned it, and then sneered. Twain says that under the circumstances he would have said nothing—to avoid making an ass of himself—but would have had the mother try to reason and caress the boy into repentance and an honest apology. If that failed, he would have promised the child a whipping, would have waited an hour or so for tempers to cool, then would have spanked the boy earnestly but not cruelly. Then the parents would have talked with the child and sent him along restored to joyfulness again. Twain then lavishes tremendous praise upon his wife, says that he almost never refers to her in print, and adds that he is mailing this reply without letting her edit it—into the stove.

[Olivia Langdon Clemens], John Junior, John Senior, Mrs. Harriet Beecher Stowe, Charles Dudley Warner.

"One of Mankind's Bores," 1871 (CG).

One of our most boring activities is writing letters. Twain hates to receive letters because he knows that he should answer them. They interfere with his work, and gradually mount up and grow so insolent in appearance that he makes an example of them in the stove. He hereby apologizes for not answering various kind correspondents, including a Wisconsin man who asked his opinion on imported brads and especially the Tennessean who asked how to become a reporter.

Rev. Mr. [Henry Ward] Beecher.

"One of the 'Polite Circle': The Prize Ring." See FW, 1870.

"One or Two California Items." See RL.

["Oneida"], 1870 (CG).

At last a newspaper—the Toronto *Globe* has been found which excuses Captain Eyre for ramming the *Oneida* with his *Bombay*. The *Oneida* must have been plying toward America stern first. Some people excuse anything. Americans have branded Cain only because he was neither Republican nor Democrat. Remember the Fiji savage? When he was told that Cain was from Fiji, he asked why Abel started messing around.

Captain Eyre.

"The Only True and Reliable Account of the Great Prize Fight . . ." See "The Great Prize Fight."

"Open Letter to Commodore Vanderbilt," 1869 (LAIFI).

Twain says that his heart goes out to Commodore Vanderbilt, the idol only of small souls who in print glorify his mean acts and praise his money. A man has to be vicious to achieve what Vanderbilt has done. Anecdotes about his stinginess, violations of the law, and spiteful revenge please only grovelers. Vanderbilt is not happy, because he is dissatisfied with what he has and wants more. Usually people laud his deeds not because of the deeds themselves but because they reflect his $70,000,000. So Twain urges him to do some unrepresentative generous act before he dies.

Astor, Commodore [Cornelius] Vanderbilt.

434 PLOTS AND CHARACTERS IN

"Origin of Illustrious Men," 1866 (CJF).

Franklin and Shakespeare are well enough publicized, Twain thinks. Now he wishes to tell us about certain fellows ignored by biographers. For example, John Smith was his father's son, William Smith was his mother's son, Edward Brown was the son of his father by a close friend, Gabriel Jones was and still is a shoemaker, Patrick Murphy was Irish, James Peterson was so poor that it was said he would inherit the earth but he did not, John Davis never arrived at maturity because he died in childbirth, etc.

Edward Brown, John Brown, Brown, John Davis, John Johnson, Caleb Jones, Gabriel Jones, Henry Jones, John Jones, William Jones, Patrick Murphy, James Peterson, John Smith, William Smith, Hosea Wilkerson.

"Original Correspondence," 1853.*

Signing himself W., Twain writes from Philadelphia to describe the healthful city, its natural setting, and its historically impressive old State House, where the Declaration of Independence was passed. The city affords many amusements, including Saturday nights in saloons and an exhibition featuring two enormous fat women and a so-called Swiss Warbler.

Jullien, Mitchell, Ole Bull, Sontag, Swiss Warbler.

*In *Mark Twain's Letters in the Muscatine Journal,* 1942.

"Orthographic Retrenchment." See FW, 1870.

"O'Shah," 1878 (WMT 29).

In June, 1873, the London representative of the New York *Herald* talks Mark Twain into agreeing to go from London over to Ostend to help escort the Shah of Persia to England. What a responsibility! So Twain gets the *Herald* to assign him Blank as a helper. Twain does not sleep well that night. He realizes that the only way England can genuinely impress the Shah is with a naval exhibition. He and Blank arise at the infernal hour of six in the morning, go by lightning-fast train through English scenery which is picture-book pretty, past Rochester and its castle, to the chalk cliffs of Dover, where they catch a little packet to Flanders. The town of

Ostend is positively full of Flounders, including ladies who deftly make lace. At every hour during his night in the hotel, porters awaken Twain in case he wants to catch an early train. By morning both he and Blank look worn and old. They board the *Lively*, alongside the *Vigilant*. The latter is to transport the Shah and his retinue. When Twain tries to set foot on the *Vigilant*, he is hustled back off its polished deck. The Shah's train arrives. A tremendous fuss is made. Twain even contributes a squeaky greeting. The imperial baggage is put aboard a third ship, and all three vessels get under way.

Soon the corps of correspondents is somewhat jaded from an excess of champagne and soda below the *Lively* deck. The Shah and his party have a sumptuous house rigged on the deck of the *Vigilant* nearby. The Persians all glitter in jewels. Twain shows a Persian aboard the *Lively* how sailors communicate with other ships by optical telegraph and feels that he should be knighted for the service. They see the *Vanguard*, the *Audacious*, and the *Devastation*—three monstrous ironclads—looming in the distance. The ships salute the Shah with their titanic guns; and their men form human pyramids in the rigging, cheer, and wave. Twain watches little of all this, however, relying instead on exaggerations by other correspondents which he can then outdo and thus gain the greatest credit of all. He does take a few notes on an old deck of cards. On his ace of diamonds he records the arrival of a fleet of men-of-war. The spectacle is impressive. At last they all sweep into the harbor at Dover, where English princes and red-coated soldiers are waiting at the pier. The seventy miles to London by train are lined with cheering citizens. Twain is glad to have fulfilled his contract to deliver the Shah to that dreary pile called Buckingham Palace, where an Oriental carpet especially made for the Shah's imperial feet had to be discarded because it contained flecks of proscribed green. Next day the Shah goes to Windsor Castle, not as you might imagine, ringing the bell, waiting, and finally being greeted briskly, but by special trains through stations converted into gardens and past regiments of cavalry. Well, next, the Corporation of the City of London gives a fancy ball at the Guildhall for the Shah, who does not dance. The immense place is divided into two corrals, one housing a glittering array of royalty, the other an enormous plebeian mob, many of whom pay for the privilege of standing for hours to glimpse the Shah a moment. A barn-

like glass house attached to the rear of the theater is jammed with
more than a thousand lunatics who have paid $1.25 to stand there,
and with a hundred special maniacs, including Twain, who have
paid $11 to stay there and also rush onto a stage to see the Shah a
minute longer. They all wait over two hours for him to arrive, surrounded by bejeweled royalty. Anthems burst forth, and it becomes obvious that the nation has gone mad. It is viewing a paltry
ruler whose subjects are starving. The Crown Prince of Russia,
also there, is relatively ignored.

At five in the morning, Twain is awakened to catch a train to
Portsmouth, to see the Shah again. Twain recalls the story of the
Russian General of Police who objected to seeing an effigy of
Nicholas of Russia at Madame Toussand's Waxworks dressed in
a mere colonel's uniform; so he wrote Emperor Alexander, who
sent over a proper general's uniform. At last Twain gets to Portsmouth, but too late to catch the Mayor's steamer; so he hires a
two-oar skiff, hitches another ride on a trim man-of-war's boat,
and just makes it. They sail through a narrow way past prodigious
old naval vessels out to the Spithead through ranks of formidable
modern ironclads which vomit out salutes from their huge guns.
Back in London again, Twain yearns in vain to attend a concert
at Albert Hall in honor of the Shah.

The Shah is now in the country, seeing a military show at Windsor. It is a bad sign when a star attraction has to go to the provinces.
The monarch grows tired. He converses via telegraph with his
Persian capital late at night. His trip will have been worth while
if he only learns from observation in Christian realms that a ruler
may be charitable. Certainly the oppressed Parsees in his land
would benefit. Baron Reuter, the telegraphic newsman, has been
granted generous concessions in Persia with respect to railroads,
mining rights, timber and well and canal operations, customs and
banking activities, and gas, road, telegraph mill, manufacturing,
forge, pavement, and other enterprises. However, one day the
Shah may so admire Reuter's head that he will order it brought
to him on a plate. At last the fatigued Shah is leaving.

> Emperor Alexander Tsar of Russia, Prince Arthur, Blank,
> the Duke of Buccleuch, the Duchess of Cambridge, the
> Duke of Cambridge, the Duke of Edinburgh, the Russian
> General of Police, the Grand Vizier, the Mayor of London,
> Princess Mary, Minister of State, Nicholas of Russia, the

Shah of Persia, St. Peter, the Mayor of Portsmouth, Queen [Victoria], Sir Henry Rawlinson, Baron [Paul Julius von] Reuter, the Crown Prince of Russia, the Princess of Russia, the Tsarina of Russia, the Duke of Teck, the Prince of Wales, the Princess of Wales, X, Colonel X, Y.

'Osteopathy,' 1901 (WMT 28).

Twain asserts that an unlicensed healer named Kellgren aided him in London and Sweden. It is strange that physicians who deal with bodies must be licensed whereas persons dealing with souls need not be. If we drive osteopaths out of the state, they will become more sought after, just like Adam's forbidden apple. Twain explains that his mother tried all sorts of unlicensed cures on him. Physicians who wish to curtail the work of osteopaths may be motivated in part by self-interest. Did Christ dispute with the doctors because they lacked licenses?

Bell, [Jane Lampton Clemens], [Dr. Henrik] Kellgren, Kneipp, Dr. Van Fleet.

'Our Children and Great Discoveries,' c. 1890 (S).

Children seem like small things to talk about, but small things often produce big consequences. Sir Isaac Newton was once attracted to an apple and produced the law of attraction. Captain John Smith was fooling around with Pocahontas when he picked his first tobacco weed. Galileo mused on a chandelier in Pisa, thought about gunpowder, and discovered the cotton gin. Those men were once two-day-old babies.

Galileo, Sir Isaac Newton, Pocahontas, Powhatan, Captain John Smith.

'Our Fellow Citizens of the Sandwich Islands.' See 'Our Fellow Savages of the Sandwich Islands.'

'Our Fellow Savages of the Sandwich Islands,' 1869-1870.*

Twain ventures to introduce himself to his audience, because he knows his own real name. He saw a statue of a skinless man in Milan once, and it reminded him of an incident from his childhood. He once ran away from home and stayed in his father's office; the creeping moonlight revealed a corpse on the floor. Twain then tells about the discovery, geography, and productivity of the Sandwich Islands. The natives are attractive, idle, good, and hospitable. They used to be superstitious, and mistreat slaves and women; but the missionaries have educated them since then. They are notorious liars in business dealings. They make pets of ugly, bushy-tailed dogs, and then eat them. It is wrong to say that the Sandwichers used to be cannibals. Twain offers to illustrate cannibalism right on stage if a member of the audience will loan him an infant. He then describes the healthy climate and magnificent scenery in Hawaii. In times of grief, Hawaiians used to be forgiven dreadfully criminal conduct; but in general they are innocent people, except that they are awful liars. They revered an especially impressive liar named Morgan, who would allow no one to outdo him in that line, especially with stories about bridges, horses, and mining explosions. (See also 'The Sandwich Islands.')

Captain [James] Cook, Morgan.

*In Fred W. Lorch, *The Trouble Begins at Eight: Mark Twain's Lecture Tours*, 1968.

"Our Italian Guide." From *The Innocents Abroad*.

"Our Precious Lunatic," 1870 (CRG).

The New York jury has been out almost two hours. The courtroom is breathless. The jury finally files in. Its foreman announces that Daniel McFarland is innocent of the charge of murdering Albert D. Richardson because he was irresponsibly insane at the time of the act. Evidence leading to the conclusion that McFarland was insane is as follows: his great-grandfather's stepfather was insane, McFarland did not adequately support his family, he drank to excess, he flirted with his sister-in-law, his wife gave public readings, two years ago he shot Richardson in the leg from behind, he told several people he was going to shoot Richardson, a doctor once called him insane, he shot Richardson from in front, and he was uneasy both before and after the shooting. When the verdict is announced, the crowd is vastly relieved. But suddenly, evidently to prove the correctness of the verdict, McFarland goes manifestly insane and kills and cripples six score persons nearby and also tears down part of City Hall. Soon thereafter the court sets him at liberty.

> Seth Brown, Charles A. Dana, Dr. John W. Galen, Marshall P. Jones, Daniel McFarland, John Morgan, Albert D. Richardson, Archibald Smith.

"Overspeeding" (MTP).

We dress convicts in unique garb, so that they may be recognized from a distance if they escape. We should do the same with the automobile speeder. Every day speeders run over people and then escape, because their license-plate numbers are too small. Twain proposes enlarging those numbers after each offense. He is personally interested because he and others of his family have been endangered by escaping speeders.

"A Page from a California Almanac," 1865 (WG).

The recent extraordinary event [San Francisco earthquake, October 8, 1865] prompts Twain to predict a few unusual occurrences which will transpire between October 17 and November 8. Expect murky air, making people melancholy. Look out (not in) for rain. Expect winds from east, north, west, or south. Prepare for balmy earthquakes followed by a falling of objects, including churches. Make out your will.

"The Pains of Lowly Life," 1900 (LAIFI).

Twain writes Sidney G. Trist, the secretary of an anti-vivisection society, to express his opposition to vivisection and his indifference to the plea that it often profits the human race. He could not even witness the vivisection of a vivisector with much satisfaction. He then quotes scientific reports on the use of curare, which prevents an animal from struggling or crying but does not anaesthetize it. He also quotes a few nauseating accounts of experiments on living frogs, rabbits, and cats, and says that he lacks the stomach to continue.

> Sidney G. Trist.

"Palm Readings" (MTP).

An editor named Stead once sent prints of Twain's palms to seven British palmists without revealing Twain's name. The resulting analyses were smooth, cautious, and vague; but one expert said straight out that the owner of those hands lacked a sense of humor. Twain told a friend that the silence of the other six on the subject seemed to be something like a confirmation. The friend theorizes that perhaps the verdict is true and that Twain has been deceiving a gullible public this quarter-century. Twain offered to tell some palmists his name and then ask whether his hand reveals humor. But his friend called the plan foolish. Yet phrenologists are aided in their readings when they know their subjects. Twain once went to a phrenologist in London, identified himself as John S. Smith, and was told that he lacked a sense of humor. Later he returned as himself and was told that his humor bump resembled a pyramid.

Fowler, John B. Smith, Stead.

"The Panama Railroad," 1897 (LAIFI).

The Panama Railroad cost the lives of thousands of laborers, because of tropical fevers. It was first and last an American project, but in between the English worked on it. The Columbian states granted rights for only a few years, after which the government of the Isthmus under President Mosquera proved troublesome and even began flirting with the English again. So the American Railroad Company sent two knowledgeable American agents down to try for an extension. They promptly got everyone drunk on champagne and whisky, started a revolution, and soon had a ninety-nine-year franchise. Or so the legend goes.

President [Tomás Cipriano de] Mosquiera [Mosquera].

["Papers of the Adam Family"], 1962 (LFE).

Methuselah records in his diary, in the year 747 after creation, that he is a blooming young sixty and that his family is beginning to urge him to marry. Being now on the threshold of young manhood, he dismisses his tutor Uz and others, celebrates the anniversary of the founding of the city of Aumrath, and enjoys the performances of certain mountebanks at court. He and others go to the theater, where the new actor Luz is performing a play on the expulsion from Eden. Old Jebel compares the show unfavorably to one he saw centuries ago. Toothless Jebel lives on and on to no purpose. Methuselah frees his Hebrew slave Zuar, who after six years has worked off his bondage. Although he does not have to do so, Methuselah also grants freedom to Zuar's wife Mahlah and to their children. The grateful couple remain to work in Methuselah's court retinue. Uz's great-great-granddaughter Zillah suddenly strikes Methuselah as beautiful. The Jabalites, tribal savages, come into town and intrigue the natives; but there is trouble periodically with these tent-dwellers, who admittedly are often cheated. Methuselah describes the curious game of baseball, which has been revived by order of his father. Next Methuselah says that rumors have it that Adam is about to visit the city of Enoch, who has therefore ordered the palace garnished by artists. The museum containing Adam's original fig leaves and Eden's deadly flaming sword grows more crowded, although Methuselah has little interest in its displays because of the fact that six other cities also sport the leaves and sword. Methuselah inveighs against the music of organ grinders, especially when they unceasingly churn out the song "O, Kiss Haggag for His Mother." It is announced that Adam will indeed visit the city in the year 787 or so.

In her autobiography, Eve explains that at first she and Adam are ignorant and happy, have to use words without being able to check their meanings in a dictionary, and go about discovering the scientific causes of phenomena. Adam discovers that water always flows downhill, for example, and later Eve discovers that cows make milk by condensing the atmosphere through their hair. One day Eve notices that their pet lion has teeth for rending meat and wonders with Adam and all his logic why this should be. Later a Voice in the woods orders them not to eat fruit from a certain tree or death will result. Not knowing what death is, they conclude that the best way to find out is to eat that fruit. However, a pterodactyl comes by and its attractive ugliness distracts them. Adam experiments to try to get fish to grow legs for fun on land. Suddenly Cain is born, and Eve quickly develops a sense of intense love for the child, in spite of Adam's initial theories as to its nature. Later come Abel and in due course seven more babies, including Gladys and Edwina. Cain studies well but spells as badly as his dictionary-writing father, whereas Eve and Abel, though slow learners, spell accurately. One day Gladys wonders off, does not return, and when found explains that she fell into the river, was carried downstream, and lived with a hospitable kangaroo family a while. About the year 920, Eve and others begin to think that, given the billions of people now in the world, war, famine, and pestilence are beneficial to mankind, and life-prolonging physicians are a menace.

A Lady of the Blood, Third Grade, records in her diary that she has just received the Mad Prophet. When he was only a poor lad, she got him a mathematics professorship. He worked hard, fell in love with Red Cloud, waited sixty years, married her, and studied that newly harnessed force called liquefied thought. This power may be the famous Lost Force, the origins of which the Prodigy, who began as a humble shoemaker, discovered among the papers of the obscure but brilliant scientist Napeer, and which the Prodigy used to conquer all enemies and finally war itself. He was able to establish a world-wide benevolent despotism lasting thirty years, until he accidentally blew himself up.

The Mad Prophet is a man named Reginald Selkirk, who reveals his real feelings about modern civilization to the Acting Head of the Human Race. The world has become a place of meretricious scientific marvels, materialism, dishonest lawmakers and officials, and vicious commercial achievements which result in luxury for some but poverty for more. We have lost the simple and reposeful life, and Noah is rightly preparing for the flood. Selkirk lectures on two important subjects, the law of intellectual averages and the law of periodical repetition. In these talks he argues that exceptional intellects are exceedingly rare and that all events repeat themselves in small or large cycles. In his diary, Selkirk records that he has had an audience with the Acting Head of the Human Race in the sumptuous and extensive Hall of Sovereigns, after which he goes to the Eden Arms for a drink with Nanga Parbat, who is a scion of the first blood through being the Eden-born grandson of the Acting Head but who has been banished from court because of his persistently malicious bitterness. It is his opinion, for example, that the accident of birth should not enable a person to lord it over others, who are in reality his equals. He is especially eloquent on the subject of nepotism.

An unidentified diarist records violent criticism of physicians for manipulating their reports on the health of the retired Head of the Race, in order to gain money for themselves—partly through stock-market fluctuations.

An historian records his former pride in his country, because of its strength, just and humane laws, liberties, and honor, and also because it is a refuge for the persecuted. But he adds that the country has recently entered upon a base war for material gain, a war which is being supported by ministers, editors, political leaders, and school superintendents. "Our country, right or wrong" is now the dreadful battle cry. Lost is the republic, corrupted by the rich, who can buy votes. The shoemaker Prodigy rises in the South and gains in power. When the professional army and navy refuse to fight him, he sweeps north and quickly destroys the patriotic but untrained civilian soldiers and sailors. Thus does Popoatahualpacatapetl seize control of the once-great republic.

In his diary for the year 920, Noah's son Shem observes that just before the flood almost everyone has become wicked and noisy. Noah and his family are ridiculed for building an ark in a dry plain. Old Methuselah comes tottering by, with his nose in the air. The truth is that he is jealous of the ark, because the Lord chose Noah and not him to build it. Methuselah is critical of Shem and his brothers, and their wives, and calls them mere children— they are only eighty to a hundred years of age or so—and hence too young to wed. When they venture respectfully to reason with him, he only cackles.

> Abel, the Acting Head of the Human Race, Adam, the Angel, Baseman, Cain, Cainan, Catcher, Edwina, Eliah, Enoch, Enos, Eve, Fielder, Gladys, Habakkuk, Haggag, the Head of the Race, Household Troops, Jabal, Japheth, Jared, Jebel, a Lady of the Blood Third Grade, Luz, Mahalaleel, Mahlah, Methuselah, Nanga Parbat, Napeer, Nines, Noah, Popoatahualpacatapetl II, the Prodigy, Red Cloud, Regina, Princess Sarah, Reginald Selkirk, Shem, the Superintendent of Public Instruction, Umpire, Uz, Uzziel, the Viceroy, a Voice, the Duke of Washoe, the Emperor of the World, Zillah, Zuar.

"Paris Notes," 1882 (WMT 19).

The narrator first explains that French waiters—represented as

"He"—speak rather good English but cannot understand a word, with the result that they make inappropriate remarks and bows. Then he explains that French sermons cite so many dates that one should take his almanac with him to French churches. For example, we should be grateful for January 13 because it made possible December 25—the former date being the birth of Adam.

> Bellows, He, the narrator.

[A Parody on Swift], 1935 (P).
> I famish for Stellakins and her beef, beer, and kisses. (In *Mark Twain's Margins on Thackeray's "Swift."*)

> Stellakins.

["A Patriarch"], 1870 (CG).
> An authenticated report has just come in from the West. An eighty-four-year-old patriarch, blind for several years, could suddenly see again. He feasted his happy vision on his children and grandchildren, then read some Biblical verses, and then went blind again and died a few minutes later. Reason and memory come back to the dying rather often, they say; but revived vision is rare.

"'Party Cries' in Ireland," 1875 (WMT 7).
> Belfast—indeed, all of Northern Ireland—is a peculiarly religious community, in which Protestants and Catholics try to proselytize. Each man is a brick-carrying missionary. If a person cries "To hell with the Pope!" or "To hell with Protestants!", he is fined forty shillings and costs. One night in a Belfast alley a policeman found a drunk shouting "To hell with." When the officer, who smelled a fine, asked him to complete his statement, the drunk, balancing sedition and economy, replied, "[F]inish it yourself—it's too expinsive for me!"

"People and Things."   See ["Several Items by Mark Twain"] and FW, 1869.

Personal, 1870 (probably by Twain) (P).

Mrs. Smith places an advertisement in a newspaper stating that Mary Jane Mahoney desires a husband. The typesetter answers the personal notice and meets the girl, who takes $10 from him and disappears with her husband, who keeps a keno shop. (In "Personal," FW, 1870.)

Smith, Mrs. Smith.

"Personal Correspondence," 1864 (MTWY).

Twain details his demand for satisfaction of James L. Laird, editor of the *Union*, for printing an editorial abusing him. Laird referred Twain to J. W. Wilmington, an Ohio army veteran of Shiloh, the actual author. Twain expressed indifference to Wilmington and repeated his challenge of Laird, to no avail. (See *Mark Twain of the Enterprise*.)

James L. Laird, J. W. Wilmington.

"A Personal Explanation," 1870 (CG).

Twain explains that he published "A Memory" when he did only to keep his hand in. Illness [the mortal sickness of his father-in-law] prevented his offering anything else in August.

"Personal Habits of the Siamese Twins." See "The Siamese Twins."

Personal Recollections of Joan of Arc, 1896 (WMT 17, 18).

Book I. By any standard, Joan of Arc was superb in character and person. By comparison to others in her brutal times, she was true, pitying, dignified, and courageous. Her work was uniquely important. Yet for her deeds, she was destroyed while the country she saved stood idly by. Her biography can be produced from data given under oath. Her present biographer, Sieur Louis de Conte, has used all known sources and also his personal recollections. It is now the year 1492. Conte, aged eighty-two, remembers being reared in the same village with Joan, being her page and secretary, being with her on that final black day. Aside from One, she was the most noble person in this world.

The Conte family lives in Neufchâteau, where Louis was born on January 6, 1410, just two years before his friend Joan of Arc, born in Domremy. After Agincourt, several of the pro-Armanac Contes are massacred by roving Burgundians, and Louis de Conte goes to live and study with a Domremy priest named Père Guillaume Fronte, whose housekeeper becomes the boy's foster mother. Thus Louis becomes acquainted with beautiful, gay-hearted, laughing Joan. They have many young friends. They tend flocks by the Meuse River near the forest, which once had a dragon in it. The children enjoy dancing around a huge old beech tree—the Arbre Fée de Bourlemont—which is the locale of fairies until Père Fronte banishes them, an act he regrets when Joan explains matters to him. The children have fun all year round: in the summer they roam over fields and through forests, and in the winter they are çozy before the fire. One winter night a ragged stranger asks for admittance, and before her father can stop her Joan gives him her porridge. In gratitude, he recites the thrilling *Song of Roland*. On the hillside one day in 1420 the children see a terrifying black flag; its bearer, their friend Étienne Roze, approaches and tells them that at Troyes the mad king, through his viper of a queen, has signed France over to Henry V of England and his French wife. When the girls say that they wish they could go fight in the wars, the boys laugh at them; but suddenly Joan proves the bravery of mere girls by talking gently to Théophile Benoist, the village lunatic temporarily loose with an ax.

The next year is dismal for France. Domremy boys fight with Burgundian lads from Maxey and are beaten up. The old king soon dies, and rumor has it that the English forces are sweeping into pockets of resistance and destroying them. Marauders slaughter many in Domremy, including harmless Benoist. Joan is aghast at sights of violence. When her friends ridicule some of the leading French generals, she defends their names. She also quietly predicts the future for some of her talkative friends. Gradually she changes, laughing less and becoming grave though never melancholy, as though she now has secrets. Then one day Conte sees her by the enchanted beech tree apparently in rapt communion with a presence whose radiance he partly sees. She tells him that Voices have informed her of her destiny: she is to lead armies which will free France and will strike the first blow in that direction a year from now. Conte is to help her because he is a literate nobleman.

She is to go with her uncle, Laxart of Burey, to Robert de Baudricourt, governor of Vaucouleurs, and ask for an armed escort to
take her to the Dauphin. Soon she goes to Vaucouleurs but is
rudely rejected and ordered back home, where her burly friend
the Paladin pretends that she promised to marry him. In the ensuing court case at Toul, she defends herself with incredible
eloquence and forensic skill. Meanwhile, Salisbury has begun the
bloody siege of Orleans, and France's future seems black.

   Book II. By January 5, 1429, Laxart thoroughly believes in his
inspired niece Joan, who soon rightly senses that Sieur Jean de
Novelonpont de Metz and Sieur Bertrand de Poulengy, cavaliers
she saw with the governor, will prove loyal to her. She bids a sob-
bing farewell forever to her village, the beech tree, the forest, the
flowery plain, and the river. She is now seventeen. Doing house-
work at Vaucouleurs, she gradually wins the respect of the villagers,
sees the governor again, is rejected once more, but suddenly makes
kneeling converts of Metz and then Poulengy. A delegation of
bishops sent from Vaucouleurs fails completely to find any witch-
like propensities in Joan, who states on February 14 that the
Dauphin is now suffering a military defeat the news of which will
be known in nine days, and further that on the 23rd she will begin
her march to him. When the disastrous Battle of the Herrings is
duly reported, Baudricourt the governor gives Joan his sword
and all possible aid. Her friends the boastful Paladin and the
initially cowardly little Nöel Rainguesson join her entourage of
of twenty five or so soldiers, also including Conte, on the road
toward the Loire River and the Dauphin. Joan miraculously survives Burgundian ambushes and threats of assassination from
within her own group. After ten difficult days and nights, they
cross the Loire and go to Gien. They get to the castle at Chinon,
where the Dauphin is practically a captive of his villainous minister Georges de la Tremouille and the Archbishop of Rheims. Also
there, however, is the Dauphin's mother-in-law Yolande, Queen
of Sicily, who is sympathetic to Joan's cause. She thinks that Joan
has indeed been sent by God to relieve the desperate plight of
Orleans. When the Dauphin dispatches some priests to worm her
secrets from her, Joan politely but firmly insists upon speaking
directly to her sovereign. She correctly assumes that, if delivered
by others, her message would be deliberately garbled.

   There are more delays. Priests must be dispatched to check into

Joan's background at Lorraine. Then one day word comes that the Maid is to see the Dauphin. At the behest of Yolande, Joan dresses in the simple garb by which she is ever after remembered. She goes to court, ignores an impostor sitting on the throne, and kneels before the disguised Dauphin, who is impressed but asks her for another sign of her inspired wisdom. When she tells him secretly that he is troubled as to the legitimacy of his claims to the throne and assures him that his blood is royal, he is satisfied. But his evil counselors cause still more delays; so she and her little retinue are sent back to Courdray. Priests come and query her to see whether she is divinely or satanically inspired. Her alternately gentle and sharp though sincere replies finally satisfy them all. Meanwhile, the Paladin buys an attractive Spanish cavalier suit, swaggers in the local taproom during several blustery March nights, and convinces everyone—himself included—that he was present at Joan's audience. Again the girl passes all tests, though the procedure consumes three valuable weeks. When the priests return from Lorraine with favorable reports, good luck begins to come in a flood: the Church gives permission for Joan to dress like a man, she is named General-in-Chief of the Armies of France, and the royal Duke of Alençon becomes her chief of staff.

Joan dictates a letter to the English commanders at Orleans, ordering them to surrender their holdings on French soil and leave the country. When old D'Aulon is named chief of her household, her young village friends fear that they will be forgotten. But she makes the Paladin her standard bearer, and all the others —Conte, Nöel, and Joan's brothers Jean and Pierre d'Arc—are appointed to good posts as well. Her friends realize all the more that she has an eye capable of penetrating to the inner worth of everyone and a spirit which brings out his best. Soon they begin a colorful march to Blois, where they stay for three days and where the soldiers under gruff La Hire are sinful and wolfish. But Joan soon transforms La Hire and his men, and they dismiss their camp followers and attend mass instead. Joan's army moves on, under the seasoned Armanac generals La Hire, Boussac, Retz, D'Illiers, and Saintrailles, none of whom initially regards their feminine leader as of more than spiritual worth. So they deceive her and approach Orleans south of the Loire, whereas she wants to come in from the north and immediately attack. Calling Dunois, the loyal Bastard of Orleans, she quickly makes him admit the blunder;

then, wasting no time uselessly lamenting, she predicts that the
wind will change to their advantage, orders her army back to a
previously passed spot, crosses the river, and enters passively be-
sieged Orleans, whose starving citizens kiss her very feet in an
ecstasy of relief. On April 30, Joan sends messengers to ask the
English for their long-delayed response to her order to evacuate,
but the only answer is a threat to capture and burn her. She therefore challenges Lord Talbot, the enemy leader, to fight it out now;
but he refuses. So she orders the Bastard to return to Orleans and
put her army into motion. Meanwhile, Conte, Nöel, the Paladin,
and their friends are briefly enjoying the society of Catherine
Boucher, whose father is Jacques Boucher, the treasurer of the
exiled Duke of Orleans, and in whose home they are billeted. As
usual, the Paladin is ridiculously but successfully boastful. In
jealousy, Conte composes a poem called "The Rose," but Nöel
recites it and the Paladin lugubriously weeps at it; so Conte gains
little attention. When an English deserter reports that the Bastard is soon to come under attack, Joan rejoices, reviews his
troops, pardons a stupendously huge French soldier—nicknamed
the Dwarf—for briefly deserting to visit his dying wife, and makes
him her man-at-arms. Wanting to attack a strategic fort on the
south shore, Joan is once again balked by her sluggish generals
and thus loses four precious days. In a tavern during the lull,
Conte reluctantly admits to fear and is praised for his honesty
by Poulengy. Suddenly the phenomenal news comes that the
French, discouraged at Orleans, have desperately begun to attack
Talbot's superior forces. Joan flies into her armor. Joined by the
Dwarf, the Paladin, and hundreds of others, she stems the devastating enemy tide, pushes it back, and miraculously succeeds
in going on to capture the British-held fortress at St. Loup. During
the onslaught she had the battle light in her eyes; afterwards, she
weeps for the wounded, for the dead, and for their mothers.

After Conte and his friends try to solve the mystery of the Boucher family ghost—they find a rusty sword and a rotten fan in a
bricked-up room—Joan gets wind of more pusillanimous delays
by the Bastard and his cohorts; so she orders an attack on the
English at the bastille of the Augustins and at Tourelles. At dawn
the French go on the offensive for the first time in years. La Hire
profanely rejoices. During the evening lull, Joan dictates a letter
telling her parents not to worry when they learn that she has been

wounded: it seems that she has long dreamed of being wounded between her neck and her shoulder on May 7. Tomorrow is the day. She quickly convinces timid, beautiful Catherine Boucher that a general cannot avoid danger but must face fate. Watching from a distance, Conte wonders why he does not embrace lovely Catherine. At dawn Joan inspires her dejected forces, leads them in an advance, and is shot between neck and shoulder by an arbalest bolt. For ten minutes the very fate of France hangs in the balance; but the Dwarf, the Paladin, and many other brave men save her. When she hears retreat sounded, she gets to her feet, countermands the order, advances, waves La Hire and his reserves into action, and Tourelles falls to her. The brave British pull out. Joan and her forces return in torch-lit triumph to Orleans.

Talbot leaves; and French delight is unbounded, especially among Orleans children, who can now leave their dingy streets and play in the grassy fields once more. Joan reports to the Dauphin back at Tours, urges him to proceed at once to his coronation at Rheims—she tells him that she will last only one more year— blushes when he offers her a personal reward, and debates angrily with wily Tremouille, who persuades the Dauphin to delay still longer. The Paladin and Nöel are downcast at news that the Dauphin has ennobled Joan and her family, because now her brothers Jean and Pierre will outrank them and therefore take precedence. The Dauphin's delaying tactics cause Joan's army to dissolve; but when the girl promises to break up enemy opposition between Tours and Rheims, the security-minded monarch gives the order to reorganize military forces, and Joan raises eight thousand soldiers by early June, marches to Romorantin and then Orleans, and promises to take Jargeau by artillery and direct assault. With rude eloquence, La Hire supports her plan, which succeeds despite the bravery of Sir John Fastolfe's troops and the stubborn courage of the Earl of Suffolk and his brothers Alexander de la Pole and John de la Pole. Joan treats a horde of prisoners humanely and rests her exhausted troops two days, during which she dictates letters to Conte, predicts a thrilling victory in four days, and then while in a trance reveals that she will die a cruel death within two years. Conte keeps this secret revelation from everyone, even Joan herself. Next, her troops advance to Meung and then Beaugency, where Joan outmaneuvers fierce Talbot and wily

Fastolfe, and accepts Richard Guétin's surrender. She catches Talbot's and Fastolfe's forces at Patay, and on June 18 manipulates her army in a victory so consequential that it erases the sting of Crécy, Poitiers, and Agincourt.

France is now like an ailing patient becoming convalescent. News of Joan's victories spreads fast, like sunlight after an eclipse. Joan has raised the siege at Orleans and won at Patay. Now she must improve the position of brave Richemont, whose daring obedience of her was technically a violation of the Dauphin's orders; and she must see to it that her monarch is crowned at Rheims. So she moves on, from Gien to Auxerre, Saint-Florentin, Saint-Fal, and Troyes, which surrenders the moment Joan orders an assault. Chalons then surrenders, and on July 16 she sights Rheims at last. The crowds there are in a frenzy of joy. Everyone kneels before her, and medals are struck in her honor. The Dauphin, who has been lodging at the castle of the Archbishop, hesitates at one point during the five-hour coronation ceremony, but finally places the crown on his head and thus becomes King Charles VII. When he offers Joan any gift she wants, she asks that taxes be remitted forever in her native village of Domremy. It is so ordered. Briefly Joan now visits and laughs with her humble father and her uncle, Laxart, who soberly tells of going to a funeral riding on a bee-stung bull. Although Joan wants nothing so much as to be permitted to go home to her mother, the King orders her back to the war council, which has been dominated by deceitful Tremouille and the foxy Chancellor of France until she enters and eloquently persuades the King to allow her to advance on Bedford at Paris.

Joan writes a courteous letter to Burgundy urging him to lay down his arms, make peace with his King, and if he must fight go fight the Saracens. Saying farewell to her father and her uncle, she then advances with the King against an ever-retreating Bedford. But then her vacillating monarch falls back toward Gien, changes his mind, and proceeds toward Paris. In spite of the efforts of pro-English Bishop Pierre Cauchon, his city of Beauvais surrenders to the King. Then Compiègne submits, on August 18, 1429. More strongholds capitulate, and Joan camps at St. Denis under the very walls of Paris. She is wounded by a crossbow but is rallied still by her Voices, which urge her to stay at St. Denis. Before she can take Paris, however, the King, whose ear is poisoned by treacherous

Tremouille, makes a treaty with Burgundy and agrees to fall back to the Loire. Joan asks to be relieved of it all, so that she can return home to her parents and her flocks, but the King, wanting her near him, refuses. She is allowed to conduct small sorties, which she does with her usual brilliance. But near Compiègne, while furiously engaging the enemy in a complex move against Marguy, Clairvoix, and Venette, she is surrounded and captured on May 24, 1430. Conte, who was wounded earlier, can only watch in agony from a wall. The Paladin and the Dwarf die trying to stave off her capture. All of Tours mourns for the lost Maid.

Book III. The summer and winter following Joan's capture are shameful. The girl should be ransomed, but her King refuses to step forward. She is to be tried by a pro-British French ecclesiastical court. Twice she tries to escape but fails. Then Cauchon, Bishop of Beauvais, enters the scene, buying her from Burgundy for 61,125 francs in gold. If Cauchon can secure a conviction, he will receive a handsome promotion. The trial is to be held at Rouen. Conte, wounded again in a minor sortie earlier, now gets a position as a clerk under a gentle priest named Manchon, who is to be chief recorder at the trial; and Nöel, who has escaped from the British at Compiègne—he also got Joan's standard out—goes along with Conte to be near Joan though unable to do anything for her good. Cauchon packs his court with fifty deeply intellectual, casuistical inquisitors—later he increases the number to sixty-two—but illegally refuses Joan any legal aid and even eavesdrops as the friendless girl confesses to a shameless churchman named Nicholas Loyseleur.

On February 21, 1431, the public trial begins in the fortress chapel. Clad in black, chained, pale, but radiant, Joan is brought before obese Cauchon. She steadfastly refuses to swear to answer all questions. Certain information from her Voices is privileged. She is often interrogated for five to seven hours in a single day. Beaupere, a doctor of theology, is a leading questioner; Joan, however, is more than a match for him and brilliantly parries his questions about grace, her Voices, her vision, the sword she found at St. Catherine's church at Fierbois, the papacy, details of her life and conduct, the beech tree back home, and the people's devotion to her. The judges hammer at her especially hard on March 3, but she resists them all. At one point she predicts that France will liberate Paris within seven years and also advises

Cauchon that he is trying God's patience. She also predicts her deliverance at the end of three months. Conte thinks that she will be rescued, perhaps by the King, perhaps by La Hire. Evidently Joan feels that she will mercifully die in her prison bed. Her Voices must in reality have been hinting at her execution.

Cauchon sees that the public trial is going badly; so he dismisses most of the judges, retains a few tigerish ones, and on March 10 resumes the sittings in secret in Joan's prison. The tired, occasionally dazed girl courageously meets all questions concerning her relationship with the Paladin, her male attire, her plans to free the Duke of Orleans (exiled in England), her abiding desire to escape her tormentors, her possible martyrdom, and her willingness to submit her words and deeds to the determination of the Church. Here she nearly demands to be taken to the Pope, a move which would surely have saved her. Conte wishes that he could so advise her, but merely to try would be a hanging offense.

On March 27 the third trial begins with Thomas de Courcelles reading a list of sixty-six charges against Joan. They distort all of the beautiful acts of her life. Then twelve judges query her on her love of the fairies near the beech tree, her pride in doing a man's work, her attire again, and the manner in which she prays. This trial too fails to produce a conviction. When Cauchon and an aide named Isambard de la Pierre visit Joan in her prison cell, Pierre daringly asks whether she would submit to a pro-French court in Basel. She immediately agrees, but Cauchon orders the man to shut up and Manchon not to record either the question or the answer.

Now Joan falls sick, is bled, and then is threatened with a denial of the sacraments unless she submits to the Church Militant. Again she refuses. Two weeks go by, and May arrives with flowers. Feeling stronger again, Joan is brought before the pitiless tribunal and queried again but responds superbly. The people of Rouen begin to decorate the city's walls with caricatures of hog-like Cauchon littering failures in court. On May 9, Joan is taken to the torture room of a nearby tower and threatened, but she resolutely says that whatever she confesses under torture she will later repudiate. When the other judges outvote Cauchon, Loyseleur, and a ridiculed master of eloquence named Thomas de Courcelles, the minority which wants Joan to be racked, she is returned to her cell victorious over her persecutors once again.

After ten days, during which Conte mopes, news comes that a committee of University of Paris theologians has rendered a damning decision on charges that Joan lied in twelve respects. So she is brought before her tribunal again, on May 23, but remains defiant. Judged guilty of heresy, sorcery, and other crimes, she must be tricked into confessing and then retracting, so that she may be burned. All this time, Conte and Nöel naively believe that absent La Hire and his hellions will rescue their Maid. Instead, Cauchon brings her before a stake at the base of which are raging coals and has her preached at. She appeals to God and to the Pope. Loyseleur whispers in her ear that if she submits she will be remanded to a Church prison. With Cauchon reading her death sentence, she submits and agrees to sign a paper to that effect. A false document is slipped in its place, and she unwittingly signs a false confession that she is a sorceress, a dealer with devils, a liar, and a blasphemer. She is then condemned to perpetual imprisonment and is returned to the English prison. The partially comprehending mob begins hurling rocks at the ecclesiasts. The English leaders fear that they have lost Joan, but Cauchon reassures them. And sure enough, Conte and Nöel are soon dazed by news that she has relapsed. When her heartless guards stole her dress, modesty forced her to resume her now illegal male attire. In addition, she says that fear of the fire made her wrongly submit, that her Voices are of divine origin, and that she prefers fire to continued captivity. She sends a brief message by Manchon to Conte: love to her family and village, there will be no rescue, she has seen the fairy tree again. On May 30, 1431, Cauchon, whom Joan severely threatens with God's justice, allows her communion and then sees to it that she is delivered to the civil judge for execution as a heretic. The English soldiers form a solid wall along the streets. The French sing a litany for pale Joan and also kneel to her. She forgives Loyseleur and prays for her King. When she asks for a cross, an English soldier gives her one of sticks. The fire kills her quickly. Twenty-three years later, King Charles decides that he got his crown by a pure girl's efforts; so he appeals to the Pope, and Joan is entirely rehabilitated, and declared spotless and perfect. She lives as a symbol of purity, unselfishness, and patriotism.

Sire d'Albret, the Duke of Alençon, the Duchess of Alençon, Catherine d'Arc, Isabel [la] Romée d'Arc, Jacques

d'Arc, Jacques d'Arc, Jean d'Arc, Pierre d'Arc, the Count
of Armanac, Franquet d'Arras, Aubrey, Dame Aubrey,
D'Aulon, the Bastard of Orleans, Robert de Baudricourt,
Beaupere, the Duke of Bedford, Madame de Bellier,
Théophile Benoist, Catherine Boucher, Jacques Boucher,
Mme. Boucher, Louis de Bourbon, Marshal de Boussac,
Gautier de Brusac, the Duke of Burgundy, Bishop Pierre
Cauchon, the Bishop of Châlons, the Chancellor of France,
the Chancellor of the University of Paris, Charles the
Bold, Charles VI, Charles VII, Charles, Regnault de
Chartres, the Children of the Tree, Sieur Louis de Conte,
De Conte, De Conte, Thomas de Courcelles, Sire de Culan,
Marie Dupont, the Dwarf, an Embassy, Guillaume Erard,
Jean d'Estivet, Sir John Fastolfe, Guillaume de Flavy,
Jean de la Fontaine, Free Companions, Père Guillaume
Fronte, Raoul de Gaucourt, Sir William Glasdale, Lord de
Graville, Bertrand de Guesclin, Richard Guétin, Bishop
Christophe d'Harcourt, Haumette, Henry V, Florent
d'Illiers, the Inquisitor, Isabel of Bavaria, Joan, Joan of
Arc, Abbot Jumièges, the French King-at-Arms, La Hire,
Martin Ladvenu(e), the Bishop of Laon, Count de Laval,
Count de Laval, Laxart, Mme. Laxart, Jean Lefevre, Cé-
cile Letellier, Du Lis, Maître Lohier, Ambroise de Lore,
Jean le Lorrain, Nicholas Loyseleur, Monsieur de Lude,
Jean de Luxembourg, Gerard Machet, Robert le Maçon,
Manchon, Marguerie, Maître Jean Massieu, Pierre Mau-
rice, Little Mengette, Sieur Jean de Novelonpont de Metz,
Nicholas Midi, Pierre Morel, the Bishop of Orleans, the
Duke of Orleans, the Paladin, Jean Pasquerel, Isambard de
la Pierre, Pierron, Alexander de la Pole, Sir John de la
Pole, Pope [Calixtus III], Pope [Nicholas V], Sieur Ber-
trand de Poulengy, James Power, Dame de Rabateau, Rai-
mond, Nöel Rainguesson, Rainguesson, Marshal de Rais,
Captain Raymond, Guillaume Renault, Sire de Retz, the
Archbishop of Rheims, Richemont, Catherine Royer,
Royer, Étienne Roze, Roze, Mme. Roze, the Abbot of St.
Corneille, the Abbé of St. Remi, Pothon of Saintrailles,
Salisbury, Thomas Lord Scales, Brother Séguin, the Earl of
Stafford, the Earl of Suffolk, Lord [John] Talbot, Georges
de la Tremouille, the Count of Vendôme, the Vicar-Gen-

eral of the Inquisition, the Vice-Inquisitor, Lord de Villars, Voices, the Earl of Warwick, the Cardinal of Winchester, Yolande.

"Petition Concerning Copyright," 1912 (WMT 7).

Mark Twain suggests that since the Constitution guarantees equal rights, including property rights, to all, and since each copyright is restricted to forty-two years, all property should be retained by the given holder for a maximum period of forty-two years. He addresses his suggestion to Congress. He adds that, given the fact that the average book does not live forty-two years, it seems absurd to take advantage of the heirs of such rarities as Scott, Burns, and Milton.

"A Petition to the Queen of England," 1887 (WMT 23).

Twain writes the Queen of England to remind her that last May Edward Bright, a clerk in her Inland Revenue Office, wrote him about an income tax due her government on royalties from his books published in London. Since he does not know Bright and is reluctant to correspond with strangers, he will write directly to her Majesty, whose son the Prince of Wales he once encountered on the street. Twain then tells her that in a weak moment he ordered his London publisher, Chatto and Windus, to go ahead and pay the tax out of his account but that he has since learned that it is not 1% for just the current year but 2½% back tax for three whole years. So he has reviewed the long tax form which Bright sent him. He incidentally advises the Queen not to let Bright use his own discretion, or the young man will discretion her right out of her palace shortly. He begs to remind her that according to the tax form authors are not officially considered under quarries, mines, iron works, salt springs, or any other listed source of income. True, Bright referred him to Schedule D, Section 14; but that part concerns trades, offices, and gas works, all again inapplicable to him. And as for deductions, his machinery or plant is his brain, which shows no signs of depreciable wear and tear. So he wishes respectfully to conclude that her Majesty should annul the letter he wrote his publisher, because he owes no tax.

Edward Bright, Chatto, Francis Bret Harte, Dr. Oliver

Wendell Holmes, the Lord Mayor [of London], Ouida, Professor Sloane, Queen [Victoria] of England, the Prince of Wales, Windus.

"The Petrified Man," 1870 (WMT 7).

It is hard to foist a truism on unsuspicious readers through satire. The author recalls the time he was an editor in Virginia City and felt obliged to ridicule the growing petrifaction mania. He had had a falling out with Mr.—, the Humboldt coroner and justice of the peace; so he described in detail the finding of a petrified man at Gravelly Point, a desolate region more than a hundred miles away, and added that Mr.— journeyed to the site and held an inquest. The jury pronounced the man dead from protracted exposure and, experiencing difficulty moving the seated creature for burial, were tempted to try blasting powder. The author included a ridiculous description of the posture of the petrified man, complete with circumlocutory mention of the fact that he was thumbing his nose; but nobody comprehended the satire, and his essay was given international publicity. He completed his insult of Mr.— by sending him bushels of newspaper notices of the petrified man.

Mr.—.

["Philippines"] (MTP).

General MacArthur says that the Philippine incident is closed. By grabbing some islands from a party that did not own them, we have earned an uncomfortable back seat in the Family of Nations. We pacified the natives by burying them, have made countless widows and orphans, and are protecting the Sultan of Sulu's concubines and other slaves. We must now bark over our possessions like a prairie dog. But our new possessions are ornamental only. When Dewey sent word that he had secured Manila, the President had to call a cabinet meeting to find out where—and what—Manila was. When the truth leaked out that the Philippines are 1,200 islands, the President ordered the Commissioners to buy them.

[Emilio] Aguinaldo, Commissioner, Admiral [George] Dewey, General [Arthur] MacArthur, President [William McKinley], the Sultan of Sulu.

"The Pioneers' Ball" (WG). See " 'After' Jenkins." (See also B., Mrs. L.; T., Mrs.; and X., Miss.)

"Playing Courier," 1891 (WMT 15).

The author and his party must go from Aix-les-Bains to Geneva and then on to Bayreuth. They have no courier. So the author decides to manage without one. He takes the party of five, including himself, to Geneva without mishap. But when he volunteers to lead it on to Bayreuth, he experiences many troubles. Two persons waiting in a Geneva pension must be added to the group, he must get seven stored trunks delivered to the hotel and seven now at the hotel put into storage, he must buy the necessary railroad tickets, he must telegraph a friend in the Netherlands, and he must draw money against a letter of credit—all between now, 2:00 P.M., and the night train. He gets incredibly mixed up with cabs, a purchase of cigars, sending the telegram, buying tickets (which turn out to be defunct lottery tickets), misplacing his letter of credit, losing sundry items, and so on. When he reports back to the long-suffering party in their hotel, the atmosphere is exceedingly chilly. The morning is no better, and they fail to make revised connections. So the author engages Mr. Ludi, a reputable courier, and rather quickly all is smooth again.

The Head of the Expedition, Ludi, the Mayor of Geneva, Merryman, Charles Natural.

'Plymouth Rock and the Pilgrims,' 1881 (WMT 28).

Twain rises to protest. Why celebrate the anniversary of the December 22 landing of the Pilgrims on Plymouth Rock? Those Pilgrims would have been foolish not to land. After all, they had been at sea three or four months, and it was bitter cold off Cape Cod in December. Oh, you say that you are celebrating the Pilgrims themselves. But why? They were a hard lot though better than their European predecessors. But so what? Everyone should be better than his ancestors. Twain boasts that he is a border ruffian from Missouri transplanted to Connecticut, and thus has Missouri morals and Connecticut culture. His early ancestors were Quakers chased out by the Pilgrims, who, after all, had braved the Atlantic Ocean for religious freedom and were therefore not disposed to let any pesky Quakers interfere. Twain's ancestors also included some Salem witches, who were even more severely punished by the freedom-loving Pilgrims. Twain adds that the first slave brought from Africa to New England was also an ancestor of his. Instead of bragging, members of New England societies should auction off old Plymouth Rock. These societies are really pernicious: they now serve milk and deadly lemonade, but it will soon be coffee and even cider. Disband, before it is too late. But seriously, Twain concludes, he reveres persons of Plymouth stock. They could be improved only by having been born in Missouri.

Elizabeth Hooton, William Robinson, Marmaduke Stevenson, Roger Williams.

Poem to Margaret, 1942 (P).

Be good, and be clever. But if you are too good, you will be lonely; and if you are too clever, you will be stepped on.

Margaret.

'Poetry, Veracity and Suicide.' See 'On Poetry, Veracity, and Suicide.'

'Poets as Policemen,' 1900 (S).

Twain recommends that policemen stop carrying clubs and revolvers, and instead arm themselves with poetry about spring and love. Tired now, Twain would serve as commissioner. He would like Howells to be his deputy and to send Chauncey Depew to the red-light district to recite poetry to all the unfortunates there. The region would soon be edified and depopulated.

Chauncey [M.] Depew, [William Dean] Howells.

"Police Court." See FW, 1870.

"Political Economy," 1870 (WMT 7).

While he is at home writing a weighty essay on political economy, the author is interrupted by a lightning-rod salesman. Not wanting to reveal his ignorance, the author airily orders the man to install eight rods and use about four hundred feet of zinc-plated spiral-twist wire. The author resumes his writing but soon is interrupted again, and again, by the persuasive salesman. In the end, the house and barn, and even some livestock, are equipped with hundreds of rods. Three days later, with the populace eagerly watching from a distance, a storm floats over the bristling house and the lightning goes for it. The place is hit seven hundred times in forty minutes. When the air clears, the author is able to sally forth and issue orders for the removal of all rods but three on the house, one on the kitchen, and one on the barn. Anyone interested in purchasing a few thousand feet of wire and innumerable silver-tipped points may address him.

Polonius' Advice to His Son—Paraphrased from Hamlet, 1866 (P).
    Speak little, be courteous, hold fast to tried friends, beware of quarrels but fight hard if need be, listen much, reserve judgment, dress as richly as you can afford to, neither borrow nor lend, and above all be true to yourself.

    [Laertes], Polonius.

"The Poor Editor." See "The 'Present' Nuisance."

"Poor Human Nature." See "Human Nature."

"Poor Little Stephen Girard." See "Life as I Find It."

["Portrait"], 1870 (authorship uncertain) (CG).
    The editor of the *Galaxy* explains that in the absence of Twain's usual "Memoranda" column this month [August], his portrait will be presented. It bears a close resemblance to the counterfeit presentiment of Samuel L. Clemens, editor of the Buffalo *Express*.

"The Portrait." See "Portrait of King William III."

"Portrait of King William III," 1871 (WMT 24).
    The author confesses that he can never look at portraits appear-

ing in the *Galaxy* without wanting to become an artist. He sleeps with some of the portraits under his pillow to study them at first light. He wants to hang them in the parlor, but his simpleton aunt says that they belong in the attic. The author has begun to study painting under De Mellville, graduating quickly from fences and roofs to cigar-store statues and at last to portraits. His depiction of William III, King of Prussia, has excited unbounded praise. Pius IX, Ruskin, Rosa Bonheur, and others have commended it. William III himself has suggested that the painter come over and stay free with Napoleon at Wilhelmshöhe, and bring the plate and the original portrait with him.

Rosa Bonheur, De Mellville, Frederick William, Landseer, Napoleon, Pius IX, Ruskin, J. W. Titian, William III King of Prussia.

"Post Mortem Poetry," 1870 (WMT 24).

Philadelphia newspapers, for example the *Ledger*, have the pleasant custom of publishing funereal verse along with death notices. The infant daughter of Ephraim and Laura Hawks (surname changed) is thus commemorated: her merry shout is heard no longer, and we give her up to the Lord, etc. A Becket boy is identically celebrated: his merry shout is heard no longer, etc. Ditto with the Wagner lad. Reading such poetry causes one depression, then suffering, and finally agony. Mothers are similarly mourned, and so are others, including consumptives. Such poetry sometimes makes one long for death. The author concludes by reproducing a genuine, earnest piece of peerless hogwash, obviously sincere, on the death by fire of the four Belknap children, whose mother wrongly left them in the house while she visited with neighbors. May she repent.

John Ball, Mary E. Ball, Sarah F. Ball, George Becket, John P. Becket, Julia Becket, Rev. Mr. T. K. Beecher, Catharine Belknap, Samuel Belknap, Belknap, Philip Bromley, Michael Burns, Burns, Samuel Peveril Worthington Doble, Doble, Mrs. Doble, M. A. Glaze, Clara Hawks, Ephraim Hawks, Laura Hawks, Catharine Markland, George W. Markland, Ferguson G. Wagner, Martha Theresa Wagner, William L. Wagner, Mary C. Welch, William B. Welch.

"The Postal Order Business," 1880.*

A few days ago, Twain received a letter from Thomas B. Kirby, the Postmaster General's private secretary, rebuking him for his recent complaint about postal service. Twain feels obliged to answer the callow secretary and tells him that he should mind his own business and stop being impertinent. Twain compares Kirby to a dog's tail: if Twain steps on the tail, it is only to arouse the dog. Then he compares Kirby to a bell: it is rung to call its owner's attention to something and should not ring itself. Then Twain likens Kirby to the fire which explodes ammunition, a faucet through which molasses runs, and a lightning rod rather than lightning. Finally, Twain warns Kirby that he has violated the law by using an official, franked envelope to send an unofficial, meddling message, then closes with a blessing.

Postmaster General [David M.] Key, Thomas B. Kirby.

*In Gus Williams, *Gus Williams' World of Humor* . . . (New York: Wehman, 1880).

"Postal Service" (MTP).

. . . Some Britisher and Frenchmen praises our postal system, and it does have merits; but it is imperfect. Twain, now in Berlin, then details lunacies past and present in the system, most of them the fault of zealous new postmaster generals. Then he explains a simple German method, such that he can be reached if addressed at Berlin 64W. German postal department workers are intelligent, well trained, and diligent. Pneumatic mail tubes are also efficient here. Twain incidentally praises Berlin's underground electric-wire complex, the inexpensiveness of its telegraph, and the excellence of its telephone service. German railway guides are easy to use. Finally, he notes that the German postal system invites public complaint and quickly responds to it.

John Brown, Stephan.

"Postscript," 1897.*

Twain begins by quoting John Fiske on the subject of coincidences in the history of scientific discoveries, especially the celebrated Darwin-Wallace one. Then Twain wonders whether inanimate objects can telegraph influences to human minds. He tells how the owner of a roll of rare wallpaper happened to visit a Hartford house which was being built and for which such a roll was desperately needed. Finally he explains that he went into a trance on his porch once and fancied that an approaching visitor had disappeared—only to find him inside the house two minutes later.

John Fiske, George.

*In *The American Claimant and Other Stories* (New York and London: Harper and Brothers, 1897), pp. 390-396.

"Postscript—Osteopathy" (MTP).

Twain first heard of osteopathy while in Europe recently. He wanted the practitioners to migrate to America and try it there, but they were too conservative. The rediscovery of osteopathy in America is timely, now that scientists have a more thorough knowledge of anatomy. In London, Twain saw the illustrious Dr. Kellgren save a man dying of dysentery. Twain visited Kellgren's establishment and admired everything. He followed Kellgren to Sweden in the summer. Kellgren is skillful with brevet corpses and is as much like an ordinary masseur as a blacksmith is like a goldsmith. Was America inspired by Europe to start up osteopathy? Mental telepathy is a more likely explanation. Kellgren and Still probably invented osteopathy at about the same time, through some sort of mental transference.

Dr. [Henrik] Kellgren, Lord Leighton, Sir John Millais, Dr. [Andrew T.] Still.

["Practical Joker"] (MTP).

Some practical jokes are forgivable because they are really witty. For example, when an important gentleman in Twain's home town asked Mr.— to recommend a suitable place to check into with his family while their house was being repaired, Mr.— recommended a place highly, offered to walk there to show the man, and strode along with him for two miles through wintry weather to—the poorhouse. Mr.— also once wrote the gas company to suggest their painting the lamp posts white because he could not see them.

George L. Martin, Mr.—.

"Preface" to *Mark Twain's Speeches*, 1910 (S).

If the author sold people a barrel of molasses and they got sick from eating too much of it at once instead of having substantial dinners, he would not feel guilty. Readers should take the nonsense contained here a bit at a time as seasoning to graver reading selected from elsewhere.

"Presence of Mind." See "Remarkable Instances of Presence of Mind."

"The 'Present' Nuisance," 1870 (CG).

Twain objects to the habit of readers of newspapers, either rural or city ones, of giving things to the editors and then wheedling those editors into printing free advertisements of the gifts by way of notices of them. When an editor once succumbs, he is often lost thereafter.

The Prince and the Pauper, 1881 (WMT 11).

In London, in the second quarter of the sixteenth century [1537], Edward Tudor was born, and so was wretched Tom Canty. Years pass, and Tom has been growing up in the slums of Offal Court, out of Pudding Lane, near London Bridge. He has fifteen-year-old twin sisters, Bet and Nan, a gentle mother, a vicious father named John, and a villainous grandmother—Gammer Canty. As solace from regular thrashings and cursings from John and Gammer, little Tom dreams of seeing a real prince; he even acts like a bookish little prince on occasion, verbosely holding petty court with his playmates. But reality is bitter.

One day he walks to Charing Village and on to Westminster, sees Prince Edward, is cuffed by a guard, but is immediately defended by the little prince, who even invites him into his private chambers. Alone, they chat not only about Tom's harsh family life but also about his fun swimming in the Thames River. Edward suggests that they change clothes for a moment, so that he can feel free of the restraint of regal raiment. But when he notices a bruise on Tom's hand and goes out to rebuke the soldier who caused it, rag-clad Prince Edward is instantly cast out to the mocking mob. His royal commands fall flat, and he is kicked and pursued to

Farringdon Street. When he comes upon Grey Friars' Church, taken by his father King Henry VIII from the monks and renamed Christ's Church, and converted to an orphanage, the children playing there scoff at his mien and set dogs on him. Concluding that the orphans need more care and better education, he wanders toward Offal Court and soon is caught by John Canty, who mistakes him for his son and drags him home.

Meanwhile, after amusing himself at playing prince in borrowed finery for a time, Tom begins to miss Edward and grows afraid in his glittering surroundings. But when he steps into the antechamber to look for his little host, the courtiers all bow. Even Jane Grey, the prince's cousin, mistakes him for Edward; and when Tom blurts out that he wants to go home to Offal Court, she flees to spread the rumor that the prince has become demented. Tom drifts through the palace until he comes upon sick King Henry, who also mistakes him for his son, quizzes him in Latin—which kindly Father Andrew has taught him, as well as to read—and then French, his ignorance of which leads his "father" to conclude that the rumor is true. But the lad shall still reign, and the king makes plans to have him installed in princely dignity on the morrow. Before the ceremony can occur, however, tainted Norfolk, marshall of England, must be executed and replaced. This dire news upsets tender Tom, who is urged to go to his uncle, Lord Hertford—dead Jane Seymour's brother—for comfort. This man coaches the lad, who learns fast and is careful not to offend any witnesses at court. Lord St. John enters with an order from the king that Tom must stop talking about his malady and denying his royal birth. after stumbling through an audience with Princess Elizabeth and Lady Jane Grey, Tom rests, while St. John asks Hertford whether it is possible that Tom is only an urchin. But Hertford, though he has his own secret misgivings, sternly warns that such talk is treasonous. At supper, Tom is attended by such hordes of solicitous servants that when he has to scratch his nose he waits momentarily for the official scratcher. Alone at last in his private cabinet, he tries on a suit of armor, cracks some nuts he filched from the royal table, and reads a helpful stray book on English court etiquette. Meanwhile, King Henry, who is quickly growing sicker, discovers that he has misplaced the great seal, with which to prepare the order to execute Norfolk. But he sends the Chancellor out anyway, for the small seal will do.

A gorgeous river pageant begins. Its fireworks are a thrill to all. But the crowd so hinders the progress of Canty and his "son" that the man clubs a person who interferes. When the two arrive at the Canty home, the father pretends to believe Edward's assertions and then beats him, and then beats the mother for trying to shield the boy. Once everyone is asleep, Mrs. Canty tests the child: when he does not flinch upon being awakened, as Tom has done ever since some powder exploded in his face, she knows—but will not admit even to herself—that her son is gone and that an identical stranger has replaced him. News of the death of the clubbed man, who turns out to be Father Andrews, forces Canty to gather his family together and rush away into the night. Edward escapes when his "father" is forced to stop and drink a toast to the prince, who is being feted on the river. The lad vows revenge upon his usurper. Simultaneously, the royal barge moves down the Thames to Dowgate, then up the Walbrook to Bucklersbury. Tom and his entourage proceed to the Guildhall banquet. While Edward tries unsuccessfully to demand entrance and is saved from the mob by a muscular ex-soldier named Miles Hendon, the midnight revelers within learn that King Henry has died. Tom's first official act is to pardon Norfolk.

Prince Edward is now King Edward VI. Miles takes him to famous, colorful London Bridge, where they meet Canty, who wants his son back. But when the little king refuses, Miles orders the ruffian away, and the two friends proceed to Miles's lodgings, a Bridge inn, where the ex-soldier vows to remain the daft lad's protector. The king orders Miles to assist at washing him, and the man humors him by complying and then entertains him with the story of his own woes: his father Sir Richard Hendon had three sons, kind Arthur, then Miles, and finally treacherous Hugh. Arthur and their cousin the Lady Edith were betrothed from the cradle. Although Arthur loved elsewhere and Miles loved Edith, Sir Richard would not break the contract. Since Hugh wanted Edith's fortune, he hid a silk ladder in Miles's chambers and spread the story that his brother was about to carry Edith off. The father banished Miles, then aged twenty, to the Continental wars for three years, but toward the end of that period he was captured and imprisoned for another seven. He escaped and is now heading for Hendon Hall in Kent. Grateful to his protector, Edward offers him a boon; Miles, forced to stand while the boy has been eating, asks the privilege of sitting. It is granted; further, the king knights Sir Miles! While Edward is asleep, Miles goes out to buy him some second-hand clothes; but while he is mending them, Canty and a fellow ruffian take the boy away. Miles vows to find their trail and rescue his little friend.

At about dawn of the same morning, Tom lies dreaming pleasantly, only to awaken to regal reality. He is elaborately dressed by innumerable servants and then turns to matters of state. When he learns of mounting debts, he surprisingly suggests economies. He hears petitions, patents, and other papers until his poor head nods. He plays with his "sisters" Mary and Elizabeth and also with Jane Grey, then admits Humphrey Marlow, his whipping boy. If the king fails in his lessons, Humphrey must be flogged. Tom remits each punishment hereafter and begins to pump his bright little companion so thoroughly that when Hertford returns to "remind" him of details, Tom can demonstrate the gradual return of his wits. The next day, he receives a splendid, dreary sequence of foreign ambassadors. A couple of days go by, and he suddenly hears a wild mob rush past the palace gates. Sending for information, he learns that a man, woman, and little girl are being led away to execution. Tom orders them into his presence, quizzes the alleged poisoner, satisfies himself that the man is innocent, and pardons him; then he queries the females, finds that they have been foolishly condemned for witchcraft, and spares them also. Kind Hertford, now Lord Protector, is pleased; but the general applause begins dangerously to thrill Tom, who next endures the ordeal of dining in public, as proof to the multitudes of his recovery, and rather enjoys the blaring, shiny fuss.

While Miles searches for Edward at Southwark, reasoning that if lost he would seek aid at Hendon Hall nearby, the king has been forced to join a robbers' gang, which is temporarily using a ramshackle barn as a roost. The Ruffler and Hugo appear to be the leaders; but Canty, who now calls himself John Hobbs and his "son" Jack Hobbs, is evidently a respected alumnus whose return is welcome. While Edward lies in the barn listening to the soothing rain and lamenting the death of his father, Canty boasts of killing a man, and others recall their various tortures at the hands of cruel authorities. Edward steps up and decrees majestically that harsh laws will be changed; but he is hooted at, and the tinker dubs him "Foo-Foo the First, king of the Mooncalves." Canty tries to strike the boy, but the Ruffler interposes and vows loyalty to Edward VI (though not to Foo-Foo). At dawn, the band heads for the highway. Hugo orders Edward to be his decoy in a plot to swindle a passer-by; but the boy soon tells the truth and, while the victim chases Hugo, escapes to wander, hungry and frightened, until night finds him near a barn. He enters and lies down amid smelly horse blankets. In the darkness he is suddenly touched by something horrifying. Overcoming his terror, he gropes and feels a warm calf. All is well as he snuggles up to it until morning. Two little girls enter the barn and take him to their widowed mother, who feeds him. Hearing Canty and Hugo nearby, the little king hides behind some hedges and then makes his way to an insane hermit's hut. The madman announces that he is an archangel but that, if it were not for Henry VIII, he might have been pope. The king has already revealed his identity; so the mad hermit trusses him up, gags him, and would slit his throat but for the arrival of Miles, whom, however, the hermit cannily leads away. Soon Canty and Hugo enter and take Edward off with them. Hugo treats the boy so rudely that the two are soon dueling with cudgels, at which the king is so adept because of training at court that he thoroughly drubs his enemy. Hugo grows vengeful and gets the king arrested as the thief of a dressed pig, whose owner—with Miles, now back on the scene, watching—takes her complaint before a judge. When that dignitary learns that the value of the pig was in excess of thirteen pence ha'penny, he says that the culprit must hang. In genuine anguish, the woman lowers the value to eight pence, which a nearby brow-beating constable secretly pays to the woman for the delicacy. Edward is then sentenced to be jailed and publicly flogged. Miles, however, requires the constable, under penalty of exposure to the judge, to return the pig and also to look the other way while Edward escapes.

Free at last, Miles and Edward proceed by easy stages to Hendon Hall, where they arrive after a few days. Miles is ecstatic, until in quick succession he learns from his younger brother Hugh that their father Sir Richard is dead, that their brother Arthur is dead, that Edith has married Hugh, and that Miles was reported killed in battle six or seven years ago. Hugh then denies that Miles is really his brother. Edith enters and also denies it. Miles tries to throttle the villainous master of Hendon Hall until the servants enter. But Miles so threatens them all that they soon back off; and he and Edward have a moment of respite, during which the king writes a letter to Hertford—in Latin, Greek, and English—which Miles absently pockets just before Edith returns. She again denies his identity but ambiguously warns him that anyone seeking to discomfit Hugh will meet a deadly fate. She offers him a purse with which to bribe the evil servants to help him escape, but at that instant the authorities burst in and drag both Miles and Edward off to a miserable jail. Here for a week the two see wretched sights, including the public burning of two Baptist women. Edward vows to reform the land within a month. Meanwhile, a loyal old servant named Blake Andrews has come to Miles, loudly upbraiding him but between taunts telling him the truth in whispers: Sir Richard pined for Miles, and Hugh penned the letter reporting his brother's death and forced Edith into marriage at his father's deathbed. Andrews also reports the coming coronation of Edward VI. The real king wonders whether the urchin who exchanged clothes with him is the impostor but doubts it. In due time Miles is tried and is sentenced to sit for two hours in the pillory for assaulting Hugh, who comes by to jeer with the crowd. When Edward tries to intercede, he is ordered flogged, but Miles volunteers to be his substitute. Hugh agrees at once, and the fickle crowd is impressed by Miles's bravery, as is Edward, who gratefully elevates the man to an earldom at once. Miles weeps and laughs, at the grisly humor of it all. Released at last, he desperately determines to go to London and see the new king, if necessary, to regain his birthright. Edward tags along. They arrive on February 19 [1547] and soon are hopelessly separated by a roiling mob, celebrating because tomorrow is Coronation Day.

Meanwhile, Tom Canty the impostor has grown somewhat accustomed to court splendors. He has remained kind, gentle, and anxious to revoke unjust laws; but at the same time he has almost forgotten both the real boy-king and also his own mother and sisters. Morning comes. London is alive with cheering people. The royal procession, a shining, endless serpent with Tom as its proud head, winds from the palace to Fenchurch Street, then to Gracechurch Street, past a pageant with effigies of Edward's progenitors, and through Cheapside, where Tom's mother suddenly bursts from the crowd to kiss his foot and identify herself. He denies her, and she is hurled away by a guard. Remorse immediately eats at the boy's heart, and his grandeurs seem to fall from him like rotten rags. When Hertford, now Somerset the Lord Protector, begs him to smile, Tom says that the spurned woman was his mother. The "uncle" thinks that the lad's fit has come again.

The scene is now Westminster Abbey. Beginning about four o'clock in the morning, crowds have been pouring into it. At dawn the peeresses are escorted to their seats. Later in come the peers. Finally Tom Canty, pale and silent, enters amid a whirlwind of applause. But then in rushes rag-clad Edward, demanding his throne. He is about to be tossed out when Tom orders him unhanded. After a long discussion, the true king proves his identity by telling where the missing great seal is: he hid it in an arm-piece of some armor just before he left his private chambers to rebuke the soldier who had injured Tom's hand. Later, Tom used the seal to crack nuts with!

Back to Miles. He tries to find Edward in the slums but fails, wanders into the country and sleeps, and then goes to the palace, thinking that his father's courtier friend Sir Humphrey Marlow might help him. Dead Sir Humphrey's son the whipping boy leads him into the palace, where Edward's letter in three languages nearly gets him into trouble. But soon he is in the presence of his king. Miles promptly sits down! Edward VI describes to the astonished courtiers Miles's brave kindnesses, affirms the man's title to be Earl of Kent, summons Sir Hugh and imprisons him, makes Tom the King's Ward for life, and puts him in charge of Christ's Hospital orphanage. Eventually Miles marries Edith, who was forced to deny him because Hugh threatened to kill him otherwise. John Canty is never heard of again. Tom lives a long life, in a quaint garb indicating that in his time he was royal, and smiles memorably upon many happy people. Because of his chastening experiences as a pauper, Edward VI rules mildly during his few years on the throne, before an early death.

Several footnotes at the end of the novel attest to the historical accuracy of various details.

> Lord High Admiral, Father Andrew, Blake Andrews, Anne Askew, the Bat, First Lord of the Bedchamber, Second Gentleman of the Bedchamber, Earl of Berkeley, Bernard, Black Bess, First Lord of the Buckhounds, Burns, Lord Chief Butler, the Archbishop of Canterbury, Bet Canty, Gammer Canty, John Canty, Mrs. John Canty, Nan Canty, Tom Canty, Lord High Chancellor, King Charles I, Lord

Head Cook, Lord D'Arcy, David, Lord De Courcy, Dick
Dot-and-go-One, Guilford Dudley, Cuthbert Bishop of
Durham, King Edward VI, Princess Elizabeth, Queen
Elizabeth, Chief Equerry in Waiting, Fathers of the City,
King of France, Gentlemen Pensioners, Lady Jane Grey,
Third Groom of the Stole, Hairdresser-royal, Halsey, Ar-
thur Hendon, Sir Hugh Hendon, Sir Miles Hendon, Sir
Richard Hendon, Lady Hendon, King Henry VIII, Sir
William Herbert, Edward Earl of Hertford, Hodge, Chief
Steward of the Household, Hugo, King James I, King John,
Head Keeper of the King's Hose, Lords of Kingsale, King's
Guard, Knight of the Garter, Chancellor Royal of the
Duchy of Lancaster, John Viscount Lisle, Margaret, Baron
Marley, Sir Humphrey Marlow, Humphrey Marlow, Miss
Marlow, Lady Mary, Queen Mary, Mary, Master of Cere-
monies, Lord Mayor [of London], Lord Norfolk, Norroy
King-at-Arms, Madam Parr, Peter, Head Ranger of Wind-
sor Forest, the Ruffler, John Lord Russell, William Lord
St. John, Jane Seymour, Sir Thomas Seymour, Great
Steward, Lord Surrey, Taster, Sir Thomas, Constable of
the Tower, Master of the Wardrobe, the Wen, Giles Witt,
Yeomen of the Guard, Yokel.

"The Prince and the Pauper: A Romance in Four Acts" (MTP).*
    St. John and Hertford talk. After a disturbance, the Prince
rescues Tom Canty; they talk alone, exchange clothes, and the
Prince is flung by guards into the rabble. John Canty carries him
away protesting. Tom acts like the Prince and is thought to be
mad. Before King Henry VIII, Tom is brought in and asks to be
dismissed. Instead, he is told to produce the Great Seal but cannot.
The King condemns Norfolk and then dies caressing the wrong
boy. In the woods, John Canty drags the Prince along as Tom, who
is drubbed and who then talks with Mrs. Canty about his royalty.
In the confusion which follows an announcement that King Henry
is dead, the Prince escapes and is befriended by Miles Hendon,
who thinks the boy is mad because he says that he is now the king.
Miles so humors him that the lad knights him and says that he can
sit in the royal presence. Miles frightens a jailor. The Prince tries
to prevent the burning of some female convicts and for his pains

is crowned in a mock ceremony by other prisoners. Miles is flogged in place of the grateful boy, who makes him an earl at once. As king, Tom Canty cancels the sentences of many prisoners. He makes his mother, Mrs. Canty, the Duchess of Offal Court. Miles is dragged in for killing John Canty and is given forty-eight hours to produce the true Prince or Tom will order his execution. In the nick of time, the true prince enters to prevent the coronation of Tom. An examination is held to determine who is the real prince, and Tom reminds the prince where the Great Seal is hidden. Miles, having failed to find the true prince, honorably returns to be hanged, sees his restored monarch, and sits down! The king defends the act and also Tom Canty.

> Bet Canty, John Canty, Mrs. John Canty, Tom Canty, Constable, Lady Jane Grey, Sir Miles Hendon, King Henry VIII, Hertford, Duke of Norfolk, [Lord William] St. John, the Prince of Wales.

*Twain's revision of Abby S. Richardson's original dramatic version.

'Princeton,' 1901 (S).

Twain says that his reading here at Princeton from his works represents a minor violation of his resolve never to appear on a platform again, unless at the request of a sheriff.

"The Printshop Version." See No. 44, the Mysterious Stranger.

"Private Habits of Horace Greeley," 1868 (LAIFI).

The narrator is able to tell about Horace Greeley's private habits through knowing a relative of the famous editor of the *Tribune*. Greeley gets up at 3:00 A.M., recites "Early to bed . . ." to members of his household, gives them their orders, and goes back to bed for eight more hours of snoring. He rises again, hums what he thinks is a hymn as he shaves with a dull razor, tills his expensive cabbages, drinks anything and everything at breakfast while he reads the *Tribune* with great satisfaction, and then writes an editorial in his indecipherable hand. It takes him hours to dress so that he will appear in an unstudied rumpled way on the street.

> Chaplin, Horace Greeley.

"The Private History of a Campaign That Failed," 1885 (WMT 15).
Twain explains that we have all heard stories about the [Civil]
War from important persons. He will tell about someone who
started out to do something in it but did not. Twain was a Mississippi River pilot in 1860, loyal to the Union but uneasily aware
that his father had owned slaves. In the summer of 1861, Missouri,
his native state, was invaded by Union forces, and Governor Claib
Jackson called out the militia. Twain and some others formed their
own military company in Hannibal, Marion County, and called
themselves the Marion Rangers. Tom Lyman was made captain;
Twain, second lieutenant; Jo Bowers, orderly sergeant; Ed Stevens,
corporal; and Peterson Dunlap, Smith, A. G. Fuqua, and others,
untitled soldiers. The herd-like group met at the Griffith place,
learned of the approach of some Union soldiers, and moved off to
Colonel Ralls's barn to have breakfast. On to Mason's farm, where
they obtained some sorry mounts. Twain's threw its rider with no
difficulty, and so did Stevens's. Bowers had his legs bitten by his
skinny horse. When Twain ordered Bowers to feed his little mule,
the sergeant refused. Nobody would cook. For a while they drilled
every morning. When they heard a rumor that the enemy was advancing over Hyde's prairie, the rangers fell back to Mason's farm.
A sudden rain that night was responsible for the loss of a good
deal of equipment. One of Mason's several dogs fastened on Bowers
and could be loosened only with scalding water. In the morning a
horseman announced that some nearby Union soldiers intended
to hang all bands like the rangers. It was time to hide again. Several
dull, still, lifeless days at the Mason place passed. The sound of its
wailing spinning-wheel was lonesome and empty. Time passed so
slowly that news of the enemy's coming again was actually pleasant.
Back to Ralls's area, where pickets were inefficiently established,
but only for a short time. Then the rangers slept in the corn crib,
with the rats. One night a Negro came to warn the men that a
stranger was approaching. There was a deep, woodsy stillness all
about. The enemy came down the road on horseback, and all of the
rangers fired at him. He fell, mortally wounded. The men crowded
around him and soon were most regretful. Twain felt that his campaign was spoiled. He fell back on one camp after another, finally
to one near Florida, Missouri, where he had been born. The rumor
that a Union colonel was sweeping toward the region helped make
Twain decide to quit. Curiously, that colonel was Ulysses S. Grant.
Thus he and Twain were within a few miles and a few hours of

each other, long ago. This view of war is somewhat different and
rarely gets into history books; yet it is certainly a part of the total
picture. After all, Twain learned something about war: he mastered
the art of retreating.

> Jo Bowers, Colonel Brown, Peterson Dunlap, A. G.
> Fuqua, Colonel Ulysses S. Grant, Griffith, Ab Grimes,
> Brigadier-General Thomas H. Harris, Hyde, Governor
> Claib Jackson, Jim, Tom Lyman, Mason, Mason, Colonel
> Ralls, James Redpath, Smith, Ed Stevens.

"Private History of the 'Jumping Frog' Story," 1894 (WMT 22).

Twain is amused when his friend Hopkinson Smith's Negro-
dialect story is criticized for having been first told by Boccaccio.
But then Professor Van Dyke of Princeton University tells Twain
that his "Jumping Frog" story is identical to a Greek tale called
"The Athenian and the Frog," which goes back two thousand
years. Twain recalls that he heard his story told by a serious fellow
in 1849. The main features of the story were that the hero was
taken in by a stranger and that it is natural for frogs to like to eat
shot. To show that here we have two independently good stories
based on fact, Twain then appends both a translation of the Greek
one and the pertinent part of his California tale. Next he tells how
his story was published in Henry Clapp's dying *Saturday Press*,
then in book form, and also in French in the *Revue des Deux
Mondes*. Finally he offers his retranslation of the French version
back into literal English, together with bits of French.

> Madame Blanc, Carleton, Henry Clapp, [F.] Hopkinson
> Smith, Professor [Henry] Van Dyke, Artemus Ward.

"The Private Secretary's Diary," 1972 (FM).

It is June, 1907. The Cabinet meets. Those present include God
the Father, S[on]., and H[oly]. G[host]. The case of Mrs. Fannie
Griscom is considered. Back in June of 1858, when she was four
years old, Fannie and her brother Georgie and their sister Hattie
were caught by their daddy breaking the Sabbath by playing circus. He scolded them, ordered them to sit silently for an hour,
and prayed for them. While so sitting, Fannie giggled. Georgie

and Hattie promised not to tell on her. God decrees that for her punishment Fannie shall be wasted by scarlet fever with delayed aftereffects, including an ear tumor. So it happens. Penalties are also pronounced against Georgie and Hattie. It is finally decreed that Fannie shall not suffer beyond June of 1907 but that her oldest son shall have softening of the brain and that his son shall become an idiot.

> Georgie, God the Father, Mrs. Fannie Griscom, Griscom, Griscom, Griscom, Hattie, H[oly]. G[host]., the Recording Angel, the R[ecording]. C[lerk]., S[on].

"The Privilege of the Grave" (MTP).

Only the dead have true freedom of speech. The living lack it, because speaking freely is too expensive. People are free to commit murder but are punished if caught. It is the same with free speech: we are punished for exercising the right. We all harbor secret beliefs which we dare not utter. It is safe to speak freely only from the grave.

"The Prodigal Son Returns." See FW, 1869.

"Professor Jenkins." See FW, 1869.

["Professor Silliman"], 1870 (CG).

Old Professor Silliman is asked his opinion about the quality of some coal from a certain hilly mine in New Jersey. He advises the owners to hold the hill forever: it will provide a vantage point from which to view the Last Day, and the coal will never burn.

> Professor [Benjamin?] Silliman.

"Property in Opulent London," 1874.*

The City of London is a mere village in the heart of greater London. By day 800,000 people work here, but at night only 50,000 sleep here. The City allows only property owners to vote. It has its own police and government. The estates of aristocrats are entailed and constitute much City property, which is rented for long terms, up to ninety-nine years, and often at ridiculously low rates when one considers recent inflation. One example, the Duke of Bedford owns seventy-five houses surrounding a scrupulously tended square. One house might rent for $150 a year, but if its lease were for sale today it might go for $1,000 a year. Twain takes a walk with a friend and learns that the Duke of Bedford owns everything for miles around. Later he learns that the Duke of Portland and the Marquis of Westminster are also owners of vast holdings in the City. Twain concludes by voicing his objection to the fact that in London taxes on real estate are trifling but that taxes on the many items which ordinary working citizens require are unjustly heavier.

The Duke of Bedford, the Duke of Portland, the Marquis of Westminster.

*In *Mark Twain's Sketches,* Authorized Edition (New York: American News Co., [1874]).

"Proposed Literary Cold Storage" (MTP).

Kids and grownups alike try to show off. If a person is untalented himself, he tries to become the tail of another's kite—or even a wad on that tail. But first, the wad must hide his true motives and pretend that what he does is for the talented person's betterment. Twain recently encountered such a Benevolent Wad, who has written him repeatedly to ask for a donation of inscribed books, which would be housed—along with gifts by other qualified writers —in a library which the Wad will later build. Twain appends the four-page request and then criticizes it: its English is juvenile; it offers no proof of sincerity; it betrays stupidity; and it is tasteless. Twain advises the Wad to abandon his idea of a book morgue and gratify his vanity in another manner. If he can sit still, the Wad may gain notoriety by accident. Some do. Even apples do. Look at Eve's, William Tell's, Sir Isaac Newton's. Those apples sat still, and fame came to them. Look at some animals even, for example, Samson's lion, Jonah's whale, and the fatted calf; they are all famous but did little.

The Benevolent Wad.

"Proposition for a Postal Check" (MTP).

In an elaborate dialogue, Wisdom Seeker tries to persuade Statesman that the postal department should abandon the sale of money orders, which take too much time to fill out, and instead offer for sale postal checks in the amounts of 5¢, 25¢, $1, $3, and $5, which a person could buy and complete by filling in the name of the person to whom he owes money and who could then collect from any post office.

Statesman, Wisdom Seeker.

"A Protest" (MTP).

Twain is tired of being criticized for local items in the Buffalo *Express* which he has not written. He was threatened by a person signing himself Venjens and praised by one Almira Roberts for writing an epic beginning "If the red slayer think he slays."

Jim Bradley, Almira Roberts, Venjens.

'Public Education Association,' 1900 (WMT 28).

Twain says that he was probably invited here so that he could see that others were busy also and in addition so that he could dramatize to others by means of contrast what good education might do them. He is alarmed that the Boxers have been criticized. All they want to do is to drive foreigners out of their country. Russia recently decided to retrench, not by recalling its thousands of soldiers from Manchuria, where they do not belong, but by curtailing public-school education. Twain is reminded of a Missouri farmer's response to the idea of closing public schools to save money. The man said that for every school that was closed an additional jail would have to be built.

The Czar of Russia.

"Public Lecturing." See FW, 1869.

'Public School Association.' See 'Public Education Association.'

Pudd'nhead Wilson, 1894 (WMT 16).

Twain begins by thanking William Hicks, a lawyer friend of his now in Florence, Italy, with him, for correcting the law chapters of his story, which begins in 1830 at Dawson's Landing, a sleepy, flowery little town on the Missouri side of the Mississippi River. The citizenry includes freethinking Judge York Leicester Driscoll, a proud man of forty from Virginia, and his childless, Presbyterian wife; his widowed Presbyterian sister Rachel Pratt, also childless; Pembroke Howard, a forty-year-old Presbyterian bachelor lawyer; and Percy Northumberland Driscoll, the judge's younger brother. On February 1, Percy's wife, who has lost several children, gives birth to a son and soon dies. On the same day, Percy's twenty-year-old slave Roxana also has a baby son and quickly takes charge of both infants. Also in February, well-educated David Wilson, aged twenty-five, arrives in town from New York state. When he happens to remark that he wishes he owned half of a certain howling dog so that he could kill his half, a group of townspeople conclude that he is witless and nickname him "Pudd'nhead." Getting no business when he advertises as a lawyer, he turns to accounting and surveying, determined to bide his time. His hobbies include palmistry and fingerprint-collecting. He even takes the tiny prints of Roxy's two responsibilities, Percy's son Thomas à Becket Driscoll and Valet de Chambre. They incidentally resemble each other although they are dressed quite differently, since Chambers is the offspring of Roxy, who is only one-sixteenth Negro.

One day when Percy sells "down the river" some of his slaves for petty pilfering, Roxy, who would have done some of the stealing herself but for a recent revival meeting, grows terrified: her own Chambers might be sold down the river. So she dresses vividly, preparing to drown herself and her son, but suddenly decides to bestow a kind of Calvinistic grace upon him by switching the two infants. She worries about Wilson's magic fingerprinting but is relieved when she has him take the babies' prints again and he seems unsuspicious. Fifteen years pass, during which Roxy's child, now called Marse Tom and terribly pampered, grows into a weak, abusive adolescent who frequently strikes his own mother, while the real Driscoll heir, as Chambers, becomes Tom's sturdy bodyguard but with a thick slave accent and no education. In the fall of 1845 Percy, about to die in poverty caused by foolish land speculation, frees Roxy and leaves Tom to become the indulged heir of his supposed uncle, the judge. Knowing that she is hated and planning now to become a steamboat chambermaid, Roxy momentarily arouses Wilson's suspicion by refusing his offer of drawings of

the fingerprints of Tom and Chambers for keepsakes. Colonel
Cecil Burleigh Essex, another leading citizen of Dawson's Landing,
also dies at this time.

   After doting upon Tom for two years, the judge's wife dies. Two
more years of spoiling follow; and then Tom, aged nineteen, goes
to Yale but quits after two years and returns home, improved only
in his fancy dress, smooth, ironic ways, and propensity to drink
and gamble. Then one hot June day, in 1853, the widow Patsy
Cooper and her nineteen-year-old daughter Rowena are thrilled
to receive an answer to their advertisement for lodgers: the Italian
twins Luigi and Angelo Capello are coming. The glowing pair
arrive: they are of a noble Florentine family, are musical prodigies,
and are well-traveled linguists. The Coopers—including two young
sons—are ecstatic, especially when the townspeople flock to see the
newcomers. Judge Driscoll drives them about town and introduces
them to fellow freethinker Wilson. Curiously, that morning Wilson
happened to look across the yard separating his little cottage and
the Driscoll home and saw a young woman in summer dress, bonnet,
and veil, in Tom's room.

   Back to Roxy. Freed at thirty-five, she worked for eight years
as a popular chambermaid on the *Grand Mogul*, between Cincinnati
and New Orleans, and became somewhat crippled but saved $400,
which she lost in a bank crash. So she returns to Dawson's Landing,
only to learn from Chambers that her son Tom is in debt because
of gambling, was "dissenhurrit" but then reinstated, and has been
put on a monthly allowance of $50. When Chambers tells Tom that
Roxy wants to see him, the spoiled young man cuffs and kicks the
messenger but admits the woman, only to refuse her plea for a
little money so insultingly that the fires of old wrongs leap fiercely.
She threatens to expose him. He does not know what she knows,
but her glittering anger chills him. So he meets her at the haunted
house that evening and learns to his horror that he is her son.
When he admits to being deeply in debt and to periodic robbing
in disguise, she offers to help. He must pay her half of his monthly
pension from the judge. She lies that she has left full particulars
in a safe place in case she is ever found shot in the back. Telling
him that noble Colonel Essex was his father, Roxy proudly leaves.
Tom laments his fate, feels cursed, mopes about for a week or so,
but remains fundamentally unchanged in character. He steals
again, pays his periodically reappearing mother, gambles, loses

heavily, and executes yet another town robbery. In fact, he was in his room disguised as a girl when he saw Wilson spying on him, which gave him pause until Roxy reported the arrival of the Italian twins. So out Tom goes on his raid after all and caps his success by robbing Mrs. Cooper's house while the twins are receiving.

Wilson entertains the judge, the twins, and Tom at his home. The twins can appreciate his calendar of dyspeptic aphorisms. Angelo rather likes Tom; but Luigi, who is darker and more violent, is suspicious. Tom foolishly needles Wilson about his lack of law work, talks of the man's habit of taking fingerprints, and mentions his liking for palmistry. Wilson reads Luigi's palm and reluctantly mentions that he sees Luigi has killed a man. Angelo gratefully explains: his brother long ago in India stabbed a man who was trying to kill Angelo, who concludes by describing the bejeweled weapon used. Tom is secretly glad, because he has stolen the knife and can sell it for a great sum. John Buckstone, leader of the local pro-rum political party, enters, and the group goes to a rally. When drunk there, Tom insultingly calls Luigi a "human philopena" and is promptly kicked by the hot-tempered Italian. A cry of fire suddenly rings out, and the raucous scene ends with anti-rum fireboys dousing the premises.

The next day proud old Judge Driscoll is returning with his friend Pem Howard from fishing when he learns that Luigi kicked Tom. Feeling the family insulted, he quizzes Tom, learns that the hangdog youth sued the Italian—unsuccessfully defended by Wilson—and won, and disinherits Tom when the cowardly fellow refuses to challenge his insulter to a proper duel. Tom mopes about, chats with Wilson regarding the suit and recent thefts in town, and learns that Luigi's missing dagger will do the thief no good since its loss has been advertised. Wilson is to run for town mayor. Tom returns home in time to see his uncle busily writing at his desk. Later Tom sneaks in and reads the document: it is a new will in his favor. He does not also learn, however, that his uncle's challenge to duel Luigi has been accepted. Tom is elated until he recalls that he needs money instantly. Discouraged, he soon goes to see Roxy, who reports that the duel, during which a bullet nicked her nose, resulted only in Luigi's being slightly wounded three times. Tom is sad that his uncle was not killed. Roxy tells her son to reform conscientiously, satisfy his creditors by paying interest for the time being, and hope that Providence will solve all by having the judge die soon.

There is now so much activity in town that everybody feels joyful. Tom cannot resist needling first Constable Jim Blake for not apprehending the stooped woman, his missing robbery suspect (really Tom in disguise), and then Wilson, whose secret scheme for retrieving the gemmy dagger—through secret advertising to pawnbrokers—Roxy guessed and thus saved Tom. He gains favor with his uncle by explaining that he could neither duel Luigi, a hired assassin, nor alert his uncle—Tom did not know of the duel in time, anyway—because both he and Wilson had pledged silence as to Luigi's having killed the Indian. Tom begins to circulate the story that the twins probably never had a fancy knife or if so still have it. Next Tom takes a boat to St. Louis to sell part of his swag but is robbed on the way. When he returns in dejection to Roxy, that magnificent mother volunteers to let him sell her as a slave up the river for $600 to clear all his debts and leave him a little extra cash. Tom agrees but in reality sells her down the river, to an Arkansas farmer, as she discovers when, on the boat bearing her to her doom, she observes the current of the Mississippi!

Next, election time comes around, and Judge Driscoll campaigns against the twins, who run for the aldermanic board. He crushes them by suggesting that no knife was ever lost and that it would turn up when needed by an assassin. Wilson is elected mayor, but the judge suddenly grows weak from his many exertions. Meanwhile, Roxy, disguised as a Negro in man's clothes, pounces upon Tom in his St. Louis room. Between sobs and scowls, she tells her chagrined son that when she was overworked by a mean Yankee overseer egged on by her new owner's cruel Yankee wife, she felled him with a stout stick, galloped to the river on his horse, stole a canoe, intended to drown herself, but chanced to drift to the *Grand Mogul*—headed for St. Louis—and so escaped. She orders Tom to confess to his uncle that he sold Roxy and beg enough money to buy her back from the Arkansan, who is now in town and whom Tom is forced to admit he has already promised to help find Roxy. Tom pretends to agree and escorts his mother to the deserted wharf where she is residing. She has a knife and threatens to stab him to death if he makes trouble and to kill herself if apprehended. On his way back home, Tom privately plans to steal, rather than wheedle, the money from his uncle. Judge Driscoll refuses Luigi's challenge—the foreigner is not a gentleman after all—but loudly promises to defend himself on the street if they meet. Wilson tried to pacify Luigi, explaining that the judge is a doting step-parent who will believe anything Tom says.

Late at night that ne'er-do-well disguises himself as a girl again, arms himself with the Indian knife, and is about to rifle the safe of his napping uncle when he awakens and screams. Tom instantly stabs him to death, drops the knife, seizes some bank notes, and escapes out the back as the Capello twins—abroad in the still night for their habitual stroll—enter the murder room from the front in answer to the judge's scream. Tom bumps into the Clarkson sisters but does not stop until he arrives at the haunted house, where he burns his disguise. He then takes furtive passage to St. Louis, wires words of comfort to his aunt—saying that he read the dreadful news in the papers—and returns to lament and be rich at last. Found by Mrs. Pratt and then two neighbors in the judge's sitting room, Luigi is indicted for murder, with Angelo named as accomplice. Wilson searches high and low for an independent murderer, to save his clients.

The trial goes badly at first. Pembroke Howard, prosecuting attorney, demands the death penalty. The people generously pity Pudd'nhead Wilson, whose main arguments are that the Clarkson sisters saw a strange woman leaving the Driscoll house and that neither twin showed any bloodstains. Tom remorselessly needles Wilson, and Roxy—free again and happily in court—eagerly awaits the verdict of guilty so that she can hoot at the twins. Then, late one night, Wilson, moodily going over his collection of fingerprints to find a set from some woman to match those found on the murder weapon, suddenly checks further and discovers that they are identical to Tom's. More research sheds light on yet another mystery. Next morning in court, Wilson repeats the evidence favoring Luigi and adds that no revenge-seeker would have remained at the scene of the murder, nor would he have dropped the weapon used. Then Wilson theorizes that robbery was the motive and that the murderer disguised himself as a woman. By this time Tom has begun to stir uneasily. Next Wilson brings out his long-preserved fingerprint collection, proves to the fascinated jury that he can identify various persons present by their prints, and finally reports in thundering rhetoric that the real

Thomas Driscoll and the real Valet de Chambre were exchanged in their cradles and that the man posing as Tom is the bloody-handed murderer—which can be proved when he puts his finger-prints on the courthouse window beside the jury. Tom's sliding unconscious to the floor and Roxy's act of kneeling are sufficient confessions.

Pudd'nhead Wilson is a grand success now. Broken Roxy joins a church and finds some solace there. The real Thomas Driscoll continues her pension. He is himself, however, a perpetual social misfit because of his gait, attitudes, gestures, bearing, and laugh—all those of a slave. The creditors of the Percy Driscoll estate do not want to be at an inordinate loss; so they recoup some funds by getting the governor to pardon the real Chambers, the murderer, and then selling him "down the river."

In a note, Twain explains that some of his plots begin as short tales and grow. Thus, *Pudd'nhead Wilson* changed into a tragedy from an original farce, about Italian Siamese twins, with one of whom Rowena Cooper falls in love. Rowena's two brothers were also characters, as was Aunt Betsy Hale. But they all became irrelevant. So when the serious book was finished, the author considered noting at Pudd'nhead Wilson's calendar entry for July 4, at the head of Chapter XVII, that Rowena went to watch the fire-works and drowned in the well. He also planned to weed out the Cooper boys, Aunt Patsy Cooper, and Aunt Betsy, by drowning them too. But since the whole book was unsatisfactory anyway, there really was no need. He did separate the twins and let them retain their foreign origin—for no good reason.

Jim Bangs, Jim Blake, John Buckstone, Count Angelo Capello, Count Luigi Capello, Capello, Signora Capello, Misses Clarkson, Dr. Claypool, [Henry] Cooper, [Joe] Cooper, Patsy Cooper, Rowena Cooper, Dobson, Percy Northumberland Driscoll, Mrs. Percy Northumberland Driscoll, Thomas à Becket Driscoll, Judge York Leicester Driscoll, Mrs. York Leicester Driscoll, Colonel Cecil Bur-leigh Essex, No. 5, No. 4, Fuller, the Gaikower of Baroda, Granger, Aunt Betsy Hale, Hale, Hanks, Billy Hatch, Wil-liam Hicks, Higgins, Holcomb, Pembroke Howard, Sally Jackson, Jasper, John Mason, Nancy, Orton, Pilligrew, Pocahontas, Mary Pratt, Rachel Pratt, Judge [Sim] Robin-son, Rogers, Roxana, No. 6, Cap'n John Smith, John

Smith, Stephens, No. 3, Valet de Chambre, David Pudd'n-
head Wilson.

'Pudd'nhead Wilson Dramatized,' 1895 (S).

Twain tells the European audience attending a dramatization of
Pudd'nhead Wilson that he has never given a speech before without some preparation. Further, crossing the ocean as he has just
done is no help in speech-making. He congratulates Mayhew for
making a good drama out of the novel. Twain has play-writing
ability himself, but no manager ever agrees.

[William Dean] Howells, Mayhew [Frank Mayo?].

"Punch, Brothers, Punch," 1878 (WMT 19).

Mark encounters some jingling rhymes in a newspaper. They end
thus:

Punch, brothers! punch with care!
Punch in the presence of the passenjare!

He finds that he can do no work—cannot add a tragic chapter to
the novel he is writing—until after a couple of days of misery he
tells his friend the Rev. Mr.— about the jingle. Then the burden
falls from Mark. But the minister is now oppressed. He can hardly
deliver an intelligent funeral sermon in nearby Boston for his
dear friend George. And how does Mark save his friend from an
asylum? By having him discharge the jingle into the ears of students at a neighboring university. Therefore if you come upon these
rhymes, avoid them.

George, Mark, Rev. Mr.—.

"Putting Up Stoves," 1872.*

First, put on a ragged old coat, to keep falling plaster off your
shirt. Then mark some soot on your nose. (No progress is possible
without your first doing so.) You, your wife, and the hired girl
must then carry the stove from woodshed to parlor. Jam your
thumbnail on a doorpost along the way. Then find the stove legs,
since you forgot them up to this point. Put the legs in place and then
let the stove fall once. Then take the stovepipe to the tin shop
for repair. Insert the mended pipe and watch the stove fall off its

legs once more. Finally, drive some nails into the ceiling to hold a wire, which is to hold the pipe elbow. Drop the hammer on your wife's head. The ceremony is concluded.

*In *One Hundred Choice Selections, No. 5,* ed. Phineas Garrett (Philadelphia: Garrett, 1872).

"Quaker City," 1927.*

In his Wall Street office, Captain Dusenberry interviews and reads testimonials concerning prospective passengers aboard his *Quaker City,* which is going to the Holy Land and on around the globe. He takes all applicants who pay the required $1,500 fare. Once on the high seas, Mark Twain, Stiggers, and Dan Sproat are disappointed and while away their time playing cards and drinking, to the annoyance of the sanctimonious Patriarchs, including Elder Homily and Sister S.

> Bascom, Beecher, Jno. Butterfield, the Committee on Credentials, Cripple, the Drummer Boy, Captain Dusenberry, Minister at the Court of France, Elder Homily, James, Gerre Washington Jones, J. B. Jones, Jno. Jones, Wm. H. Jones, Livingston, Livingston, Maid, Maggie Mitchell, Patriarch, Deacon Pendergrass, Elder S, Sister S, General Sherman, Jno. Smith, Jno. H. Smith, Jno. Potter Smith, Jno. W. Smith, Dan Sproat, Stiggers, Mark Twain, Sister Whistler.

*The Quaker City Holy Land Excursion (New York: [M. Harzof]), 1927.

"The Quarrel in the Strong-Box" (MTP).

One day in a banker's strongbox a Nickel and a Copper start arguing about the Declaration of Independence, the Constitution, and discrimination. Copper believes in the equality of money, but Nickel feels that he is more welcome in society, that copper-colored people belong in the kitchen, and that Copper has a rank— that is, a smell—of its own. When a thin old Half Dollar urges Nickel not to be conceited, Nickel insults him for losing value. A Ten-Dollar Gold-Piece says that any coin used for a tip is offensive to him. A Hundred Dollar Bill and a Thousand Dollar Bond complain of being crowded; but when they start arguing, the

Bill hits the Bond and leaves some green on his snowy face. Such a jangling fight then breaks out that the police take the entire box to court, where his Honor opines that although each piece of money is created equal, it is a law that nature's children are unequal, in both appearance and reality, regardless of any Constitution, and that equality means only the same right to try with what one has: after all, each piece of money can earn 5% a year, whether his talent is large or small.

Copper, Half Dollar, his Honor, Hundred Dollar Bill, Nickel, Ten-Dollar Gold-Piece, Thousand Dollar Bond.

'Queen Victoria,' 1908 (WMT 28).

Twain feels honored to be asked to speak in celebration of the birthday of Queen Victoria, now justly imaged as a star which has fallen to extinction but whose light still shines upon us. She was peerless as a beneficent moral force. In her office she was without reproach, which cannot be said of any monarch preceding her on her throne or any other. In heart and character, she was admirable and memorable. A righteous mind—that of Prince Albert—was beside her. War between England and America is unthinkable while the son of Albert and Victoria rules England.

Prince Albert, [King Edward VII], Queen Victoria.

"Queen Victoria's Jubilee," 1909 (WMT 29).

A parade is valuable as a spectacle and as a symbol. A Mardi-Gras march is merely a show. The post-Civil War march up Broadway by regiments of New York veterans, with gaps in their ranks to indicate their fallen comrades, had memorable symbolic value. Queen Victoria's Jubilee procession may be regarded as a fine show but more importantly as a unique symbol. There has always been a London. Five thousand years ago its tribes wore skins, and their chiefs warpaint. London was not much when Alfred burned those cakes, nor even when the Conqueror first saw it. But all of London glowed in 1415, when England celebrated the gigantic victory at Agincourt, during which 15,000 Englishmen routed a French army of 100,000 soldiers, killing 8,000 noblemen and taking the remaining 1,500 of the nobility as prisoners to march in a stupendous parade through the English capital in December.

A young man of the time, who would have been a correspondent if he had been born five hundred years later, communicated his impressions to the author through a spirit medium. The young fellow rose with a pass from the Tower to the city and through it to his seat at St. Paul's. Windows, balconies, and roofs were colorfully crowded with people. A distant roar announced the coming of the procession. At last King Henry V appeared, tall, handsome, and brilliantly armed. His robe-clad prisoners were escorted by 3,000 English knights in glittering armor, followed by 5,000 men-at-arms, all veterans of Agincourt, and then that godless ruffler Sir John Falstaff. As Henry and his vast entourage passed St. Paul's, they bowed and simultaneously raised their shining shields. Queen Victoria's pageant is an impressive contrast. Between 1415 and now much moral progress has occurred. Criminal laws have been modified, liberty broadened, the modern newspaper introduced, the international copyright instituted, women considerably liberated, workingmen's unions organized, and the working day reduced. Scientific inventions have multiplied, to render life both happier and more accursed. During Victoria's reign, British rule has been vastly extended. The meek shall indeed inherit the earth! The author is now at his seat in the Strand. Houses on each side as far as he can see are packed, like beds of flowers. Soon the procession has no visible beginning or end. Bodies of soldiery, each unit in a different color, move splendidly past. The whole thing allegorically suggests the Last Day. Yellow soldiers, then black, then brown all troup by, with samples of white. Fifty thousand•soldiers are in London now. Present also is Prince Rupert of Bavaria, to whose Stuart mother, Princess Ludwig, Jacobites pay unavailing homage. Whitelaw Reid is there, to represent the United States. The excitement mounts. Then a landau approaches, drawn by eight cream-colored horses. It is preceded by Lord Wolseley and followed by the Prince of Wales. The Queen Empress is there! She *is* the British empire. Individuals and representatives of certain groups are absent. They include capitalists, manufacturers, laborers, religious dissenters, speculators, Cecil Rhodes, and Doctor Jameson. When one sees a rainbow, he enjoys it but need not forget the forces behind it.

Captain Ames, [Barnett] Barnato, the Lord Chief Justice of England, Sir John Falstaff, King Henry V, Doctor [Sir Leander Starr] Jameson, Knight Templar, Princess

Ludwig, the Lord Mayor [of London], the Premier, Whitelaw Reid, Cecil Rhodes, Prince Rupert of Bavaria, the Speaker of the House, Queen Empress Victoria, the Prince of Wales, Lord [Garnet Joseph] Wolseley.

["The 'Raft Passage' from *Life on the Mississippi*"]. See ["The Suppressed Chapter of *Life on the Mississippi*"].

"A Railroad Mint—What the Legend Says." See RL.

"Rambling Notes of an Idle Excursion." See "Some Rambling Notes of an Idle Excursion."

["Randall's Jew Story"], 1972 (FM).

Some old men are talking intemperately about Jews, until Randall the bank president begins to tell about a fine young Jew he once saw years ago, back in 1850. He was on a steamboat heading for New Orleans. A slave trader named Hackett was gambling with old Fairfax, a courtly old Virginia planter. Fairfax was losing so heavily that a handsome, alert Jew named Rosenthal asked to take his seat until his luck might change. When Hackett objected, Rosenthal said that he always hated to see an honest man robbed. Hackett grew offensive but was faced down, and the game continued. Later Fairfax sat in again but lost disastrously, until finally he even bet and lost his beautiful daughter's terrified servant, a pretty mulatto named Judith. The trader demanded payment on the spot, whereupon Rosenthal interfered again, offering to buy the trembling girl back for the Fairfaxes for $1,500. Spurned with a sneer, Rosenthal slapped Hackett resoundingly and was immediately challenged. Randall was the brave Jew's willing second. The dueling party put ashore, and Rosenthal shot Hackett to death. The Jew had been temperate but when reason failed resorted unflinchingly to courage and thus saved Judith. Randall concludes his tale by saying that ever since the event he has weighed Jews in unloaded scales.

Fairfax, Miss Fairfax, Hackett, Judith, Randall, Rosenthal.

'Reading-Room Opening,' 1900 (S).

Twain declares the reading room at Kensal Rise, London, now formally open. Communities should provide intellectual food and willingly tax themselves to do so. Beginning with newspapers, which are important in spreading accounts of disaster, and working on up, one can use a reading room to gain an introduction to a library. A little New Zealand girl gave Twain confidence recently by writing to tell him that she knew his name as Mark Twain and not Clemens because Clemens was the name of a patent-medicine man whose first name was not Mark, and further that Mark and Twain are in the Bible.

"Real Estate versus Imaginary Possessions, Poetically Considered: My Ranch," 1865 (SS).

Twain reads a poem called "My Kingdom," by Paul Duoir, is momentarily taken in by it, but then realizes that the poet's kingdom is only the heart of his beloved. It cannot be rented, armed, or sold; and—like most kingdoms—it may be densely tenanted. Twain composes his own poem, called "My Ranch": kingdom becomes ranch; treasures and wealth, turnips and oats; strength, fence; sky and clouds, stones and clods; and speaking queen, squeaking sow.

Paul Duoir.

The Reason Why, 1869 (probably by Twain) (P).

A mother explains to her daughter that men start to propose and then go away because they start to think about the cost of the girl's clothes.

["A Recently Discovered Twain Letter"]. See RL.

"The Reception at the President's," 1870 (CG).

The narrator drifts into the White House with a flood of other visitors, waits in a long reception line until he reaches President Grant, and then talks at great length even though a tactless man behind him seems anxious to have his chance to shake hands with the general. The narrator has to rebuke the fellow repeatedly, because he really wants to continue telling about Governor Jim Nye's more gaudy receptions thrown for the Indians out in Nevada. Finally he moves on, shouting the last of his Nevada news.

Tom Fitch, Mrs. [Ulysses S.] Grant, President and General [Ulysses S.] Grant, the King of Darkness, Governor Jim Nye, Bill Steward.

"The Recurrent Major and Minor Compliment," 1972 (FM).

Twain explains that a beautiful woman is complimented on her beauty, an orator on his oratory, a strong man on his strength, and so on. These are all major compliments, of the sort that individuals who know themselves expect and therefore are not especially pleased by. Each individual has several traits which he thinks might earn him compliments. But he is deeply pleased only when exceptionally astute persons praise him for a trait which he knows he has but which most observers do not notice. For example, says Twain, he was once solemnly complimented by an illustrious European sage for being utterly serious. Twain thinks that his seriousness should be obvious and sets up an imaginary dialogue between himself and the sage. The conversation should lead anyone to conclude that every sane person over fifty years of age has known pain, disappointment, shame, and grief, and that he ought therefore to be regarded as serious.

He.

"Reflections on the Sabbath," 1866 (WG).

God should have created the world in three days, because that would have doubled the number of Sundays in the week. However, we should not question providential wisdom but instead take things as we find them. Twain is a brevet Presbyterian and a brevet member of Dr. Wadsworth's church. The Presbyterian hell and heaven are best. Presbyterian hell is all fire and brimstone; so you know where you stand. And Presbyterian heaven is all happiness, because there is nothing to do. Wildcat religions have different, less satisfactory conceptions of heaven and hell. In one, it is all study and progress; in the other, merely remorse of con-

science, which is hardly a punishment at all. Dr. Wadsworth
preaches ably but often frowns after he makes a good joke.

Michael Reese, Dr. [Charles] Wadsworth.

"The Refuge of the Derelicts," 1972 (FM).
George Sterling, an idealistic young poet, is discouraged. He
tells his bluff old friend David Shipman that when he approached
Admiral Abner Stormfield about his project he was summarily told
to go to hell. George explains to kindly old David what his project
is: to erect a monument to Adam, for which he naturally needs
funds. But the Admiral did not let him in or even ask his name.
David regards this as fortunate because now George can try again.
David tells the naïve fellow that each person has a weak spot and
can be bribed through it. With some it is greed, with others vanity;
still others are compassionate or dote on their children. As for
the Admiral, he thinks that he knows a lot, especially about the
Bible, is religious and believes in temperance, and fancies that he
can sing. But the avenue to his purse is through his cat. David,
who knows most of the people on George's proposed subscription
list, telephones the Admiral and arranges an interview. Off George
goes.

Stormfield is called Admiral only through courtesy. He was born
on a whaler, spent seventy years at sea—none in any navy—and has
now been retired for a decade. He is hearty and rough, bald-headed
and of a varicolored complexion. George enters, is ordered to
take an uncomfortable chair, and the inquisition begins. When
asked to expound on any miracle, George brilliantly declines,
saying that David Shipman warned him that the Admiral could
outtalk him on that score with incredible eloquence. Highly
gratified, the Admiral is about to take another tack when his
gloriously beautiful cat—Bagheera, nicknamed Bags—slinks in, and
George wisely snatches him up, drapes him across his lap, and
strokes him ecstatically, murmuring poetic praise of him the
while. Moist-eyed, the Admiral is thoroughly won over and orders
his guest to take a softer chair. Soon the old fellow is chatting
affably about his companion Aunt Martha—only a kind of second
cousin often removed—and his grand-niece Jimmy Fletcher Stormfield, no relation but in reality a waif whom he and Martha have

reared, and then about the unique independence of all real cats. The two men watch as Bags does a trick: he paws the fire out of a little lamp. The Admiral easily drifts into some gossip about Martha, who he says is sixty years old, profane, and bad-tempered, and once loved a sailor named Eddy who was swallowed by a whale. For years she loved his memory and hoped that he would return. Then as she aged she began to think of him as her absent son, and later as her grandson. Still, Presbyterian as she is, she hopes that he will reappear. George ventures to doubt that he ever will, and the Admiral readily agrees. Meanwhile Bags has started to stalk the Admiral as though he were a bird to catch. The Admiral turns his back, to play the game; and Bags comes closer and then leaps like a rocket onto his shoulder. In comes Martha, all sweetness, soft voice, and silky white hair. When she says that she wishes to advertise for a lodger, though they do not need the money, George volunteers and is quickly invited to come.

The happy poet delivers his belongings to the Admiral's lame old nautical butler—a man named Tom Larkin and nicknamed the Bos'n—then goes to report his progress to David Shipman, who is pleased and explains that the Admiral had a sadness fifty years ago. He was so embarrassed by Father Matthew's temperance campaign in New Bedford on one occasion when he returned from a long voyage that he signed the pledge and sent in his name to join the Society. He then shipped out for three years, remained grogless the whole time though sorely tempted by his reeling Kanaka crew, and finally returned to New England. He roared thirstily into the Society and demanded that his name be stricken from the rolls, only to be informed that he had been blackballed and therefore had never been made a member. David and George agree that nothing happens by accident, that the Admiral was so saddened by the experience that it influenced him much later to convert his residence into what David describes as "The Haven of the Derelict" and "The Refuge of the Broken Reed."It seems that his home is always open to life's varied failures.

And now excerpts from George's diary. The poet is back at the Admiral's in time for supper, which is also attended by Martha, Jimmy, and a loud middle-aged lady called the Marchesa di Bianca, the middle syllable of whose title the Admiral pronounces "cheese." Bags sits in a highchair at dinner but plans to eat by himself later, according to the Admiral, who also explains certain

theological principles which the cat allegedly has discussed with
him. Adverting to Adam, the Admiral further startles George by
expressing his concern for Satan, who after all—like Adam—figures
prominently in the Bible, which is entirely sacred; it follows that
Satan, also in it, is likewise sacred. The Admiral reasons that
Satan has been trying unsuccessfully to tempt the world ever since
he offered kingdoms to Christ; so he deserves our pity. The Bos'n
announces eight bells; and divine service follows, with the Admiral
intoning prayers and hymns most reverently. But then he prays that
God will save a certain unnamed one. Is the Admiral egocentrically
alluding to himself?

A week later, George is still there, according to his diary. He is
modifying his opinion of mankind. Everyone is interesting, if only
a person can understand what is going on secretly. George meets
a former mailman named Smith, there at the Admiral's refuge.
While George paints his portrait, Smith gradually opens up and
tells about himself. He had a happy boyhood, was a journeyman
machinist at age nineteen, met Mary, married her, and was ecstatically happy for a year. But then he made the mistake of becoming a
mailman and was soon envied by his old friends. He got supercilious and tried to develop more exalted friendships. He and his
wife began to spend above their means; and he stole from the
mails, was caught, and was jailed for two years. Mary fell, hurt
her spine, and lost her mind. Smith now owes his salvation to the
Admiral. All the same, he is bitterly pessimistic. When George
mentions his plan to build a monument to Adam, Smith says that
he hates Adam, because he gave mankind life, but also loves him,
because he brought restful death into the world. When Smith
leaves, the old Bos'n comes in to sit for his portrait and chats
with George about Smith, who he says cannot help his pessimism.
He was born that way, and the wretched news of the world oppresses him constantly and unbearably. The Bos'n reads the headlines to George and makes that young man miserable with their
catalogue of disasters.

Days pass. George finds his senses growing brisk, and life is all
full of substance for him. He is beginning to sympathize with
others and thus to know himself better. Various derelicts sit, and
he paints them. While he works on the Admiral's portrait, that
gruff old man lectures on the subject of Adam to several derelicts,
including Uncle 'Rastus, a strong, freethinking, bent old Negro,

and to Aunty Phyllis, an old black Methodist, who runs a nearby boardinghouse. The Admiral feels that Adam was both man and child, and God should have warned him more sympathetically, as one does an erring child. 'Rastus and Phyllis want Adam to have his monument, which pleases George. Then the Admiral discusses Adam's greatest accomplishment—naming the animals. Adam would have named the ornithorhyncus and the pterodactyl, too, except that the alphabet was then so new that he was in danger of running out of letters. The marchesa interrupts to complain that the Bos'n has insulted her, simply because she has championed the cause of poor Rev. Caleb Parsons. It seems that the Bos'n accused her of being so nearsighted that she could not hear thunder. The Admiral weighs the evidence carefully and then renders his verdict: Bos'n, not guilty of intending slander; marchesa, guilty of resenting the intention; Bos'n, innocent of accomplishing slander since what he said is not actionable—God causing both nearsightedness and thunder—and marchesa, innocent of being able to convict him of slander. Case dismissed. George is impressed but puzzled. The marchesa starts in again on the Bos'n, this time accusing him of saying that she said lack of money is the root of evil. While the Admiral ponders his verdict, George gazes at the collection of derelicts: Strother the drunkard, the Twins—Jacob, who had money but lost it, and Curry, his coachman, who inherited wealth, with the result that Jacob became Curry's coachman, but then Curry invested his money and lost it—the ex-Senator, the General, and Peters the frustrated inventor who turned forger. The Admiral judges that both money and lack of it are roots of evil; then gently beseeching the marchesa to simmer down, he returns to the subject of Adam, summarizes Darwin's theory, and urges everyone to be kind to Adam, a relative easier to identify with than germs and pterodactyls are. George's dream of a monument to Adam seems to be possible now, because of the Admiral's support.

Ten days pass. George comforts various derelicts by lending a fresh ear to their tales of disappointment and failure. He and the Bos'n agree that the derelicts are sorry not only for their sins but sometimes also for good deeds which have caused ruin. For example, Henry Clarkson, one of the Admiral's guests, was a rising poet and the assistant editor of a religious magazine when he happened to notice a fraudulent advertisement in proof stage,

showed it to Haskell the aging editor, but learned from him that
it was planned as a trap to lure unwary investors. Clarkson resigned from his post, went to his fiancée to explain that honor
was more important than money, but was rebuffed and soon became an expensively honorable derelict. George concludes that the
story is tragic, even though Clarkson was always relatively insignificant.

Every day or so a new person comes by. George enjoys meeting
them all. The Bos'n has a theory that everyone has at least one
good point and also is slightly insane. He explains, for example,
that the marchesa loves children and once rescued a child from a
raging fire. Even Satan, a flitting derelict who occasionally drops
by and thinks he is *the* Satan, is good in one sense: he is intensely
charitable. The Bos'n says that even George has his good side,
though as yet it is unrevealed; and as for his insanity, look at his
plan for an Adam monument. At this, George grows huffy and
walks away.

George explains that 'Rastus and Phyllis have argued intermittently about an event which occurred thirty years ago. 'Rastus
stopped a runaway horse and buggy, and thus saved a wealthy
man, his beautiful wife, and their lovely child from certain death.
In gratitude the rich man gave 'Rastus $1,000, with which he
bought a farm; then he took out a mortgage, worked himself to
death until rheumatism stopped him, and finally drifted into the
Admiral's circle. Phyllis argues that the horse, buggy, harness,
and the clothes of wife and child came to $1,014; so 'Rastus was
cheated. When she adds that a special providence placed him in the
road to effect the rescue, he counters by wondering that such a
providence could spook the horse in the first place. Then there is
Governor Stanchfield Garvey, now eighty years old, with kind
eyes which betray a visionary and unstable nature. He was a
printer's apprentice; studied to be a scholar, a lawyer, a minister,
and a Christian Scientist; was alternately a prohibitionist and a
whiskey supporter; edited a weekly paper and bought a business;
became engaged simultaneously to two girls but married only
No. 2; became Secretary—and even Acting Governor—of a new
territory but was not practical enough to get on any party ticket
when the territory became a state; and finally returned home to live
on the charity of considerate friends until his wife died a few
years ago. Now, like the poet Clarkson, Garvey constantly wishes

that he could go back and have his best chance to make good. Now it is time for an entertainment at the Admiral's haven for derelicts. Rev. Caleb Parsons gives a lecture on the benevolence of nature, with motion pictures provided by an amateur naturalist named Edgar Billings and flashed on a big screen. Parsons wishes to show nature's love and concern for all her creatures, even the tiniest. He tells how a spider eats her mate and then produces baby spiders which attack her. Then he goes on to explain how a wasp drags the spider off to its hole and feeds her alive and piecemeal to its larva. All this time Billings's pictures graphically illustrate the ennobling lecture. The audience regards nature's plan as intelligent and grand, but decides not to eat for a week.

> Adam, Bates, Benson, Benson, the Marchesa di Bianca, Edgar Billings, Henry Clarkson, Cully, Derelict, Eddy, Eve, Aunt Martha Fletcher, Jimson Flinders, Governor Stanchfield Garvey, Mrs. Stanchfield Garvey, the General, Haskell, Henry, Jacob, Tom Larkin, Louise, Mary, Father Matthew, Member, No. 1, Rev. Caleb Parsons, Peters, Mrs. Peters, Aunty Phyllis, Uncle 'Rastus, Satan, Satan, the Senator, David Shipman, Mary Smith, Smith, Mrs. Smith, Smith, Smith, Smith, Son of Temperance, George Sterling, Admiral Abner Stormfield, James Fletcher Stormfield, Stormfield, Mrs. Stormfield, Strother, Mrs. Strother, Strother, Mary Walker, Walker, Mrs. Walker.

'A Rejoinder by Mark Twain,' 1887.*

It seems wrong for Matthew Arnold to criticize the grammar of General Grant's memoirs, when Arnold's criticism contains a number of errors itself. It is a fact that many reputable authors write ungrammatically, as Henry H. Breen's *Modern English Literature: Its Blemishes and Defects* shows. Besides, Grant's book is great and unique, has thunderous military phrases in it which will thrill Americans as long as America lasts, and also shows its author's admirable love of peace.

> Matthew Arnold, Henry H. Breen, General [Ulysses S.] Grant.

*In *General Grant by Matthew Arnold with a Rejoinder by Mark Twain,* ed. John Y. Simon (Carbon and Edwardsville: Southern Illinois University, Press, 1966).

"Remarkable Gold Mines," 1880 (LAIFI).

The author replies to a newspaper article about gold-bearing water out at Calistoga Springs by reporting that he once owned the springs. He used to extract gold by giving an old uncle of his drinks of water, then attaching him to a machine which sucked the gold through his pores. Better though is the gold-bearing wind whistling along Catgut Canyon. To precipitate gold from the breezes there, set out persons heated by passion and let them sigh or swear dividends of gold dust. Soon Catgut tradewinds will appear on the New York stock market.

William Abrahams, John Harbison, Aleck Norton.

"Remarkable Idiot" (MTP).

In San Jose lives a middle-aged idiot named W. Frank Strewitt (or Street). He wants to aid mankind. So he predicts earthquakes. The newspapers let him run prophecies and descriptions, which, to be sure, often scare out-of-town visitors when they read them. Poor Strewitt is always wrong. One night he was looking through his telescope for signs of a predicted moonquake when an earthquake, which he had predicted to occur seven months later, came early and knocked him into his own cellar.

W. Frank Strewitt.

"Remarkable Instances of Presence of Mind," 1866 (CJF).

On one of her voyages from San Francisco to the Sandwich Islands, the *Ajax* meets a storm so severe that for two days and nights everything is jumbled together and no table can be set. At one point when a particularly rough sea knocks a group of people together, over a praying voice can be heard a card player asking his companions to remember that he played the three. One pitchy night a passenger named Lewis L. . . . mistakes an order about bearing a hand aft for a warning that some caged bears are after him. He runs in fright but, learning the truth, puns about not bearing the experience well and barely escaping.

Captain F. . . . , Lewis L. . . .

"A Remarkable Stranger." See "About a Remarkable Stranger."

"A Reminiscence of the Back Settlements" (CRG). See "The Under-taker's Chat."

"Reminiscences of the Back Settlements." See "The Undertaker's Chat."

Report from Paradise, ed. Dixon Wecter (New York: Harper, 1952). See "Captain Stormfield's Visit to Heaven" and "Letter from the Recording Angel."

[*Republican Letters*], 1868.*
   "My Trip on the Henry Chauncey." Twain charters the *Henry Chauncey* in New York, lets hundreds of other passengers on as his guests, and steams past Hatteras and Cuba to Panama, where they change to the *Sacramento,* bound for San Francisco. A group of easy-going passengers enjoys everything: heavy seas, cold, tropical heat, shopping ashore, food aboard ship, and lively punning. The night before they reach their destination, they have a party and read poetry of their own composition.
   "Captain Ned Wakeman." In Panama harbor, Twain sees Captain Ned Wakeman aboard his *America.* The salty fellow explains that he has been stuck here for six months and hates the ordeal more than anything in his life except for the time an apparently sweet old captain first wooed him—and a few other childish cronies—to sea and then abusively treated them during the whole voyage.
   "My Return to Virginia City." Twain visits Nevada, where he lec-tures and also compares May Day in a howling snowstorm there to his memories of May in the balmy Mississippi Valley. He visits a modern silver mine and contrasts its operation with methods back in 1864, when he dangled down into mines by rope and windlass, and carried a candle between his teeth. He describes a crooked mine superintendent whose illegal mill was providentially washed away by a flood.
   "One or Two California Items." Twain rambles through a discus-sion of the migration of unemployed Easterners to the West, the wheat crop in California and Oregon, the methods used to find new-comers employment, California speculators, and local politics.
   "A Railroad Mint—What the Legend Says." It costs more to travel the forty-five miles of the Panama railroad than to take a train from

New York to Chicago. Ten thousand men died building the Panama line. Twain discusses the ephemeral quality of Panamanian governments. According to legend, a pair of ingenious Americans once saved the railroad right-of-way franchise by getting certain local officials drunk—including President Mosquera.

"Hartford." Twain praises Hartford, which he recently visited, as a handsome financial and insurance center.

"Up Among the Clouds." Twain describes traveling by train and stage from balmy California to snowy, blustery Nevada. He wanted to go with the cordial California and Nevada delegates to the Chicago convention in June but will stay longer in the West.

"Novel Entertainment." Twain describes the hanging of a callous Frenchman named John Melanie, who killed a woman, sold her clothes, and almost killed another woman but was caught.

["A Recently Discovered Twain Letter," 1867]. Having read that friends of Colonel Burke, a Fenian patriot, tried to rescue him by exploding a barrel of gunpowder near his Clerkenwell jail cell, Twain suggests removing Secretary Stanton from the Cabinet by touching off some powder under him. If blowing him up would elevate him enviably, let him be blown down.

Augustus William, Johnny Barker, the Rajah of Borneo, Colonel Burke, the Captain, Cohen, [Schuyler?] Colfax, Captain Cox, Daniel-come-to-judgment, Edward, "Greaser," Governor Haight, Augustus William Mayberry, McIlerson, John Melanie, President [Tomàs Cipriano] Mosquiera [Mosquera], St. Paul, Riley, Sister of Charity, Secretary [of War Edwin M.] Stanton, Captain Edward Wakeman.

*Edited by Cyril Clemens (Webster Groves, Missouri: International Mark Twain Society, 1941)

"A Restless Night." From *A Tramp Abroad*.

"Rev. H. W. Beecher: His Private Habits," 1869.*

Twain reveals that the great preacher does not sleep with his clothes on, does not wear his hat to dinner, never swears, promptly retires between nine and three o'clock, and does not collect advertising for his religious pamphlet called *Plymouth Pulpit*. He farms by the book, and grows hay, hogs, strawberries, watermelons, and dried apples, and gathers eggs only in accordance with information in his expensive agricultural library. His sermons are inspiring, progressive, and intellectual.

Rev. H[enry]. W[ard]. Beecher, [Horace] Greeley.

*In Buffalo *Express,* September 25, 1869.

"Rev. Henry Ward Beecher's Farm," 1872.*
Mr. B. farms his thirty-six acres by the book. The trouble is, sometimes a crop fails while he is looking for his book. His wheat is superb but loses money. His hogs eat lots of corn but make him money; of course, he loses more on the corn. His strawberries are fine, for the robins. But his main trouble is that he plants watermelons, which then grow up to become pumpkins; similarly, his potatoes come up carrots. When he first bought the farm, he gathered a pile of eggs and put them under the most experienced hen. She failed to hatch them, since they were porcelain. He can find no partner rich enough to share profits and losses. All the same, with persistence he will rise from affluence to poverty.

Henry Ward Beecher.

*In *Mark Twain's Sketches* (London: Routledge, 1872).

"Review of Holiday Literature." See FW, 1870.

"A Rich Decision." See "The Great Landslide Case." (See also Bunker, [Benjamin B.]; Rust, Tom; and Sides, Richard [D.].)

A Rich Epigram, 1865 (P).
Why did Tom Maguire light on McDougall and pommel him so? Now Vestvali, the gentle Jewish girl, has little left but bones.

Tom Maguire, McDougall, Vestvali.

"Riddle—What is it?" (MTP).
I talk all the -ologies, on all subjects, in one language as easily as in another. I speak truth, lies, wisdom, foolishness. I treasure every-

thing I say, never forget it, can repeat it a century later. But no subject interests me. I am such good company that people hate to see me leave.

"Riley: Newspaper Correspondent," 1870 (WMT 7).
Riley is one of the best men in Washington or anywhere else. He is a correspondent for a San Francisco daily. He is humorous and ironic in conversation; yet he writes soberly out of fear of losing his position. He is full of stories about his trip via the Isthmus to California and about a variety of jobs he held there. He was a baker, pin-setter, lawyer, and interpreter for Chinese in the courts (without knowing any Chinese words), and once established a newspaper in Alaska when it was only a wandering iceberg. Riley is a reliable enemy and a generous friend. He is a master of deadpan humor. When his landlady in Washington lamented the death by fire of a Negro servant and asked Riley to suggest an epitaph, he solemnly offered this: "*Well done,* good and faithful servant."
    Riley.

"River Intelligence," 1859.*
    Sergeant Fathom is one of the oldest cub pilots on the Mississippi River. He is always extremely careful, and he is much admired by ancient Southern dames, who pronounce him charming. He reports from Vicksburg in May, 1859, that the river is the highest it has been since 1813, but that since it rises less each year it will eventually cease to rise at all. Back in 1763 he went down the river with a Chinese Captain and a Choctaw crew, and steered with a window shutter. Long ago, when he and DeSoto discovered the river, it was so narrow that one could wade across at Donaldsonville.
    [Hernando] DeSoto, Sergeant Fathom.

    *In *Selected Shorter Writings of Mark Twain,* ed. Walter Blair (Boston: Houghton Mifflin, 1962).

["Robert Collier"] (MTP).
    His friend Robert Collier sends a letter to Twain in which he says that he has bought him a baby elephant for Christmas [1908]. Collier

knows that the letter will be opened and read by Miss Lyon [Twain's secretary] and will throw her into instant panic. It does. She advises with Ashcroft, and the two plan a strategy whereby they will suffer and spare their employer. She telephones Collier, who strings her along and even says that the little elephant will enjoy playing with the Clemens pony. Ten days pass. Collier telegraphs to blame the untoward delay in the elephant's arrival on his inability to find a car to ship it in. Then Collier sends ten bales of hay, followed by a man supposedly from Barnum and Bailey, but really Collier's butler. Lounsbury, one of Twain's employees, chats with this "agent" and learns that he is a fraud. However, the butler gets to Miss Lyon and Ashcroft, and urges them to make the loggia the pet's abode. All the time, Twain is being shielded from this confusion. The elephant arrives: it is a wheeled vehicle, and the hay is for the pony.

[Ralph W.] Ashcroft, Billy Brisbane, Robert Collier, [H. A.] Lounsbury, Miss [Isabel] Lyon, Hank Roberts.

'Robert Fulton Fund,' 1906 (S).

Twain begins by announcing that this will be his last paid speech. Hereafter he will speak only gratis until he is buried; then he will keep still. In the audience he sees many friends. Strangers there he also regards as his friends. Together all these people in the audience seem to him to represent the entire nation, to which he thus bids farewell. He begs the people to donate generously to the victims of the San Francisco earthquake. But now he must praise Robert Fulton, the inventor of the telegraph, the sewing machine, and the dirigible. Twain knew Fulton personally and loved to see him gallop through town on a broncho. Twain cannot remember where Fulton was born, but it does not matter. A friend once advised Twain to confuse interviewers; he did so, therefore, by telling one reporter that he was born in Alabama or Alaska or the Sandwich Islands, further that he was a twin—Samuel was the name of the other twin—but that one twin drowned but that the family perhaps buried the wrong one. Twain recalls his story of an old man whose grandfather dropped a dime in front of a ram; Twain never found out what happened because the story teller kept getting distracted and even told about a man named Reginald Wilson who went into a factory one day, got caught and twisted into the machinery, and was woven into sixty-nine yards of three-ply carpet which his widow therefore bought and buried under an explanatory tombstone.

Samuel [Clemens], Robert Fulton, Reginald Wilson, Mrs. Reginald Wilson.

Rock Him to Sleep, 1868 (P).

Twain urges Ball to stop boring the public with poor rhymes [such as occur in the poem "Rock Me to Sleep, Mother"]. If he does not, Twain will tell certain Westerners to get revenge by really rocking him to sleep.

Ball, Westerner.

"Rogers," 1874 (WMT 19).

The narrator meets Rogers in southern England. The cool fellow criticizes the narrator's hat and then his coat, both of which seem admirable enough, whereas Rogers's greasy hat is mashed and his coat is ripped and napless. Later, in London, Rogers invites the narrator to dress formally and accompany him to the residence of the Earl of Warwick. The two men stop at Rogers's miserable room for some champagne. But Rogers is unable to arouse any of his alleged servants; so they have no drink, and moreover Rogers must leave for the Earl's in ordinary attire, because no valet is there to garb him. The two men take a cab to see the Earl; in front of an old house Rogers alights first but quickly returns with the news that the Countess is there and he must not be seen. Rogers later takes a voyage and, giving his name as the Earl of Ramsgate, dies.

Anglesy, the Duke of Argyll, the Emperor of China, the Countess, Morgan, Lord Palmerston, Sir Richard, Rogers, Sackville, Tailor, Theodore, Thomas, H.R.H. the Prince of Wales, the Earl of Warwick.

'Rogers and Railroads,' 1909 (WMT 28).

Twain is delighted to hear Rogers praised for his part in developing the Virginian Railroad. Yet should he be compared to the great road-building Caesar, when the Virginia line is not even complete? Twain knows lots of things about Rogers's private life. The financier helped support the education of Helen Keller, the most marvelous woman since Joan of Arc. When the Webster Company failed and left Twain deeply in debt, Rogers protected his copyrights and arranged with creditors to allow Twain to lecture around the world to pay dollar for dollar. See Rogers there, with his white moustache and his hair turning whiter so as to resemble Twain's.

[Olivia Langdon Clemens], President [Grover] Cleveland, Helen Keller, [Henry Huttleston] Rogers, Mrs. [Henry Huttleston] Rogers, Charles L. Webster.

"Romance of the XVIth Amendment." See FW, 1870.

'Roughing It,' 1871.*

Twain begins by introducing himself as a learned, truth-loving man who is discommoded by compliments, then adds that since he is tired of repeating his fond old lecture he will try a talk about his new book. Some years ago, he traveled by stagecoach from Missouri to Nevada over plains covered with sand and dead cattle, to a land of few people but much silver. He then tells about sagebrush, mountains and passes, Salt Lake City, Western horses (including a kind known as the Mexican plug), Lake Tahoe and its wondrous atmosphere, and the vagaries of silver mining. When he became a reporter for the Virginia City *Territorial Enterprise*, he gratefully wrote up stories of Indian attacks on wagon trains and gunfights involving local desperadoes. Next Twain tells about nabobs Colonel Jim and Colonel Jack who in New York saw an empty omnibus and fancied that by tipping the driver extravagantly they were hiring it for a long ride; when others boarded as passengers, Jim and Jack graciously invited them to stay as their guests. In conclusion, Twain tells a story Artemus Ward told, about a man in danger of losing his girl friend because he stammered; so he went to a doctor, who cured him by teaching him to whistle instead of stammering, but then he lost his girl anyway.

President Angell, Higby, Colonel Jack, Colonel Jim, Johnny, Artemus Ward.

*In Fred W. Lorch, *The Trouble Begins at Eight: Mark Twain's Lecture Tour*, 1968.

Roughing It, 1872 (WMT 3, 4).

Twain happily agrees to be secretary to his brother, who is now the Secretary of Nevada Territory, and to accompany him to Nevada. After a dull trip by steamboat from St. Louis to St. Joseph, Missouri, they buy overland coach tickets, repack to have less weight, and arm themselves. Soon they are swinging away through Kansas. A woman passenger swats dozens of mosquitoes and leaves them dead on her arms. After a thoroughbrace breaks, they dump part of the mail, lie on the rest, and soon enter Nebraska. At sunset they see a jackass rabbit run prodigiously and then note the curious lilliputian sage-brush. Wherever the coach stops, the epic driver is envied. Station buildings are filthy but picturesque. Served to all passengers is slumgullion—tea plus dish-rag, sand, and bacon-rind. No coffee yet. They exchange their six horses for six miles and fly on, soon arriving at Fort Kearney—three hundred miles from St. Joe in fifty-six hours. (A decade later the lush railroad covers the same distance in fifteen hours.) They thrill to the vernal West but soon see that disgusting eater of offal, the coyote. Twain now describes the functionaries of the coach line: superintendents, conductors, drivers, hostlers, and station-keepers. Then he tells the story of Ben Holliday, an able superintendent to whom an admirer while in the Holy Land said that Moses leading his people three hundred miles in forty years was nothing, that Ben could have hauled them out in thirty-six hours. The coach stops at Overland City on the South Platte on the fifth day, 470 miles out. They transfer to a mud-wagon and stall next morning, 550 miles along. The party goes on a buffalo-hunt, and Bemis, a fellow-passenger, tells of being chased up a tree by a buffalo, which he lasooes, shoots, and hangs. All this reminds Twain of an impressive British liar named Eckert in Siam. Now Twain pauses to picture the pony-rider who can carry letters 1,900 miles in eight days! Beyond Scott's Bluffs Pass, Twain and his group see alkali water and plan to boast of the rare sight. He recounts the tale of the 1856 Indian mail robbery and massacre nearby, from which only one person, a man named Babbitt, survived. On the seventh morning, they pass Fort Laramie and enter the Black Hills, 676 miles out. They begin to worry about hostile Indians. From within the darkened vehicle that night they hear a violent conversation, then they rattle off again. No explanation ever follows, but a station later the name of J. A. Slade is mentioned. Twain now tells the story (partly out of Thomas J. Dimsdale's book *The Vigilantes of Montana*) of the notorious Slade, who was a coach-line manager, a murderous gunman, a sadistic torturer, and finally the victim of Montana vigilantes. Twain has coffee with Slade at a station but does not enjoy it, since he fears that Slade may repent of his generosity in giving Twain the last cup and therefore shoot him. Twain journeys on, overtaking some Mormons when he is eight days and 798 miles out, and now in the Rocky Mountains with snow in summer and the Great Divide ahead, on the summit of which they encounter an emigrant-train with a former friend from home—John, on whose head Twain once dropped a watermelon from a third-floor window. Over perilous mountains and past lonely graves and the glowing skeletons of animals. On the tenth day, Green River. Then Fort Bridger, 1,025 miles along, and finally Salt Lake City.

Twain admires the wide streets, the health and extreme probity of the citizens, and the setting of Salt Lake City, and in addition a local drink called "valley tan." He has an amusing audience with the king—i.e., Brigham Young. A fellow named Johnson tells Twain many humorous stories about roll-calls in crowded Mormon homes, meals there, jealousy among wives, bedding down, snoring in unison, etc. Next Twain ridicules the Mormon Bible for being poorly written and tedious. Pondering high prices (for a shoeshine, for example), currency variations, and Western fun-poking at Eastern tenderfeet, Twain leaves Salt Lake City after two days and starts his last six hundred miles. About a hundred miles west, they enter a fearful alkali desert—a waveless ocean, dead and ashen, taking ten hours for the mules to cross. Sixteen days from St. Joe, they are 250 miles west of Salt Lake and begin to encounter the squalid aboriginal Goshoot Indians, whom Twain calls carrion embezzlers. Then he rebukes James Fenimore Cooper for ennobling any such savages. On the nineteenth day out, they cross a forty-mile desert. Twain discusses Nevada's lakes with no outlets. Then he recalls hearing four times the story of Horace Greeley's trip from Carson City to Placerville in a coach driven by Hank Monk so fast that Greeley was almost shattered. Twain refused to let a wanderer tell the story again, and the poor man died straining.

On the morning of the twentieth day they arrive at Carson City, a wooden town of two thousand people, gunmen, fearful dust, a violent daily wind called the "Washoe Zephyr," boardinghouses with basted flour-sack partitions, and Governor Nye and his Irish

Brigade of fourteen wild retainers. For fun these men turn tarantulas loose in Mrs. O'Flannigan's boardinghouse. Feeling gloriously idle, Twain and a friend named Johnny K— late in August explore Lake Tahoe, where for two or three weeks they revel in its beauty, row their boat, cook, camp out, fence a timber claim, drift on the surface of the deep clear lake as though in a balloon in air, fish, swim, play cards, and then accidentally set part of the woods on fire, and finally shiver through a tempest. Back in Carson again, Twain resolves to buy a horse, goes to an auction, and successfully bids for a Genuine Mexican Plug, which bucks fiercely and cannot be permanently loaned, or sold, or even easily given away. Twain now sketches Nevada's brief history: Mormons, silver in 1858, Congressional organization of the Territory, high cost of living, dense parsimony in Washington, the troubles of his honest brother ("The Secretary"), and Nevada legislators' idiocy.

Now Twain is smitten with the silver fever, recounts rumors of sudden riches, quotes from the *Daily Territorial Enterprise*, and decides to go to the Humboldt mines (rather than to the Esmeralda). So in December Twain, two lawyers (Claggett and Oliphant), and an old blacksmith named Ballou (who mangles the language with unwitting humor—for example, the coffee tastes too technical) get a wagon, horses, provisions and equipment, and in two weeks go 250 miles through an alkali desert into freezing Humboldt County. They build a cabin, and Twain soon greedily pounces on some glittering rocks, only to learn that they contain worthless mica. They prospect, stake a claim, sink a shaft, tunnel, trade feet with other men beginning to mine in the region, and go broke. Twain sells his interest and goes back to Carson with Ballou and a Prussian named Ollendorff, planning to go on to the Esmeralda with his brother to look into his investment there. They stop at a way-station, are told by Indians that a huge rainstorm is coming, pay no attention since the skies are clear, and then are flooded that night and have to remain cooped up in a log stable for eight days. A ruffian named Arkansas picks on the landlord until the latter's wife quells him with a pair of scissors. After eight days Twain, Ballou, and Ollendorff press on across flooded streams and then get snowbound and lost. They try but fail to build a fire, weep, and prepare to die. The morning light reveals a stage-station a few feet away. Back in Carson soon, where Twain attends the trial of the landslide case of Hyde *vs.* Morgan. Judge Roop (former

Governor of Nevada) decides in favor of Tom Morgan, whose ranch slid onto that of Richard Hyde (unsuccessfully represented in court by General Buncombe, a pretentious U.S. Attorney from the East) and buried it. Buncombe gets the elaborate joke two months later. Next Twain travels a hundred and twenty miles to Esmeralda with Governor Nye's talkative brother John. His investment at the Esmeralda mines proving worthless, Twain starts working—for a week—as a laborer in a quartz-mill, the intricate process of which he observes and records. Next he tells the story of Whiteman's cement-mine. It seems that Whiteman learned from the one survivor of three German brothers where—near Mono Lake—a vein of gold-bearing cement was located. Now everyone follows Whiteman around, including Twain himself one whole disappointing night. He decides to vacation at Mono Lake for a week and explore it thoroughly. The area features worms, flies, ducks, sea-gulls, vaporous streams, alkali waters, and rapid changes in the weather. One day Twain and Cal Higbie, his new partner, now fifteen miles on Mono to a little ashen island, carelessly let their boat drift away and retrieve it only after a close call, and return to safety and the others just before a storm. Soon they go on to the Sierras and enjoy August trout-fishing there. Back in Esmeralda, Twain is almost killed when his hired Indian lights a stove in which some gunpowder was hidden. Twain and Higbie are envious of the Wild West Mining Company for a very rich strike until Higbie discovers that the ore is coming from a blind lead which is public property and stakable. He and Twain and the Wild West foreman—A.D. Allen—stake claims. But Twain goes to nurse sick John Nye, Higbie follows Whiteman in a long search for the cement-mine, and Allen is called out of town by a telegram. So, not working their claim within ten days, they lose it. But for a few days they were millionaires and dreamed of brownstone mansions and European travel.

Twain opens the second half of *Roughing It* with a brief summary of his varied life to date: clerk, law student, blacksmith, printer, steamboat pilot, secretary, and silver-miner. Now he becomes city editor of the Virginia City *Territorial Enterprise,* under Mr. Goodman. His competition is the rival *Union* reporter, Boggs, who gets the exclusive monthly school report but who one night lets Twain copy it for the *Enterprise* but then gets drunk and does not file it for his own paper. Genially blaming Twain, Boggs next month lowers him into a ninety-foot mine-shaft about which the two are to report, gets the school news alone, and prints an exclusive.

Suddenly Twain describes flush times in Virginia City, its traffic, income, population, honeycombs of mines under the slanted town, nearby stamping mill, habit of giving feet of mines to reporters for free newspaper advertising, and trick of "salting" mines by putting silver ore (and, once, melted half-dollars) into otherwise barren shafts. Money is more plentiful than means of spending it. Once, Reuel Gridley was defeated for mayor of Austin, Nevada, and was given a fifty-pound sack of flour by the Republican victor; Gridley auctioned and reauctioned the flour in Austin, Virginia, Carson, and various places in California, and donated the proceeds—$150,000—for the comfort of wounded Union veterans back east. Next Twain tells fantastic stories of fortunes made and lost through luck, ingenuity, and conniving, and of the gaucherie of the resultant nabobs—for example, Colonel Jim and Colonel Jack who boarded a bus in New York, gave the driver twenty dollars, and imagined that they had hired the vehicle even after other "sociable" people got on. Now comes the story of Buck Fanshaw's funeral, which was arranged with a slowly comprehending preacher by Buck's devoted, slangy, but sincere friend Scotty Briggs. In Virginia City, distinction is gained fastest by killing your man. Such murderers go free because of the stupid system of trial by jury. Typical desperadoes slouch and shoulder their way through ordinary mortals and, fortunately, fight among themselves usually. Twain names several desperadoes and quotes from contemporary newspaper accounts of violent shooting frays. Such stories remind him of tough Ned Blakely, a sea-captain off the Chincha Islands. When his favorite Negro mate was brutally shot by a bully named Bill Noakes, Blakely resolutely captured and hanged him. Tediously, Twain now summarizes a foolish round-robin novel which he, Mr. F. (witty editor of the Virginia City *Weekly Occidental*), Mrs. F., and a periodically drunk stranger write about a French duke, a virtuous blonde, a mysterious Rosicrucian, and a brilliant lawyer. Then Twain appends his ridiculous poem "The Aged Pilot Man," about an Erie Canal boat whose passengers are rescued during a storm when a farmer puts a plank aboard from shore. Next Twain provides details on high freight charges between Virginia City and California, the Comstock lode, the veritable city of busy miners under the streets of the town, the cost of timbering, and cave-ins. For a long time Twain has been urged to go listen to Jim Blaine tell about his grandfather's old ram. One evening Blaine is symmetrically drunk and starts his story, but reminiscences interrupt his memory so much that he rambles and falls asleep before he describes the ram at all. Next Twain discusses the Chinese in the West: their virtues, the acts of intolerance committed against them by policemen and politicians, the vividness of the Chinese quarter in Virginia City, and the Chinese love of their homeland and desire to be buried there.

Gradually Twain tires of Nevada, of reporting, of failing to make a fortune, and so he decides to go to San Francisco. California scenery and weather have a monotony of sameness which makes New England preferable. He pictures San Francisco, Mono, Fort Yuma, Sacramento, and ghost cities where mining once flourished. Then he tells stories of the rarity of females in the West. Twain is idle for months in San Francisco but refuses to sell his soaring Nevada mining stocks until a crash wipes out their value completely. Then he narrowly misses a chance to join Dan and Marshall, two reporters, in a scheme to sell mining stock in New York. Next he witnesses a severe San Francisco earthquake. He continues to write literary pieces, but now for magazines (including the *Californian,* edited by Bret Harte) which fail. So he slinks into poverty. He meets a fellow luckless person, named "Blucher," who when broke found a dime once, met a starving beggar, fed him at a nice restaurant on credit, and then went elsewhere and bought a veal cutlet for himself with his dime. Then a friend rescues Twain by having him go to a ghost town at Tuolumne, California, to do some pocket-mining there. One pocket-miner, Dick Baker of Dead-Horse Gulch, once had a cat, named Tom Quartz, which was good at pocket-mining but was insulted when it got blown sky-high during some unaccustomed shaft-mining. After three months of unsuccessful prospecting, Twain returns to San Francisco for a five-month stint with the *Enterprise* there, then delightedly agrees to go to the Sandwich Islands and write letters back to the Sacramento *Union.* Among the thirty passengers aboard the *Ajax* are "The Admiral," who is a salty, retired whaleman turned colorful liar, and Williams, who smoothly accepts the Admiral's lies concerning the secession of South Carolina only to cap them.

When Twain arrives at Honolulu, he compares it favorably with

San Francisco as cleaner, closer to nature, more virginal and vernal. Twain examines a Hawaiian prison, hires a lazy, sleepy horse (named Oahu) to widen his scope of activity, and observes groves of cocoanut trees, native cottages, ruins of temples, and old battlegrounds of Kamehameha the Great. Then he digresses informatively on Hawaiian horses, native girls, poi, awa root, the fish market, the hula hula dance, missionary work, the falling population, the national government, the place of women in Hawaiian life, luxurious funerals, the Great Shark God, rural bathing, the foolish effects of the missionaries on native habits of dress, and finally the over-organized retainers of Hawaiian royalty. Next he describes the lavish funeral of Princess Victoria, the King's sister, and contrasts it with that of Kamehameha, a native account of whose death in 1819 Twain quotes. Next he and a friend sail for Hawaii aboard a tiny schooner loaded with rats, cockroaches, and fleas. They land and ride horses through orange groves, peach orchards, and sugar-cane fields, then visit Simon Erickson, a crazy preacher from Michigan (now at a Hawaiian plantation), who mumbles about his correspondence with Horace Greeley concerning turnips. (Twain's purpose here is presumably to satirize incomprehensible handwriting.) Then Twain describes a mountain of lava, Kealakekua Bay (where Captain Cook was killed), the ruined temple of Lono (the last Hawaiian god), then a bevy of nude native girls bathing (Twain sits on their clothes to keep them from being stolen), next Lono's history (Cook's appearance was at first interpreted as Lono's return), and finally the breaking of the tabu that prohibited a king from eating with a queen (Christianity arrived shortly thereafter, to supplant dead paganism). Twain and his friend hire a native to take them by canoe to the ruins of Honaunau: they see coral, porpoises, surf-bathers, and the ancient stone city of Refuge. Then they return to their schooner and sail to Kau, obtain horses, and go to the gigantic and awesome volcano of Kilauea, the floor of which Twain and a stranger named Marlette wanderingly visit at night. Next Twain rides on horseback all around the island of Hawaii and then sails to Maui for several weeks: he picnics, explores the volcano Haleakala, and sees a spectacular storm below the crater rim. He also meets a man named Markiss who is such a liar that when he later killed himself and left a suicide note the authorities suspected murder.

After half a year in the Sandwich Islands, Twain returns by a boring ship to San Francisco, where he hires a lecture hall and some helpful laughers and is fortunately successful. So he hires an agent named Mike and lectures elsewhere in California, and also in Nevada. Near Virginia City, Twain is terrifyingly robbed by former friends as a practical joke. Giving up a dream of lecturing in Japan and then going on around the world, he instead takes a steamer to New York via the Isthmus. Thus ends a period of seven years in the West.

Roughing It has three appendices. Appendix A briefly sketches the history of Mormonism. Appendix B describes the Mountain Meadows massacre, in which more than a hundred emigrants from Arkansas and Missouri were butchered by Mormons, partly disguised as Indians, in September, 1857. Twain uses Mrs. C. V. Waite's book on Mormonism as his main source. Appendix C, called "Concerning a Frightful Assassination That Was Never Consummated," is largely a collection of quotations from Conrad Wiegand, an editor from Gold Hill, Nevada, who in print maligned an aristocratic miner on hearsay evidence, was horsewhipped for it, and then published his verbose and melodramatic account of the episode.

The Admiral, Ah Sing, A. D. Allen, Arkansas, Babbitt, Dick Baker, Ballou, Bascom, Beauregard, Mrs. Jackson Beazeley, William Beazeley, George Bemis, Colonel Bilgewater, Bill, Billings, Widder Billings, Billy, Jim Blaine, Captain Ned Blakely, Blucher, Bob, Boggs, Brewster, Mrs. Brewster, Scotty Briggs, Sam Brown, Brown, McKean Buchanan, General Buncombe, [Anson] Burlingame, Captain, Claggett, [Orion Clemens], Cradlebaugh, Abe Curry, [Sam] Curry, Dan, Dollinger, Deacon Dunlap, Mrs. Dunlap, Eckert, Johnny El Dorado, Simon Erickson, Buck Fanshaw, Deacon Ferguson, Filkins, Captain Fish, F., Mrs. F., Gardiner, Mrs. Gardiner, John James Godfrey, [Joseph T.] Goodman, Gould, Granger, Horace Greeley, Seth Green, Reuel Gridley, Parson Hagar, Hank, General Harney, [C. C.] Harris, Jack Harris, Harris, Bret Harte, Sile Hawkins, Calvin H. Higbie, Miss Higgins, Mortimer Highie, Squire Hogadorn, Ben Holliday, Richard Hyde, Bob H—, Colonel Jack, Jack, Stonewall Jackson, Jacobs, Mrs. Jacops, Miss Jefferson, Colonel Jim, Jim, John, John, Baldy Johnson, Johnson, Johnson,

Mrs. Johnson, John Jones, Jones, Jules, David Kalakaua, Kekuanaoa, Heber C. Kimball, Kimball, Johnny K—, L., Uncle Lem, Joe McKee, Jack McNabb, Maria, Markiss, Marlette, G. M. Marshall, Becky Martin, Mike, Hank Monk, John Moody, John H. Morgan, Johnny Morgan, Tom Morgan, Judge [Gordon N.] Mott, Muckawow, Billy Mulligan, Nixon, Bill Noakes, Governor [James W.] Nye, Captain John Nye, Bridget O'Flannigan, Captain Ogden, Oliphant, Ollendorff, Owens, Parson, Farmer Pease, Captain Perkins, Captain Phillips, Pock-Marked Jake, Reeder, Rigdon, Robbins, Governor [Isaac] Roop, Captain Saltmarsh, Sawyer, Scotty, See Yup, Phil Sheridan, Sing-Sing Tommy, Six-fingered Pete, J. A. Slade, Mrs. J. A. Slade, J. Smith, John Smith, Joseph Smith, Smith, Stewart, Street, Sugarfoot Mike, Sutro, Archibald F. Thompson, Tom, Tom, Jim Townsend, Valentine, Van Dorn, General Van Valenburgh, Princess Victoria [Kamamalu Kaahumanu], Miss Wagner, Waite, Miss Watson, C[harles]. H. Webb, Welch, William Wheeler, Mrs. William Wheeler, Whiteman, Conrad Wiegand, Sarah Wilkerson, Prince William, Jack Williams, Williams, Winthrop L. Willis, Wong, General W., Bill Yates, Thankful Yates, Brigham Young, Mrs. Brigham Young.

'Roughing It on the Silver Frontier.' See 'Roughing It.'

"A Royal Compliment," 1870 (CRG).

Twain notes that a recent *Tribune* article has suggested that the Spanish throne should be offered to an American and hinted that it has just the candidate in mind. Why the *Tribune* should single Twain out for this compliment he does not quite know. True, he has an intimate knowledge of Spanish history and is proud of various Spanish achievements, such as Cortes's victory at Thermopylae. Twain will insist that his royal salary be paid quarterly and in gold. The Spanish people must learn to wash more regularly and get along with fewer quarantines. Marshal Serrano's rank must be reduced to constable at most, and the late Queen Isabella must be chased out of France. Twain interrupts to report that he

has just learned he was not the American hinted at in the *Tribune*.
Very well, he did not care anyway.

> Vasco Nunez de Balboa, Don Caesar de Bazan, Hernando
> Cortes, George, the Duke of Wellington.

["A Royal Funeral"]. See LSI.

"Running for Governor," 1870 (WMT 7).

Mark Twain explains that a few months earlier he ran for
governor of New York on the independent ticket against John
T. Smith and Blank J. Blank. His grandmother warned him not
to descend to the low level of such opponents. Soon the newspapers accused Twain of perjury in Cochin China, petty theft in
Montana, lying about Blank's dead grandfather, drunkenness in
his hotel, filthy corruption, and loathsome embracing. He could
not answer the baseless charges, because new ones came at him too
fast. So he withdrew.

> Blank J. Blank, Handy Andy, Catty Mulligan, Michael
> O'Flanagan Esq., Pol. Pry, Snub Rafferty, John T. Smith,
> Mark Twain.

"A Rural Lesson in Rhetoric." See FW, 1869.

'Russian Republic,' 1906 (S).

Twain applauds the efforts of the persecuted Russian people to
wrest freedom for themselves from the hands of the Tsar. They
should use violence if necessary. All Americans should support
the movement with money. Russians are seeking the same independence from oppression that Americans once sought.

> Hunter, the Tsar of Russia.

'Russian Sufferers,' 1905 (WMT 28).

Twain is sad to have to follow a speech given in flowing French,
because it sounded so expressive. He did not understand what was
said, however. He then expresses his delight at meeting Madame
Bernhardt. He remembers an anecdote about her. Two cultivated

ladies named Jones—widow and daughter—wanted to see Bernhardt at Hartford but felt guilty at spending the required $6; so
they sent $6 to two poor people named Smith whom they knew
and who needed bread. But the Smiths bought tickets to see Bernhardt with the money. Next Twain tells about a young sailor who
liked his grog but was socially ostracized until he signed a pledge
in order to apply for membership in Father Matthew's popular
temperance society near New Bedford. The sailor soon returned
to sea for a three-years' voyage, during which he kept his pledge,
though in agony. Ashore again, he rushed to the society, asked
that his name be taken off the membership list, but was told that
it was not necessary to do so since he had been blackballed anyway.

Madame [Sarah] Bernhardt, Mrs. Jones, Miss Jones,
Father Matthew, Smith.

"S. Browne Jones." See *Mark Twain's San Francisco*.

"Sabbath Reflections," 1866 (WIM).
The narrator notes that today is the Sabbath. His calm and serious meditations, however, are interrupted by the cackles and
braying of countless fowls and brutes here in San Francisco.

Brown.

"Sabbath Reflections" (in *Mark Twain's San Francisco*). See "Reflections on the Sabbath."

"A Sad, Sad Business" (CG). See the second third of "An Entertaining Article."

Saint Joan of Arc. See *Personal Recollections of Joan of Arc*.

"Saint Joan of Arc," 1904 (WMT 22).
Evidence confirmed by oath concerning Joan of Arc reveals a
marvelous life. She lived in the dull, backward village of Domremy until she was sixteen years old, then successfully contested in
court at Toul a false charge of breach of promise of marriage, and

then went to the Vaucouleurs commandant for soldiers to win back the crown for the King of France. She appeared before an academic congress at Poitiers to prove the divine origin of her commission. At seventeen Joan became commander-in-chief, carried Orleans, was then delayed because of the King's instability and the treachery of his advisers, but next took Jargeau, Meung, Beaugency, and Patay. She went on to Troyes, crowned her monarch at Rheims, and soon proceeded to Paris, where she was wounded. After passing some time in the frivolous court, she fought at Compiègne and was captured there when she was eighteen. John of Luxembourg demanded the princely ransom of 61,125 francs; but ungrateful France did not pay, and eventually Cauchon, Bishop of Beauvais, bought her for trial. The charge was wearing male attire and committing other impious acts. Though ignominiously imprisoned and mistreated at Rouen, she remained dauntless, intelligent, fluent, dignified, and patient. Cauchon confessed her but then used her confidential revelations about her Voices against her. She innocently signed a false paper but then repudiated it, thus sealing her doom. It was an English soldier, not a fellow Frenchman, who gave her a cross of sticks to kiss as she burned. Twenty-five years later, the rehabilitation of Joan of Arc began. A cloud of witnesses testified. Gradually the world realized that she was the wonder of the ages and also a riddle. Her performance cannot be accounted for by her environment. She had courage, military genius, a brilliant and logical mind, eloquence, statesmanship, the gift of prophecy, and a profound religious sense. We should remember her not as a typical peasant woman but as spirited, lithe, and youthful. She was unique, the most extraordinary person mankind has yet produced.

> The Duc d'Alençon, Cauchon, the Commandant of Vaucouleurs, [Sieur Louis de Conte], [Jean, Comte de] Dunois, King [Charles VII] of France, Joan of Arc, John of Luxembourg, [John] Talbot, Voices.

'The St. Louis Harbor-Boat "Mark Twain,"' 1902 (S).

Twain offers his thanks that the St. Louis harbor boat has been named after him and also thanks the Countess de Rochambeau for presiding at its christening. Then he notes that it was La Salle's exploration of the Mississippi Valley which resulted in the gathering of the vast Louisiana territory. But, Twain adds, he would have done it himself for half the price.

Countess de Rochambeau.

"St. Pierre" (MTP).

The narrator is cooling himself in the solitude of his mountain house 2,000 feet in the air. Fortunately his family is all away, on a trip to Jamaica. Suddenly the earth crinkles like a shivering emotion. Cendrillion, an old servant, is not disturbed; but within hours eight more shakes come on, and by nightfall the mountain top is smoking. Next day, jets of steam erupt hoarsely, and the night which follows is lit by belching red shafts. Falling ashes dim the next dawn. Suddenly the narrator sees snakes, which have been frightened down from the mountain. The narrator wants to descend to the safety of the town and to the comradeship of his friends there; so he sends a servant to St. Pierre for a shoulder chair and a bearer. The next night the people huddling in the house hear a terrifying crackling sound, caused by the advent of land crabs. Utter silence suddenly ensues, unbroken even by the punctual Martinique cricket. In the morning, the quakes cease and everyone but Cendrillion expresses relief and hope. Below them in the distance lies tinted St. Pierre, safely nestled by the sea. But suddenly a subterranean roar shakes the entire mountain, and vast quantities of smoke and steam burst from the crater. St. Pierre disappears under an ocean of red-lit inky blackness. The narrator's mind is instantly a confusion of thoughts of the newly dead down there in the obliterated city. Visions of lost mementoes of six generations of his family sweep through him uncontrollably. Volcanic steam continues to ascend, but blobs of lava begin to fall like a bombardment. Fires erupt everywhere. Then the narrator finds himself alone, in the woods, lost. He should stop and wait for help, but he stumbles on and on, aimlessly, powdered by ghostly ashes, until he drops at a spot where he is finally found.

Cendrillion, Felix, Josephine, Marie, Maximilien, Mimi, Saunders, Alice X.

["St. Valentine's Day"]. See W 1868.

"Salutatory." See "Two Mark Twain's Editorials."

"Samuel Erasmus Moffett," 1923 (WMT 29).

On August 1, 1908, the author's nephew Samuel Erasmus Moffett, aged forty-eight and in superb physical and mental health, drowned while sea bathing in a strong surf. He had been a journalist for nearly thirty years and had a high place on the staff of *Collier's Weekly* when he died. Years ago the author had obtained a position for Moffett on a San Francisco daily. Weak eyesight had prevented him from attending school as a regular pupil; so he learned by listening to the recitations of others. He had a phenomenal memory and allowed his encyclopedic learning to be imposed upon often. He is survived by wife, daughter, and son. In a sordid epoch of our national history, Moffett was a gentleman of dignified character and high ideals.

Samuel Erasmus Moffett, Mrs. Samuel Erasmus Moffett, Moffett, Miss Moffett.

'San Francisco Earthquake,' 1906 (S).

Twain recalls that he was a reporter in San Francisco for three or four years in the 1860's and that the city had a population of 118,000 then. He has not been back there since 1868. He remembers that on a sleepy Sunday afternoon he was walking down a street in San Francisco when he saw a building collapse up ahead, was thrown into the side of a building, and felt stunned. No other damage was done. He always thought that it was an earthquake—no one else said so—and that it had been gotten up just for his entertainment.

"A San Francisco Millionaire," 1866 (WG).

A millionaire named M. loans some money to his friend S., who speculates in coal, loses, is shadowed and dunned by M., and finally commits suicide. M. is remorseful, treats a few friends to some beer, confesses to them that he is sad and intends to be more generous with his money in the future, and pays for the beer—damn the expense. But soon thereafter he repents and becomes stingy again.

M., S.

'The Sandwich Islands,' 1866 (WMT 28).

For some reason, Providence placed the Sandwich Isles 2,100 miles west of San Francisco. Their Kanaka population is declining. Kanakas lie dreadfully, cheat, but are hospitable. They know how to lie down and die when they wish. They are fonder of their puppies than they are of their children. They feed their dogs tenderly and when they are fully grown eat them. Old Kanehameha had fierce warriors, but the natives are peaceable now. They are fond of their horses and ride them well. The women ride astride, as they should. Kanakas are cruel by nature. They disprove the maxim that if one is virtuous he will be happy. The Kanaka king used to be sacred, and could execute whomever he wished and could put taboos on places and persons. Next in authority came the high priest, then the chiefs, then ordinary men, then the poor, degraded women. The missionaries arrived and changed things. The scenery is magnificent, especially the mountains. Curiously, the natives are unafraid of volcanic eruptions and their blazing showers.

[C. C.] Harris, Kanehameha [V], Secretary of Navy, Secretary of War.

'The Sandwich Islands,' c. 1877 (LAII I).

Twain tells his audience that the Sandwich Islands are 2,100 miles southwest of San Francisco, are twelve in number, and have about the area of Rhode Island and Connecticut together. There used to be 400,000 natives, but the advent of white civilization and diseases has halved that figure. King Kamehameha wielded absolute power. Under him, in order, came priests, chiefs, plebeians, and women. The missionaries taught everyone to read and write. The natives are hospitable but are also tricky traders. They can die when they wish, by simply lying down and willing it. They are not cannibals, but they do have a cruel streak. They do everything backwards; so, if we take them into the United States, they will elect incorruptible congressmen. A typical white politician on the islands is Harris, who is brainless and vain. The lovely islands lull one to a forgetfulness of all toil and anxiety.

[C. C.] Harris, King Kamehameha [V].

'The Sandwich Islands.' See 'Our Fellow Savages of the Sandwich Islands.'

'Sandwich Islands! A Serio-Humorous Lecture Concerning Kanakadom.' See 'Our Fellow Savages of the Sandwich Islands.'

["Satan and Shakespeare"] (MTP).
There is a remarkable parallel between the histories of Satan and Shakespeare. Details about both are lacking. Neither earned his reputation. There is no evidence that either ever wrote anything much. Satan's known act as Tempter in the Wilderness is on a par with Shakespeare's one known piece of writing. As the Owner of the universe, Satan was inept to offer Christ merely a parcel of it.

Satan, [William] Shakespeare.

["Saturday in Honolulu"]. See LSI.

'The Savage Club Dinner,' 1907 (WMT 28).
Twain expresses his joy at learning that Harold Frederic's last hours were made easier by someone's reading from Twain's works. Stanley found Twain's books pleasant and stole one to take to Africa. Twain says that an interviewer reported his describing Birrell's recent Pilgrims' Club speech as "bully." Not so. Twain does not use slang. Interviewers should be more careful. He then apologizes for his white clothes, which he says he wears to make himself conspicuous. One must be clean to wear white. He is naturally clean, cleaner, in fact, than members of his present audience. He is glad to be here at the Savage Club in London, though because of his age he may never get back again. When he arrived on English shores this time, the stevedores cheered him warmly. Those hardhanded workers build empires and civilizations, in which others can live comfortably, until Savages destroy things.

Birrell, Harold Frederick, [Dr. David] Livingstone, [Henry Morton] Stanley.

[Says Gossip One to Gossip Two], 1869 (probably by Twain) (P).
Mrs. Pry's story that Smith bought his goods from Brown is

exaggerated as it passes from Gossip One to Gossip Five, until it becomes a story of robbery.

Brown, Gossip Five, Gossip Four, Gossip One, Gossip Three, Gossip Two, Mrs. Pry, Smith.

"Scenery." See *Mark Twain in Three Moods.*

"School of Journalism" (MTP).

Asked whether Yale should start a journalism school, Twain replies by first offering a story. A man's father wrote a bad play based on one of Twain's books; and the son, who is employed in the *Tribune* drama department, sent Twain a letter offering to help get the thing produced. Thus we have a pirate whose son wants to share the swag! When Twain declined, the pirate family criticized him in the newspapers. Well, then, why not have a journalism school? It could teach neophyte reporters some basic standards of fair play.

"Schoolhouse Hill," 1969 (MSM).

It is fifty years ago in St. Petersburg, Missouri. The morning is icy. Boys and girls are climbing up Schoolhouse Hill and sliding back. Finally they arrive at the school door. Sid Sawyer, the model boy, is prompt. Tom Sawyer brings his sled. Huck Finn walks with him but does not enter. The new bully, Henry Bascom, whose father is a slave dealer and who has a miniature slaughterhouse for puppies and kittens, suddenly sees a new boy, apparently about fifteen years old, handsome, and charming, challenges him to a fight, throws a fist at his face, but misses and tumbles down hill. Archibald Ferguson, the kindly old Scotch schoolmaster, calls the boys and girls to order, begins some lessons, notices the new lad and asks him his name, is accorded a polite reply in French, and learns that the stranger knows no English. The graceful boy recites the lessons he has just heard, word for word, even echoing the accents of the original speakers. Dumbfounded, Ferguson queries him further, is courteously informed that the lad learns instantly, gives him a thick English-French dictionary and watches him read every page in a few minutes, and listens as the boy now answers a spate of questions in English. The stranger quickly learns Latin, Greek, shorthand, and mathematics in the same fashion. Pronouncing it all a miracle, the teacher asks where the boy came from. As is his habit when he chooses not to answer or dispute, the boy merely bows; but he reports his name as Forty-four and his temporary residence as the home of the compassionate Hotchkisses, who took him in out of the cold the night before. Ferguson leaves, thrilled and humbled, for noon recess.

The girls rush home to tell what they have seen. But the boys wait near the schoolhouse for Bascom to challenge Forty-four. Tom Sawyer warns the gentle stranger, shows him a few tricks in the art of fisticuffs, and then watches with the others as Bascom tries repeatedly to hit his hated rival but misses, slips, and falls amid jeers. He practically orders Forty-four to hit him and for his pains is felled again and again. When the bully turns to hit a laughing witness, Forty-four knocks him senseless. Bascom's father the slave trader rushes up with his whip, but Forty-four seizes the man's wrist and crushes it. Mrs. Bascom wants vengeance upon Forty-four, but he has suddenly disappeared.

At the Hotchkiss house a crowd gathers. In addition to mercurial old Oliver Hotchkiss, his steady Presbyterian wife Hannah, her lovely niece Annie Fleming, and the family slaves Rachel and Jeff, there are the widow Mrs. Dawson, Mrs. Guthrie, Dr. and Mrs. Wheelwright, Miss Pomeroy the schoolteacher, and Judge Taylor the magistrate. They tell each other things about the strange new boarder, who paid rent in advance in gold, magically produced a wax candle, talked with the cat Sal and fed it out of an apparently bottomless pocket, and has already displayed several changes of clothes and yet brought no baggage. When they search his room, they pour a mound of gold coins out of his coat pocket. Dr. Wheelwright concludes that the strange lad is extraordinary, and the others agree.

Darkness descends, and with it comes a terrifying blizzard, which kills twenty-eight people during the night. Rachel alarms her master Hotchkiss by reporting that Forty-four is missing. Old Jeff goes to look for him but is instantly lost in the choking clouds of powdery snow. But when Forty-four enters and learns what is wrong, he rescues Jeff and then disappears to save the lives of thirteen other people. Suddenly Hotchkiss wants to conduct a spiritualistic séance, orders everyone—including a guffawing neighbor named Crazy Meadows and the two frightened servants—to hold hands, and calls up the spirits of Lord Byron, Napoleon, Shakespeare, and several old Romans. Forty-four's voice accompanies some mysterious rappings and frightens everyone until the handsome lad reveals that he is not dead. Then he and contented old Hotchkiss sit by the fire, have a drink and a smoke, and have a chat. When food is mentioned, Forty-four magically provides luscious, smoking dishes, brought by velvety little red imps with short horns and spiked tails. Forty-four explains that they are servants belonging to his father, whose name is Satan.

Hotchkiss is embarrassed and begins to apologize for thinking bad thoughts about Satan, but Forty-four mildly interrupts, saying that he does not admire Satan and is not a devil himself. He adds that he is almost five million earth years old, saw many planets created, watched the drama in Eden with interest, blames his father for the Fall, and feels that the forbidden fruit conferred not merely a knowledge of the difference between good and evil but also a disposition to do evil. Forty-four provides Hotchkiss with a devilish little servant, whom the old man names Edward Nicholson Hotchkiss after his dead brother. While Hotchkiss takes his rest, Forty-four will travel around the world, learn some things, and return in the morning. Then the two will put into operation a plan for ameliorating the human condition.

In the morning, Hotchkiss explains to worried Jeff and Rachel that the fiery little stranger named Edward is a good devil, a kind of slave who will run errands for them. When Rachel wishes that there were cream on the breakfast table for Marse Oliver, Edward fetches some in a twinkling . . . .

Henry Bascom, Bascom, Mrs. Bascom, Crazy Meadows, Mrs. Dawson, Archibald Ferguson, Huck Finn, Annie Fleming, Forty-four, Mrs. Guthrie, Edward Nicholson Hotchkiss, Edward Nicholson Hotchkiss, Hannah Hotchkiss, Oliver Hotchkiss, Jake, Uncle Jeff, Miss Pomeroy, Aunt Rachel, Sid Sawyer, Tom Sawyer, Henry Slater, Jack Stillson, Margaret Stover, Judge Taylor, Becky Thatcher, Dr. Wheelwright, Mrs. Wheelwright.

'Die Schrecken der Deutschen Sprache' (WMT 28). See 'The Horrors of the German Language.'

"Science vs. Luck," 1870 (WMT 7).

The Hon. Mr. K— explains that Kentucky was once so strict in enforcing its law against games of chance that John Wheeler and ten or so other men were arresting for playing seven up. The successful and wily lawyer Jim Sturgis was retained to defend them. He had the brilliant idea of maintaining in court that seven up is not a game of chance but a game of science. Most of the audience had a good laugh, and then the judge challenged Sturgis to prove his assertion. So he suggested that six deacons and dominies, who had been contending that seven was a game of chance, be locked up with six old cronies from among his cloud of witnesses, and the dozen play until one side won. This curious jury of a dozen men retired to the jury room. Soon one of the deacons sent out for a loan. Then a dominie asked to borrow a stake. More deacons asked for small sums. Finally the jury returned the verdict that seven is a game of science, on the grounds that the chance men lost consistently and the science players won all the time. K—winds up his account by saying that the verdict is a matter of record and holds good to this day.

Deacon Burke, Deacon Job, Deacon Johnson, Hon. Mr. K—, Dominie Miggles, Deacon Peters, Jim Sturgis, John Wheeler, Dominie Wirt.

"A Scrap of Curious History," 1914 (WMT 26).

The murder of the President of France in 1894 by an Italian assassin inspires Twain to record a coincidence. He is now at the village of La Bourboule-les-Bains, France. The assassination has just occurred. An irate French mob the night before surrounded his hotel demanding that the Italian waiters he sent out to be drubbed and then exiled. Back in 1845 Twain was in another village, Marion City, Missouri, on the Mississippi River. He remembers that the Missouri equivalent of a modern European anarchist was Robert Hardy, the first abolitionist in the village. He was a pale New Englander, thirty years of age, a bachelor and a reader. He worked as a cooper. Suddenly he began to yell out his belief in abolition. The Methodist minister, a man named Damon Williams, saved him from a lynch mob. But then Hardy helped a runaway slave over to Illinois, and in the fight preceding the man's escape Hardy killed the town constable. The local paper published a biography of the murderer, who became an object of intense interest. His hanging was the occasion of much celebration and even of picnics. Now comes the change. Martyrdom plus notoriety is fascinating to some. Within a week four young men—Ed Smith, Dick Savage, Will Joyce, and Henry Taylor—proclaimed themselves abolitionists. They made the town uneasy for a couple of months. Then a house was blown up. It had belonged to Rev. Hiram Fletcher, a Presbyterian minister who had denounced the quartet of abolitionists from his pulpit. Although a coroner's jury returned a verdict of death by the visitation of God, Joyce confessed that he was the assassin, witnesses corroborated details of his story, and he was soon executed. From the gallows he made such an incendiary martyr's speech that riot and war soon followed. This is the way of reform in our world.

President [Marie François Sadi Carnot], Cesario [Caserio], Rev. Hiram Fletcher, Robert Hardy, Henry Hart, Will Joyce, [Luigi Luccheni], George Ronalds, Dick Savage, Ed Smith, Henry Taylor, Damon Williams.

"The Scriptural Panoramist," 1865 (WMT 7).

Mr. Nickerson explains that a fellow was traveling around in that country with a moral-religious show, a panorama of scriptural scenes. To liven the exhibition, he hired a piano player who was nimble enough but whose selections did not seem to jibe with specific biblical scenes passing at the time. So the showman lectured the old slab narrowly and decided to try him again. Evening came. Middle-aged and old people flocked in, because of their interest in the Bible; and so did plenty of young people, who were anxious to taste each other's complexions in the dark. First scene: the Prodigal Son; first musical number: "Oh, we'll get blind drunk/ When Johnny comes marching home!" Next: Christ walking on water, accompanied by "A life on the ocean wave." Finally, the raising of Lazarus by our Savior, to the tune of "Come rise up, William Ri-i-ley, / And go along with me!" Old people leave in a huff, younger ones rattle the windows with laughter, and the panoramist dismisses the house.

Nickerson.

"The Second Advent," 1972 (FM).

Black Jack, Arkansas, is a small town in the wilds, full of mud, hogs, and sloth. Nancy Hopkins, a comely young girl there, falls in love with a blacksmith named Jackson Barnes, and they plan to marry. But before they can do so, gossip has it that she is pregnant. A crowd gathers and is about to demand that the girl name and marry her betrayer or be tarred, feathered, and banished, when Jackson walks serenely up and informs the group that Nancy was overshadowed by God, is still virginal, and will bear a divine son. It seems that an angel told her all this—a modern angel in straw hat, jeans, and boots. While Nancy was telling Jackson the marvelous story, he fell asleep and in a dream was assured by God that it was so and was told to stand by the pure girl. The child will be named Jesus Christ, for this is the Second Advent.

The people do not believe the story; so the Hopkins family and Jackson avoid their acquaintances while the marvelous tale spreads. Some wise men, presidents of eastern colleges and editors of eastern newspapers, hear of it and follow the planet Venus in the West through Pittsburgh and Louisville to remote Black Jack. They decide to examine all the evidence, interview the girl, select a little jury, and render a verdict. After much haggling, it is decided that the jurors must be members of orthodox churches. Then the wise men interview Nancy, her husband, and her parents. The religious faction believes their story; the editorial faction does not. But the packed jury calls it all a miracle and accepts the resulting infant as Christ. When Horace Greeley, one of the editors, voices his strong objection to lightly calling the event a miracle, since the future of Christian nations may well be at stake, a religious zealot named Talmage from the opposition rebukes the editor and says that all the evidence is divinely inspired and further that this event parallels in all essential ways Christ's first coming.

The Holy Family lives quietly in Black Jack for thirty years but then suddenly comes into notice when Christ begins to teach in churches and perform miracles. Twelve disciples—including Talmage—start miraculous works as well, which please everyone at first, but then come murmurs of discontent. A drought threatens nearby Tumblinsonville, and Talmage prays hard for rain, and it comes in such a deluge that crops are flooded, livestock drowned, and bridges washed out. A sick man asks for some cold weather to abate his fever, and the resulting ice freezes to death two old men and six children. An esteemed weatherman feels so threatened that he attempts to kill Talmage. A dying youth is prayed for, recovers, murders a man, and is hanged; his mother is upset with Talmage. Christ raises a rich latter-day Lazarus from the dead, only to create animosity among his already-paid heirs. The Lazarus sues to repossess his assets, but his complaint is declared inadmissible since he was recently a corpse. The disciples are all accused of disturbing the order of nature. But they go on and finally save a dying man named Marvin, who is a brutal, loathsome drunkard, liar, thief, and arsonist. The people are so distressed to see him hale and hearty again that they pass laws making it illegal to ask so that one may receive, to pray for the sick or for peace or rain. The official Arkansas prayer will now be for the Lord's will, not the individual's, to be done.

All is well again, until those meddling disciples pray for the sun and moon to stand still to help a posse. The result, of course, is a lethal disruption of the tides, and millions of persons are drowned. One after another, the Savior and all of his disciples are tracked down and crucified—except one. Talmage gets thirty pieces of silver from some detectives, for services he performed. The Second Advent, 1881, is ended.

The President of Andover, Jackson Barnes, Mrs. Nancy Hopkins Barnes, Beach, Bennett, the Twelve Disciples, Horace Greeley, Hopkins, Mrs. Hopkins, Jesus Christ, Lazarus, Marvin, Mary, the President of Princeton, St. Talmage, the President of Yale.

"The Secret History of Eddypus, the World-Empire," 1972 (FM).

Book I. In the year 1001 A.M. (Anno Matris), or 2901 A.D. by old reckoning, the narrator writes a letter in cipher to a trusted friend to explain that Christian Science history should not be confused with real history. Mary Baker G. Eddy, so-called Mother, fourth person of the Godhead but second in rank, was really born naturally, more than a thousand years ago. Presently forbidden evidence, prepared in 30 A.M. (1898 A.D.) by Mark Twain, the Bishop of New Jersey, hanged 47 A.M. (1912 A.D.), documents everything. So does the introduction to Mary Eddy's first edition of *Science and Health*, now in one extant copy and locked in the Vatican at

Eddyflats (formerly Boston). Her bull, called *Jubus Jorum Acqui-lorum*, says otherwise, and further erroneously states that Popes now wear female apparel and call themselves "She" in her honor. All Christian Science Popes since Mrs. Eddy are called Her Divine Grace Pope Mary Baker G. Eddy II, III, IV, etc. She always planned for female Popes. Anyway, the last female Pope was Mary XXIV, ending 226 A.M. She weakly desired to stop the rivalry between her church and the Roman Catholic one; so she favored a merger. When she died, Pius XII abolished his papacy, started to wear clothes like Mary's, and became mistress of the world and of Christian Sciencedom, as Mary XXV. From 226 A.M. forward to 1001 A.M., 103 Popes named Mary have reigned, but none has been either female or Christian.

In a second letter, the narrator promises to send his friend in invisible ink a private true history of Eddypus, which though perilous to compose will counteract the romantic nonsense which passes for the official history of the centuries of rule by the holy Marys. The long history now follows.

Holy Eddypus is a world empire, governing the entire globe except China, where an enlightened culture uniquely survives. Eddypus = *Eddy* + *pus*, that is, a religion with priests full of sanctifying pus. Other words deriving from Eddy include Eddymaniac, Eddymas (formerly Christmas), Eddyville (formerly heaven), Eddycation, and Eddycant. In the sixth century A.M., the Pope ordered all books burned. A few survived, however, including an invaluable ancient one, by Mary Twain, Bishop of New Jersey. It was discovered twenty years ago and is entitled *Old Comradeships*.

The destruction of libraries and books, beginning a century after the first Mary, was nearly total. But in China culture survived. Few books of any kind were written for the next four centuries. Eddyraids were conducted against them. But *Old Comrades* escaped. Its author made arrangements to hide it for five hundred years, but actually it lay unread for a thousand. Most of the few extant books are histories, inaccurately preserving oral traditions. This is what we know. There was a Christine Empire. Columbus and Uncle Remus discovered America. The Greek Empire was located in Dublin or Dubling. England had the following kings, in order: Louis XIV, William the Conqueror, Saxton Heptarky, George III, Peter the Hermit, and Charles the Bald. During Charles's reign, George Wishington in America cut down a cherry tree, thus precipitating the Declaration of Independence and a temporary democratic and freedom-loving fervor.

After England and America separated, the nineteenth century transpired. It was a remarkable epoch, commercially and scientifically, and included the birth of Mary I and Her church. Then came the splendid, nightmarish twentieth century. The first big era in human history was pre-Christian; the second, Christian; and now, since 1865 A.D. or so, the time of Eddy. Some officially discredited scholars say that Mary I stole Christian Science from a man with a name something like Quim. After a busy life, during all of which Mary I was depicted as never aging, she was translated directly into heaven.

We speak of the dawn of a civilization. The advent of Christian Science was more like an eclipse. The fault was Mary I's, but also that of so-called civilization, with its so-called progress. Where we now live, the United States once flourished, with between fifty and a hundred states, each with a legislature or asylum. The national legislature, called Congress or the Head Asylum, was filled with idiots. In Eddyflats there was a copper statue supposedly of Mary I; but really, according to Twain of New Jersey, it was of Charley's Aunt, a once-puissant republican leader now forgotten.

Book II. Since the chief authority for most of the following historical information is Mark Twain of New Jersey, a brief sketch of that great man may not be amiss. He is the most ancient surviving writer; hence he is called the Father of History. In addition to his multi-volumed Old Comrades, he wrote philosophical studies. It is thought that he was hanged sometime between 1912 A.D. and 1935 A.D. He had a wife and family, and also twenty-six illegitimate children, including Huck Finn and Tom Sawyer, of whom he often wrote with immoral fondness. Clergymen in those days must have kept harems. Twain read widely. He especially liked the following books: Innocents Abroad, Tramp Abroad, Puddnhead Wilson, Joan of Arc, and Prince and Pauper. Twain sadly lacked a sense of humor. For example, he once wrote that the truth is so precious that we should economize it. Obviously, he should have said the truth is so precious that we should not be careless with it. He set down several hundred such blundering, incongruous maxims in his Appendix. Twain founded the Smithsonian Institute and invented such things as the phonograph and the telephone. In his Old Comrades he attempts to describe unimportant acquaintances as well as illustrious ones, in order that a nakedly honest history of his age would flow from his pen. At first he planned to delay its publication for a hundred years, then a thousand; but he realized that if publication waited too long the work would prove as indecipherable to future readers as *Beowulf* was to his contemporaries. His book was typewritten, bound, and deposited in a vault in the presidential palace. He left instructions that it should be retrieved in five centuries and published. The proceeds were to be used to educate specialists to devise a sensible copyright law. But his book, sadly, lay undiscovered for a thousand years. It was found by shepherds digging for water only three years ago. The narrator's uncle bought it for three eddyplunks, gave it to the narrator, and its translation has just been completed.

To the reader of his book, Mark Twain, Bishop of New Jersey, addresses a few words. His skeleton comes to the reader and invites him to feel the page, warmed once by Twain's own hand. Don't shiver. Death is nothing but peace and rest. Twain once delivered fine speeches, his eyes once flashed from what are now empty sockets, his bony hands once shook those of all kinds of people, his bamboo legs once danced gracefully. Twain now drinks a clinking glass of wine. It does not matter that the liquid wets his spinal column. He has an umbrella, a gift from kind old Howells. Embrace your wife and children while you can. As the clock strikes midnight, Twain squeaks off, with a promise to meet the reader later, in wormland.

It is next reported that early in his first volume Bishop Twain explains that in London on April 1, 1900, he read a poem by Joseph B. Gilder praising the Giant of the West. Is this giant America or Twain himself? Reading the laudatory verses, Twain finds his head swelling. So he wraps it in a turban, and goes to Briggs and Pollard, phrenologists. When he identifies himself as a broker named Johnson, the two feel his skull bumps and characterize him as a poltroonish, fiendish, lascivious, thieving liar. Later, Bishop Twain returns with chaplain and canonicals, and is adjudged this time by Briggs and Pollard to be noble, courageous, angelic, humble, and honorable. Conclusion: phrenologists determine character from clothes.

We are now asked to imagine that we are standing on the threshold of the nineteenth century in America. How does everything we see differ from aspects of the thirtieth century, in the time of

Eddypus? Not much. No science, no civilization, but a dozing land. And Negro slavery, sluggish transportation, Sunday as a day of rest and worship (Monday, for Motherday, will be Sabbath later), slovenly whites, wooden agricultural tools, coarse wool and cotton and linen cloth, meat and vegetables for a diet, cider and beer for drink, and tea and coffee (which will be unknown in the thirtieth century), and in the towns churches, prisons, gallows, and slave pens (but no Inquisition as in the thirtieth century). Here in the nineteenth century, there are also newspapers, big ships, and pestilential land wars, but no religious persecution—since various religious factions police each other unknowingly. In the thirtieth century, there will be no papers, boats, or wars, but plenty of religious burnings. Yes, America reposed in peace back in those days. Did Eddypus civilization, which burst upon America a few years later, come from heaven or hell?

Early in the nineteenth century a series of extraordinary scientists, inventors, and financiers were born. From Bishop Twain's *Old Comrades* and other books which miraculously escaped Eddyraids, the author now summarizes some of the accomplishments of these geniuses. Sir Izaac Walton discovered the law of gravity and received the Victoria Cross for so doing. Tycho Bruno theorized that the world was spinning. John Calvin Galileo proved Bruno's theory by applying Walton's law to the moon and the sun, but Galileo's great-great-grandson was burned as a heretic because according to Eddygraphs the world stands still. Herschel invented the telescope by fiddling with two eyeglasses and soon discovered Uranus. Leverrier used a telescope on some stars, accounted for their wobbles by applying Walton's law out there, and in the process discovered Neptune. Bessel then measured the distance of stars from the world. Mankind began to realize at this point that the lid had been removed from the universe by these momentous discoveries. It was as though people who had been foully imprisoned all their lives were taken into flowery fields bathed by healing sunbeams.

Then came Priestley, who discovered oxygen and terrified everyone by saying first that oxygen was necessary for combustion and second that oxygen was everywhere. People thought that the world would surely burn up soon. Priestley then proved that oxygen was necessary for life by putting more than a hundred people into the Black Hole of Calcutta, drawing out the oxygen, and sure enough they died. Lavoisier proved that the world was not getting smaller because of oxidation. He burned everything, even his neighbors' socks, weighed the ashes, added the lost oxygen, and the total was the same as the original weight of the object burned. Kirchhoff and Bunsen invented the spectroscope and proved that distant astronomical objects were composed of the same things we are. They searched the heavens for new materials and found helium. They established a company called the Heavenly Trust to search the skies, and they put the renowned explorer Henry M. Stanley in charge. This was the first trust. Billionaires followed. Dagger of Salem—or Dugger, or Daguerre—invented a method of making pictures called tintypes. At first these pictures frightened everyone and thus occasioned the Salem Witch Trials, but later he learned how to make tintypes very profitably, especially near Niagara, where people would pose in front of his camera looking sick and happy. Next was invented a process for printing one picture in thousands of copies; then came motion pictures, and photographs of stars invisible even through telescopes.

The nineteenth century had growing pains. The French Revolution was followed by Henri IV, Cologni, Charles IX, Louis XVI, the Duke de Guise, Marat, and Charlotte Corday. Meanwhile, Martin Luther, the Father of Geology, was so happy when he found some fossils that his students, aiming only to please him, helped him find some more, including fake ones, which they had planted, of tiny animals. Luther theorized that they were God's models for various species. Finally, his pupils planted a model of woman for him to find, and the game was up. He knew that God had created Eve out of Adam's rib. So the students confessed, were sentenced to be beheaded, and would have been except that Luther got them pardoned by Emperor Henry IV at Canossa. Luther had planned a book on his geological notions but suppressed it.

Luther gave up his theories of models but continued to study fossils. How could they have bored their way into rocks? At first it was decreed that they had been created dead and hard, at the very same time all living things were being created. The church discouraged further inquiry for a long sleepy time, but by and by Lyell reasoned that things died and were then deposited as fossils in geological layers over eons. Then Darwin explained the descent of species, and Spencer posited the law of evolution. Each of countless circumstances contributes its mite to onrolling, inevitable change—without plan. No individual makes events; accumulations of circumstances do. But every once in a while a bright person discerns the power of certain accumulations and gets undeserved credit.

In the nineteenth century all of this intellectual ferment generated a material revolution and was beginning to cause slavery to become unprofitable. But then Awkwright's spinning machine, Watt's development of steam power, and Whitney's cotton gin combined to give slave labor a new value. So slavery was extolled by press and pulpit. And the blind force of unplanned circumstances rolled on.

Aldrich, Awkwright, William Bacon, Napoolyun Bonyprat, Briggs, Tycho Bruno, Buffon, Mary Ann Bullion, Bunsen, John Calvin, Charles IX, Charles the Bald, Charley's Aunt, Cologni, Columbus, Charlotte Corday, Richard Croker, Cuvier, Dagger, Darwin, Dick, Dontchutellim, Mrs. Mary Baker G. Eddy I, Mary Baker G. Eddy II, Mary Baker G. Eddy III, Mary Baker G. Eddy IV, Mary Baker G. Eddy XXIV, Mary Baker G. Eddy CII, Mary Baker G. Eddy CIII, Mary Baker G. Eddy, Ralp Waldo Edison, Huck Finn, Flinders, Charles Frohman, John Calvin Galileo, George III, Joseph B. Gilder, Goethe, the Duke of Guise, Harry, Henri IV, Emperor Henry IV, Saxon Heptarky, Herschel, Howells, Judge Jaffries, Kirchhoff, Lavoisier, Leverrier, Linnaeus, Louis XIV, Louis XVI, Martin Luther, Lyell, Marat, Rev. Cotton Mather, Mirabeau, Parcelsius, Old Parr, Peter the Hermit, Pope Pius XII, Pollard, the Pope, the Pope, the Pope, the President of the United States, Priestley, Quay, Quim, Sir Walter Raleigh, Tom Sawyer, Scientist, Servetus, Sir Francis Shakespeare, F. Hopkinson Smith, Herbert Spencer, Henry M. Stanley, Tom, Mark Twain the Bishop of New Jersey, Wat Tyler, Uncle Remus, Sir Izaac Walton, Watt, Eli Whitney, William the Conqueror, George Wishington, Witch, X.

["Senator Chandler's Party"]. See W 1868.

"Sending Him Through." From *Roughing It.*

"Sending Them Through." From *Roughing It.*

"Ye Sentimental Law Student," c. 1863.*
    Twain explains that he found a letter on Sugar Loaf Peak. It is a combination of sentimental and legalistic phrases, and must have been written by the Unreliable. It is addressed to Mary Links, is signed Solon Lycurgus, and verbosely advises her as party of the first part of the feelings of himself, the party of the second part.
    Mary Links, Solon Lycurgus.
    In *Wit and Humor of America,* ed. Kate M. Rabb, Vol. 5 (Indianapolis: Bobbs-Merrill, 1907).

"Servant-Girl ism." See FW, 1870.

'Seventieth Birthday,' 1905 (WMT 28).
    Twain asserts that he remembers his first birthday. He had no hair, teeth, or clothes, and went to his first banquet just that way. Villagers swarmed in because he was the first thing that had happened to the place in years. He was the only innocent creature there. He told them so, in his first after-dinner speech. That was his cradle song. Now he will deliver a swan song. He says that he has achieved the age of seventy by a regimen which would kill others. So his maxim is that we cannot reach old age by another person's road. Twain goes to bed when no one is still up to sit with, and he gets up when he has to. He eats nothing after a breakfast of coffee and bread for a period of eleven hours, and then has dinner. He advises everyone to live as he pleases and not simply to prolong his life. Twain smokes only one cigar at a time and never while he is asleep. He seldom takes any medicine, perhaps because when he was young his father was paid a drugstore in lieu of a debt and the family thus inherited nine barrels of cod-liver oil, which therefore became cheaper for them than other breakfast foods. Twain never exercises. He has led a moral life. Not that he was born with any morals. But he acquired a moral, developed it, then watched it lose ground and therefore sold it to Leopold the piratical king of Belgium. After three score and ten years, your statute of limitations has run out, you owe no active dues, you are emancipated, and the only bugle call that remains for you is Lights Out. You can stay home if you please and not lie about previous engagements. You

do not have to go on tiptoe to keep from waking up your friends, because you can never disturb them any more. When you arrive at Pier No. 70, step aboard your ship and head for the setting sun with contentment.

King Leopold of Belgium.

["Several Items by Mark Twain"], 1853, 1869, 1870.*

In the Hannibal *Daily Journal*, 1853, Twain replies to Grumbler, who objected to Twain's poem "Love Concealed: To Miss Katie in H—1," on the grounds that no poet should address a lady in Hell; Twain says that H—1 means Hannibal, calls Grumbler a lunatic, and signs his protest Rambler. In 1870, Twain writes F. P. Church, editor of the *Galaxy*, accepting his offer to let Twain run a "Department of Agriculture" in that magazine. He knows nothing about the neglected subject, but he will make a reaping hook blossom and curdle the blood of his readers. "Adventures in Hayti," 1869, describes a traveler's arrival at Port-Au-Prince, with its poverty, narrow streets, cool estates, and tropical trees and plants. The *Quaker City* is off the northern coast bombarding Fort Picolet. For $40,000, the narrator happily sells a citizen his field glasses for use in watching an incipient battle near Bejar but then he learns that prices have skyrocketed so dreadfully that he must pay a hotel bellhop $900 for carrying his valise. He retires to his bedroom to recite figures and poetry to make sure he is not insane. A distraught American widow bursts in upon him with a tale of woe. She needs his help to get home. Will he pay her food bill? When he agrees and then asks the sum, she says that it is only $60,000. He leaps out his window and soon is wandering about the town, crazy and desperate. He returns to his hotel and is flabbergasted when he learns that his bill is $285,400. So he sneaks out and hides between decks on his ship. In a postscript he explains that he now understands: Haitian currency is so inflated in wartime that a dollar in gold costs $1,800 or more in local greenbacks. Extracts from Twain's 1869 Buffalo *Express* column called "People and Things" deal with many subjects, including geography, art, politics, money, virtue, sickness, oddities (including archeological finds and a two-headed girl), old people, and death.

Euphrosyne Braatz, Charley, F. P. Church, Ellen Durkee, Eddes, the Editor, Gen[eral]. [Ulysses S.] Grant, Grumbler, John Holland, George Hollister, M. de Lamester, Pere L'Epingle, Rambler, Henry J. Raymond, Vinnie Reams, Second Adventists, John Smith, W. Frank Stewart, Mrs. Stewart, Brigham Young.

*In Merle Johnson, *A Bibliography of the Works of Mark Twain* . . . (New York and London: Harper, 1935).

"A Severe Stab at Women's Rights." See FW, 1870.

"Shackleford's Ghost" (MTP).

Two men are discussing the disappearance of rich Benson, who, says one, was experimenting with a way to make people invisible, bribed a stranger to let him try it on him, made him disappear, and now Benson is scared and has run away. The two talkers leave, and the Invisible Man enters, annoyed that he cannot find work. Negroes Jim and Sally enter, discuss the probable murder of the young man, and step on a cat also rendered invisible by Benson. The cat howls. Suddenly the Invisible Man has an idea: he can hire himself to haunt places, in return for room and board. Next we see him working for a medium, helping her fabricate messages from the dead on slates. Later he writes love messages on the slate to Miss Benson, the absent inventor's eligible daughter. Soon the Invisible Man persuades her to kiss and hug him, and tells her that though invisible he is also immortal. At the last scene, an innocent man, caught and tried for murdering the stranger, is about to be hanged when the Invisible Man shouts that he is the spirit of Benson, who died a suicide, and that the accused is innocent. At this, the real Benson appears and announces that no one has been murdered, gives the Invisible Man an antidote to make him visible again, and accepts him as a son-in-law.

Benson, Miss Benson, the Invisible Man, Jim, Sally, Shackleford.

"Short and Singular Rations." Part of "Forty-Three Days in an Open Boat." See "My Début as a Literary Person."

"The Shrine of St. Wagner." See "At the Shrine of St. Wagner."

"The Siamese Twins," 1872 (WMT 7).

Chang and Eng have clung to each other with touching fidelity. Even as children they were inseparable. Whenever they got lost, their mother knew that if she found one, the other would be near. Now that they are men, there is still a bond between them. Yet they are different. Chang usually gets up an hour before his brother, does the indoor work, and is a Baptist. Eng runs the errands and is a Roman Catholic. They fought on opposite sides during the Civil War, took each other prisoner, and were mutually exchanged. On one occasion they fought bitterly, and no one could separate them. They both fell in love with the same girl; but Chang, who does not drink or smoke, won the girl after a curious courtship. By and by, Eng fell in love with his sister-in-law's sister, married her, and all live happily. When Eng gets drunk, so does Chang, which makes the latter's efforts among the Good Templars confusing. People have concluded that Chang gets physically but not morally drunk. It is of interest to note that one twin is fifty-one years old and the other is fifty-three.

Chang, Eng.

"The Signal Corps," 1866 (WG).

Twain watches two Signal Corps "mediums" silently transmit messages to each other. The pair, named Wicker and Jerome, were active in the Civil War. They signal messages by moving their canes, hands, fingers, and eyes. Twain has Wicker successfully transmit two messages, about General Jackson and cholera cases, to Jerome. The process seems more baffling than spiritualism. In the recent war, such signals—with flags and torches—were exceedingly efficient and reliable.

Conway, the Acting General, General Jackson, Jerome, General Shields, Colonel Wicker.

"Simon Wheeler, Detective," 1967 (SB).*

The backward little Missouri village is named Guilford. Its two wealthiest families are the Griswolds and the Burnsides. "Judge" Griswold, aged sixty, tall, thin, and intellectual looking, was born in Kentucky of a proud Virginia family. He is a gentleman of honor, whose word is his bond. His wife Ruth, about fifty, is loving, patient, and acquiescent. They have buried all their children but Milly, who is sixteen, sweet, and beautiful. Mrs. Mary Burnside is a gracious old lady, whose life is wrapped up in her two remaining children. They are Clara, twenty-one, delicate, refined, and plucky; and Hugh, twenty, giddy, thoughtless, sappy, and poetic. One spring day the Griswolds are discussing the arrival in town of Mrs. Burnside's nephew, young Hale Dexter from Kentucky. The Judge begins to reminisce about a feud between the Dexters and the Burnsides, interrupted by the death of Mrs. Burnside's husband before he could be killed by Hale's fiery father Edward Dexter, Mrs. Burnside's brother. Edward came to Guilford for that purpose but returned home to Kentucky without even sending a message to his sister. Instead, he hoped that his son, Hale, would grow up and kill his cousin Hugh. The Judge now announces that he must befriend Hale, who is at this moment on his way to Guilford to resume the feud. This news saddens Mrs. Griswold, who likes Mrs. Burnside and has nothing against foolish Hugh. At this point Milly Griswold enters the room; so the talk abruptly changes. The girl embroiders a bookmark with the name "Hugh" spelled in it.

Hale Dexter has been riding his horse for a day and a half, when it dawns on him that he has wandered from the Drytown road and is lost. He is meandering about aimlessly when a talkative young man and a remarkably pretty girl canter up and offer to help. As they lead him to his road, Hale catches the girl looking at him approvingly. He thinks enviously that she is probably the young man's sweetheart, when suddenly that fellow calls her his sister. Soon Hale is on his way again, without, unfortunately, exchanging names with his helpers. Shortly after dark he arrives at a tavern in Drytown and aids a husky man of about fifty, with yellow-red hair, who is having a fight with three roughnecks. Once victory is determined, the two new friends introduce themselves. The older man is Cap'n Simon Wheeler, amateur detective, who is sad when Hale reveals his name, because Wheeler would rather have detected it and everything else about the newcomer. After supper Hale reads in the miserably printed Guilford newspaper that desperado Jack Belford was prevented from breaking out of jail by Major Hoskins, the Boggsville sheriff. Hale is more interested in thinking about a certain girl's beautiful form.

Next evening Hale presents himself at the Griswold house and is made most welcome. Mrs. Griswold likes him at once. Milly is pleased when he relays stories he has heard about the California gold rush and when later he sings for her. And the Judge admires the apparent firmness with which his young guest, once the ladies have retired, speaks of continuing his dead father's feud. The Judge urges him to prepare a will, in the event he inherits Humphrey's fortune and then is killed. Suddenly absent-minded Martha Griswold brings news which obliges her brother the Judge to take his wife to her gravely sick sister at Hoxton. Major Barnes, a distant relative of the Judge, must act as Hale's second.

Hale writes his will, pens a pleasant letter to his mother, wonders why he must continue a meaningless feud, and in the morning shrinks guiltily from Milly. Wheeler greets him on the street, and then Hale bumps into the two young people who befriended him on the prairie. They turn out to be Hugh Burnside and his pretty sister Clara. They take him into their home and introduce him to their mother, who expresses her sense of relief that her nephew Hale is not going to feud with her son Hugh. The two young men go wolf-hunting and find some poisoned meat spread in the woods. Hugh mopes about because he and Milly have argued over the bookmark she made him. Wheeler follows the men and, concluding that Hugh wants to kill Hale to have their relative Humphrey's legacy for himself, sends the supposed victim an enigmatic note cautioning him not to eat beefsteak. Hale reads the ridiculous message after supper. Then illiterate Toby, his assigned Negro servant, enters and asks him to write a letter for him to his mother Betsy, a slave down in Arkansas. To Hale's delight, Toby confesses that the letter he was to deliver from Judge Griswold to Major Barnes accidentally fell into the kitchen fire and was destroyed. Hale copies a foolish form letter from a girl to a rejected suitor, which Toby then happily prepares to send to his mother. The slave steals Wheeler's letter to Hale, puts it with the Judge's unburned letter to Barnes, and asks the Judge's sister to mail everything in a packet to Toby's brother Jim, a cotton-field worker. Hale later goes downstairs, sees gloomy Milly, and brightens her evening by suggesting that they walk over to the Burnsides' house, where a reporter named Tom Hooker and a store clerk named Lem Sackett are calling on Clara. When Milly and Hale enter, Hugh morosely leaves. Clara seems so aloof that Hale is embarrassed and soon departs with Milly. Only then is Clara sorry. On their way

home, Hale and Milly encounter Wheeler disguised as a fortune-
telling gypsy. He warns perplexed Hale to avoid beefsteak. Next
morning Hale and Hugh go hiking, and Hale advises Hugh to regard himself as in love with Milly; but the fellow loquaciously
explains that he has now talked himself out of love. Next day they
go hunting, and Hale reveals himself to be a poor shot. Several days
pass. Then the two talk about Clara. When Hugh says that he
thinks his sister is in love, Hale becomes so depressed that he
resolves to go to her and announce that all is over. But when he
arrives, she says that she is very happy to see him. Soon they play
chess, sit on the sofa together, and decide that they are engaged.
Days now fly by as in a blissful dream. They are amazed at the pro-
fundity of their unique love. Meanwhile Hugh, who has dreamed
of saving ungrateful Milly's life, has his chance. A group of pic-
nickers, excluding the young poet, goes up a hill north of town for
an outing, after which, growing impatient, Milly drives a horse
and carriage too fast down a twisting road. Hugh happens to be
walking near a dangerous bend, seizes the frantic horse's bit, and
thus prevents disaster. He becomes a hero in the local press. But
soon he spoils it by publishing some atrocious personal verse celebrating his love for Milly and Hale's for Clara. The result is that
Clara rebukes him and so does Milly, to whom he says he will kill
himself. Hale, who is there at the time, jokingly says he will gladly
feed Hugh's remains to the worms. Judge Griswold happens to
return at this very moment, hears the remark, and assumes that
Hale still intends to duel with Hugh and kill him. Having to leave
the house again, instantly, to care for his sick wife, the Judge
merely drops Hale a note urging him to complete his mission
and rely on Barnes for help in getting away afterwards. Puzzled,
Hale concludes that reports to the Judge must have miscarried;
surely the man would want to thank Hugh for saving his daughter
Milly, not hope that Hale will shoot him. Meanwhile, Baxter, Billings, and Billings, three detectives from Inspector Flathead's
detective agency in St. Louis, have arrived on the scene in pursuit
of notorious Jack Belford, who, it seems, has escaped from jail
on the eve of his execution and is thought to be in the area. Wheeler
is enormously impressed by their professionally apt questions.

The Judge returns to Drytown, this time with his sister Martha,
to care for his wife, who is too sick from fatigue in connection with
his sister's death to return to Guilford at this time. Mrs. Griswold

is afraid that Martha will bring news of dreadful tragedy at home, but the woman instead explains joyfully that Hugh saved Milly's life and wants to marry the girl. When the Judge hears this report, he leaps on his horse to gallop back home and save Hugh from death at Hale's hands.

Meanwhile, back in Guilford on this very night, two drugstore clerks, Bob and Jimmy, have just sold Hugh a sleeping potion which the sad young poet thinks will kill him. The clerks tardily repent of their act, realizing that Hugh might become sleepy and fall into the river or otherwise hurt himself. They agree to keep mum. Next, Wheeler stumbles on sleeping Hugh, mistakes the big figure for a log, sits on it, and lectures about his prowess as a detective. Next, drunken reporter Tom Hooker sees Hugh and regards him as a corpse, takes him home in a wheelbarrow to hide him for next week's newspaper, and frightens his sleeping roommate Lem Sackett. The two fight and get blood on the "corpse," which they therefore carry back to the spot where Tom first found it. The two young men feel certain that they will eventually be hanged for murder.

At dawn Hugh awakens, is glad that he is not dead, but decides to disappear for a while so that his mother, his sister, and Milly will feel sorry for abusing him. Jack Belford the desperado happens by, disguised as an organ grinder with blue goggles and false whiskers. Hugh persuades him to exchange clothes with him for a lark. Belford is only too willing and soon is plunging through the woods in Hugh's attire, when Hale, out hunting wolves, fires at him in the uncertain light. Belford falls face down, pretending to be dead until the hunter goes away for assistance. Hale walks closer, mistakes the "corpse" for Hugh, and staggers through the woods to the Drytown road, down which Judge Griswold is galloping at this moment. Hale tells the Judge that he shot Hugh by accident, and the two go to the Griswold house to consider matters. Meanwhile, the three St. Louis detectives are approaching the thicket where Belford has now concealed himself. On the theory that their quarry has disguised himself as a cow, the sleuths are following cow tracks to a tree. After listening to their maunderings a while, Belford emerges, introduces himself as a country detective by the name of Bob Tufts, tells them that he recently saw a cow climb a tree and wants to shoot it, but allows himself to be persuaded instead to take letters of introduction from them on his way supposedly to Illinois to seek out a desperado named Belford. Baxter, Billings, and Bullet laugh at his retreating form. While all of this is transpiring, Wheeler and his admiring wife Jenny are on their way to the Burnside home. He tells her to ask certain leading questions about Hugh. When she does so, she learns that Hugh has not been missed but then alarms Mrs. Burnside and Clara. The Wheelers proceed toward Mrs. Higgins's house, near which they find the wheelbarrow left by Tom and Lem. Wheeler examines it and some leaves from a nearby tree, then announces his deduction: Hugh decided not to kill himself, climbed the tree, plotted to murder his mother, went to sleep, fell, and landed on a burly stranger who in anger killed Hugh with the wheelbarrow. Jenny is tremendously impressed by this theory. Then Wheeler sees a man scratching his head with his left hand, sends Jenny home, and trails the suspicious fellow, who, however, turns out to be harmless Crazy Hackett. Hugh in his disguise next appears, and Wheeler without recognizing him asks him several leading questions. His bewildered answers arouse Wheeler's suspicions; so the detective hires Hugh to saw wood for him so that he can keep an eye on the obviously dangerous fellow.

Almost as soon as the Judge and Hale return home, Clara and her mother burst in. The two men can hardly comfort them, but gradually the Burnsides begin to encourage themselves to hope that Hugh will soon reappear. They tell Hale that he must come and stay with them—and even occupy Hugh's room. He should eventually even marry Hugh's sister. When the visitors leave, Hale slowly decides not to confess that he shot Hugh, not to run away, and not to kill himself. He must comfort Hugh's mother and sister. The Judge commends him. Hale then writes a full explanation to his mother, but Toby secretly sends the letter to his mother and brother Jim. In the morning strangers oppress Hale by asking him his theory as to Hugh's whereabouts. Hale goes to the Burnside women to comfort them some more. Walking home at midnight, he hears the three detectives theorizing on Hugh's disappearance, and the next thing he knows Milly is showing him a newspaper extra with Hugh's probable murder headlined.

For four days Hale suffers terribly. He hypocritically comforts the Burnside women. Then Milly late one night finally forces him to admit that he believes Hugh is dead. Telling him that she thinks Hugh was murdered, she reveals her plan: Hale must offer $1,000

of her money for the killer, whom she suspects to be Crazy Hackett.
Hale reluctantly agrees and goes to bed feeling that he is the un-
happiest, most perplexed person in the world.

It seems that Captain Simon Wheeler has tried various occupations, including that of traveling showman. When his father died,
he freed all their slaves and in other ways continued his advanced
thinking. One night he dreamed that he died and went whizzing
off through darkness and cold, past flaming suns for many years,
and finally landed in an enchanting region of supernal loveliness.
A Beautiful Personage stood under a huge and glittering arch, told
a Quaker to join other Quakers, then a Mohammedan to consort
with others of his kind, and finally beckoned to Wheeler, who
advanced, dropped his hat, sweat profusely, and at last knelt in
fear. But happily the Personage gave him the freedom of the whole
territory. To return to earth—Wheeler alternately farms and
plays detective. In fact, he has been a would-be sleuth ever since
reading *Tales of a Detective*. He has the confidence born of ignorance and self-appreciation. In his former slaves' quarter, he has
set up an office, where he pretends he is a chief of detectives. He
also has a showy little museum of costumes and waxworks. Hugh,
in his disguise, is now living with Wheeler but out of sight of his
wife Jenny, who, Wheeler explains, would disapprove of the expense of a hired man. The arrangement pleases Hugh, who one
night sneaks into his employer's office, reads the dispatches
Wheeler has written for his imaginary men, and even visits the
room full of wax dummies. A little later Hugh and Wheeler converse about the newsworthy murder of young Burnside . . .

Abble, Inspector Adams, Bagley, Detective Barker, Major
Barnes, Baxter, the Beautiful Personage, Jack Belford,
Betsy, Billings, Bishop, Bob, Bullet, Clara Burnside, Hugh
Burnside, Mrs. Mary Burnside, Burnside, Burnside, Conk-
lin, Edward Dexter, Mrs. Edward Dexter, Hale Dexter,
Ding, Buck Farley, Father of a Young Lady, Fire-eater,
Inspector Flathead, Martha Griswold, Milly Griswold,
Mrs. Ruth Griswold, Judge Griswold, Griswold, Griswold,
Crazy Hackett, Aunt Hanner, Hassan Ben Ali, Mrs. Hig-
gins, Tom Hooker, Hooker, Abel Hopkins, Major Hoskins,
Hubbard, Humphrey, Uncle Jim, Jim, Jimmy, Jones,
Larkin, Hank Miller, Morgan, Morgan, Mucker, Mulatto
Bob, Archibald Skidmore Nickerson, Nobby Bill, Lem

Sackett, Elizabeth Sapper, Suitor, Toby, Johnny Tompson, Waxy, Mrs. Jenny Wheeler, Captain Simon Wheeler, Colonel Whiting, Whitlow, Young Gentleman of Fortune, Young Lady.

*The text used supersedes *Simon Wheeler, Detective,* ed. Franklin R. Rogers (New York: New York Public Library, 1963), also excellent.

"Simon Wheeler, the Amateur Detective." See "Simon Wheeler, Detective."

"A Simplified Alphabet," 1917 (WMT 26).

Twain confesses to having a cousinly feeling toward simplified spelling but adds that it is really only the substitution of one inadequacy for another. What we need is a new alphabet. He favors Burnz's phonic shorthand, which is based on Isaac Pitman's scientific phonography. Adopting it would result in accurate spelling—based strictly on sounds—and also a reduction of labor. To write *through* requires twenty-one pen strokes; the simplified form *thru,* twelve; but the phonographic form, only three. Twain can copy about twenty-four words a minute. Using the phonic form, he could easily copy three times as fast. It has taken us five hundred years to simplify some of Chaucer's rotten spelling; but many words spelled in simplified forms still look awkward, although in time the publik ma get rekonsyled to simplified kombynashuns. On the other hand, phonographic spelling looks like Arabic or hieroglyphics, that is to say, is fascinating because of its mystery.

["Simplified Spelling"], 1962 (LFE).

Here the narrator is, in Egypt, in an earlier reincarnation. A faction is in revolt against cumbersome hieroglyphics. A debate is taking place even now at Astarte's temple between the Simplifiers and the Opposition. Uncle Cadmus, an uncle of Cadmus, takes the floor, moves up to the blackboard, and spends forty-five minutes drawing a bunch of skinny Egyptians, saws, skeletal birds, a house, a king spearing a lion, and a pair of fighting armies. He explains that it is all a hieroglyphic for the Lord's Prayer, which he then writes out in four minutes in Italian script. He reasons that Egyptians are wasting man-years learning hieroglyphics, which he admits are attractive and venerable. But for the sake of future generations, he urges the adoption of the alphabet, even though, he adds, it is monstrously imperfect in English, the spelling of words in which language—for example, *bow*—is often insane. When Cadmus sits down, the Opposition begins to tear into him.

Uncle Cadmus, Cadmus, Croesus, the Khedive, the Opposition, a Revolter, the Simplified Committee, a Simplifier.

The Singer Holds the Flag-watch in the field (MTP).

The battlefield Singer rests at night, singing a song about the lady he worships but will not name. He fights for freedom and the light. In the morning he strews the field with corpses and beseeches the unnamed lady to come.

The Singer.

"A Singular Episode" (MTP).

Mark Twain is singularly tired. The train journey is ending, after what seems months. The fatal shout is heard. The train has arrived at New Jerusalem and will go on to Sheol. Parties wishing to transfer should get into the next car forward. Twain exchanges tickets with the late Archbishop, snoozing in the adjoining seat, and with his pass ostentatiously displayed in his hat, then steps into the next car and rides to the pearly gates. When the Archbishop gets off, St. Peter notes his pass—really Twain's—is not amused, and tells the prelate to stop masquerading as the deceased ecclesiast whose spirit all heaven is awaiting when in reality he is only Twain. The offended archbishop would protest but for the sudden, boisterous arrival of the Reverend Sam Jones, a hosannahing Southwesterner with a slouch hat and a plug of tobacco. He wants to shake St. Peter by the hand but gets nowhere until he presents his credentials. All is in order; so St. Peter admits him though by the back door. Seeing this, the Archbishop is agreeable to going off to the other place. St. Peter returns to an examination of the real Mark Twain, still posing as the Archbishop. His pass is genuine. So, although angels No. 1, No. 2, and No. 3 begin to gossip about the apparent interloper, St. Peter reluctantly lets him through. Twain stays a week but is snubbed; so is Rev. Jones.

Soon there is a general exodus for hell, and by Saturday night the Texan has heaven all to himself.

> Pope Alexander VI, Borgia, the Archbishop of Canterbury, Rev. Sam Jones, Catherine de' Medici, No. 1, No. 3, No. 2, St. Peter, Torquemada.

"1601: Conversation, As It Was at the Social Fireside, in the Time of the Tudors," [1880].*

Queen Elizabeth's cup-bearer, who is a person of noble and ancient lineage, reports in his diary that just one day earlier the Queen invited to her closet several authors, including Lord Bacon, Sir Walter Raleigh, Ben Jonson, young Francis Beaumont, and the famous Shaxpur. Women present included the Duchess of Bilgewater, the Countess of Granby and her little daughter Lady Helen, and two aged maids of honor named Lady Margery Bothby and Lady Alice Dilbury. The cup-bearer had to remain, but he did so reluctantly because he objected to the law converse held. In the midst of the scandalous talk, someone broke wind mightily. Amid the ensuing stink, many laughed full sore. The Queen commended the wind instrument and identified it as surely male. Lady Alice confessed that she certainly was not the cause, since she lacked requisite room in her ancient bowels. Lady Margery said that had she contained such a volume of gas she would have dribbled it forth all evening, because launching it of a sudden would have rent her weak old frame. The Queen then opined that such a blast would have put dainty Beaumont into orbit and that Helen's wind would doubtless only tickle. Jonson denied all responsibility but suggested that only a veteran could have done the foul deed. Bacon argued that his own entrails were too lean. Shaxpur proclaimed his innocence, then poetically described the stench as issuing from hell and the noise from admiring heaven's artillery. At this point, everyone turned to look accusingly at Raleigh, who with smiles and simpers confessed that he did the deed but added that it was fragile compared to some of his better effusions. He did it only to clear his nether throat, as it were. He then punctuated his modest comments with a godless, rock-shivering blast, blushed through the accompanying suffocation, and commented that even his second performance was unrepresentative of his true powers.

Next, the offended cup-bearer records in detail the courtiers' distasteful talk about manners and customs. Shaxpur spoke of a passage in Montaigne describing the habit of Perigord widows of wearing in their headdresses jeweled simulations of a limp phallus, whereupon the Queen noted that English widows wear such things elsewhere. Shaxpur then spoke of Montaigne's account of a potent emperor, until Countess Granby detailed ways in which the ram out-performs even Montaigne's hero. Raleigh then told of certain abstemious American natives, whereupon the Queen hinted that perhaps little Helen might like to be sent to the New World for the preservation of her innocence. Helen neatly replied that she would happily follow the Virgin Queen's example anywhere. At this point, Beaumont expressed a sense of his own sexual modesty. Then the Queen repeated Rabelais's story to her of a man with a double pair of bollocks, at which the court paused to wonder how the word should be spelled until Lady Granby reminisced to the effect that amatory male explorers grow quickly and enormously indifferent to lexicography. Raleigh then told a bawdy tale from Boccaccio about a priest, a maiden, and a nimble abbot. Conversation turned to the topic of Luther, then poetry, at which Shaxpur read part of his abominable *King Henrie IV* and also a portion of his "Venus and Adonis." The cup-bearer's attention was weakened when Raleigh took to additional zealous blasting. When talk turned to Nicholas Throgmorton's defense back in Mary's time, the Queen leveled a glare at Raleigh, well known as once a lover of Throgmorton's daughter. The cup-bearer feels that the Queen should not pretend to object to debauchery in this licentious age. After all, Shaxpur's wife was with child when she wed the poet. Nor was the Duchess of Bilgewater stainless ere her marriage. And was not little Helen born on her mother's wedding day? Next came talk of Cervantes and Rubens. A grandiose speech then issued from old Alice which was so labored that the Queen, growing impatient with euphuisms, mincingly delivered herself of a brief, sibilant expletive. Raleigh changed the subject to a degree by recalling a story told by Margaret of Navarre about a maiden who kept herself from rape by urging her aged would-be attacker anaphrodisiacally to make water first.

Lord [Sir Francis] Bacon, Francis Beaumont, the Duchess of Bilgewater, Lady Margery Bothby, Lady Alice Dilbury, Queen Elizabeth, the Countess of Granby, Lady Helen, Ben Jonson, [John] Lillie [Lyly], Margaret of

Navarre, [François] Rabelais, Sir Walter Raleigh, [William] Shaxpur [Shakespeare], Nicholas Throgmorton, Miss Throgmorton.

*Edited by Franklin J. Meine (Chicago: Mark Twain Society, 1939).

'Sixty-Seventh Birthday,' 1902 (WMT 28).

Twain wants permission to talk as long as he pleases, since he has cancelled all other engagements for the entire winter. He is glad that the chairman did not introduce him with compliments, because he might then have found it hard to respond. He looks about and sees innumerable old faces, including those of John Hay, Tom Reed, and Reverend Twichell. When he first met Wayne Mac-Veagh, at Charles A. Dana's place, Twain could hardly get in five words to MacVeagh's one. Twain dreamed of traveling to heaven, exchanging tickets with the Archbishop of Canterbury—who did not object, because he was dead—and when arriving not being able to get in because MacVeagh was occupying the entire region. Howells nicely commended Twain by saying that the humorist attacked people's conventions rather than their convictions. Twain revisited Hannibal, Missouri, last June; and he and his boyhood friend John Briggs roamed through old haunts and renewed old memories blessedly. Twain closes by mentioning his wife and saying that she and Twichell made him what he is. Twichell is such a good minister that when he moves to a new church all the property values around it rise sharply. Out of one heart, Twain and his wife thank all present.

> The Archbishop of Canterbury, Bangs, John Briggs, [Olivia Langdon Clemens], Charles A. Dana, Chauncey [M.] Depew, Colonel [George] Harvey, Secretary of State John Hay, [William Dean] Howells, John, Sam Jones, St. Clair McKelway, Wayne MacVeagh, Mitchell, Saint Peter, Tom Reed, Dr. Rice, [Henry Huttleston] Rogers, Rev. [Joseph H.] Twichell, Dr. [Henry] Van Dyke.

"Skeleton Plan of a Proposed Casting Vote Party," 1923 (WMT 29).

The author proposes a plan to improve government by compelling the two major parties to nominate their best candidates

always. A Casting Vote Party should be organized, composed of
non-political persons who pledge always to cast their entire vote
for the one candidate they agree is better. They should never deal
with minor parties. They should organize from the ward level
upward to the presidential election. They should ordinarily remain small, aiming at quality rather than quantity membership.
At the local level, a membership of fifty might be sufficient to
swing the desired result. They should begin secretly, like all con-
spiracies, and through canvassing pyramid their influence. Local
lodges of their members should send delegates to meet with higher-
level lodges; when the decision as to which candidate is better has
been reached, all members should vote for that one. If the reader
thinks well of this proposal, let him organize a small group to test
its feasibility. American political conditions must and can be
improved.

Jones, Smith.

S'klk! G'lang!, 1963 (P).
When trouble looms, don't mope. Instead, cast off and take a
ride, like Mon[t]golfier, Columbus, Stephenson, and 'Lijah.

["A Sleeping Lion Aroused—Gideon Rampant"]. See W 1868.

"A Small Piece of Spite," 1864 (MTWY).
Twain opines that the action of Coroner Sheldon and his under-
strappers is spiteful. It seems that some practical joker stupidly
wrote on the morgue bulletin board that a certain person had died
who had not. Reporters printed the false news. The coroner's men
were so outraged that they have irrationally refused to give reporters legitimate news. Twain says that the public has a right to
read obituary notices.

Coroner Sheldon.

"Small-Fry Congressman" (MTP).
When a backswoods Congressman arrives in Washington, D.C.,
he ceases to be an eagle and turns into a bug. He thought that he

was a local Demosthenes, but no one listens to his eloquence in Congress.

Congressman.

"Smith Brown Jones." See *Mark Twain's San Francisco*.

"Smoking as Inspiration," 1882 (LAIFI).

Twain reports that drinking merely a glass of wine dulls his pen. Smoking, however, is different. He has smoked cigars immoderately most of the time since he was eight years old, and his health has been perfect. He quit a few times, once when he happened to be writing *Roughing It*. He felt obstructed, burned what he had written, resumed smoking—sometimes as many as three cigars an hour—and wrote the book in three months.

"The Snow-Shovelers" (MTP).

The peaceful Sabbath silence of the New England village, recently blanketed by snow, is broken by the shouts of Morgan's Negro snow shoveler Aleck and Newton's Negro shoveler Hank. The two men agree not to be paid by the job but to ask 30¢ an hour instead. They discuss the Negro ball they attended the night before. Aleck went on to meetings held by "Anerkis" and "Socialis," where the talk was all about politics—that is, having everyone get along without working. Hank interrupts to praise work as noble. Aleck agrees, adding that it keeps a body healthy and soun', but he goes on to explain that de Anerkis complain about the unfair distribution of wealth, part of which they intend to take by foce. On the other hand, the Socialis' plan to get some of that wealth by 'suasion in Congress. Hank wonders what the world is coming to. It would seem that work is growing disrespectable. At this point, Morgan and Newton tell the two Negroes to get busy or leave.

Aleck, Hank, Higginson, Morgan, Newton.

"Society for the Confusion of Intelligence." See FW, 1869.

'Society of American Authors,' 1900 (S).

To the society Twain observes that it seems hard for people to say anything uncomplimentary about him. Perhaps he is simply charming. Judge Ransom just now spoke almost enviously of Twain's modesty. But in truth Twain has a wicked side. People really want to lead lives of undiscovered sin. The Judge seems to have all the virtues he ascribes to Twain, but in reality the two are alike. Twain certainly lives two lives, and doing so keeps him busy. He says that he has more vanity than modesty; most of all, however, he has veracity. Recently a man introduced Twain at the Press Club and started off sincerely enough; but when he said that he had never read anything by Twain, it was obvious that he lied, because he could not have shown such wit without having read Twain! Twain concludes by saying that he likes compliments, takes them home to repeat them there, and dreams about them.

Judge Ransom.

"Sold to Satan," 1923 (WMT 29).

Mark Twain decides to sell his soul to Satan, since all the stocks are down in value; he can raise a stake and make his fortune. The midnight bell booms, and Satan shimmeringly enters, with his Mephistophelian smile and attractive stage bow. After a hot toddy and some chat about the weather, the author chances to ask what his visitor is made of. Satan explains that he stands six feet one and is composed of nine hundred pounds of radium inside a skin of polonium. Divining that Twain wants to kidnap him, incorporate him, and make a fortune by sharing shares, Satan laughs heartily, commends his host's Cavour cigars, praises the stunning little nine teenth century, and predicts that the twentieth will be staggering because of power. He explains that everything needs power, that coal and steam power are wasteful and limited, but that radium—which Madame Curie has just discovered on earth—is spontaneously and eternally luminous, self-charging, and hot. When polonium, freed from bismuth, can be used to shield radium, obtained from barium, scientists will have an endless source of power. Then Satan gives the narrator a lecture on chemistry, involving explanations of molecules, atoms, and electrons, and concluding with two revelations: that the source of light in the firefly is a single radium electron inprisoned in a polonium atom, and that fireflies go to a certain snow summit of the Cordilleras to die. Satan demonstrates his power by lighting a cigar with his finger and then disintegrating an iron letterpress by a single touch. He tells Twain to wait until

Madame Curie has isolated polonium, then clothe himself in a skin of it, and take possession of the Cordilleras radium mine. Satan thus has earned possession of the soul of Twain, who announces that stock in his venture is now for sale.

Blank, Satan.

"So-Long," 1866 (MTWY).

Twain bids farewell to the West by writing to the editors of the *Alta*. He asks them to say goodbye for him to the people who robbed him near Gold Hill and to inform them that he has the last laugh: A.D.N. telegraphed him from New York and authorized him to go to Nudd, Lord & Co. and collect the equivalent of the sum taken.

Lord, A.D.N., Nudd.

["The Solons at Work"]. See LSI.

"Some Fables for Good Old Boys and Girls." See "Some Learned Fables, for Good Old Boys and Girls."

"Some Learned Fables, for Good Old Boys and Girls," 1875 (WMT 7).

Forest creatures hold a convention and decide to send a commission to explore beyond the woods. Earlier, Dr. Bull Frog found a northwest passage and Sir Grass Hopper sought the source of the swamp rill. But now the real work begins. After three weeks the well-equipped procession comes upon a plain with a hill beyond it. Muscular Tumble-Bug calls it tilted land but is rebuked for thinking by Professor Snail. Professor Bull Frog, the late doctor's nephew, theorizes that the hill is the wall enclosing the entire earth. Snail verbosely calls the hill vapor. Professors Angle-Worm and Field-Mouse laud his learning. Next day at noon the expedition comes upon some railroad tracks, which Professor Mud Turtle labels parallels of latitude. A train shrieks by, and the geographer calls it the verbal equinox, and carries the day in spite of some objections. When another train rumbles past, Lord Grand Daddy, Duke of Longlegs, after tolerating Professor Woodlouse's interruption, calls it the transit of Venus. Tumble-Bug enters, obviously drunk, and reveals that the second train dropped off an object with a rounded summit and a woody stopper. Norway Rat, chief of the sappers, dips his tail into its contents and thus provides drinks all around. The next day is devoted to rest and recovery; then the explorers sally forth and find tree-like poles strung with wires which they theorize are the webs of a giant spider.

A week later the expedition camps in the midst of some cave-like houses containing web-festooned corpses. The scientists draw some geological conclusions from the strata of red sandstone near-by, then find many printed and illustrated signs, and also a wax museum with man-like creatures which, judging from their insides, once fed on straw. The conclusion is inescapable that the creatures belong to the extinct species of reptile called Man, about whose animal companions, eating habits, weapons, and spiritual beliefs Woodlouse writes quaintly.

Near the great river the scientists find a stone telling of a flood in 1847 which overflowed the town and destroyed hundreds of cattle. Woodlouse mistranslates the inscription and receives praise for doing so. The expedition finds a round, flat mass, which Snail inspects and orders sent home on the backs of four tortoises. As winter approaches, the group visits the museum one last time and finds an exhibit labeled "Siamese Twins." Obviously one half slept while the other kept watch in the dangerous country the pair came from. Finally, Woodlouse finds a book in which proof is written of the curious supposition by extinct men that lower creatures might reason. King Bullfrog XVI is begged to appoint a new commission to look for these previously unsuspected beings. The procession arrives home to ovations. Tumble-Bug remarks that science needs only a spoonful of supposition to build a mountain of fact and further that God surely meant certain secrets to remain unexposed.

> Professor Angle-Worm, Dr. Bull Frog, Professor Bull Frog, King Bullfrog XVI, Professor Dogtick, Professor Field-Mouse, Grand-Daddy-Longlegs, Sir Grass Hopper, Jones, Chief Inspector Lizard, the Mayor, Professor Mud Turtle, Norway Rat, Professor Snail, Herr Spider, S.T., the Tumble-Bug, Varnum, Professor Woodlouse.

"Some Life Insurance." See FW, 1870.

"Some National Stupidities," 1923 (WMT 29).

The slowness of nations to adopt each other's valuable ideas is curious and unaccountable. Examples include the convenient and economical German stove, American overshoes, typewriters, fountain pens, photographic film processing, railroad efficiency, and even the courtesy of Boston cabmen. Americans generally improve on ideas borrowed from Europeans, who on the other hand borrow our ideas backward. The American postal system is admirably efficient and was as far back as the time when the Spaniards first arrived; see Prescott's account in his *Conquest of Peru.*

"Some Rambling Notes of an Idle Excursion," 1877 (WMT 19).

The narrator in May goes with his minister friend (an ex-army chaplain) to New Haven and then by boat to New York. Restless before retiring, the narrator harmlessly eavesdrops on William and John, two brothers. William persuades his brother to buy a certain cemetery lot and then chuckles to himself that John is booked for sandy soil. Next day the narrator and his friend the Reverend board a steamship for Bermuda and soon are far out on the cool sea. An old whale-ship master named Tom Bowling reminisces about a callow, youthful sailor who became Governor Gardner of Massachusetts. Tom once spied Governor Gardner in the fancy dining-room of the Revere House and bet a fellow mariner that he would go up, shake hands with him, and take grub with him. And he did. At the end of the story, a grave, pale young man (later identified as "the Ass") asks if he had ever met the governor before! Just after ships' chronometers are discussed, the Reverend recounts the shipwreck of Captain Rounceville and members of his crew. They had given up all hope, after vainly trying to wave at occasional passing vessels. On seeing another ship in the sinking sun, they pray, and the ship immediately comes about and rescues the castaways. When the Reverend points the moral that God's chronometer is unerring, the Ass asks what the chronometer of God is! During dinner the second day out, with seasickness diminishing the group, the Ass discomfits the brawny captain by opining that the engineer cranks the ship forward by hand. The Ass is then about to interrupt Captain Bowling, but that garrulous fellow orders him to shet his head and continues by pointing out that poetry is wrong which portrays the sailor's lot as hard: the women who stay behind face manifold miseries, while their husbands are comfortable on the sea. He cites Captain Brace, aboard now as a passenger, for one example, and then launches into a character sketch of Captain "Hurricane" Jones, an ignorant, tatooed, wild, Bible-misreading captain who argued once with Rev. Mr. Peters that Isaac was a lone Presbyterian among the prophets of Baal. The narrator lands at Hamilton, Bermuda, of which he extensively describes the people, onions, white coral architecture, roads, and cats. He chats with Mr. Smith about litigation over Bermuda cats. Next we are given information about music in Bermuda, churches there, the fast-answering hotel waiter, trees, quail, insects, flowers, and the unvarying happiness of the islanders. At the hotel at St. George's the narrator and his friend have trouble eating a hellishly peppery soup and baked but iron-clad chicken. Telling briefly about the climate, the narrator then explains that after four days they return to New York and get through the so-called health inspector in thirteen seconds by paying the usual fee.

The Ass, Captain Tom Bowling, Captain Brace, Mrs. Brown, Calvin, Captain, Governor Gardner, Si Higgins, Hooper, Hosea, Deacon Jackson, John, John, Gran'ther Jones, Captain "Hurricane" Jones, Mrs. Jones, Mariar, Rev. Mr. Peters, Rev. Mr. —, Johnny Rogers, Captain Rounceville, Seth, Deacon Shorb, Maria Smith, Smith, William.

"Some Random Notes of an Idle Excursion." See "Some Rambling Notes of an Idle Excursion."

"Some Remarks on the Science of Onanism." See 'Some Thoughts on the Science of Onanism.'

'Some Thoughts on the Science of Onanism,' 1879.*
Twain agrees that we are properly warned against adultery, which is a social evil. But there is also a recreation called self-abuse, about which ancient and modern authors have written much. Homer asked to be given masturbation or death. Caesar called it the friend of the foresaken and the penniless, and admitted that at times he preferred it to sodomy. Robinson Crusoe acknowledged

his debt to the gentle art. Queen Elizabeth called it virginity's bulwark. A certain Zula observed that one jerk in hand is worth two in bush. Franklin extolled it as good policy and a source of inventiveness. Michelangelo and other old masters—the phrase is a contraction—were of the same mind. There have been decriers of the practice, for example, Brigham Young, who likened the difference between it and the real thing to that between lightning bug and lightning. Solomon could praise only its cheapness. Galen said that he preferred amputation to ignoble use of the *os frontis*. Smith followed a statistical bent and complained that masses of children have been wasted in this manner. Darwin's theory is reinforced by the fact that the monkey is man's only brother in the animal kingdom to practice the science—and with ecstatic facial expressions which are almost human. Over-indulgence in the practice is detected by such signs as a tendency to eat, drink, smoke, joke, meet convivially, tell dirty stories, and paint pictures. It is really too brief an entertainment, too debilitating a hobby, and too profitless a public performance. It is really too private as well, although among consenting males it often leads to conviviality. Twain closes by advising gamblers to avoid playing the lone hand too much and by urging would-be revolutionaries not to jerk down the Vendome column.

> Brown, [Julius] Caesar, Cetewavo, Robinson Crusoe, [Charles] Darwin, Queen Elizabeth, [Benjamin] Franklin, Galen, Homer, Pope Julius II, Michelangelo, Smith, Solomon, Brigham Young.

> *(Charlottesville?, Virginia: Privately Printed, 1964).

"Some Unpublished Literature of Paten Mecine." See FW, 1870.

"Something about Doctors" (MTP).

When Twain was seven years old and in Hannibal, he almost died; but Dr. Meredith saved him with cups of castor oil. Doctors were paid annually in those days—an advantage, because in that way they did not invade the sickroom after the patient was well and make him worse just for more fees. Patients are afraid to fire doctors. In Elmira in 1895, Twain got a carbuncle and his doctor lectured him on carbuncles to great ends; yet Twain's ex-slave cook, Aunty Cord, knew more than the doctor about treating them. The doctor visited his patient too often and overcharged him. When Twain started his world-lecture tour, his carbuncle was thriving and had children. It took an Australian doctor twenty-four hours to cure the whole brood. Twain advises people to avoid the habit of getting sick. The best way to cure a cold is not to call the doctor but to get the cough to bark itself to death. In London when Twain's Ceylon and Bombay cold got worse, he called a doctor who did him no good, continued to make social calls, and overcharged him.

Aunty Cord, Dr. FitzGerald, Charles Meredith, Dr. Meredith, Dr. Sidney Smith, Dr. Taft.

["Something about Repentance"], 1962 (LFE).
Twain notes that too many people repent of their sins and too few repent of their good deeds. The few people alive who do good and fail to repent should go on to heaven, since they are only in the way down here. Twain has committed millions of sins but has been lingeringly sorry for only one of them. On the other hand, he has done eleven good deeds and repents of the four which he can recall most vividly.

Sorosis, 1869 (probably by Twain) (P).
At night a blooming girl with "Sorosis" on her crest passes through an eastern city. She is warned to remain away from the polls. But on the following evening she appears on a high rostrum, with blazing eye and pale lips shouting "Sorosis!"

[Horace] Greeley.

'Speech,' c. 1884 (WMT 28).
Twain wishes to report, very briefly—well within his allotted ten minutes—to the International Congress of Wheelmen that on May 10 he confessed to age by putting on spectacles, and at the same time he renewed his youth by riding a bicycle for the first time. The spectacles stayed on.

'Speech at the Scottish Banquet in London,' 1875 (WMT 7).
At a festival of the Scottish Corporation of London, Mark Twain

responds to a toast to the ladies by observing that perhaps the word "women" is preferable since the Bible calls Eve a woman, not a lady. Then he begins to recite a poem apostrophizing women but soon quits. He alludes to Joan of Arc and her defeat at Waterloo, Sappho of Israel, the longed-for ministrations of Lucretia Borgia, the absence of extravagance in Eve's modified Highland costume, Cleopatra's victory over George III and her poetry about dogs, a few celebrated men and then more women, then the unselfishness of Florence Nightingale, and finally the devotion of the typical wife and of the typical mother.

'Speech of Samuel L. Clemens,' 1881 (WMT 28).

Twain is proud to address a reunion of the Army of the Potomac and suggests for his text the propriety of the civilian's telling the soldier how to fight. When Twain was invited to address the group, he realized that he lacked the requisite knowledge and therefore decided to go to West Point and have the cadets fill him up with military lore. They did so. Now he knows and can tell everyone that before a battle it is best to feel the enemy—at night, that is, because in the daytime he can be seen and therefore need not be felt. Grant always sent young redoubts to reconnoitre. Sheridan advised getting to a given battle by any train, not simply a siege train. See that hod carriers are connected with mortar batteries. It is curious that generals regularly have horses shot under them. Why does the enemy not shoot the horses directly at those generals instead of always under them? The French at Waterloo were wrong to keep their whole army under fire. Why did they not light small fires at the rear, for warmth, instead of placing vast bodies of men under huge fires? Wellington opened fire on Napoleon with a battery of vivandières. Camp followers generally inspire the enemy with dread. Finally, Twain advises privates to avoid making suggestions to their superiors but instead to resign if the battle appears to be conducted badly.

> General Burnside, General Grant, Napoleon, General Sheridan, General Sherman, General So-and-So, Wellington.

'Speech on Accident Insurance' (WMT 7). See 'Accident Insurance.'

'Speech on the Babies.' See 'The Babies.'

'Speech on the Weather' (WMT 19). See 'The Weather' (WMT 28).

'Spelling and Pictures,' 1906 (WMT 28).

Twain appeals to the members of the Associated Press to help simplify spelling. If they will use simply spelled words in their dispatches for three months, the world will be reformed. Why write "pneumonia" and "pterodactyl"? Twain was indifferent to the simplified-spelling movement when it started in 1883, but no longer. At that time he wrote for magazines at 7¢ per word. One day he had an assignment to produce ten pages on "subterranean holophotal extemporaneousness of the conchyliaceous super-imbrication of the Ornithorhyncus," went to Jackson the editor to demand more money for the long words, was denied, and swore at him in long words. Jackson died within two hours. The function of language is to convey ideas and feelings; so we should use the simplest forms possible. Twain wants not to help himself but to aid the 82,000,000 people here who are prevented from having spelling simplified, just because of the conservativeness of a mere million, who like to see words spelled the way Chaucer and Shake-speare spelled them. Twain closes by saying that he is so old that nothing is left for him but his age and righteousness; then he blesses his audience and hopes that they will always keep their youth.

[Grace Donworth], Jackson, Rudyard Kipling.

"A Spicy Correspondence." FW, 1870.

"Spiritual Insanity," 1866 (WG).

Twain has been watching with concern the spread of the spiritu-alism madness. The newspapers report stories about it. The Board of Supervisors meets, and its ordinarily able members recite jingles like "Fee, Faw, Fum" and "Three Blind Mice." To think that those men stayed out of the asylum on various pretexts and now are heading there merely because of spiritualism.

Ashbury, the Board of Supervisors, Laura Cuppy, [Ada Hoyt] Foye, the Mayor [of San Francisco], Supervisor McCoppin, Dr. Rowell, Shrader.

"Statement of Captain Murchison" (MTP).

Captain Murchison says that his knowledge of Samuel Langhorne Clemens has come about as follows. One day the fellow asked the sick captain for a job as mate and was signed aboard in desperation. The captain then told him to weigh anchor. Clemens reported the weight at 1,264 pounds. Told to go to hell, Clemens disappeared to begin shouting oddly phrased orders to the hands, for example, to climb the middle pole and smooth the shirtfront. The bos'n rushed to the Captain and expressed fear that they were heading for the devil. After ordering the bos'n to save the ship and throw Clemens down to him, Murchison fell into a sick sleep, out of which he awakened to notice his new mate sitting nearby, placidly reading. Murchison was won over by the fellow's touching, silly face. Clemens had the appearance of a man in the thirties, but for his white hair, which was that of a sixty-year-old. Further, he was dressed like a stage sailor. Clemens explained that he was reading his own book on navigation. When asked why an incompetent like himself offered his services as Murchison's mate, Clemens asserted his belief that he was a very able sailor indeed. Murchison took up Clemens's book and read some nonsense from it, for example, that the anchor watch watches the anchor so that it won't fall out of the main truck into the water in rough weather. When Clemens offered to recite some of his poetry, Murchison rebelled.

Samuel Langhorne Clemens, Captain Murchison.

'Statistics,' 1899 (S).

In response to MacAlister, chairman of the Savage Club, who said that Twain was really a statistician rather than a humorist and that it would be easy for him to count his real jokes, Twain observed that, yes, he was good at figures. He had counted the number of words in MacAlister's speech just now: 3,439. And the number of lies. Also, 3,439.

Chairman MacAlister.

["The Steamship *Ajax*"]. See LSI.

"The Steed Oahu." In *Roughing It*.

"Still Further Concerning That Conundrum," 1864 (SS). (See also "Concerning the Answer to That Conundrum," and "A Notable Conundrum.")

The author boasts of his ability as a writer of opera reviews. The work is important, because too often the wrong people have been getting the applause. For example, *Crown Diamonds* was performed last Monday and Signor Bellindo Alphonso Cellini was insufficiently appreciated for his superb carrying of the bandit chief's valise, his watching of a camp stool, his mashing of a mosquito, and his placing of the Queen of Portugal's chair. Moreover, he leaned on the chair and smiled bewitchingly over the Queen's head. Yet the uncomprehending audience called only others before the curtain. In a postscript, the author explains that he has no answer yet to his conundrum of last week, about Napoleon's resemblance to cheese.

Signor Bellindo Alphonso Cellini, Hill, Jenny Kempton, Peakes, the Queen of Portugal, the Prime Minister, Caroline Richings, Seguin.

"Stirring Times in Austria," 1898 (WMT 22).

The political atmosphere here in Vienna in 1897 is stirring. No one can guess what will happen, except that there will be no revolution. This is so because Austria-Hungary is fragmented and polyglot, and its official policy is tranquillity. The press censor holds down activity too, and so do the Catholic Church and the army. Talent is discouraged. To secure a majority vote, Count Badeni had to make a deal; so he passed a law making Czech, not German, the official language in Bohemia. The Germans in Austria sought revenge by manuevering against the *Ausgleich,* that is, the renewable arrangement binding Austria and Hungary.

Then during the evening of October 28, Dr. Lechner was granted the floor in the Parliament by the chairman, Ritter von Abrahamowicz. In spite of the deep-throated protests of an opposition fighter named Wolf, who demanded the right to introduce a formal motion and even threatened revolution, Lechner spoke continuously for twelve cruel, heroic hours.

So the government side was mortified, and the Left was jubilant. The author next discusses the earned title of doctor, anti-Semitism, and parliamentary manners. Deputies Gregorig, a roosterish man, and Iro had a dispute which led to Iro's referring to a soda-siphon-squirting incident involving Gregorig's wife. Iro then denied it. Sides were taken, and many insults were shouted back and forth. Deputy Dr. Lueger took Gregorig's side, and ultimately Iro resigned. The gallery was vastly entertained. The author wonders how it is that such deadly insults regularly go unavenged.

Things went from bad to worse through November. One night there was a fist fight in Parliament, but the combatants seemed not really to be in earnest. Then Badeni's government thought of a strategem. Count Falkenhayn read a motion giving the President the power to suspend disorderly deputies. All in favor stand up! The noise was such that few standing knew that they were voting passage. The *Ausgleich* could now be put through easily. But next day the opposition, under Wolf, simply pressed around the President's desk, scattered his papers, swarmed around the man and Vice-President Fuchs, and swept them physically out. Unfortunately sixty policemen, all efficient ex-soldiers, were summoned to drag and tug the riotous representatives into the street. What a tremendous episode! The final result was the downfall of Badeni, outbreaks in Vienna and Prague, persecution of innocent Jews and Germans, and still no peace. All the same, the government did get itself out of the frying pan.

> President Ritter von Abrahamowicz, the Emperor of Austria, Count [Kasimir Felix] Badeni, Count Falkenhayn, Vice-President Fuchs, Gessman, Glöckner, Deputy Gregorig, Frau Gregorig, Holansky, Deputy Iro, Kletzenbauer, Vice-President Dr. Kramarz, Representative Dr. Kronawetter, Dr. Lang, Representative Dr. Lechner, Deputy Dr. Lueger, Dr. Mayreder, the Minister-President, Dr. Pattai, Dr. von Pessler, Prochazka, Saltpeter, Dr. Scheicher, Schneider, Schönerer, Deputy Schrammel, Strohbach, Vielohlawek, Deputy Wohlmeyer, Representative Wolf.

"The Stolen White Elephant," 1882 (WMT 19).

The narrator, an official in the Indian Civil Service, is assigned the mission of accompanying a white elephant named Hassan from Siam to England, where the Queen is to receive it as a pledge of newly established peace between the two countries. But in Jersey City, on the way to London, the elephant is stolen. The narrator reports the theft to Inspector Blunt, the chief of the New York detective force. He carefully takes down Hassan's description, suggests to the narrator that he post a $25,000 reward—gradually raised to $100,000—and marshals an army of detectives. Other detectives telegraph clues from various parts of the northeastern United States. The elephant is seen here and there, and occasionally stampedes and kills people. P. T. Barnum offers $4,000 to use the sides of the elephant to plaster circus posters on. Blunt insists on $7,000, and the offer is accepted. Hassan is wounded by cannon-balls, but a dense fog prevents his capture. Three weeks pass. Blunt tries to deal with two notorious thieves "Brick" Duffy and "Red" McFadden—whom he suspects—only to receive word from their widows that the two men have been long dead. Blunt takes the $100,000 anyway and soon leads the narrator through the basement of the police station, where many detectives are sleeping or playing cards. There they find the corpse of the missing elephant. The narrator is tremendously impressed with the ability of the chief of detectives, and so are most of the newspapers.

Alaric, Baker, P. T. Barnum, Bartholomew, Bates, Inspector Blunt, Boggs, Brant, Brent, Brown, Burke, Captain Burns, Cross, Dakin, Darley, Davis, "Brick" Duffy, Halsey, Hawes, Higgins, Hubbard, Jones, "Red" McFadden, McFlannigan, Mrs. Bridget Duffy Mahoney, Moses, Mulrooney, Murphy, O'Donohue, Mrs. Mary McFadden O'Holligan, O'Shaughnessy, Rogers, Stumm, Tupper.

["Story Laid in Hawaii"] (MTP).

It is 1840 in the Hawaiian Islands, which are lying asleep on tropical Pacific waves, far from the fretful world. Vegetation is lush, and temperatures vary from hot summer to snowy cold as you climb the tall mountains. You see sinuous gorges, varied scenery, and always the ocean. . . . The King, moved by the brave sincerity of the boy, grants life to Aloha as well as the boy. The disappointed priest mutters critically. . . . The King is depressed: someone has stolen his spittoon and will now try to pray the monarch to death. As word of the calamity spreads, the natives grow morose. . . .

Aloha, Kalama, the King, Manly, Puna.

The Story of a Gallant Deed, 1870 (P).

Twain rhymes the gallant 1865 indenture between Mr. and Mrs. Philip Gray, the party of the first part, and O. B. Johnson, the party of the second part [see "A Memory"].

Joanna S. E. Gray, Philip Gray, O[rrin]. B. Johnson.

'The Story of a Speech,' 1877, 1907, 1910 (WMT 28).

Twain finds the present occasion [the dinner in Boston, 1877, celebrating the seventieth anniversary of the birth of John Greenleaf Whittier] appropriate for digging up literary reminiscences. Thirteen years ago he was tramping through the mines in southern California and knocked at a miner's log cabin at nightfall. The jaded fellow heard Twain's *nom de guerre*, admitted the writer reluctantly, gave him bacon, beans, coffee, and whiskey, and explained that his guest was the fourth literary man in twenty-four hours. Longfellow, Emerson, and Oliver Wendell Holmes had been there last night, on their way to Yosemite. Emerson was a tiny, red-headed chap. Longfellow was built like a boxer, had bristly hair, and a flattened nose. Holmes must have weighed three hundred pounds and had double chins to his stomach. They had been drinking, recited their poetry, played cards with a greasy deck, and drank the distraught miner's whiskey. When Twain ventured to opine that the three were impostors, the miner countered by asking if Twain were also.

Twenty-nine years later Twain received a letter from Mrs. H. reminding him of his embarrassing speech. He obtained a copy from the Boston newspapers, reviewed it, and concluded that it is wonderfully funny and not in the least vulgar. Twain recalls that in Italy in 1888 some friends, Mr. and Mrs. A. P. C., of Concord, Massachusetts, were indignant that his audience did not think the speech funny. Time passed, and then Mrs. H.'s letter permitted him to reconstruct that evening in Boston. Fifty shadowy people were feeding. Emerson was grave. Whittier's spirit illuminated his face. Longfellow seemed benignant. Holmes flashed smiles and good fellowship. Willie Winter of the New York *Tribune* read a vivacious little poem for the occasion. Then Twain got up, began his carefully prepared speech, but soon detected a sort of black frost in the unamused audience. He went on, all the same, even though his listeners seemed to think that he was insulting the

Trinity. Finally he sat down, feeling dead. [William H.] Bishop, the recently successful novelist, was to follow; but, being inexperienced at speaking, he could only stammer a while and then collapse in a mush. The rest of the program was canceled. [William Dean] Howells helped Twain out and remarked that the speech would inevitably ruin Bishop's career. Nonetheless, Twain has just reviewed it and pronounces it good, smart, and humorous. Everyone should have laughed, including the three literary deities. Perhaps Twain lacked the confidence to carry it off.

[William H.] Bishop, A. P. C., Mrs. A. P. C., Mr. Chairman, [Ralph Waldo] Emerson, Mrs. H., Oliver Wendell Holmes, [William Dean] Howells, [Henry Wadsworth] Longellow, [John Greenleaf] Whittier, Willie Winter.

["Story of Captain Cook"]. See LSI.

"The Story of Joseph." From *The Innocents Abroad*.

"The Story of Mamie Grant, the Child-Missionary," 1967 (SB).
    Mrs. Wagner asks her nine-year-old niece Mamie Grant if she will have cream and sugar in her coffee, and if she wants some batter cakes; but the sweet child, who adores Sunday School, is more concerned about the condition of the woman's soul. Someone rings the door bell. It is the census taker, whose questions Mamie ignores because she wants to forsake vanities, and read about drunkards and gamblers instead. He leaves, but the bell soon rings again. It is the newspaper boy, who wants to collect 40¢ due but who instead is urged to fold religious tracts into his papers. He leaves. Martin then comes to pay Mamie's uncle $1,000 borrowed a month ago; but her lectures on sin, materialism, and blasphemy soon drive the man away. Then up comes Phillips, who holds the mortgage on the uncle's house. He wants $1,000 at once but receives instead a discussion about a periodically reformed drunkard named William Baxter who during brief relapses murders his successive families. Phillips leaves. In the evening, Mamie's uncle Wagner is distressed: his newspaper is stopped, he is posted as a delinquent, the census taker has black-marked him, a debt of $1,000 to him remains unpaid, and his mortgage is foreclosed. But Mamie happily reports that the various persons who called are

all now in the vineyards sowing for the hereafter. Wagner only groans. But Mamie puts a happy head on her pillow that night.

> Edward Baker, William Baxter, Mrs. William Baxter, Baxter, George Berkley, [John Ballantine] Gough, Mamie Grant, Roger Lyman, Martin, Phillips, Wagner, Mrs. Wagner, James Wilson.

"The Story of the Bad Little Boy," 1865 (WMT 7).

The bad little boy is named Jim. Usually bad little boys in Sunday-school books are named James and have consumptive mothers who pray in plaintive tones. But Jim's mother regularly spanks her bad little boy to sleep. Jim steals jam and does not repent. He climbs Farmer Acorn's apple tree, does not fall, takes lots of apples, and when the dog comes to bite him knocks him endways with a brick brought for the purpose. He steals his teacher's penknife and puts the blame on good George Wilson, who is not rescued by the testimony of a passing witness. Jim goes boating and fishing on Sundays, and is neither drowned nor struck by lightning. He hits his little sister in her temple, but she does not die. He runs off to sea and returns home not repentant but drunk. He marries, later brains his whole family with an axe, eventually grows wealthy, and is now a legislator.

> Farmer Acorn, Jim, George Wilson, Widow Wilson.

"The Story of the Good Little Boy," 1870 (WMT 7).

Jacob Blivens is a good little boy. He always obeys his parents, studies diligently, and attends Sunday-school on time. He does not rob birds' nests or give hot pennies to organ-grinders' monkeys. He wants to live and die like a hero in a Sunday-school book. In fact, he wants to be written up in one. He has his dying speech all ready. But things always go wrong. For one example among many, he tries to warn some boys who have gone sailing on Sunday but nearly drowns and is sick for nine weeks. Finally, one day he begins to lecture Tom Jones and some other bad boys, who have tied nytroglycerin cans to the tails of fifteen dogs, all tied together; but an alderman comes up and rebukes slow Jacob with a whack, whereupon boy and dogs sail into the sky like a kite. Four townships must hold inquests over Jacob's scattered remains, and his dying speech goes unspoken.

Jim Blake, Jacob Blivens, Blivens, Mrs. Blivens, Tom Jones, Alderman McWelter.

"A Strange Dream," 1866.*

Late in the evening, Twain and a friend at the volcano house near Hawaii's Kilauea, the world's mightiest volcano, decide to hike out and view it. Soon they are looking down upon an ocean of fire from which burst shocks like thunder and huge jets of lava. The narrator's friend reveals that when old King Kamehameha the First died, an enormous band of mourners took his corpse down to a plain near the volcano. Suddenly the funeral torches burned blue and went out, and the corpse disappeared. According to Wiahowakawak's prophecy, it will be found again when sea water miraculously disappears from Aua Puhi, the sacred cavern on Molokai. Last month, Twain notes, that cave did go dry. He wonders whether the prophecy will now come true. A little later, restless from his walk, he finds a book and chances to read about revelations in dreams. When he falls asleep at last, he dreams the same dream three separate times: a muffled figure beckons him to walk down through piles of blackened lava and suffocating sulphur fumes to a chamber below the cliffs of Kilauea. Suddenly he is alone, near a boulder, which he tilts over. Beneath are the crumbling bones of Kamehameha I. A groan then awakens Twain. In the morning he goes to the wall, and walks down and down, recognizing everything exactly as it was in his repeated dream At last he comes to the huge rock, tips it over, and finds—nothing. This only shows that one should not trust dreams.

King Kamehameha the First, Wiahowakawak.

*In *The Celebrated Jumping Frog* (New York: Webb, 1867).

"A Strange Story." See FW, 1870.

"The Stupendous Procession," 1972 (FM).

At the appointed time, a gigantic procession begins to move

across the world. The twentieth century enters first, as a drunken girl in Satan's arms, with public and private robbers as her honor guard. Then comes a gory but victorious Christendom, supported by Slaughter and Hypocrisy. Chamberlain and Cecil Rhodes represent England. Spain has nothing but broken Inquisition tools, bulls, and bullfighters left. The Russian float shows a Bear hovering over mutilated Finland and Manchuria. France sports effigies of Zola, Dreyfus, and Tonquin, among many other figures. Germany is shown violating Shantung, with German missionaries idly standing by. And now for America. She is depicted as aided by Greed and Treason, and simultaneously caressing and stabbing Filipino Independence, while Tammany sells indulgences at one side. The American Eagle is shown bedraggled, while the American Army is drafting Filipino recruits and signing up foreign-born white American volunteers. A Frivolous Stranger bothers the Adjutant General by figuring that it may well be the year 1946 before we have our army up to desired strength, at the present slow rate of enlistment. Along comes the Constitution, wrapped in a ragged blanket labeled the Declaration of Independence. The spirit of Washington is visibly distressed when he hears that Filipino prisoners are being called rebels. Cuba, Patriotism, and the Paris Commission parade by next, all in ruins. Then comes a float illustrating the opprobrious conduct of Tammany Hall, with "What're going to do about it?" for its motto. The American Flag and the Pirate Flag are next revealed as conversing easily. The torch of the Statue of Liberty is depicted as extinguished and held upside down. Lincoln's spirit broods in pain above the entire stupendous sequence.

> Adjutant General, Otto Allerheiligenpotstausenddonnerwetter, Allessandro, Bjjwkp, Jokai Borowackovitch, Jefferson Davis, a Frivolous Stranger, Joblokoff, W. J. Lampton, [Abraham] Lincoln, Duncan MacGregor, Master of Ceremonies, Denis O'Hooligan, Kanaka Okahana, O'Shaunessy, Mahomet Osmanlie, Sancho Panza, Head of the Spanish Inquisition, Tcherniejoosky, the Three Hundred, Villeneuve, [George] Washington, Arthur Wellesley Wellington.

["The Sugar Industry"]. See *Letters from Honolulu.*

["Sunday"] (MTP).

Twain proposes revoking all laws and ordinances in which the word "Sunday" imposes limits on individual liberty not imposed by non-Christian Sabbath laws and ordinances.

"The Sunday-School." See "Misplaced Confidence."

"A Sunday in Carson," c. 1863.*

Having arrived from Virginia [City] by Layton's express, Twain goes to church at Carson [City]. He hears the Rev. Mr. White recite the long-meter doxology while the choir accompanies him with a short-meter tune. Then Twain goes to Sheriff Gasherie's handsome jail, where the solitary prisoner, Swazey, who murdered Derrickson, is writing something.

> Derrickson, Sheriff [D. J.] Gasherie, Layton, Horace Smith Esq., Swazey, Rev. Mr. [A. F.] White.

*In *Wit and Humor of America*, ed. Kate M. Rabb, Vol. 5 (Indianapolis: Bobbs-Merrill, 1907).

["The Suppressed Chapter of *Life on the Mississippi*"], c. 1910 (LAIFI).

Twain says that when he revisited the South he noticed that Negroes are free but whites are as enslaved as ever. The solid South votes for only one political party. Southerners are neighborly and honorable. The myth that they are unusually hot-tempered is incorrect. But it is true that ruffians can terrorize Southern towns more easily than they could in the North, because Northerners band together for justice more readily. In the South, often juries fail to convict, individuals take the law into their own hands, and masked men conduct lynchings. A movement is now afoot in the South to arouse an apathetic public to provide more protection for judges, juries, and witnesses.

A Sweltering Day in Australia, 1897 (P).

Coolgardie breezes die. Timaru shade diminishes. The Worrow Wanilla is in pain. Penola's prayer seems scorned. Tungkillo Kuito is in sables. All is hellish from Onkaparinga to Oamuru. Even the Goomeroo sinks to death.

"Switzerland, the Cradle of Liberty," 1892 (WMT 26).

Twain was in Switzerland years ago, and here he is again, in 1891. One can enter Switzerland by carriage or by boat. The latter mode takes longer but is much the better. Then one can step with head uncovered and clean into the presence of the Jungfrau, the most impressive mountain on earth. Interlaken is flooded with active sunlight. This fine country has known no taint of slavery for six hundred years. Rutli and Altorf are holy places, because freedom is associated with them, the latter the more so because of William Tell. From the Victoria Hotel one looks across some flat land to a mountain barrier, and beyond it is the aptly named Jungfrau. According to legend, it was called the Jungfrau by Fridolin, a saintly missionary from Ireland. While in the region of Sackingen, on the Rhine, Fridolin was given some lands by the Frankish king. When a local citizen named Urso died, Fridolin claimed his land too. Urso's brother, Landulph, protested and demanded papers as proof of ownership. Fridolin could produce none, but did call a talking skeleton—perhaps Urso's—into court to testify for him, and won the verdict. Twain amuses himself by noting that shadows across the white front of Jungfrau resemble a human nose. Those shadows were there before puny man entered the scene. One day the King of Greece was traveling incognito when he met a German-born American brewer who quizzed him, admired his deportment, took pity on his evidently uncertain economic situation, and offered him a job back home in Rochester.

> The King of the Franks, Saint Fridolin, Gessler, the King of Greece, Landulph, Stauffacher, Frau Stauffacher, Willaim Tell, Urso.

"The Synod of Praise," 1972 (FM).

Various animals stand around praising their God the Elephant, who occasionally knocks over an innocent or steps on him for glory or a lesson or to over-punish an unknown offense. The narrator reasons that God is an ungracious host who invites creatures into His house only to make slaves of them by force. The brutes are all in pain and cannot enter heaven; yet they thank the Elephant for their afflictions. The Cow attempts to moderate by saying that the Elephant is their loving father, but the Monkey offers the last word: it is good that they do not have two of him.

Brute, the Caterpillar, the Cow, the Elephant, the Fish, the Giraffe, the Goat, the Grasshopper, the Rabbit, the Spider.

"A Tale for Struggling Young Poets," 1880 (LAIFI).

A young man who thinks that he is a poet has difficulty convincing anyone else until he enters a poetry contest in Buffalo. The local newspaper is offering $10 for the most original poem on spring. The poet turns his title page into a bank draft for $10, wins first prize, and begins his career.

George P. Bissell, Mrs. David Gray.

"A Tale of Rats."* See *Mark Twain's Travels with Mr. Brown.*

*In Edgar Wakeman, *Log of an Ancient Mariner* (San Francisco. Bancroft, 1878).

"The Tale of the 'Bird of a New Specie.' " In *Mark Twain's Travels with Mr. Brown.*

"Talk about Twins," 1895 (LAIFI).

Twain explains that two years ago an exhibition of Italian Siamese twins in Philadelphia inspired him to put similar characters in a book [*Pudd'nhead Wilson*]. But soon the pair went their own way. Luigi proved devilish; Angelo, kindly. The pair became troublesome. Twain feared that Luigi would go to hell; though the author did not mind, he did not wish to be responsible. So he separated the pair but then lost interest in them.

Angelo [Capello], Luigi [Capello].

"Taming the Bicycle," 1917 (WMT 26).

Thinking that he can surely do it, Twain buys some liniment and a bicycle. An Expert comes to teach him in the privacy of his back yard. The bicycle is only a colt, not full-grown, and with shortened pedals. The Expert says that learning to get off can come last, but Twain surprises him by showing that he can get off easily, and often. He falls on the Expert time and time again. The man soon prudently hires some assistants. The machine seems never to get hurt by the falls. Five days later, Twain is well enough to visit the Expert in the hospital and to try again. The bicycle wobbles. It is hard to learn, against one's instincts, to turn the tiller in the direction that one is falling. Twain can mark stages of his progress with the bicycle, though he never could do so when he was studying German. It is a pity one cannot fall off German, hurt oneself, and thus train oneself to pay attention. Twain soon learns to mount his steel-webbed steed, then pedal, and finally dismount voluntarily. He frequently dismounts involuntarily. Riding uphill is an ordeal, especially since Twain has few muscles. His instructor inspects his biceps and compares it to an oyster in a rag. On his own finally, Twain decides one Sunday to try a back street. A boy on a gate post shouts ridicule, and a passing girl giggles. Stones in the way bother Twain, but the worst part is turning around. The granite curb proves inhospitable when he lands on it. Next he runs into a horse pulling a farmer's cabbage wagon. But within five more days Twain can outdistance the jeering boy. Though Twain has read that dogs can dodge a bicycle, he runs over them regularly—no doubt because he is trying to avoid them, and they become puzzled. Twain longs for the day to come when he can run over the laughing boy.

The Expert.

'Tammany and Croker.' See 'Edmund Burke on Croker and Tammany.'

'Taxes and Morals,' 1906 (WMT 28).

Twain says that he has come here to police Choate, who fortunately has improved of late. America can be thankful that it has produced both Choate and Twain, but soon—sadly—they will be passing away. There are two kinds of Christian morals, private and public. On all but two days of the year, the typical American citizen is true to his private morals. But he demonstrates his public morals when he goes to the polls and foolishly votes according to party rather than for the more meritorious candidate, and when he goes to the tax office and swears that he has no personal property. When Twain first learned that millionaires were cheating on their taxes, his own moral integrity crumbled—in about fifteen minutes. At Tuskegee Institute people think that gentlemen never swear. Even Dr. Parkhurst thinks so. But millionaires certainly swear, and falsely. The wife of historian John Fiske informed him that their son thought his Aunt Mary was a fool and that his Aunt Martha was a damned fool. Fiske replied that the distinction was about right. Thus, Fiske came close to swearing. Twain closes by hoping that [Booker T.] Washington will teach his Tuskegee students to apply the wisdom he has just imparted.

[Joseph Hodges] Choate, John Fiske, Mrs. John Fiske, Fiske, Aunt Martha, Aunt Mary, Dr. Parkhurst, [Booker T.] Washington.

"Telegraph Dog" (MTP).

The time is a quarter of a century ago. Forty-five men of Company C, 7th Cavalry, are on an island in the South Platte under attack by six hundred Indians. Three weeks pass. One man offers to sneak out to learn the plans of the suddenly silent Indians, who are now advised by a pair of renegade whites, named George and Peter; but the volunteer's friends say that wounded Captain Johnson would not hear of the foolhardy plan. A dog named Billy begins to bark in short staccato bursts. His friend, Corporal Sandy McGregor, believes that Billy barks in a certain way if Indians are lurking about. The barking ceases, and the men conclude that the Indians have killed the dog. Meanwhile, down among the cottonwoods Sandy is kissing Billy and sending him off, with certain orders. When Captain Johnson calls him in, Sandy explains his activities so badly that for punishment Sandy is demoted to private. But when he volunteers to go reconnoitre the enemy, Captain Johnson is impressed and somewhat forgiving. Off Sandy goes. Soon, Billy starts barking and Sandy returns to report that the renegades have persuaded the Indians to attack at 2:00 in the morning. Lieutenants Burr and Taylor prepare to frustrate the maneuver, and the soldiers mow down the Indians, who retreat, mourn their dead, and execute a person identified by the frightened renegades George and Peter as the traitor in camp who must have informed the enemy. Next evening Sandy receives permission to spy again, listens to the dog's message again, and reports the imminence of a second attack. It happens, with a repetition of the slaughter. Captain Johnson promotes Sandy to captain. In the enemy camp George and Peter save their necks by sacrificing another "traitor" and devising another scheme. But Billy barks out its details to Sandy: at noon on the morrow forty-one redskins, disguised as decrepit squaws, will approach with hidden weapons. Sure enough, in the morning the cavalrymen see a stream of hags advancing, and beside them George and Peter—and faithful Billy. The renegades tardily grow suspicious of the dog, which seems diabolical to them. They toy with the idea of shooting him, decide not to, and plan to escape by the lower ford if their latest scheme for the Indians backfires. Suddenly they hear a barrage of shots, Indian wails, and white men's shouts of victory, followed by Billy's barked message about the ford in Morse code, which the renegades can understand. They change plans, see faithful Billy, shoot him in the leg, and get away. Next day Sandy finds the dog in misery and kills him with a final shot.

> Billy, Jack Burdick, Lieutenant Burr, Phil Cassidy, Jack Foster, George, Tom Hackett, Captain Johnson, Corporal Sandy McGregor, Peter, 'Rastus, Lieutenant Taylor.

"A Telephonic Conversation," 1880 (WMT 24).

A telephone conversation is a solemn curiosity, when you hear only one end of it. The other day the author was writing on a weighty subject when he was asked by a female in his family to ring up the Bagleys. Then he heard that female speak mysteriously of an event, cooking, sewing, the Bible, a hairpin, music, an occurrence in church, candy, and buying food. The talk was confusing.

> Bagley, Mrs. or Miss Bagley, Central Office.

"The Temperance Crusade and Women's Rights," 1923 (WMT 29).

The women's crusade against rum sellers is sweeping the country. The crusaders condemn force but instead camp before bars, sing hymns, pray, and force the owners to capitulate. These women have won three thousand such victories already. Surely it is the sidewalk position of those who pray rather than the content of their prayers which does the job. The crusaders are young girls and women, the best in various village communities. They meet in church, make speeches, pass resolutions, collect purses, and appoint praying bands. Their conduct is not lawful, but it is thoroughly justifiable in those who are without the franchise but who are instead represented by foreign-born savages turned local politicians. These women see their fathers, husbands, and brothers sit inanely at home and not vote. We have many laws but much improper enforcement of them. These women are plucky but unfeminine. Sadly, they are heroically striving to save men not worth saving. When women are permitted to vote, the cause of morality will advance. Women must be raised to the political altitude of Negroes, foreigners, and thieves, and allowed to vote. Then Congress will improve. Or if not, then God help us. We should have a women's political party now. In a moral fight, women are dauntless; and most men, ever since Adam ate the apple and told on Eve, have been cowardly. With the clergymen who are leading these crusading women the author has no sympathy. Soft-hearted preachers, however, frequently lose their soft heads.

["The Ten Commandments"], 1972 (FM).
    The Ten Commandments were made for people not animals. There would be no point in commanding a mouse or a butterfly not to kill, because they cannot do so anyway. It would be just as foolish to order a tiger not to kill, because his temperament is such that he will automatically kill under certain circumstances. Penal laws do not mete out justice to convicted killers but only protection for the public. The circumstance of a law against murder will not stop some murderers, like Slade the western gunman and Holmes the Chicago butcher, whose temperaments compelled them to kill when circumstances permitted.

    Holmes, [J. A.] Slade.

"A Thanksgiving Statement" (MTP).
    We are thankful that our Republic is the godfather of the Congo Graveyard, first recognized its piratical flag, and became responsible through silence for King Leopold's atrocities there for the past twenty years. We are thankful that Leopold, overdue in hell, is alive and working. Finally, let us pray that at the Last Judgment he will be as quiet about us as we have been about him.

    King Leopold of Belgium.

"That Book Agent." See FW, 1871.

"That Burial Lot." See "Some Rambling Notes of an Idle Excursion."

"That Day in Eden (Passage from Satan's Diary)," 1923 (WMT 29).
     The time is long ago, and Satan is in the bushes watching Adam and Eve near the Tree of Knowledge. They are slender, young, and lovely to look upon. They are puzzling over such words as good, evil, and death, and then decide to ask Satan to explain. He asks whether Eve knows what pain is. She does not. Satan explains that she cannot, because it is outside her experience. How about fear? She knows nothing of that either. Satan says that therefore he cannot tell her about death. Still, he tries. It is like sleep. Eve is delighted, because she likes sleep, and the longer the better. When Eve wonders what good and evil are, Satan replies that she cannot understand because she has no moral sense and hence happily has no morals. Every act that she and the other animals perform is right and innocent. When she wonders how she and Adam can acquire the moral sense, Satan says that they can do so by tasting the apple. Adam indifferently says that he has understood nothing Satan has said. Eve tastes the apple, grows confused, is ashamed of her nakedness, and begins instantly to age. Adam notices and then loyally tastes the apple too. He changes as well. They cover their nakedness and walk away together, bent with age.
     Adam, Eve, Satan.

"That Dog of Smiley's." See "The Celebrated Jumping Frog of Calaveras County."

'Theoretical and Practical Morals,' 1899 (WMT 28).
     Twain begins by saying that it is difficult but never exceedingly so to respond when people compliment him; however, it is more than difficult when they compliment his wife, who is better than he is. Since Grossmith, who introduced him tonight, was unusually humorous, Twain wants to respond with gravity. He distinguishes between theatrical—no, theoretical—and practical morality. To become truly moral, one must commit all the sins. Twain wanted to

become professor of practical morality at St. Paul's school, but the headmaster was away; so Twain probably must earn his living in his same old way. Glories and grandeurs are as nothing compared to Twain, an example of perfected morality.

[Olivia Langdon Clemens], Grossmith.

"Things a Scotsman Wants to Know," 1973 (WIM).

Signing himself Beruth A. W. Kennedy of Augusta, Maine, Twain on August 31 [1909] writes Harper's Weekly to reply to the Scotsman who earlier in Harper's [July 24, 1909] asked certain questions. Kennedy wants to help with the answers. God is probably personal. He created evil, because He created the conditions which make evil unavoidable. Man owes God no allegiance. Evil falls from heaven on the world. We get Christmas presents all year round in the form of diseases. Let us give thanks that God's ways are not our ways. God gives us these things to make us love Him, we are told. But He dumps these gifts on snakes, birds, animals, and insects; and they eat each other day and night. It makes no sense. Even a prejudiced cow would agree. God is not in His right mind.

[E.] Kaufman, Beruth A. W. Kennedy, [David Ross].

"The $30,000 Bequest," 1904 (WMT 24).

In the pleasant little western town of Lakeside live Saladin ("Sally") Foster, aged thirty-five; his wife Electra ("Aleck"), thirty-three; and their daughters Gwendolen ("Gwen") and Clytemnestra ("Clytie"), who are thirteen and eleven. Sally, an able bookkeeper in the leading store in town, has progressed over a period of fourteen years to a fine salary ($800 annually), out of which Aleck, a shrewd and practical woman, regularly saves, has purchased their comfortable home, and enjoys an income of $100 a year from investments in land. The one day comes stunning news. A distant cousin named Tilbury Foster, a crusty bachelor of seventy, writes Sally that he is mortally sick, that he is bequeathing him $30,000 not out of love but because money is a curse and he wants it to continue its destructive work, and that Sally may have the cash only if he neither inquires into Tilbury's demise nor attends the subsequent funeral. The Fosters begin to dream about the money.

Aleck plans skillful investments, while Sally wants to buy some things for a change. When he mentions that they might get a buggy, a cutter, and a winter lap robe, Aleck rebukes him and announces that they will never touch the capital—only part of its earnings. In her mind she builds fortunes in coal, oil, wheat, and other investments, while in his mind he spends modestly and even gives a big sum to charity. They take out a subscription to the *Weekly Saga-more*, the newspaper in Tilbury's town, and wait many days for the issue which they hope will report his death. The old man dies, but by an accident his obituary is crowded out of the next issue and is omitted after that. Weeks and months drift by, and the Fosters conclude that Tilbury must unfortunately be immortal. When Sally suggests disguising himself and going to Tilbury's village to ask around, Aleck vetoes the plan as dangerous. She subscribes to the *Wall Street Pointer* and makes a staggering amount of imaginary money in the market. Wanting to celebrate their good fortune but reluctant to expose it, they decide to have a party to memorialize the Discovery of America. Gradually the two become discontent with the attentions of common men toward Gwen and Clytie. Professional men would be more suitable sons-in-law for millionaires. Perhaps a lawyer and a dentist, the pork-packer's son and the banker's son, or even the sons of the Governor and the Congressman? The Fosters deliberate over an imaginary bottle of champagne. In two years they reckon their worth at more than two billion dollars. They begin to break the Sabbath in order to find big blocks of time free from their real work—as accountant and homemaker respectively—to take account of their imaginary stocks, by the light of candles which Sally steals from the store. They begin to pilfer a little food now and then as well. Their $2,000 house in their garden acre gives way first to a fictitious brick dwelling, then to one of granite, finally to a private dream palace in Newport. Aleck in her imagination exchanges her original Presbyterianism for Episcopalianism and then Catholicism, and also builds universities, hospitals, hotels, churches, and a cathedral, and even founds a feminist association and supports the W.C.T.U. But then Sally playfully accuses her of aiding bogus Christians in their efforts to wreck good Confucianism abroad. She is hurt and sulks. But when he stops and realizes that all this time he has been getting vicariously drunk three times a day, he feels ashamed, apologizes, and all is well again. Yet in time Aleck begins to regard Sally as bloated and repulsive, as they fictitiously recline on their imaginary yacht. Five years pass in all. Gwen and Clytie are still un-married, because their ambitious parents are holding out for the sons of the Senator and the Vice President of the United States. Finally Aleck confides in her husband that she wants their daughters to marry royalty. Next, unfortuntely, Aleck's imaginary investments are all wiped out in a devastating stock-market crash. They are paupers. But Sally comforts his distraught wife: after all, she never invested any real money but only its unmaterialized future; hence the bequest from Tilbury is safe. Aleck's swift tears of gratitude are interrupted by the entrance of the editor of the *Sagamore*, in town combining some business and a little grief. He is wondering why the Fosters have not paid their subscription recently. In the course of conversation, he reveals that Tilbury Foster died five years ago, so poor that the town had to bury him, and that the editor's little obituary got crowded out. The man leaves, and Sally and Aleck are disconsolate. They now long only for death, which arrives for both of them on the same day two miserable years later. At the end, Sally mutters about the snare which sudden wealth weaves and also about the unkind, ungenerous act of revenge perpetrated on the Fosters by Tilbury, whom money had made miserable.

Rev. Mr. Eversly Bennett, Mrs. Eversly Bennett, His Royal Highness Sigismund-Siegfried-Lauenfeld-Dinkel-spiel-Schwartzenberg Blutwurst, Bradish, the Congressman, Hosannah Dilkins, Hosannah Dilkins Jr., Clytemnestra Foster, Mrs. Electra Foster, Gwendolen Foster, Saladin Foster, Tilbury Foster, Dr. Fulton, the Governor, Adelbert Peanut, Flossie Peanut, Gracie Peanut, the Senator, the Vice President of the United States, the Woman with the Hatchet.

"Thomas Brackett Reed," 1902 (WMT 29).

Tom Reed was frank, sympathetic, affectionate, sturdy, logical, articulate, and humorous. He made a speech at the author's birthday dinner and suddenly died a few days later. It seems incredible that he is gone. The author will not indulge here in reminiscence but will simply praise Reed and say farewell.

Thomas Brackett Reed.

Those Annual Bills (A parody on "Those Evening Bells" by Thomas Moore), 1875 (P).

The things I bought have passed away, but those annual bills are now trilling their discordant song.

"Those Blasted Children," 1864 (WG).

The narrator likes his pleasant room in the Lick House in San Francisco, but the children in the place bother him while he tries to write. They kick at his door, charge up and down the hall pretending to be the infantry and then the cavalry, and argue loudly. They tease a Chinese laundryman. The narrator offers the following remedies for children's ailments: for measles, saffron tea and arsenic; brain fever, remove brain; worms, administer catfish; fits, soak in rain water and vinegar; stammering, saw off lower jaw; and cramps, boil in tureen or, if necessary, parboil. He could go on, but thinking about children reminds him of his own halcyon childhood and brings tears.

> Susy Badger, Sandy Baker, Baker, Washington Billings, Thane of Cawdor Scotland, Chollar, Charles Creed, Oliver Higgins, Florence Hillyer, Hillyer, Johnny Kerosene, Kerosene, Mrs. Kerosene, Johnny Leavenworth, Zeb Leavenworth, Flora Low, Governor [Frederick F.] Low, J. W. Macbeth, Mary, Bob Miller, Mr. Smarty, Tom.

"Those Extraordinary Twins," 1894 (WMT 16).

In a prefatory note, Twain explains that when he starts a piece of fiction, he has some characters in mind, a few incidents, and a scene, but not a story for a novel. Then the tale grows, and the original motif gets lost. That happened to him with *The Prince and the Pauper* and again with *Pudd'nhead Wilson*. The latter started as a farce with Italian Siamese twins, a couple of aunts, some boys, and a lightweight heroine named Rowena who loved the sober twin, who got drunk when his twin drank. But the tragic story of Wilson, Roxana, and Tom Driscoll eclipsed the farce; so he drowned most of the foolish characters down a well.

The farce should read as follows. Aunt Patsy Cooper receives a letter from the Italian twins Luigi and Angelo Capello, who want to rent her advertised room. Her lovely daughter Rowena is curious and falls half in love with Angelo, she thinks, by the time the two—or is it one?—arrive on Thursday at midnight in a drenching rain. The twins make up a double-headed person with four arms, a pair of legs, and but one body. They quickly say goodnight to go up to their room, leaving mother and daughter agog. Rowena soon expresses her admiration of Angelo, for his blonde hair, blue eyes, and creamy skin. Luigi, on the other hand, is dark, aggressive, and inconsiderate of his brother. In their bedroom, the two have difficulty undressing, and soon Luigi oppresses his twin by smoking and drinking and refusing to participate in a goodnight duet.

In the morning, down they both come to breakfast and tremendously impress Patsy by their conversation but especially by their eating habits. It seems that one brother's arms can be enlisted to feed the other's mouth. They explain that they save money by traveling single, occupying one theater seat, buying one bath ticket, and so on; however, they must pay double at peep shows. Luigi is tougher; once, after their aristocratic parents died and they were forced into freak-show employment, he ate the foul food they were given since it was revolting to Angelo's fastidious taste. Patsy shakes all four of their hands and begs leave to call them by their first names. Then Judge Driscoll asks them to accompany him on a drive, which is punctuated by the clamor of dogs. At noon the Judge returns them to their residence and momentarily offends Angelo by expressing pleasure that Luigi will be coming in the evening to the Freethinkers' Society, when Pudd'nhead Wilson will be present. It seems that Angelo is quietly proud; and, although he would hate to be separated from his fiery brother and be like other monstrous and lonely human beings, there are times when being dragged along at Luigi's whim—as, for example, tonight—is a torture. Luigi explains to Patsy and her chum Betsy Hale that for one week to the minute (ending each Saturday at midnight) one twin has absolute control over their joint body; then authority transfers. When Angelo begins to doze, Luigi explains to the awestruck old women that he is six months older than Angelo, since he had hair and teeth and solid food half a year ahead of his brother. A visitor comes to talk with the twins in the parlor, and the two women discuss Tom Driscoll and his shiftlessness.

The twins quarrel. Angelo seeks the truth and therefore changes religions frequently. He now inclines toward the Baptist faith. Luigi seeks excitement and therefore wearies and embarrasses

Angelo, as, for example, when he takes his blonde twin to an anti-temperance meeting and vigorously kicks Tom at one point. At last Wilson has a case. He is to represent the Capellos, charged by Tom with assault and battery. A jury is sworn in before Judge Sim Robinson, who would rather see justice done than quibble over legal niceties like the Fifth Amendment. Neither twin can be forced to admit that he was in charge of their legs on the evening of the kick in question. The Judge is outraged when Wilson demonstrates that although an assault was committed by one of the twins, their identities are so merged that the guilty one cannot be identified. Harkness, Wakeman, Rogers, Buckstone and all try to testify in support of the case being developed by Robert Allen, Tom's lawyer; but Wilson adroitly reduces all of their evidence to a shambles. Patsy also provides testimony, which might damage Luigi, who she reports was in charge of the legs at kick time, but for the fact that her evidence proves inadmissible. She is then naïvely happy at the verdict of innocent, and the courtroom dissolves in shouts and whoops, even though the Judge warns that dire consequences will follow such a ridiculous precedent. Wilson's entry into the arena of trials ends in victory and free drinks.

The popular fellow is soon asked to run for mayor. Tom avoids challenging the twins to a duel. Therefore Judge Driscoll calls out Angelo, who refuses; so Luigi accepts in his place. Wilson acts as Luigi's second; Howard is the Judge's. Dr. Claypool attends, with a bag of bandages, the sight of which causes Angelo to swoon against Luigi, who orders him to straighten up, since no bullets are meant for him. The two principals bang away at each other, miss, but in the process wound Howard, Wilson, and Angelo slightly. Suddenly the bells chime midnight. Sunday has begun. Angelo takes charge of the twins' legs and scampers off the field of honor.

Dr. Claypool soon reports to Patsy's house, where Angelo is nursing his wound and the others are milling about for a look. The doctor verbosely describes his patient's dangerous condition and prescribes a vile mixture of medicine, which Luigi grudgingly offers to swallow for his dainty twin. When the doctor orders Angelo to remain in bed for several days and nights, the young man declines, vowing that if death spares him he will be baptized by Baptist authorities this very afternoon. Claypool thought Angelo was a physical coward at the duel but now admires the man for his moral courage. By nine in the morning the town is buzzing with news of the duel and of the imminent baptism ceremony. People are divided into those who admire Luigi for fighting and those who admire Angelo for running away to avoid fighting on Sunday. People from the surrounding farms crowd the river banks at Dawson's Landing for the gayest event in years. The baptism occurs on schedule, after which the twins are hustled back into bed. Angelo naps. Patsy spoons the vile medicine into reluctant Luigi, who now has a head cold from his dunking in the Mississippi.

While the doctor is around, Angelo and Luigi grow steadily sicker. But then he is called out of town; so the twins get on their feet again. It is now time for political campaigning. Wilson, Luigi, and other drinkers are on the Democratic slate; Angelo and other Whiggish teetotalers oppose them. Campaigning is awkward for the twins, because neither can control their legs for long. At the end, Luigi is in charge, drinks a good bit to get Angelo drunk, and walks him with disgraceful unsteadiness to the Teetotalers' Union. That destroys his chances with Rowena, who was in love with him before. Luigi wins the election but cannot sit as an alderman because his brother lost and is therefore denied admission. All local government comes to a standstill. The citizens gather and decide that there is but one course of action. They hang Luigi.

Robert Allen, John Buckstone, Jack Bunce, Count Angelo Capello, Count Luigi Capello, Count Capello, Countess Capello, Dr. Claypool, Mrs. Claypool, Henry Cooper, Joe Cooper, Aunt Patsy Cooper, Rowena Cooper, Tom [Thomas à Becket] Driscoll, Judge [York Leicester] Driscoll, Aunt Betsy Hale, Harkness, Rev. Mr. Harkness, [Pembroke] Howard, Jack Lounsbury, Parson Maltby, Nancy, Mrs. [Mary or Rachel] Pratt, Billy Price, Judge Mr. Justice [Sim] Robinson, Rogers, Roxana, Job Turner, Wakeman, [David] "Pudd'nhead" Wilson.

"Thoughts of God," 1972 (FM).

When God invented the fly, He used intelligence but no morals. No man would ever want to invent such a filthy creature. It has been explained that the fly exists to remove garbage, but why was garbage ever introduced? The fly's mission is to cause suffering in people and animals, and to spread disease. The inventor of the fly is less brave and charitable than suffering mankind is.

"1002d Arabian Night," 1967 (SB).

King Shahriyar commends Queen Scherezade for an interesting story and then gently tells her to report to the headsman. But she starts another tale, about a lovely Persian princess, to delay her execution. Shahriyar frequently interrupts her, to hurry up the account.

The Sultan of the Indies is in Bagdad when a roc flies over the city and drops a huge egg, which blocks a whole street. The Sultan goes on to his imperial bath, but a ferocious dog breaks in upon his reflections. He draws a magic scimitar, and the discomfited beast vomits forth a silver plate with a symbol on it and then howls off. The Sultan asks Bahram Bahadoor, his chief soothsayer, for an interpretation, and the magician is obliged to call for reinforcements. The Sultan meanwhile is comforted by Alida, the sister of his favorite Sultana, Shakahgah, and by some of his many pretty children.

Wise men interpret the mysterious portents. The roc egg means that Shakahgah will bear a beautiful son and that Bashi Bazouk, the Grand Vizier, will become the father of a lovely girl. To interpret the plate symbolism, it is decided to found a college and train scholars to copy the symbol and send the copy to distant wise men. Ali Mahommed ben Mahoud ibn ben Ali wins the highest honors in the college. But when Shakahgah and the Vizier's wife have their babies, an invisible witch parts the hair of the boy—Shakahgah's child—in the middle like a girl, and the hair of the girl—the child of the Vizier's wife—on the side like a boy. Both the Sultan and Vizier are disconsolate but gradually grow reconciled and even happy with their respective offspring, in spite of the fact that the Sultan's line will end with his "daughter": if "she" weds and bears a child, both mother and baby must be executed, according to law.

Baby-naming time comes, and the Sultan's "daughter" is called Fatima-Noor-Sitt el-Hosn-Bab-en-Nasr-el-Jawalee, and the Vizier's "son" is called Suleyman-Mohammed-Akbar-ben-Selim-ben-Ali-ibn-Noormahal-ben-Saladin-Badoorah-el-Shazaman-Aladdin-ben-Yusef-ibn-Kismet-el-Emir-Abdallah-ben—"Selim" for short. The two children play together, and their singing is a wonder. But their parents are puzzled because Fatima, supposedly a girl, plays with a tiger cub and wants to hear tales of war and harems, while Selim, supposedly a boy, fondles dolls and whining kittens.

The time eventually comes for the two devoted children to be separated. Years then pass. Fatima turns thirteen but shows interest only in manly pursuits. More years pass. Selim, now seventeen, is surpassingly beautiful but likes nothing so much as to hide in the nearby lush garden, which is full of fruits and flowers. One day Fatima sees Selim there and swoons while spying secretly upon "his" nice high bosom, smooth cheeks, slim waist, and large hips.

Days lag by. Fatima takes his telescope to some high ground near Selim's garden to peep at the girl, who is taking target practice there one day. Suddenly she sees Fatima, kneels before "her," and leaves some flowers. Fatima rushes away through the forest, then sits musing on his closely seen love. He returns, finds the flowers, and treasures them. He goes home, does masculine things like energetic handsprings out of sheer joy, and thus worries his parents. Meanwhile, Selim has been pierced by the arrow of abiding love. She goes back to the target ground, but Fatima is gone. Then one day he is out riding when he comes upon Selim and rescues her by killing a gigantic serpent with his javelin. He wants to hug Selim but decides against such unmaidenly aggressiveness. So off he goes; but Selim follows, kneels before him, and volunteers herself as his boy friend. They confess their mutual love. Selim kisses Fatima's hand, takes his breastpin, and wears it next to her heart.

More time passes. The Vizier finds his Selim writing sonnets, while the Sultan is distressed at the frequency with which he observes his Fatima before the mirror. Now, the numerous palace buildings are situated around a square, across a part of which the windows of Fatima and those of Selim look toward each other. Selim plays her harpsicord toward him, and Fatima answers with flute music in her direction. What rapture! The two also meet in an intricate garden maze.

In the year when the lovers turn eighteen, a rude day comes. Fatima is sitting in the garden summarizing a poem to his Selim when they hear a noise. It is a duenna from the Vizier's harem. She discovers their transgressions and refuses all bribes to keep their secret. Soon the Vizier himself enters and is about to strike his "son" Selim when he sees the Sultan's "daughter" Fatima, who generously forgives the man and asks his help in securing the Sultan's permission for the young lovers to wed. A dim smile flickers vaguely across the Vizier's countenance, and the man agrees. Astral signs are also propitious.

The party seeks out the Sultan, who when he learns that Fatima and Selim wish to marry turns visibly pale and then explains the law. If Fatima has a child, "she" must die. But the young couple agree to take their chances. The Sultan then explains that he once vowed that only the man who will slay the huge serpent periodically plaguing his domain can have his daughter. At a sign from Fatima, Selim modestly asseverates that she has already killed the creature. The royal entourage journeys to the site and confirms the death. The marriage ceremony is set for the day the pair turn nineteen. Fatima clothes "herself" in a samovar of sackcloth and ashes of roses, then a cyclone trimmed with cylindrical, celluloid, and flatulent algonquins, then a scarlatina banshee which is a riot of colors trailing off into radiant gangrene. The couple stand before the holy archimandrite and his croziered parasites. Fatima is erect and proud; Selim, graceful and demure. The ceremony finished, husband and wife begin their wedding excursion.

Months pass. Fatima and the Sultan spend what time they can together, because, having possessed Selim, Fatima feels certain that his execution will be necessary in due course. But it is Selim rather than Fatima who miraculously produces the royal offspring—and not one but twins. The ecstatic Sultan sees for himself: the "husband" is the mother. The Sultan then names the red-haired baby Ethelred and the bald one Ethelbald. The babies dance for the crowds outside the palace, and all is well: no execution will occur, nor any civil war as a consequence of it.

Scherezade thus finishes her tedious story, and King Shahriyar gratefully calls for the headsman to execute her. But the headsman has died. Scherezade remembers a circumstance of moment in the tale and resumes her account, at such length that the new headsman dies and so does the king. Thus did Scherezade obtain revenge for the execution of so many of her predecessors.

> Alida, Ali Mohammed ben Mahoud ibn ben Ali, Bahram Bahadoor, Bashi Bazouk, Ethelbald, Ethelred, Fatima-Noor-Sitt el-Hosn-Bab-en-Nasr-el-Jawalee, Shah Safet ibn Jan, Queen Scherezade, King Shahriyar, Shakahgah, Suleiman Ben Daoud, Suleyman-Mohammed-Akbar-ben-Selim-ben-Ali-ibn-Noormahal-ben-Saladin-Badoorah-el-Shaza-man-Aladdin-ben-Yusef-ibn-Kismet-el-Emir-Abdallah-ben—, the Sultana, the Sultan of the Indies.

"Tramp to Boston" (MTP).

After a tiring walk of thirty miles, Twain, numb with exhaustion, and his energetic pastor friend enter an inn at Duffield, where they encounter two seated men spitting at a hot stove. The Reverend asks the younger spitter a question about local horses. The man replies amiably and at length, but his speech blazes with lava jets of profanity—all harmless but desolating. The Reverend is appalled, appeals to Twain for help but without success, and therefore returns to the profane ostler with a question about local roads. The ostler replies with a new volley of lurid language. When the Reverend queries him about the crops, he is hailed over by more profanity. So the Reverend tells the older spitter, evidently the village bummer, about Twain's lameness, whereupon the codger recommends a local remedy but couches his comment in Vesuvian blasphemy. The ostler seconds the recommendation, mephitically. The Reverend then leaves a letter on the bar showing that he is a preacher. When the ostler sees it, he profanely says that the Reverend should have identified himself, rousts the cook out, seats his divine guest comfortably, and blasts amiably at him with an indelicate account of religion in Duffield. In the morning the two visitors hear the same ostler telling the mild landlady about the frozen pond—and all in the same innocent, sulphurous language.

No. 1, No. 2, the Reverend.

Three Aces: Jim Todd's Episode in Social Euchre, 1870 (probably by Twain) (P).

Aboard the *Natchez Ranger* Jim Todd plays three-card poker with a stranger named Cap. Jim has three aces and bets heavily, only to lose to Cap's three-card flush of clubs. (In FW, 1870.)

Carl Byng, Cap, Jim Todd.

["Three Statements of the Eighties"], 1973 (WIM)

Twain announces that he believes in Almighty God but not in divine intervention, eternal punishment, or any certain hereafter; further, he believes that moral laws are the result of human experience. Also, though he believes that no religion can influence one's hereafter, it may be a comfort to one; in addition, some aspects of the

Bible (parts of which are atrocious) help teach humaneness to modern society. Finally, if a great, wise, experienced person wrote a book, it would be full of consistent common sense, whereas the Bible is so full of contradictions—for example, about adultery, being a good Christian, and having children—that God could not have written it.

Three Thousand Years among the Microbes, 1967 (WWD).

This account is by a microbe, who also added several notes seven thousand years later. It was translated from the original microbic in 1905 by Mark Twain, who in a preface states his belief that the work is true history, unembellished by fancy and having only a few divergent passages.

The narrator was once a human scientist but was transformed by a magician into a cholera germ. He soon became eagerly germy and now enjoys observing the other germs from their own point of view. Ten human minutes are the equivalent of a microbe year; a human day, 144 microbe years; a week, 1,008 years; etc. By human standards, microbe families multiply and die fast.

The narrator was introduced three human weeks ago into the hoary body of an old Hungarian tramp named Blitzowski, now in America. The narrator felt at home immediately. His new planet seems as vast as the world does to men. In Blitzowski are more than a thousand republics and at least thirty thousand monarchies. Twenty-five thousand microbic years ago the Pus family established a dynasty in him, and its reigning monarch is Henry CMX. In a note, the narrator reports that he and a friend have discussed the moral sense, which teaches the difference between right and wrong, hence creates wrongs, and thus makes life more exciting. Foreigners in Blitzowski are tolerated. His stomach is a fertile land, which imports happiness and pus. Nearby is the rancid Great Lone Sea. The narrator enjoys paleontology in the pleasant region he occupies. He digresses on the relativity of sizes, then on the animation and self-sufficiency of all things, from ocean to drop of water to molecule to atom.

Next he reports a pleasant conversation held long ago on these topics with his friend Bblgxw. For simplicity, let us call him Benjamin Franklin. Memory of human life is fading. Human mathematical problems are hard to perform when one is in a microbic state: $4 \times 9 = 42$ is as far as the narrator can easily go now. Well, Franklin assured him that all things are alive—trees, rocks, and horses, for example. Oxygen furnishes temper to each thing. Water is an animal. Remove hydrogen, and that is an animal. The oxygen remaining is an animal. Combine the two into water, and you make a third individual; yet the first two continue as individuals. Is this not like the Trinity? Franklin explained that though all is mysterious and troublesome, and we go we know not whither, evanescent life is not the end, and even the humblest will be cared for. But the narrator feared that Blitzowski might die soon and abandon him to the fate of oblivious disintegration. Pretending that he did not want the plaudits of crowds outside, the narrator finally let Franklin leave by the door alone; but then he stepped out onto his balcony to be photographed as though caught in embarrassed poses. What hypocrisy! Everyone, from babe to king, has an appetite for publicity. It is our nature.

The narrator recalls the reason for his fame as a microbe. He was poor and unknown when he arrived in Blitzowski, so he got a cheap room, and hired a hand organ and a monkey. He sang in English— "Bonny Doon," "Buffalo Gals," and other songs—prospered, associated with the Taylor family and their two million or so children, pretended that he had come from an infection in one of Blitzowski's molars, dreamed repeatedly of lovely Margaret Adams back in America and curiously associated her with microbe Maggie Taylor, and recalled a number of confusing human historical events like Napoleon at Marathon and Washington the commander of the Hessians.

The narrator, who now calls himself Huck, has lots of friends among the microbes. But when for some reason he does not age as they do, they grow suspicious and then ignore him. So he invites two of his closest semi-aristocratic pals, Lemuel Gulliver and Louis XIV, to his humble quarters, gets them mellow on hot punch before his fire, and confesses that he has invented no elixir of life but rather was not always a cholera germ. Huck tells them that his former name was B. b. Bkshp and lectures to them about his former world, with its incredible size, round shape, oceans, ice and deserts, rains, and system of evaporation. He even describes the sun, moon, and stars. Louis regards the whole discourse as inspired poetry; Lem, as a supernatural life.

By now it is two o'clock in the morning. The visitors leave, to spread word about Huck at the site of archeological diggings around a recent flea-fossil find. To his quarters comes the girl who records his thoughts. He is writing the history of the world and now wishes to dictate some thoughts—not words—on Japan. Earlier, when he was recording English history and mentioned Catherine of Aragon, the girl affectedly changed her name from Kittie Daisybird Timpleton to Catherine of Aragon. She is bright, because she has some energizing cancer blood in her system. Entering now, she strikes Huck as changed: she has been reading "Science and Wealth, With Key to the Fixtures," confesses that her flesh is changing to spirit, and lectures to the effect that substance is a mere delusion of moral minds and that pain does not exist—except in the teeth. Huck tolerantly observes to himself how odd it is that each creature thinks he knows it all and everyone else is foolish. Then he wonders whether heaven has room for creatures smaller than microbes. He wants to include dogs, cats, and horses, and—in spite of his dislike of them—even mosquitoes. He once asked a clergyman friend of his, who replied that the biblical message to Christians is clear: they are to preach the gospel to every creature. Huck remembers and is able therefore intelligently to discuss this and related matters with Catherine, whose vocabulary is fuddled by "Science and Wealth" and who rattles on about Rev. Brother Pjorsky, her former spiritual adviser, about the countess, a rank-conscious appendicitis microbe, and about the dignity of labor. A theory is widely held in Blitzowski that working for one's bread soils it. Pjorsky shares this belief and hence looks down on the Soiled-Bread Eaters. While he and Huck chat, they eat an SBE baby microbe and enjoy it. Then Pjorsky puts some of his scientific slides under one of Huck's microscopes and demonstrates that microbes have microbes. Lecturing in black-plague dialect with what resembles a French accent, he explains that without microbes to break down excretions and carcasses, it would be impossible for plants to get back their foods again and soon the whole planet of Blitzowski would become rock and sand. Microbes therefore obviously deserve a place in heaven, he concludes benevolently. Huck knew from scientific studies under Professor H. W. Conn back in the world that microbes were vital, but learning that the microbes of microbes are also essential to miniscule life cycles is startling. He now wants to see these little microbes; so his visitor rigs up an exhibition, and they soon peer down at a fierce battle about to take place in a drop of Huck's blood. Militant masses leave their tents for war in defense of their royal family. Huck and Pjorsky drown the conceited family with boiling water. Unfortunately, the microbic army is also extinguished.

When his guest leaves, Huck draws the momentous conclusion that we all have something to look down on. Human beings look down on microbes. Microbes look down on their own germs. And they in turn do the same, and so on down to the bottom atom of the universe. Huck now reviews a paper he once wrote on Blitzowski currency. As he looks at the faded sheets, he thinks of Catherine three thousand microbic years ago. By comparison, human time has been shorter between the founding of Rome and the world when Huck was translated out of it. Suddenly Catherine is there again, reminding him that his class in theological arithmetic is about to arrive. He dictates some thoughts on the history of Japan, turns his class over to his assistant, and rushes off to the fossil field, where Lem and Louis have been reporting his depiction of the world. Friends, including Sir Galahad, his favorite and brightest pupil, urge Huck to spin more poetic lies about the world. So he rattles off statistics on the Spanish-American War and the Jap-Russian War. Lem bets that Huck cannot repeat them accurately, but he does. Only Galahad believes him and goes off to get Catherine to play back the recording of Huck's history of the world. Calling Huck an impressive liar with a perfect memory, Lem wants to incorporate his lies and sell them. Huck suggests that they call the corporation Standard Oil. But then he realizes that if he is labeled a notorious liar, his college of morals will be jeopardized; so he decides to hint at the existence of a gold mine up in the region of Blitzowski's major molar. Everyone makes plans to go mining and forgets the lying company. Now Huck begins to recall a recurrent dream of a gold- and cement-filled hole in one of Blitzowski's teeth. He muses. It will be a veritable Klondike. More. Should he reveal all and let his friends share? Should they have half? Perhaps only a third? A fourth? It might undermine their morals. He probably should keep the gold and let them have the cement. He goes to bed.

Margaret Adams, Angel of Death, General Assfalt, Uncle Assfalt, Blitzowski, Sam Bowen, Butters, Catherine of Aragon, Professor H. W. Conn, David Copperfield, the Countess, Cuvier, Darwin, Dogberry, the Duke of Donnerklapperfeld, Grand Duke, the Founder, Benjamin Franklin,

Benjamin Franklin, Sir John Franklin, Sir Galahad, John
Garth, the General, Ggggmmmdw, Lemuel Gulliver, His
August Majesty Henry D. G. Staphylococcus Pyogenes
Aureus CMX, Henry MMMMMDCXXII, Henry the Great
861, King Herod, Huck, Ignoble, Lord of Creation, Louis
XIV, Lurbrulgrud, Guy Mannering, Master, Napoleon,
Tom Nash, Noble, the Observer, Sancho Panza, Rev. Broth-
er Pjorsky, the President, Pus, Don Quixotte, Grovernor
Rossfelt, Colonel Mulberry Sellers, Socrates, Soiled-
Bread Eater, Sooflasky, Ed. Stevens, the Swink, Maggie
Taylor, Taylor, Terry, Thompson, Mark Twain, Mike
Burbank Twain, Rip Van Winkle, General Washington,
Wzprgfski.

"A Tide of Eloquence," 1863 (WG).

Asked to speak, Twain though unprepared bursts forth in an
eloquent tide. The audience soon fancies that it is hearing
inspiration. Twain soon thinks it best to avoid being alone any
longer and therefore joins the others in dissipation.

"To Correspondents," 1870 (CG).

Twain urges readers who have offered to send odd obituary
poems to do so, and adds that he has already received several
samples of this neglected branch of literature. To the few readers
who have asked whether his connection with the *Galaxy* is permanent, he refuses to reply; if he says yes, they will cancel their sub-
scriptions.

"To My Missionary Critics," 1901 (WMT 29).

The author has received much criticism for his attack on the Rev.
Dr. Ament, missionary to China. The Rev. Dr. Judson Smith, Cor-
responding Secretary of the American Board of Foreign Missions,
for example, accused Mark Twain of charging Ament with bully-
ragging and extortion, and said that following violence by the
Chinese the missionaries did not demand indemnities amounting
to thirteen times the losses but only one-third more than the losses;
therefore Twain should apologize. Far from doing so, however,

he admits that "1-3d" in a cable was wrongly converted to "13" but then exhibits evidence supporting his general criticism. Chamberlain, a New York *Sun* correspondent in Peking, reported in a Christmas Eve dispatch that Ament collected indemnities from the Boxers, demanded head for head for 680 Catholics killed, criticized the Americans for being soft, and praised the Germans for using the mailed fist on the Chinese. In addition, George Lynch, an experienced war correspondent, reported that the missionaries looted the Chinese. Sir Robert Hart leveled the same charge in a British magazine in January, 1901. Twain writes Smith challenging him to try to persuade Chamberlain to confess that his dispatch was false and unauthorized. Next, Ament explains that the extra third collected was for church expenses. Twain then details nine factual errors in a letter to him from Smith asking Twain to withdraw his criticism. Twain refuses and follows by reporting that he has been criticized for writing to China to get the facts. He wonders whether it would be considered better form to grope about without the facts. He asks whether Ament forced innocent people to pay any of the damages. Any extra money so collected would be loot from theft and extortion. If only one-third extra, it could perhaps be called the result of modified theft. He is reminded of an illegitimate child's mother who rationalized by arguing that her baby was small. The fact that the collection of indemnities was approved by Chinese officials does not excuse the Christians. Twain then tells two stories. One story concerns an Oriental king who squeezed his treasurer for money; the treasurer then squeezed the village leaders, and so on. The other story explains that back in antebellum days some Negroes stole three watermelons from Twain's adoptive brother. So a white friend—a kind of Board understudy—took four melons at gunpoint in retaliation from an innocent Negro's patch and gave them to Twain's brother. But the judge called the act theft and extortion, ordered the melons returned, and rebuked the boys for basing their conduct on inferior slave morality. Twain concludes by first praising virtually all missionaries as men of quixotic hearts and then criticizing the American Board for deficiency in the region of the head.

> Rev. Dr. Ament, Chamberlain, Rev. Dr. Washington Gladden, Sir Robert Hart, the King, George Lynch, Macallum Martin, Rev. Dr. Sheffield, Dr. Judson Smith, Rev. Mr. Tewksbury, the Treasurer, Ward.

"To Raise Poultry," 1870 (WMT 7).

When the Western New York Poultry Society conferred a complimentary membership upon the author, he replied in a courteous letter, reporting as follows. From early youth he has been an expert in raising poultry. By the time he was twenty, he had raised more poultry than anyone else in his region. In summer, he did the raising by lighting a match in front of a hen and leading her with it into a handy bag. In winter he raised poultry by heating a plank and then insinuating it under a sleepy chicken's feet. He recommends raising the donkey-voiced Shanghai rooster by lasso because he must be choked quickly, and the costly Black Spanish by lifting him coop and all. Members of the Society may call for the author any evening after eleven o'clock if they need his help.

To the Above Old People, 1900 (P).

The sun rises and marks off one more day of life. The cup of youth is empty. Can its wine revive age? We should drown what might have been. We pay for every joy with grief. Pleasures give way to pains. Eventually old age finds everyone. Germs house in our bodies. Teeth fall out, and mouths are filled with dust. We are afflicted with coughs, chills, bunions, and neglect. Every fine must be paid. Voices of the past fall silent. The magic bowl is my medicine, and I will welcome death. (In "My Boyhood Dreams.")

"To the California Pioneers," 1869 (LAIFI).

Twain sends his regrets to the California Pioneers that he cannot attend their New York dinner. He reminds them that he once staked claims in California, paid high prices for food, owned mines until they failed, studied extensions of main leads, was the victim of salting, paid assessments, and worked in mills. He hopes that when the Pioneers return to the East they will not find delusion and death there.

> California Pioneer, Forty-Niner, Hale, Norcross, Returned
> Prodigal, Simonton.

"To the Person Sitting in Darkness," 1901 (WMT 29).

The essay begins with three quotations. The New York *Tribune* reports that Christmas [1900] will dawn over cheerful, optimistic Americans. The New York *Sun* on the other hand deplores East Side New York political corruption, police villainy, prostitution and white slavery, disease, and crime. The *Sun* also reports that American Christian missionaries after the Boxer rebellion in China are demanding heavy indemnities in taels and even Chinese heads for the murder of Christians. Americans in China seem too soft. The Germans and French are more systematic looters.

Mark Twain bitterly rejoices at such news just before Christmas, adding that we can now joke: taels I win, and heads you lose. He offers to collect designs for a monument in honor of Mr. Ament, spokesman for the American Board of Foreign Missions. But when that man says that indemnities collected from poor peasants are to be used to propagate the faith, the blasphemy is inconceivably hideous. Then Twain quotes from the Tokyo correspondent of the New York *Tribune* to the effect that religious invasions of the Orient are menacing and should be suppressed. Twain wonders whether we should continue conferring our civilization on people sitting in darkness. What they have already seen of our civilization has enlightened them more than was judicious. They now suspect that civilization is apparently a package of virtues but is really something which they must buy with blood, land, and freedom. For example, England, like an elephant charging into a nest of field mice, goes after the Boers mercilessly. Germany loses some missionaries in Shantung and demands crushing reparations. Russia robs Japan. And America, after behaving admirably in Cuba, proceeds to the Philippines and plays the European game through greed. After the Spanish fleet was destroyed, the American forces should have left the Archipelago to the Filipinos; but instead we joined forces with the natives to free Manila and then took it for ourselves, alienated [Emilio] Aguinaldo, and provoked incidents leading to war. We can speak of our gift of civilization to the unenlightened victims, boast of our military prowess, and even contend that lies, treachery, and debauched American honor are all properly in the service of civilization, progress, and business. But what we really should now do is take our formerly inspiring flag, paint the white stripes black, and replace the stars by a skull and crossbones.

Rev. Mr. Ament, Macallum.

To the Velocipeed, 1869 (P).
Why make such a fuss over a broken wagon?

'To the Whitefriars,' 1899 (WMT 28).

Twain begins by greeting the brethren who have taken the Whitefriars' vow and says that the only thing that is more fun than making
a big vow in public is going out and breaking it. At a Whitefriars'
dinner twenty-five years ago, a man was to introduce Twain but
forgot to come; so when George Augustus Sala came in, someone
asked him to do so, extemporaneously, and he did, and well too.
Then Twain contrasts Senator Depew and Ambassador Choate.
Twain then praises persons who can give impromptu speeches.
He can do so only because he rehearses them and even writes in the
places for applause, so that the reporters will know. Dr. Hayes
was once lecturing about the beauties of the arctic region when a
janitor interrupted first to ask Mrs. John Smith to go home because her husband had broken his leg—innumerable women left—
and then to ask Mrs. John Jones to go. In order to close on a wise
note, Twain recommends that when one is in doubt he should tell
the truth.

> [Louis F.] Austin, Robert Buchanan, Ambassador [Joseph
> Hodges] Choate, Senator [Chauncey M.] Depew, Dr.
> [Isaac Israel] Hayes, John Jones, Mrs. John Jones, George
> Augustus Sala, John Smith, Mrs. John Smith.

Tom Sawyer: A Play, 1969 (HHT).

Act. I. Gracie Miller and Amy Lawrence hint that they can tell
each other some secrets, then argue, then kiss and make up. They
discuss Amy's engagement to Ben Rogers, Gracie's imagined widowhood, the arrival of a new boy from St. Louis, and the latest battle
in the war between Tom Sawyer's Bengal Tigers and Joe Harper's
Bloody Avengers. Grace admits that she loves Joe. Amy leaves a
piece of cake for Tom, with a love letter inside. Exit both.

Jim, a Negro lad, enters soliloquizing on Tom's being out of
favor and on goody-goody Sid. Jim finds Amy's cake and eats it,
letter and all. Muff Potter comes along, repairs Jim's comb-and-
paper musical instrument, and learns that Injun Joe was last seen
walking toward Dr. Robinson's place. Exit both.

Aunt Polly and Mary come looking for Tom. Polly says that if she punishes Tom for scaring her just now with firecrackers, her conscience will bother her, but it also will if she does not. The two go back into the house. Tom enters, playing with a dead rat and some worms. He is sad when he cannot find Amy's cake and note. Alfred Temple, the new boy, approaches; and soon they have a fight, and Tom beats him up. Polly emerges again, criticizes Tom, learns through Sid that Tom has been swimming without permission again, and orders him to whitewash the fence. He is disconsolate until he decides to persuade a gang of his friends—including Huck Finn—to regard the chore as a pleasure. They pay him for the privilege of doing his work for him. Meanwhile, Dr. Robinson, Potter, and Injun Joe enter and discuss their nocturnal plans.

Act II. Tom and Huck enter a moonlit graveyard. Huck timidly reveals that he alerted Jones the Welshman, who saved the Widow Douglas from Injun Joe. The boys then discuss cures for warts, exchange a tick for a tooth, and dig for treasure. They find a small box of coins and put it in a handy sack they find nearby. They hide just before Injun Joe enters. He picks up his sack—with the money—and leaves. Dr. Robinson and Potter enter, arguing over grave-robbing. The doctor knocks Potter down; and Injun Joe, seeing his opportunity, kills the doctor with Potter's knife.

Act III. At the village schoolhouse Amy sees Alfred pour ink over Tom's spelling book. She tells the sneak that she will not tattle on him because she now dislikes Tom. (Tom never acknowledged receiving her cake and note, obviously, because Jim ate both.) Amy and Alfred leave. Becky Thatcher, a new girl, and Tom come in. He gives her a bite of his apple, draws some pictures for her, tells her he loves her and gets her to return the compliment, and they kiss to seal their engagement. When he lets slip the fact that he enjoyed his recent engagement with Amy, Becky cries and storms out. Amy returns, fools with the desk of Dobbins, the teacher, and accidentally breaks his bottle of whiskey. Tom sees her do it. They argue. School resumes, and concerns history, grammar, arithmetic, and declamation. Dobbins finds Tom's inky spelling book and flogs the owner. When he asks who broke his bottle, Tom—to save Amy—names Alfred as the culprit, and the sneak is flogged. Amy calls Tom a darling.

The schoolhouse has been converted into a courthouse large enough to accommodate everyone interested in attending Potter's trial. Tom and Huck talk outside, deciding that they must not testify for the accused because Injun Joe would surely kill them. They go in.

The Judge quickly pronounces sentence: Muff Potter must hang on August 14. Tom can contain himself no longer. With Huck's approval, he blurts out the truth. Injun Joe proves his guilt by breaking through the crowd and escaping.

Act IV. Separated from the other children during a picnic, Tom and Huck are lost in a cave. But Tom, who figures that the villagers would ordinarily have found them by now, regards the adults as lost themselves and prepares to search for them. As the boys wander off, Amy and Becky come in. They are also lost and hope that Tom will rescue them soon. The girls fall asleep, and the boys return and find them. The girls are happy until they learn that all four are really lost. Dragging his money sack behind him, Injun Joe now enters, see the children, and tries to stab Tom and Huck, who jump over a plank-bridged chasm onto a ledge. Injun Joe follows but falls through the rotten planks to his death far below. The children leave. Hordes of townpeople, led by Judge Thatcher, enter. They are about to give up the search when the children return. Once the embracing is all concluded, the Judge adds to the general happiness by revealing that it was Huck who saved the life of the Widow Douglas, who therefore hugs the boy. The Judge has respected Huck's fear, but now it is safe to tell the truth because Alfred recently found a drowned Indian answering Injun Joe's description. But Tom reports that Injun Joe was in the cave and has just died. Tom also shows everybody the money from the dead man's sack, and he ridicules thoroughly discomfited Alfred. Finally, Tom announces his intention of marrying both Amy and Becky, but Aunt Polly talks him out of it and orders him to kneel in prayer. He stands on his head instead.

> William Bacon, Johnny Baker, Mrs. Beesom, Bill, Dobbins, the Widow Douglas, Huck Finn, Pap Finn, Mrs. Finn, R. L. G., Joseph Harper, Jim Hollis, Tom Hooker, Mother Hopkins, Injun Joe, Jim, Jones the Welshman, the Judge, Amy Lawrence, Mrs. Lawrence, Miss Lawrence, The. Lawson, H. M., Mary, Gracie Miller, [John A.] Murrell, Johnny Patterson, Muff Potter, Dr. Robinson, Mrs. Robinson, Robinson, Benjamin Rogers, Sarah, Mrs. Polly Sawyer, Sid [Sawyer], Thomas Sawyer, the Sheriff, Bob Tanner,

Alfred Temple, Becky Thatcher, Jeff Thatcher, Judge
Thatcher, Mrs. Thatcher, Miss Thatcher, Bessie Thompson, Edward Tompkins, J. B. W., William. Hoss Williams.

Tom Sawyer Abroad, 1894 (WMT 19).

Huck Finn explains that Tom Sawyer is not satisfied after all
of his adventures down south, even though he is able to brag more
than the postmaster Nat Parsons, who once had to go to Washington, D.C., and receive a pardon from the President for accepting
an undeliverable letter without postage. So Tom offers Huck and
Jim a chance to accompany him on a crusade; but when the two
are critical of making war on strangers to recover land belonging
to those strangers, Tom calls it all off and plans other ineffectual
activities until finally the three decide to go down to St. Louis to
see a balloon described in the newspapers. Nat goes also. When
they arrive, a crowd is jeering at a dreamy-looking professor and
his contraption. He tries to argue back, but since he is only a
genius he cannot do so very well. Tom, Huck, and Jim look through
the boat-like part of the balloon and are about to follow Nat out
of it when the whole thing begins to ascend. Up, up they go, until
the city is only a scar on the earth below. The professor shows Tom
how to fly and steer his balloon, which he boasts is powered mysteriously. But when he grows dangerous, brandishes a revolver,
and threatens to crash and drown them all, they become fearful.
Dawn arrives, and they all have some breakfast. As they speed
eastward, Tom convinces Huck and Jim that they are passing over
different states—Illinois, Indiana, Ohio, Pennsylvania, and then
New York —even though the land below is colored the same and
not differently as on maps. He also lectures on time changes as they
cross different lines of longitude. Then they spy the monstrous
city of New York and head over the vast Atlantic. That night during a violent storm the professor takes out a bottle, gets roaring
drunk, shouts about England as his goal, and lunges at Tom to
hurl him overboard but falls instead to his death.

About midnight the storm ceases and moonlight bathes the
scene. The three inspect the stores laid in by the late professor.
Tom sets watches and writes Aunt Polly a descriptive letter, dating
it in the welkin approaching England. The three argue about words
and then birds. In the morning they spy land, but it is a desert.
When they descend and walk on the hot sand, a lion charges and

they barely escape in their faithful balloon. In the cool upper air again, Tom lectures on "Grinnage time," concludes that they are over the Great Sahara Desert, and drops down again to observe a long caravan of men and camels. Suddenly it is attacked by robbers; after a violent skirmish, the marauders break off but one of them kidnaps a wailing mother's baby. Tom takes control of the balloon and with it knocks the man off his horse. Jim steps down, rescues the infant, and the trio of aeronauts returns it to the ecstatically grateful mother.

Tom, Huck, and Jim drift along. Tom lectures on the relative strength of fleas and tells his friends a tale from *The Arabian Nights* which though finished ends too soon to suit Jim. Huck gets to liking the laziness and absence of "good" people in their lives now. They fly over a group of dead men, women, children, and camels, go down and examine everything, and help themselves to some rusty swords, pistols, and a little inlaid box of gold coins. Later they resist the temptation to return these items on the grounds that other people might come along and steal them, which would be a sin. Soon they grow thirsty, test their water supply, find it spoiled, and spot an oasis which turns into a "myridge." So they follow a flock of birds to a real oasis and go swimming. Unfortunately a crowd of lions gallops up and destroys their clothes. But they know that Jim can fix up suitable togs from the dead professor's left-over wardrobe. They haul up a small lion carcass and that of a cub tiger, bait hooks with some of their flesh, and go fishing. The resulting meal of steak, fish, and corn pone is memorable. After two days there, they fly away from the lovely oasis, saying goodbye to it as though it were a friend. Then they discuss the size of the Great Desert, theorize as to how it was made, and consider the relative importance of things of different size. Next Tom tells his admiring friends a story from *The Arabian Nights* about a dervish who encouraged a selfish rich man with a caravan of a hundred camels to let him put salve on his right eye to enable him to see treasure in a hill. Then the two loaded and divided the camels. But the rich man persuaded the dervish first to give him back the camels and then to put some more of the salve on his left eye, even though the dervish warned that it would blind him. Sure enough, he was blinded, and the dervish marched off with the entire caravan. Tom and Jim argue over the moral of the tale and the usefulness of lessons in real life, but Jim soon falls asleep and begins to snore most volubly. Later Tom leads the others to the very hill in the story, and they praise him for his astuteness even though they do not check for treasure at the spot.

They fool along for a day or so, and when they see another caravan they tag along behind and get to feeling friendly toward some of the individuals in it. When a sudden windstorm buries all of the people under ten feet of sand, they mourn as though the dead were relatives. Tom momentarily considers selling the sand in their balloon-boat until he happens to realize that duty on Sahara sand in the United States would be confiscatory. Then they go to work shoveling the mess of sand overboard. Jim is discontent when Tom suggests that each boy shovel a fifth and Jim the rest. He feels better when the boys agree to do a tenth each. They continue to fly along, now on a northeastern course, until they come upon the Pyramids, then the Nile. Huck is astonished at seeing these things in reality after all of his dreams about them. Suddenly they encounter a frightening face, but Tom explains that it is only the Sphinx. Tom and Huck land Jim on its head and sail back for the perspective, when suddenly they see tiny people shooting at Jim and trying to get at him with ladders. They fly to the rescue, and soon Tom is lecturing about the flying horse of bronze. But Huck flatly denies that there is any truth to such a tale and logically refutes Tom, to Jim's immense delight.

Next Tom and Huck tell Jim to float along while they explore the Pyramids and then visit Cairo. Its streets, crowds, and shops are intriguing. They see the Sultan and some whirling dervishes; then Tom wants to locate Joseph's granary and other revered buildings. They pick up an English-speaking guide, and Jim returns for all of them. They fly over the Red Sea, and Jim is thrilled. Suddenly Tom's corn-cob pipe breaks, and the boy orders Jim and the guide to whiz straight west across the Atlantic to Florida, then aim for the Mississippi, locate St. Louis on it and then their village, get his other corn-cob pipe, and bring it back, while he and Huck wait on Mount Sinai. The round trip should take only from Thursday to Saturday afternoon, local time. Jim is to sneak in and out, and leave a note for Aunt Polly. In due time, he returns but reports that she caught him and wants them home again. So they shove off, unhappily.

Uncle Abner, Bushrod Butler, Judge Jeremiah Butler, a Whirling Dervish, the Widder Douglas, Huck Finn, Jim,

Harryet McDougal, Colonel Jacob McDougal, Nat Parsons, Aunt Polly, the President of the United States, Adaline Robinson, Elexander Robinson, Tom Sawyer, Hen Scovil, the Sultan, Bill Thompson, Lance Williams, Hank Wilson.

Tom Sawyer, Detective, 1896 (WMT 19).

Huck Finn explains that it is now the first spring after he and Tom Sawyer set Jim free when he was chained as a runaway slave on Tom's uncle Silas's farm down in Arkansas. The frost is gone, and the boys are looking forward to summer and swimming. They mope about. They are suffering from spring fever and want to get away. Suddenly Aunt Polly tells Tom that he and Huck are wanted by Sally and Silas to comfort them. It seems that ever since his pretty daughter Benny refused to marry the widower Brace Dunlap, things have gone badly for old Silas, who is growing ill-tempered and also unpopular, even though he hired Brace's worthless younger brother Jubiter Dunlap to placate the disappointed suitor. Tom tells Polly that Jubiter, so named because of a set of moles above his left knee resembling the planet and four of its satellites, is a twin of Jake Dunlap, an escaped convict now thought to be dead. Tom pretends that he does not wish to visit in Arkansas, so that Polly will be certain to order him to go. And so it happens.

On the stern-wheeler heading south, Tom and Huck question a waiter who is suspicious of a passenger insisting upon hiding and wearing his boots day and night. Tom bribes the waiter to let the two boys serve the man his meals. The instant they see him, they recognize him as Jubiter's twin Jake. They gain his confidence, and soon the rough but friendly fellow tells them a long story of jewel robbery and duplicity. He has tricked his two partners in crime, Bud Dixon and Hal Clayton, by substituting his boots for Bud's, in the heels of which two stolen diamonds are secreted. But Bud and Hal are now on this very boat waiting their chance to waylay, rob, and kill him. Tom and Huck tell Jake the Dunlaps down south, as well as all of their neighbors, including Silas and Sally, think that he is dead; and the boys help him steal ashore a few miles north of his old home in the dead of night. He hopes to disguise himself in goggles and whiskers, and hide out with his brothers Brace and Jubiter. But soon the boys see Bud and Hal skip off the boat and follow their quarry.

Tom and Huck plan to meet Jake in a certain grove of sycamores at sundown after reconnoitring the Dunlap farm. But their boat is delayed. Late the following afternoon they head directly for the woods, only to see two men rush into the sycamores ahead of them. They hear screams, then see two more men rush in, then see a pair scamper out again, followed by two others. The boys hide, quaking, in Silas's tobacco field in deepening darkness, until they finally see emerging from the grove what they regard as the ghost of disguised Jake, goggles and all. They discuss ghosts, then eavesdrop on Bill and Jack Withers, then on Lem Beebe and Jim Lane, as they amble in pairs along the road. It is Saturday, September 2, a day Huck will never forget. But then Tom remarks that since Jake's ghost had its boots on the thieves could not have gotten the diamonds. Huck praises Tom for his detective ability and wonders why they do not therefore go at once and report everything to the authorities. Tom, however, prefers an inquest, jury twaddle, and auction of effects to pay for burial, because at that point he and Huck can buy Jake's boots and hold the jewels for reward.

So Tom and Huck walk to the farm home of Sally and Silas, who make a great fuss over them. When details of the untrue explanation of their delay in arriving happen to include mention of Beebe and Lane, their talk of Jubiter's dog, and of Silas and Jubiter spading some ground, Silas looks sharply at the boys and then lapses into sighing moroseness. He seems changed from the happily addlepated preacher-farmer of the previous mixed-up summer. Benny too looks sad and appears to be worried about her father. Brace's Negro servant comes and seeks news of Jubiter from Silas, who snarls and then apologizes, saying that he knows nothing of the man's whereabouts. When she can, Benny whispers that her father is upset and has taken to sleepwalking. Soon the boys skip out into the darkness, feed on some watermelons, smoke, discuss the puzzling events, and then return to the house. Tom remarks that Silas's old green work clothes with a white patch are missing. Benny is restless in her room next to that of the boys. They look out and see a man in a patched work gown with a shovel. They assume that it is Silas sleepwalking again. They are awakened at dawn by a lashing rainstorm. Tom remarks that it is curious no one has raised the cry of murder in all this time. The men who chased Bud and Hal should be doing so. Broad daylight soon comes, and with it the rain ceases. Tom theorizes that the four men who left the sycamores might all have killed each other and that Jake's corpse might still be there. So they scurry to the grove but find nothing. Tom is disgusted. The diamonds are gone.

At breakfast everyone is glum, especially Silas, whom pretty Benny comforts even while she nods to the boys to leave. So they strike for the woods and soon encounter Jake's ghost again. Tom guesses that Jake, now close-cropped, is really alive and boldly addresses him, but he only gesticulates and makes the goo-goo noises of a deaf mute. The boys assure the man, who remains curiously distant, that they will be cooperative and not reveal anything he told them. Then they go to the schoolhouse at recess time and renew acquaintance with several pupils there, including the Henderson brothers. It is hard to keep mum under these circumstances.

Several days go by, and the supposedly deaf-and-dumb newcomer is most popular. On a slate he writes comments which only Brace can decipher. It seems that "Dummy" belonged away off, was swindled, is now poor, and has no means of livelihood. Brace is praised for being good to the stranger. More days pass. Jubiter is still missing, and gangs hunt of evidence of him but fail and give up. Suddenly Tom decides to borrow the blacksmith Jeff Hooker's bloodhound and look. He and Huck soon find the corpse in the tobacco field. Instead of being relieved, Silas is utterly downcast and soon confesses that he argued with Jubiter, felled him with a stick, and watched him get up and run into the woods—only, doubtless, to die there. Tom tries to comfort him and wonders who buried the corpse. At this time Silas lapses into silence. So Tom urges him to believe that his reputation will surely protect him. But then they all hear the sheriff shouting at the door for Silas, wanted for the murder of Jubiter Dunlap. Tom vows to help his uncle escape or—better—to prove his innocence.

The month which passes before Silas's mid-October trial is difficult. Sally stays with the jailer's wife. Benny manages at home, with the children. Tom and Huck try to prove the old man's innocence but cannot. His lawyer is hardly more effective than a mud turtle. The lawyer "for the prostitution" is more skillful. First it is shown that there was bad blood between Silas and Jubiter. Beebe and Lane testify that as they walked past the sycamores on the fatal night they heard the prisoner's voice say that he wanted to "kill you," and saw a club rise and fall, and then heard groans. Later they saw that the victim was Jubiter. Bill Withers then takes the stand, testifying that he and his brother Jack saw what they thought was a Negro stealing a big sack of corn and then recognized that it was really Silas carrying a body, which they thought at the time must have been drunk Sam Cooper. Then Brace Dunlap tearfully, and effectively, reveals that because of uneasiness over his brother Jubiter on the night of September 2 he went into Silas's field and saw the prisoner digging a grave and burying his victim. At this point Silas leaps to his feet and confesses everything! He says that Jubiter was wrong to force his attentions on Benny, that he hired the worthless young fellow to placate the man's rich and vengeful brother Brace, that he struck the victim with murder in his heart, and that in the dead of night he returned to bury him.

Tom dramatically jumps up, tells Silas that he is innocent, and vows to explain everything. Then he histrionically brands Beebe, Lane, and the Withers brothers perjurers and reveals everything that happened. Jake Dunlap stole two diamonds from a pair of confederates, who followed him into the grove of sycamores and bludgeoned him to death. Beebe and Lane saw part of the murder, true enough, but Silas was uninvolved. Then Jubiter and Brace came along, also heard the fatal fight, chased the killers away, and returned to the scene to examine it. Jubiter put on the goggles, whiskers, and countrified Sunday clothes, all of which were to have been Jake's hometown disguise, pulled off the dead man's boots, put them on, and placed his own ragged ones on the corpse's feet. He waited there a while and then walked away in a ghostly fashion. Meanwhile, Brace lugged the body off in the twilight and later, disguised as Silas in his old work robe, buried it in his tobacco field. The Withers brothers saw Brace carrying the body. The culprits had been planning that Jubiter should disappear, hoping to enmesh Silas with the law after he hit his enemy; but when they stumbled upon the battered corpse of their own unrecognized brother, they modified their scheme, as now revealed.

Tom is a hero. He reveals that Jubiter, now in disguise and fidgeting in court, gave himself away during the hearing of testimony by drawing an imaginary cross on his cheek with his finger in a way which Tom observed last summer. He even unscrews the heels of the unsuspecting and repentant fellow's borrowed boots and recovers the stolen diamonds, for which the judge later obtains a reward of two thousand dollars for him. Tom divides the sum with Huck. Meanwhile, Silas is back in favor with his neighbors again and preaches a uniquely jumbled and hence treasured sermon in return.

> Lem Beebe, Billy, Hal Clayton, Sam Cooper, the Court, Bud Dixon, Brace Dunlap, Mrs. Brace Dunlap, Jake Dunlap, Jubiter Dunlap, Huck Finn, Jeff Hooker, Jim, Jim Lane, Mary, Steve Nickerson, Nickerson, Benny [Phelps], Mrs. Sally [Phelps], Parson Silas [Phelps], [Phelps], Phillips, Aunt Polly, Tom Sawyer, Sid, Bill Withers, Jack Withers.

"Tom Sawyer's Conspiracy," 1969 (HHT).

Huck Finn explains that when he returned he began to live again with the Widow Douglas and get civilized some more, and Jim began to work for her for wages in order to buy the freedom of his wife and children. Frozen winter yielded to slushy spring, and now summer is here and has brought with it much activity. Huck, Jim, and Tom Sawyer go to Jackson's Island one Saturday morning to plan something to do—that is, Tom will plan. He suggests getting up a civil war, but Jim opposes it on the grounds that it would not be civil. Tom suggests a revolution in which they would not depose a king but put one in, but Jim and Huck object because they had their fill of royalty last summer. Tom then suggests a conspiracy, defines what one is, and while the others rest thinks up a good one in about an hour of walking and head-wagging.

The plan is to worry the abolitionist-fearing villagers. So Tom, Huck, and Jim go to their island cave—a rendezvous, one of several —plan to establish a Council of Ten and a Council of Three—in spite of Huck's ignorant protests—and then hear Tom reveal his intention of pretending to be a runaway Negro slave so that he can hide and be betrayed by Huck and sold to Bat Bradish the local slave trader. Jim delays matters by suggesting that they take out a license to do all of this; but when Tom convenes his Council of Ten and grants the permit, all is regular.

The three paddle back to town. Jim goes home. The boys talk with some men patrolling the streets for abolitionists, then take some material from the printing shop—leaving a couple of quarters in payment—for a runaway-Negro poster, and Tom writes out a wanted bill on which he describes himself as he will look when disguised in minstrel-show costume. When they can, they paddle down river to Hookerville, get some reward posters printed, and wait until a rainy night—when the patrol will be under cover—to tack one up near the post-office door. On their way back to their room, they notice that Sid is sitting in his window watching them. So Tom waits until the sissy is asleep and then hangs his clothes in the rain to soak them so that he cannot tattle about their being out late at night without compromising himself. Next Tom must get Sid and Mary out of the house for a while, to work the conspiracy in safety; so he crawls into bed with Joe Harper, supposedly sick with the measles. Aunt Polly learns about it, puts him to bed at home, and packs Sid and Mary off to their Uncle Fletcher's farm thirty miles up country. But it develops that Joe has scarlet fever, which Tom also contracts. He is desperately sick for two weeks, gets worse, nearly dies, but then slowly recovers—probably because Huck, who could safely hover nearby because he had the disease earlier, ladled water into Tom contrary to the do

While Tom was sick, Huck borrowed some type, a s rule from Baxter the printer, for the boy, who amused himself in bed setting type. Tom soon is well enough to be up and about. It is now real summer. The boys go to the island, and Tom takes a pine block, carves a warning on it to the town that the Sons of Freedom are about to strike—the signal will be a certain number of blows— and prints it on some printer's paper. When the message comes out backwards, Tom is puzzled but then all the more pleased because of the mystery of it all. Jim makes a horn out of a hickory sapling, for the warning blows. Late at night the boys post copies of their notice all over town. In the morning Jake Flacker the town detective looks wise but keeps mum. Colonel Elder is elected Provo Marshal and establishes martial law. Tom and Huck are appointed as spies and are issued special passes. They order Jim to mingle with the other Negroes to see what information he can pick up. In the night the boys put up some more of their alarming signs, to the effect that no house is to be harmed which has a sign on its door. In the morning the people on whose doors such notices are tacked grow smug, and those without them are crestfallen. Tom is thrilled with his success.

Tom judges that it is now time to post his printed reward bills for the runaway slave. Huck is to surrender Tom, disguise, chains, padlock, and all, to Bat Bradish for part of the reward, and tempt Bat to try to claim it. Then Tom will take his spare key, unlock himself, wash off his greasepaint, and go free. Meanwhile Jim is to blow his signal, which will scare the town into believing that Tom was freed by abolitionists. But when Huck goes to Bat, the man tells him that he already has one runaway and that he cannot handle another until a little later. Huck tells Tom, who is abashed and momentarily blames Providence until he decides to check on Bat's runaway. The boys go to the man's log house, and Tom reconnoitres in a thoroughly detective way. He finds that the husky runaway snoring inside is really a disguised white man. Another team is playing the same game! Tom's faith in Providence is restored. They must seek out a stranger in town, wait and find his undisguised partner in this swindle, and follow them for the glory of it all. After briefly voicing his realistic objections, Huck decides to let his romantic friend have his way. So they find Jim and have ⸱⸱ ⸱⸱ his horn—horrifyingly.

⸱n uproar again, before dawn. Tom sends Jim to ⸱olly not to worry, that he is out on spy duty. Then he ⸱⸱ Huck return to Bat's place for clues but find him murdered and the lean-to empty. The boys follow the tracks of two men, one limping badly from a fall at a hidden jumping-off place near a river branch. Tom reasons correctly that the men might be hiding in the haunted house in which he planned to change out of his minstrel disguise. Huck timidly waits behind while Tom verifies his theory. He hears two men talking there. Huck wonders what his ingenious friend will conjure up next, but he knows better than to ask. The boys are returning to town when a one-legged slave hops up to them and reports that Jim has been arrested for Bat's murder. Tom is ecstatic. He goes to the jail and interviews Jim, who is terrified at the prospect of getting hanged. But Tom encourages him to be easy in his mind, although the poor fellow has a motive: it was Bat Bradish who persuaded Miss Watson to plan to sell Jim down the river a year ago. Tom is still more pleased, because the charge against Jim may now well be first-degree murder.

The boys are sure that Jim will not be lynched, because Ben Haskins, the resolute sheriff, is guarding him and Colonel Elder is outside the jail keeping the mob quiet. So Tom revels in his plans for a dramatic, last-minute exoneration of Jim during the darkest time of his upcoming trial. The boys go to the haunted house again to check on the real criminals, but the men are gone. Tom upbraids himself terribly, and both boys cry now. Jim will be hanged for sure. Tom realizes that the limping man did not have a broken leg but only a sprain of some sort, and that now the two criminals might be headed for the next town. So the boys catch the steamboat to intercept them. Tardily, Tom abandons this plan, reasoning that since the man did not break his leg he and his partner could easily now be in the Illinois woods. To comfort him with talk of any kind, Huck suggests that perhaps the men are part of Burrell's gang, with headquarters on Fox Island more than a hundred miles away. If the boys can quickly get there by the steamboat, they can alert a sheriff and have them arrested. Hoping to sight them in their stolen canoe up ahead, Tom and Huck separate to watch. Huck immediately stumbles over the King and the Duke, the memory of whose earlier shabby treatment of Jim down south prompts him to tell them that Jim is in jail and due to hang for murder. The rapscallions listen to Huck's careful story and then ask whether the boy would prefer to have Jim hang or be sold down the river.

The Duke explains that he and the King have a friend in St. Louis who can print a warrant for Jim's arrest for murder down south and that they can use the warrant to take the Negro away from town here. Huck tells them to count him in. He rushes to tell Tom, who is thrilled also and who wants to see the rapscallions, whom he glimpsed in Arkansas but only after they were completely hidden by tar and feathers. By the time the boys return, however, the men have already disembarked. So Tom and Huck hop off too, and soon they return home to get spanked by worried Polly and then listen to Flacker the detective reveal that he suspects the Burrell gang and further that he has found their provisions and even their printing equipment.

First thing in the morning Tom and Huck cross the river to search for suspicious footprints. They still would rather find the murderers than have to rely on the Duke and the King. But they come across no clues. Suddenly Tom has the bright idea of letting the rapscallions serve their paper and take Jim to Cairo, Illinois, in free territory, and then buying him from them. If the men cannot realize more money by taking Jim farther south, they will quickly accept Tom's offer. Providence must have sent the Duke and the King up north at just this time, the boys reason. That night they draw $800 each from Judge Thatcher, who is puzzled but cooperative. When the rapscallions do not reappear, the boys search for them in St. Louis jails and slums, but to no avail. Home again, they try to encourage poor Jim. Two weeks pass. It is now time for the trial.

Everybody, even the quality, is there. Lawson, the lawyer for the prostitution, calls Captain Haines and Buck Fisher as witnesses. They found Jim hovering over Bat's body. Jim's young lawyer performs in a rather sickly fashion but calls Huck, who tells his story very briefly, and then Tom, who tells everything about his elaborate conspiracy. The people appear to believe most of his account until he comes to the part about following the real murderers from Bat's hideout. When the judge asks Tom why he did not warn the sheriff, the boy can hardly say that he wanted to play detective for glory. He breaks down and cries. The jury quickly returns a verdict of guilty. Suddenly the Duke and the King enter the courtroom and announce that they have some business concerning the prisoner. Tom instantly recognizes their voices as those of the real murderers, produces his drawing of the King's heelprint, and flourishes the Duke's false teeth, which he filched from the supposed runaway slave while he was snoring in Bat's hut.

> Baxter, Oliver Benton, Bill, Bat Bradish, Burrell, Claghorn, Day, the Widow Douglas, the Duke, [Brace] Dunlap, [Jubiter] Dunlap, Colonel Elder, Huckleberry Finn, Buck Fisher, Jake Flacker, Fletcher, Jimmy Grimes, Captain Haines, Simon Harkness, Joe Harper, Captain Harper, Mrs. [Sereny] Harper, Captain Haskins, Higgins, Jim, the Governor of Kentucky, the King, Pete Kruger, Lawson, Mrs. Lawson, Mary, the Governor of Missouri, Paxton, Silas [Phelps], Plunket, Aunt Polly, Captain Sam Rumford, Thomas Sawyer, Sid, Judge Thatcher, Mrs. Thatcher, Jake Trumbull, Abe Wallace, Miss Watson, [Joanna] the Hairlip [Wilks], Mary [Jane Wilks].

["Tom Sawyer's Gang Plans a Naval Battle"], 1969 (HHT).

The narrator [Huck Finn], Tom Sawyer, and twenty other boys catch part of a floating raft, and Tom plans a naval battle. Let it be the Battle of the Nile. He will play Nelson. John Riggs is elected to be the French admiral but prefers to let Tom fight the Nile while he fights as Van Tromp against British frigates in the time of Charles II. Dick Fisher so sarcastically objects to mixing history that the others reduce him to be a Dutch commander named Van Wagner for insubordination. The boys count their fleet. They have twenty-two rafts, barn doors, planks, and the like. They divide them into British and Dutch vessels but then notice that they have more ships than men. So they reduce their fleets to two flagships and two canoes.

[Huck Finn], Dick Fisher, John Riggs, Tom Sawyer, Jimmy Todd.

"Tom Sawyer's Whitewashing Job." From *The Adventure of Tom Sawyer.*

"The Tomb of Adam." From *The Innocents Abroad.*

"Tom's Aunt." From *The Adventures of Tom Sawyer.*

"The Tone-Imparting Committee," 1871 (CRG).

When he grows old and respectable, Twain wants nothing so much as to be put on tone-imparting committees sitting on platforms when obscure lecturers deliver sounding emptinesses. He remembers Horace Greeley, Peter Cooper, and others on such platforms imparting tone to public lectures in 1799, 1812, 1824, and 1848. Such officials bolster many dull events but some progressive ones as well.

Peter Cooper, the Four-legged Girl, Benjamin Franklin, the Great Egyptian Sword Swallower, Horace Greeley, John Hancock, Thomas Jefferson, the Old Original Jacobs, Red Jacket, the Remains of the Old Red Sandstone Period, the Siamese Twin, the Siamese Twin, Tone-imparter.

"A Touching Story of George Washington's Boyhood," 1864 (CJF).

The narrator advises the reader to be patient when a neighbor tortures his ears by practicing on the trombone. The narrator used used to go burn out neighbors who played the violin, the clarionet, the cornet, the bugle, the bassoon, and drums. But he has since learned patience. He realizes now that such persons cannot control their ambition toward musicianship, because he himself suddenly fell victim to the urge to play the accordion. He practiced only "Auld Lang Syne," so badly that he was evicted from room after room by offended landladies—first Mrs. Jones, then Mrs. Smith, next Mrs. Brown. He was practicing in his room in a house run by an Italian named Mrs. Murphy when an old fellow-resident stumbled in, announced that he was grateful because the music had reconciled him to death, and very shortly died. So the narrator now advises the reader to be reconciled and would get at once to the main body of his sketch—an anecdote about George Washington—but his space is all used up.

> Mrs. Brown, Mrs. Jones, Mrs. Murphy, Mrs. Smith, George Washington.

"The 'Tournament' in A. D. 1870," 1870 (CRG).

An item recently appeared in the newspapers announcing that a telegraph station has been established on the site of the Garden of Eden. Equally apt is the recent news that the knightly tournament has been revived in Brooklyn. A tourney in Virginia might have attracted the chivalric, but Brooklyn? Imagine, in Brooklyn, heralds and pages, plumes and ruffles, steeds, and knights, and all in broad daylight. Nothing but an insanity plea before a New York jury could save latter-day Bois-Guilberts and Front-de-Boeufs. Earnest medieval chivalry was absurd enough. Why reproduce it in tinsel and mock pageantry?

> The Disinherited Knight, "Sir" Jones, Knight of Maryland, Knight of Shenandoah, Knight of the Blue Ridge, Knight of the Secret Sorrow, "Sir" Smith, Queen of Love and Beauty, Ashby de la Zouch.

The Tragedy of Pudd'nhead Wilson. See *Pudd'nhead Wilson.*

"Train Up a Child and Away He Goes." Partly in FW, 1871.

A Tramp Abroad, 1880 (WMT 9,10).

Planning a walking trip through parts of Europe with Mr. H. Harris as companion, Twain sails in April, 1878, to Hamburg and proceeds to Frankfort-on-the-Main, so named by Charlemagne, after he forded the river there. Twain retells the story of the executioner of Bergen who after dancing masked with the Queen of Germany saved himself from the King's wrath by asking to be knighted—the Knave of Bergen. Next the group goes to Heidelberg, taking quarters at the Schloss Hotel, above the castle near the Neckar River. Twain wanders into the dense woods and is laughed at by two ravens. This reminds him of Jim Baker's bluejay yarn. Thinking a log house with a hole in the roof had a ceiling, a bluejay once tried to fill the hole with acorns, until one of a crowd of visiting jays peeked through the door and saw tons of acorns all over the floor. Twain now tells about students at Heidelberg: their corps, beer-drinking, classes, dogs, and freedom. Twain saw five bloody duels in the whitewashed dueling-room, and gives details, statistics, and sundry information on student-dueling. Next he describes being fat M. Gambetta's second in his duel in France with M. Fourou. After much haggling, the adversaries decide on dainty pistols with tiny bullets at thirty-five yards. It is foggy; so the combatants have to whoop to locate each other. They fire, and Twain is fallen on by the unhit Gambetta and sustains glorious injuries. Then Twain briefly describes seeing *King Lear* at Mannheim and in detail the torture of sitting through *Lohengrin* there and also other Wagnerian operas in Munich and Hanover, often sung by artists long past their prime. He approves German punctuality at the theater but criticizes delayed applause. In the summer, after completing an art course in Heidelberg, Twain and Harris dress up to walk along the Neckar via Wimpfen to Heilbronn. Mr. X and Mr. Z plan to go along. But the party proceed by train and garbage cart instead, and stop before dark at the rickety inn at Heilbronn where Götz von Berlichingen stayed. They inspect the *Rathhaus*, the Square Tower, the main church, and a hill called the *Weibertreu*—hallowed by a legend. When an angry duke forced the castle there to surrender, he vowed to kill all the men but to let the women carry out their most valuable possessions. Each wife carried her husband away safely, for the duke kept his word. In the night Twain is restless, gropes for his clothes in the vast room, and gets lost until, knocking a pitcher on the sleeping Harris, he rouses the landlord. As the group leaves Heilbronn next morning, Twain sees the Neckar and charters a raft to Hassmersheim and Hornberg: floating down the river he and his friends see swimmers, steamboats, keel-boats, and scenery, and they picnic on the

raft gloriously. Below Hornberg is a cave which was occupied by
Lady Gertrude, who ran from home to stay faithful to her first
love, Sir Wendel Lobenfeld; when he returned from the Crusades,
he mistook her for a cave specter and killed her with his cross-bow.
As for the Lorelei—Lore used to sit on a rock called Lei. Count
Hermann fell in love with her, sang wretched songs to her, and
was drowned by Lore. A spectacular ruin above Eberbach has a
legend: after many knights failed, Sir Wissenschaft succeeded in
killing the fire-breathing dragon of the area by shooting it with a
fire-extinguisher. When the Emperor asked him to name his
reward, the hero wanted to have the monopoly on spectacles, only
to reduce their price (therefore many Germans wear glasses now).
As Twain and his friends float on their raft down the Neckar, they
are showered with stony rubbish from a series of explosions set off
by Italians blasting for a new German railroad. After a comic storm,
the party lands at Hirschhorn and spends the night at a tidy tavern.
Suddenly Twain launches into an essay on misinformation in Germany and then courtesy there. The travelers go by raft to Neckar-
steinach and the Dilsberg Castle, which has an empty well, a huge
old linden, and a legend. Young Conrad von Geisberg was persuaded to believe that he had slept in a haunted chamber of the
castle for fifty years. He was even told that his girl friend, who was
in on the trick, was dead. But after the pranksters took off their
disguises, Conrad continued to believe he was half a century older,
and soon died. The raft bears the group to Heidelberg and is
wrecked against a bridge there. When his trunk comes from Hamburg, Twain unpacks and gives part of his collection of ceramics
to the Grand Ducal Museum in Mannheim—he says. In Baden-
Baden he meets his friend Rev. Mr.— but cannot talk much with
him because huge, white-clad Cholley Adams, who is studying horse-
doctoring before returning to New York state, intervenes and talks
interminably. Twain expatiates on the insolence of Baden-Baden
shop-clerks and waitresses but praises its curative baths. He describes the clean but noisy hotel, the gabbling American tourists,
the quaint cemetery, and the weird Favorita Palace. Soon the party
enters the Black Forest and visits a typical farmhouse there, notable
for its huge dimensions and big pile of manure—the latter an important item of currency. Twain sketches the outline of a Black
Forest novel, in which Paul Hoch loses Gretchen Huss to Hans
Schmidt because of stealing from his prospective father-in-law's

immense inheritance of manure. Walking out of Ottenhöfen, Twain
observes an idiotic Black Forest ant and proceeds to debunk at
length the legend of the ant's steady intelligence. Next appears
sylvan, craggy Allerheiligen, with its ruined convent and brisk
hotel. Walking with Harris to Oppenau, Twain talks about mis-
used perfect infinitives, dentistry, skeletons, and then a sixteen-
year-old friend of his youth named Nicodemus Dodge, a practical-
joke victim who, however, sold the skeleton of Jimmy Finn which
pranksters put in his bed. Then Twain and Harris see a boy named
Peter tumble down a steep hill and cut his head; their seeing him
makes them feel heroic. Back in Baden-Baden at church, Twain
feels sorry for a dowdy-looking woman who he thinks probably
cannot put much in the collection plate, until she turns out to be
the Empress of Germany. Twain expatiates on being idle on the
Sabbath, then on popular music, and finally on Turner's paintings,
which he could not appreciate until he became dishonest like
Ruskin. With a courier to aid them, Twain and Harris go by train
to Lucerne, where Twain is evidently attacked by fleas, which he
pretends to confuse with the celebrated chamois. Then he jokes
about alpenstocks. Next he accepts Harris's dare at the table d'hote
of the Schweitzerhof to chat with a strange, pretty girl of about
eighteen. Soon he is entangled in lies, because the girl, seeing his
game, pretends to know him and leads him on. He returns to Harris
and confuses him out of exasperation. After discussing the Hof-
kirche organ concerts, Twain turns to the Lion of Lucerne, which
reminds him of Louis XVI. This leads to his conclusion that some
contemptible personages are lucky to be martyred and hence treated
gently by history. Twain hates cuckoo clocks so much that he buys
one for an enemy back home. Watching unsuccessful fishermen at
Lucerne reminds him of the story of an impatient San Francisco
schoolteacher named Lykins who asked Riley in Washington to
help him obtain a postmastership in a matter of hours. Riley proceeded to tell Lykins about a claim-seeker in President Jackson's
time who was still in Washington trying to get his claim. Lykins
did not get the point, nor did he get the post-office. Twain describes the Glacier Garden at Lucerne, the beautiful lake amid
the Alps there, then a boat trip to Fluelen before going up to Rigi.
On the way he encounters an unbelievably talkative American who
asks questions, forgets the answers, and asks again. Twain and
Harris disembark at Wäggis and supposedly take three days to

climb by inn-marked stages and past yodelers and along the steep railroad tracks to the Rigi-Kulm hotel. Next day they awake and rush out to see the celebrated Rigi sunrise, but the sun is going down. Though roused by the hotel horn-blower next morn, they miss the start of that sunrise through watching the dark western sky where the sun set before. But they see the world below in miniature relief and soon creepingly descend the mountain by cogged railway-car past Kaltbad to Vitznau.

Fatigued by Alpine pedestrianism, Twain rests in Lucerne at the outset of the second volume and dispatches Harris and their courier to the Furka region, the Rhone Glacier, the Finsteraarhorn, the Wetterhorn, etc. Harris returns in a week and submits a long written report full of fine descriptions but also innumerable foreign words—not only German and French but Zulu, Choctaw, Chinese, and the like—for which Twain stingingly rebukes him. The weather is so fine that, instead of walking, Twain and Harris hire a carriage for the ten-hour drive to Interlaken. Twain discusses chalets, Mount Pilatus, St. Nicholas, tidy fruit-selling children on the road, harnessing horses (this thing through a ring and over that thing, etc.), and a stalwart British tourist named Neddy and his wine-bibbing bride near the Brünig Pass. The travelers fall asleep and thus miss Meiringen from the Pass. They put up at the Jungfrau Hotel at Interlaken. This place features a bewhiskered waitress in a pretty peasant costume (which Twain ludicrously describes— pâté de foie gras backstitching, etc.), a wretched piano on which an American girl plays "The Battle of Prague" formidably, and a view of the Jungfrau. Twain digresses on the subject of couriers—their honesty or lack thereof, and their function. Next he discusses the serene effect on him of the Alps, especially the Jungfrau, a symbol of immutability. Then he satirically describes invalids existing on whey or grapes. He and Harris plan to walk to Zermatt but instead take for the first leg a two-horse buggy (with a drunk driver), stopping for the night at peaceful Kandersteg. They throw logs into the stream of a torrent and watch them tumble away, and next day they hire an old guide and climb slowly past a high-altitude pig-farm and close to the Great Altels mountain. While Harris is hiring guides for a climb over Altels, Twain reads Hinchliff's *Summer Months Among the Alps,* with an account of scaling Monte Rosa so breathtaking that when Harris returns, Twain begs off. As they pick their way through the Gemmi Pass, their guide tells them about a young French countess whom he saw fall there in 1861 from her saddle to her death. They stop at Leukerbad and are amused to watch a drunk guest try to fill his glass with a corked wine bottle. Then Twain sees another guest, a seven-foot lady of perfect form. Next morning, a carriage to the Rhone valley, a train to Visp, and a rainy walk to the village of St. Nicholas. The guests at the hotel all send their clothes down to the kitchen to be dried, and the subsequent redistribution of garments is confusing. Twain gets an undershirt with pockets for his shoulder-blades. As the two Americans walk on toward Zermatt, Harris protestantly complains that everything is dirty in this Catholic canton; even the Catholic glacier is unwhitewashed. When a little girl slips and nearly falls forty feet into the Visp, Harris expresses gratitude that she has been spared, whereas Twain laments the loss of a literary plum. Soon they see the Matterhorn, the Napoleon of mountains. At Zermatt, Twain reads up on mountain-climbing again and quotes Whymper's description of his near-fatal fall off the Matterhorn. Twain next treats us to a long fictive yarn about his 154-man expedition which climbs the Riffelberg. After three nights out, the party becomes lost. Twain ties almost a mile of rope to a guide, who instead of warily seeking a pass defects and ties the rope to a ram. In spite of dosing his worried men with paregoric and consulting a barometer which he scientifically boils before using, Twain has difficulty dynamiting a path toward the Gorner Glacier for his party. Next he meets the grandson of a supposedly notable American; the young man affectedly calls himself an old traveler and a man of the world. Twain and party press on intrepidly, and after a total of five nights out, they arrive at the Riffelberg Hotel. Twain boils a thermometer, takes a reading, and importantly discovers that the higher he climbs the lower the altitude actually is. He sees the Monte Rosa and beyond it the Matterhorn, with snowy sides down low, vaporous clouds above, and its finger-like wedge above all—and all unimaginably beautiful. Determining to proceed to Zermatt by riding the Gorner Glacier, Twain orders Harris to descend from the hotel to the glacier by using an umbrella as a parachute; Harris as a favor to the guide urges that man to take the honor; the Latinist next refuses. So they march down and get aboard the glacier, but it does not appear to move. Next morning they rig a sail on the glacier, but it is aground and also leaking. Learning from a guidebook that the glacier travels only an inch a day, they walk down and arrive at Zermatt next day. Twain now describes glaciers, their thickness, violent shapes, awesome crevices, moraines, and inconceivable power when they are in motion. He quotes Whymper on this subject and summarizes material from Stephen d'Arve's *Histoire du Mont Blanc*. Next he devotes a whole chapter to reprinting the narrative of Whymper on how he and seven other mountain climbers in July, 1865, scaled the Matterhorn but how four of the group, including Lord Francis Douglas, were killed in a fall on the way back to Zermatt. Twain briefly discusses Swiss graves; then he and his friend leave rainy Zermatt by wagon for St. Nicholas and walk on to Visp, noting the violent effects of the rain, also the way children pretend on manure-piles to be mountain-climbing, and at Visp the pretty waitress. By train to Brevet, then by boat to Lausanne. Twain voices no sympathy for the prisoner of Chillon, since his chamber was spacious and he might have amused himself by reading autographs—Byron's and Hugo's, by example—on the walls. By train to Martigny, and afoot to Argentière, where they look up to iridescent mountains whose colors are like those of soap-bubbles. They proceed to Chamonix in a wagon managed by the monumentally drunk "king of the drivers." Twain is profoundly impressed by the moonlight on Mont Blanc but quickly gets funny again and tries to buy a diploma certifying that he has climbed the mountain; then he theorizes that the moonlight cannot climb higher than 12,200 feet above sea level (because of gravitational refraction, refrangibility of the earth's surface, etc.) and says that the roar of the torrents gives the Swiss permanent headaches. Using one of the many telescopes at Chamonix, Twain observes stages of the journey up to the summit of Mont Blanc; he then advises others who wish to climb Mont Blanc by telescope not to pay the owner of the instrument in advance, since he might abandon them up there. Then Twain recounts the story of three amateurs, Sir George Young and his brothers, who foolishly climbed Mont Blanc in 1866 and fell two thousand feet: one died of a broken neck, but the others miraculously survived unhurt. Twain goes on to tell about women mountain-climbers and then (following d'Arve) about a party of eleven men who in 1870 tried Mont Blanc, got lost in a week-long snowstorm during their descent, and froze to death five steps from a path to safety. Uneventful is the slow ascent of Twain and Harris to a hotel near the Glacier des Bossons, then next day the journey to a hotel on the Montanvert and along the Mer de

Glace to the Mauvais Pas, where they meet a hog which forces them back. Next they take a crowded diligence to Geneva, where Twain resists a pestering shop-lady, watches rude pedestrians (and praises Americans by contrast), and then boards a train to Chambèry (old and sleepy), then Turn (big, wide, and ponderous). He sees a puppet show and is asked to put less money into the collection made afterwards; so he revises his prejudices concerning Italy, the more when he is not cheated on a bus in Milan. Twain feels wiser concerning art and the Old Masters (it is time, not human genius, which makes their works beautifully mellow) than when he was in Italy twelve years before. This is all owing to his art lessons in Heidelberg. He gives us a rollicking satire on aestheticians: a forty-foot Bassano in Venice he now knows is not really important for its Pope and Doge; it exists for the portrait in it of a hair-trunk, painted in flawless early Renaissance and sirocco Byzantine style. Next Twain analyzes the charm of St. Mark's: it is harmoniously old and ugly, like a warty bug out strolling. He recounts the story of Stammato, who four centuries ago systematically stole a treasury of jewels out of St. Mark's until he was denounced by a friend and hanged. Twain demonstrates his homesickness by unfavorably comparing European food with American. Then he gives several satirical recipes, concluding with one for German coffee, which is incredibly diluted. Finally he lectures on contemporary fig-leaf censorship of statues and literature but the lack of censorship of obscene nudes by such painters as Titian, who, however, he adds, painted a magnificent Moses. Twain's fatigue is betrayed by his cursorily saying that the group then went to Rome, Munich, Paris, Holland, and Belgium, and then gratefully returned to New York.

Six appendices follow. Appendix A discusses European portiers and the eminently just Continental tipping system. Appendix B describes the Heidelberg Castle, with its stupendous lights and fireworks, grounds, Heidelberg tun, and museum of antiquities and curiosities. Appendix C contains a description of the Heidelberg College prison, in which wild students are briefly jailed; Twain visited it. Appendix D, called "The Awful German Language," describes Twain's discontent with German and includes suggestions for reforming it, a translation to show oddities in German pronoun use, and an oration in English and "German" on brotherhood. Appendix E is called "Legend of the Castles" and is about a scholar named Franz Reikmann who is saved from financial ruin by supposedly stingy twin brothers bidding against each other at the auction of the scholar's books. Finally, Appendix F unflatteringly compares German newspapers with American ones and closes by translating the German news account of a child murder and giving samples of German newspaper humor.

> Cholley Adams, Grand Duchess of Baden, Grand Duke of Baden, Jim Baker, the King of Bavaria, Boots, Count Bruno, Captain, Captain of Mont Blanc, Paul de Cassagnac, Catharina, Chung-a Lung-Fung, Crioni, Darley, Dietz, Nicodemus Dodge, Duke, Duke, Jimmy Finn, Fourtou, Frances, Gambetta, Gay, Conrad von Geisberg, the Emperor of Germany, the King of Germany, the Queen of Germany, Lady Gertrude, Givenaught, Hans Gross, Hämmerling, H. Harris, Hertless, Count Hermann, Paul Hoch, Gretchen Huss, Huss, Professor H—y, Jimmy, John, George Jones, Miss Jones, Joseph William, King of the Drivers, Knave of Bergen, Sir Wendel Lobenfeld, Lore, Lykins, Tom McElroy, Mary, Müller, Neddy, Noir, Peter, Pontius Pilate, Herr Doctor Franz Reikmann, Hildegarde Reikmann, Rev. Mr.—, Riley, Hans Schmidt, Schumann, Stammato, Susan Amelia, William Tell, Thomas Henry, Henry Thompson, Tom, Professor T—l, Ulrich, Joseph N. Verey, Vogel, Wilhelm, Sir Wissenschaft, X, Z.

"Traveling with a Reformer," 1893 (WMT 22).

In the spring the author plans to go to Chicago and see the Fair. In New York, first, he meets a major in the regular army; the man is handsome, soft-spoken, built like a gladiator, and destitute of a sense of humor. He stands for citizenship. His hobby is to reform petty public abuses. The author must take the railroad to Boston and back before going to Chicago. The reformer agrees to accompany him and soon explains that diplomacy is usually better than force, which should be used only in extreme cases. Rudely treated when he wishes to send a telegram, the Major composes a new one, to the president of Western Union, hinting that he wants to complain; when the skylarking clerk reads it, his manners mend. Learning that the Major does not know the company president, the author begins to rebuke him gently for lying; but the reformer remains bland and says that lies are bad only when they injure

another or profit the liar. On a horse car going uptown that evening, the Major objects when three roughs board and begin to
curse. He tells the conductor that he will help throw them off;
when the roughs charge at him, the Major deftly knocks them unconscious and hurls them into the street. He tells the author that
in this instance he used force, not diplomacy. On the way to Boston
the next day, the Major forces a burly brakeman to apologize for
rudely treating a meek old passenger, by threatening to report the
incident to his (non-existent) brother-in-law director of the line.
The Major does not want the conductor to discharge the rude
brakeman but only to see that his manners improve. Firing him
would only cause his wife and other dependents to suffer. The
author and the Major return to New York and then start for Chicago. On Sunday morning, the reformer encounters two fellow-
passengers playing cards; he joins them, and when the conductor
tries to enforce certain nebulous company rules against breaking
the Sabbath, the Major talks him out of it but then threatens to
report the official for not reporting the alleged infraction. Once
in Chicago, the author promptly gets sick and misses the Fair. On
the way back, still with the Major, the two see a line superintendent
in the dining car eating chicken, which is not on the menu. So the
reformer demands—and gets—his chicken, but only as a matter of
principle, because he really dislikes chicken.

    Bliss, the Major.

[*Traveling with the Innocents Abroad: Mark Twain's Original Reports from Europe and the Holy Land*].* First version of *The
Innocents Abroad*, which see.

    *Edited by Daniel Morley McKeithan (Norman: University of Oklahoma
Press, 1958).

"A Travelling Show." See "The Scriptural Panoramist."

'A Tribute,' 1884 (WMT 28).
    Twain offers a funeral tribute to the dead partisan, that person
who worked so hard to place political party over the good of the
country that he overdid it and died. We should draw the veil of
oblivion over his minor faults. True, his zeal left widows and

orphans destitute, he was a slave to party and had no opinions of his own, and he sought to enslave others. But he did work hard—so hard, blessedly, that he ruined his cause. Now, fortunately, there are some who prefer state to party.

"A Tribute to Anson Burlingame." See "Two Mark Twain Editorials."

"The Triplets" (MTP).

Near the Hudson River is the Van Spuyten Duyvel mansion. Four recluses live there: eccentric Madame Van Spuyten Duyvel and her eighteen-year-old identical, dress-alike triplet granddaughters Annice, Harmony, and Stephanie. The old woman brought them up herself, and they now do all their own work, with the aid of an old deaf-and-dumb servant. Access to the Van Spuyten Duyvel mansion is barred by a precipice above the river on one side and high walls on the others. But one day the servant leaves a gate ajar, and Edward Armstrong happens by and enters. Annice sees him, is enthralled, and wishes that her sisters were able to see him. When he turns to leave, she confronts him. He apologizes, explains that he is a wandering artist in search of a house in his region where he might stay for the summer, and accepts her invitation to sit in the library while she rushes off to inquire—that is, to tell Harmony and Stephanie. They agree to hide him from their grandmother and deceive him into thinking that there is only one of them, not three. Stephanie goes down to Armstrong and tells him that her grandfather is away, their grandmother is confined to her room, and he may stay. He is thrilled. When he asks terms, she has to go and consult again. Armstrong is transported by her beauty but puzzled at Stephanie's speed when he almost instantly sees Harmony approaching from a different direction. She tells him that the charge will be $10 a month. He gallantly offers more. She goes to ask about this, and Annice continues the conversation from behind his back. He grows dizzy. When she leaves to see which room he is to occupy, another triplet emerges to tell him that his room is on the second floor, northeast. He agrees to follow her, although he would prefer to rest his spinning head.

Edward Armstrong, Annice Van Spuyten Duyvel, Harmony Van Spuyten Duyvel, Stephanie Van Spuyten Duyvel, Madame Van Spuyten Duyvel.

Tropic Chidings, 1884 (P).

He (also called Mark) fans her cheek incessantly, but She only complains of the continuing heat. When She suggests that they sever their love forever, to effect a cooling, He is willing.

Mark, She.

"The Trotting Season." See FW, 1870.

"A True Story," 1874 (WMT 7).

One summer evening at twilight, the Clemens family is sitting on the porch of their farmhouse, chaffing their tall, vigorous Negro servant Aunt Rachel, sixty years of age and perpetually laughing. But when the author asks her how it is that she has never experienced trouble, Rachel quickly sobers and says that she will tell him and then leave it all to him. She was born into slavery, had a loving husband, and seven children. Though raised in Virginia, she had a proud Maryland mother, who delighted in repeating that she was not born in the mash to be fooled by trash. She blurted out her favorite line one day as she cleared the kitchen and cared for Rachel's little boy Henry, when he tore his left wrist and cut his forehead. Then one day Rachel's mistress went broke and sold her slaves at auction. Crowds came by and felt the Negroes, and one by one Rachel lost husband and children, at last even little Henry, who whispered to his mother that he would escape, work, and buy her freedom. Rachel was sold as a cook to a Newbern man who became a Confederate colonel during the Civil War. He lost his mansion, which was finally occupied by Union officers. One night a platoon from a Negro regiment came by and put on a dance in Rachel's huge kitchen. A spruce young black danced wildly with a yellow wench. When the Negro band put on airs, Rachel rebuked them, announcing that she was not born in the mash to be fooled by trash. The young dancer heard her and frowned, soon came to her, and stared into her eyes. Suddenly Rachel knew! She saw a scar on his left wrist and another beneath his hair line. He was her son Henry, who had indeed escaped, gone north to become a barber, and eventually enlisted in the Union army to go south and look for his mother. Oh, yes! Rachel concludes; she has known trouble—and joy!

[Miss Clara] Clemens, [Miss Jean] Clemens, Mrs.

[Olivia] Clemens, Misto [Samuel Langhorne] Clemens, [Miss Susan] Clemens, Gen'l, Henry, Jim, Aunt Rachel.

"A True Story Repeated Word for Word as I Heard It." See "A True Story."

"Tupperville-Dobbsville," 1969 (HHT).
The scene is a village in Arkansas on the bank of the Mississippi River years ago. The houses are very modest. The town looks lazy and neglected. The river keeps eating at it. Since there are no sidewalks, the streets are often full of dust or mud. People loaf about until a dogfight rouses them. One of the largest dwellings is the home of Mrs. Bennett, a widow, and her family. At the back of the town near the corn and cotton, the house has a sitting room with fireplace, spinning wheel, table, eight-day clock, splint-bottom chairs, and guns, a dining room, and bedroom. Separate from the house are a log kitchen and small cabins for slaves.

Mrs. Bennett.

'Turncoats,' 1884 (WMT 28).
Twain objects to being contemptuously called a turncoat by Republicans, simply because he has refused to support [James G.] Blaine and has joined the Mugwumps. Twain has not deserted Republican Party principles but has merely changed his opinion concerning Blaine. But so did other Republicans, until Blaine was nominated; therefore, they are double turncoats.

[James G.] Blaine, Mulligan.

"The Turning Point of My Life," 1910 (WMT 26).
The topic is the change in Mark Twain's life which introduced the most important condition of his career. Such a link in the circumstantial chain is only the last, most conspicuous one; and each of its predecessors is just as important. Caesar's decision to cross the Rubicon was momentous, but perhaps a noble fellow's snatching a trumpet and blowing it, thus helping Caesar make up his mind, was as crucial. When Caesar crossed the Rubicon, certain Roman

events followed, leading to Christianity, the discovery of America, the western migration, the settlement of Missouri, and the birth of Twain. The most important aspect of his life is the literary. The following events form a chain: when Twain was twelve, his father died and the boy caught the measles. Soon he was apprenticed to a printer, began wandering, grew ambitious to explore the Amazon but became a Mississippi River pilot instead, went west during the Civil War, tried newspaper reporting, went to Hawaii, returned to lecture, went to Europe, and was asked to write a book about the voyage. So he became a literary man because he had the measles. Circumstances must have a partner, which is man's temperament. Twain has a temperament of a sort making it impossible for him to have things come out according to plan. A man is like a watch, except that a man is conscious and tries to plan things. A nation is only an individual multiplied. Its plans go only so far, and then circumstance intervenes to carry events beyond plans. Columbus did not plan to discover a new world. God commanded Adam's temperament, which caused the act of disobedience. If Adam and Eve had been postponed, and if Martin Luther and Joan of Arc had come first, the apple would be intact today. And the old scheme of making Twain a writer would have been defeated.

["Twichell and the Profane Ostler."]. See "Tramp to Boston."

"Two Little Tales," 1901 (WMT 23).
Early in 1900 the author is talking with a friend in London who complains that a friend of his could not get government recognition of a light, cheap, durable boot he invented for the troops in South Africa. The author's friend adds that he too failed to interest officials in the boot. He wrote the proper agent, called on him, wrote again, went to his office and waited, and so on. The wise old author is not surprised and by way of showing his friend how really to get things done tells him how the chimney sweep got the Emperor's ear. Everyone was sad one summer when dysentery swept the land and even the Emperor lay dying. His physicians could do nothing, although they emptied drugstores into him. Tommy, a sixteen-year-old cleaner of cesspools, learns from his closest friend, Jimmy the chimney sweep, that eating a slice of ripe watermelon is a sure cure of dysentery. Tommy then explains that the way to

alert the Emperor is not to write him a letter—he and his father cart away eighty thousand unread letters a night from the palace—but to tell a close friend, who will tell a friend, and thus the message will get to the Master of the Household and to the Emperor's pet page. The scheme works. When the Emperor recovers, he orders his Grand High Chief Detective to trace the whispered solution to its source. Learning about Jimmy, he sends him a pair of used boots as a reward. The author's friend follows the advice implicit in the tale, and soon the government adopts the inventor's boot.

> The Admiral of the Blue, [the Admiral of] the Red, [the Admiral of] the White, the Chief Equerry, the Director-General of the Shoe-Leather Department of the War Office, the Emperor, the First Lord of the Admiralty, the Grand High Chief Detective, the Head Groom of the Stables, Jimmy, the Lord High Chamberlain, the Lord Mayor, the Master of the Hounds, the Master of the Household, the President of the Council, the Rear Admiral, the Speaker of the House, Tommy, the Vice [Admiral], Zulu.

"Two Mark Twain Editorials," 1879, 1870 (WMT 29).

In his "Salutatory," Mark Twain explains that since he has suddenly and violently assumed the associate editorship of the Buffalo *Express*, he owes it to his public to say a few things now. He will not deliberately hurt the newspaper. He will introduce no reforms. He will do his duty when he cannot get out of it, will work when privation compels him to do so, will tell the truth unless it is inconvenient, will rebuke crimes other than his own, and will use profanity only when commenting on rents and taxes. It is foolish to present his platform, but custom requires such salutatories. Valedictories are even worse. His predecessor refused to issue one, saying that it would be like a corpse commenting on the funeral.

"A Tribute to Anson Burlingame" extols its subject as true, brave, and just. Burlingame was big and handsome, was always interested in others, and had chivalric generosity. His Brooks-Sumner speech and his espousal of the cause of Italian liberty helped to make him better known. He became a distinguished diplomat. He was envoy to China, where he cleaned up consular inefficiency and corruption, insisted upon justice to both American and Chinese citizens, established the

Imperial College, improved trade, induced China to close her ports to vessels of the Southern Confederacy, and simplified diplomatic documents. His biography reads like a fairy tale: he was a surveyor out west, attended Harvard, became a Boston lawyer, entered Congress, became an Old World magnate, and then went to the Orient as an ambassador. His influence for good was enormous. He died at the age of forty-seven.

Anson Burlingame.

"Two Poems: By Moore and Twain." See "A Couple of Poems by Twain and Moore."

"Two Sisters" (MTP).

Medea and Saffa are peasant sisters on the estate of the Count of Taormina, whose huge castle is nearby. One day Medea, who is dark and beautiful, tells quiet Saffa that she has set her cap for the Count's major-domo. Saffa is awestruck. But Medea succeeds, gloats, and begins to prize the envy of others. Saffa is not jealous, in fact is happy for her smouldering sister. Medea rankles: she must make Saffa jealous. Finally she devises a plan, which involves the Count himself. Just after the wedding supper, he walks in. The humble guests are aghast, then envious of Medea, who steals a glance at Saffa now. The lack of jealousy there poisons fiery Medea's cup. Worse, when the Count chances to see demure Saffa he asks for a dance, then another, and finally the rose from her hair. Medea becomes jealous, sees little merit in her husband, and imagines that without him she might have become a countess. She tries to dissuade Saffa from thoughts of any future with an aristocrat, but Saffa softly replies that she and the Count are in love and that true affection abolishes rank. In desperation, Medea begins to slander Saffa, but the Count pays no heed.

Medea, Saffa, the Count of Taormina.

"An Unbiased Criticism," 1865 (SS).

The narrator explains that the Editor of the *Californian* ordered him to review the California Art Union exhibition. He knows nothing about art and anatomy but admits to his enjoyment at looking at pictures. So, he reports, he went over to the Union rooms, about which he had read much while in the Calaveras mining camps. Up there in the camps, he digresses, they used to read anything they could find, even religious tracts, patent-office reports, and dictionaries. Political factions were organized on the basis of loyalties to rival safe and sewing-machine companies. Campaigns were heated. But the narrator must return to his review. Yes, he went over to the Art Union, collected admission fees from a few other visitors, met an old mining crony who introduced him to a man named Brown, exchanged intimate family yarns with Brown, and then walked out with him to have a drink.

> Admiral Ambrose, Brown, Mrs. Brown, Coddington, Coon, Tom Deer, Dyer, Editor, Martha, Morgan, Murphy, the Opposition, 'Lige Pickerell, Dick Stoker, the Superintendent.

"Unburlesquable Things," 1870 (CG).

Some events cannot be burlesqued, because accounts of them use up all the materials and leave nothing out of which to fashion burlesques. Examples include the Byron scandal, the Boston peace jubilee, Henri Rochefort's boast that he could not be arrested, the McFarland murder trial (with its ridiculous insanity plea), and the Fenian invasion of Canada (with its irrational appeal to the minority vote and its foolish news leaks).

> Governor Alcorn,[George] Cruikshank, the Fenian General-in-Chief, [Patrick] Gilmore, Graham, the U.S. Marshal, [Daniel] McFarland, President McThis, General O'That, the Recorder, [Albert D.] Richardson, Henri Rochefort.

'Unconscious Plagiarism,' 1879 (WMT 28).

Twain says that when a person first receives a letter from a great man, he will always remember it. Dr. Oliver Wendell Holmes was the first such person to write him. It seems that a friend told Twain that the dedication page of his *Innocents Abroad* was identical to that in Holmes's *Songs in Many Keys*. When they checked and proved the fact, Twain wrote Holmes to apologize and to explain that the theft had been accidental. Holmes so gently replied to the effect that we all unconsciously plagiarize that Twain grew almost glad that he had

committed the crime. He closes his speech with the hope that it will
be years before people can truly say that Holmes is growing old.

Dr. Oliver Wendell Holmes.

'An Undelivered Speech,' 1895 (WMT 28).

Twain praises the new steamship the *St. Paul,* about to be launched,
and explains that he is going to start across the Atlantic Ocean again
two days hence in the *Paris,* another ship of the same line. He has
crossed so often that he knows all the whales, waves, and sunsets
along the way. He prizes safety and speed. The new American ships
are admirably water-tight, and they take you from New York to
London with a minimum of dockside delays. He is unsure whether
the *St. Paul* was named after the city or the hero who killed Goliath.

Goliath, St. Paul.

"The Undertaker's Chat," 1870 (WMT 7).

The undertaker pats the folded hands of deceased and calls him a
brick. The corpse wanted a roomy box rather than something styl-
ishly metallic but cramped, his name daubed on with a blacking
brush rather than an engraved silver plate, a simple planting rather
than a funeral with flummery, and a modest eulogy and a choir singing "Pop Goes the Weasel" rather than a highfalutin performance.
Actually deceased was rehearsing that song when he was suddenly
snuffed out. The undertaker adds that he would follow such a person's last requests to the letter if he could. Then he cracks his whip
and lumbers away with his ancient hearse. The author's moral is that
cheerfulness is possible in any occupation.

"The Undertaker's Tale" (MTP).

In the year 18—, the narrator, a boy of fifteen, homeless and forlorn has been pushed and kicked from door to door, when a lovely
girl accosts him, learns his plight, and takes him into a cheery-
looking house, where he is given food and a bed. His benefactress
is Grace Cadaver, aged eighteen. Her parents are the local undertaker Cadaver and his cheerful wife. They also have a son Jimmy
and another daughter, Mary. Weeks pass, and the boy is lovingly

treated. He learns the family business. He and Grace decorate coffin interiors together, singing the while. Grace's fiance is Joseph Parker, the village sexton and grave digger, and a fine young man. Mr. Cadaver mortgages his house to Marlow in order to help Joseph buy the local graveyard. A good season will enable them to pay off the debt quickly. The changeable weather augurs well. Grace commends her patient father for never betraying anguish during recent nice weather when nobody died. He kisses the flattering girl. Then comes trouble: business slackens even though it is still wintry. The family grows apprehensive. Warm spring ensues, with its unfortunately healing zephyrs. Then just before the advent of summer, the happy news comes that cholera has hit the seaport. The Cadaver household brightens. But the disease totally spares their village. Cadaver bows to God's will. Disaster hovers. Marlow wants his mortgage payments. Cadaver begs for more time, showing his harsh creditor a list of sick neighbors as proof of solvency. But Marlow derides the list, predicts that the sick people will recover, and gives Cadaver two days to pay or move. The Cadavers and the narrator sit about staring into space. Then the narrator goes out, paces through the night, and finally visits house after house of the Cadavers' potential customers. Bad news: they all seem better, or at least no worse. The next day the narrator posts friends in those same houses with orders to report any good news to him at once. Back at the Cadaver residence, Marlow paces, gloats, and then orders the family to pack up its rotting coffins and clear out. Silently the narrator's friends come gliding in, whisper to him, and leave. Just as Cadaver is about to surrender, the narrator announces that five neighbors are no more and that the cholera is even now in town. Cadaver is transported with joy. Joseph and Grace hug one another fervently. The narrator advises Marlow to depart. Cholera ravages the village. The Cadavers are busy, and so is Joseph, who in time marries Gracie. Their wedding procession is graced by old Marlow in a $60 casket.

> Grace Cadaver, Jimmy Cadaver, Mary Cadaver, Cadaver, Mrs. Cadaver, Mrs. Hale, Marlow, Philip Martin, Joseph Parker, Samson, George Simpson, William Thompson.

"An Unexpected Acquaintance." From *A Tramp Abroad*.

'The Union Right or Wrong,' 1872 (S).

Twain reminisces about his days as a reporter in Nevada. He worked for the *Enterprise;* Boggs, his alcoholic rival, was on the *Union.* Boggs could always get the school report; but Twain could not, because the school principal hated the *Enterprise.* One snowy night Twain met Boggs on his way to the principal and talked himself into accompanying him. After they got the report, Twain enticed thirsty Boggs into the *Enterprise* office for some hot punch, and the *Union* was scooped. Boggs seemed to hold no offense. Later the two reporters visited the Tennessee Mine. Boggs lowered the unsuspecting Twain by windlass into the ninety-foot shaft to inspect it and left him there, to go get the latest school report. The *Union* printed it next day, but Twain's paper did not.

Boggs.

"'The Union—Right or Wrong?'" From *Roughing It.*

"The United States of Lyncherdom," 1923 (WMT 29).

After eighty years of honorable conduct, Missouri has now joined the ranks of lynchers and therefore, because of a handful of villains, has had its deservedly good name besmirched. The tragedy happened near Pierce City, where after a white woman was found murdered three Negroes were lynched and many others were driven into the woods. Regardless of provocation, people should not take the law into their own hands. Why do people engage in lynching? It is because strange, publicized events are imitated. A murder committed by a Negro will be imitated, and a notorious lynching will produce other lynchings. Individuals will join a mob through aversion to being conspicuous if they do not; such fear is moral cowardice. Our moral sense teaches us what is right and also how to avoid it when it is unpopular. One daring man can lead 10,000 others. A man will risk his life to save another in a burning building, for approval and because no one will disapprove. We hate to be unpopular, to have our neighbor's disapproval. Yet one brave man—for example, Savonarola —can quell and scatter a mob. Perhaps we should station such a man in each lynch-prone town. Although there are plenty of physically brave men, there are few morally brave ones. American missionaries should return from China and go where lynching is prevalent. After all, they are converting only two Chinese apiece per annum against an uphill birth rate of 33,000 pagans a day. Moreover, each such convert runs the risk of being infected by our civilization. Chinese reading news of our lynchings should prefer to remain uncivilized. If all of our lynch victims were immolated at one time, their shrieks might reach the Throne. Missionaries, who are experienced in facing violence, should leave China and convert Christians here at home!

'University Settlement Society,' 1901 (WMT 29).

Twain praises the University Settlement, where one can have a dancing lesson for a penny, pawn things for a moderate 1% a month, and receive charity without humiliation. In San Francisco Twain once helped an impoverished poet who wanted to commit suicide. As the poet was attempting to drown himself, a wave washed in a life preserver, which he and Twain pawned for a derringer, which sent a bullet through the poet's brains cleaning out the gray matter and poetic faculty. Now the poet is a useful member of society.

Mrs. Hewitt, Mrs. Thomas.

"The Unreliable," c. 1863.*

The narrator offers to the editors of the *Enterprise* a letter addressed by the Reliable to the Unreliable, but the narrator says that it was really to him from the Unreliable. The letter accuses the recipient of stealing journalistic ideas and makes a threat. The narrator then reports that he challenged the Unreliable to a duel with bootjacks at a hundred yards and thus terrified the fellow. The Unreliable threw away his demijohn and tried to poison himself by drinking water, but Dr. Tjader saved him by prescribing brandy. The narrator bought the Unreliable a coffin, and then reports attending the wedding of Miss Emma Curry and Hon. James H. Sturtevant.

Father Bennett, Abe Curry, Judge Dixon, Mrs. Emma Sturtevant, Hon. James H. Sturtevant, Dr. Tjader, the Unreliable, the Unreliable.

*In *Wit and Humor of America*, ed. Kate M. Rabb, Vol. 5 (Indianapolis: Bobbs-Merrill, 1907).

"Up Among the Clouds." See RL.

"The Upper Mississippi." See FW, 1870.

"Valedictory," 1871 (CG).

Twain explains that he has written for the *Galaxy* a year now. For the last eight months he has been associated with doctors and sick people, and recently death claimed two members of his family circle. His humor has therefore been rather funereal of late. He is dropping his "Memoranda" column and will now write a book. What immediately follows here ["My First Literary Venture"] simply dropped from his pen: it was his first attempt at writing for a periodical.

"Vanderbilt—Mark Twain Sends an Open Letter to the Commodore." See FW, 1869.

"Venerubel Fogee." See FW, 1869.

"A Victim to Jeremy Diddling Trustees . . ." See "The Latest Sensation."

["The Victims"], 1972 (FM).

Johnny Microbe begs his mother for permission to go to the picnic. Mamma Microbe tells him to be careful, put his faith in the good spirit, and be home before sundown; then she hunts for a white corpuscle for their supper, finds Willie Molecule, takes his head home, then kneels and thanks the good spirit for being provident. Peter Anthrax obtains permission from his mother to go to the picnic and trots off while his mother, foraging for supper, gets Johnny Microbe's face. And so it goes: Peter Anthrax is eaten by the mother of Robbie Typhus Germ, who is eaten by the mother of Davy Itch Germ, and so on, involving Red-Speck Spider and his mother, Ant and mom, Gray Spider, Pitch-Bug, Sparrow, Weasel, Fox, Wildcat, Lion, Tiger, Elephant, and on up to little Jimmy Gem-of-the-Creation Man and his father, who shoots Jumbo Jackson Elephantus and trades his tusks to an Arab for black slaves to be sold to a Christian planter who will teach them Christianity and hard work and thus extend our civilization. When the sun goes down, broken-hearted mamma Molecule says that the good spirit has deserted her son Willie, who will return home no more.

Fanny Ant, Ant, Peter Anthrax, Anthrax, Jumbo Jackson
Elephantus Ichthyosaurus Megatherium, Elephantus Ich-
thyosaurus Megatherium, Jacky Fox, Fox, Davy Itch Germ,
Itch Germ, Robbie Typhus Germ, Typhus Germ, Caleb
Sierra Lion, Sierra Lion, Jimmy Gem-of-the-Creation Man,
Gem-of-the-Creation Man, Johnny Microbe, Microbe,
Willie Molecule, Molecule, Sammy Pinch-Bug, Pinch-Bug,
Dora Sparrow, Sparrow, Gray Spider, Phoebe Gray Spider,
Tommy Red-Speck Spider, Red-Speck Spider, Sissy Bengal
Tiger, Bengal Tiger, Harry Weasel, Weasel, Sophy Wildcat,
Wildcat.

"Villagers of 1840-3," 1969 (HHT).
    The author reminisces about Hannibal villagers, their home life,
employment, religious beliefs, ambitions, travels, sins, crimes, sor-
rows, entertainment, and the like.

Bright Alforata, Jesse Armstrong, Mrs. Jesse Armstrong,
Bart, Beebe, Bence Blankenship, Tom Blankenship, Blank-
enship, Mrs. Blankenship, Miss Blankenship, Miss Blank-
enship, Blannerhasset, Mrs. Blennerhasset, Bart Bowen,
Captain S. A. Bowen, Mrs. S. A. Bowen, Sally Bowen, Sam
Bowen, Mrs. Sam Bowen, Jenny Brady, Dana Breed, Letitia
Richmond Breed, Artemissa Briggs, Bill Briggs, Carey
Briggs, John Briggs, Bob Buchanan, 'Gyle Buchanan, Joe
Buchanan, Joe Buchanan, Robert Buchanan, Burton Car-
penter, Han Carpenter, Hartley Carpenter, Joanna Carpen-
ter, M. Carpenter, Oscar Carpenter, Priscilla Carpenter,
Simon Carpenter, Judge Carpenter, T. K. Collins, Collins,
Ben Coontz, Coontz, Cross, Becky Davis, Lucy Davis, Davis,
Davis, Davis, Dawson, Judge Draper, Eliza, Dr. Fife, Jim
Foreman, Garth, Glover, Mrs. Mary Green, Green, the
Hanged Nigger, John Hannicks, Dick Hardy, Ben Hawkins,
Jeff Hawkins, Laura Hawkins, Sophia Hawkins, Mrs. Haw-
kins, Mrs. Hawkins, Miss Hayward, Urban E. Hicks, Mrs.
Holiday, Lavinia Honeyman, Letitia Honeyman, Mrs. Horr,
Dick Hyde, Ed Hyde, Eliza Hyde, Jackson, John, John, Ro-
berta Jones, Josephine, Helen Kercheval, Kercheval, Bill
Kribben, Mary Lakenan, Lakenan, Mrs. Ella Lampton, Jim
Lampton, Kate Lampton, Bill League, Mrs. Bill League,
Clint Levering, Levering, M(a)cDonald, Wales McCormick,

Dr. John McDowell, McManus, Pet McMurry, Charley Meredith, John Meredith, Dr. Meredith, Miss Meredith, Miss—, Priscella Moffett, W. Moffett, Moffett, Neil Moss, Russell Moss, Mrs. Russell Moss, Mary Nash, Tom Nash, Nash, Mrs. Nash, Miss Nash, Miss Newcomb, Ouseley, Pavey, Mrs. Pavey, Miss Pavey, Dr. Peake, Bill Pitts, Pitts, Prendergast, Jim Quarles, Mrs. Jim Quarles, Quarles, Quarles, Quarles, Colonel Ralls, Ratliffe, Mrs. Ratliffe, Dr. Ratliffe, Ratliffe, Ratliffe, Dr. Ray, Sam Raymond, Rev. Mr. Rice, Richmond, Clay Robards, George Robards, John Robards, Mrs. John Robards, Sally Robards, Captain Robards, Dick Rutter, Sam, Charley Schneider, T. R. Selmes, Miss Selmes, Margaret Sexton, Mrs. Sexton, Shoot, Mrs. Shoot, Simon, Smar, Lot Southard, Mrs. Lucy Southard, the Stabbed Cal[ifornia]. Emigrant, Dick Stevens, Ed Stevens, Stevens, Margaret Striker, Striker, Mrs. Strong, Miss Torrey, Rev. Tucker, Ustick, Will, Jim Wolfe.

"A Visit to Niagara." See "Niagara."

"A Visit to the Savage Club," 1907 (LAIFI).

Thirty-five years ago (in 1872), Twain says, he went to England to study the country and while on the train from Liverpool to London was distressed to see a fellow passenger reading *The Innocents Abroad* without laughing or even smiling. When Twain got to London, he was entertained by the family of his publisher Routledge. Edmund Routledge took him to the Savage Club, where everyone had a good time but Twain mislaid five five-pound notes. He looked high and low, and his friends helped him; but only when he returned to his hotel did the notes turn up: a servant found them in Twain's dress-suit tail-coat pocket. The Savage Club in London and New York's Lotus Club then enjoyed—and perhaps still do—membership exchange privileges. Twain closes by reporting that about 1900 he was made an honorary Savage member. The Prince of Wales, and the explorers Nansen and Stanley were then also on the honorary list.

Frank Buckland, [King Edward VII], Tom Hood, Harry Leigh, [Fridtjof] Nansen, Edmund Routledge, Routledge, [Henry Morton] Stanley.

'Votes for Women,' 1901 (WMT 28).

Twain advises Mr. Meyer, president of the Hebrew Technical School for Girls, to urge people to contribute money on the spot, and not to rely on promises. Twain had $400 in his pocket in a Hartford church one day and wanted to give it all, but the fever of giving cooled because the plate took too long to come, and instead of giving anything he stole a dime. As for women's rights, he feels that women are always right. If women had the ballot and could therefore help make the laws, the government of the city [of New York] would be clean rather than shameful, as it is.

[Jane Lampton Clemens], Meyer.

["Voyage by Canoe"]. See LSI.

"A Wail and a Protest" (MTP).

Twain protests that, although he is only a proprietor and an editor of the Buffalo *Express,* he is frequently attacked by persons imagining themselves to be abused in its columns—even though he neither writes nor commissions the items.

Stephen Massett, Jeems Pipes.

"The Walt Whitman Controversy" (MTP).

Only one argument justifies leaving old obscene books uncensored but giving new ones the axe, and that is that the old masters aimed to mirror their times and not to sully their readers' minds. However, we should not enact laws against the alleged purpose of obscene writing but only against its probable effect; we should condemn all indecent literature, not merely recent filth. Compared to Fielding, Shakespeare, Casanova, Rabelais, Balzac, and the *Satyricon,* recent indecent items such as Swinburne, Wilde, and *Leaves of Grass* seem refined and vapid.

Editor, Oliver Stevens, Walt Whitman.

"Wanted Them Sorted Again." See FW, 1869.

"Wanted to See a Woman." From *Roughing It.*

"Wapping Alice" (MTP).

Alice is called Wapping because she comes from the Wapping district in London. She is employed as a servant to the Jackson family and lives in an annex off the main part of the house, near a laundry-room exit. A month after she starts working there, the burglar alarm at the Jackson house rings, and its wiggling metal tab shows danger in the laundry room. Jackson returns to bed, because there is nothing of value in that room. But in the morning the alarm rings again. The Negro servant George happens to explain to Wapping Alice what a burglar alarm is, and it does not ring again. When the family returns from summer vacation, Jackson learns from Mr.—that the Jackson home has been robbed. George only laughs at his employer's ensuing concern, explaining that no burglar would rob a house with an alarm. When Jackson explains that he found the front door open on his return, George rushes to check for $1,500 hidden in his mattress. It is safe. He explains that he won the sum at the races and further that he lied to Mr.—about the house being robbed. It seems that one day he returned from an outing, after leaving Wapping Alice in charge; soon thereafter he saw a strange man race past the front door. George adds that he has been investigating and has concluded from much evidence that Wapping Alice disguises herself in men's clothes and sneaks out for a drink now and then. Jackson suggests that they check the laundry-room wires. Sure enough, they are disconnected.

Jackson concludes that Wapping Alice is harboring sneak thieves; so he questions her, and she confesses that she has been hiding a young Swedish carpenter named Bjurnsen Bjuggersen Bjorgensen. Relieved that no thief has been about, Jackson forgives Wapping Alice, but she expresses the fear that Bjorgensen will not marry her now. So Jackson arranges to have the Reverend Thomas X. officiate, and orders Wapping Alice to entice the young Swede to the house and leave the rest to him. He and George arrange a festive reception. Bjorgensen arrives, and Jackson talks to the uneasy but honest-looking fellow, then suddenly accuses him of betraying poor Wapping Alice, who has befriended him. He denies everything and refuses to marry her. So Jackson threatens him with prison for unlawfully entering the laundry room, which Wapping Alice says he did. The young man blusters until Jackson tells him that a policeman is waiting on the premises even now. Bjorgensen gives in, Jackson summons Wapping Alice, and the Reverend Tom performs the rites and tells Bjorgensen to kiss his bride, which he does—but without

much taste. The ensuing banquet is interrupted when George staggers in to report that Wapping Alice is a man. She—that is, he—
accused Bjorgensen as she (he) did just for theatricality of it all.

> Alice, Major Archibald, Bjurnsen Bjuggersen Bjorgensen,
> Bridget, Dennis, Dickson, Gen'l—, George, Hubbard, the
> Reverend Joe, Mr.—, Rogers, Wapping Alice, the Reverend
> Thomas X.

"War and 'Wittles.'" See FW, 1870.

"The War Prayer," 1923 (WMT 29).
   It is a time of war. Flags flash, and volunteers march before admiring crowds. Patriotic oratory evokes applause and tears. The few
rash spirits who disapprove of the war are frowned upon severely.
Sunday comes. Next day the battalions will leave for the front. In
church, after a war chapter is read from the Old Testament, the organ
throbs and the minister offers a long prayer for victory. Suddenly, an
aged, robed, white-haired stranger ascends to the pulpit and, motion-
ing the minister to step aside, tells the congregation that he comes
from God and that He will grant both their spoken prayer and the
unspoken one, if they truly understand what they are praying for. He
tells them that they are asking God to deliver to the enemy death,
hideous wounds, and widowhood, and homelessness, hunger, rags,
bloody feet, and misery to little children—all in the name of Him
Who is the source of Love. Afterwards, the people decide that the
stranger was a lunatic, because his words were senseless.

"Warm Hair," 1888.*
A lady in Milwaukee has such red hair that she is frequently kidded
about it. She regularly shoots people now who offer stale witticisms
on the subject of red hair. But recently she heard a new one. A friend
from the East said that he liked Skaneateles hair. She asked what
Skaneateles hair might be. When he said that Skaneateles is forty
miles past Auburn, she maimed him and put him in the hospital.

   Mrs.—.

*In *Mark Twain's Library of Humor* (New York: Charles L. Webster, 1888).

"Was It Heaven? Or Hell?," 1902 (WMT 24).

In the family are four persons: Margaret Lester, a thirty-six-year-old widow; her sixteen-year-old daughter Helen; and Mrs. Lester's twin aunts; Miss Hannah Gray and Miss Hester Gray, aged sixty-seven. In spite of Mrs. Lester's grave illness, the two aunts righteously force Helen, who has just told a harmless lie, to march to her mother and confess. The patient's doctor, a rugged, leonine, former sea-faring man, affectionately called The Christian by his friends and The Only Christian by his enemies, enters the sick chamber just as Mrs. Lester is affectionately forgiving her weeping daughter with a loving embrace. The doctor quietly hurries the sanctimonious old aunts out, since their presence is making his patient worse, tells them that her disease is typhoid, then lectures them at length on their selfish habit of telling only the truth. When they insist that they could not lie even to save a friend's soul—because doing so would jeopardize their own—he scoffs, accuses them of often fibbing wordlessly, and urges them to reform by learning to tell lies. They must take turns nursing their sick niece. Moreover, young Helen has also come down with typhoid; The Christian lied when he looked at her tongue and pronounced her sound. Twelve days pass, and mother and daughter hover on the brink of death. When Mrs. Lester asks Hester how Helen is, the aunt hesitates, then says that the girl is well, which is a lie. Later, when Hannah is asked, she repeats the lie. They lie each morning and then confess their sins in prayer. They even forge little notes from the dying daughter to the dying mother, who is comforted ineffably by the loving messages. Helen grows delirious, calls for her mother, blindly embraces Hester—who addresses her as "my child"—and dies. When Mrs. Lester hears noises—those of persons making funeral arrangements—in Helen's room nearby, the aunts explain that the girl is entertaining friends and is even playing the organ for them. When the woman dies, in peace, her aunts agree that it was a blessing that she never knew of Helen's death. That night an angel visits the sorrowful aunts. They confess that if it all had to be done over again, they would be so weak as to tell the same lies once more. The angel says that he must report to heaven to learn the verdict for such sinners. He returns and whispers it to them. Was it Heaven? Or Hell?

The Christian, Mrs. Foster, Hannah Gray, Hester Gray, Higbie, Helen Lester, Mrs. Margaret Lester, Nancy, Sloane, Tilly.

"Was the World Made for Man?," 1962 (LFE).

Twain wishes to add his comments to the welter of scientific and theological remarks devoted to the subject of whether the world was made for man. Most experts believe that it was; Twain, however, thinks it likely but feels that the evidence is not yet all in. [Alfred Russell] Wallace has argued on astronomical grounds that the world was created for man and further that the universe exists for the steadying of the world. Now for some geological considerations. It evidently required 100,000,000 years or so to develop the earth but only the last 32,000 years, roughly, to evolve man. First came the invertebrates, some falling extinct along the wayside; then encrinites, stalacites, and even blatherskites, and at last in Cambrian times the mighty oyster, which probably reasoned that the whole show had been at pains to produce him. Like men, oysters are conceited. Next fish and coal had to be created, so that the one could be fried by the other, and then sandstone to store fossils in. Making coal is a sickeningly slow process. Ganoids and asteroids were left over from this development. In Paleozoic times came the reptiles and also big saurians of various sorts, including Arkansawrians. Then the intriguing pterodactyl burst upon the scene. He undoubtedly reasoned that everything to date had been staged just for him. He had the makings of birds and mammals in him. In order then came bird, kangaroo, mastodon, Irish elk, and then Ice Sheet, which chased all creatures up and down from one climate to another. Volcanoes exploded for their entertainment. At last the monkey appeared, and man had to follow soon. We have now been here 32,000 years. The fact that 100,000,000 years preceded man seems to be proof that man was the predestined end product, just as the knob on the top of the Eiffel Tower is obviously the thing for which the tower was built.

Lord Kelvin, [Sir Charles] Lyell, Herbert Spencer, [Alfred Russell] Wallace.

[Washington in 1868], 1868 (W 1868).*

["Congressional Poetry"] Twain quotes some poetry by William Mungen, a Congressman from Ohio, about his absent wife, and then criticizes its inconsistent and inaccurate imagery, and its pretentiousness. He resolves that the poem shall be amended after its third line. Congress should sail into political economy, not soar into poetry.

["Kalamazoo"] Twain goes to the Judiciary Committee to await Senator Trumbull there. Soon a breezy young fellow with a wisp of a moustache bounces in from Kalamazoo. Twain gives him the impression that he is the committee clerk, and soon Kalamazoo profanely rushes out. Later the two meet at Colfax's reception, where Kalamazoo is an enviable social success. The Capitol police must be replaced, since they cost $30,000 a year and appropriations for them have been cut to $5,000. Colorado is petitioning for statehood and may now get it since 30,000 inhabitants out there want it and only two—a disappointed office seeker and his loud brother—oppose it. Fashions are of such interest that Twain attends General Grant's reception and takes notes to report to his readers. Mrs. G. C. wears a long train and has, among other accoutrements, a plaited pony tail canted upwards by a velvet crupper hooked by a half hitch around a hairpin on her poop deck. Her complexion is rosy at the outset, but she squeezes past Twain in the crowd and leaves it on his shoulder.

["Defeat of the Impeachment Project"] Twain reports that on February 13 our beloved Impeachment died, at his lodgings in the House Reconstruction Committee. Fear came upon his physicians, and his most assiduous nurses fell asleep. Mrs. Farnsworth, Mrs. Boutwell, and a woman named "Thad" Stevens were especially anxious to keep Impeachment alive; but Mrs. Bingham, among several others, said that the doctors were troubled and wanted their patient to die. And so it came to pass.

["Senator Chandler's Party"] Knowing what it means to his readers, Twain wishes to describe as vividly as possible the dresses Senator Chandler's wife and daughter wore on the occasion earlier this week of the girl's flower-drenched coming-out party. Mrs. Chandler wore a dress a rep silk with empress waist and border of satin with beaded fringes. Miss Chandler, who is a fair brunette with golden hair, wore a chignon and silk-tunic dress. Twain confesses that he never really saw a fair brunette with yellow hair; so there must be a mistake in his writing here—owing, no doubt, to haste in composition.

["St. Valentine's Day"] Twain confesses that for the last sixty years he has watched St. Valentine's Day approach with great feeling. He regularly receives loads of dainty notes, addressed in crude, manly-looking handwriting—obviously to conceal the fact that doting women have sent them. Once again he has received ostensible advertisements from Box & Plant, undertakers; Blister & Carve, cancer eradicators; Peg & Hoop, artificial-leg manufacturers; and others, offering everything from chewing gum to tombstones. But each letter was really written by a girl secretly burning for him. Oh, here is one from Bridget, his washerwoman, telling him to pay up.

["Curious Legislation and Vinnie Ream"] When legislators seem unable to impeach the President, they deny him private secretarial help. How childish! Vinnie Ream is a shrewd politician. She has wheedled permission from Congressmen to use a room in the crowded Capitol as a studio, in which she is now daubing together an ugly statue of Abraham Lincoln. Nine territorial delegates are in need of office space, but this clever woman will not budge.

["The Illinois State Association"] Colonel Chester and his lovely daughters, from Chicago, have just held a pleasant reunion, or at home, or something of the sort. It cannot be called a reception, for such affairs are usually too funereal. Twain relished going to the Chester party. While there he met a woman from Dubuque and regarded her as practically a neighbor. Unfortunately he also met an icy old Congressman, who replied to a mild comment about the weather by saying that he was indifferent to weather at a time when his country was rapidly approaching its doom. Twain vows to gather unpleasant things about the foolish man, print them, and make him wince. Twain had a list of those present at the Illinois function, but a vile chambermaid burned it. That dead creature Impeachment has been called up like Lazarus from its sepulchre. The date of Congressional action on the matter is February 22. Congress sits at night, and the galleries are packed with breathless spectators. Behold emaciated Thaddeus Stevens; see the Speaker as he demands strict silence. It is an historic scene. Three days later, the Capitol is still jammed with crowds wanting to be on hand when the fatal vote is taken. Twain goes over to the White House, to see the Chief in his castle. Early in the evening the President looks simple and good-natured enough, like an old farmer; but fatigue conquers him at last.

["A Sleeping Lion Aroused—Gideon Rampant"] By February 26 testimonies of approval and promises of help for the embattled President are pouring into Washington. Gideon Welles is standing by with four hundred marines. The Irish offer a regiment. A Chinese from California suggests that a few hundred of his west-coast cohorts could come and "smach 'em Congress." A man named C.

Green Iceberg started to send proceedings from a mass meeting in Alaska, but a bear ate his messenger. And so on.

["Mr. Justice Field"]Twain reports that a resolution passed the House a few days ago to consider impeaching U.S. Supreme Court Judge Stephen Field, because rumor had it that he had said Reconstruction acts would be ruled unconstitutional. The rumor was false. Dignified old men do not gossip about official business.

> Bangs, Mrs. Beaman, Beauregard, Mrs. Bingham, Blister, Mrs. Boutwell, Box, Bridget, Mrs. Brooks, Mrs. G. C., Carve, Senator [Zechariah] Chandler, Mrs. [Zechariah] Chandler, Miss Chandler, Colonel Chester, Miss Chester, Speaker [Schuyler Colfax], Colfax, Congressman, Congressman, Garret Davis, Mrs. Farnsworth, Judge Stephen [J.] Field, Governor [John W.] Geary, General [Ulysses S.] Grant, Hong Wo See Yup, Hoop, Mrs. Hulburd, C. Green Iceberg, Congressman from Illinois, Representative from Illinois, Impeachment, John, President [Andrew Johnson], Kalamazoo, Hans Von Kraut, General Logan, Senator from Michigan, Senator from Michigan, Honorable William Mungen, Mrs. William Mungen, [Richard J.] Oglesby, Mrs. Paine, Peg, Perkins, Plant, Pub. Func., Vinnie Ream, Secretary, John Smi[th], [Edwin M.] Stanton, Thaddeus Stevens, Mrs. Thad Stevens, George Francis Train, Senator [Lyman] Trumbull, Gideon Welles, Weston.

*Edited by Cyril Clemens (Webster Groves, Missouri: International Mark Twain Society, 1943). The titles of individual items in this book are not listed in my Chronology above but are interspersed through this alphabetized sequence of summaries for reference.

"Washoe: Information Wanted" (WG). See "Information for the Million."

"A Washoe Joke," 1862 (MTWY).

A petrified man was recently found near Humboldt City. Preservation is perfect. He is seated against a wall of stone, right thumb against side of nose, left thumb supporting chin, left forefinger pulling left eye partly open, right eye closed, fingers of right hand spread.

Judge Sewell comes out to hold an inquest. Verdict: death by exposure. Some men want to bury him; but, since he has been glued to the wall by limestone trickles down his back and dynamite would be required, the judge refuses permission. Three hundred people have visited him in the past six weeks.

Judge Sewell.

"Washoe Wit." See "Concerning Notaries."

'Water Supply,' 1901 (S).

Twain thanks the Albany legislators for their hospitality and then says that if he were allowed to offer a suggestion it would be for them not to worry about the measure which is to supply the citizens of New York City with water. Twain lives there and knows. People do not drink water there.

"Watterson and Twain as Rebels,' 1901 (S).

Twain is happy to introduce the speaker Colonel Henry Watterson in celebration of Abraham Lincoln's birthday anniversary. Watterson is well known as a versatile former rebel. Twain was also a rebel soldier and had a plan—fortunately ignored, and the Union was saved—to drive General Grant into the ocean. Northerners and Southerners alike fought for what they thought was right, but it is good that the Union has been preserved. Lincoln is the greatest American after Washington.

[John Marshall Clemens], General [Ulysses S.] Grant, Abraham Lincoln, Colonel Henry Watterson.

'The Weather,' c. 1910 (WMT 28).

God made everything but New England weather. It is made by apprentices in the weather factory who experiment, perfect their techniques, and then go to work elsewhere. Spring is the season for especially varied weather in New England. Weather prophets are timid in New England and suggest, for example, that the wind on a given day will probably be northeast to southwest and also varying. You can be sure of one thing: there is so much New England weather that it sticks out and influences other regions. Its lightning is potent, and its thunder terrifies visitors. It produces the bewitching autumn foliage, and also the miraculously beautiful ice coats on wintry trees.

Old Probabilities.

A Weaver's Beam—or Handle of a Hoe—(unpublished poem).*

This was once like a hoe handle but is now doughy, and its former master laments at night the change.

*Original in the Collection of American Literature, Beinecke Rare Book and Manuscript Library, Yale University, New Haven, Connecticut.

'Welcome Home,' 1889 (WMT 28).

Twain greets a baseball team returning home from a world tour by way of Hawaii. He says that there is something incongruous about the Sandwich Islands and baseball. The one is a constant sleepy Sabbath, the other all nineteenth-century energy and rush. In Hawaii they do everything wrong, from getting off horses to milking cows and recovering from having babies. That is why everyone there is left-handed and cross-eyed. Natives wear few clothes and feel overdressed if they simply smile. Their language is soft and liquid, most unsatisfactory to swear with. Everyone is educated; yet out there the ten takes the ace. What a bewitching land it is. Twain can still smell the breath of Hawaiian flowers which perished twenty years ago. One who dies there goes from paradise to paradise. Yet we should not envy men who played baseball there, because their run around the world was earned. Before the baseball tour, travelers could not see the equator. Now it is a line around the globe plowed by fellows stealing bases on their bellies.

'Welcome Home,' 1900 (WMT 28).

Twain begins by thanking everyone for the compliments, which a mere Missourian does not deserve. Yet, Twain notes, there are several good Missourians here at the Lotos Club tonight. Whether the kind words for him are deserved or not, he is grateful. Ninety-five of the ninety-six creditors of the bankrupt firm of Charles L. Webster & Co. treated Twain beautifully, told him not to worry, not to hurry. They were so considerate that he is almost sorry to be out of debt again. America has done many things since Twain left:

it nobly freed Cuba; it started to free the poor Filipino, but the righteous purpose soured; it performed creditably in China, though we must watch out for the Yellow Terror; it worried the President and popularized the office of the Vice President by putting Roosevelt in it. Rough Riders are now so popular that Twain would like to be one, by automobile, however, not unreliable.horse. The only Mugwump left is Twain himself. The Daughters of the Royal Crown are positively insane. Well, Twain is glad to be back. When he left the country seven years before, he was old and despondent. Now he is young and ready for life again.

> Daughters of the Royal Crown, Senator Chauncey [M.] Depew, Hendrix, [St. Clair] McKelway, President [William McKinley], Odell, Tom Reed, Vice President [Theodore] Roosevelt, Charles L. Webster.

"The Whaling Trade." See *Letters from Honolulu.*

["What Cheer Robbery"], 1865 (MTWY).

Twain is critical of Smythe, the *Alta* reporter who is blaming every crime, including the recent robbery of the What Cheer boardinghouse (where Twain hints that Smythe himself resides), on that unknown villain—"The Mysterious"—who slugged Myers, robbed his father's pawnshop, robbed the mayor's clerk, and half-murdered a detective named Rose near Santa Clara. At this rate, Smythe, who wants to be a detective himself, will solve all crimes by irrationally naming some one fellow as the some perpetrator.

> The Clerk, the Mayor, Myers, Myers, "The Mysterious," [George] Rose, Smythe.

"What Have the Police Been Doing?," 1866 (WG).

The San Francisco police take good care of the city, by arresting Chinese chicken thieves, leaning on lamp posts, keeping their hands soft, caving in the head of a suspected robber, and doing duty as nurses for their own captain when he broke a leg. Why must everyone criticize the police? They will get their reward hereafter—no doubt.

> Chief, Captain Lees, Dr. Rowell, Shields, Supervisor, Ward, Ziele.

"What He Really Said." See FW, 1869.

"What I Don't Know of Farming." See FW, 1870.

What Is Man?, 1906 (WMT 26).

By means of questions and answers, the Old Man begins to persuade the Young Man that man is nothing but a machine without control over his traits. True, Shakespeare was a Gobelin loom compared to whom most people are mere sewing machines or engines made of rocks. The Old Man argues that everything we do is motivated by our desire to secure our own peace of mind and spiritual comfort.

Acts of charity, violence, patriotism, and parental love, to cite a few varied examples, are all undertaken for our own approval. We are sorry that we have inflicted pain upon others only when the memory of the act gives us pain.

To demonstrate that self-approval is behind all action, consider the case of the Adirondack lumberman who neglects father, young sister, and schoolboy brother, in order to preach Christ's gospel, on a gamble that he might convert otherwise lost souls. He does all of this not for Christ's sake but for the approval of self and fellow gospelers. When the Young Man suggests that tipping is an unselfish act, the Old Man quickly persuades him that we tip to get good service, that when we tip too little we are made to feel uncomfortable, and that when we tip too much we scold ourselves. The two discuss the *Berkeley Castle*, a ship loaded with women and children and a thousand soldiers. When the ship sank, there was room in the lifeboats only for the women and children, and so the soldiers drowned without a murmur. The Old Man ascribes their supposed self-sacrifice to training and a reluctance to face the pain of any alternative to so-called duty.

The Old Man lectures his young friend on the subject of training, by which he means study, instruction, lectures, sermons, and much more, in fact all outside influences. A person is predictably trained by the environment into which he happens to be born, but unique accidents of fate may change him suddenly and profoundly. People get their perceptions of good and evil from outside, as well. The Young Man asks why he scolds his servant when he has been trying for years to control his temper. The Old Man explains that there are two pleasures, primary and secondary. When his young friend scolds his servant, he is yielding to a whim which gives him momentary pleasure, but then he repents because learning to control his temper yields him secondary and longer-lasting pleasure. The Young Man wonders if he will ever be perfect in controlling his temper, to which the Old Man says that he will reform only up to his limit. This introduces the topic of temperament, which is as significant as training. Temperament is the disposition one is born with, which one can put pressure on but never fully control. The Old Man admonishes the younger one to train his ideals upward so that he will have more self-approval. This is an old gospel, but its phrasing here is uniquely candid. Live a charitable and decent life, but do not misunderstand your motives; do not be like the ordinary man who is generous but pretends that he is a duke being generous. Best of all is so living that, while contenting yourself, you do good to your neighbors and your community. A good man does not succumb to temptation right away but only at the end of a series of trials, just as gold is not melted by a few blasts of steam but may be crumbled by repeated blasts of steam and vaporized quicksilver.

Man the machine cannot even control his own mind, which works diligently day and night in spite of his orders to it to stop. It thinks its own thoughts, mulls tiresomely over completed chess games, hums old ditties like "I saw Esau kissing Kate,/And she saw I saw Esau...," and dreams uncontrollably. A person can tell himself to read a certain dull book and ignore a nearby pleasant one or a pretty picture, but the mind does as it pleases. Trains of thoughts are likewise capricious. Inventors and poets are no more responsible for their work than is the rat, which incidentally is relatively more moral than man. Everything follows combinations of chance influences and instincts. The Old Man confesses that he is no longer a truth-seeker; in fact, nobody seeks truth after he—mistakenly—thinks that he has found it.

Part of the next lesson ends with the Young Man obliged to admit that there is no essential difference between the intellect of man and that of cows, chickens, and ants. Instinct is petrified thought; and when non-human creatures are confronted with unusual circumstances, they do not fall back on unsatisfactory instinct but reason matters out and then act. Ant hills are relatively superior architecturally to any domestic construction by a savage race. We cannot learn animal talk, but some animals can be trained to understand human talk. Surely this is an indication of superiority in animals, which also are superior to men in not having the moral sense. We do not have free will; instead, our minds freely tell us which of two options is the better choice, but our choices are predetermined. Cowards knew that it would be better to go out and kill Goliath; but only David, who also knew, did it. All covetousness is ultimately spiritual, never material, because things are coveted to satisfy the master within us. What is the I which is the master of the whole person I am? Is it physical, mental, spiritual? Perhaps the I is the soul. But no one knows what the soul is. The conscience is a mysterious, colorless autocrat within one, compelling him to satisfy the master passion driving him to self-approval. At their final meeting a few days later, the Young Man says that he thinks the Old Man has been tempted to assemble, write up, and publish his doctrines but that outside influences have not yet determined that he will do so. The Old Man agrees. The Young Man concludes that his mentor's philosophy is desolate and degrading, since it robs man of glory, pride, heroism, and so on, and converts him into a mere coffee mill which neither provides the coffee to be ground nor responsibly turns the crank doing the grinding. The Old Man agrees and then says that traits, for example, holiness and heroism, which we admire in another person he was in reality born with, and that God is therefore the author and deserves the praise. When the Young Man feels that such a philosophy should make its believer wretched, the Old Man says that he is never sad, because it is his inborn temperament to be cheerful, that his depressing convictions cannot alter that temperament, that two temperamentally different people can go through precisely the same experiences and remain true to their respective temperaments. So with whole nations, which eternally feel and do not think. So with mankind, which is constantly cheerful. Therefore the Old Man's philosophy, if published, would alter nothing.

> Henry Adams, Burgess, [Benjamin] Franklin, George, Henry, Holme, Holme, Holme, Miss Holme, the Infidel, Jane, Sir John Lubbock, the Old Man, Sally, the Young Man.

"What Ought He to Have Done?" See "On Training Children."

"What Paul Bourget Thinks of Us," 1895 (WMT 22).

The author takes an interest in Paul Bourget's comments on Americans but questions the critic's qualifications to teach 70,000,000 people spread over a vast land. His training is French and his method that of a naturalist observing bugs. A naturalist cannot teach a bug new ways which it will prefer to its own. The French can tell Americans nothing about transportation, the postal service, journalism, government, religion, or novel-writing. Perhaps deportment? But Bourget failed in that regard at Newport. The only way to learn what a group of people is like is to live among them for years and absorb their ways. Novelists know this. Bourget wrongly fancied that he could learn about the American soul by observing Newport showiness briefly. No human characteristic can be safely called "American." When Bourget imagined that he had understood the American type of coquette, he was simply the victim of rather cruel practical jokers. When he revealed that he was taking notes about Americans, they resented his intention to ridicule. The only thing distinctly American is fondness for ice water. Love of money is certainly not uniquely American although opportunities for quick profit are more frequently found in America than elsewhere. An example of ineffective analysis by Bourget is his conclusion that married American women are seldom pursued by seducers because of Puritanism and the ease of obtaining divorces in America. The real reason, of course, is that American marriages usually have a love basis rather than a commercial one. Next comes an objection to Bourget's statement that he does not believe in anecdotes but rather in statistics: his conclusions about coquettes were based on anecdotal jokes perpetrated on him, and his conclusions based on divorce statistics are in error. The essay ends in praise of Bourget for using a grandfather joke. But the present author used a similar chestnut against Napoleon. When Napoleon said to the present author that a bored American can always while away some time by trying to find out who his grandfather is, the author replied that a Frenchman can always improve his idle hours by trying to find out who his father is. Bourget should have read some American novels before coming over.

Paul Bourget, Giordano Bruno, Bret Harte, Napoleon, [Mark Twain].

"When I Was a Secretary." See "Facts Concerning the Late Senatorial Secretaryship."

'When in Doubt, Tell the Truth,' 1906 (WMT 28).
Twain did invent the motto about telling the truth when in doubt, but he meant it as advice for others. When he is in doubt, he uses

sagacity. Mr. Putzel is related to Twain through the tax office. Twenty-five years ago Twain went to Putnam's bookstore, saw Putzel clerking there, and picked up a $4 book on fourteenth-century friars in England that he wanted. To be funny, he asked the clerk for a 40% discount as a publisher, 40% more as an author, 20% as a ministerial student, and 10% as a member of the human race. Putzel soberly allowed it all, and gave Twain the book with a bonus of 40¢. Years later Twain met Putzel working in the New York tax office, swore to a certain statement there, and was touched by the man's tears. Putzel sensed that after a brief immersion in New York morals Twain had no more conscience left than a millionaire.

Grout, Judge Leventritt, George Haven Putnam, Putzel.

["Whenever I am about to publish a book"] (MTP).

Twain explains that just before publishing a book, he grows curious to know what kind of work it is. So he does two things: he reads it to a group of friends of varied personalities, and they tell him; and he waits for the professional reviewers to inform him definitively.

"Whereas (Love's Bakery)." See "Aurelia's Unfortunate Young Man."

"Whereas, or Love's Bakery." (SS). See "Aurelia's Unfortunate Young Man."

Which Was It?, 1967 (WWD).

Alison Harrison explains that she has been married eight years, is now twenty-six, and adores her thirty-three-year-old husband George Louisiana Purchase Harrison and her daughters Alison, a blonde aged six, and Margery, a brunette aged five. George has repeatedly promised to write his autobiography; but only tonight, the night of little Alison's birthday party, has he started—because his girls have asked. Later—the party is almost finished. Alison goes to the study and sees her husband struggling and nodding over his manuscript. Soon the party will be breaking up.

It is now fifteen years later. George Harrison takes up the narrative. That fatal night of the birthday party the mansion caught on fire, burned his wife and daughters to death, and also Harry, one of the Osgood twins. Only his little son Tom was left to George, who decides now to tell the story of his wretched later years, and to write it in the third person because of shame.

Indiantown is a sleepy village in corn-growing country. Andrew Independence Harrison, his forty-eight-year-old son George, and George's twenty-two-year-old son Tom—a lawyer who works under attorney Gilbert—live in a house by the Harrison mill near Jake Bleeker's little place and have done so ever since the big Harrison mansion burned. Old Squire Fairfax, Andrew's quality friend, died five years after the fire and left his extensive estate to his high-tempered son Squire Walter Fairfax, a seemingly conceited Virginia college graduate who became the devoted and reformed husband of a charming Virginia bride. She bore him a daughter named Helen, became an invalid, and later died. Well, on Saturday, November 3, Fairfax summons old Andrew, tells him that the $4,000 he paid Fairfax for the note on his mill was counterfeit money, and that he must make out a new note under threat of exposure. If Andrew dies, then his son George must pay. If Fairfax dies, then his daughter will hold the note. Andrew sullenly agrees. Later Bridget Bleeker, the mill hand's Irish wife, enters, demands her wages as Helen's sewing helper, and quits because Fairfax has described her hot-tempered but ineffectual husband Jake as a sentimental German jackass. Putting the counterfeit money in a drawer, Fairfax absently pays the woman, and she goes home to argue with befuddled Jake. Meanwhile, Andrew reluctantly admits to his gentle son George that the money was indeed counterfeit, then adds that Fairfax was threatening and abusive, and that George must never speak to him again until the debt is settled. Not comprehending, George nevertheless promises. Alone, the sad man is trying to puzzle it all out when young Dug Hapgood enters, bringing snowflakes and gossip with him. Dug is a deaf handyman and quickly explains in great shouts that Andrew sent his new note to Fairfax by a Negro whom Dug intercepted. Dug then delivered the note himself, first mastering all its details. George is distressed because Dug, an inveterate gossip, will spread the whole story all around Indiantown. Dug reveals that Fairfax has taken to solitary drinking again and further that George's son Tom has returned from an errand to New Orleans for his employer. What the two men do not know is that Tom is secretly engaged to Fairfax's daughter Helen.

Still on November 3, Miss Fairfax's maid Emly tells Liza, the aged Negro servant of the family, that her mistress must be sick, since she is dressing so carefully. Liza flies to comfort the girl and hears a happy whispered secret. Tom enters, and he and Helen embrace fondly. The handsome young man reveals that it will be announced a couple of days hence in court that he is going to be Gilbert's partner. He must not publicly release the good news yet, nor should Helen. They can be theatrical about it all later. Tom has already heard the town gossip that his grandfather Andrew's note to Helen's father was questioned and that a new mortgage has been executed with the mill as security. But that will all be cleared up soon, Tom hopes. Then Fairfax enters, learns that Tom and Helen are engaged, hands the young man the canceled note on Andrew's mill, and asks him to tell his grandfather to come see him since he has something for him— meaning the bogus money. But Tom is too happy to be able to hear the entire message. When he gets home, his father George rejoices to see him again but soon breaks down, lectures vaguely on the subject of honor, says that Fairfax has a new note payable at a day's notice, and adds that he wants to see Andrew. Tom says that Fairfax told him he wanted to see Andrew and is tempted to produce the canceled note but wants to be theatrical and delay until all of his revelations can make an enormous impression at one time. That night he hears George pacing restlessly, tardily decides to tell him the good news at once, but by the time he gets up his father has evidently retired. So he lays the papers by George's plate at breakfast, but in the morning Martha the Negro cook moves them. That afternoon some workers dare Jake to insult Fairfax, who is riding by. The German rushes up to him but gets a cowhiding for his pains and vows dire revenge. Andrew returns to his son George and tells him that Fairfax must be intending to call in the note, take the mill, and expose him for trying to pay with counterfeit money. By evening, George, laughing at his sudden absence of honor, has decided to burn the mill, collect the insurance, and pay back the note.

George sneaks off to the mill under cover of darkness, but shortly after he arrives he hears footsteps. Hiding, he eavesdrops as Jake and Bridget enter for their routine evening inspection but also talk about revenge against Fairfax. Jake wants to burn the man's mansion. But Bridget prefers to have him rob the rich squire, who, she says, has bundles of dollars in his desk drawer in the downstairs study. Jake agrees. Commenting on the general rottenness of the world, George quietly returns to his home to muse in front of the sputtering fire. He decides to rob Fairfax at once, instead of burning the mill for insurance. Meanwhile, Tom is back visiting Helen. He tells Fairfax that he delivered the message to Andrew, through George. When Fairfax wonders why Andrew has not therefore come for what he wants to give him, Tom admits that he said only that Fairfax wanted to see the old man. Fairfax admits that Helen was a distraction to the young man, who leaves—just as his masked father enters downstairs to rifle the study desk. But Jake now enters for the same purpose, and George takes Fairfax's stout cane, which is handy, clubs the German viciously with it, and rushes home ahead of sauntering Tom. When George gets there, he quickly sees both that the money he stole has been labeled counterfeit by Fairfax and also that the canceled note from Fairfax is on the mantel. He burns the bogus money and falls into terrible anguish, which is made worse when Tom comes in and confesses that he would have told his father the whole story, including news of his engagement, but for wanting to be theatrical in a day or so. Dug now bursts in with the news that someone has killed Jake at the Fairfax mansion. Tom flies to Helen's side. Demented Andrew enters and mutters insanely that after supper he forced Fairfax to cancel the note and return the counterfeit money under threat of death. George speaks gently to the old man and gets him off to bed. Dug returns later with fresh news: Fairfax is in jail for murder, Bridget organized a lynching party, Tom got knocked down by a flying brick but will recover at the Widow Wilkinson's house now that he is being cared for by Helen and her servants Liza and Emly, someone in the mob shot and killed Doc Stevens the kindly old town physician, and the inquest is set for eight in the morning. George bitterly lectures himself on the disastrous fruits of false pride.

For a few hours, George is drugged by troubled sleep, then awakens to grim reality again. He wonders what happened to his mask, now missing. Bowles the tavern keeper is happy to give him a ride to the inquest, where he sees Jake's gory corpse and hears the verdict go against Fairfax. George returns home by way of the Wilkinson place, where Helen greets him gently but pierces his conscience by begging him to find the real murderer so that she can stare at the villain pitilessly. George talks with his injured son Tom briefly, then begs leave to go, saying that he does not want to describe the depressing inquest but does wish to go comfort Fairfax. Friends standing about understand and applaud. George tells Fairfax in jail that he must be cleared. The accused man says that he heard Jake yell, evidently at another intruder, "You godless villain!" (George knows that the man really shouted *"Um Gottes willen!"*) Fairfax asks George to find a stranger in town whose language is educated, even Shakespearean, then beseeches him to go to his study, take the big roll of money from the desk, and give it unexamined to old Andrew. But George feels obliged to reveal that the official inventory of the murder room listed no such money. Fairfax immediately surmises that the literary murderer collared it. Suddenly deaf Dug bursts into the jail and confidentially yells that George's father, knowing that he is dying, has quietly sent for the district attorney Randall and his clerk to take down a statement.

At the Harrison home mourners softly come and go, pitying George the noble son. The old man dies. Two days later all three funerals are held, for Jake, Dr. Stevens, and Andrew. After the parades and the graveside services, George remains at his family plot, musing bitterly. His old friend Frances Osgood comes up to comfort him by saying that the loss of her lovely son Henry, whose twin Allen is idle and alcoholic, has been uniquely sad; but George counters with the remark that he is glad mourners cannot recall their sacred dead back to life. He leaves, and Frances silently admits the truth of his remark but wonders how he could have come to such wisdom without suffering more than he has. That night George sits tussling with his lacerated conscience as Dug enters to gossip. Deathshead Phillips, who once dressed in a sheet and dough face to scare his fiancée but frightened her into permanent insanity, glides in and stands behind Dug's chair—a sure indication that the fellow will die soon. Meanwhile Dug reports that Gilbert the lawyer just got a letter asserting that George's rich Memphis uncle died and left his nephew wealthy. Such news only makes him more miserable.

In the morning came sympathetic visitors, including erect old General Landry, Gilbert, the Presbyterian minister Swinton Bailey, and Sol Bailey, his useless, supercilious, intermittently canny failure of a younger brother, also called Hamfat and the Idiot Philosopher. Landry praises dead Andrew. Gilbert tells bewildered George that his Memphis inheritance includes $45,000 in ready cash. When the minister reveals that Andrew once confessed that he had committed an undiscovered crime in youth and caused an innocent man to die of misery, George falls to the floor and must be cared for by several women, including the widow Bridget, whose dead husband's wages he pledges to pay her in triple measure for life. Dr. Bradshaw enters, bleeds his patient, and prescribes some medicine so awful that Dug, who has just entered to cheer George by yelling that Deathshead's visit bodes ill for the sick, gulps it instead and soon writhes in temporary pain. The humor of it all revives George, who invites Dug and Sol to remain for supper. George feels almost happy again, especially when Helen comes by to report that Tom is feeling better. When the two are alone, Sol pries out of his host the fact that the rich, dead uncle in Memphis had a housekeeper named Mrs. Milliken, who had a little boy. In the night, George's sleep is disturbed by nagging worries again, and the uneasy man is visited by Deathshead once more. Meanwhile, at the local ice-cream parlor Sol looks up Allen Osgood, whose fiancée Asphyxia Perry's parents are resentful of the young fellow's idleness, and rather quickly persuades him to join forces and go to Memphis to encourage Mrs. Milliken to sue for the Harrison estate as the rich dead man's wife and rightful heir. Sol's clinching argument is that all human motives are selfish. Late that night, as the two step into a black night of raging snow, a dark mulatto named Jasper, who is Fairfax's gardener, skulks into the establishment, moves about with silent familiarity, and soon is in deep talk with the cowering owner, Templeton Gunning, whom he orders to explain to the authorities if told to that as he was returning from a catering assignment on the night of Jake's murder he passed behind the Fairfax mansion, heard a scream, saw a man whom he recognized rush past, then saw Jasper run out, chased and caught the first man, but was tempted by him to keep silent through a promise of money. Now his conscience obliges him to tell all. Jasper leaves, and Templeton hurls a silent curse after him into the night. The huge mulatto is soon caught, jailed for not having his freedom papers, mercilessly lashed at dawn, then released, all of which prompts hideous maledictions against the entire white race.

At eight the next morning, Templeton is still in bed, pale and sad with thought. His mother Charlotte Gunning enters, pets him, tells him that she heard everything Jasper said the night before, and then decides to disburden herself of her long-held secrets. In great detail she explains that she was Mrs. Milliken, dead Harrison's abused housekeeper near Memphis, and that Jasper was the vicious man's slave, bought his freedom, lost his papers in a fire, and was forced to work himself free again. While doing so, he generously loaned his friend "Mrs. Milliken" $300 to start a business in Memphis. The business was an elaborate mail fraud that ultimately backfired in part. Becoming greedy, she—as Miss Lucy Wallace—amassed $20,000, decided against repaying Jasper, was robbed of much of her loot, escaped with less than $6,000, and was after seven years located by Jasper, who had been jailed for alleged conspiracy with her, had then at last earned his liberty, and is now systematically blackmailing Mrs. Gunning. She and her son, whose real name—she now reveals—is Templeton Ashes, have been in Indiantown only a short while and may soon have to move on again, since Jasper though legally free is periodically threatened by men who would like to sell him back into servitude.

Ten days poke along, and a thaw comes. Tom is better, then worse again. George visits him and also looks in on Fairfax, still in jail. George feels periodically easier and is given a tremendous boost when Sol Bailey comes calling one day, as he frequently does, and professes to be such a firm friend that George is so grateful that Sol forgets his scheme with Allen, now down in Memphis, to ruin George and instead vows to champion him against the dead uncle's alleged widow. George puts Sol on salary to shield him from that fictitious woman's machinations. Back home with his wife Ann, Sol reveals his scheme. At first she rebukes him; but when he tells her about his salary and the possibilities of future financial security, she joins him in his dreams. Soon, tardily worrying about Allen's incompetence, they decide to consult Charlotte Gunning, who not only helps manage the ice-cream parlor but is currently enjoying a local success as a spiritualist. She can give the Baileys the name of a better aide than Allen. But a letter comes from Allen explaining that he has learned that Mrs. Milliken, alias Lucy Wallace, is now wanted by the law for fraud. Allen has gained the confidence of Simon Bunker, the Memphis post-office clerk who innocently collected her mail, and that bitter, untrustworthy man, who is now county clerk, has agreed to cooperate for a share of the proceeds. Ann Bailey is alarmed at this turn of events and repeats her fixed opinion that Allen is a half-done doughnut.

Meanwhile, in Memphis, Simon Bunker is pumping callow Allen for information about Sol and George, and concludes that both are only temporary little obstacles in his path to the money. So he inserts an enigmatic advertisement in the newspaper which he hopes will be reprinted and will lure Lucy Wallace out of hiding. Back at the séance, Mrs. Gunning goes into her customary trance; her son Templeton then takes messages from Sol and Ann, relays them to his mother in Chinese, and receives replies—from Confucius through her—which he translates. Confucius suggests that a reliable confederate for the Baileys would be Templeton. Financial terms can easily be arranged. Sol and Ann are thrilled. Sol reports to George, who has been comforted spiritually by Swinton Bailey. But Sol undoes all that good by lecturing so mightily on man's selfishness and ruinous moral sense that George begins to snore.

A letter from Sol lowering their percentages reaches Allen and Bunker in Memphis. Chuckling to himself, shrewd Bunker persuades Allen to agree to accept the worse rates, also to believe that Sol plans to bilk the lost widow secretly and then share everything with George, and finally to send to Sol for an assistant—since Sol is probably planning to dispatch a man to spy on them anyway. Allen writes Sol as directed. When Allen returns to his room in a Memphis tavern, he finds Templeton already there. The following evening, the two report to Bunker, who indirectly persuades Templeton to volunteer to follow the trail of Mrs. Milliken and gives him the newspaper advertisement which may produce a reply leading to her location. Templeton gloats about all of this in a letter to his mother back in Indiantown. Bunker, with Allen as his unsuspecting assistant, is now free to produce dead Harrison's "widow." Bunker obtains from Floyd Parker, a postal worker, some old letters written by the late Harrison and forges a couple of new letters from him in his handwriting to his brother Andrew. The fake letters are dry and dutiful except where they say that Mrs. Milliken is really Harrison's wife, who is unwanted and not to be acknowledged, and whom in a temper he branded and turned out, along with their son. Parker, whom Bunker has taken into his confidence, now puts Templeton— to get him out of the way—on the trail of one Sally Archer, who left Memphis, stopped at various places, and finally died in a New York pest house. Parker's next assignment is to proceed disguised to Indiantown to snoop around.

A week passes. One day Ann goes slumming among the poor, returns home happy, but finds Sol steeped in grief, cast down by letters from Memphis reporting no progress. She quickly brightens him up by explaining that so long as he is on salary with George it does not matter if the uncle's alleged widow is never found. Sol happily goes to cheer up George, who after his first visitor leaves has another. He is Jasper. The two talk, and George treats him to some typical white-supremacist language until Jasper stops him. The huge mulatto coolly explains that on the night of the murder he heard Jake scream, saw the murderer rush out, and has blackmailed a white witness—

whose testimony would be legal—to stand ready so to testify. He now produces the initialed, bloodstained, missing handkerchief which George used as his mask! George wilts. He soon writes out papers— one making Jasper his nominal servant and the other confessing to the murder—and agrees to support Jasper for the rest of his life, paying him $10 a week to start, and even to play the part of his slave when the two are alone. Revealing at this time that the late Harrison of Memphis was his father, Jasper vows to use his present power without pity and then leaves to deposit his deadly evidence with his white witness. In the morning Jasper returns with his possessions, begins to flirt with old Martha, and insists on serving Marse Hahson a steaming breakfast, which behind locked doors he himself eats while the quaking white man acts as servant. Dug roars up, reports the presence of a gifted, fortune-telling stranger (Parker) in town, and suggests that George hire him to ferret out the facts of Jake's murder. Dug soon leaves to spread word of Jasper's redemption and happy employment, and soon crowds of townspeople flock in to commend kindly George. Jasper stores up their flattery and later turns it sarcastically against his victim.

Sally Archer, Templeton Ashes, Charley Axtell, Mrs. Ann Bailey, Sol Bailey, Mrs. Sol Bailey, Rev. Mr. Swinton Bailey, Mrs. Swinton Bailey, Bailey, Mrs. Batterson, Ben, Billy, Mrs. Bridget Bleeker, Jake Bleeker, Bowles, Dr. Bradshaw, Simon Bunker, Agnes Burley, Catlin, Ben Chapman, Confucius, Emly, Evans, Helen Fairfax, Squire Walter Fairfax, Mrs. Walter Fairfax, Squire Fairfax, Billy Fletcher, Miss Fox, Miss Fox, Hank Frisbee, Sally Furniss, Jim Gatewood, Gilbert, the Governor, Mrs. Charlotte Gunning, Templeton Gunning, Dug Hapgood, Mrs. Alison Harrison, Alison Harrison, Andrew Independence Harrison, George Louisiana Purchase Harrison, Margery Harrison, Tom Harrison, Harrison, Rube Haskins, Burt Higgins, Hodgson, Holme, Holme, Holme, Miss Holme, Mrs. Hopkins, Jasper, General Landry, Liza, Martha, Allen Osgood, Mrs. Frances Osgood, Harry Osgood, Osgood, Floyd Parker, Parker, Asphyxia Perry, Solar Plexus Perry, Perry, Mrs. Perry, Perry, Sidney Phillips, Randall, Mahaly Robinson, Park Robinson, Dr. Stevens, Mrs. Stevens, Miss Stevens, Buck Thompson, Ben Thurlow, Tom, Joseph B. Wallace, Wallace, the Widow Wilkinson.

"Which Was the Dream?," 1966 (WWD).

Mrs. Alison (Alice) Sedgewick X. writes in her diary for March 1, 1854, that it is going to be a busy day. Tom, her husband, and some others are rehearsing a play composed by their young daughter Bessie. He has also promised to write a sketch of his life in honor of the girl's birthday. Alice later sees him in his study nodding over the chore.

Major General Thomas X. now explains that he was born in Pawpaw Corners, Kentucky, in 1820. Alice was born there in 1826. When he was eleven and she was five, they first met, shared an apple, became engaged, and sealed the event with a kiss. In 1841 he graduated from West Point. In 1845 he and Alice were married. Bessie was born a year later, and soon thereafter Alice's father died and then coal was discovered on his land. The X. family became wealthy. Next Lieutenant X. left for the Mexican War, fought bravely, and rose like a meteor to the rank of general—the youngest in the army. He became a senator, and the family moved to Washington. Jessie was born in 1849. Bessie is thoughtful, haunted by dreams, intense, considerate, inquisitive, and truth-loving. Jessie is stoical and adventurous.

A great number of glittering guests have come to the first dress rehearsal of Bessie's play. Suddenly a shriek rings out. The house is on fire. A young West Pointer name Grant happens to be at the party and skillfully marshalls the crowd to safety. The X. family moves into a hotel. Tom notices that Jeff Sedgewick is missing. Jeff is his wife's cousin and has been handling all of Tom's financial matters, in spite of Alice's pleas that he be dismissed as untrustworthy. Tom is telling another of his interminable fairy tales to his daughters when the marine band considerately comes by and serenades him at the window. He goes out and makes a mechanical speech. Then Simmons, one of his bankers, enters with the dire news that Tom is dangerously overdrawn at the bank and also at other banks. Next day after a little work Tom returns to the hotel and makes extravagant plans for rebuilding his house. Then, a couple of days later, Simmons and three other bankers call on him with the stunning news that he is completely ruined and further that his house insurance was never renewed. Tom blames Jeff and is obliged to explain that Jeff had his power of attorney and even his permission to execute documents in exact imitation of his hand. Of course the bankers cannot believe that a general and a senator would be a party to such irregularities. One of them adds that Jeff was last seen leaving the country. They accuse Tom of swindling. When one goes so far as to call him a forger, he springs at the man and then loses consciousness.

When Tom comes to, he is lying in a homemade bed in a rude log cabin. He hears the voice of Jake, his devoted Negro servant. Tom looks about in sleepy bewilderment. Everything is neat, clean, and cheap. He is wearing blue jeans and an old army shirt. Bessie timidly looks in. When he recognizes her, she jumps forward for a kiss and then brings Jessie. He learns from them that they are at Hell's Delight, California. They tell him that his new name is Edward Jacobs. Bessie is nine and a half! He has been asleep for eighteen months. Alice enters. By the clock Tom has been separated from her for only an hour but in the true sense for a year and a half. She explains that their friends in Washington were very understanding. She got work as a copyist. Jake and his sister Maria refused to leave, and Jake earned money which kept the X. family alive. The newspapers treated Tom decently, and so did the bankers. Army men believed his story, feeling that a West Pointer might be a commercial fool but never a lying rascal.

> [Thomas H.] Benton, [Henry] Clay, Collins, Billy Dent, Judge Dent, Fulton, Lieutenant Grant, Jake, Jimmy, Johnny, the Governor of Kentucky, Maria, President [Franklin] Pierce, Riggs, General [Winfield] Scott, Jeff Sedgewick, Sedgewick, Simmons, General [Zachary] Taylor, Senator Walker, Mrs. Walker, [Daniel] Webster, Mrs. Alison Sedgewick X., Bessie X., Jessie X., Major General and Senator Thomas X., Mrs. X.

"'White Man Mighty Onsartain.'" See *Mark Twain's San Francisco.*

"Wicked Mark Twain," 1867 (SS).

It is sad that Mark Twain was ever sent to the Holy Land. His Christianity is of the inferior Mississippi-pilot type. Beecher might have toned him down but decided not to go with the other pilgrims. So Twain demoralized them. The *Californian* vows not to republish his wicked letters and is sorry that the *Tribune* did so.

A kindred spirit for Twain to seek out in the Holy Land would be that of Ananias, the arch-liar whom Twain popularized a while back in San Francisco by suggesting that Ananias was probably even then swapping lies with Fitz-Smythe in hell.

Ananias, [Rev. Mr. Henry Ward] Beecher, Fitz-Smythe.

"The Widow's Protest," 1870 (WMT 7).

Dan Murphy of Corning enlists in the army as a private, fights bravely until badly wounded, then becomes a sutler, but finally dies and leaves his wife a hard-pressed widow. Mrs. Murphy, who knew poverty for years, has taken in washing and grown miserly. When Dan's fellow soldiers wire her to ask whether she wants his corpse embalmed, she replies in the affirmative, thinking the job might cost only two or three dollars. The bill for $65 comes during the wake. She screams at such a charge for "stooffin' Dan" and wonders whether anyone has imagined she would start a museum of "expinsive curiassities." Not a dry eye is left in the house.

Dan Murphy, Mrs. Dan Murphy.

"The Wild Man Interviewed," 1869 (CRG).

There has been so much talk about the hairy, long-limbed, strong Wild Man out west that Twain decides to go and interview him. He finds Old Shep, as the Wild Man is called here, and the suffering creature says that it will soon become clear why he is willing to unbosom himself to a journalist when he had been anxious to avoid talk with other people. He confesses that he is the son of Cain; that he is the father of the Wandering Jew; and that he was with Caesar, Mahomet, Godfrey the Crusader, Columbus, Warren Hastings, Cornwallis, Washington, Napoleon, and Lincoln at key points of their careers. The Wild Man's long life has been stirring; he has been at robberies, celebrations, murders, races, and all sorts of notorious events. Twain says that he begins to understand and asks the creature his real name. "Sensation" is the answer. Then, with a sigh, the Wild Man says that he is off now to dig up the Byron family.

Sensation.

"William Dean Howells," 1906 (WMT 26).

Twain asks whether it is true that a person's mentality is best at age forty and then declines. An exception is certainly William Dean

Howells. His charming *Venetian Life,* which was published more than forty years ago, is no better than his recent paper on Macchiavelli. Howells's English is a sustained exhibition of clarity, compression, felicity, and precision. His ability with words must have been born in him. Twain quotes an example of prose by Howells on Macchiavelli; it flows easily and yet is compact. Then Twain quotes descriptive passages from Howells's *Venetian Life* and his *Undiscovered Country.* His humor is delicious but unobtrusive. Another notable feature is his stage directions, those little touches which make us visualize the scene and understand the conversation.

Alfred, Arkwright, the Earl, Evelyn, Gladys, William Dean Howells, Richard.

"Wit Inspirations of the 'Two-Year-Olds,'" 1870 (WMT 24).

The narrator is dismayed by the permissiveness of adults toward infants who utter what are called witty remarks but which are really imbecilities. When he made smart remarks as a child, he was snubbed or spanked. His stern father hated precocity. Only once did the author try a clever remark in his presence. The narrator was teething at the age of two weeks, and his parents were thinking of a name for him. Abraham? Isaac? Jacob? Chewing an India-rubber ring, the child approved. But when his father suggested the name Samuel, he announced his refusal to wear it. The father explained that Samuel was a prophet and that the Lord called him with His own voice. When the narrator replied that He had to call Samuel a couple of times before he would come, the father chased the baby outside, thrashed him, and named him Samuel. If his father could hear the witticisms of two-year-olds today, infanticide would be on the increase.

Abraham, Ephraim, Samuel.

'Woman,' 1867 (SS).

During a banquet of the Washington Correspondents' Club Twain rises to reply to the toast of woman. He loves all women. They sew on buttons, take us to church fairs, gossip to us, bear our children—generally ours. They are bricks. Twain then mentions numerous illustrious women, including Cleopatra, Desdemona, Joan of Arc, Eve—a delight before the fashions changed—and Lucretia Borgia. Wherever they are, they are ornaments. People would certainly be scarce without them. Each of us knows the best woman of all—his own mother.

'Woman: A Eulogy of the Fair Sex.' See 'Woman.'

'Woman—An Opinion' (WMT 28). See 'Woman.'

'Woman, God Bless Her!,' 1882 (LAIFI).

Two opposite types of women are the savage from central Africa and the modern civilized woman. The first dresses only in her complexion, which always fits and is ready, and is easily laundered. The second type would lose most of her charm without her wardrobe and accoutrements, which come from all over the world. If you find a hairpin on a train and hold it up, no woman present will ever admit that it is hers. Women play many roles in life. We have, for example— but time has run out.

'Woman's Press Club,' 1900 (S).

Twain begins with the statement that America is an ungrammatical nation. In this very audience, you will hear people say things like "She don't" and "They would have liked to have gone." When such speakers write, they use better grammar. Then he tells of his daughter summarizing her knowledge of the reindeer which drew a sled hundreds of miles in an hour and then died. Finally he says that he might have amounted to something if he had been able to shut out distractions and concentrate, as his beautiful friend Helen Keller can do.

Helen Keller.

"A Wonderful Pair of Slippers," 1890 (WMT 29).

In October, 1889, Mark Twain writes a little girl named Elsie Leslie to tell her how he and Gillette together got the bright idea of embroidering and sending her a pair of slippers. Gillette finished his slipper with facility and splendor, but Twain took longer with his. There is no key to his many-colored design, since he improvised as he went along, just as he would with the plot of a story. He invents two or three people, turns them loose, lets things happen, and it takes the rest of the book to get them out of the consequences. Dr. Root came by and did a suture or two of embroidery in the slipper. Every stitch cost Twain some blood, but it is only a testimony of his affection. [Elsie gratefully replied, commented on Twain's big words, and sent her love to his family.]

Mrs. [Olivia] Clemens, Elsie Leslie [Lyde], [William] Gillette, Dr. Root.

"A Word of Encouragement for Our Blushing Exiles," 1923 (WMT 29).

To a voluntary exile who is a member of the American colony in Paris and has just written that he is ashamed of his country, the author offers these comments. The exile's shame is evidently owing to our meddling in the private affairs of another nation under a sham humanitarian pretext in order to filch Cuba in a novel, base, brutal, dishonest maneuver. Then the author wonders if we will lose respect in Europe. In Russia, perhaps, whose history includes episodes in Manchuria, Siberia, and Port Arthur? France, which deserted the brave girl who saved it, and which contributed Bartholomew's Day and the Reign of Terror to history, imprisoned Dreyfus, and insulted Émile Zola? Spain, which chained Columbus, enslaved West Indians, murdered the Incas, drove its Jews out, instituted the Inquisition, and today delights in bull fights and starving prisoners? The author concludes that his Parisian friend has no occasion for shame.

"The Wounded Soldier." Part of "How to Tell a Story."

["'Wuthering Heights' and Her 'Language'"]. See "Kaltenleutgeben."

"Yaller Dogs." See FW, 1869.

"The Yacht Races," 1903 (LAIFI).

The narrator explains to the interviewer that he is sometimes interviewed without knowing it and now charges high rates for interviews. His trade is to talk and write; so he should be paid when reporters get words from him. He likes facts. His yacht the Kanawha goes thirty-seven knots an hour, that is, forty-five. Patrick Clancy measured her speed and knows. Clancy has been with the Kanawha since she was thirty feet long, and now she is 127. Rogers owns her. The narrator superintends her and has a thankless job, no salary, just neglect and ingratitude. He admits that during the race last Sunday he was steering and suddenly offers the interviewer an intemperate drink. The narrator complains that they set the anchor watch once and lost two minutes winding it. Also they measured the boat and found she was short an inch, which meant that she could not arrive at the homestake fast enough. Then when they broke out the spinnaker, it remained broken. Clancy advises the narrator as to bets. The narrator would rather have a weakened intellect than bad teeth, because he does not eat with his brains. He explains that his prose style is superb because he uses only short words and lots of them, for the good reason that unlike German writers he is paid by the word not by space. He is sailing soon for Italy, on account of his wife's health.

Patrick Clancy, Leeds, Lord Roberts, Rogers, Sir Thomas.

'Yale College Speech,' 1888 (WMT 28).

Twain has delayed until now coming to Yale College to thank everyone for his master's degree. He would have arrived earlier, but he has been far from home and also he had to find out what his new duties at Yale are. Now that he knows he is head of the college, he has come to report what he has done. The faculty has obstructed him unduly. Respect for authority is at a low ebb. He told the Greek professor to stop writing with Greek letters, because it is hard to spell with them and they are generally illegible anyway. He ordered the mathematics professor to simplify things, especially conundrums. When he found the astronomer searching for more comets, he told him to stop piling up new items until he had worked off the present stock of stars and asteroids. To make reform complete, Twain plans to move the astronomer into the law department and replace him with a cheaper student. Twain will not specify other changes at this time.

A Yankee at the Court of King Arthur. See *A Connecticut Yankee in King Arthur's Court.*

"Ye Cuban Patriot . . ." See "Cuban Patriot . . . , Ye."

Ye Equinoctial Storm. See Equinoctial Storm, Ye.

"Ye Sentimental Law Student." See "Sentimental Law Student, Ye."

"You've Been a Dam Fool, Mary. You Always Was!," 1972 (FM).

At a crossroads seventeen miles from Charleston, South Carolina, James Marsh and Thomas Hill go into partnership. Marsh is a breezy, confident Georgian and becomes a storekeeper. Hill is a plodding Connecticut blacksmith and provides all of the capital, a sum of $800. Each man is twenty-three years old. They prosper until the Civil War threatens a collapse of their over-extended joint establishment. They part, and the four tragic war years follow. Then Marsh writes to his former partner, but his letter is returned since Hill cannot be located. So Marsh starts on a long trek to find him, learns that typhoid kept him out of the army, and traces him from Connecticut to Indiana and then to Freeman's Flats, Ohio, where Billy Samson the town loafer shows him Hill's grave. It seems that Hill was a good blacksmith but was too tender-hearted to collect money due him, and that shortly before he was going to auction his possessions to satisfy his creditors he burned to death. When Marsh introduces himself, Billy recalls that Hill always spoke kindly of him—he said that he knew one Southerner who would never go back on a debt—and suddenly reveals that Hill escaped the fire which consumed his dwelling place and is now living in Rocky Hill, Wisconsin. Marsh explains that he has $800 with him in cash and $4,000 more in the bank back home. Half of it all is Hill's. Then Marsh and Billy decide to dress up like tramps, go to Wisconsin, and surprise Hill, who, according to a clipping he sent Billy, must auction off his shop and holdings to satisfy a hundred-dollar debt.

Meanwhile, up in Rocky Hill, Hill has been working hard at blacksmithing but cannot collect his bills. His sweetheart, Mary Lester, is beginning to waver, mostly because her rich and childless old uncle, Jacob Lester, who owns the sawmill, has loaned Hill the $100 and wants Mary to drop Hill for Charley Hall, the son of a store owner in a nearby town. Hill asks Jacob to go partners, collecting his bills and even sharing whatever his long-lost Charleston partner, Jimmy Marsh, may eventually pay. But with a sneer Jacob refuses, says that Hill must auction his things, tells Mary that if she weds the plodding failure she will inherit nothing, and thus persuades her to drop Hill in favor of Hall. Hill slumps and then leaves. Mary is momentarily saddened; so, when her uncle gives her $300 for a trousseau, she tells Hall, who has arrived, that she wishes to spend it at the auction to get Hill out of debt. This will salve her conscience. Hall agrees to bid also, to aid poor Hill.

That same afternoon two tramps enter town. They are Marsh and Billy, and they soon learn from various outcasts the gossip about Hill. His Mary has apparently stuck by him, though her uncle wants her to marry Charley Hall, who is going to be worth $30,000 eventually; all the same, according to gossip, Hill will lose his shop at auction to-morrow. Marsh and Billy look up forlorn Hill. His ecstasy knows no bounds when he sees them, especially Marsh. But the two newcomers do not reveal that Marsh has plenty of ready money and will finance Hill. Instead, the three celebrate their coming together with whiskey, some of which poor Hill goes out and trades his last coat to obtain. Marsh suggests that he will become Hill's bill collector and thus save his shop, which they will then rename Hill, Marsh and Samson. When Hill objects that he needs $20 in cash tomorrow to satisfy Jacob's immediate demand, Marsh urges him to rest easily and promises to come up with an idea to get that sum in the morning. Soon the three men are snoring peacefully.

Shortly after breakfast, Marsh reappears looking worried, then goes out again, and returns with just enough money to make up the essential cash payment, obtained—as he explains—from impoverished persons in debt to Hill. They conclude that the poor are always with us so that they can help persons in trouble. Meanwhile, Billy is figuring out how to capitalize the new firm, sell stock, pay large dividends, and make millions on Wall Street. Now the auction begins. When Mary enters and seems not to notice Hill, the unsuspecting people are pleased, reasoning that a demure fiancée should keep her eyes averted from her true love. Marsh and Billy agree to bid against each other on the anvil and thus raise its price astronomically. Mary asks an old widow sitting next to her to bid. And Hall bids too. The price of the anvil rockets from $5 to $1,000, then $3,000, $50,000, and finally $600,000—this from histrionic Marsh, still in his tramp's disguise. He tears open his valise and dumps out bonds, and then reveals himself and tells in great detail the story of the old Charleston partnership of Hill and Marsh. Marsh collected the firm's debts, invested in cotton, and became a millionaire. After the war he tried to write Hill and when unsuccessful traced his path on foot here to Wisconsin. He happily presents the loyal fellow with $600,000—his half of the old firm. Hill stumbles through a heartfelt little speech praising the loyal Southerner and sits back down. Jacob tells his niece Mary that she has been a damned fool and always was.

In a note, Twain explains that his plot is based upon a real-life event, embroidered on by tradition. George W. Williams of South

Carolina sought out his old partner Daniel Hand of New England, after the Civil War, and saved him at an auction of his goods with a check for $600,000. Much later Hand established an educational fund for Negroes. All of this shows that probity is not a sectional American trait but a national one.

Henry Addicks, Mrs. Henry Addicks, Collins, Irish Dennis, Mrs. Foster, Charley Hall, Hall, Daniel Hand, Harvey, Thomas Hill, Jenkins, Jacob Lester, Mary Lester, James Marsh, Mat, Billy Samson, Abel Smith, Sam White, Mrs. Sam White, George W. Williams.

["Zola's 'La Terre'"], 1962 (LFE).

Twain says that he has just finished reading Zola's *La Terre*. Is it a hideous nightmare, the product of a diseased mind? No, it is all as true as a photograph. A review reported that the story was too odious for the French to stomach. How odd. That is like saying a meal was so tasty that the French did not want it. *La Terre* is an example of sustained filth, but we must all admit that things have happened in America similar to everything in the book. And even more awful things have occurred here. We have been asleep, and Zola has aroused us.

[Émile] Zola.